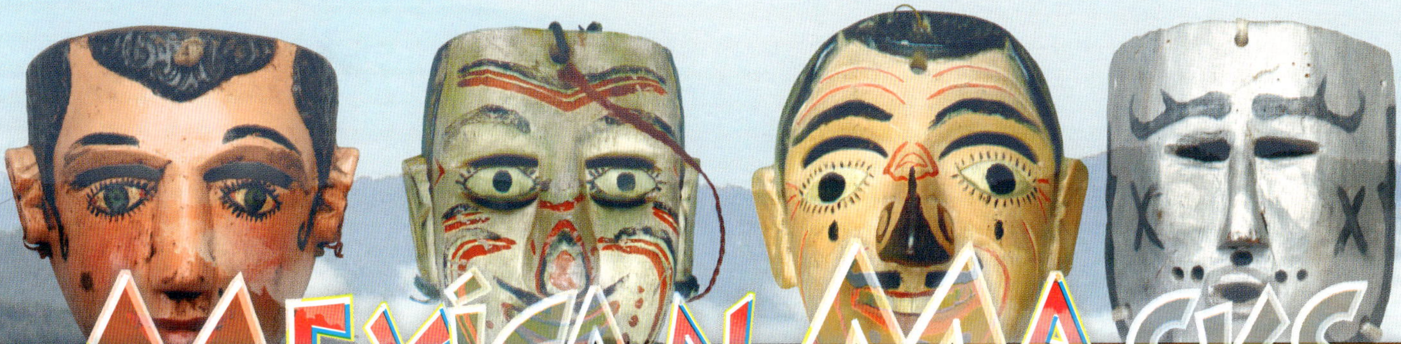

Mexican Masks & Puppets

Master Carvers of the Sierra de Puebla

Bryan J. Stevens

Schiffer Publishing Ltd
4880 Lower Valley Road • Atglen, PA 19310

Schiffer Books are available at special discounts for bulk purchases for sales promotions or premiums. Special editions, including personalized covers, corporate imprints, and excerpts can be created in large quantities for special needs. For more information contact the publisher:

Published by Schiffer Publishing Ltd.
4880 Lower Valley Road
Atglen, PA 19310
Phone: (610) 593-1777; Fax: (610) 593-2002
E-mail: Info@schifferbooks.com

For the largest selection of fine reference books on this and related subjects, please visit our website at **www.schifferbooks.com**
We are always looking for people to write books on new and related subjects. If you have an idea for a book, please contact us at proposals@schifferbooks.com

This book may be purchased from the publisher.
Please try your bookstore first.
You may write for a free catalog.

In Europe, Schiffer books are distributed by
Bushwood Books
6 Marksbury Ave.
Kew Gardens
Surrey TW9 4JF England
Phone: 44 (0) 20 8392 8585; Fax: 44 (0) 20 8392 9876
E-mail: info@bushwoodbooks.co.uk
Website: www.bushwoodbooks.co.uk

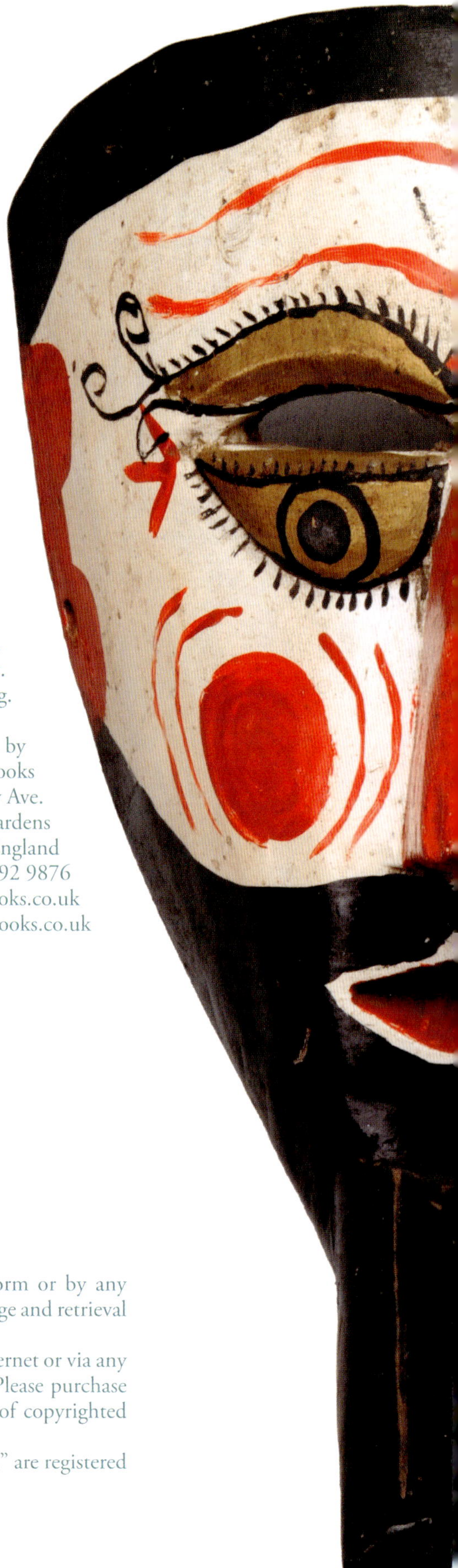

Library of Congress Control Number: 2012936442

Designed by RoS
Type set in Adobe Garamond Pro

ISBN: 978-0-7643-4027-7
Printed in Hong Kong

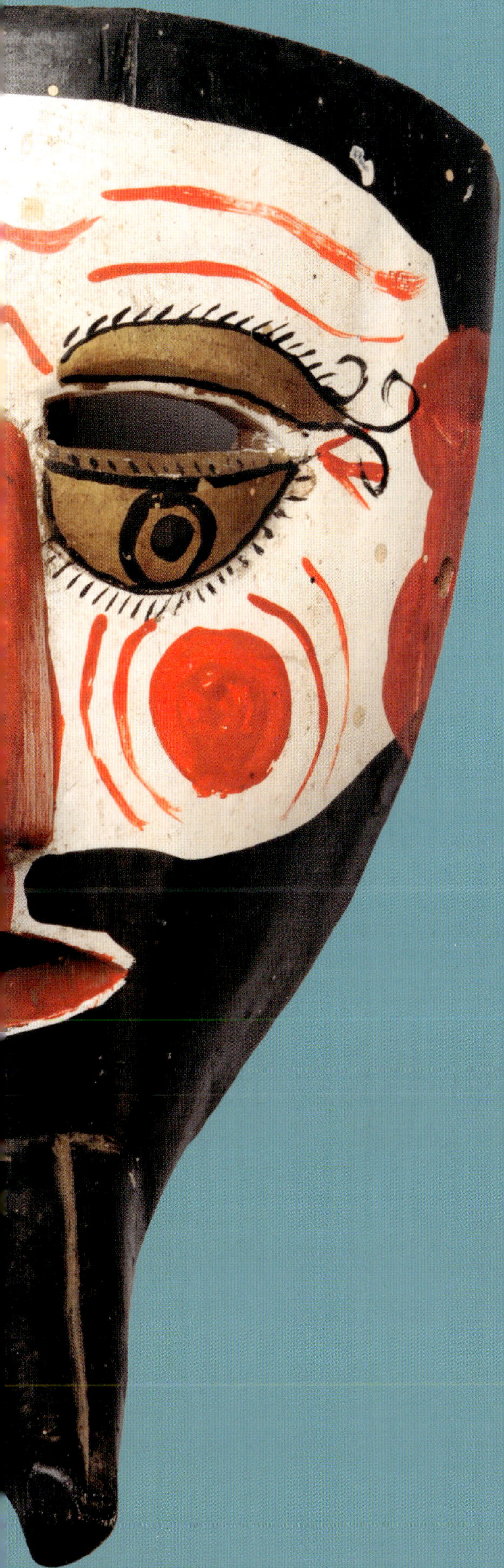

This book is dedicated to the memory of the master carvers of the Sierra de Puebla.

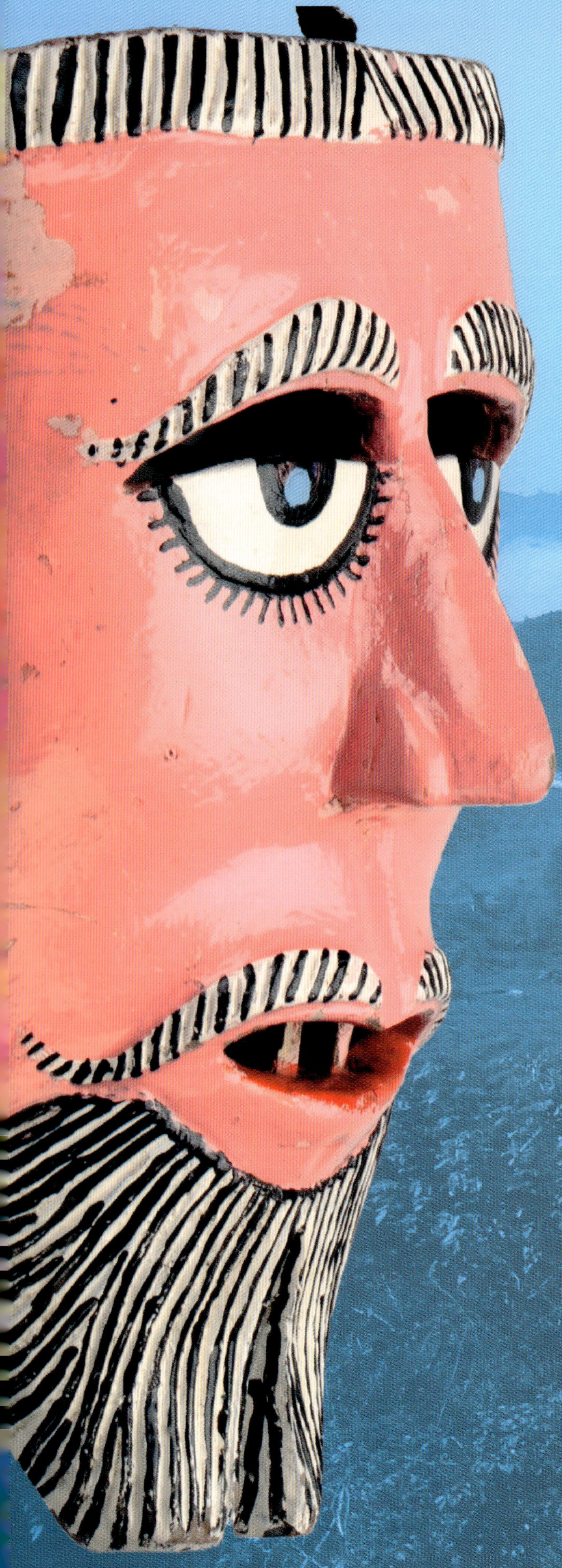

Contents

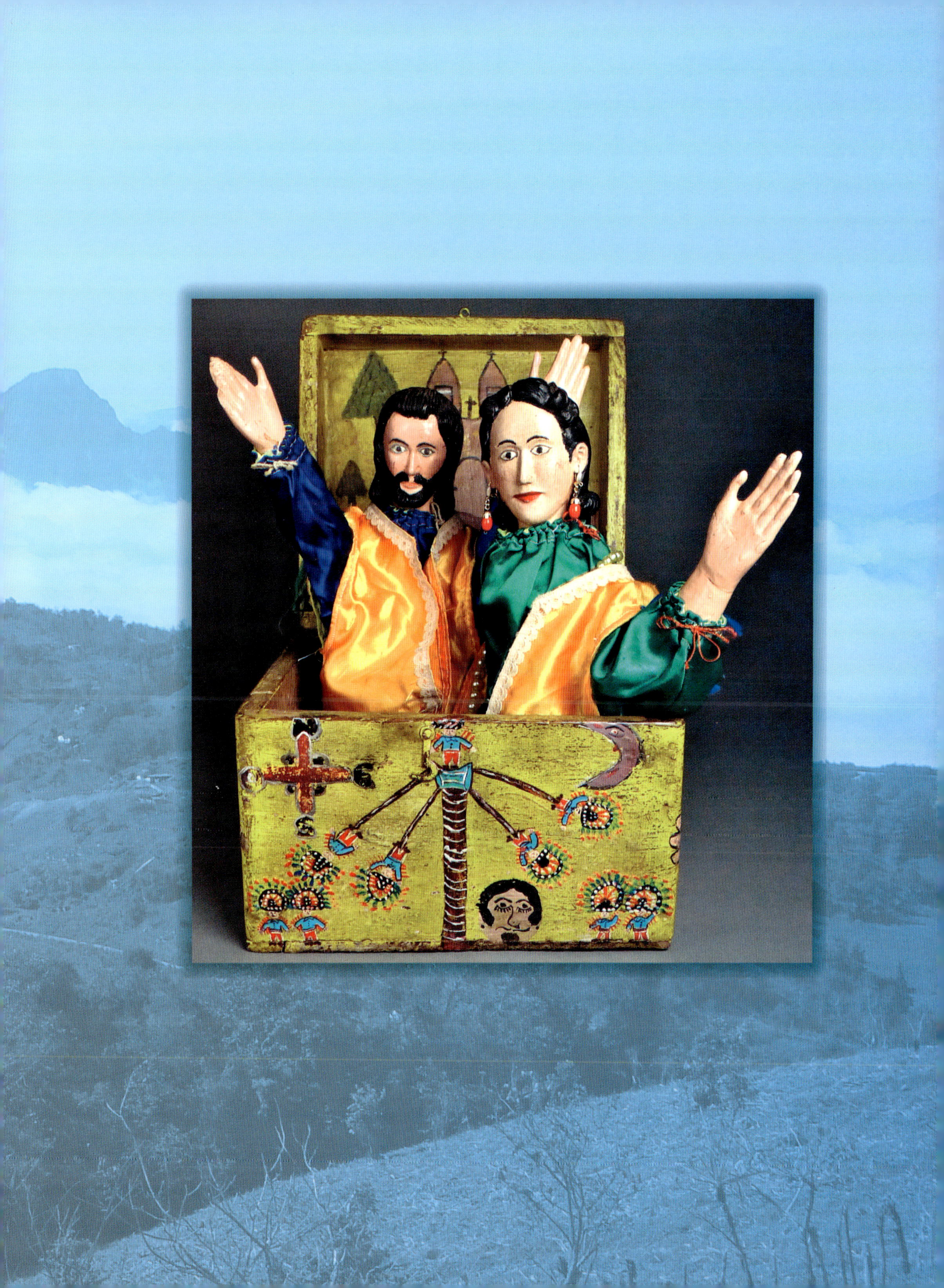

Acknowledgments

This book would not have been possible without the help and encouragement of many people over the years.

During the period of five years when I occasionally traveled in the Sierra de Puebla in preparation for this book, there were many carvers, dancers, musicians, and their family members who responded with grace and enthusiasm to my request for explanations, demonstrations, and the opportunity to take photographs. To all these individuals, I owe my hearty thanks.

My education in the appreciation of Mexican masks began in 1987, when my mentor and friend, Barbara Cleaver, insisted that I should learn everything possible about this subject if I planned to collect, due to the emerging recognition of decorative masks. Little did she suspect that I would take this advice so literally. I also benefitted from the infectious enthusiasm of Robin Cleaver, Barbara's husband, for Mexican folk art in general and masks in particular. I will never forget the excitement of my early visits to their house, where one was suddenly surrounded by the most amazing collection of masks, saints, paintings, furniture, and pets.

In 1989, I went to Tucson, Arizona, to learn about masks; there I had a remarkable experience. I had contacted James ("Big Jim") Griffith for directions to the Yaqui dances. Jim introduced me to Larry Evers and Joe Wilder, both of them referred me to others such as Richard Felger, and within several days I had met a network of scholars, collectors, folk art dealers, and museum curators in that community. I was shown some impressive collections. More important, I acquired some additional mentors and friends. One of these, who remains a curator at the Arizona State Museum, is Diane Dittemore, who has welcomed my annual visits over the last 20 years.

Richard Felger has been another very important mentor, as a scholar and a collector of masks. Richard's wife, Silke Schneider, has also become a good friend.

Later I also met another important Tucson friend and mentor, Tom Kolaz (see Chapter 5). Tom's serious commitment to learning about masks and carvers is quite similar to mine, and we learn from one another about the complexities and facts of this endeavor. I am greatly in his debt.

Museums play a major role in the education of a mask collector. I want to thank the following additional museums for their willingness to open their collections for my inspection: the American Museum of Natural History, the Arizona State Museum, the Field Museum, the Heard Museum, the Lowie Museum (now the Phoebe A. Hearst Museum), the Museo Nacional de Antropología of Mexico City, the Museo Rafael Coronel of Zacatecas, the Museum of the American Indian (Heye Museum), the National Museum of Mexican Art, the Smithsonian National Museum of Natural History, and the Southwest Museum. I want to especially thank Barbara Mauldin of the Museum of International Folk Art, where I have also been a frequent flyer.

In Chapter 4, I will describe at some length the many things that I have learned from Bruce Lane and his films.

Dealers in Mexican folk art have been helpful, exposing me to thousands of masks. I want to recognize a short list of friendly, honest, knowledgeable, and helpful dealers who became friends: Rene Bustamante, Shari Cavin, Joe Ferrin and John Kania, John Isaac, and Spencer Throckmorton.

Primarily collectors but also dealers who have been helpful friends include Bob Ibold, the late Jaled Muyaes and Estela Ogazon, and their daughters, Kena and Karima.

Fellow collectors who have been friendly and helpful include Jim Annis, Joel Brown, Jerry Collings, the late Gary Collison, Helmuth and Terrie Goede, the late Burt Lazar (Tucson), Bill LeVasseur, Joris Miller, Jim and Jeanne Pieper, Jim and Leslye Roby, Chuck Thurow, and the late Dale Hillerman (Chicago). I thank Jim Annis, Bill LeVasseur, and Joris Miller for providing some necessary photos for this book.

My friend David Lippman is neither a collector nor a dealer, but he has been remarkably steady in his support of my interest in masks.

I want to thank all those at Schiffer Publishing, Ltd., who were so kind to me during the authoring process. I am especially grateful for the dedicated and energetic assistance of my editor, Douglas Congdon-Martin, and my designer, Ro Shillingford. Together they transformed my material into an unexpectedly beautiful book.

A few other individuals deserve special mention. As will be obvious from the text, Vernon Kostohryz has played a very active role in the research that led to this book; he declined my offer to be a co-author. Then in the final phases of writing he was most reliable as a source of urgently necessary facts and photos. Carlos Moreno Vásquez has likewise played a very important supporting role, particularly during my jaunts in the Sierra over the past five years. I could not have written this book without the help of these two friends.

I also want to single out my friend and neighbor, Sandy Twitchell, who generously provided a great deal of assistance in the final phase of editing and organizing the book. I wish that everyone had the benefit of such friends.

I feel fortunate to have enlisted Elise Meyer-Bothling to prepare the index for this book. She did a great job.

I want to express my extreme gratitude to my wife, Lucy, for her extraordinary level of support and encouragement over a period of many years, particularly during the final year's work on this book. In particular, Lucy helped me to translate many interesting references from the original Spanish. My children have also been supportive and understanding. My brothers, Peter and Tom Stevens, have encouraged my efforts. Finally I thank my parents, Henry and Jean Stevens, for all their help and encouragement throughout my life.

Introduction

Masks and Puppets of the Sierra Norte de Puebla

In January 2006, I bought an interesting mask on eBay™ and was thereby reintroduced to the seller, Vernon Kostohryz, a retired teacher living in San Miguel D'Allende, who is a collector and dealer in Mexican masks and antiques. I had seen his website in the past, but hadn't visited it for a year or so. To my surprise, he had acquired a large number of very high quality masks from the Mexican states of Puebla and Veracruz in the interim. We began corresponding about these masks. He explained that he had been disappointed in the quality of masks that were available from pickers, so he began to personally comb remote mountain villages in the Sierra de Puebla. He discovered that it was useful to identify mask carvers, as they often had older masks for sale, along with the new ones that they had made. Sometimes these carvers directed Vernon to dancers who might have their masks, which they might sell. So Vernon had begun to learn about the carvers in this region.

By that time I had developed an interest in the broader context of Mexican masks. I liked seeing groupings of masks from a particular dance or from a particular *mascarero* (carver). I was fascinated by the remarkable range of styles in Mexican masking, which involved local traditions and also the visions of individual carvers. So I wanted to learn everything I could about some of the unknown master carvers. It happened that Vernon's approach and subsequent discoveries about mask carvers was providing exactly the sort of information that I wanted to learn.

I began to discuss such things with Vernon and a natural collaboration developed. Together we began to sharpen what was known or could be learned about individual carvers and their masks. Often one discovery would quickly lead to others, as we developed the ability to identify mask features that could suggest the identity of the carver. Vernon had noticed that each carver tended to develop an individual style for carving the ears on a mask. Other features like this included the use of painted designs, the handling of the eyes and vision slits, and the carving of the back of a mask. We began to develop an identification system.

We were greatly aided in this process by Carlos Moreno Vásquez. Carlos is a Mexican national who has been working as an antiques dealer in rural Puebla for many years. He had proven to be invaluable to Vernon as a guide and intermediary in this rugged and confusing terrain. With his help, tasks that would have been impossible became merely difficult and ultimately achievable.

What emerged from all this was an appreciation that there had been many very talented carvers in this region; some were still carving and a number were long deceased. We encountered many older masks that seemed to be masterpieces, yet they remained the work of anonymous folk carvers in the eyes of many. It was shocking that so little was known or remembered about these men, though they had been dead for only a few years. Virtually none of these carvers had achieved the sort of prominence that might have led to their inclusion in such books as *Great Masters of Mexican Folk Art* (Fernández de Calderón 1998) or Donald Cordry's *Mexican Masks* (1980). Yet they showed that level of talent.

Prior to my involvement, Vernon and Carlos had surveyed an area of the Sierra de Puebla and the adjacent coastal plain in Puebla and Veracruz, specifically looking for dance masks and related material. Through this effort they had identified a band of towns where the use of masks and dances remained a vigorous part of the culture, and it was there that they began to identify carvers and to link specific masks to those artisans.

The work of Vernon and Carlos thus provided me with what we might call a "convenience sample," and I decided to take advantage of this body of knowledge, as the basis for further research, which then followed over a period of five years.

Chapter 1

The Region of the Sierra de Puebla

In the remote past, distinct areas of Mexico were associated with particular indigenous peoples. Following the Spanish conquest, these areas continued to carry the names of their respective former rulers, even though the populations of these regions gradually shifted. Such an area is the Totonacapán, formerly the kingdom of the Totonac Indians. According to Harvey and Kelley (1969, 638–641), the main body of the Totonacapán occupied much of the northern portion of the modern state of Puebla and then extended across Veracruz to the Gulf of Mexico, essentially between the Rio Cazones to the north and the Rio Tecojutla on the southern boundary. Then there was another Totonac enclave lower down on the coast of Veracruz.

Prior to the arrival of the Spanish, the Totonac nation, or Totonacapán, had become a vassal state of the Aztec or Nahua peoples, and over the last five centuries there has been a steady increase in Nahua in-migration along with a growing use of Náhuatl as the trade language for this region. Other native speakers have come in smaller numbers, but the major Indian populations are Nahua and Totonac. As elsewhere in Mexico, there has also been a growing mestizo presence throughout this region (Harvey and Kelly 1969, 639).

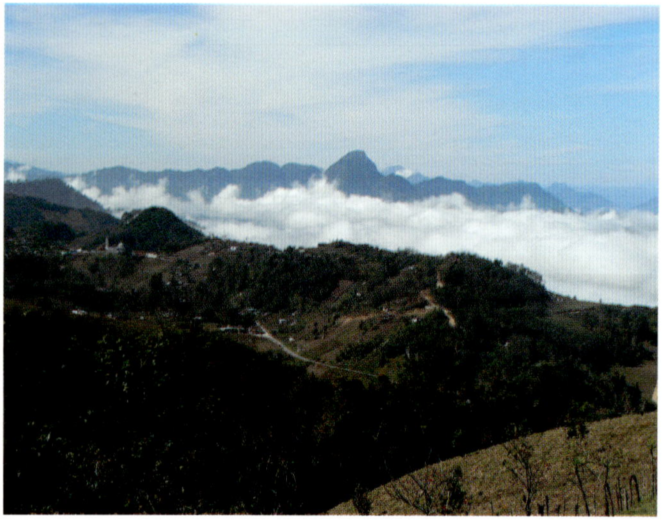

The cultures of this region have been the subject of study by many investigators, and a rather broad literature is available, although largely in Spanish. Most of the writings about the dances and related cultural aspects of this area are quite local in their focus. The advantage of this is that one can obtain a broad view of the entire arc of this area, from Ichon's work (1973) in the gulf slope and Sierra Norte of northwestern Puebla, through Stresser-Péan's investigations (2009) slightly to the south in the Sierra Norte in the municipios of Huachinango and Xicotepec and extending to the Otomí Indians in neighboring Hidalgo. A number of authors have written about the area of this book's focus, which is further south and straddles the border between the states of Puebla and Veracruz.

A possible advantage or disadvantage of this fragmented and collective picture of the region is that it exposes the diversity that truly exists. This will become apparent in the next chapter and those that follow, when the range of beliefs and the variation in the dances are considered. We will see that our ability to generalize is limited by this diversity, and yet larger patterns also emerge with reasonable clarity.

The area that Vernon Kostohryz and Carlos Moreno Vásquez identified as particularly rich in masks and masked dances lies within the main body of the Totonacapán, so that area provides a boundary for this study. The villages and carvers within this area of focus have been for the most part either Náhuatl or Totonac speakers. For the remainder of this book, the study area will often be referred to as either the Totonacapán or the Sierra de Puebla, but it should be remembered

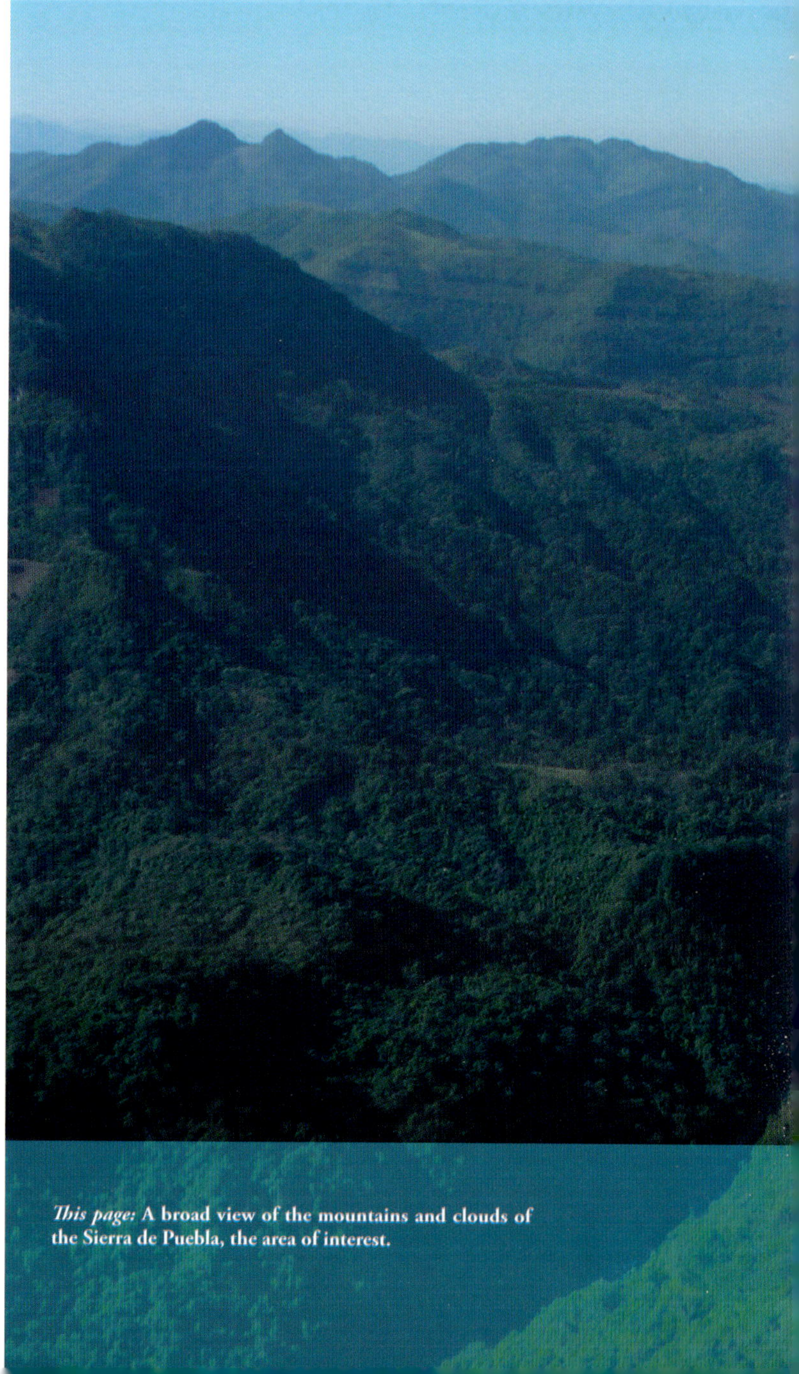

***This page:* A broad view of the mountains and clouds of the Sierra de Puebla, the area of interest.**

that in these dance traditions we will be encountering equal numbers of Totonacs and Nahuas, along with occasional Otomís and Mestizos, across this band.

There is much to consider in the discussion of this region regarding the geography. The northern portion of the Mexican state of Puebla lies along the coastal slope of the Gulf of Mexico. Just below or adjacent to this region the state is crossed diagonally by the Sierra Madre Oriental mountain range, defining an area known as the Sierra Norte de Puebla. The Totonacapán actually includes a portion of the coastal slope as well as a strip of the Sierra de Puebla proper along the western edge (Fuentes Aguilar 1972, 24). The area of the Sierra is of course dominated by alternating mountains and valleys. This has greatly limited travel within or across the region, contributing to the isolation of local communities from one another within the mountains and also from the adjacent hill country of the coastal slope. Thus there are significant variations in cultural practices within the region, even from one town to the next. With the building of roads, which did not occur until recent decades, all this is gradually changing.

Such variations in terrain are of course associated with significant differences in climate and to some extent crop selection. The area is cold in the winter months, and also, a rainy season, punctuated by tropical storms from the Gulf of Mexico, extends from May through November. Agriculture there has focused on subsistence farming, mainly involving corn and related crops—chickpeas, beans, chilies, and squash, grown on steep hillside plots (Arizpe Schlosser and Kandt 1972, 96–97).

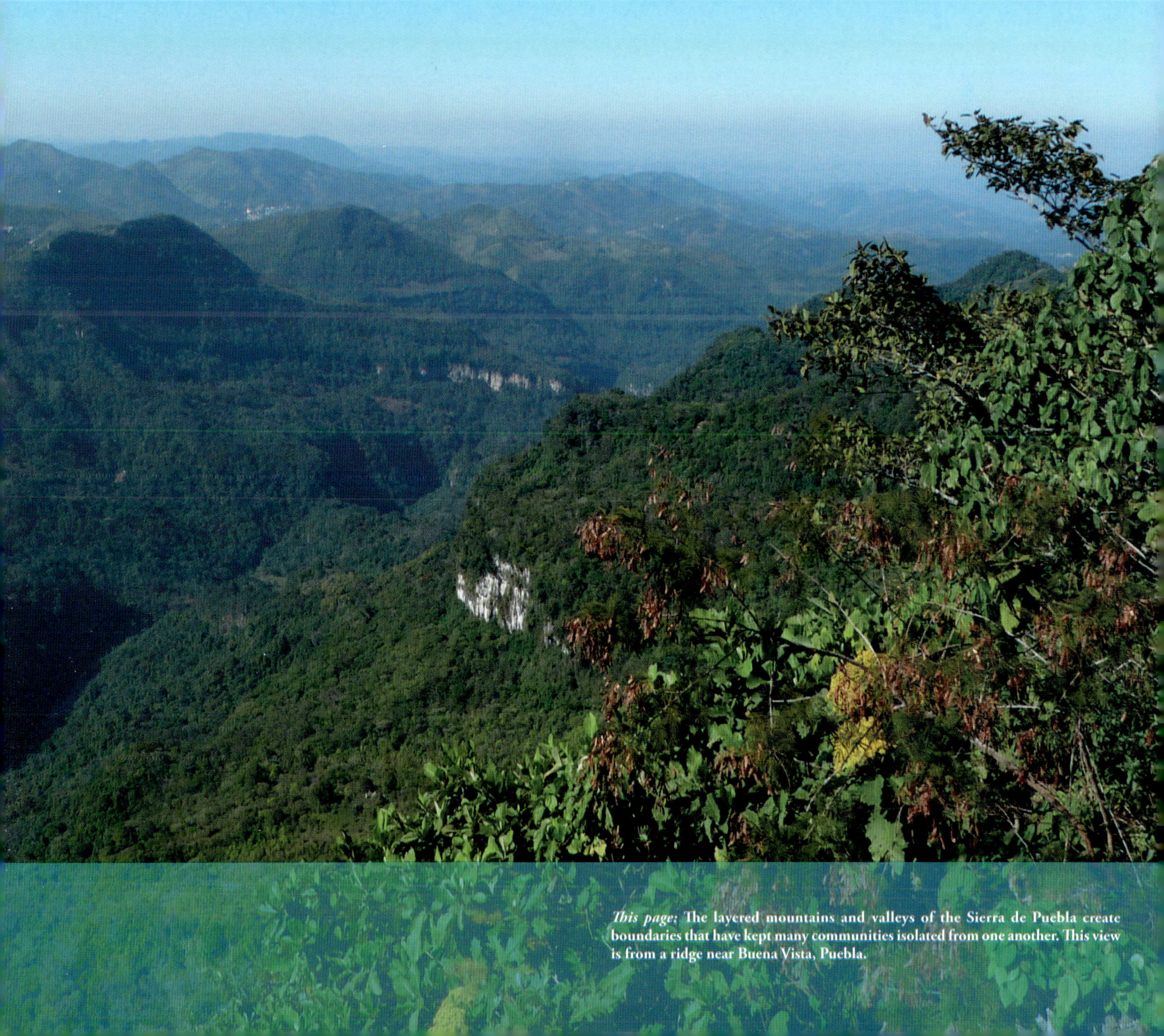

This page: The layered mountains and valleys of the Sierra de Puebla create boundaries that have kept many communities isolated from one another. This view is from a ridge near Buena Vista, Puebla.

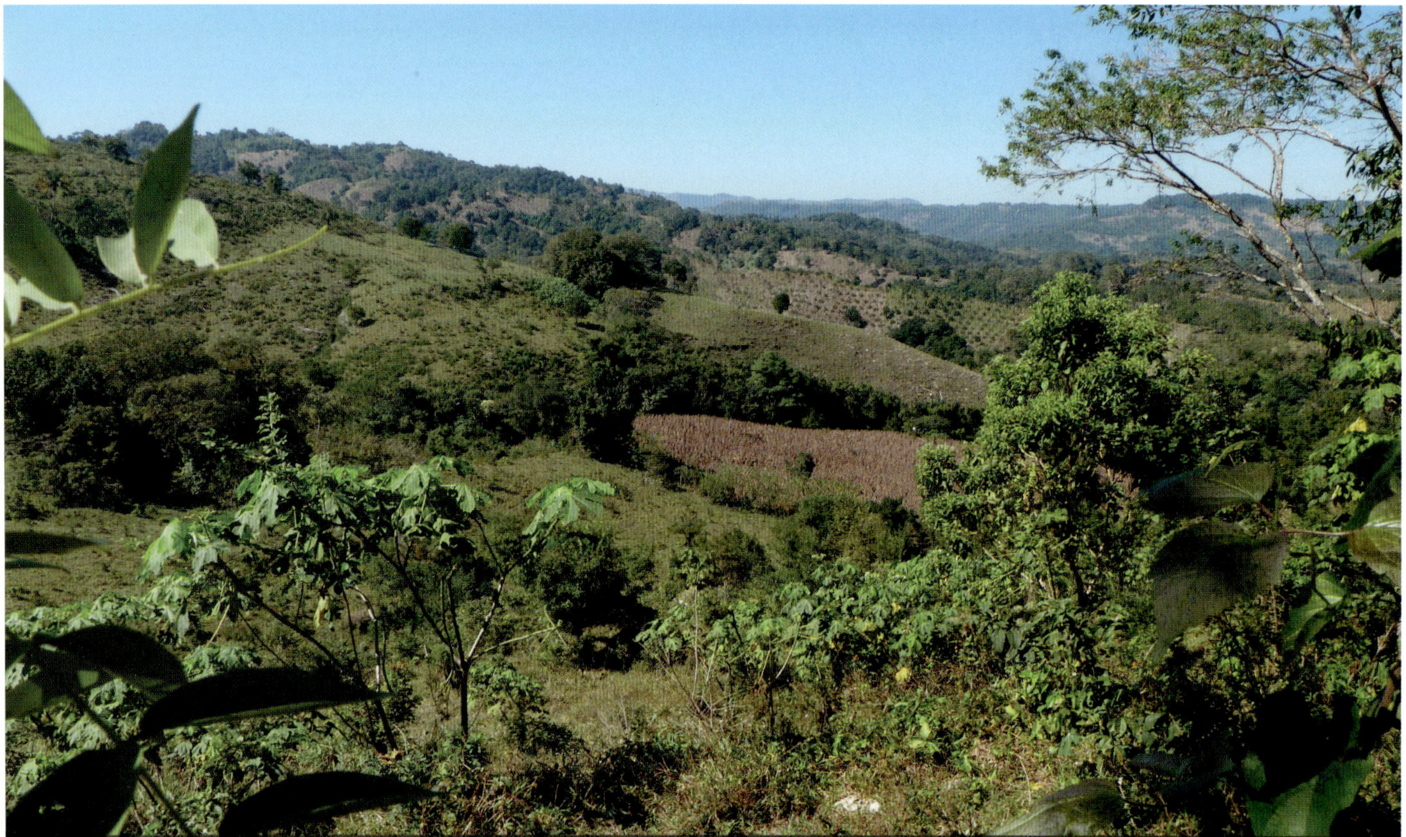

As will be seen when the religious perspective of this region is discussed, the growing of corn has long been culturally important, having been viewed in effect as the manifestation of an enduring contract between the Indians and their gods, a perception that extended down to the modern era, and which may only now be diminishing.

For most of the Totonacapán, the climate also permits the growing of coffee, sugar cane, and temperate zone fruits including apples, pears, and plums. Communities located in lower altitudes ("tierra caliente," the hot country below 800 meters) also grow oranges, limes, bananas, and other tropical fruits (Fuentes Aguilar, 115; Arizpe Schlosser and Kandt 1972, 97).

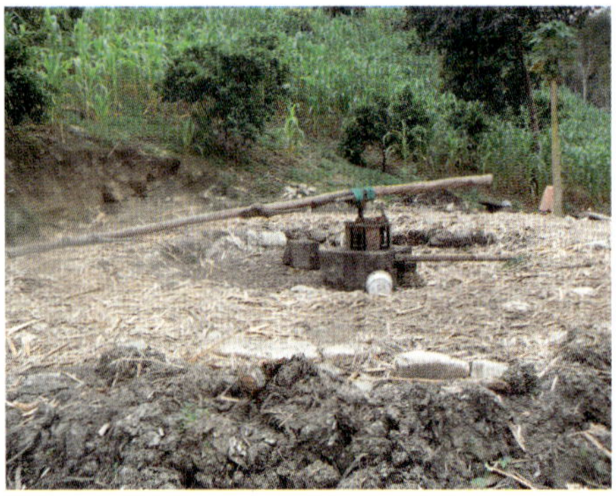

Top photo: On sloping fields, papaya in the foreground, a tan cornfield in the middle distance, and further out, a grove of limes, in Puebla.

Bottom photo: A working *trapiche*, or sugar mill, constructed of wood and iron and driven by a horse, near San Antonio Rayón, Puebla. The pipe going to the right drains off the juice that is pressed, delivering it to a container. The juice must be boiled down to produce sugar. *Photo courtesy of the owner of the trapiche.*

In the narrow true coastal plain along the Gulf, the major crop was historically sugarcane, usually grown on large plantations. This was squeezed through the rollers of a *trapiche* (sugar mill) by the Totonac Indians and African slaves who labored there. In such a mill, sugar cane is fed between the rollers, and the juice falls into an ingenious arrangement of collecting pipes below. These are constructed by splitting bamboo stalks in half lengthwise to form open troughs or pipes; these are laid side by side. Other split stalks are inverted to cover the gaps between the parallel troughs so that any juice that falls on the collecting system will trickle into one of the pipes. At one end these all empty into a collecting vessel.

It is said that in early colonial times the work on the sugar plantations was so exhausting that many Indians and African-American slaves died from the effort. This history is believed to have led to the development of the Dance of the Negritos, which you will have the opportunity to read about in Chapter 4.

The experience of driving in a car across the Totonacapán bears description. One must begin with an expression of gratitude, because there are paved roads linking most of the towns, a condition that has only emerged in recent decades. But these roads are less than ideal. Due to the terrain, roads climb and descend though what seem almost endless switchbacks, and since most of the roads have just two lanes, one's progress is as rapid or as slow as the vehicle one is following. This leads to dramatic efforts by some to pass slow-moving vehicles, which efforts are apparently far more successful than one would have predicted, based on common sense.

A particular hazard associated with the roads of this region is that they tend to wash out on the edges during the rainy season, creating small or larger voids along the edge of the road.

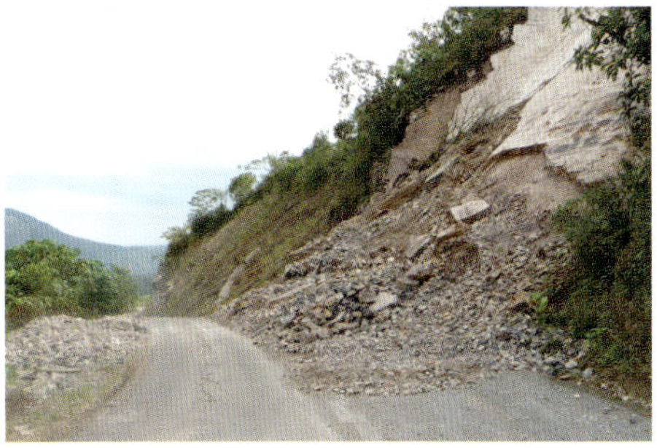

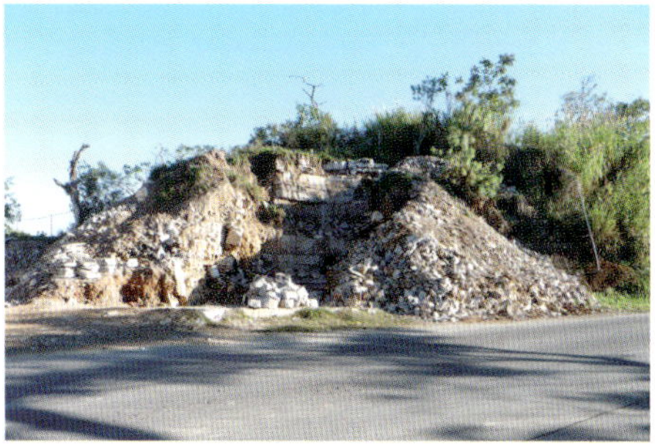

Right photo: A rockslide caused by heavy rains obliterated both lanes of this two-lane road near Hueytlalpan, Puebla. One lane has been opened by hand, but the other remained seriously blocked in December 2010.

Far right photo: In contrast to the hazards of unstable rocks, roads in the Sierra also provide access to roadside quarries like this one. These are a common sight.

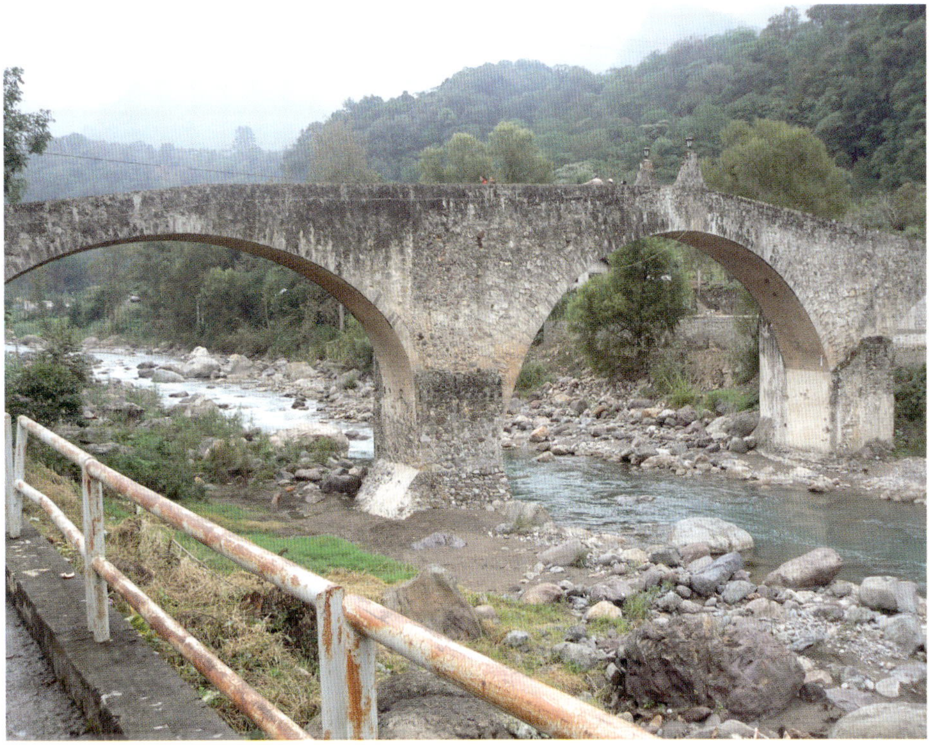

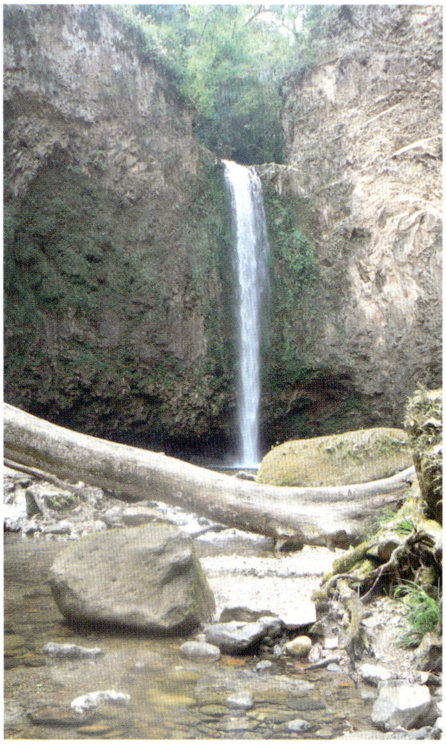

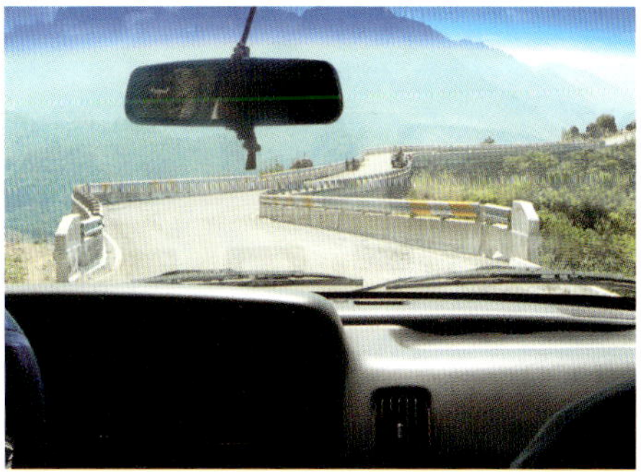

The fruit of such driving efforts arrives when the road climbs to a high stable ridge, permitting one to view remarkable vistas. I have often traveled there at the end of the rainy season, and the lush green landscape frames beautiful waterfalls and wonderful rivers.

Looking off at one's destination, within what seems a palpable proximity, one soon discovers again how indirect the roads must be to negotiate these slopes and valleys. But just as one begins to feel sorry for oneself, several industrious teens appear on the road ahead, traveling somewhere on their bicycles.

One discovers that no matter how isolated a setting may seem, in a moment one will encounter some sign of human activity, be it livestock, a fence, or a spring. As wild as the forested mountains (the *monte*) appear to be, there doesn't seem to be any area that has not been claimed for some use.

Then there are the towns themselves, remarkable for their own topography, as they have been constructed along ridges and valleys. On a flat spot one might find an ancient church, a pole for the Voladores dance, or a miniature pyramid. The cobblestone streets climb steeply from one level to the next.

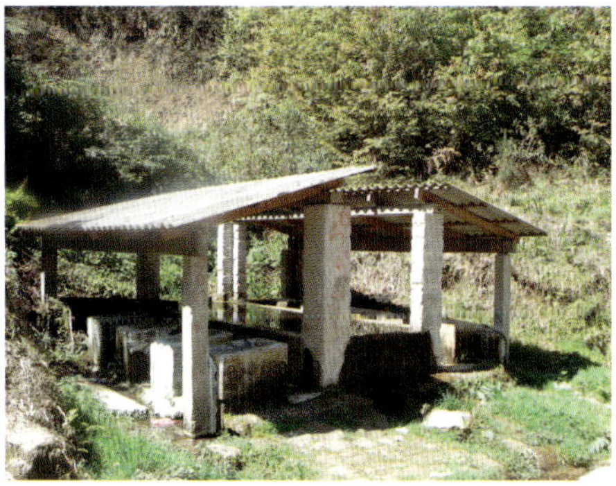

Center left photo: The beautiful stone arched footbridge at Zapotitlán, Puebla, rebuilt in the 1890s, after an earlier bridge was destroyed by a flood.

Center right photo: A picturesque waterfall near Huahuaxtla, Puebla.

Lower right photos, top: A curving bridge spans a ravine to connect two portions of a rocky ridge on the road between Hueytlalpan and Zapotitlán. In the middle of this little-traveled bridge, two men have arranged to meet to transfer firewood.

Lower right photos, bottom: On a small gravel road through mountainous terrain, we suddenly came upon a community washhouse, connected by a trail to the settlement above. One must carry one's wash to the source of water.

In the towns, as in the *rancherías* (small rural settlements), many householders have their own animals, such as chickens and turkeys, which roam freely along the roads.

The Catholic churches are in the towns. The carvers live nearby to carve wooden saints for the church sanctuary, along with smaller ones for home altars. The church grounds are the sites of fiestas; the place in front of the village church is the dance space.

Coming into El Espinal, Veracruz, in the darkness of late evening, we saw burning candles for the celebration of el Niño Perdido. This refers to the story in Luke 2:41–52, when twelve-year-old Jesus is apparently lost for a period of three days and then Joseph and Mary find him in the temple. Each year during the evening of December 7, candles are set out at 7 p.m. to line the sidewalks, roads, and fences; these are meant to light the path to the lost baby Jesus. Families walk through the illuminated streets, eventually converging on a replica of the infant Jesus, of wood or plaster.

Descending from the sierra, one enters the hilly slope that had been rain forest in the past, although now much of this has been cleared for pasture. This area is beautiful as well, although less dramatic. Sometimes one sees an isolated hill instead of rolling terrain and wonders if this might be an undiscovered pyramid.

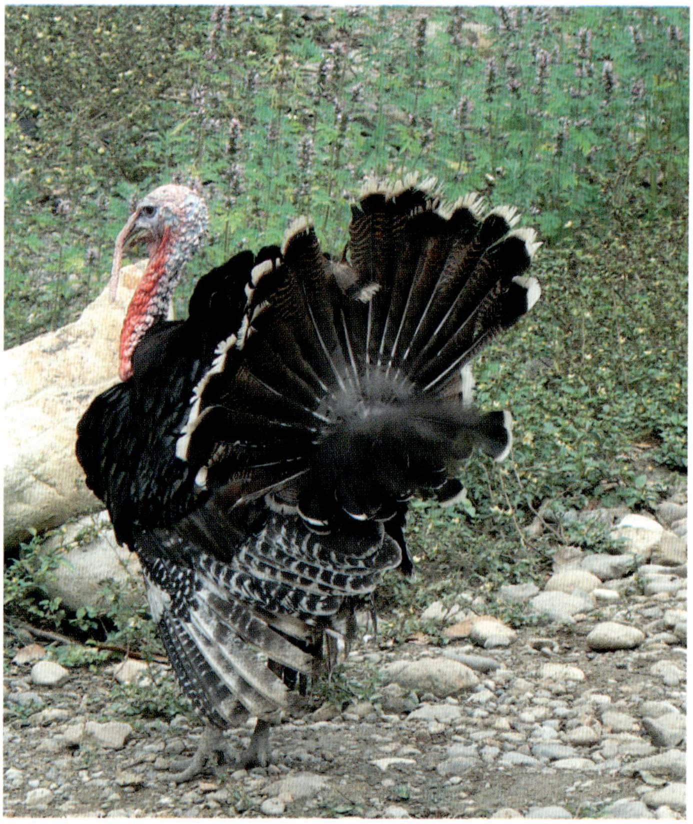

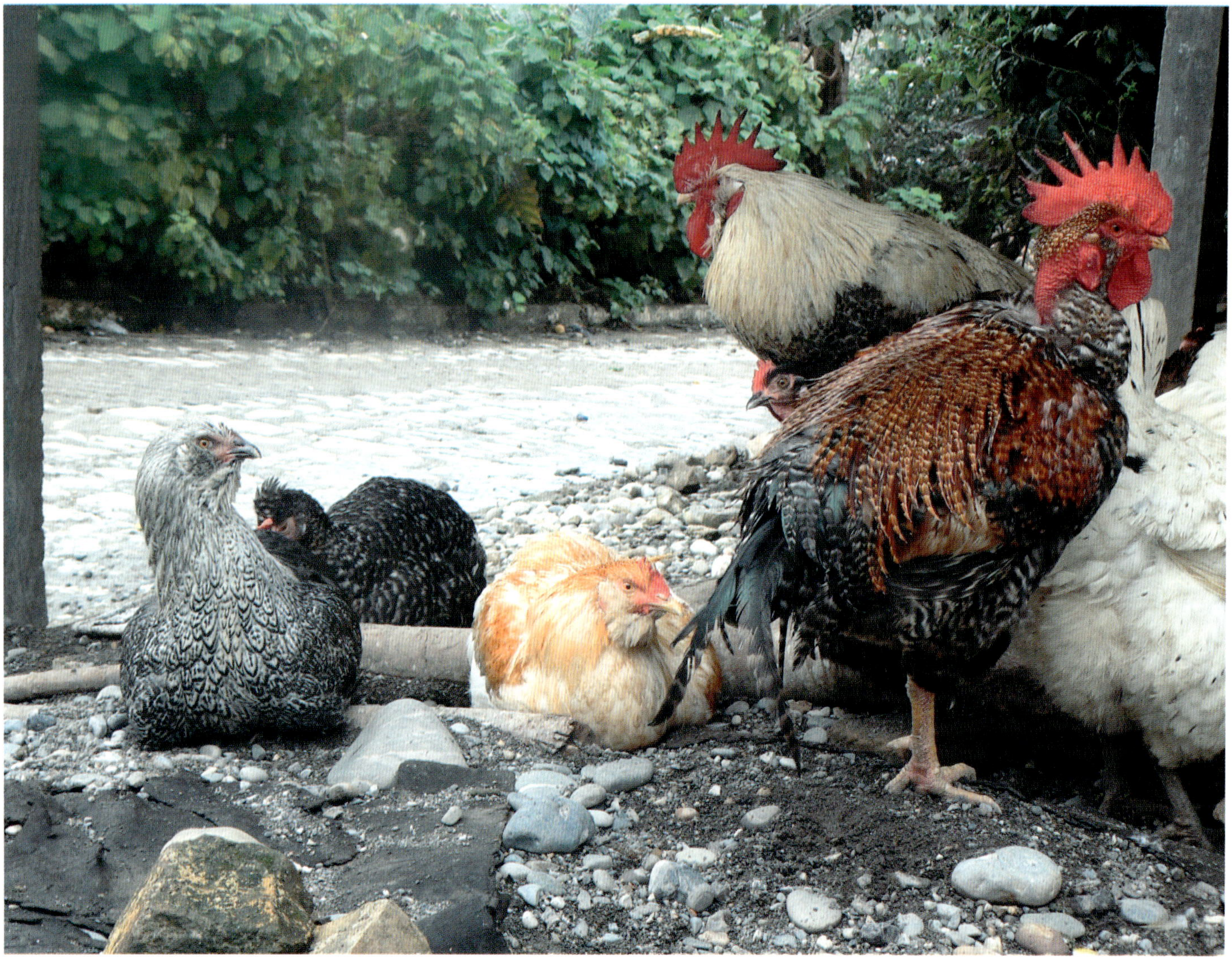

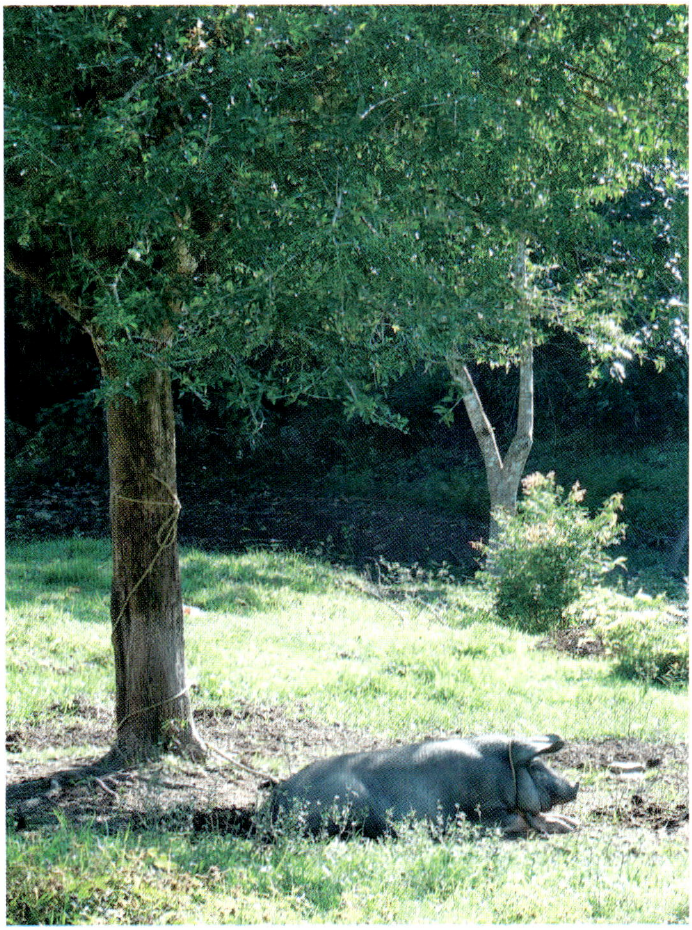

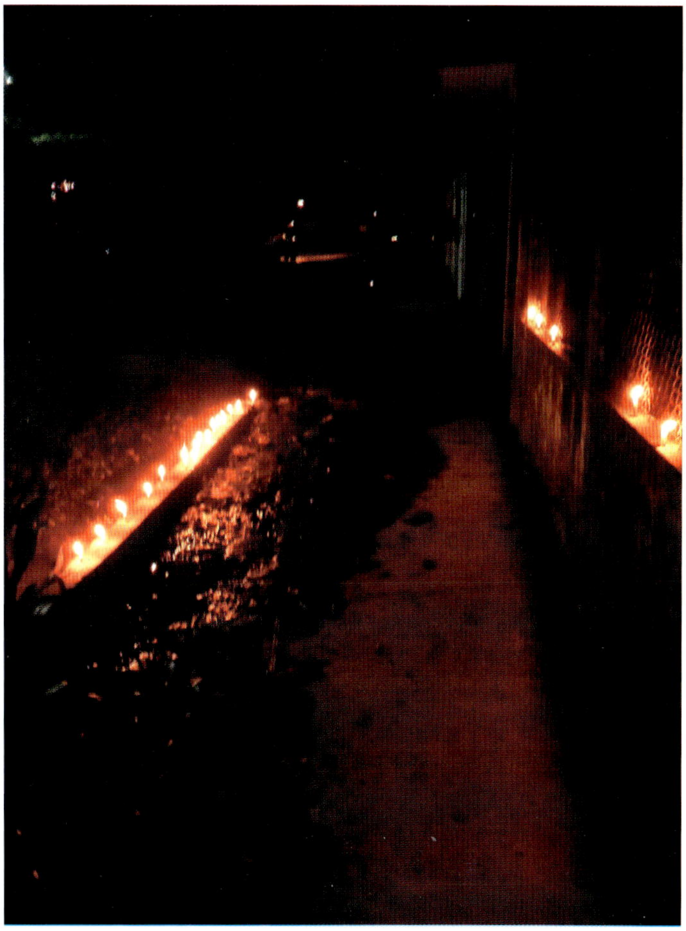

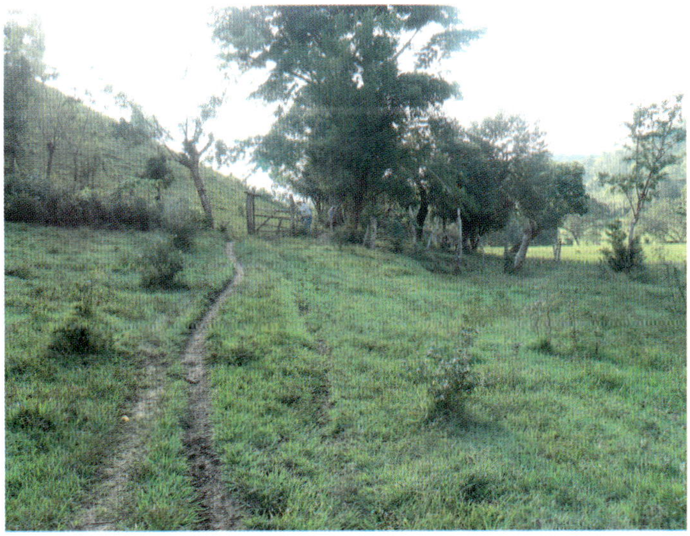

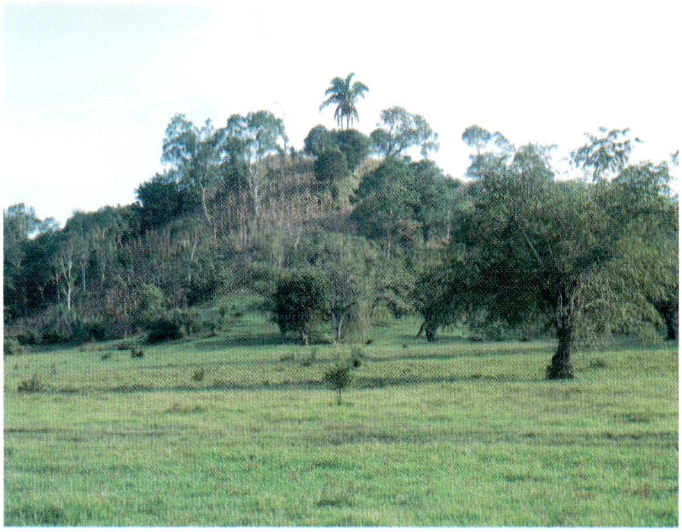

Opposite, top: A strutting tom turkey in Buena Vista, Puebla.

Opposite, bottom: A flock of chickens, each one beautiful and different from the rest, perch in their roadside yard in Chumatlán, Veracruz.

Top left: A pig loafs in the shade of a tree near Coxquihui, Veracruz.

Top right: Lights line the streets and sidewalks on the evening of December 7 to illuminate the search for the lost Jesus, *El Niño Perdido*.

Bottom left: The pasture leading to the home of mask maker Don Simón in Tuncuhuíni, Veracruz, on the coastal lowlands.

Bottom right: A hill near Don Simón's house. Is this an unexcavated ruin of a pyramid?

Chapter 2

The Religious Context

Any attempt to explain the dances in the Sierra Norte requires an understanding of their religious foundations. Guy Stresser-Péan has made a great effort to document and draw together this aspect in his book, *The Sun God and the Savior: The Christianization of the Nahua and the Totonac in the Sierra Norte de Puebla, Mexico*. So I will start with an overview of the religious beliefs of the Nahua and Totonac peoples in this region, based on his extensive review.

Although the belief systems of the Nahuas and Totonacs of the Sierra may have been more distinct in the distant past, these religions became increasingly similar over the centuries due to proximity related to the conquest of the Totonacs by the Aztecs (Nahuas), the subsequent exchange of ideas, and an increasing tendency for the Totonac speakers to adopt Náhuatl as their primary or secondary language. Stresser-Péan points out that there are Totonac*s* who still speak that language, others who have become "Náhuatlized" and speak only Náhuatl, and others who are traditional Nahuas (2009, 48–49).

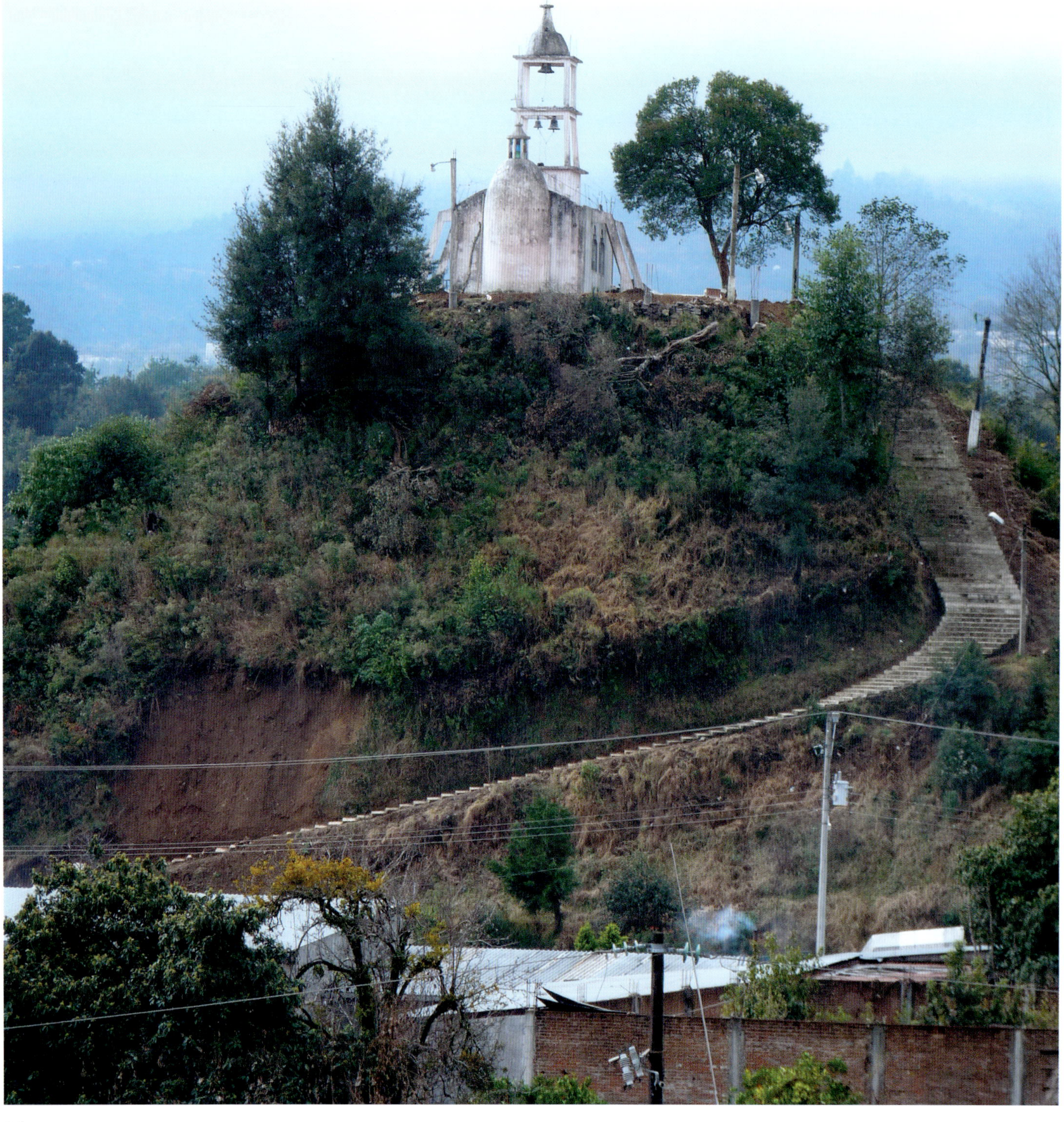

With this melding, Stresser-Péan describes an increasingly shared religious perspective among the peoples of this region. For example, the Náhuatl name for a village or town, *altepetl,* means "water-mountain;" the Totonac name for town, *chuchut-sipij,* has the same meaning (2009, 130). This reflects the traditional belief that each town had a related sacred mountain, which held within it a spring of water to supply the people of that town. In some villages small pyramids were constructed in a central location to represent the sacred mountain (152). By its height, a mountain approaches the sky; some mountains are so tall that they have been perceived as causeways, permitting desirable or undesirable spirits or Gods to descend to earth (129). As will be seen, imagery alluding to great height is a dominant theme in some dances, apparently conveying the desire to reach towards heaven and to join with God.

The Indians of Mexico believe that the world has passed through a series of ages or "suns," each dominated by a different god. According to the Nahua (or Aztec) accounts, four ages have already passed, and we are presently living in the fifth age, the age of agriculture, when the sun is considered to be the dominant god. The ruler of the first age was Tezcatlipoca; that age is said to have ended when, in the form of a jaguar, Tezcatlipoca devoured all of mankind, who were giants in that era. Although the order and specific details of these ages vary with the region and speaker, the overall concept of successive suns is widely accepted (Stresser-Péan 2009, 419).

However, Stresser-Péan reports that when he collected information about these ages in the area of the Sierra de Puebla where he was working, his informants blurred or compressed the usual history, emphasizing aspects that were apparently of particular local interest. As a result, their chronology does not differentiate so many different eras, but instead focuses on the world before, during, and after the creation of the sun by the Spirit of Corn (or Spirit of Maíze), yielding the sequence described in the paragraphs that follow (Stresser-Péan 2009, 421–453).

In the beginning, the world was believed to have been ruled by giants, on the theory that only giants could have built the ancient meso-American pyramids; the fossilized bones of mastodons were perceived as the bones of these builders. They were thought to have lived in darkness. That world ended due to a great flood. According to Stresser-Péan, Tezcatlipoca receives little emphasis in the accounts of the informants from his region of study.

After the flood, according to this chronology, only one being survived, carried in some form of floating craft. The myths vary as to whether he was a man or a monkey. He was accompanied by his dog, which magically turned into a woman. They married and together they re-peopled the earth.

Before the flood, the world was said to have been ruled by Old Thunderbolt, the Great Lord of Thunder (Aktzini, in Totonac), and his assistants, the Little Lords of Thunder. It was under his reign that the natural world flourished, to support a hunter-gatherer culture among the humans. In his youth, this god was a positive leader, but as he grew old, "he became a brutal colossus, a boisterous drunkard whose screams made little children die. He abhorred the sun, which came to replace him as the Master of the World" (Stresser-Péan 2009, 428–429). Due to the decline of Old Thunderbolt, the Little Lords of Thunder rebelled against him and managed to imprison him at the bottom of the Eastern Sea, under a huge pile of rocks. Then they managed the world.

A Catholic church has been erected on the summit of a pyramid in San Juan Xiutetelco, Puebla, reflecting a long-standing strategy of the Roman Catholic Church to co-opt the sacred space of a prior religion to the service of Christianity.

The Spirit of Maíze appeared and further transformed the world. His story is discussed later. This is the present era, an age that is predicted to end in an earthquake (Stresser-Péan 2009, 431–442, 453).

"For the Indians of the Sierra," says Stresser-Péan, "the supernatural world is formed primarily by the spirits of nature, to whom we owe everything: life, food, air, light, and heat. Humans have constant relationships with these spirits…based on the principle of reciprocity." The Indians receive all these gifts from the spirits, and they respond with offerings of food in gratitude. While the offerings may seem small, they have souls, which reflect the sincerity of the giver; "it is said that the spirits eat the soul of the food that is given to them" (Stresser-Péan 2009, 522).

It is believed that there are mountain, water, and forest spirits; other spirits are the souls of the dead. Healers attempt to make contact with such spirits if someone falls ill (Stresser-Péan 2009, 363).

Stresser-Péan describes other enduring supernaturals; many "are the equivalent of ancient gods of Aztec mythology. Nonetheless, in general, people today avoid calling them 'gods.'" This is because they have accepted the Christian teaching that only the members of the Trinity (Father, Son, and Holy Ghost) are God. The most important of these additional supernaturals include the "supreme primordial couple"—Tonacatecutli and Tonacacihuatl—and their children, the four great Aztec gods (Camaxtli, Tezcatlipoca, Quetzalcoatl, and Huitzilopochtli) (Stresser-Péan 2009, 418). Additional important deities include the sun, the moon, and the earth; the mermaid or Siren (108), capable of provoking floods; the Lady of Salt (474), or spirit of saltwater, somehow an alter ego to Malinche; Old Thunder, Great Thunder, Aktzini, or Saint John the Baptist (see later); and "the God of Maíze, great culture hero of the Sierra de Puebla," whose identity merges with that of Quetzalcoatl (524–543).

Legends about the God or Spirit of Maíze are echoed in several of the dances. The Spirit of Maíze is so beloved among the Totonacs that they call him the God of Maíze. (We will see later that this is not a contradiction of the earlier statement about using God's name only for God.) In the Sierra, he has various names including el Niño (the child) and 9 Wind (a reference to Ehecatl or Quetzalcoatl) (Stresser-Péan 2009, 536–543, 570–571).

According to the myths, this personage was born to parents who were hunter-gatherers in a time before agriculture. Sickly as an infant, he soon died; his mother buried his body, and Maíze sprouted from his tomb. His mother cooked the corn but found it sour tasting, so she threw the grains in the river. One of the grains turned into a baby, who rode safely to the riverbank on the back of a turtle. Meanwhile his father, who invented music, was killed by those in charge because they feared that his music might have some special power; later the son found his bones and brought his father back to life. His father subsequently ran off and became a deer, as if psychologically trapped in a world of hunters and the hunted. In contrast, Stresser-Péan reports, "The young god's purpose was to teach men the art of agricultural life to allow them to escape the chronic shortage of food resulting from the uncertainties of hunting, fishing and plant gathering" (Stresser-Péan 2009, 433). He actually condemned hunting, as if he was also a protector of the animals.

Then the Spirit of Maíze searched for his mother. He found her with the aid of hummingbirds and told her, "You shall henceforth be the grandmother of all men; you shall know how to heal them ritually, you shall teach them the chants and music of all the ceremonies." The Spirit then invented the harp and the violin and taught his mother how to play religious music.

The prevailing powers, the Little Lords of Thunder and Clouds, engaged the young Spirit in a contest of magic, meaning to kill him. Instead he bested them and so became their master. He distributed them among the clouds and empowered them with thunder and lightning. Thus these Lords "became the assistants of agriculture" (Stresser-Péan 2009, 434). Subsequently, says Stresser-Péan of the relationship between the Spirit of Maíze and the people of that time, he "lifted them to a spiritual plain by introducing them to religion, for religious practices made them feel they could contribute to maintaining the natural world as it was, ...able to request the intervention of supernatural beings."

The preceding paragraphs describe one of many variations of these myths. In others el Niño somehow creates Maíze, then stores it in a mountain or releases it from storage to establish the first planting. But a new series of myths describe the next step, in which our young hero throws himself into flames, soars to the heavens, and becomes the sun. A rival for this honor, reluctant or delayed, comes after to become the moon (Stresser-Péan 2009, 442–450).

Stresser-Péan explains that, although this was not a belief from the earliest colonial times, those in the Sierra have come to believe that Jesus, 9 Wind, and the sun are one and the same, and that all are together God. So the Spirit of Maíze has become the God of Maíze, and the belief has spread that, following the Resurrection, Christ himself became the sun (Stresser-Péan 2009, 515).

The Spirit of Maíze is regarded as an aspect of Quetzalcoatl, one of the principal Aztec gods. Stresser-Péan's writings show that he was particularly impressed by the emphasis in this region on the role of the Spirit of Maíze, while Quetzalcoatl was mentioned less often. Earlier we noted a parallel loss of focus on Quetzalcoatl's mythical adversary, Tezcatlipoca, the ruler and destroyer of the first sun or era, in the accounts of other regions. Writings that focus on the religion of the Aztecs at the time of the conquest have underscored the importance of these two gods and the duality that seemed to define their relationship. Among Stresser-Péan's informants, the concept of duality failed to receive major emphasis.

Apparently these differences reflect a regional perspective, illustrating the way that particular ideas can grow or fade in the context of such extreme geographic isolation. But later, when we turn to the literature on the Totonac dances in Veracruz, we will see that those writers focus heavily on the concept of duality, and they also express curiosity regarding the possible influence of beliefs regarding Tezcatlipoca. So it seems necessary at this point to turn to some other sources to enrich our understanding.

Much of what is known about the Aztec/Nahua beliefs regarding Tezcatlipoca was initially documented by Bernardino de Sahagún in the 16th century. A Franciscan friar, he spent nearly 50 years gathering information about Aztec culture, with the purpose of being better able to convert the people to Catholicism. The result was his *General History of the Things of New Spain*, also referred to as the *Florentine Codex,* comprising 2400 pages in twelve heavily illustrated books, containing over 2000 drawings. This document was originally collected in the language of the Aztecs and then translated into Spanish. I will draw on the English translation by Arthur J. O. Anderson and Charles Dibble.

In Book I, *The Gods*, there is a brief account of Tezcatlipoca. A most powerful god, his potential influence spanned all domains—"in the land of the dead, on earth, [and] in heaven." When he came to earth he was likely to have a negative influence: "He quickened vice and sin. He introduced anguish and affliction." He sowed "discord among people," apparently by trickery. He was called "the enemy on both sides." He might create great things or destroy them. "He cast his shadow on one, he visited one with all the evils which befell men; he mocked, he ridiculed men." Although he was viewed as capricious and unpredictable, capable of such evil and malice, he might also elevate, empower, or enrich a supplicant. So he was described as if he were a god of extremes (Sahagún 1970, Book 1, 5).

In Book 2, *The Ceremonies*, Sahagún sequentially listed and detailed the feasts and spectacles dedicated to the various gods over the period of 18 months and 5 days that made up the Aztec year. In Toxcatl, the fifth month, there was a feast in honor of Tezcatlipoca, who is described as supreme, "one they held to be god of the gods" (Sahagún 1981, Book 2, 9). A young man would impersonate this god for one year; then he was ritually killed and another impersonator took his place. Human sacrifice was a prominent feature of ceremonies dedicated to many other gods and goddesses over the period of the 18 months of the Aztec year.

Later in Chapter 19, Sahagún discusses the period of five remaining days that completed the year, days that were considered unlucky and barren, when a movable feast was held in honor of Tezcatlipoca, "who was the great god." On this occasion quail were sacrificed, their heads manually twisted off. "All prayed and besought of this god that he grant them favors, for [it was thought] that he was almighty." During this period of the five unlucky days, quail were also sacrificed to honor other gods; that is, their sacrifice was not specific to the worship of Tezcatlipoca (Sahagún 1981, Book 2, 37).

Book 3, *The Origin of the Gods*, includes a chapter that provides much additional information about Tezcatlipoca. He was also called Titlacauan and many other names as well. He was said to have created "the heavens and the earth. All these in truth he made. And he gave to men all that which was necessary." He was described as "invisible—like the darkness; [like] the wind. When sometimes he called out to one, he spoke like a shadow." He could read one's thoughts. People constantly prayed to him for help or relief. He could give one riches or afflictions (Sahagún 1952, Book 3, 11–12).

In Chapter 4 of Book 3 (Sahagún 1952, 15–16), Titlacauan (Tezcatlipoca) is described as being one of three demons or sorcerers who traveled to Tula to disempower that city-state. Titlacauan "took the form of one who was much bent and whose hair was very white, very silvery." He visited Quetzalcoatl, but the servants were suspicious and described him as "one who seemeth like a net, like a trap for thee." Nevertheless Quetzalcoatl agreed to see him, whereupon Titlacauan offered him a healing potion, which Quetzalcoatl drank. It was wine from the maguey plant, and he became intoxicated. He realized that "the devil had tricked him." (Here we see direct evidence that Sahagún equated the devil with Tezcatlipoca.)

Other stories follow, to further illustrate Tezcatlipoca's ability to change form in order to trick others and to foment conflict. In Chapter 5, (Sahagún 1952, Book 3, 17–18) he became a Huastec Indian, a seller of green chiles. He had a large penis, which he did not cover with the usual loincloth. He claimed that it was not customary to cover the genitals in his homeland. The daughter of the king became "inflamed [because of] her desire of the stranger's member." In response she was somehow made ill, but when her father permitted them to marry, and the seller to lie with his daughter, she immediately recovered.

In Chapter 6 (Sahagún 1952, Book 3, 19–20), the other Toltecs mocked the king for permitting such a bizarre marriage, and a plot followed to enlist the stranger in an expedition of war; he was to be abandoned on the field of battle, where the enemy would kill him. Leading a corps of dwarfs and hunchbacks who had been left with him, Tezcatlipoca used his magic power to kill or capture the entire enemy force. So the nobleman and his fellow Toltecs had to acclaim Tezcatlipoca as a hero.

In Chapter 7 (Sahagún 1952, Book 3, 21–22), a celebration followed, and many Toltecs gathered around the new hero. Tezcatlipoca sang and drummed. Apparently all present fell under an enchantment from the music; they danced for an entire day. "And as all danced, [as] the movement was vibrant and most intense, very many then fell on the crags in the canyon. All died there, and then were turned into rocks." Even as they died, the Toltecs lacked understanding of what had developed: "It was as if they were besotted."

Other tales follow in the subsequent chapters, describing how Tezcatlipoca would assume some other form or disguise, then he would kill all those who were drawn to him.

In Book 4, *The Soothsayers* (1957, 33–36), Sahagún described the calendar system used for divination. The day "One Death" was assigned to Tezcatlipoca, who was honored on that day, "for this was the time to pray for favors."

It was believed that he empowered the humble and disempowered the haughty: "He whom he had favored and honored, and to whom he had revealed his sweetness, fragrance and mercy, from this same one he might withdraw and remove it." Individuals born on that day (One Death) were given one of the many names that referred to Tezcatlipoca. One Death was considered to be the day sign of all slaves, so they were well treated on that day, as if they were representatives of the god. If any person was so unwise as to mistreat a slave on that day, it was expected that no end of calamities would follow him for the rest of his life, punishment from Tezcatlipoca himself.

In Chapter 9 of Book 5, *The Omens*, one reads of the omen of the skunk (Sahagún 1957, 171). If this animal entered one's house and sprayed its scent, this event was regarded as a visit by Tezcatlipoca, and the owner of the house was expected to soon die.

Chapter 11 (Sahagún 1957, Book 5, 175) describes the omen of the towering man, referring to the experience of seeing a gigantic figure in the night, thought to be Tezcatlipoca in disguise. One could either bravely pursue and capture the figure to demand a gift or face the prospect of ruin.

Chapter 12 of Book 5 describes the omen of the bundle of ashes, a "rolling, groaning and billowing" cloud that was thought to be another apparition of Tezcatlipoca (Sahagún 1957, 177–178). As with other signs, this was a portent of the coming death or ruin of the observer. However, the brave warrior would take action to counter this threat, seizing the wraith of ashes until it granted what he wished.

Chapter 13 (Sahagún 1957, Book 5, 179–180) describes several other omens that might appear at night; these involve images such as a severed head, the walking dead, or a coyote, all of which might taunt the viewer but evade pursuit or capture, as if Tezcatlipoca in yet another strange form was warning or tormenting the traveler.

Another, more recently published, book may greatly extend our understanding—*Mockeries and Metamorphoses of an Aztec God: Tezcatlipoca, "Lord of the Smoking Mirror,"* by Guilhem Olivier. This has been translated from the French by Michel Besson and was first published in English in 2003.

Olivier notes that Sahagún and his colleagues had engaged in a campaign to reduce the native gods to the status of mere men, then to "demonize" them. Citing Sahagún (1970, Book 1, 67–69), he reports: "After describing the attributes and ornaments of the main figures of the Mexican pantheon, the Franciscan strove, in an appendix, to deny the divinity of each of them, taking the Holy Scriptures as his basis for argument. To him, the Mexican god Huitzilopochtli was a mere man, a sorcerer friendly with the devils, just as Quetzalcoatl was nothing more than a mortal and corruptible man who deserved eternal tortures, although he did have some appearance of virtue" (Olivier 2003, 15). Sahagún identified Tezcatlipoca with Satan (1970, 67–69): "This is the evil Lucifer, father of all meanness and lies, very ambitious and proud, who tricked your ancestors;" evidently the two were perceived by the Franciscans as one and the same. These ideas immediately became part of the message of conversion (Olivier 2003, 15–16).

Here we might note something of great interest. It seems that Indians wishing to covertly retain their traditional gods, in the face of forced conversion, had the option of renaming their gods with the names of similar Christian saints. For example, "the ancient Aztecs venerated a mother-goddess named Tonantzin (Our Mother) who after the evangelization was soon Christianized as one of the manifestations of the Virgin Mary" (Stresser-Péan 2009, 516). Eventually she was accepted by the Catholic church as the Virgin of Guadalupe. In the case of Tezcatlipoca such Christianization or renaming was essentially unnecessary, because the equivalence of the devil and Tezcatlipoca was explicitly provided by the Christian fathers. It is suspected, therefore, that the presence of the character of Satan in a dance might have once signaled the presence of the god Tezcatlipoca. We shall encounter this hypothesis in the writings of Mexican authors regarding the dances of the Totonacapán, described in later chapters.

Sahagún perceived Tezcatlipoca as the devil and interpreted the things that he learned about this god from that perspective. This negative slant leaves one to wonder what there was about this god that might have inspired positive feelings on the part of his worshippers. Olivier had set himself the task of understanding this god at a broader level. Tezcatlipoca had many names. Each name referred to a distinct aspect of the god, and these various aspects presented different faces to the Aztec worshipper (Olivier 2003, 14–44).

Olivier introduces the idea that Tezcatlipoca's positive and negative actions towards humans might be understood in a new way: "There was seemingly a link between the laughter of the deity, his penchant for mocking men, and the revelation by the god of a specific destiny" (2003, 19). The apparently cruel and "malicious" treatment of humans by Tezcatlipoca might "constitute trials at the end of which individuals can discover the fate that is theirs" (20), the fate that they had already inherited by being born on a certain day. From this perspective Tezcatlipoca did not arbitrarily endow suffering or privilege on humans; rather, he made manifest by his behavior the fate that they already possessed or that they had earned by remarkable folly.

One of the god's names was Yohualli Ehecatl, or Night Wind (Olivier 2003, 20). As described by Sahagún, Tezcatlipoca was "invisible, like the night and the wind" (22). "During their appearances on earth, Huitzilopochtli and Tezcatlipoca acted under the guise of 'owl men' (*tlacatecolotl*), sorcerers (*nahualtin*)" (23). He points out that in the Sierra de Puebla the night wind is perceived as a potential cause of illness and death (24). It was to Yohualli Ehecatl that people confessed their sins, begged forgiveness, and engaged in acts of penance, such as fasting and bloodletting, notes Olivier (24–25).

Olivier quotes Durán, who observed the feast dedicated to Telpochtli (a manifestation of Tezcatlipoca) in the fifth month. After the young man who impersonated the god had saluted the four directions with his flute, "all those present and those who were absent but could hear him placed a finger on the ground, smearing it with earth, whereupon they placed it within their mouths and ate the earth which had stuck to their fingers. Then all prostrated themselves, weeping, invoking the darkness of the night and the wind, begging not to be forsaken, forgotten, or killed, begging that the labors of this life be alleviated" (Durán 1971, 101). Having confessed and demonstrated penance to Yohualli Ehecatl, those present were reinstated with another aspect of the god—Telpochtli (the young man).

Apparently the Indians had made their own connection between Telpochtli and Saint John the Baptist. Telpochtli was described by Jacinto de la Cerna as a "very handsome young man…who used to walk on the slopes of the volcano, that young virgin and penitent man, covered with the skin of a deer, and he used to eat wild fruit and grasshoppers" (Olivier 2003, 26). It is not surprising that some converted Nahuas made their own connection between Telpochtli and Christ (26).

The name Telpochtli refers to the state of puberty—a young man who is pubertal (Olivier 2003, 26). Temple schools to prepare young men to be warriors were called *telpochcalli*, and these were dedicated to the gods, including Tezcatlipoca. These warrior schools reflect another one of Tezcatlipoca's names, *Yaotl* (enemy) (28), reflecting his status as one of the gods of war.

One dimension of being a warrior was that warriors were privileged to seduce women; according to legend, Tezcatlipoca was the seducer-in-chief. We have encountered this aspect already in the account of his actions to destabilize Tula. So here we have a god to whom people confess their sins— in one personification he is pure and virginal, and in his warrior mode he may be the chief sinner.

Olivier investigates the many manifestations of this god in detail, while also paying close attention to the interaction between Tezcatlipoca and Quetzalcoatl, the "enemy brothers" (2003, 274). In the limited space available, it is impossible to provide an appropriate review of this remarkable analysis. Sketching the briefest of summaries, however, may be helpful and encourage the interested reader to consult this work in its rich entirety.

Olivier examines the role of Tezcatlipoca in various alleged events, such as the fall of Tollan (Tula), and the efforts of many historians to organize this history. He concludes that the history of these actors and the associated alleged events is so complex and so difficult to decipher because it does not reflect an actual sequence of events; instead we encounter a story or plot that has apparently been successively rewritten by the cultural groups whose history it claims to represent. For this reason it has seemed impossible to place the alleged events in one coherent sequence (Olivier 2003,129). One must turn to a mythical interpretation of this history (130). In a section of the book where Olivier draws some of the evidence together to support this perspective, he begins with the following introduction:

> The often-repeated failure to reconstitute the "history" of the Toltecs is due to insoluble chronological problems, to which is added a puzzling variety of narrations related to them. Far from being trustworthy historical testimonies from which the Toltec past could be reconstituted, the chronicles that have survived belong to a set of mythical constructs quite common in Mesoamerica. In fact, these tales perpetuate the myth of the creation of the sun, while being variations on the theme of the exile from Tamoanchan. Thus, in order to understand the many versions of the events retold by the chroniclers, it is necessary to place the "Toltec history" within a wider mythical environment (162).

For example, the Aztecs wished to portray themselves as the spiritual and cultural heirs of the Toltec empire. So, speculates Olivier, much of the material in Sahagún regarding Tezcatlipoca's role in the fall of Tula can be best understood as formulaic invention, long after the alleged events, to integrate various gods within the cosmology of the Aztecs and to "explain" (justify) their ascendancy (2003, 151, 162–164). The Spanish seemed to engage in the same techniques, promoting their spiritual values through emphasis on the positive aspects of Quetzalcoatl versus the darker side of Tezcatlipoca.

The broader truth, which comes into focus for Olivier after ten years of investigation, is that Tezcatlipoca and Quetzalcoatl have complementary roles within a cosmic drama, such that one ascends to power when the other falls into a state of moral collapse. The period when either reigns defines an era or sun. That era ends with a reversal, so that the god who was ascendant then falls from grace, to be replaced by the other as the new ruler of the universe (Olivier 2003, 274–277). Each of these gods has positive and negative aspects, and then each in turn assumes other more temporary qualities. Occasionally they cooperate to bring about some cosmic event. The current sun is under the charge of Quetzalcoatl (el Niño), so Tezcatlipoca is cast in the role of the underdog.

With the assistance of Olivier, we can take advantage of a long tradition of scholarship to assist us in our understanding of this blend of history and myth. However, the average Totonac or Nahua Indian, living centuries ago in the Sierra de Puebla, would have felt compelled to accept all of these contradictory ideas as a confounding yet genuine account of the powerful deities that had to be worshipped and placated. Thus the main purpose of the preceding summary was to spell out the remarkable powers and personality ascribed to Tezcatlipoca in the past, so that we might better understand why he might have required extraordinary attention from the people through worship and dance. A second purpose was to introduce the concept of duality, so richly demonstrated in the relationship between the enemy brothers, Tezcatlipoca and Quetzalcoatl.

Dualidad (duality) is a word frequently used in Mexico, but English speakers apparently prefer a related word, "dualism." According to the *Catholic Encyclopedia* (www.newadvent.org/cathen/05169a.html), "dualism" refers to a "religious or theological system which would explain the universe as the outcome of two eternally opposed and coexisting principles, conceived as good and evil, light and darkness, or some other form of conflicting powers." The article explains that in the Christian tradition there is believed to be one God, unopposed by any second power; in Christianity the principle of dualism has been rejected. Evil intention or behavior is seen as a product of free will and human frailty, not as reflecting the influence of a competing power. God alone is said to be all-powerful and beneficent.

In my opening remarks about Sahagún, I referred to his campaign to reduce the native gods to the status of mere men and then to "demonize" them. We see now that these efforts reflected an extremely fundamental tenet of the Roman Catholic Church. In keeping with the Christian church's rejection of dualism or duality, Satan is described as a positive creation of God who, with his angels, subsequently rebelled. The devil and his minions are *not* perceived by the church as an opposing power to God (www.newadvent.org/cathen/04764a.html).

In contrast, the gods of the great religions of Mexico were viewed from the perspective of duality or dualism. On the one hand, a god was considered to have a dual or mixed nature. So each god was perceived as having the potential for a range of possible responses, depending on the mood of the god or on the context. For example, we have seen that Tezcatlipoca might appear in one manifestation or another, and ultimately he represents the sum of his manifestations. Quetzalcoatl might behave as the most holy creator or he might drink too much and engage in inappropriate acts. On the other hand, justice or injustice was not necessarily expected to flow in a predictable manner from any particular deity, but rather might be the result of the interaction between deities or powers. In some cases, it seems that gods were deliberately described in pairs, to emphasize the idea that their combined efforts would determine the outcome. Here is one of the confusing aspects of the Mexican view of duality, that it operated on several different levels—within each god or power and then between them as well.

Francisco Acosta Báez and Zeferino Gaona Vega (2005, 94–102) point out that in the Miguelitos dance the devil is perceived as one of two opposing powers; the other is Jesus. Each has a dual or mixed nature *and* they are two agents in a duality, *"los dos son necesarios para sustentar, de manera dynámica, el equilibio del universo mismo"* [both are necessary to sustain in a dynamic manner the balance of the universe itself] (95).

The subtle implications of this may, on reflection, seem a little shocking to the orthodox Christian understanding. One is accustomed to thinking of Jesus in purely positive terms and the devil in the opposite way. But in the Mexican Indian perspective, Jesus and Satan are believed to need one another in order to achieve balance. It may or may not be the case that Jesus has lost status, but certainly the devil has been elevated. Both have been incorporated into the Indian worldview, it seems, but, in turn, each has become subject to the expectations of duality. That is to say, both have been co-opted!

One important theme of this chapter (and beyond) concerns the possibility that the Indians of the Sierra de Puebla might have chosen to attach a particular Christian deity, saint, or power to an existing pre-conquest god, as either an accommodation or a feigned response to the conversion process. One possible marker for such an attachment or conversion is that the incorporated figure became subject to duality, thereby demonstrating a change in his or her status.

Earlier it was noted that Jesus had lost his aura of omnipotence in a subtle fashion, which can be explained by the fact that he has become identified with the sun and the Spirit of Maíze, and thereby subject to the apparent Mexican view that no god is perfect but all are on an equal footing. Still left to explain is the apparent elevation of the devil's status. Has he been included in the pantheon merely as a courtesy or accommodation to Christianity or has he also been attached to some existing Indian deity? My working theory is that one gains status by attachment to a powerful deity, and that an elevation in status would never have resulted from courtesy or accommodation alone. Earlier we noticed the likelihood that the devil might have become identified with Tezcatlipoca. We will be considering such matters further as the evidence grows.

Stresser-Péan reports that the Indians of the Sierra recognize a number of supernaturals from the Christian tradition, including, of course, the Holy Trinity. Stresser-Péan notes that the Indians are aware that the Trinity includes the Holy Ghost, yet they don't find that concept easy to understand, and they tend to equate the Trinity with the Holy Family: "the Mother, the Father, and the Son" (Stresser-Péan 2009, 514).

When they speak of God, the Sierra Indians are consciously referring to the Eternal Father and his son, Jesus Christ. They perceive Christ as the more approachable and compassionate of the two, and it is to Jesus that the prayers of the people are usually addressed, rather than to God the Father. The death and subsequent ascent of Christ has become attached to the Indian myths regarding the birth of the sun: "In fact, what is essential is the identification of Jesus Christ with the sun," according to Stresser-Péan (2009, 515).

The cross as a symbol of the crucifixion of Christ is commonplace, and one addresses the cross, on the Day of the Holy Cross, as a symbol of Christ. However, says Stresser-Péan, "The Indians regard the rites of this festivity as a prayer for rain, perhaps because a cross has equal branches evoking the four cardinal points" (2009, 515). This is a wonderful example of what is often observed in various parts of Mexico, including the Sierra: there can be such a powerful condensation of Christian and indigenous beliefs, which has the potential effect of strengthening both traditions.

As alluded to previously, in the discussion of members of the Holy Trinity, another important Christian personage is the Virgin Mary, or Santa María. In Mexico there are actually believed to be many incarnations of the Virgin, based on local experience and interpretation. Cassidy (1958) provides a tour of some of these local or regional expressions of the Virgin. The Virgin de Guadalupe appears to carry the projection of an important pre-conquest Nahua goddess—Tonantzin (Our Mother)—and she has become widely worshipped in the Sierra (Stresser-Péan 2009, 516).

In Jonotla, Puebla, a chapel dedicated to the Virgin of Guadalupe is constructed around a spot on a rock that appears to bear the image of this saint. The *Capilla de Guadalupe* contains a number of beautiful carvings of saints.

Echoes of the Virgin are encountered in various regional dances, where there is almost inevitably some Maringuilla (Little Mary) or Malinche/Malintzen figure, as if her presence is more or less required in some form. Max Harris has pointed out that Malintzen and Malinche are names that refer back to members of the Aztec royal lineage, and that this is likely to be the point of reference when a dance character bears one of these names, despite the apparent reference to the consort of Cortez (Harris 1996, 149–177). As with Jesus, the Virgin Mary, then, may have become associated with multiple deities or important pre-conquest figures, which would enhance her status.

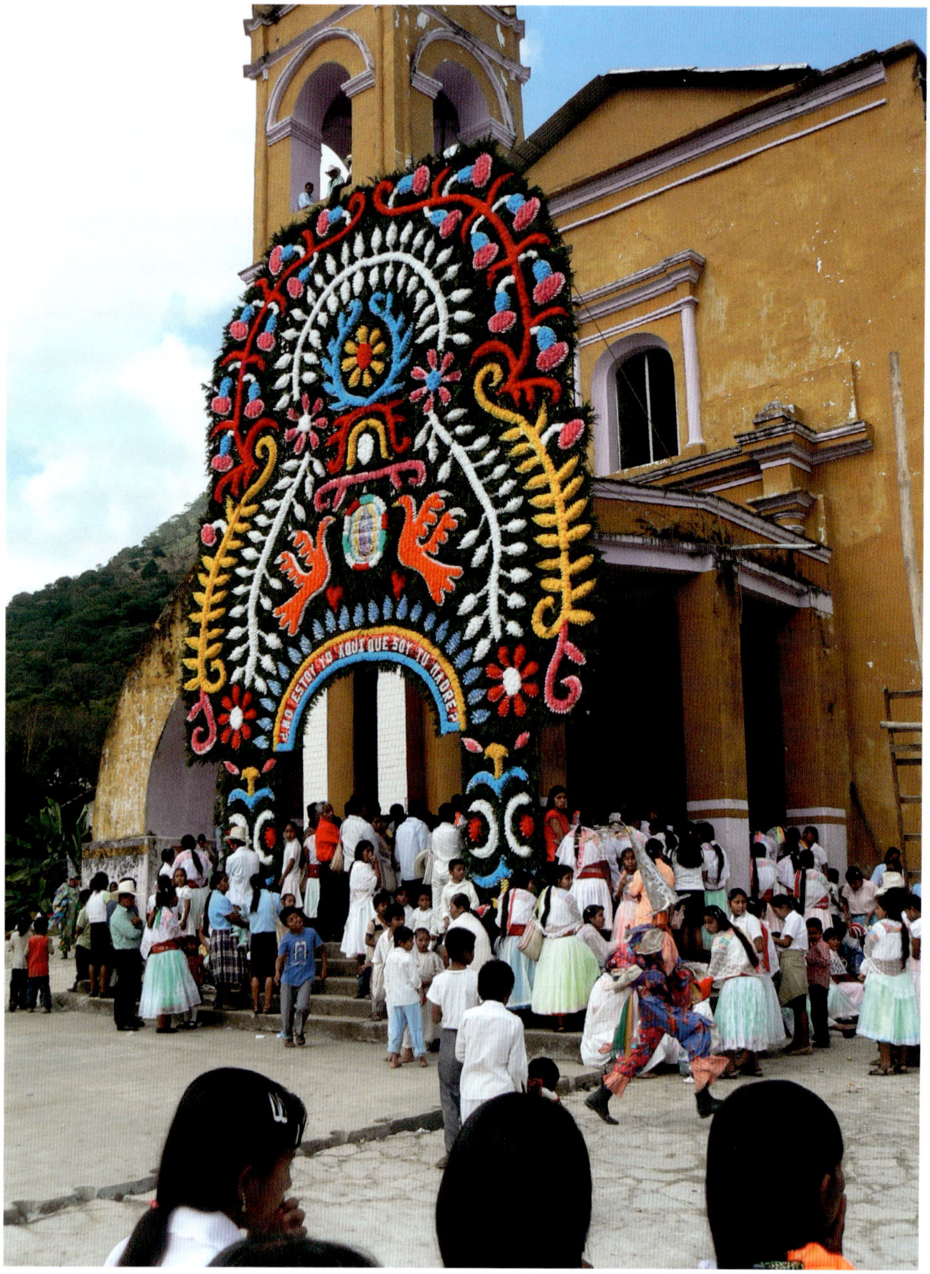

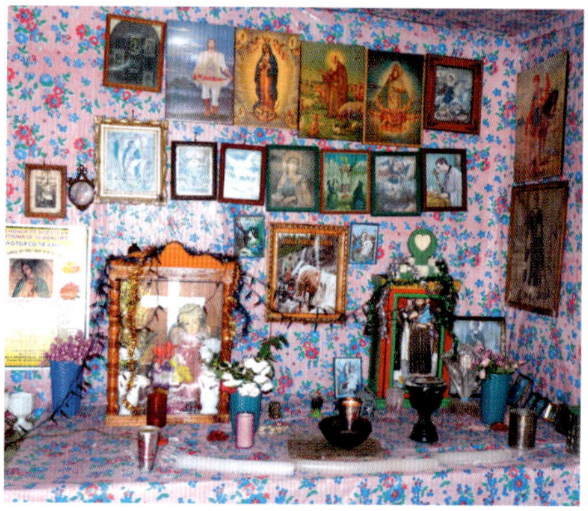

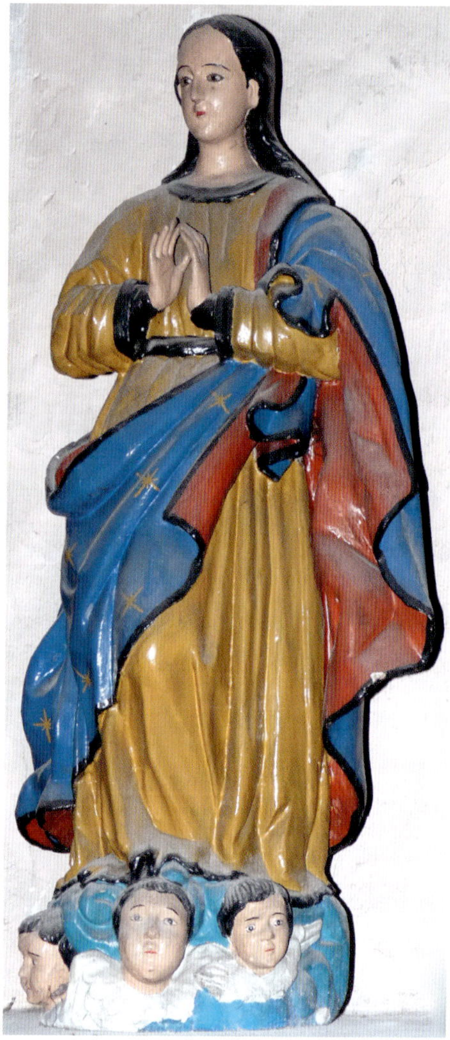

Above: The church in Huehuetla, Puebla, decorated to honor the Virgin of Guadalupe in December 2006. In the foreground a Huehue clown performs for the crowd.

Top right: An altar in the home of Guadalupe Ortiz González in Buena Vista, Puebla. This is a rich example. On the altar two wooden boxes with glass doors display the saints inside. Such a box is called a *nicho*. The nicho on the left holds the Santo Niño de Atocha, and the one on the right reveals Saint Anthony of Padua, who is always depicted as holding Christ nestled on his left arm. There are many images of Saints, including the Virgin of Guadalupe, Saint Francis of Assisi, the *Virgen de Concepción* (the Virgin of the Immaculate Conception, wearing her crown) *Santiago Apóstol* (Saint James the Apostle), San Miguel (Saint Michael, archangel), San Martín de Porres, and Saint Martin of Tours. Under the second row of images is a large portrait of Pope John XXIII.

Bottom right: A representation of the *Virgen de la Asunción* (The Virgin of the Ascension, supported by angels below her feet) in the chapel dedicated to the Virgin of Guadalupe, in Jonotla, Puebla.

In December 2006, when my wife and I were traveling east towards the Sierra de Puebla, we saw many trucks and buses going in the opposite direction that were decorated with references to the Virgin of Guadalupe. I was told that they carried pilgrims who were going to the Basilica of Guadalupe in Mexico City. When we reached the Sierra towns, we saw many more similarly decorated vehicles that were preparing to depart on this pilgrimage.

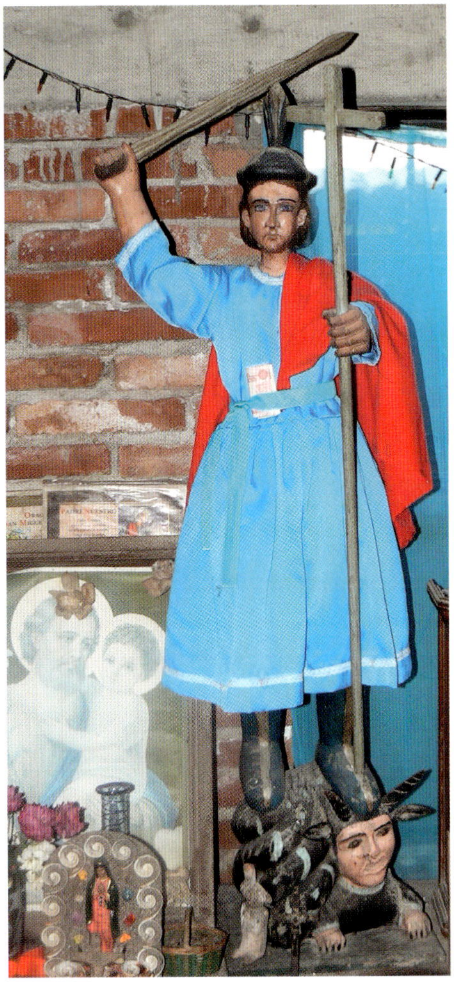

A 20th century wooden carving of San Miguel from a home altar in El Espinal, Veracruz. He stands on a dragon or serpent that represents Satan. Offerings of money have been tucked in the saint's belt.

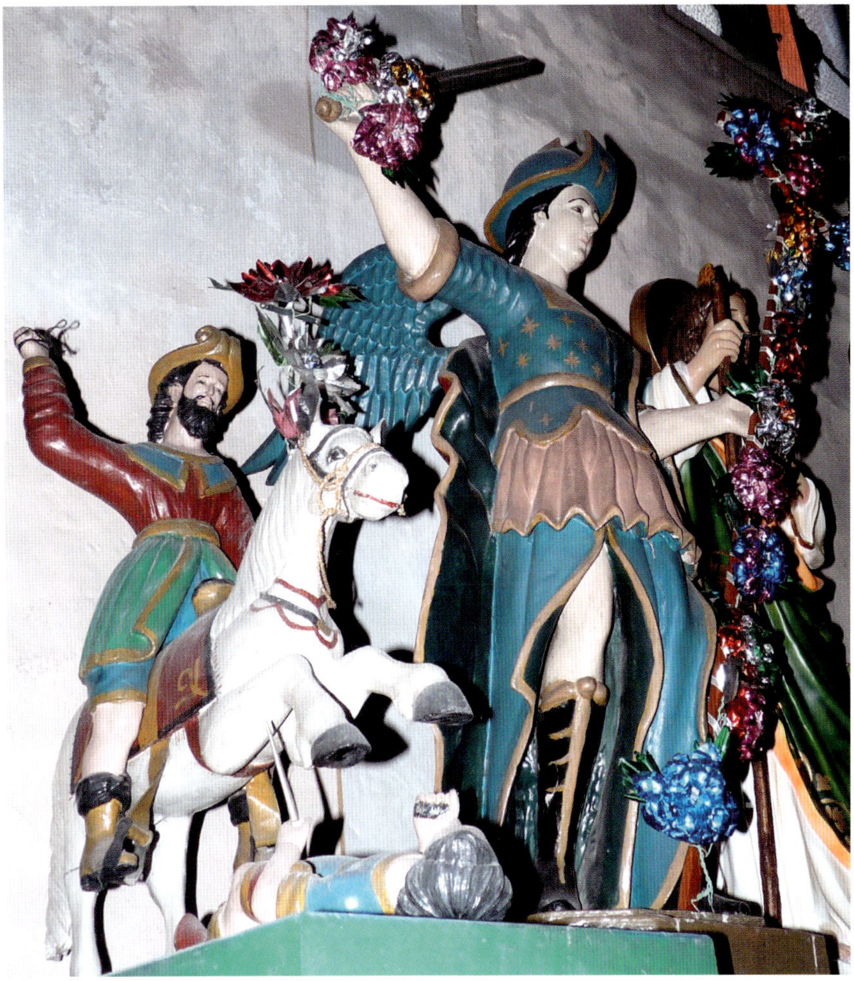

An image of San Miguel flanked by Santiago Apóstol and an angel in the chapel at Jonotla, Puebla.

Stresser-Péan reports that three archangels are important to these Indians: Miguel, Raphael, and Gabriel. San Miguel (Saint Michael) is described as "the leader of the heavenly militia in the eternal war against the demons" and he is perceived as the hidden commander of the Migueles or Miguelitos dancers, who subdue the devil in the dances to which they give their names. The other two archangels are not directly involved in the dances (Stresser-Péan 2009, 518).

Stresser-Péan lists many Christian saints who play their roles in the annual worship cycle of the Catholic church. Of these a few bear specific mention, because they appear to have taken on altered meanings in this region, beyond the usual European descriptions. Stresser-Péan notes that the choice of a patron saint by a village was sometimes based on the inhabitants' perception of similarity between that saint and some pre-conquest god who was particularly revered there, permitting one personage to be covertly folded into the other (Stresser-Péan 2009, 59).

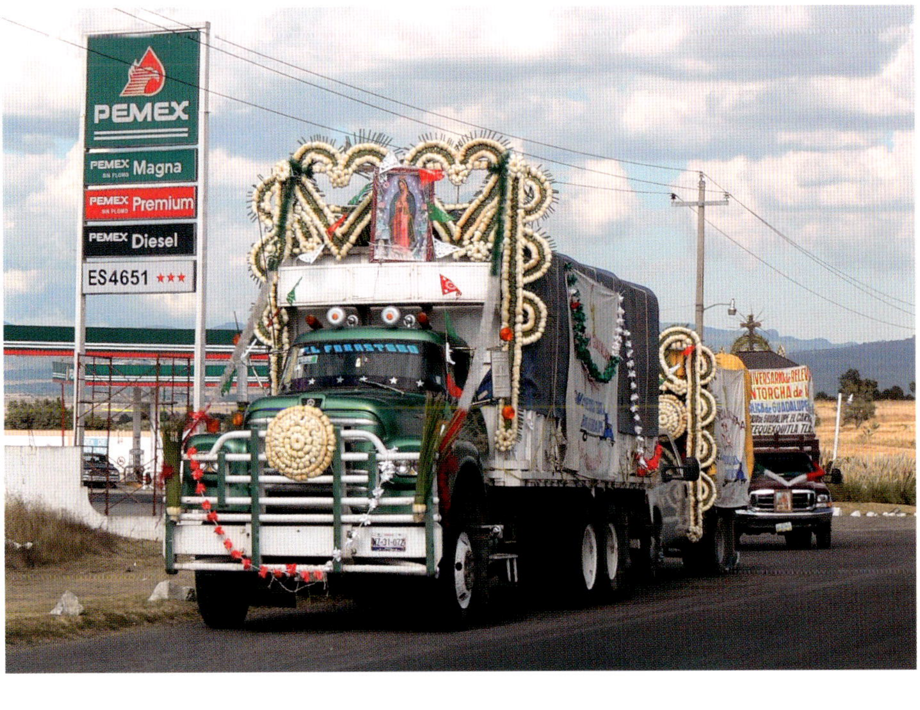

A truck carrying pilgrims to the Basilica of Guadalupe in Mexico City in December 2006.

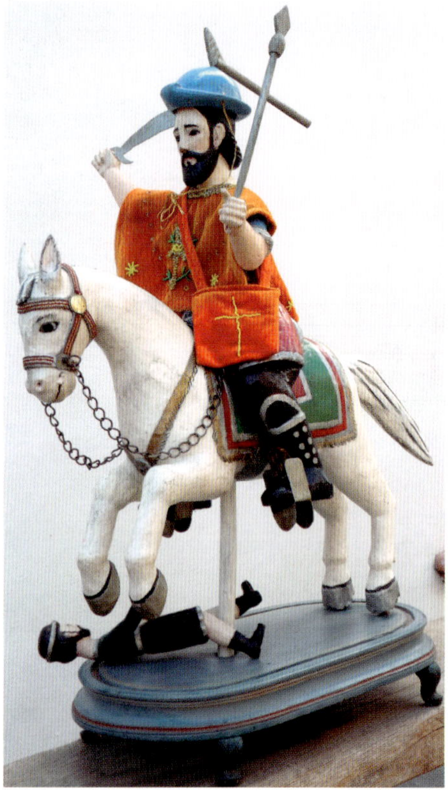

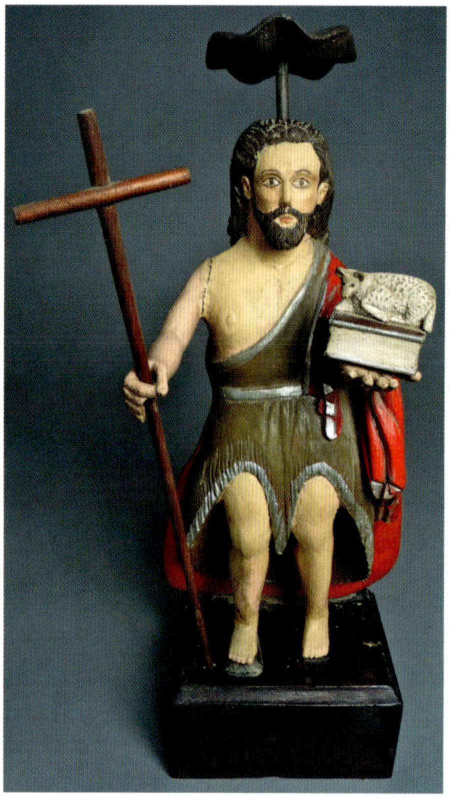

Far left: Santiago Apóstol (Saint James), from Puebla. *Collection of Vernon Kostohryz.*

Left: Carved santo of John the Baptist, by Roberto Villegas Santiago, c. 2006. Height is 16" including base and halo. *Collection of the author.*

Saint Francis of Assisi was widely regarded in the Middle Ages as the second Christ, due to his stigmata, and this idea has carried over to the Sierra Totonacs, "who often refer to the sun by the Christian name Francisco" (Ichon 1969, 39).

Saint James the Apostle (Señor Santiago Apóstol or Santiago Caballero) was perceived as the power behind the Spanish Christians in their defeat of the Moors. In a Totonac myth, Santiago lent his powerful horse to the God of Maíze, to accelerate his ascension to Heaven to take his place as the sun. (Stresser-Péan 2009, 520).

Saint John the Baptist, through his association with baptismal water, has become identified in the Indian view with the mythical "great Master of Water and Lightning" (Great Thunderbolt or Old Thunderbolt), a Nahua deity, whom the Totonacs refer to as Aktzini and who is believed to be confined to the bottom of the Eastern Sea (Stresser-Péan 2009, 520). It is further believed that the souls of those who drown must go to live with him (506). There is a Totonac myth that, due to jealousy, Great Thunderbolt attempts to prevent the sun from rising in the morning, since the sun's path must pass over the Eastern Sea, but the sun passes safely with the help of Venus, the morning star (527).

Then there are the devil and his demons. It is believed that Christ permits the devil "to control the night hours," but that God is invariably more powerful than the devil. In Náhuatl the devil is referred to by the name Tlacatecolotl (Owl Man), but for those Nahuas in Chicontepec, north of the Sierra, "Tlacatecolotl is a very complex, indigenous devil, patron of *Carnaval* and endowed with a dual nature in which good and evil coexist" (Stresser-Péan 2009, 521–522). So here, again, Satan, in his re-definition as Owl Man, has become a creature whose nature demonstrates duality. But to what prior god has he become attached to bring this about? According to Olivier, Tlacatecolotl is a name applied to Huitzilopochtli and Tezcatlipoca. It is becoming increasingly clear that Satan and Tezcatlipoca have merged, at least in the thinking of the Indians of this region.

Stresser-Péan recounts a common myth that the devil "created sugarcane and invented the manufacture of alcoholic spirits" to better enslave sinners. Furthermore, the devil "has in his service innumerable evildoers called *Judíos* (Jews), *Pilatos* (little Pilates), *Judas, Chichimecas, Mecos, Comanches,* and so forth" (Stresser-Péan 2009, 522). In Sahagún's account it was Tezcatlipoca who used the fermented juice of the agave plant to intoxicate Quetzalcoatl, and now Satan is described as the inventor of liquor made from sugar cane; we continue to see commonalties between Satan and Tezcatlipoca.

Stresser-Péan reports that when churches were built in the Indian communities in Mexico, the parishioners were eager for their churches to be equipped with bells. This was because of a European teaching that bells chase demons (245). The Santiagueros wear bells; one may wonder whether this is their purpose.

When the Spanish conquered Mexico they intermarried with Indians, and an ever-increasing population of Creoles and Mestizos followed, all Spanish speakers. Calling themselves the "people of reason" (*gente de razón*), as if superior to the Indians who remained, the Mestizos came to dominate the commerce of the rural towns, to the disadvantage of the indigenous population. Stresser-Péan comments that "The Indians, within the framework of their traditional religious beliefs, tended to think that their Spanish-speaking adversaries—both mestizo and Creole—owed at least part of their success to the fact that they were, at least to some degree, attached to the infernal but powerful world of the devil" (2009, 480–481). By now this sort of idea comes as no surprise; we have already learned about the earlier beliefs that Tezcatlipoca was the power who conferred wealth or who took it away.

The friars taught the Indians traditional Christian history and beliefs, but it is difficult to measure, 500 years later, the extent to which the religious orders themselves might have softened or modified these teachings in order to achieve wider acceptance.

Although the initial conversion of the Indians was carried out by the members of various religious orders from Spain or elsewhere in Europe, there was a tendency on the part of the church to move quickly towards lay leadership and teaching, due to very limited numbers of clergy. This policy created a remarkable opportunity for Indian Christians to remodel important Christian teachings to some extent, perhaps in a direction that permitted some earlier beliefs to more readily co-exist with those of Spanish Catholicism. That this occurred will be readily apparent in the description of *Todos Santos* and *Carnaval*, in the chapter about the dances. Furthermore, as religious teaching was based on memory and not on written texts, the lay teachers were unusually vulnerable to the risk that they might inadvertently or purposely distort their teachings based on individual values, beliefs, and invention (Stresser-Péan 2009, 61).

So we have reason to speculate that, despite the apparent wholesale conversion of the Sierra Indians to Christianity in colonial times, many earlier beliefs and powers lingered in the memories of the converts and may have been deliberately maintained, whether cloaked by or incorporated within the body of Christian beliefs.

In this context, Stresser-Péan (2009, 61) reports, "a Christian oral tradition began that was popular in origin and folklore-like in character. This explains the pious stories circulating today in which the lives of Christ, the Virgin, and Saint Joseph are sometimes strangely transformed." For example, "the current idea began to form that God our Lord went to heaven and became the sun."

In an article about the Danza de Los Negritos, by Rocío Aguilera Madero (*Entre los Hombres y las Deidades* 2005, 117–120), there is a particularly spectacular example of a myth like those described by Stresser-Péan. *"Se piensa que todas las danzas se formaron cuando Jesús iba a morir. A cada una de las danzas le dan un representante, así en la de los negritos "Pilato" representó a José, el "caporal" a San Miguel, la "Maringuilla" a la Virgen María y los demás como discípulos y arcángeles de Dios"* (120). [It is believed that all the dances were formed at the time when Jesus was about to die. To each one of the dances He gave a representative of himself, thus in the case of the Danza de los Negritos, Pilato represents San José, the "Caporal" corresponds to San Miguel, the "Maringuilla" to the Virgin Mary, and the rest are thought to represent disciples and archangels of God.]

Before the arrival of the Spanish, the propitiation of important powers involved human and animal sacrifice along with other rites. It was considered vital to honor the gods appropriately by such measures. In Sahagún's writings about Tezcatlipoca, the manual beheading of live quails was already customary in feasts dedicated to that god and to many other gods as well. When the Spanish condemned the practice of human sacrifice, animal sacrifice continued or expanded.

Stresser-Péan reports that more generally, by 1530,

> Most of the Indians of Central Mexico changed the superficial appearance of some of their former practices, condemned by the missionaries as demonic. Many ceased to keep idols of their ancient gods in their homes. Henceforth, followers of the old religion kept their activities secret or dissimulated to protect themselves. Anyone who practiced pagan rites after being baptized was considered to have relapsed and ran the risk of harsh punishment" (Stresser-Péan 2009, 21).

The Inquisition process was activated in the New World due to such cases, so the danger was well known and could be extreme.

In his book *The Devil in the New World: The Impact of Diabolism in New Spain*, Fernando Cervantes provided some additional perspective. He observed that European writers had a long history of speculation about the as yet undiscovered areas of the world and from these writings "Europeans had grown accustomed to expect the unusual and the fantastic to be the norm in the remote corners of the world" (Cervantes 1994, 6). Observations by visitors to the Americas were therefore immediately embroidered, either towards the ideal of the noble savage or to the other extreme, the assumption that all was corrupt and reflected the work of the devil himself. Cervantes would say that the latter view prevailed, with little evidence to support it, in the attitudes of the Spanish clergy (13).

So when the Franciscan priests arrived they preached that the Indians had been previously under the control of Satan, but now they could elect the religion of the Spaniards, who presented themselves as "the children of the Sun" (Cervantes 1994, 13). How powerfully this must have resonated with the Indians, given the central focus on the sun as God that was already in place. There was "a growing conviction among the missionaries that satanic intervention was at the heart of Indian cultures." This perspective provided a lens through which every aspect of traditional Indian beliefs was to be challenged or considered suspect.

The ceremonial use of masks, costumes, dance, and drama was well established in these indigenous religions, such that the Spanish insisted on the destruction of a great body of ceremonial masks, costumes, and religious documents, and only a few of these documents and objects survive to the present day. Cervantes includes a drawing of the burning of idols (1994, 15, Plate 5).

In public fiestas, the worship of old gods could be incorporated in disguised forms. This danger was explicitly recognized in colonial times and certain of the friars, most notably Ruiz de Alarcon, de la Serna, and Durán, made great efforts to detect and manage this (Stresser-Péan 2009, 30; Durán 1971, 20–21).

Stresser-Péan (2009, 375-408) had an intense interest in the possibility that ancient customs and practices might have survived into the 20th century, so this was a major focus of his research. He discovered that there had been uncommon Totonac and Nahua communities in Puebla that continued to use the ancient calendar system as an instrument for divination and planning. He learned that there were tradition keepers in these villages, men who had spent their lives learning and then passing on ancient teachings. That is, the belief that the day sign of one's birth determined one's fate had apparently been maintained.

Following a civil war called the Mexican Revolution (c. 1910–1920), there was a phase of religious repression during which many routine Catholic practices were condemned by the government, even baptism and marriage within the church. These rural, traditional societies were literally turned upside down for a period of years!

There then developed what Stresser-Péan calls a crisis, when these indigenous sages or learned men and their ideas had abruptly lost their former prestige during the second quarter of the twentieth century (2009, 351–361). Apparently the old belief systems were swept aside as these formerly isolated villagers were increasingly exposed to modern ideas, either because new roads were built or because travel to distant places became necessary to find work. Researching all this, decades later, Stresser-Péan had to search diligently to identify a few individuals who still could recall some of the knowledge that had been routinely maintained over so many centuries.

Chapter 3

Dance Complexity in Mexico

The published descriptions of the dances in the Sierra de Puebla often seem contradictory and confusing. Fortunately such mysteries have inspired other writers to develop theories and explanations that might prove helpful for an understanding of the dances of this area.

James Scott, in his book *Domination and the Arts of Resistance: Hidden Transcripts* (1990), provides a very helpful perspective. In his study of a Malay village, he had encountered contradictory reports. He discovered "that the poor sang one tune when they were in the presence of the rich and another tune when they were among the poor. The rich too spoke one way to the poor and another among themselves" (ix). The result was that an informant would provide at least two versions of some statement of fact or belief, based on the political or social context; this variation was common in many situations where there was a disparity in power between two groups. Scott developed a lengthy and comprehensive analysis of the uneasy relationships between the powerful and the less powerful members of any society, considering colonial settings as well as the workplace, slavery, and hierarchies based on caste. He notes that the interactions between members of dominant and subordinate groups "are forms of personal rule providing great latitude for arbitrary and capricious behavior by the superior. An element of personal terror invariably infuses these relations—a terror that may take the form of arbitrary beatings, sexual brutality, insults, and public humiliations" (ix–xi). Scott does not claim that the members of various subjugated groups are all the same in some way. Rather, he believes that "to the degree that structures of domination can be demonstrated to operate in comparable ways, they will, other things equal, elicit reactions and patterns of resistance that are also broadly comparable" (xi).

It is Scott's hypothesis that "Every subordinate group creates, out of its ordeal, 'a hidden transcript' that represents a critique of power spoken behind the back of the dominant" (1990, xii). This is something that can be studied, because "the hidden transcript is typically expressed openly—albeit in disguised form. I suggest, along these lines, how we might interpret the rumors, gossip, folktales, songs, gestures, jokes, and theatre of the powerless as vehicles by which, among other things, they insinuate a critique of power while hiding behind anonymity or behind innocuous understandings of their conduct" (xii–xiii).

Scott recognizes that the imbalance of power between members of a ruling class and their subjects can be extreme. To "speak truth to power" can be dangerous, while keeping silent may be humiliating or stifling. Scott sets out to study, in a generic way, the history of how the subjugated peoples in such situations might have managed their humiliating experiences by resisting in any way that seemed safe, such as by maintaining covert group discussions of their felt injustices (1990, 1–16).

Scott elaborated on the idea that those in power might also have their own hidden transcripts. The public transcript is unlikely to reflect the full belief set of those in charge, Scott tells us; rather, it probably represents an idealized statement of the ruling perspective, laundered of less seemly aspects. He notes that this is in itself advantageous for the oppressed because, when it suits their purposes, they can humbly appeal to the rulers to behave according to those rulers' published values (1990, 18).

One purpose of a hidden transcript, says Scott, is "to call down a curse on the heads of their aggressors... The curse is an open prayer—even if confined to the backstage audience—embodying an intricate and lovingly ornate vision of revenge. From the perspective of magic, the curse, if properly prepared and recited, will bring about the wish it expresses" (1990, 42–43).

What Scott does not say, but something that I have come to suspect, is that dances like those of the Sierra de Puebla may sometimes represent nonverbal curses or prayers, expressed in plot action rather than in words, to pantomime the desired intervention by God or by indigenous powers. Such requests might involve the gifts of sun and rain or the correction of past injustices and the punishment of the wicked. We will have further cause to speculate in this way as we examine the dances in Chapter 4.

Scott (1990, 58–60) notes that a parade or ceremony will ordinarily have a public transcript involving a purpose or message that leads those in authority to initiate or to permit the event. Perhaps the performance is promoted simply to reinforce the power of the authorities. Scott later discusses a special case, that of Carnival (or Mardi Gras): "As the occasion for rituals of reversal, satire, parody, and a general suspension of social constraints, carnival offers a unique analytical vantage point from which to dissect social order... we can assess it as an institutionalized form of political disguise... there are scores of festivals, fairs, and ritual occasions that share many of the essential features of carnival itself." He elaborates, "For our purposes, what is most interesting about carnival is the way it allows certain things to be said, certain forms of social power to be exercised that are muted or suppressed outside this ritual sphere... carnival is the 'people's informal courtroom' in which biting songs and scolding verse can be sung directly to the disrespected and malefactors" (172–173). Scott tells us that "One of the first pieces of legislation passed during the Spanish Civil War by General Francisco Franco's government was an act outlawing carnival" (179).

When public performances include actors from the oppressed group, then this situation permits the overt or covert expression of ideas from a hidden transcript, empowering the underclass to mock their oppressors or to symbolically portray a reversal of their oppression. The hidden transcript is meant to be enjoyed by observers or players who are in on the secret. Although disguised, presented as a metaphor or as only a passing joke, the hidden transcript is offered in full view, so it can be detected by an outsider through observation for discrepancies, reversals, and the unexpected. If questioned by those in authority, however, it can be disavowed.

The issue of ownership of a fiesta or dance drama might also bear discussion. Although an event might have been introduced by some civil or religious leader to serve a particular purpose, the survival of this ceremony might have resulted from the popularity of an embedded hidden transcript, so that the performance is maintained by the less powerful for their own purposes. In Mexico, the Spanish no longer rule, the Roman church's power has been diluted, yet the populace carries on the old dances in rural Indian settings, either due to their agreement with the public transcript (for example, to honor Jesus and the saints), or due to their pleasure in some part of a hidden transcript, or perhaps due to some combination of the two.

As if this is not complicated enough, there is another potential level to be considered, the conscious or unconscious collusion of some segment of the ruling class with the oppressed. More specifically, it is possible that the clergy, in their work to convert the Indians to Christianity, may have provided the Indians with theatrical themes or practices that were sympathetic to their plight. When a hidden transcript is encountered, the possibility that the priests may have made a major contribution, based on their own idealistic beliefs, should be considered.

Here is an example to demonstrate the application of these ideas. Frances Gillmor (1983) visited various villages in the state of Jalisco, Mexico, during the 1930s. There she observed La Danza de los Tastoanes. Although this particular dance is not performed in the Sierra de Puebla as such, its study provides us with a palpable example of a hidden transcript, perhaps layers of hidden transcripts, in an unusually well-documented Mexican dance performance.

Tastoanes is apparently derived from *tlatoani*, a Náhuatl word that means "speaker." This was the title, Gillmor explains, for the Aztec rulers. The Tastoanes dancers wear dramatic masks that have exaggerated and distorted features; they may be decorated with snakes or scorpions. (In all this they resemble the masks of *Diablos* in other parts of Mexico.) The faces of the Tastoanes may or may not suggest that the characters in the drama are human, and, if unaware of the meaning of tastoanes, one would have no way of knowing that these characters were Indians. Gillmor comments that their faces remind her of the faces of gods in the Aztec codices (1983,106–109). This ambiguity or dissonance should already make us consider whether we are encountering blatant misdirection, possibly the mark of a hidden transcript.

Gillmor surveyed the use of masks in several villages. She reports that the masks from San Juan Ocotán are made of leather, with hair from horses' tails for the attached wigs. The neighboring village of Jocotán borrows the masks from San Juan Ocotán as the two villages dance on different days (Gillmor 1983, 107).

The dance has two distinct phases. In the first, the *farsa* (farce), the Tastoanes are described as Chichimecas, Indians from the north. Chichimecas, Mecas, or Mecos occur in various Mexican dances; they represent stock outsider figures or barbarians, who behave in a manner that would be unthinkable for more civilized people. The Mecas engage in combat with Santiago Caballero (an individual who depicts Saint James, riding a live horse), and after some fighting Santiago is pulled from his mount and apparently killed. In a comical pantomime, the Saint is skinned, castrated, and disemboweled by his opponents under the cover of a blanket; fruits are extracted from the site of the surgery to represent the victim's organs, all with great hilarity on the part of the Indian audience (Gillmor 1983, 106–107).

Then, with no apparent explanation, the Santiago actor rises to his feet for the second phase—the *juego* (game). Mounting his horse, the

A Tastoanes mask from San Juan Ocotán, Jalisco; 7" × 7" (mask), 36" overall. Note the very long wig made of horse tail and formed over a straw hat. The mask is made of heavy leather that is folded together and stitched with string at the base. Carved wooden features are attached with string. Each mask is decorwated by its owner, and there can be dragons, devils, or cartoon characters on the cheeks. In this case there are two representations of the Virgin Mary. This is, of course, unexpected on a mask of such an allegedly negative character. *Collection of the author.*

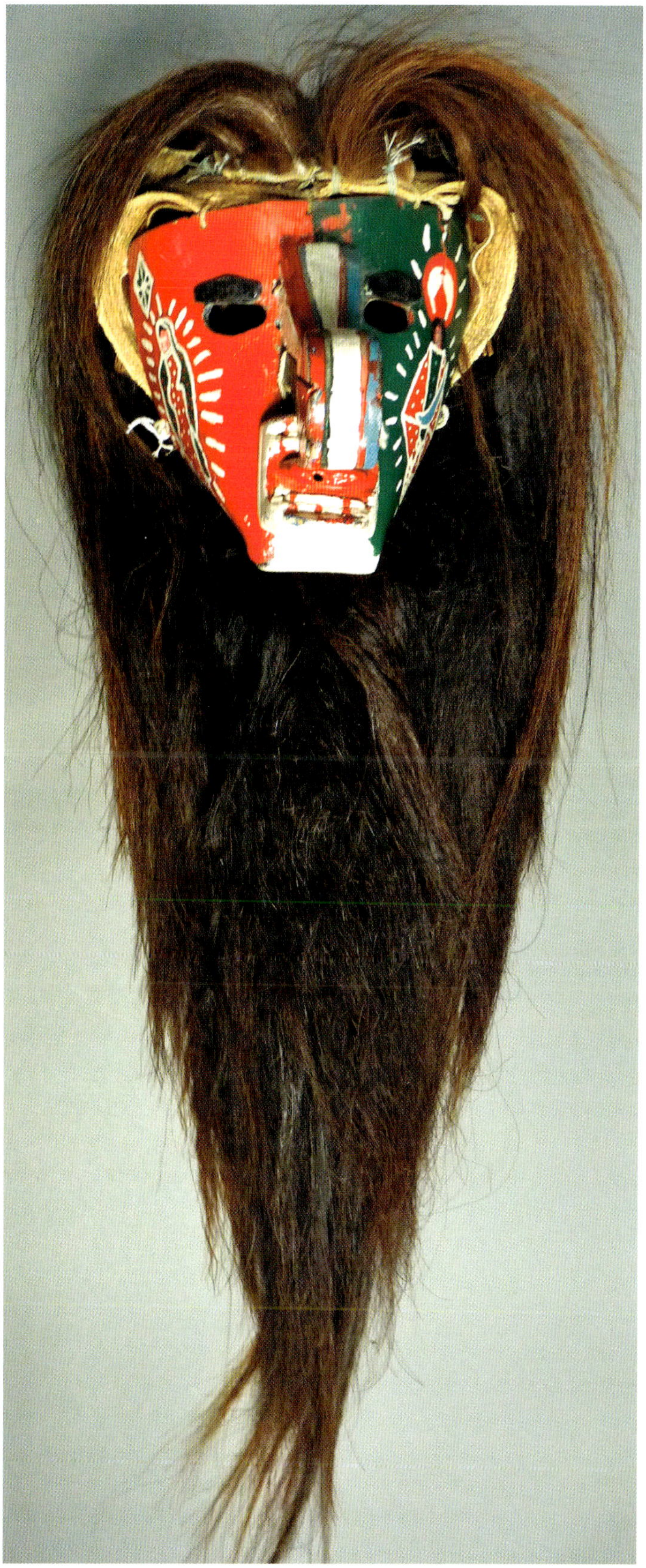

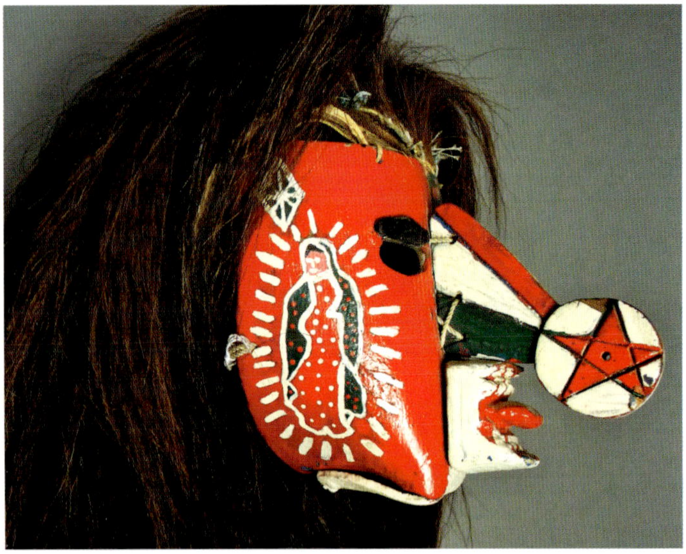

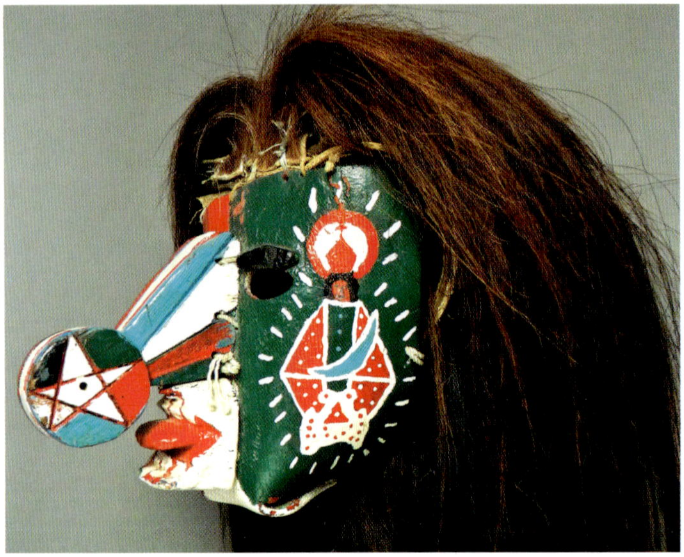

Top: On the right cheek there is an image of the Virgin of Guadalupe, surrounded by her characteristic rays of light. This view shows how the two sides of the leather mask overlap at the base, then the front flap also folds under the chin.

Bottom: On the left cheek there is the image of the Virgin of Zapopán (Cassidy 1958, 86–91). These side views show the wooden elements, the nose and the mouth, with great clarity.

actor resumes combat, defeats the Tastoanes (who are now described as various enemies of Christ), and converts them to Christianity. It is as if the farsa was indeed a passing joke, the meaning of which is negated by the action that follows. Gillmor was provided with the names of these second-phase Tastoanes: "Anás, Caifas, Herodes, Pilato, Satanás, Barrabas—names from Christian tradition and known easily to the Tastoanes from the New Testament" (1983, 107–108). According to that source, these were characters whose actions were collectively responsible for the crucifixion of Jesus. So in this phase, Santiago punishes or converts the killers of Christ, just as in the Santiagueros dance.

In the play, Santiago's identity is somewhat blurred. In one dance script reviewed by Gillmor, Santiago was described by a Tastoane actor as "Apostle, King of Spain and King of Nueva Galacia, Conqueror in battle, who has done us much harm" (1983, 106). This reminds us that Saint James is considered to be the reincarnation of James the apostle.

Between rounds of the dance, the Santiago figure behaved as if he were the Saint, visiting. He blessed the people of the town by laying his sword on a petitioner's shoulder. In this manner he engaged in healing of the sick and afflicted. So this was, in effect, a third phase of the drama and actually a direct extension of the outcome of the second phase (Gillmor 1983, 108).

Of this dance, Gillmor commented that the Aztec practice of flaying a sacrificial victim seemed to have been inserted into the dance drama, so that Santiago was ritually skinned. This would represent a remarkable reversal of the plot. In fact, when the dance director described for Gillmor the action of the Chichimecas/Tastoanes against Santiago, he used the words "sacrifice" and "crucify" (1983, 107–109).

In this example from Jalisco puzzling reversals and paradoxical developments are observed, which appear subversive but in the guise or context of a joke. The masks used in this farsa are allegedly caricatures of barbarians; it is they who are portrayed as killing and dissecting Santiago when he appears to be a stand-in for the King of Spain. However, my mask has two Virgins on its cheeks, suggesting another polarity entirely. The farsa phase of the dance literally carries the plot in the opposite direction from what was expected. Instead of the glorification of Santiago as the conqueror in battle who defeated the Moors, barbarians are glorified.

But if the skit about killing and dissecting the Saint is an obvious and amusing aberration, it may also serve to distract the observer from the more radical action that follows. This is the more significant insertion of a hidden transcript.

Another observer makes this clear. Olga Nájera-Ramírez (1997) has written about the Tastoanes of Jocotán, Jalisco, in *La Fiesta de los Tastoanes: Critical Encounters in Mexican Festival Performance*. She states her impression that this dance represents a hybrid adaptation of the Moors and Christians dance, one that permits the Indians or Mestizos to accept Santiago as a native healer, *while simultaneously* opposing him as a representative of the Spanish Conquest. Likewise, the Tastoanes are uncivilized barbarians *and* heroic defenders of their Náhuatl culture. Nájera-Ramírez concludes that "La Fiesta de los Tastoanes is both indigenous and Christian, allowing Jocoteños to accept the framework of Christianization and conquest, yet infuse this framework with subversive elements" (1997, 7–9).

Nájera-Ramírez includes an explanation of the Tastoanes dance by one of the principle dancers, who stated that God sent Santiago to Mexico to evangelize the Indians. Instead Santiago was drawn into violent behaviors. The people did not trust him, and so he was killed. God resurrected the Saint, but with the injunction that he was to avoid further bloodshed; instead he was to convert the people through the use of his supernatural powers for healing. This then occurred, so now Santiago is a revered healer among the Jocoteños (Nájera-Ramírez 1997, 92–93).

Santiago's resurrection leading into the second phase of the dance, then, is based on a powerful but largely inapparent reframing of Santiago and his mission. However, because the overall action involves Santiago's conquest of the "Moors" or Tastoanes after all, the observer would hardly be aware that such a radical hidden transcript has been embedded.

Although Nájera-Ramírez describes the dissonance within this performance as reflecting a hybrid form (1997, 7–9), one can see that these paradoxical combinations of ideas also reflect the insertion of a hidden transcript, in which the Indians and/or the priests had provided their own description of God and his purposes, and then they accept this God and his agent, Santiago Apóstol. This counterscript has become embedded in the performance, and the reframe has actually established Saint James in a positive and living role within this community, along with his dance. What may have once seemed subversive has become a profound truth known by all and celebrated in the dance.

Nájera-Ramírez also attempted to answer another question: Why do the townspeople continue to invest so much time and energy to continue this dance performance? She concluded that participation in this performance is at least partly meant to honor the Indian traditions of the Mestizo inhabitants of the town, who wish to retain a feeling of connection to their indigenous origins. They participate in order to maintain or to reclaim their identity as Indians (1997, 74–75).

Govers (2006) explored such issues for a Totonac community in the Sierra de Puebla—Nanacatlán, Puebla. This is relevant to us because not only is Nanacatlán located within our area of study, but also it was the home of several of the greatest mascareros from this region. These include Benito Juárez Figueroa, his father, and his paternal grandfather, along with Daniel Ramos Ramos and his father Felix Ramos. Govers provided some history about Felix Ramos which will be included in Chapter 6. She also describes the interaction of the inhabitants of Nanacatlán with the dances and fiestas in neighboring towns. Thus she illustrates how Nanacatlán had been part of a regional Totonac tradition of masks and related dances (225).

Govers offers much information about several of the questions that have been considered in this chapter. Two areas are of particular interest. The first concerns the link between the performance of traditional dances and the maintenance of identity. The second is her observation of a disconnection between the dances and their earlier levels of meaning, which seemed long forgotten. Thus an explanation for inconsistencies in the dance descriptions may be that they have become fragmentary and perhaps increasingly invented.

Govers reports that there had been a long and rich tradition of the usual dance performances in Nanacatlán. Some dances had been maintained and others abandoned by the time she began to study this village in 1989. In fact, the Voladores dance was first performed again that year after a long absence (Govers 2006, 219). Then, in the 1990s, most of the other abandoned dances were also revived. It had become increasingly necessary for residents of the town to migrate to Mexico City for part of the year, in order to find work. Some of these workers subsequently chose to build new lives there; other migrants wished to maintain their identity as residents of Nanacatlán, planting and harvesting crops in fields there and also visiting for special holidays. Some from the latter group became particularly interested in strengthening and expanding the holiday dance traditions of their home town; this involvement enabled them to more strongly experience themselves as part of a stable community, in contrast to the unstable and turbulent context of Mexico City (196–197, 232–233).

As noted above, one of the dances that were revived after an absence of many decades was the Voladores. A dance troupe from nearby Hueytlalpan visited to train the local flyers. Bernadino, the initial leader of the reconstituted Voladores dance group in Nanacatlán, had to relearn its meaning from a course he took from the Roman Catholic priests in Huehuetla (Govers 2006, 195).

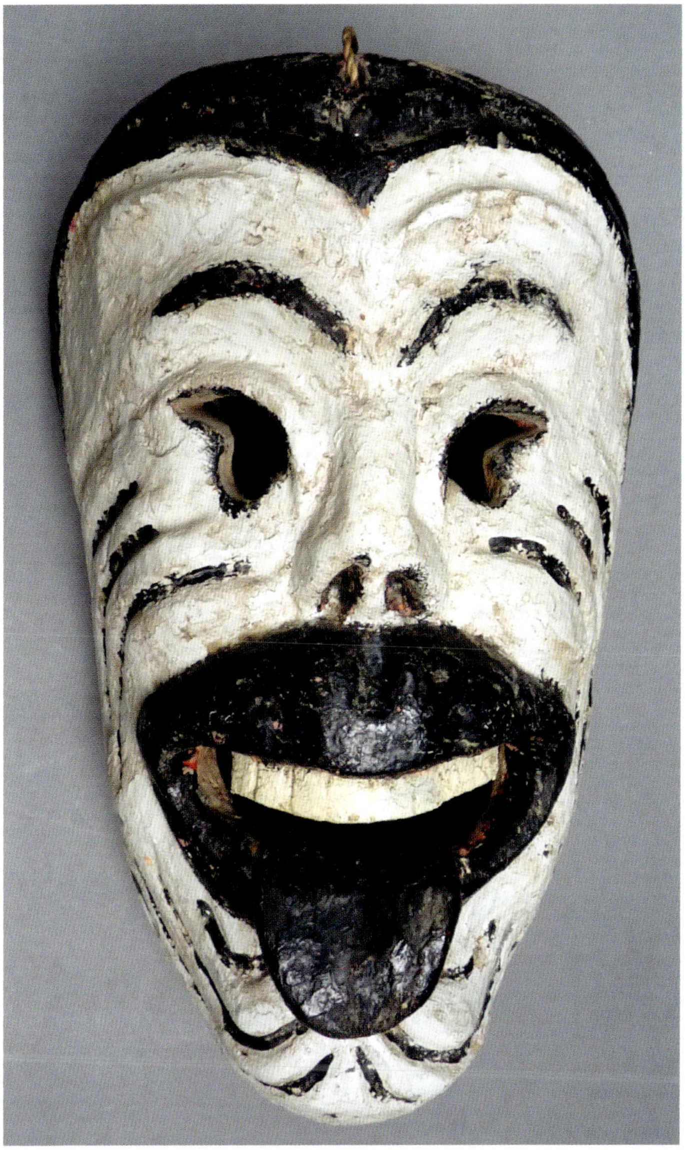

This is a mask worn by a Meco character in Calnali, Hidalgo; 7" × 11". It has deliberately distorted eyes. It is very dramatic in white, with black lips and tongue. One can see that it was previously painted pink with red lips. *Collection of the author.*

Govers was interested to note that the villagers seemed relatively less concerned about the meaning of a particular dance: "The meaning, recitations or dance passes are not what counts, but rather their spectacle and drama as an expression of local customs that need to be preserved and continued" (2006, 296).

In her remarkable paper, "Confronting Looking Glass Men: A Preliminary Examination of the Mask," Marjorie Halpin (1979, 41–61) postulated a generic mask type, characterized as "the negative of ourselves." She described Tsimshian Indian masked characters that seemed to personify the nether side of the society's idealized values. When a Tsimshian assumes such a masked role, she explained, he is essentially acknowledging the possibility that he might behave in a particular negative manner like the portrayed character. In this case, the characterizations seemed to portray the tension between one's natural inclinations and the rules of society, as if to serve moral teaching.

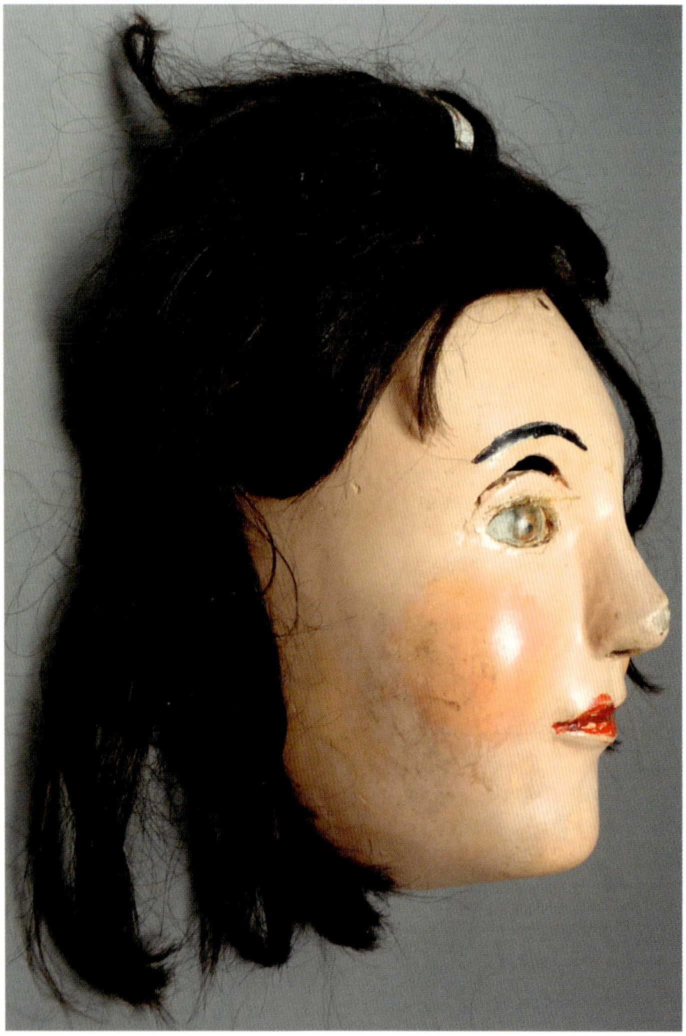

Little Mary, or *Maringuilla*, an example of a "beautiful" character from the Tarascan town of Nuevo San Juan Parangaricutiro, Michoacán; 6" × 7". *Collection of the author.*

Halpin wondered whether this type of mask might be used elsewhere, in this or some other way.

In my observation of mask use in Mexico, I have been impressed that Halpin's concept has often seemed very useful. But in contrast to the use of such a mask among the Tsimshian to portray the moral dilemma within a person, Mexican Indians appear to use such masks to project a negative identification onto an outsider for dramatic purpose. The outsider (or other) is described as having negative traits that the insider group members allegedly lack. For example, the Chichimeca/ Meco masks seem to clearly personify "the negative of ourselves," allowing the Jocoteños to disavow their involvement if they wished to attack the King of Spain through his representative, Santiago.

More generally, I have observed that Mexican masked characters very frequently represent outsider figures; it is rare for a masked figure to represent someone from the wearer's culture. Mexican Indians put on masks to portray Spaniards, Mestizos, Afro-Mestizos, Orientals, gods, death, devils, Mecos, and animals, but hardly ever themselves. This is of course very convenient, to cloak a hidden transcript within the alleged bad behavior of some outsider. There is a style of Meco mask, in Hidalgo, that underscores the outsider status of the Meco character by requiring the masks to have distorted eyes (Barbara Cleaver, personal communication, 1988).

In various publications, Janet Brody Esser has described her observation that, in the mountain towns of Michoacan, masked characters seem to represent polar extremes—the "beautiful" and the "ugly." By beautiful, she refers to noble, idealized figures that personify right behavior. In contrast, other figures act in an ugly fashion, through intoxication, promiscuity, lack of cleanliness, and chaotic behavior; they are literally called *feos* (uglies). The performance of dances that compare these contrasting styles is apparently meant to teach a moral lesson to the young. (Esser 1978, Vol.1, 10, 71)

The beautiful/ugly dichotomy suggested by Esser's observations has proven to be another very valuable tool for me in my understanding of masks from all over Mexico. I have noticed that there are virtually no masks that represent the common man as a neutral figure; a dance character is either noble or badly behaved. Occasionally one does encounter a character that teeters between these two poles. For example, Bartolo, the foolish shepherd in the Shepherds play, is tempted by the devil to give up his journey to see the newborn Jesus, but a friar preaches to him and he comes to his senses, rejecting Lucifer by the play's end (Rael 1965).

Combining some of the insights derived from the writings discussed here, it is evident that the assignment of otherness to a character is a common feature in Mexican masking, and this can have various purposes. From the discussion of the Tastoanes dance we observed that one purpose might be to present a forbidden idea or action while disclaiming any direct ownership of this; it is the Chichimecas who are the enemies of the King of Spain. Another related purpose seemed to be that of providing misdirection, in the manner of a stage magician, to divert attention from some more significant subterfuge. Thus the joke about Santiago's death at the hands of the Chichimecas diverts us from his hidden redefinition. Halpin and Esser raise the use of polar opposites as also a tool for moral teaching. So we see that the use of such stereotypes appears to be widespread and probably over-determined.

A dance may present layers of meaning. There are contemporary reasons to maintain a dance, such as to build or maintain cohesion within the community. But underneath this level are hidden themes or beliefs, ideas that would have been forbidden by the civil or religious authorities when they were first introduced. There are portrayals that may represent prayers or curses, appealing to God for restoration of justice or for revenge. Over the centuries, although the social framework itself has changed, some of these alterations have remained a part of the dance, becoming embedded in the performance. The social and religious forces that might have prevented such portrayals in the past are no longer so powerful, so the presentation of these once radical themes can now be more openly acknowledged. Nevertheless, when these dances are described to outsiders, it is still customary to provide the simplest of descriptions. Is this merely through force of habit or tradition? Have new layers of subterfuge been introduced to make necessary still the language of misdirection? Or, perhaps, are the explanations so simple because the old meanings have been forgotten?

With this introduction in mind, we should be better prepared to understand some of the dances found in the Sierra de Puebla.

Chapter 4

The Dances

The dances of the Sierra Norte of Puebla and the coastal slope of Puebla and Veracruz can be placed into some major categories.

The first category includes dances that appear to be, in large part, survivors of indigenous performances dating from before the arrival of the Spanish. In particular, the Voladores dance seems to be a clear example of this type, along with two apparently closely related dances, those of the Quetzales and the Tejoneros.

Dance performances in the second major category reflect or have grown out of historic events, such as the Dance of the Moors and Christians, the Dance of the Santiagueros, and related combat dances.

A third category includes those dances that portray Christian teaching, such as the Shepherds play found in other areas of Mexico, or dances associated with Lent, the Crucifixion, and the Resurrection of Jesus.

A fourth major dance type is that of Carnaval (in English, carnival), or Mardi Gras, referring to dances held in the immediate pre-Lenten period. These may demonstrate a level of license that the Roman Catholic Church authorities ordinarily considered inappropriate for public performance at other times of the year. Because most dance performances in Mexico are related to Christian holidays, including Saint's days, the approval or disapproval of the Church was and is a relevant factor.

Dances in the fifth major category are somehow syncretic, combining pre-Hispanic and post-conquest themes. Just which dances fall into this category will prove to be a matter of opinion and observation; perhaps this is the predominant category. Furthermore, one may wonder whether these prior underlying ideas or meanings linger in the minds of the current dancers or their audience as part of the living theme of the dance.

The dances that interest us are those in our area of focus that actually or potentially involve the use of masks. That is, this is meant to be primarily a book about masks, puppets, and master carvers, and the discussion of related dances is specifically meant to enhance our understanding of the masks and puppets themselves. It is beyond the scope of this book to discuss the broader universe of dances that can be found in this area, apart from those with masks. Ironically, there is enough variation regarding the use of masks that I have included some dances that may or may not use masks, depending on local traditions, along with those that involve stable but limited mask use and others that use masks heavily.

The complexity of some of the dances is impressive, and the published descriptions often seemed confusing or contradictory. Hopefully the ideas and theories reviewed in the previous chapter will serve as tools for better understanding of this ambiguity.

This chapter is meant to provide information that seems necessary to understand these dances. The descriptions will demonstrate that their complex and contradictory nature probably reflects a layering of meanings, because the dances were apparently modified over time to reflect the changing cultural context. It now seems axiomatic that these dances would be complex and multi-layered, because that process of adaptation was undoubtedly a major factor in the survival of these customs.

Finally, a word about the naming of these dances. According to Stresser-Péan (2009, 281), writing about the Dance of the Scarlet Macaws, "In Mexico, dances do not have names in the Native languages; one speaks of them only as the dancers. Those that concern us are called *cuezali* in Náhuatl (plural, *cuezaline*, *cuezaltini*, or *cuecuezaltini*) and *lak'a* or *lak'a lukxni* in Totonac." Such names have led to Hispanicized forms; thus we will read of Quetzales dancers or of the Dance of the Quetzales. We will encounter other dances that refer to an occasion rather than to the dancer, such as the dances of Carnaval (Carnival or Mardi Gras). This tradition is the opposite of North American practice, where a dance has a name and then the dancer performs that dance—for example, the waltz, the polka, the square dance, and the twist.

La Danza de los Voladores

The *Voladores*, or flyers, is a famous example of a pre-Columbian dance spectacle that has continued down to the present time, seemingly because it was perceived by those in authority as a dramatic entertainment. Stresser-Péan (2009, 259) believes that the dance originated in Mexico by about 1200 AD and spread south to Guatemala, El Salvador, and Nicaragua, where it survives in some communities in what appears to be an early form.

Durán observed the Voladores during the 16th century (1971, 297): "They also used to dance around a tall flying pole. Dressed as birds and sometimes as monkeys, they flew down from it, letting themselves go with ropes which had been wrapped around the top of the pole." Of the performance of the one who remained on top, he wrote (313): "Nor is it less wondrous to see an Indian standing on the top of the 'flying pole' (for so they call it) anywhere between one hundred eighty and two hundred forty feet in height! … And after having performed a thousand turns and tricks, he descends with an expression as serene as if he had done nothing!"

The centerpiece of the Voladores dance is the *palo volador* (Volador pole), a tall pole or "tree," perhaps 80 feet high in modern times; at the top is a rotating wooden hub. The hub supports a suspended square frame, made from four poles that are lashed or bolted together at the corners; ropes from the corners rise to attach securely to the hub. So the frame rotates with the hub like a playground merry-go-round.

Stresser-Péan (2009, 265–266) notes that in modern times the Pemex™ oil company provided iron poles to many Mexican communities for the dance, and that these poles were significantly taller than those traditional ones of wood—35 meters high compared to 25 meters for those made of wood.

The Voladores begin by dancing on the ground, usually around the base of the tree. Sometimes one encounters a dance group that dances only on the ground, but yet they call themselves Voladores.

In the normal Voladores performance, dancing on the ground is an introductory phase, then four flyers climb to the top and sit on the arms of the frame; they can brace their feet against footrests that are attached to the pole. Four additional ropes have been attached to the pole and then wound around it together in a band; each flyer ties one

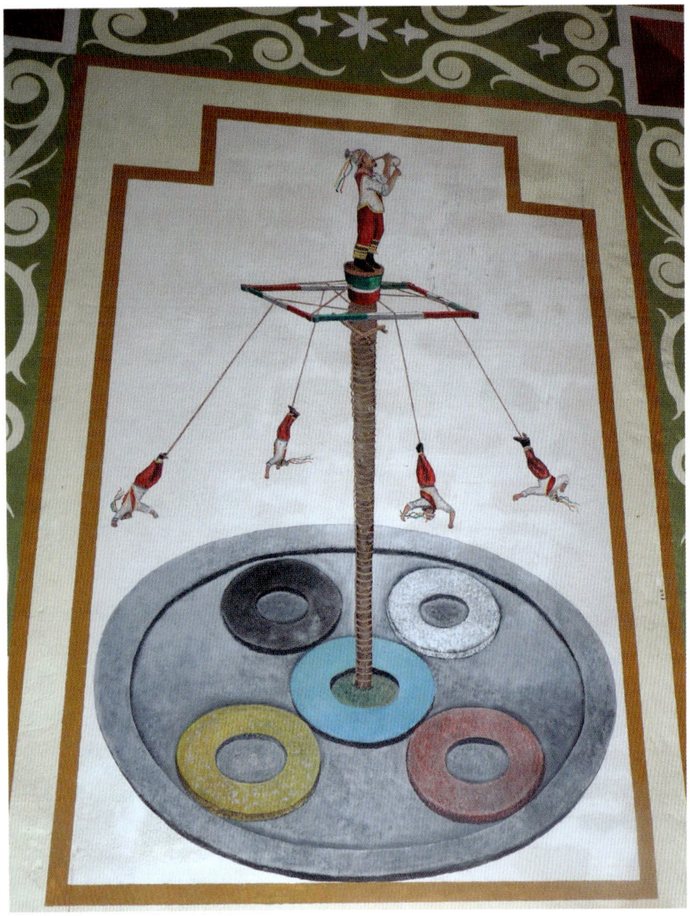

of the rope ends around his waist. A fifth flyer, the *Caporal* (captain or leader), then ascends to stand on the hub; the platform provided by the top surface of the hub is about 24" in diameter, and there he dances while playing a flute and a small drum. He salutes the four cardinal directions. He is not attached to any part of the wooden structure, and if he were to lose his balance, it is highly likely that he would fall to his death. In fact, such deaths have sometimes occurred over the years.

Then comes the descent of the flyers. The Caporal sits on the hub, tucks his feet under two of the corner ropes, and leans back, balancing. He continues to play the flute and drum. Each of the Voladores "kicks back," deliberately tumbling backwards from his seat. Their ropes, which had about 5 feet of slack before this action, tighten over the places where each had been sitting; then the pressure of the ropes on the seat timbers causes the hub and frame to rotate, unwinding the ropes. As the ropes unwind the flyers descend in a growing arc. They maintain a vertical position, heads down, by hooking one foot around the rope. As they near the earth, each flyer swings to an upright position and hits the ground running. The descent of the four together is ordinarily safely accomplished, but on occasion one of the ropes may break, so that the dancer falls and is killed. When I observed the Voladores in Huehuetla, Puebla, in 2006, I was told of such a death in that locale, just several years earlier.

The Caporal could climb back down the pole after the others have landed, and indeed this is often what one sees in modern performances. However, the traditional technique is for him to slide down two of the ropes, which are being held taut and parallel by those on the ground to form a rung-less ladder. The Caporal lies on his back, with the ropes under his shoulders and his feet pointing up towards the sky; his arms grip the ropes at his sides and he positions his feet to maintain each rope wrapped in a turn around its respective ankle and foot. This arrangement will ordinarily permit the Caporal to make a safe and controlled descent, by letting himself down, hand over hand, while the ankle loops provide what amount to brakes. This is the most alarming part of the performance.

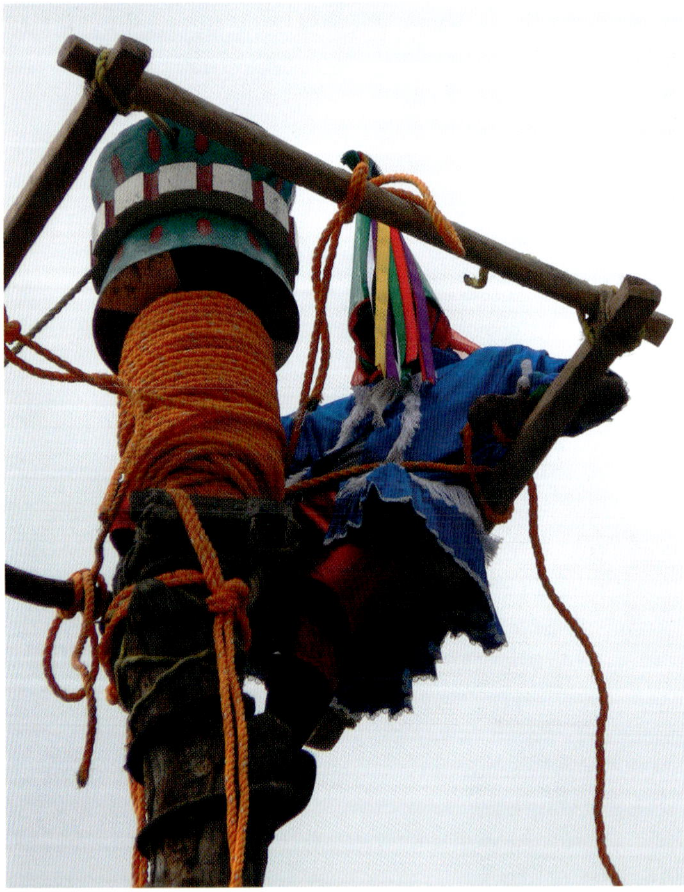

Above: A mural in the church at Olintla provides an excellent view of the construction of the Palo Volador pole and its use. We see the hub at the very top of the pole. Ropes from the hub support the four corners of the frame. Below the hub four ropes have been wound around the pole in a band together. There is a footrest just below those ropes. Vines lashed around the pole, from the ground up to the footrest, provide hand and foot holds so that the flyers can climb to the top. The mural compresses two phases of the Voladores performance into one view. In practice the Caporal dances on the top of the thimble; then he sits securely braced by the corner ropes and the flyers begin their descent.

Right: In Huehuetla, Puebla, a flyer has climbed up the pole. He is clambering onto one of the seats on the frame. We see the ropes that have been wound around the pole in the space between the footrest and the hub. Eventually the Volador will tie one of the loose rope ends around his waist.

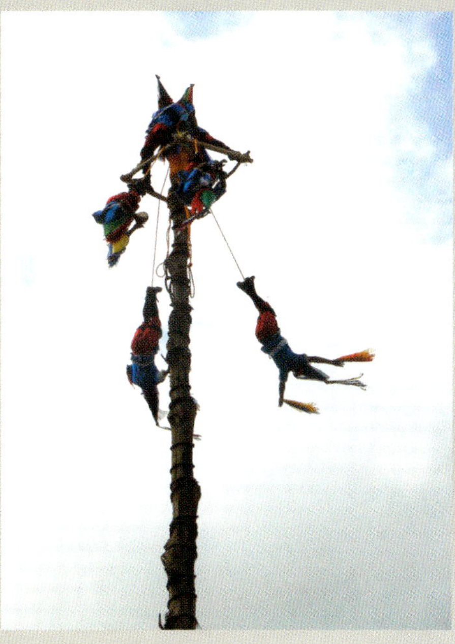

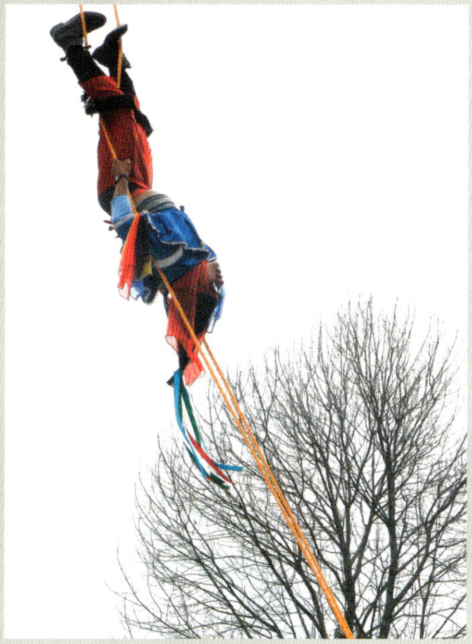

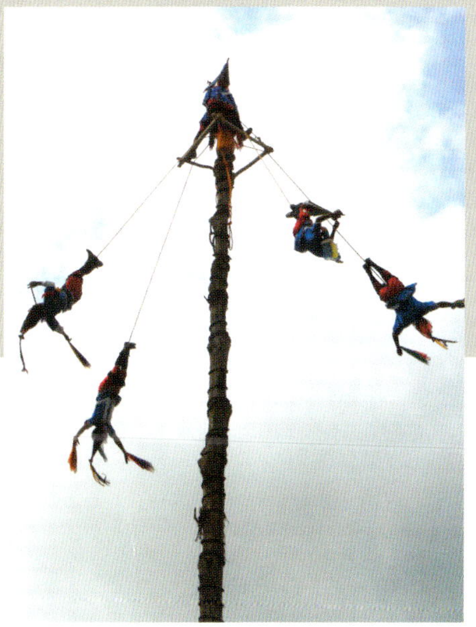

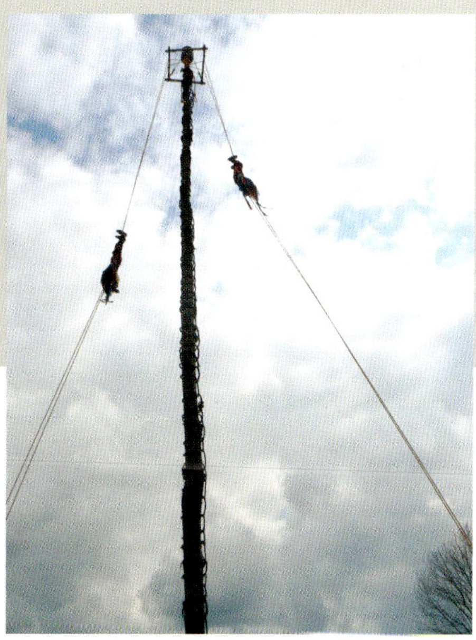

Top left: In this dramatic photo the Voladores have suddenly tumbled off their seats and their slack ropes have been drawn tight. The hub is just beginning to turn. The two remaining on top can be seen bracing, shoulder to shoulder against the sudden revolution of their seat, the hub.

Bottom left: A moment later the Voladores have settled into stable flying positions. One has begun playing his flute. This photo provides a good view of the somewhat tattered vines wrapped around the pole for climbing.

Top right: A close-up view of one of the Caporales descending. The ropes pass under his shoulders. Note how the dancer's feet are hooked around the ropes.

Bottom right: At Huehuetla in December 2006, both Caporales are descending at the same time.

Over the centuries, sometimes the Voladores have worn masks, for instance masks of eagles. In the state of Hidalgo, in the Huasteca, some Otomí dancers have revived this custom in recent years, apparently for commercial reasons, after a long period when the flyers in that area were unmasked (Stresser-Péan 2009, 273). Otomí flyers in the area of San Bartolo Tutotepec/ El Nante, Hidalgo, have worn Viejo masks, which are sometimes called *macho cabrillo* masks by collectors (274).

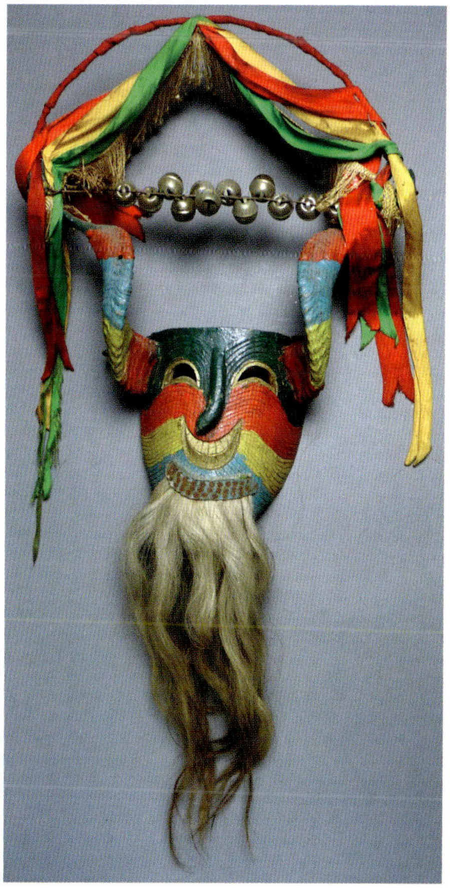

This is a *Macho Cabrillo* (billy goat) or Viejo mask, worn at Carnaval by Otomí Indians in Hidalgo; 12" × 15", plus 13" beard. Circa 1970. These masked dancers perform on the ground and as flyers. *Collection of the author.*

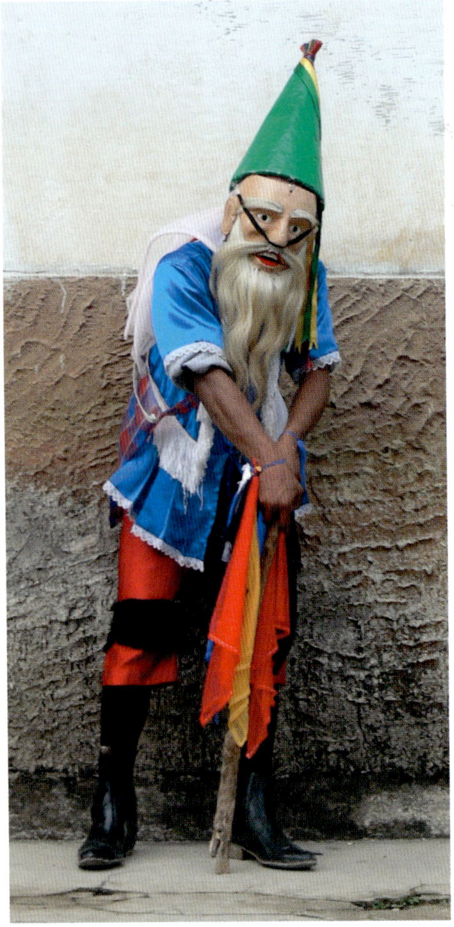

This Voladores character, who is called Pilatos or el Viejo, was photographed at Huehuetla, Puebla, in December 2006. Note that his costume is identical to that of the other Huehuetla Voladores.

In the Sierra de Puebla, those who ascend the pole don't usually wear masks, but it seems that there has sometimes been a masked Viejo figure on the ground as part of the Volador group. According to Aguilera Madero and Cano González (2005, 36), his name is Pilatos. I encountered one of these figures at Huehuetla, in December 2006. More recently Carlos Moreno Vásquez was told by the leader of the Voladores in Huehuetla that sometimes these masked Viejos do actually participate in the flying.

In December 2007, Vernon Kostohryz and Carlos Moreno Vásquez had observed a dance in a church in Zacapoaxtla, Puebla. The dancers identified themselves as Voladores but they had no pole. Two of the dancers wore jaguar masks, and they claimed that such masks had been used in the Voladores dance in pre-conquest times. We found this puzzling, but I purchased one of the masks and Vernon purchased the other. One of these is shown in Chapter 6, the work of Odilón Pérez Ciriaco.

In 2005, Vernon Kostohryz met Jesús ("Chucho") Arroyo Cerón, a retired Volador who was living in Zozocolco de Hidalgo, Veracruz. Chucho showed Vernon his collection of Tejonero masks, and he said that he wore these masks when he was a Volador who performed at El Tajin, near Papantla, Veracruz. Most of the masks had been modified with double vision slits, openings above and below the eyes to permit a wider field of vision during the more dangerous aspects of flying. Having been retired for 10 years, Chucho was willing to sell his masks to Vernon, although he expressed greater ambivalence about parting with his favorite mask, of the style worn by a Payaso in the Tejoneros dance.

On March 20, 2006, within a year of selling the masks, Chucho Arroyo abruptly resumed his old role as the Caporal of the Voladores de Zozocolco, at El Tajín, so he was the one who stayed on top while the others flew down. Then he attempted to descend on the ropes, but fell to his death.

Near the one-year anniversary of Chucho's death, the Voladores group from Zozocolco de Hidalgo performed at El Tajín to honor his memory. In this context a newspaper reporter interviewed some older Totonacs there who revealed a secret. They expressed the view that Chucho Arroyo's death was due to divine retribution, because Chucho had violated an ancient taboo. In 1972 Chucho had permitted his adolescent daughter, Isabel Arroyo Cepeda, to train and then participate as a Volador. Subsequently he also allowed his three sisters to become *Voladoras* (female flyers). Women had always been forbidden to participate; it seems likely that Chucho had introduced the use of masks to conceal the fact that he was permitting women to fly. At the time of the anniversary tribute, a twenty-year-old woman named Viviana Guerrero García was openly participating as a flyer with the Voladores de Zozocolco group, and the reporter was told that there were also female flyers in Cuetzalan, Puebla (http://www.jornada.unam.mx/2007/03/26/index.php?section=espectaculos&article=a18n1esp).

In *Mexico Magico*, a book of dance photographs that was printed in 1974, there is a photo of four Voladores sitting on the platform and ready to descend, while another stands on the center hub and plays the flute. One of the sitting flyers is wearing a Tejoneros mask; I like to think that this masked figure is Jesús Arroyo's daughter in her early days as a Volador. Unfortunately the location and participants are not documented in the book (Gutiérrez and Gutiérrez 1974, np).

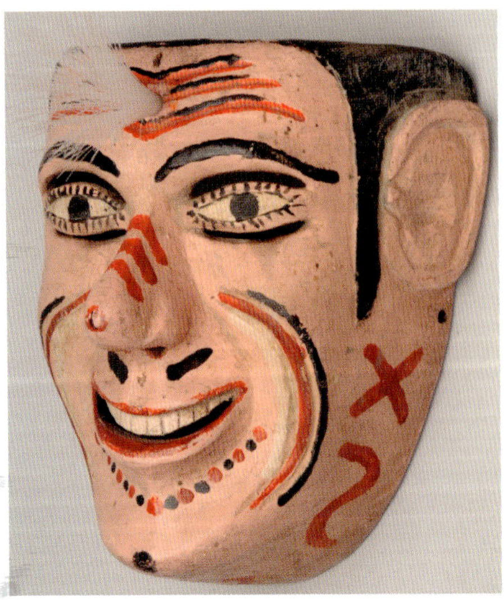

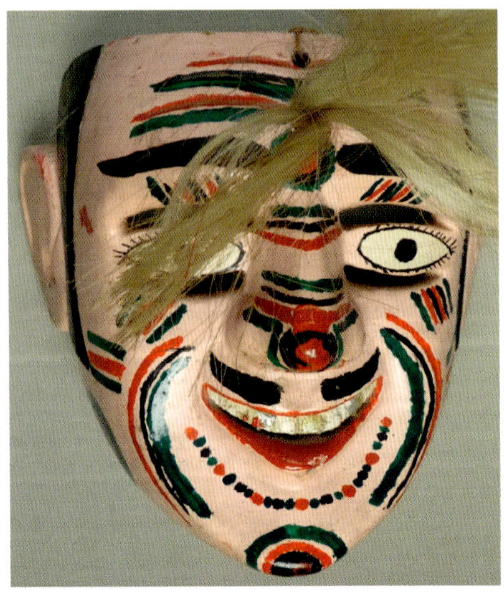

Right: This Payaso mask with double vision slits was obtained from Jesús "Chucho" Arroyo in 2005; 6¾" × 7½". Circa 1975. He stated that it had been his brother's mask, and that it had been used in the Voladores dance. The usual vision slits had been carved over the eyes and a second pair were cut underneath the eyes. Vernon Kostohryz and I have concluded that this mask was made as a copy of Chucho's favorite mask and that both were carved by Mateo Luna Vásquez, more commonly known as Luis de Luna. *Collection of the author.*

Far right: This was the favorite mask of Chucho Arroyo. Like the preceding one, this Payaso mask was carved by Luis de Luna; 7" × 7". Circa 1975. It is very thinly carved, and the face is quite expressive. This mask was famous in Zozocolco de Hidalgo, where it was thought of as a masterpiece, although for many years no one could recall who carved it. *Collection of Vernon Kostohryz.*

Recently Carlos Moreno Vásquez has discovered several masks from Xochitlán, Puebla, said to have been carved by Francisco de Aquino, that were used in the Voladores dance there. One of these was a *tigre* or jaguar mask that was reportedly 50 years old. A Santiaguero mask, with ears in one of the typical De Aquino designs, even has double vision slits, like those from Zozocolco. Both of these masks are shown in Chapter 6, with the work of Francisco de Aquino.

Many have speculated about the meaning of the Voladores dance. Bruce "Pacho" Lane (2002, 1–5) has written about his struggle to understand the complexity of what he had filmed in Huehuetla, Puebla, in the early 1970s, regarding the Voladores performance. Very few of the most helpful resources available to us had been published at that time, and he felt compelled to develop his own theories.

Lane discovered some Náhuatl poetry that had been collected by Sahagún, and which he read in Spanish (he does not name his reference). Several of these poems referred to *el arbol florido* (the flowering tree). In other unnamed references he learned that "there are five flowering trees—one for each direction, and one in the thirteenth heaven, from which Ometeotl and Omecihuatl (two god and two goddess), the dual male/female gods, rule the cosmos. Human beings are conceived as flowers on this tree and descend to earth to be born" (Lane 2002, 1).

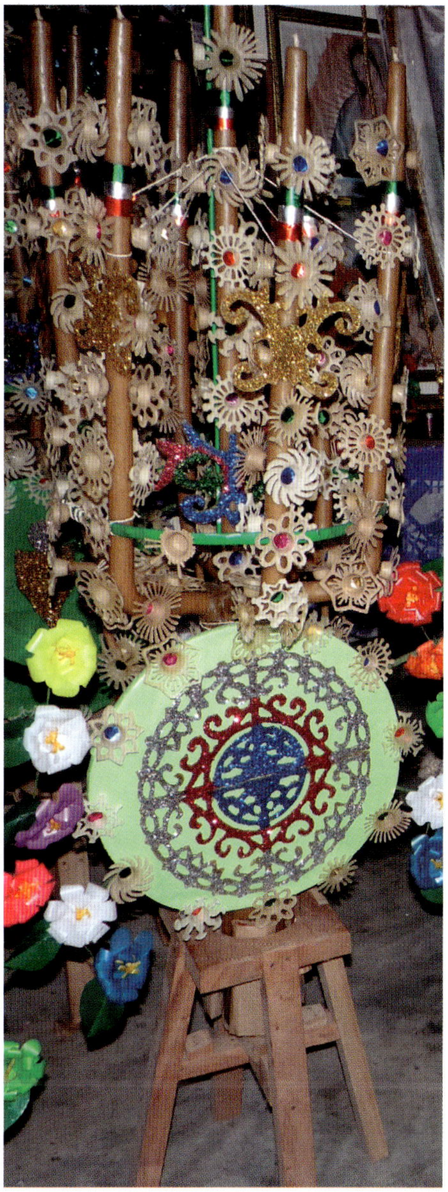
Seen in a chapel at Zozocolco de Hidalgo, Veracruz, these candelabras are very similar to those described and filmed by Lane. There is a taller central candle surrounded by six candles in a ring, rather than four.

During the making of his documentary *The Tree of Life* (Lane 2005), he had filmed the making of an elaborate candelabra, consisting of a central candle with four more candles around it. The candle in the center was taller than the rest, and all five candles were decorated with wax flowers. Lane wondered whether the candelabra used in Huehuetla was likely to represent the five flowering trees. If this was the case, then did the Volador tree symbolize the central flowering tree that was said to extend to the place where the gods lived (Lane 2002, 1–2)?

In his reading, Lane (2002, 1–2) had also discovered a legend that "Warriors who are sacrificed on the altar, or die in battle, are reborn to live in the Eastern tree, in the paradise of Tamoanchan. They are reborn as hawks and other predator birds…, and each day they follow the sun to the zenith, when they descend to receive the offerings and to bring the sun's blessings to earth in exchange." Lane wondered, Do the Voladores represent these "messenger birds of the sun"?

Lane (2002, 2) explored these ideas with his Volador informants. He was interested to learn that "They agreed they represented birds in the ritual, that the candelabras were trees, and that they used the same Spanish word for the wire pole on the candelabra as they did for the hub and frame on the Volador pole. They got very excited, and made a drawing of it."

Lane's film *The Tree of Life*, initially released in 1976, is now available on DVD (Lane, *The Tree of Life* 2005). It offers important views of the process of erecting the volador pole, the training of the young to participate, and the actual Voladores performance. But then there is more. The viewer can observe that the members of the Totonac community are heavily invested in this performance. For instance, when a tree is selected to be cut down for the volador pole, first there are prayers, and offerings of liquor are made to the spirit of the tree. Then 300 men cooperate to fell the tree and drag the trunk from the forest to the church plaza over stone roads. In front of the church, they work together to raise the pole to a stable position. It then shows how the Voladores performance is integrated into a community fiesta, which involves a procession of wooden saints, special handmade candles, and a number of related dances, all surrounded by a majestic landscape of mountains, trees, and sky.

Leyenaar (1988, 193) pointed out that, in pre-conquest times, it may have been traditional for the four voladores to each make 13 turns around the pole before landing, for a total of 52 cycles. This would have symbolized the 52-year-cycle of the native calendar.

Stresser-Péan (2009, 276) recalled one myth that underscores the sacred nature of the Voladores dance: "The first voladores accompanied and aided Christ-Sun on his first ascent into the heavens. Their mythical rising is symbolically represented every time the dancers of today go to the top of their pole."

In another myth (Stresser-Péan 2009, 278–279), a man had many sons, but only one of them was his natural son. That son stood apart from his brothers; he spent much of his time playing his flute. Actually this was a magic flute. At this young man's direction, his brothers erected a Volador pole, climbed to sit on the benches, and launched themselves into flight. "There were so many of them starting the flight that in the air they seemed to form 'a great flower' about to bloom." At that moment their brother began to play his flute, causing them to be "taken up to the heavens in the direction of the rising sun, with their cords and terminal block. They disappeared forever, for they had been changed into spirits of thunder and storms. The one who sent them to the clouds was the famous mythical hero called 9 Wind, Chicnaui Yeyecatl, who was able to command the spirits of thunder and is also the Master of Maíze." You may have recognized this story as being a variant of others that were reviewed in Chapter 2 about El Niño or the Spirit of Maíze.

One is impressed by certain related themes that have been evident in these writings about the Voladores. There is repeated reference to one special god, who is described as an amalgam of Christ, the Sun, and the Spirit of Maíze; the Volador pole is apparently one of his instruments. More specifically, the Volador pole is repeatedly described as a launching pad. By its height it rises to proximity with the layers of the sky where the gods live. From the vantage point of the top of the pole some mythic characters are transformed into rising spirits or related beings, such as those who accompanied Christ-Sun in order to assist his ascent into orbit. The more ordinary human Voladores are launched towards the earth; possibly they symbolize messengers from the gods.

Expanding on an idea introduced in Chapter 3, one could say that there are two kinds of prayers. Some prayers are based on words, such as those that were offered to Tezcatlipoca by the Nahua Indians (Sahagún 1981, Book 2, 37) during the five unlucky days at the end of the Nahua year. But other prayers are conveyed by symbolic action, as when the devotees of Tezcatlipoca placed dust from the ground into their mouths when they heard the voice of the human who portrayed that god. Such nonverbal prayers are more commonly called rituals. Rather than stating a feeling or desire in words, the supplicant demonstrates or mimics the content of the prayer. As another example, in Chapter 2 we reviewed the belief that an offering to the spirits has a soul that reflects the sincerity of the giver; the receiving spirit is said to eat the soul of the offering (Stresser-Péan 2009, 522).

Could the flight of the Voladores be an example of this symbolic type of prayer, in which the simulation of bird messengers bringing blessings to those on earth would represent a prayer for such blessings? All this is entirely beyond my expertise, yet I can't resist asking the question.

Lane's latest film about the Voladores, *Warriors of the Sun,* was released in late 2011. There, Salvador, the Caporal of the dance in Huehuetla, Puebla, testifies regarding the persistent sacred meaning of the dance to the Totonacs. It is indeed a prayer, addressed to God and Christ, for the blessing of the Totonace people. Like Lane's other films, this one provides vivid images of the dance, the people, and the beautiful region of the Totonacapán.

The Voladores dance seems to be part of a dance complex, one of a group of pre-Hispanic dances often performed together, and with some sharing of themes. The other dances in this group are the Dance of the Tejoneros and the Dance of the Quetzales. Both dances were also closely related to agriculture, although more contemporary meanings have been added onto the Dance of the Tejoneros.

The Dance of the Guaguas, Guacamayas, Quetzales, Quetzalines, or Scarlet Macaws

Illustrating the diversity that one encounters in this area, largely due to the physical isolation of one community from another, there are many local names for the same dancers, yet there are many shared aspects. The dancers can be called Quetzales, Quetzalines, Guacamayas, or Scarlet Macaws (Stresser-Péan 2009, 280–282). They can also be called Guaguas (Croda León 2005, 58–59). In general, it seems that these dancers are all named for some variety of parrot. To keep things simple I will standardize on Quetzales to refer to these dancers, as if all these names were interchangeable, when really they are not.

In this dance none of the Quetzales dancers are masked, but Stresser-Péan (2009, 283) reports that there can be one or more masked buffoons attached to the dance, whose purpose is to maintain order. He had read of such a buffoon who performed at Papantla, Veracruz, in 1938, and in 1986 he had observed two such characters in Yaonáhuac, Puebla.

The Quetzales dancers wear dramatic conical caps, surmounted by large colorful wheels of ribbon or paper, perhaps a yard in diameter. In Spanish this headdress is called either a *corona* (crown) or a *penacho* (crest); in Náhuatl it is called a *cuesalin* (red macaw feather) (Stresser-Péan 2009, 283). (In contrast, the Voladores usually wear small conical caps, with small fans on top.)

The Quetzales dance in two parallel lines that move forward and back; they loop around the outside or through the inside, demonstrating a generic form that one sees in dances throughout Mexico. From my observations, the model for such dances is the Matachines dance (Champe 1983), but I am not aware of any formal research that would tie together all the variations of this form.

A second phase of the dance might involve a "flying" device, although some dance groups perform only on the ground and lack this added feature. Like the Voladores, the Quetzales dancers are considered to be flyers, but instead of rotating in a spiral, the Quetzales may rotate vertically on something like a miniature Ferris wheel. According to García García (2005, 52–54) the present version is called a *cruceta* (cross), because it is composed of four arms of equal length in the shape of a cross, which rotate around an axis through the center of the intersecting arms. It can also be called a *molinete* (mill). A dancer stands clinging to each post, with the support of crossbars for the arms and legs. By shifting their bodies, the dancers induce the cross to rotate, so that each dancer tumbles forwards headfirst to an upside down position and then rises up again to the top. Sometimes these dancers are called somersaulters, due to the nature of this movement (Stresser-Péan, 2009, 282).

At the time of the conquest of Mexico, such dance structures were already in use, although there were then just two arms on one rotating timber (Stresser-Péan 2009, 286–289). The rotating mechanism is often installed on the top of a tall pair of poles, to underscore the symbolism of the movement. Stresser-Péan reports that "The dancers believe they are in the heavens, so the axis must rise as high as possible" (281, 284).

This dance also resembles the Voladores dance in terms of the music that accompanies the dance; several tunes are played on the flute along with a small drum, just as for the Voladores. However, Stresser-Péan (2009, 282) was told by a Nahua musician in Xicotepec that "the melody for the 'flight' (*son de la volada*) should be played with the flute alone because only the flute has true supernatural power." According to Salas García (2005, 56), one of the songs played for the Dance of the Guaguas is "la Guasanga." According to *Cassell's Spanish Dictionary* (1969), the meaning of *guasanga* in Mexico is "noisy mirth." If you have ever heard the raucous sound of parrots flying overhead, then you will probably agree that this would be an apt description of their song.

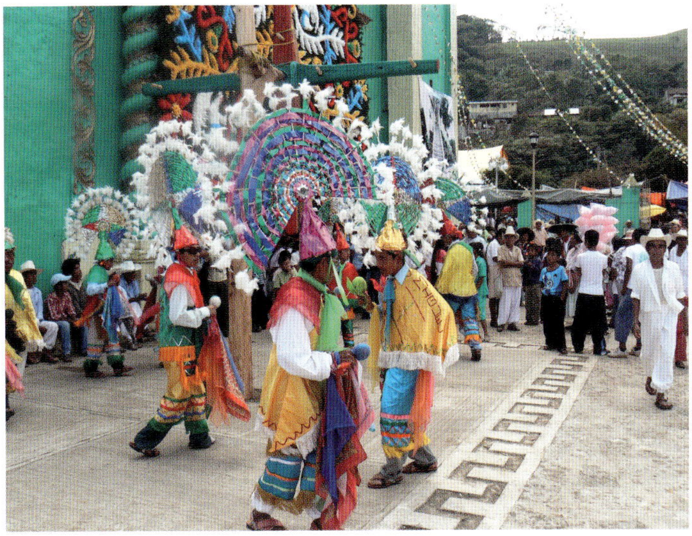

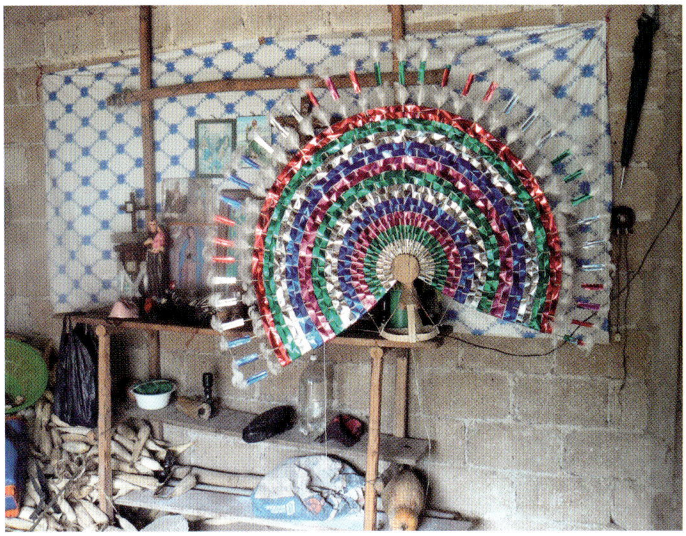

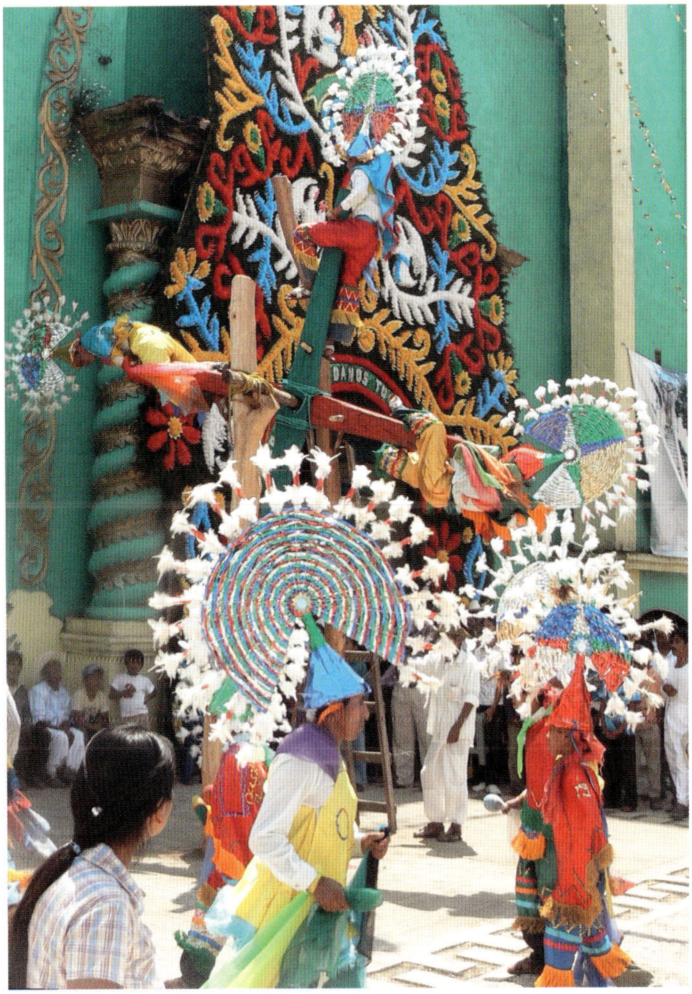

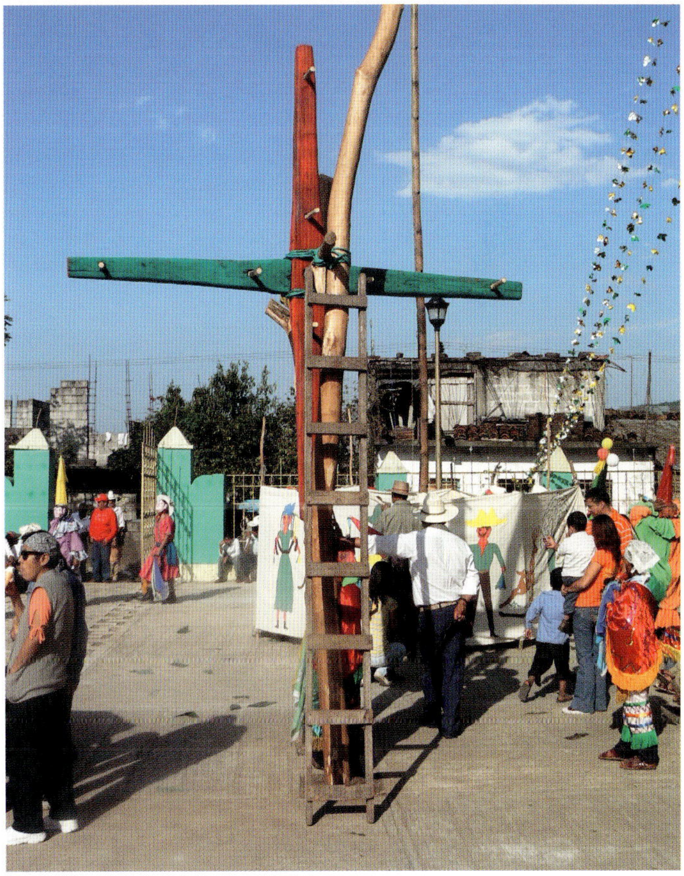

Top left: Quetzales Dancers in Olintla, in March 2010.

Bottom left: In this photo notice that the Quetzales dancers on the wheel are in different postures. The flyer who is descending has already extended his body; the ascending flyer will extend as he reaches the apex. Extending one's posture at the top and drawing in at the bottom provide the energy to accelerate the wheel. The process is something like that of pumping a swing on the playground, although the swing has a pendulum motion and the *cruceta* a rotary motion.

Top right: Quetzales headdress in Huahuaxtla, Puebla.

Bottom right: A view of the *cruceta* (cross) between dances. The dancers climb the ladder and mount the wheel at the top.

The meaning of this dance has been explored by various writers. Briefly, it is noted that, just as the Voladores rotation symbolizes the passage of years in the 52-year cycle, the Quetzales dancers' rotation symbolizes the rising, shining, and setting of the sun, and then its passage through the underworld, during its daily cycle. Furthermore, *"a medianoche se encuentra de cabeza en el mundo de los muertos"* [at midnight it encounters the leader of the world of the dead] (Croda León 2005, 58–59). Likewise the dancers are said to fly (in their rotation), just as the Voladores fly in their descent. The first Voladores were carried to heaven by a magic wind, and the Quetzales rotate as if flying towards heaven. Also, the dancers wear elaborate headdresses and colorful costumes to mimic the scarlet macaw or some similar bird, because legends suggest that these birds were the original owners of the cornfields, and farmers are able to raise corn because they honor these birds (Medina Jiménez 2005, 43–44). So it is readily apparent that there are overlapping themes with the Voladores dance.

Alberto Popoca (2005, 49) has something interesting to tell about the dance steps: *"Los danzantes bailan de norte a sur y de poniente a oriente, señalando la dirección de los puntos cardinales: avanzan en complicados pasos, dibujando con los pies el signo de la cruz, mientras hacen sonar sus sonajas."* [The dancers make it a point to dance from north to south and from west to east, signifying the four cardinal directions; as they dance, they form the sign of the cross with their feet, all the while sounding their rattles.] As Stresser-Péan had earlier explained (2009, 515), the cross itself is viewed as a symbol of the four cardinal directions, and the Indians regard the Rite of the Holy Cross "as a prayer for rain." I have seen dancers use this step (of inscribing the cross with their feet) in other parts of Mexico; possibly this was something that the priests encouraged them to do, without realizing this potential hidden meaning.

Despite considerable research on my part, and attendance at several different performances of the Quetzales dance, I have yet to see either an image of a payaso or an actual payaso associated with this dance. In retrospect, there was absolutely no mention of payasos associated with this dance in any other reference besides that of Stresser-Péan, including those about the Papantla area. Yaonáhuac, Puebla, currently has its own website, which features a description of the Quetzales dance, but there is no mention of payasos and no evidence of them in the accompanying dance photos. On the one hand, this illustrates once again the extreme diversity of this area, that the details of a dance performance are ultimately so local. Maybe there are still communities that do use masked payasos in the Quetzales dance, but they are uncommon. On the other hand, my failure to find these payasos reminds us of the cultural change process described so eloquently by Stresser-Péan, of elements dropping out that were prominent in the past in the context of rapid social change.

Don Lillo recalled (personal communication, March 2010) that there were formerly clowns in the Quetzales dance in El Espinal, Veracruz, but this practice has not been maintained; in his community there were never clowns for this dance.

It should be noted that although clowns may play uncomplicated roles as entertainers in North America, such figures are often more multi-dimensional in Mexican dance dramas (see Chapters 3 and 8).

The Dance of the Tejoneros, Green Woodpeckers, Chéncheres, Huehuetones, Huehues, or Matlachines

Like the Dance of the Quetzales, this is another dance that goes by many names, based on regional preferences. In the area of Puebla around Huehuetla and Cuetzalan it is called the Danza de los Huehues or occasionally Matlachines, while it is usually called the Tejoneros dance in Veracruz. Guy Stresser-Péan (2009, 291–294) has concluded that the original name was the Dance of the *Chéncheres* (Green Woodpeckers). As discussed later, it can be argued that the Huehues dance may be an even earlier form than the Chéncheres.

The dancers are referred to by their local names, generally Huehues in Puebla and Tejoneros in Veracruz. From my experience the masks, the puppets, and the dance vary little despite the differences in names.

To the casual observer, this appears to be a relatively simple and modern dance. Four, six, or some other number of couples dance in a square or circle. All the dancers are male, but they wear male and female masks and costumes. The masks are invariably of idealized Caucasian faces, handsome men and attractive women. All except, perhaps, one of the dancers wear Mestizo clothing. The one wearing traditional clothing is sometimes called El Cotón, which refers to a traditional hand-woven cotton poncho worn by men in the Sierra, according to Arizpe Schlosser and Kandt (1972, 109); apparently such a garment is a defining element of his costume. He may be the hunter, although in the absence of such a character one of the clowns will usually take that role.

Within or outside the dance circle, depending on local custom, there are two or more masked Payasos (clowns) whose apparent role is to amuse or divert the crowd if necessary. They wear tall conical hats of shiny paper over a split bamboo frame, and costumes that resemble those of circus clowns. The classic Huehue or Tejonero Payaso mask, which is male, differs from a male Huehue mask in two respects. The mouth of a Payaso is always open, showing either

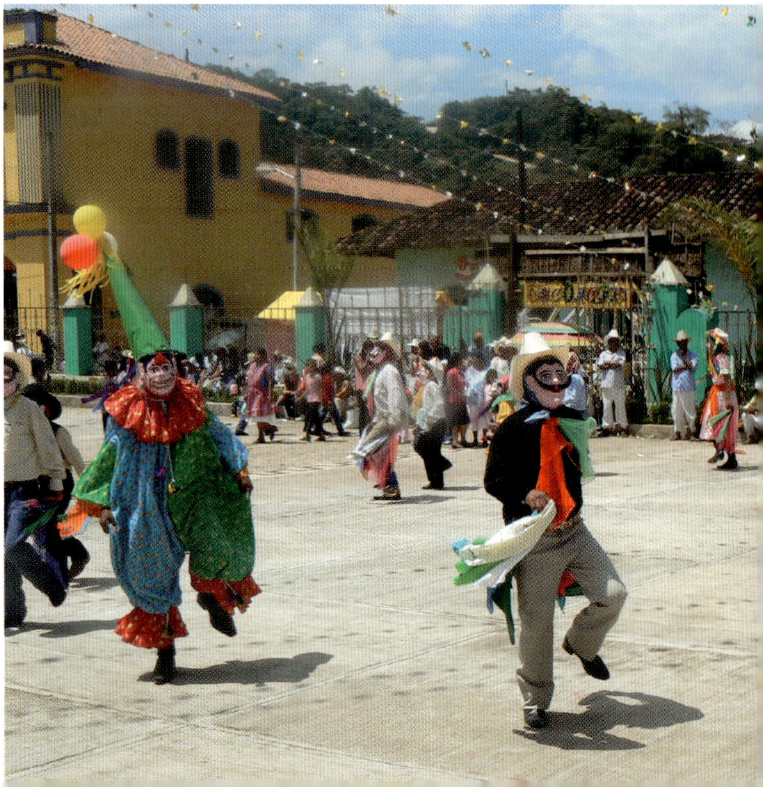

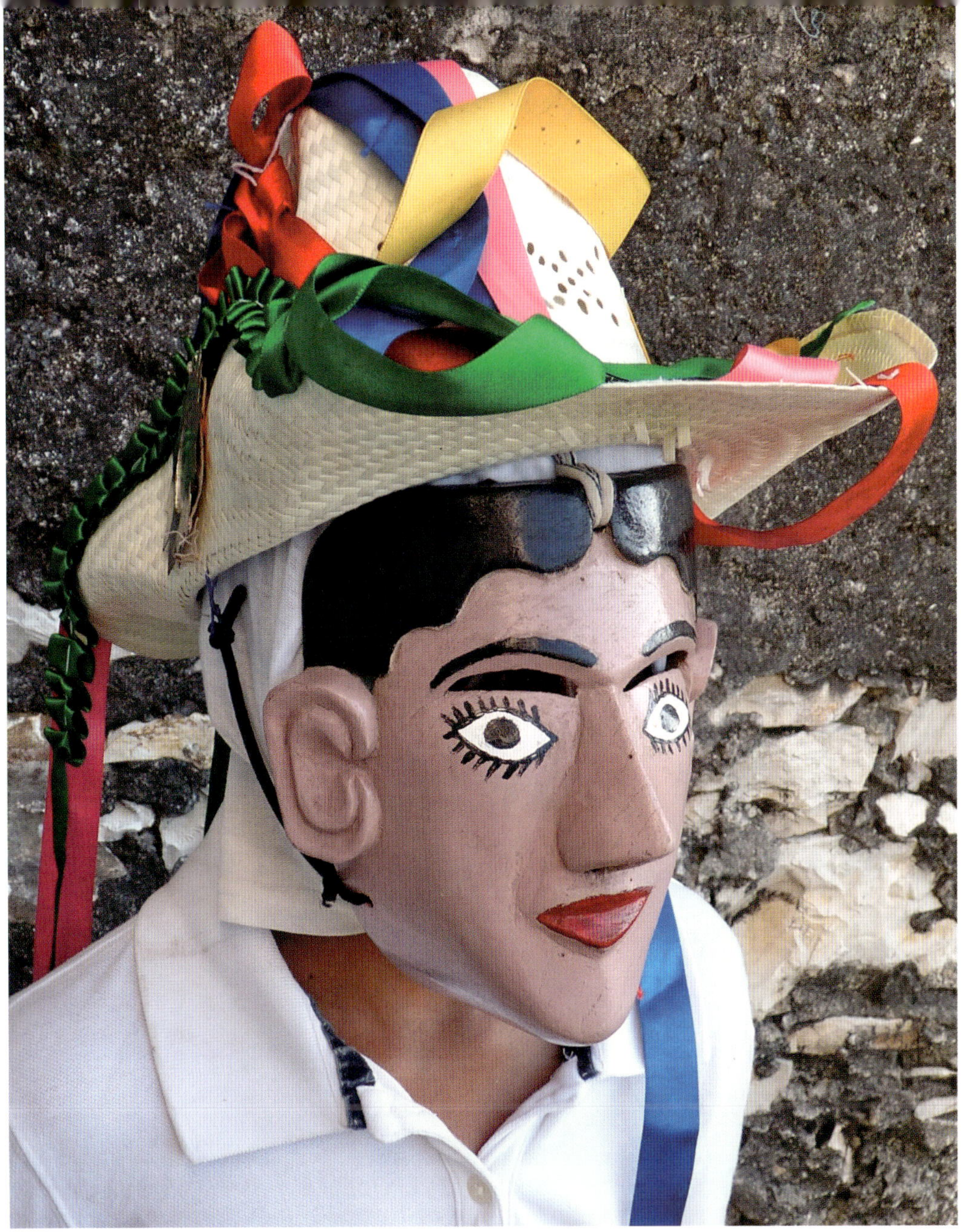

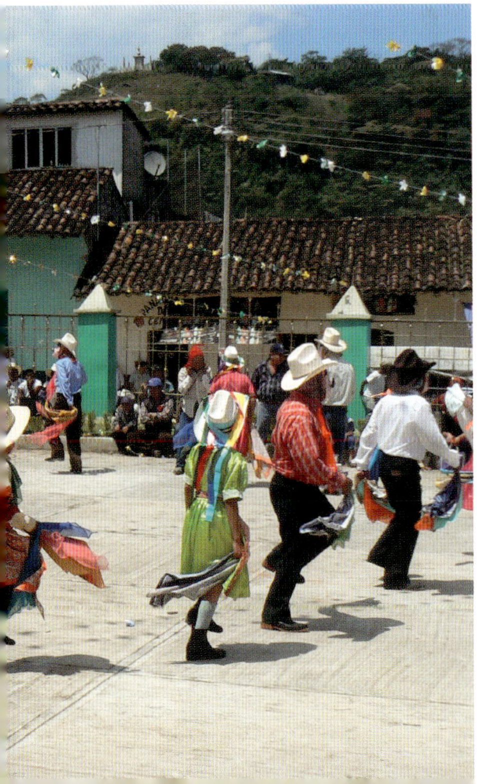

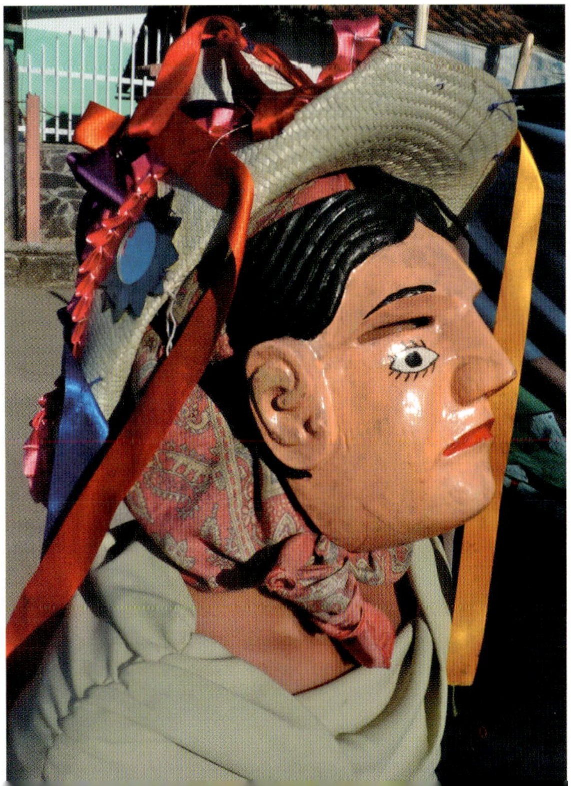

Bottom left: The Huehues are dancing in a large circle at Olintla, Puebla, in March 2010, including male and female Huehues, large and small, along with one Payaso. Note that every one of the dancers has his left foot in the air; they will all step to the beat in unison.

Above: A female Huehue at Xonalpú in December 2010.

Bottom right: Again at Xonalpú, an old female Huehue mask by Lorenzo Ciriaco García, whose nickname was El Kalimán. Note the remarkable ear design. Also notice the expression on the face of this mask, so somber. Vernon Kostohryz and I often see Huehue masks that appear to be modeled on the faces of the life-sized wooden Saints in the church. This mask has that appearance.

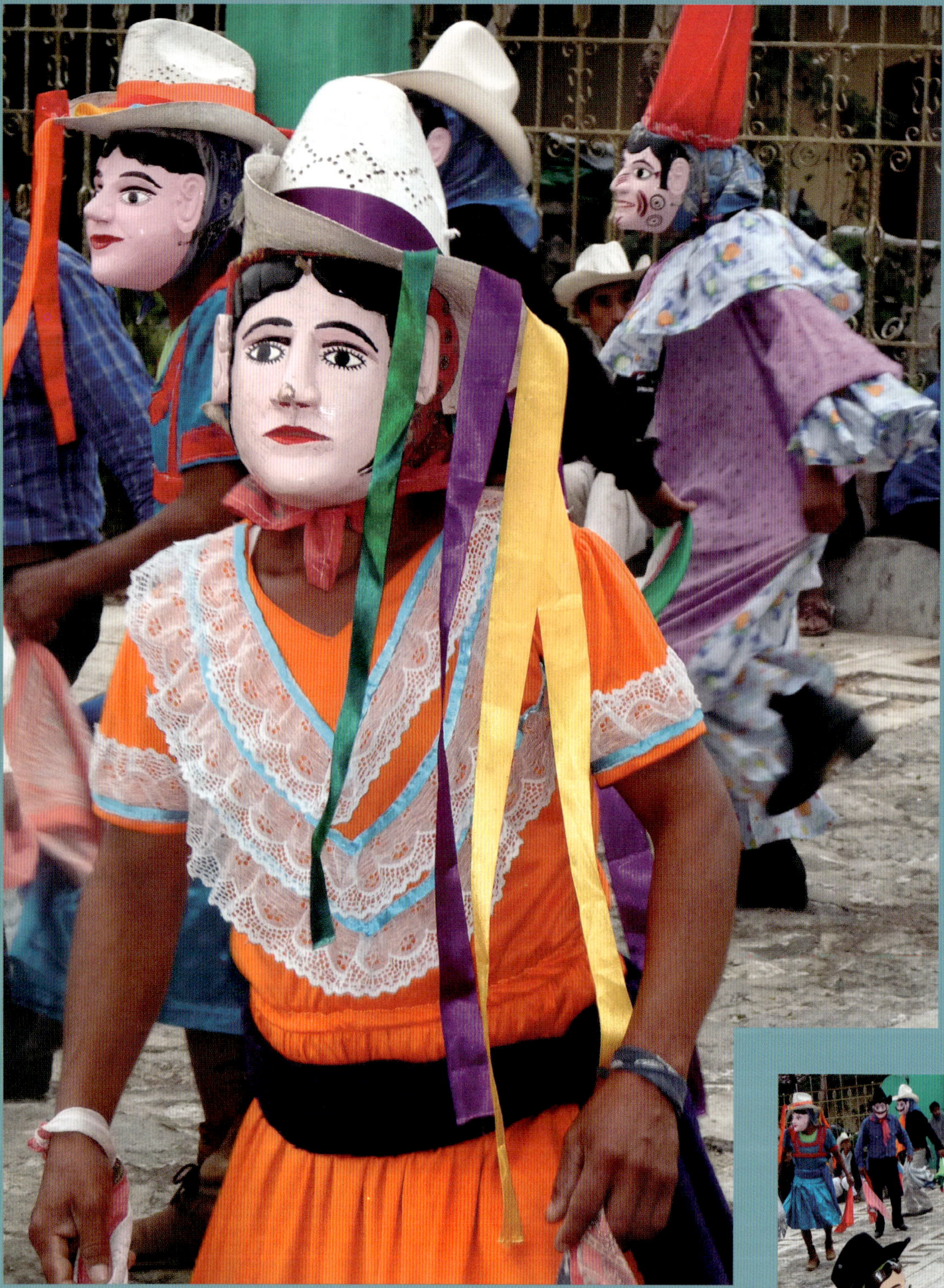
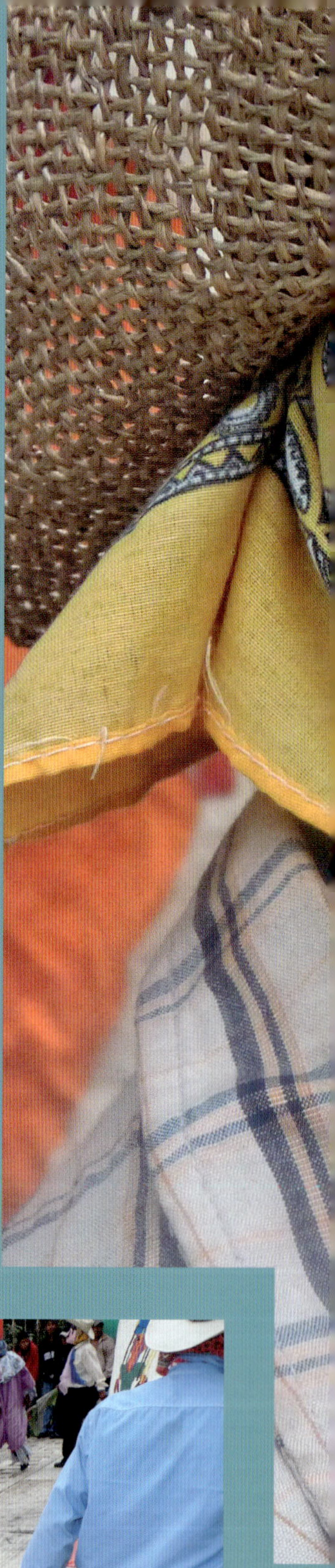
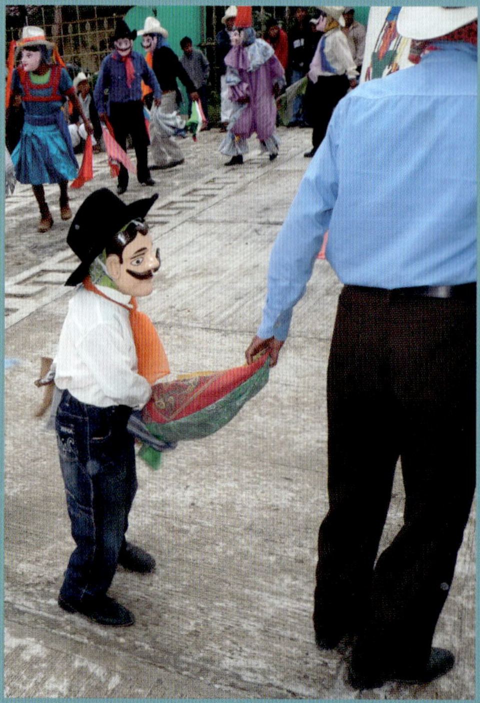

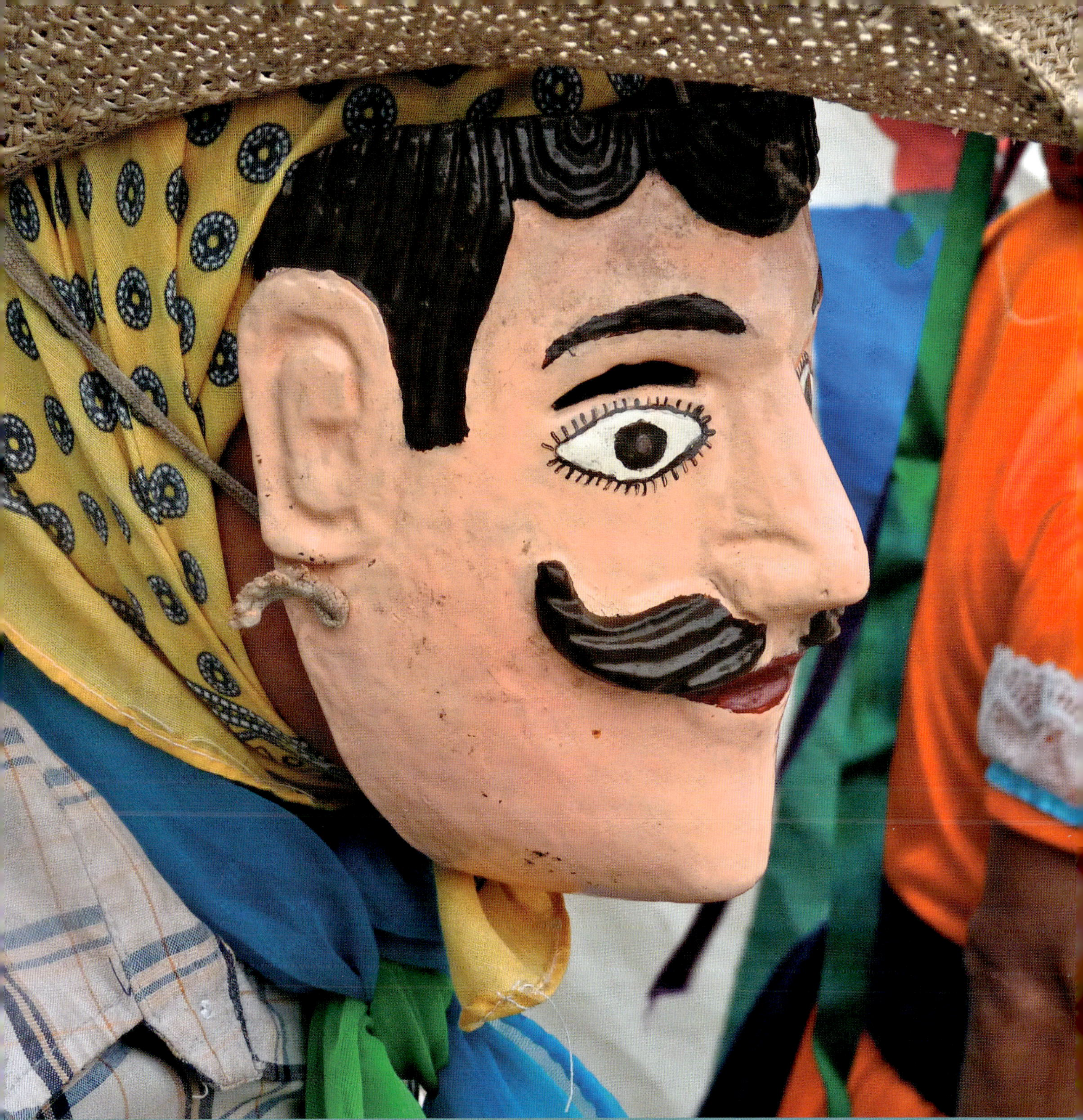

Opposite page, left: At Olintla in December 2010 we see two female Huehues in the foreground. I find them very convincing, even though I know that they are men or boys wearing masks.

Opposite page, inset: We see a very young Huehue at Olintla, probably dancing with a relative. He is wearing a handsome mask.

Above: I took photos of this mask, hoping to identify the carver. The carving is wonderful, the mask is old, but I don't recognize the ear design.

the upper teeth or nearly all of the teeth. Also the face of the mask has decorative elements or "face paint." At Olintla, Puebla, in March 2010, an early-elementary-school-aged boy demonstrated a wonderful level of energy as one of the payasos. He gave a truly charismatic performance.

Sometimes one sees female clowns. It took me a while to recognize these masks because they are less stereotyped than the male Payaso masks, and often lack the usual face paint. The female Payaso masks do usually have open mouths, with or without prominent teeth. In Chapter 6 several examples will be presented by Lorenzo Ciriaco García, Miguel Juan Marquez, Andrés Juárez García, and Germán Vega Pérez. Here I've included a dance photo of the one by Andrés Juárez García (p. 42).

There are a few other characters in the dance. There is a Perro (dog), who pretends to assist the character who portrays the hunter. Sometimes these Perro masks look more like jaguars than dogs.

In the usual Huehues or Tejoneros performance, the dancers will have set up a small, four-sided enclosure that is about 6 feet high and perhaps 10 feet square. This consists of four corner poles and four more poles midway between the corners on all four sides. The poles support a cloth curtain, the *telón*. On each of the four sides of the telón there is a painting of some scene; these scenes appear to be related to the dance or a related legend. In Olintla, in March 2010, we saw an eight-sided telón. The designs vary, but usually one scene is of a hunter shooting at the coati in a tree or on the bamboo pole. Stresser-Péan (2009, 296) reports that in the past the walls of the enclosure were constructed of woven palm mats.

As part of the Huehues or Tejoneros dance, hand puppets gesture and clap their oversized hands over the top edge of the curtain, to the amusement of the crowd. They are usually named San José and the Virgin María. An in-depth discussion of the puppets will be found in Chapter 7.

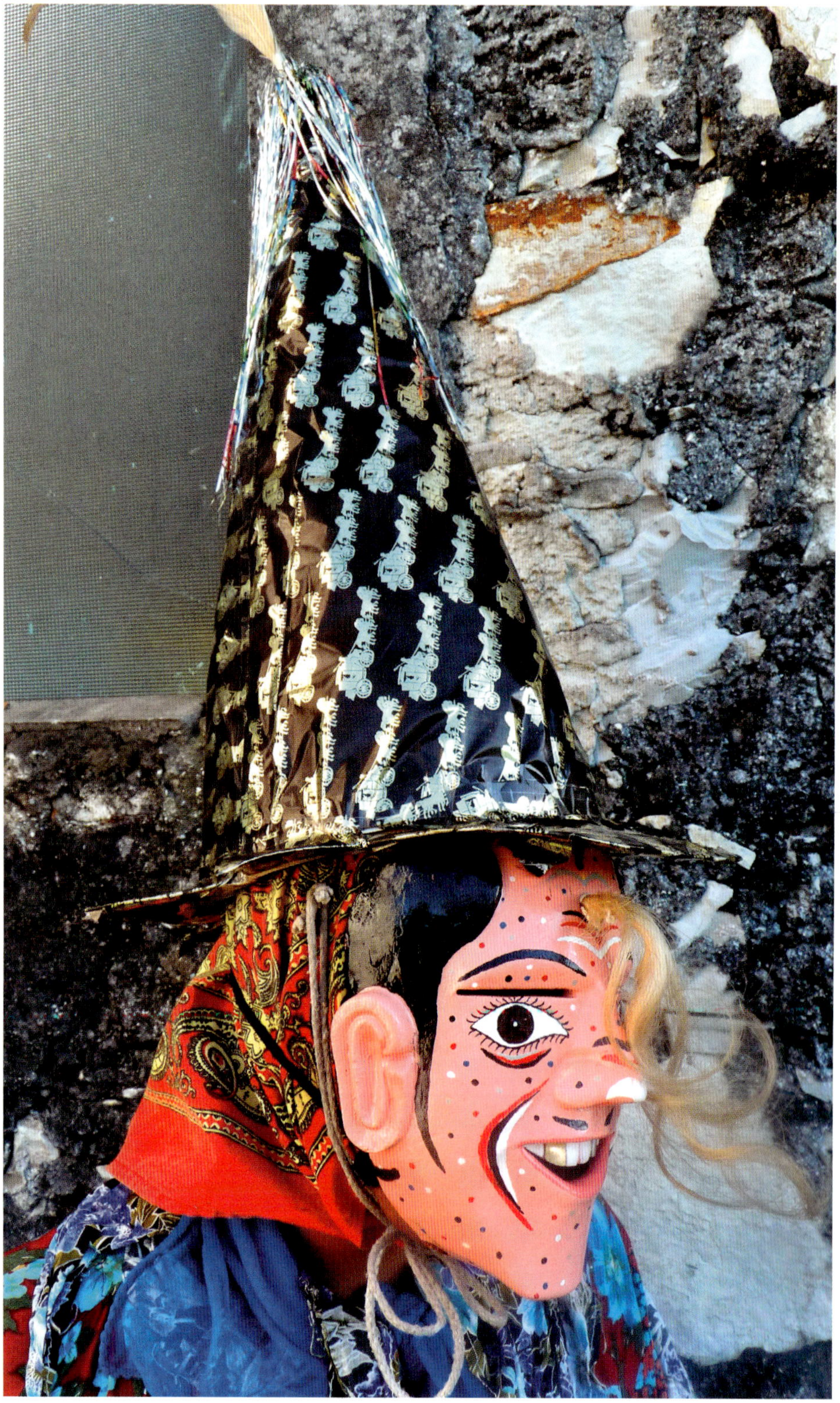

A male Payaso dancing at Xonalpú. His beautiful mask was carved by Andrés Juárez García.

Opposite:
Here we see the young but highly energetic Payaso at Olintla, dancing between two slightly older boys who are dressed as girls. Look at his right leg, positioned for action, compared to the demure postures of the two "girls." In the background the onlookers watch with obvious interest because his enthusiasm was infectious.

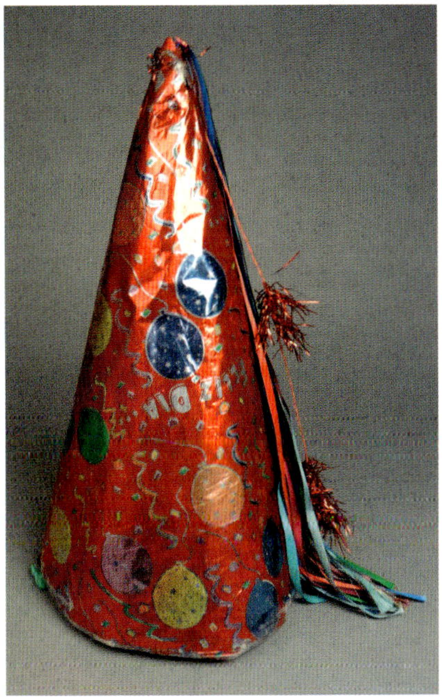

Left: Clown's hat purchased in Sabanas de Xalostoc, Veracruz, in 2007; 8" in diameter, 13" tall. Circa 2000. This one is brimless. Note the use of birthday wrapping paper to cover the hat. *Collection of the author.*

Below: The inside of the clown's hat, showing the framework of split bamboo.

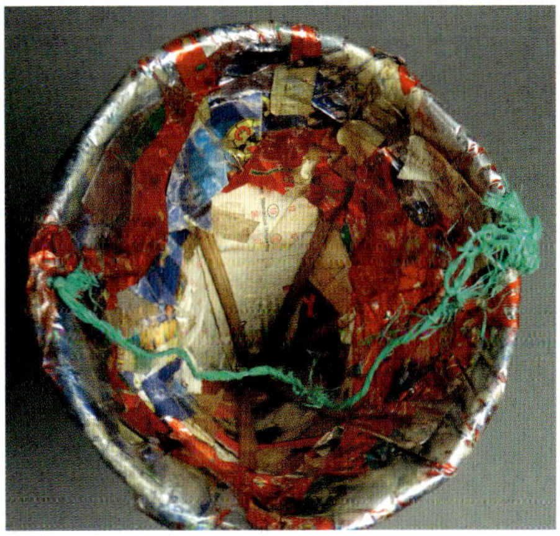

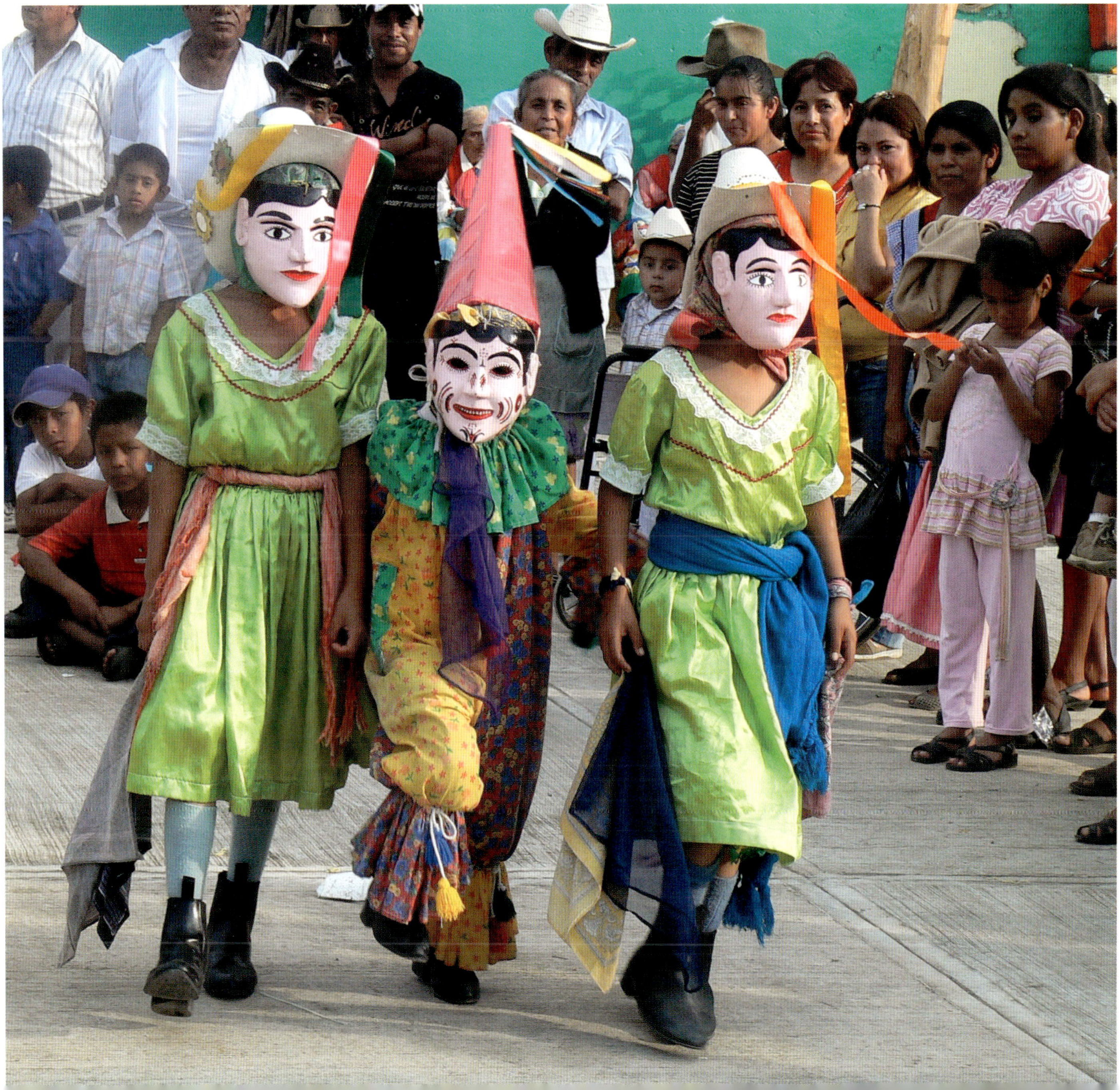

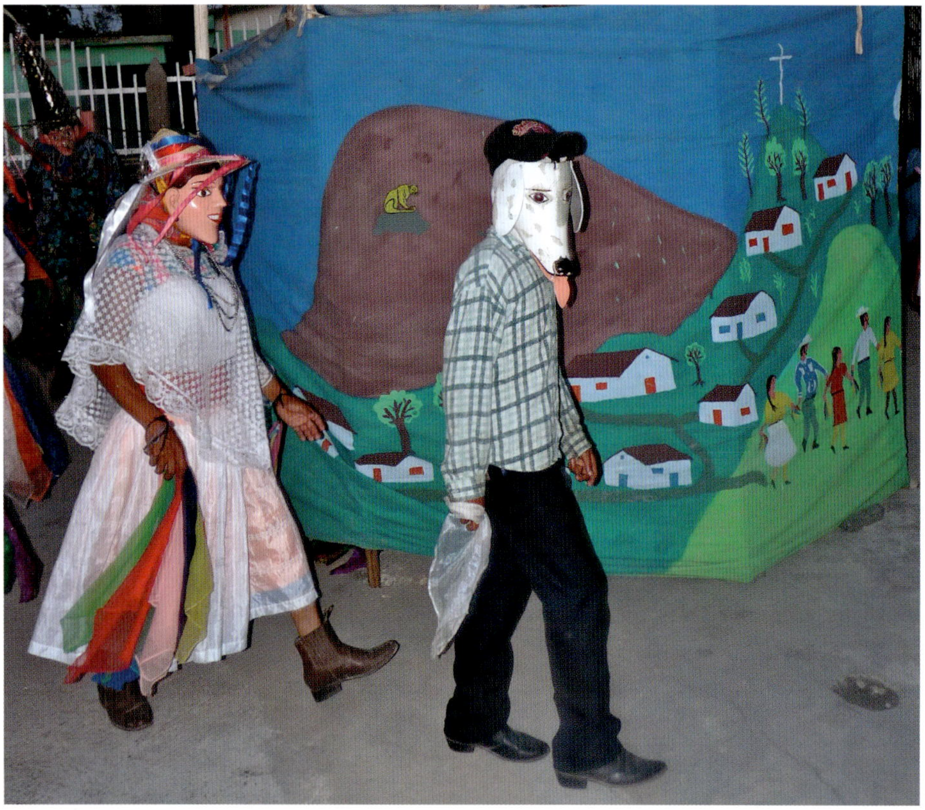

Top left: At Xonalpú, Puebla, in December 2010, a Perro and a beguiling female clown, both masks recently carved by Andrés Juárez García, are dancing. Behind them we see a *telón* (curtain) that was painted by Leonel Lecona. The female clown is wearing the typical dance boots (*botines*).

Bottom left: Inside the telón, the enclosure functions as a refuge for the dancers during quiet intervals. Here we see some familiar dancers unmasked in December 2010 at Olintla.

Below: In this scene from March 2010, the male and female puppets appear over the telón and clap their hands. We can see the shadow of the operator on the telón; simultaneously we see his black cowboy hat behind the puppets. On the telón a Perro carries the dead Tejón. Huehues dance while the puppets perform.

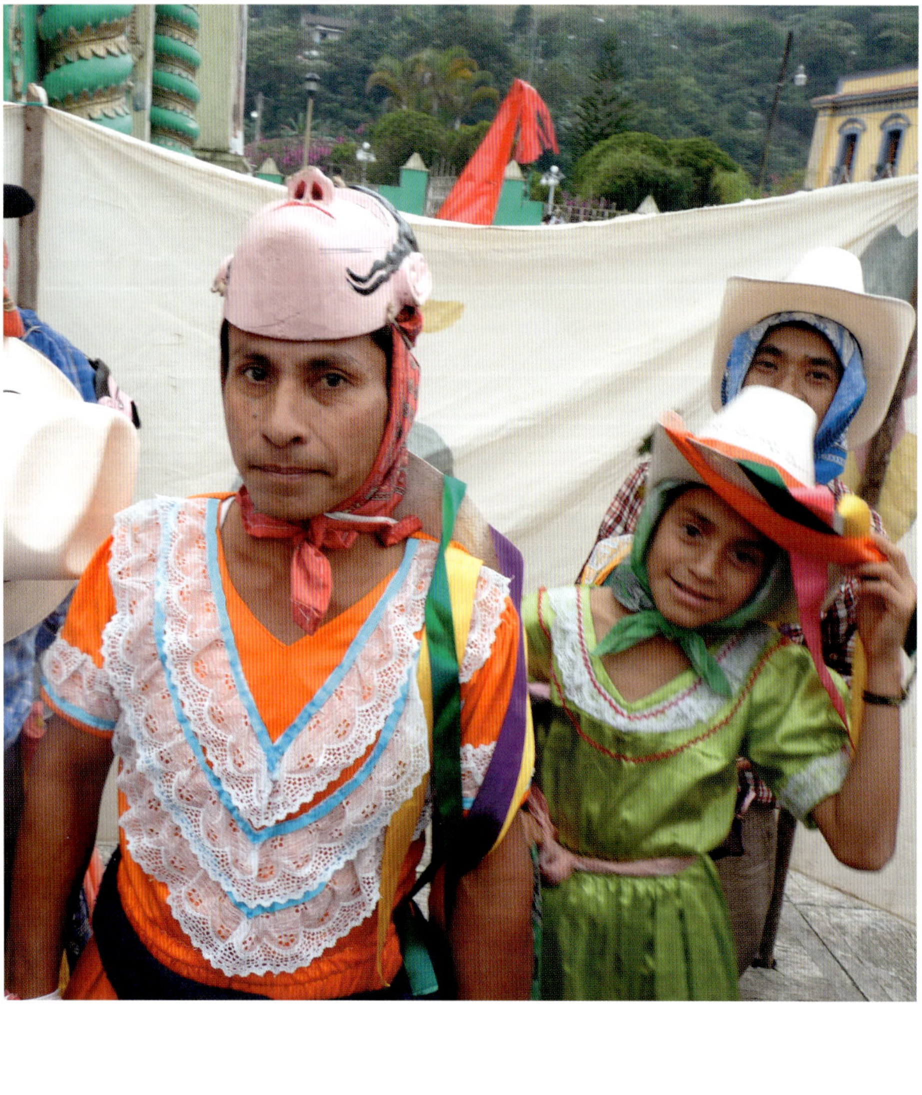

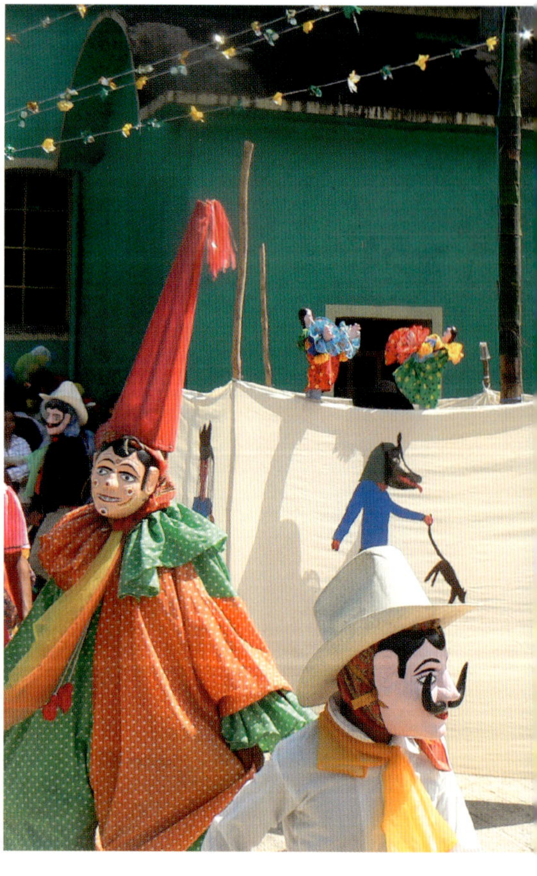

A tall bamboo pole is erected in the middle of the enclosure. It has been specially prepared; holes at every joint have facilitated the removal of the partitions inside the bamboo, permitting a rope to pass up through the interior space to the top. This rope then spirals down around the outside of the pole to the ground, where it is available to hoist the Chénchere and later the Tejón. First the woodpecker puppet is hoisted up the pole; as it rises, it gives the appearance of pecking. Because the hoisting string is wrapped around the pole it holds the Chénchere more firmly in place, facilitating the manipulation of the bird's neck. When the Chénchere reaches the top, a container (the *Guajillo*) opens and a flag or ribbons unfurl. As the Chénchere descends, it appears to strip the banana leaves that have been tied around the pole; this illusion is accomplished with yet another string. Next, a stuffed coati (or *Tejón*) is likewise maneuvered up the pole and "shot" with a blank cartridge, whereupon it falls to the ground. Then it is carried around as a trophy.

There can be a Viejo figure in the Huehues dance. I have seen only one of these characters dance, and that was in a film (Lane 2005). I have a danced Viejo mask, identified by the carver. It is identical in appearance to the Viejo or Pilatos masks used in the Dance of the Voladores, and I suspect that the same mask can be used in either role.

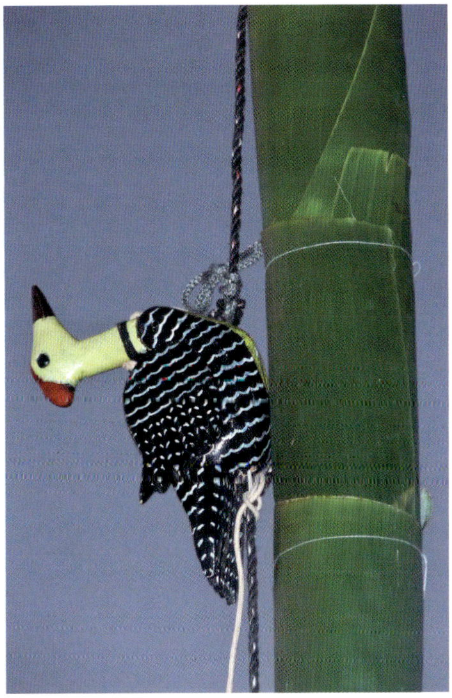

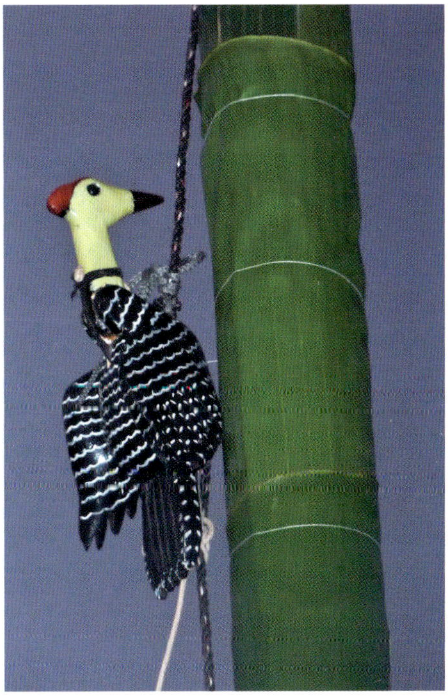

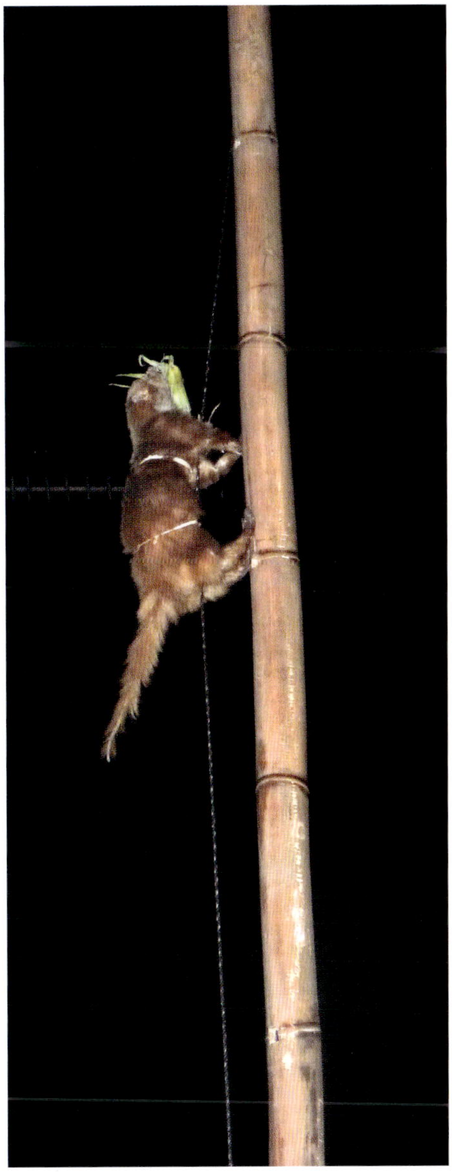

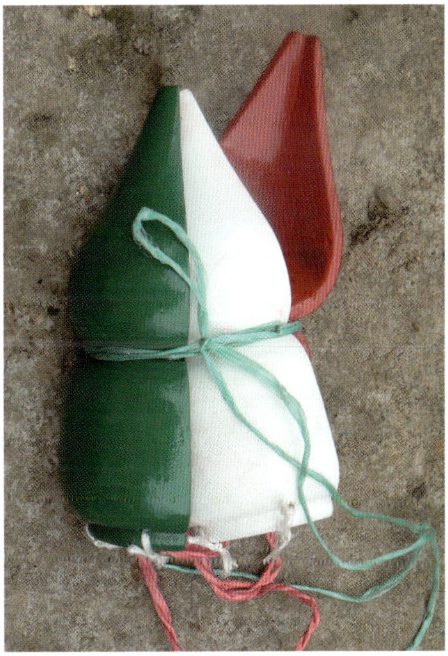

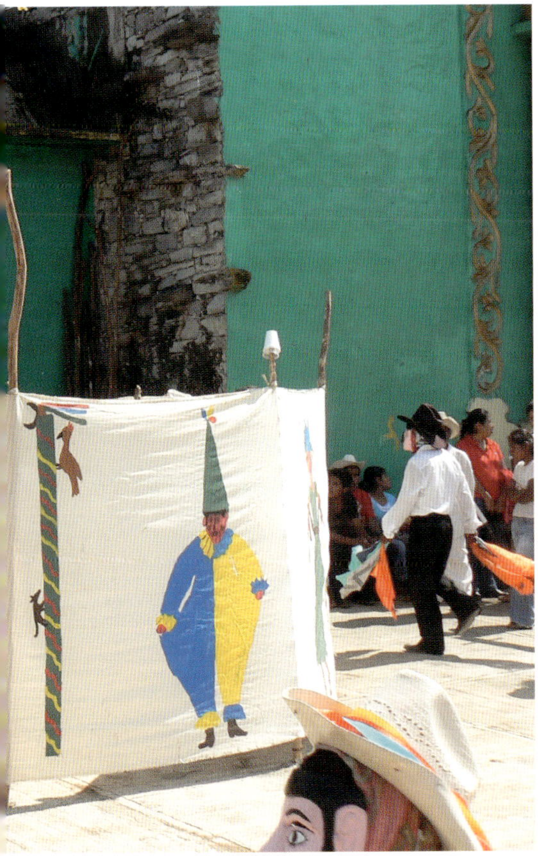

Top left: At Xonalpú in December 2010 the Chénchere is going up the pole.

Top right: The Chénchere's neck is extended, giving it the appearance of pecking.

Bottom right: The Guajillo used in Zoatecpan, Puebla, is painted in the colors of the Mexican flag; 12" tall. It is a wooden container, carved in the general shape of a chili pepper, with three sections. A string tied with a slipknot holds the Guajillo closed; when the string is pulled the container falls open, releasing the Mexican flag.

Bottom left: The (stuffed) Tejón "runs" up the pole at Xonalpú in December 2010. It has an ear of corn in its mouth.

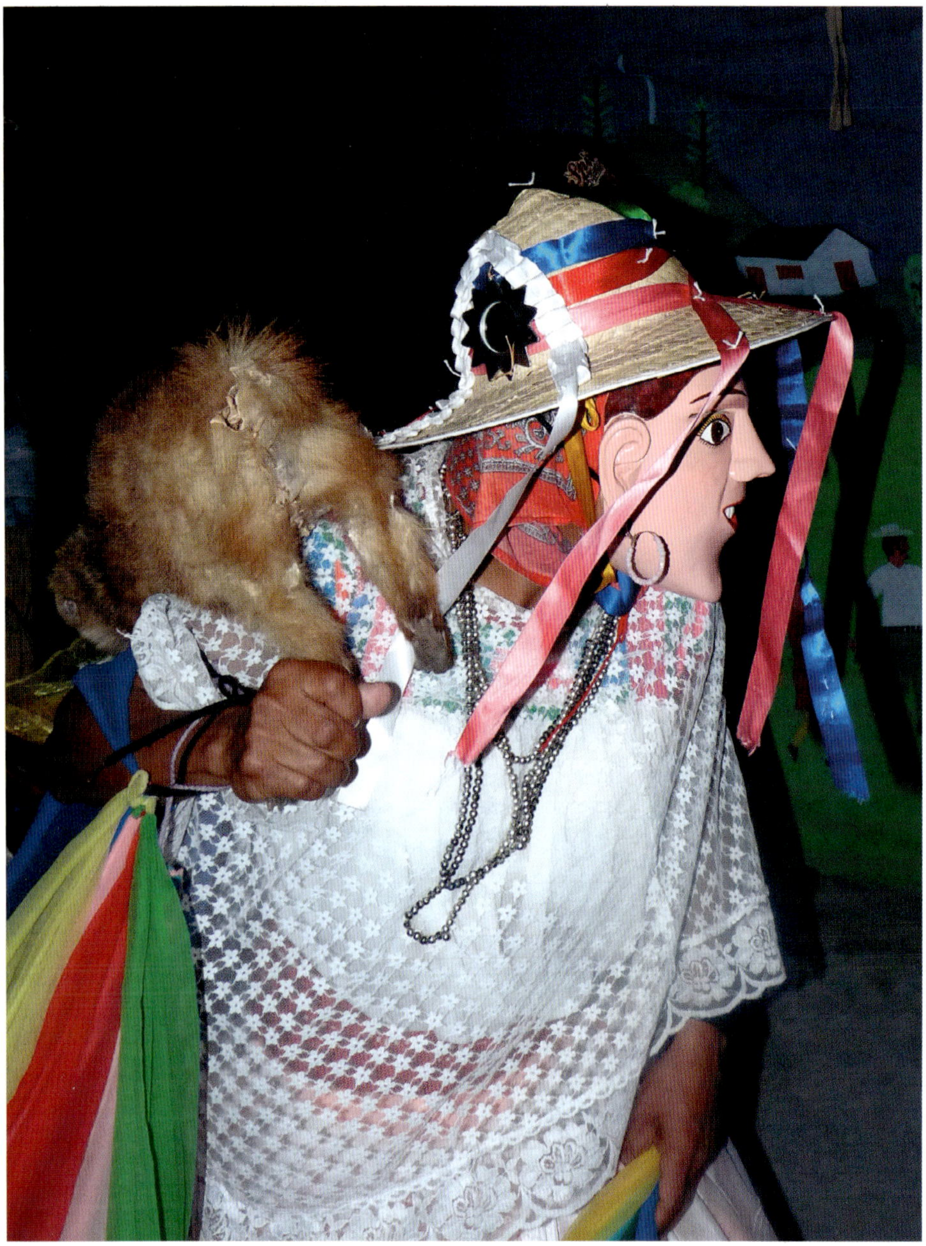

At Xonalpú in December 2010, the female clown carries the carcass of the Tejón in triumph. Note the remarkable carving of the ear on this mask.

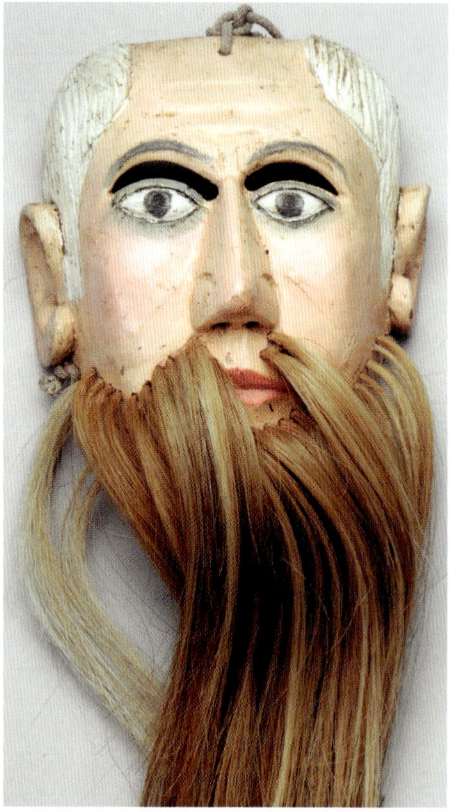

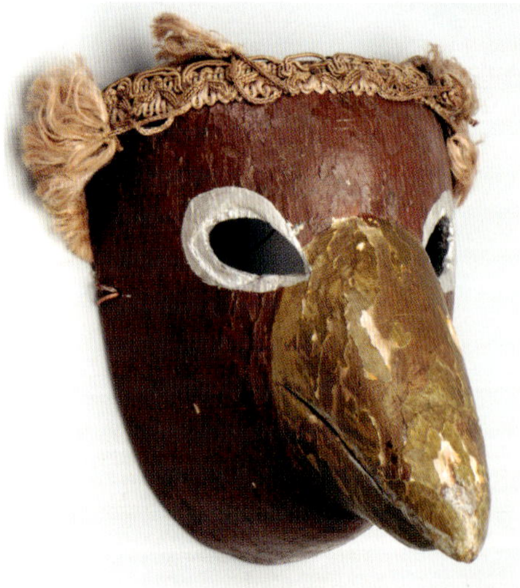

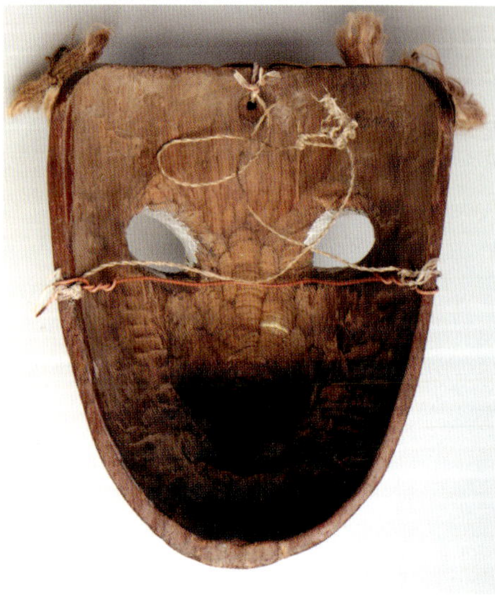

Right from top:
Vernon Kostohryz purchased a number of Huehue masks from a dance group in 2005. This was one of those masks. All had been carved by Roberto Villegas Santiago. When Roberto was later shown a photo of the mask, he acknowledged (personal communication 2007) that he had carved it and said that it was a Viejo mask for the Huehues dance; 6½" × 8", 20" with beard. Circa 1975. *Collection of the author.*

The Pájaro mask seen from the front; 6" × 7½". Circa 1975. At one time the beak was bright yellow; more recently it was painted gold. A braid is attached across the top of the mask. *Collection of the author.*

The back of the Pájaro mask shows good evidence of wear. We have no idea *why* it was dancing, but it was definitely dancing.

Completing the list, it seems that there can be a Pájaro or bird mask in the Huehues dance. Vernon Kostohryz collected such a mask in 2005, in Tuxtla, Puebla. It was said to have been carved in about 1975. I have not found any specific reference to explain it. In the legend of El Niño planting the first cornfield, which will be discussed later, many different animals and birds threaten the cornfield (Medina Jiménez 2005, 63–66). Perhaps this mask portrays one of those thieving birds? But really we know nothing else about it.

As I traveled through the Sierra with Vernon Kostohryz and Carlos Moreno Vásquez, we were always looking for special informants such as dancers, carvers, or dance leaders. In Hueytlalpan, Puebla, we met a Perro who was performing on the street. In the area around Entabladero, Veracruz, Carlos and I were fortunate to visit the homes of two Caporales who graciously shared their knowledge about the Tejoneros dance.

Near Entabladero we met Omar Jesús Fajardo González, who lived with his wife and children in the house of his parents. The house itself was distinctive, with balusters out front in the form of seahorses. Omar could not have been more gracious. He put on the mask and costume of a Tejonero, then dressed his son as a Perro. He hung the telón used by his group on the fence next to his house. He showed us other masks and shared old dance photos. Then we drove to another house nearby where there were more masks and a set of beautiful puppets. Omar demonstrated how the puppeteer must wrap his fingers with an elastic bandage to permit a more stable attachment of the puppets on the hands. Our guide on this visit was Don Chico, another friendly gentleman from Entabladero who has even more masks at his house.

Top left: This Perro character was with a Payaso on the street in Hueytlalpan.

Bottom left: A closer view of the Perro mask. As you can see, this is another fairly old mask.

Center: Our host, Omar, modeling his Payaso outfit. Note the image of the Virgin of Guadalupe on his cap.

Below: Omar's son dressed as a Perro.

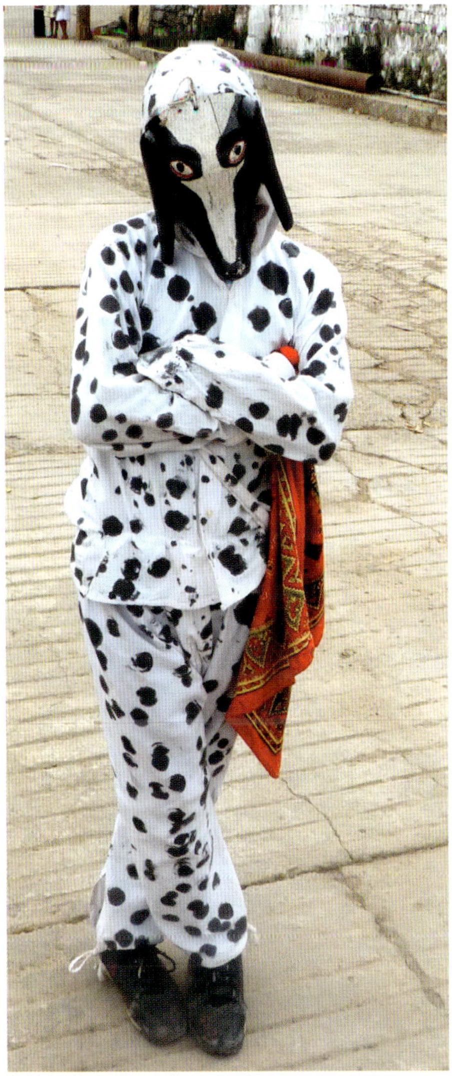

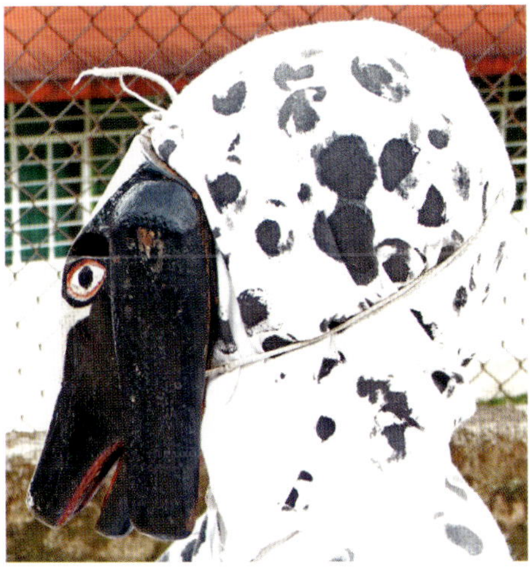

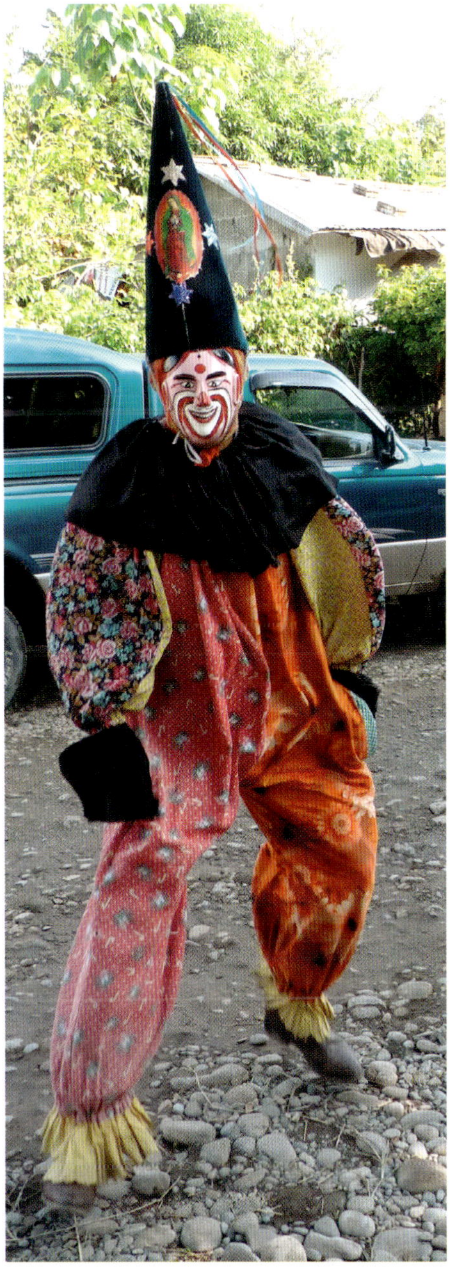

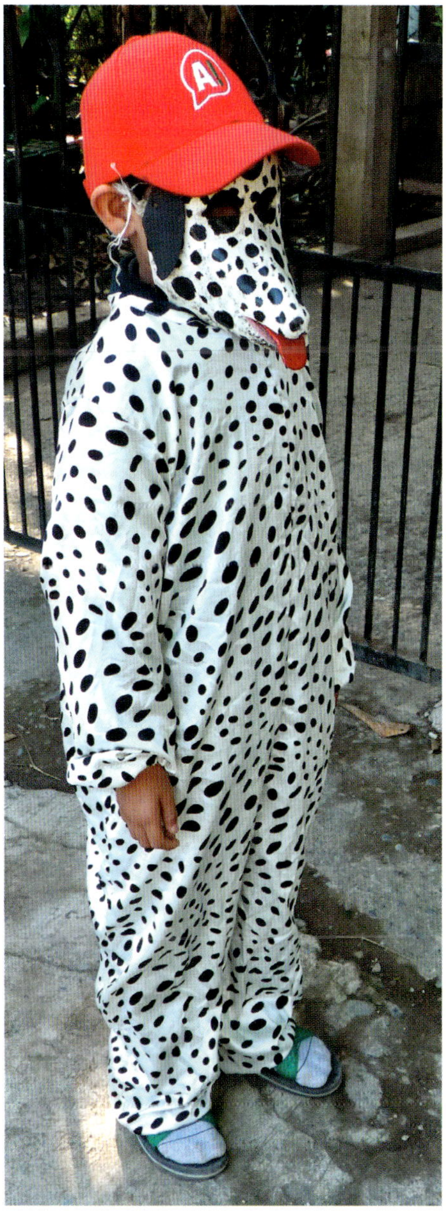

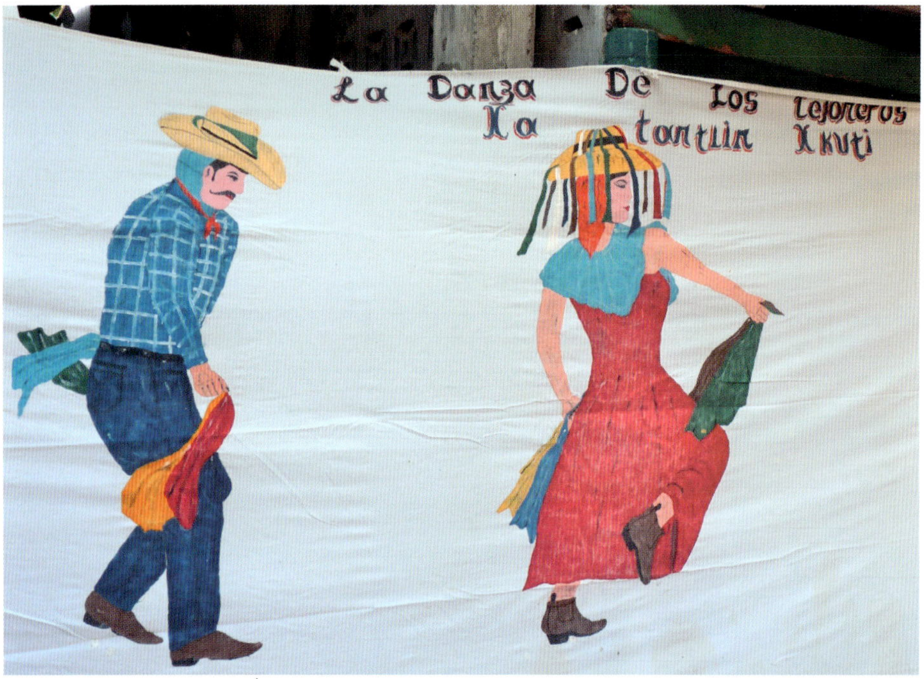

Left:
On Omar's telón we see two Tejoneros. At the top of the banner, under the name of the dance, we see the Totonac word *Xkuti*, which refers to the Tejón.

Below:
Omar wearing the mask and very elaborate headdress of a female Tejonero in his locale. Note again the image of the Virgin of Guadalupe on the headdress.

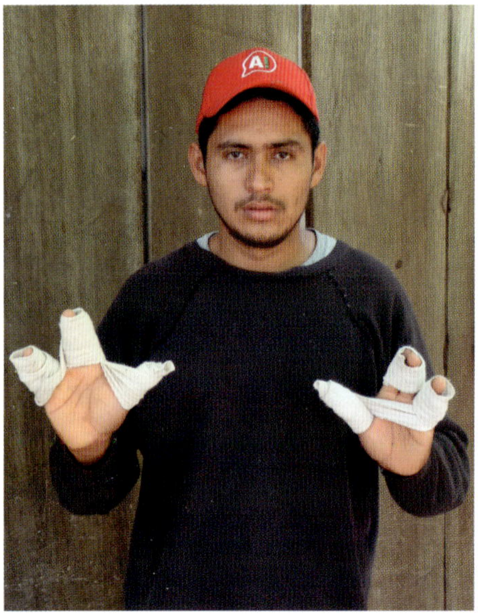

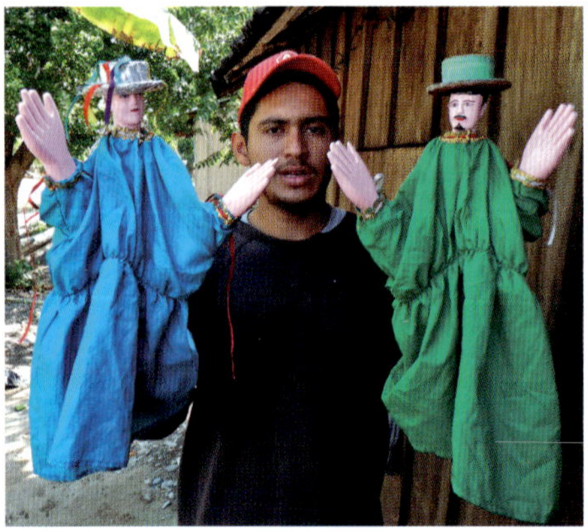

Above:
Omar, without a mask, demonstrates how the fingers are wrapped with an elastic bandage so that the puppets will fit more snugly. The thumb supports one arm, the middle and pointer fingers hold the torso, and the fourth and little fingers control the other arm.

Omar has installed the puppets on his hands. These are very beautiful puppets with elegant costumes.

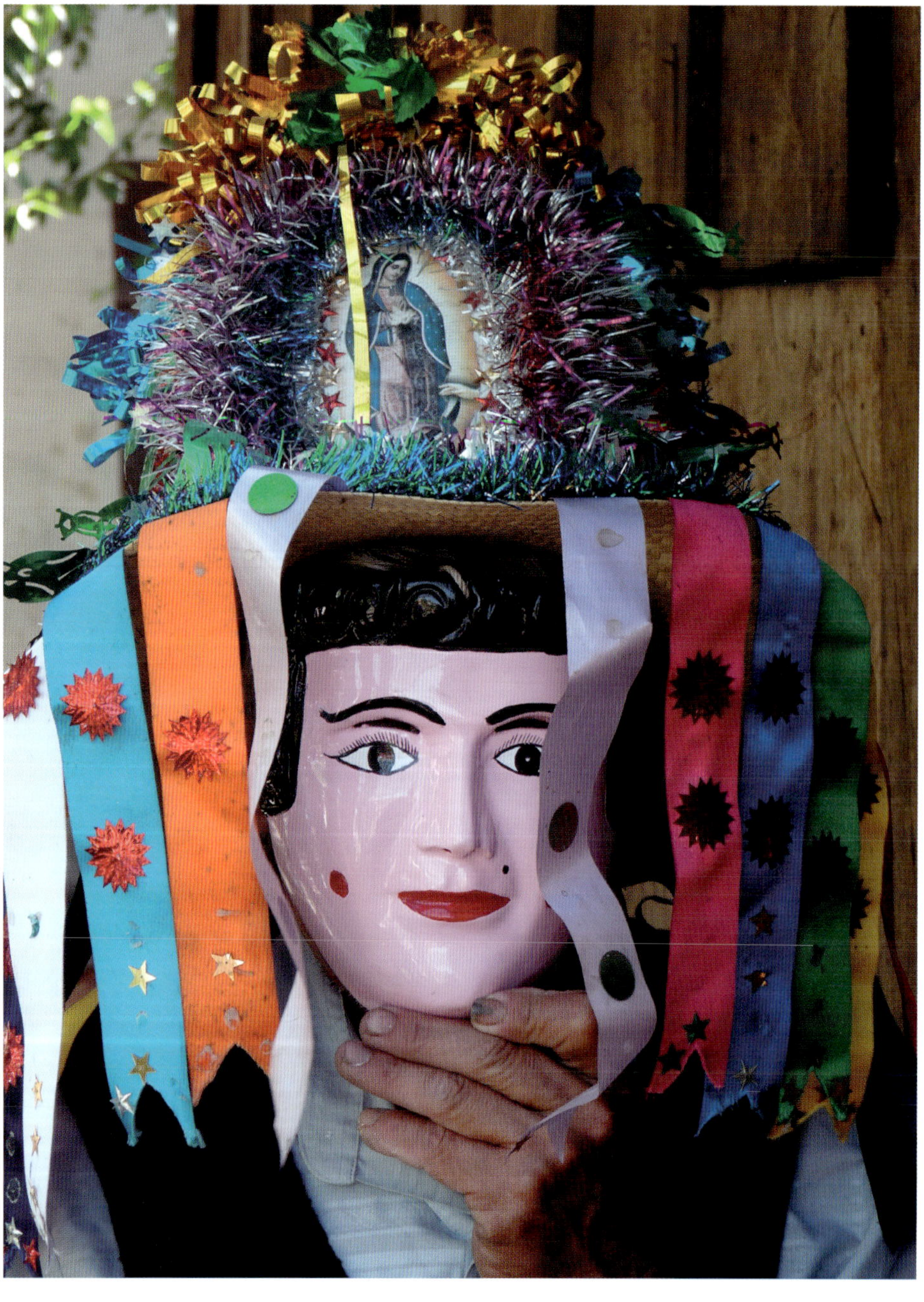

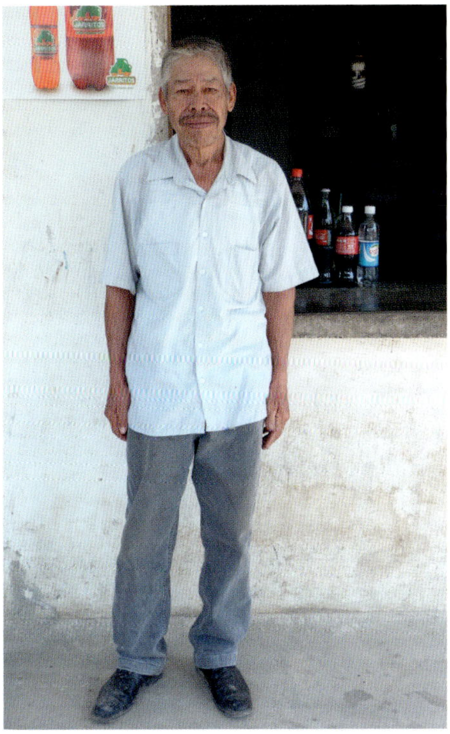

Don Chico, known to Carlos Moreno Vásquez from prior dealings, was our guide in finding Omar and arranging to visit him.

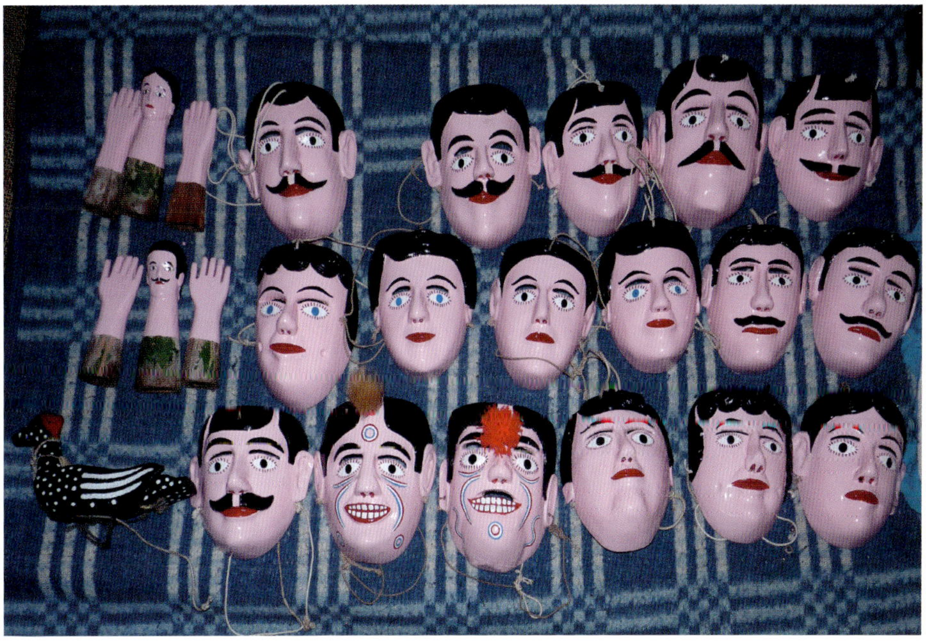

We saw many Tejonero masks at Don Chico's house. On the left is an old set of puppets. In the front row the male and female Payasos stand in sharp contrast to the Tejonero masks. Don Chico told us that these masks were carved by José Pérez or José Pascual of Coyutla, Veracruz, about 40 years ago, and that the carver is now deceased. Everything is newly painted, creating an impression of homogeneity that is misleading, as the masks are certainly the work of several carvers. The mask on the upper left, next to the female puppet, is probably the work of José Juárez, the grandfather of Benito Juárez Figueroa, so it may be 100 years old, based on two features of the mask: the delicately carved ear design and the knobbed chin of that carver.

We traveled from Entabladero to Sabaneta, a nearby town in the municipio of Coxquihui, Veracruz. Don Salvador Mejorada Romero, who lives there with his sister and other relatives, rode up on his bicycle just after we had arrived. He proceeded to unwrap a parcel that had been tied to the rack on his bike. To our surprise, what emerged was the Tejón, a stuffed animal with an ear of corn in its jaws. There was more to follow, as Salvador put on masks and costumes to demonstrate aspects of the Tejoneros dance.

This dance probably has had many different levels of meaning over the years, and these have persisted to some degree.

Bruce Lane returned to Huehuetla, Puebla, in the late 1970s and made a second film there; this one included discussion and images of the Huehues dance. He called this film *The Tree of Knowledge*; it was initially released in 1981. Now it is available on a DVD (Lane, *The Tree of Knowledge* 2005). The film has many charms. In the opening sequence the camera reveals the appearance of the town and the mountainous terrain around it from the air. Then one has the remarkable opportunity to observe Lorenzo Ciriaco García, otherwise known as El Kalimán, unmasked and rehearsing the dance (Leonel Lecona, personal communication 2006). We also see examples of his masks and puppets.

For the camera, Lane's colleague Mary Fukumoto interviews a Mestizo resident of Huehuetla, Manuel Leonel Lecona (Lane, *The Tree of Knowledge*: English text nd); she asks him whether he could "tell us the story of the Huehues dance?" A rich dialogue follows, which is interwoven with images in the film to supplement what we are seeing.

In the film (Lane, *The Tree of Knowledge* 2005) the narrator says, "These are the puppets in the dance." We are then shown two puppets. The female puppet is very similar to one of Kalimán's puppets in chapter 7, particularly in her hairstyle. Soon the film shows two other puppets and many masks on a home altar; that female puppet also has a near duplicate in the puppet chapter, again the work of Kalimán. Later the narrator says, "Of course, in the dance, one Indian wears Totonac clothes." At that moment we are shown El Kalimán himself, wearing a red printed handkerchief around his head and putting on a sombrero. He is wearing a bag made from an armadillo shell. He carries his mask in one hand. (Around him we see other dancers with masks by other carvers.) Still later the narrator reports that "In the summer they hunt, in the fall it rains, and in the winter it's cold so no one goes out." Then we see the Viejo character from the Huehues dance; he appears to be a clown, walking stooped with a cane. A boy apparently asks to be picked up and we see the Viejo carrying that boy on his back. The film then proceeds to show the entire process related to the puppets, including the hanging of the telón, the erecting of the bamboo pole, the woodpecker's climb up the pole, and the shooting of the stuffed Tejón. Towards the end of the film, just after the principal of the school reports that the students will "reenact the proclamation of independence," a procession is shown that includes Santiaguero dancers and Señor Santiago wearing a wooden horse at waist level.

Meanwhile the dialogue in the film provides information about the possible meaning of the dance. In a related document, the author adds to these points. Both documents are readily found on the Internet, so I'll simply repeat a few of the most important ideas. A description of the Huehues dance was provided to Manuel by his teacher, but it contains explanations that seem more puzzling than revealing. For example, the puppets are described as Spanish or Mestizo personages who have come to teach the Indians how to live—how to hunt, how

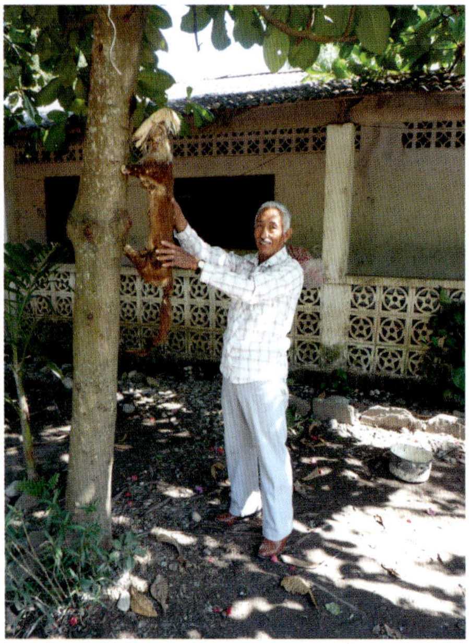

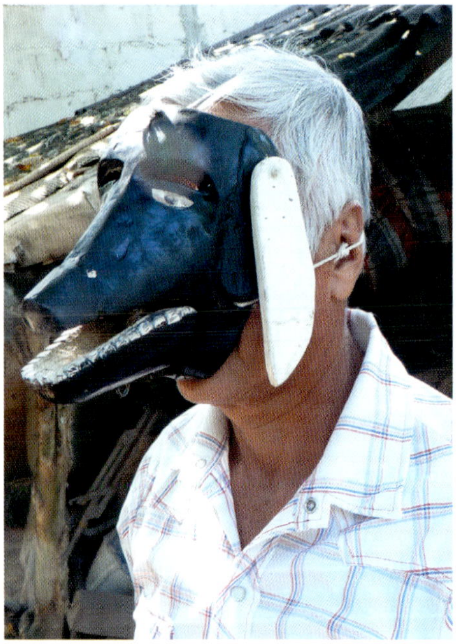

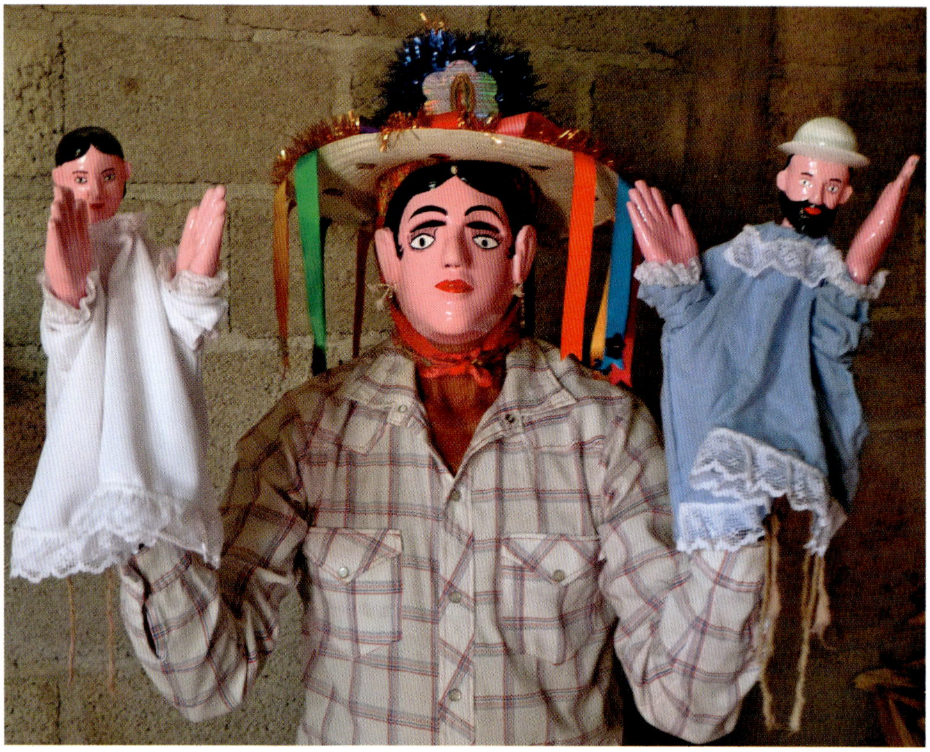

Above left: Don Salvador holds up the Tejón as if it is running up a tree.

Left: Salvador models an old Perro mask. It has an articulated jaw, meaning that the mouth opens and closes. The screw eye under the lower jaw should have a string attached; rubber bands hold the jaw shut, but pulling the string would open it. The mask has ears that are carved in relief, but it also has another set of ears that were added later.

Above:
Salvador has put on a female Tejonero mask and the appropriate hat for the female Tejonero character. Again the hat has an image of the Virgin of Guadalupe on the crown. Salvador is holding a beautiful pair of puppets.

to adapt to the seasons, and how to dress like Mestizos. These teachers live in the woods while their Indian students live in the town. But the Indians were hunters, they had their own calendar, and traditionally it was the Indians who lived in the forested mountains while the Spanish lived in the towns. The "explanation" represents a reversal of facts known to everyone. Then as the film ends the Totonac violinist is quoted as saying that "the Huehues dance is about trees. The dancers are not really who are dancing. They're just moving. The real dancers are the masks, because they're made of wood. They too are alive. They have hearts and can speak. Not just us. That's where the dance began" (Lane, *The Tree of Knowledge*: English text nd). Lane adds (*Notes on the Text of The Tree of Knowledge* nd) that "The Huehue violinist went on to explain to me that what the Indians saw in the woods were trees who had died, but whose hearts were still good, who had stood up and were dancing. The puppets are those trees—as are the 12 posts, the masks, and, most of all, the central pole."

Lane concludes (*Notes on the Text of The Tree of Knowledge* nd) with a summary of his understanding:

One of the most important things about this film, I think, is how it shows the use of ritual drama as a dramatic teaching device—a way of transmitting beliefs and values in a non-verbal, intuitive manner. The story of the Huehues *danza* is instructive, but both viewers and dancers can experience the important messages of the story even if they don't know it in words. It is especially important because we can see how the *danza* has been reworked to deal with two and perhaps three different layers of meaning. It seems possible to me that the original *danza* was about trees as animate beings.

As an ancient, pre-conquest ritual, the focus of the Huehues dance may have involved such spirits of the natural world as the trees, and perhaps others too. We may recall Stresser-Péan's discovery that healers attribute illness to spirits: "These spirits are called *teuyome* (divine beings) and can be mountain, water, or forest spirits, as well as souls of the dead" (2009, 363). In areas directly adjacent to the Sierra de Puebla, in the Huasteca, the primary meaning of the Huehues dance still is that the spirits of dead people visit the village and then leave again.

There must have been a subsequent shift in the focus of the dance because we find another layer of meaning that reflects agriculture and the cultivation of corn. Medina Jiménez (2005, 63–67) provides a legend about El Niño (the Spirit of Maíze), concerning his efforts to provide corn to humankind. An old woman lived in the woods with her grandson. One day they observed mule-ants (also known as leaf-cutter ants) carrying unfamiliar seeds on their backs. They picked up some of these grains and ate them; this was of course corn and they liked its taste. Following the ants, they saw that the corn was being carried into a hole in the side of the mountain. They recruited a woodpecker to help them dig open the entrance. The storehouse of corn was exposed but a falling stone injured the woodpecker's head so that it bled; this is the reason that the woodpecker has a red crest. The Niño went on to plant the first cornfield, keeping its location a secret from his grandmother; he apparently had a premonition that she would interfere. She searched out the field and was shocked to find birds and animals walking between the stalks of corn. They had not discovered that the corn was edible, but the grandmother didn't know this. She waved her arms and yelled, hoping to drive them off, but her actions were perceived as an invitation to a fiesta. The encroaching animals searched for the fiesta food and discovered the corn. Next the grandmother invented scarecrows to guard the crop. In this way the cultivation of corn was established and El Niño was able to pass this crop and these agricultural techniques on to the Indians for their use. When the grandmother died she was reborn as a coati (El Tejón).

In a subsequent paper, Medina Jiménez (2005, 68–69) provides some interesting information about the puppets. He notes that each year when the Huehues dance they have a ritual to remove the male and female puppets and the woodpecker puppet from the wooden box where they have been safely kept since the last fiesta. The dancers address the puppets as if they were living spirits and ask for their blessing. The puppets are kept on a home altar during the period of time that they are out of their storage box. The author describes the puppets as *"Duendes, dueños del maiz y la naturaleza"* [Spirits, proprietors of the corn and of nature].

Medina Jiménez (2005, 68–69) ends this second paper with an explanation of the meanings of all the separate elements in the dance:

> *Un tarro forrado con hojas de plátano representa a la milpa; el "Chénchere" es el pájaro perjuicioso que picotea los jilotes; el "tejón" es el que come los elotes; los danzantes representan a los espantapájaros; el "payaso" mata a los animales perjuiciosos; el "chichimeco" es el perro que delata dónde andan los animals perjuiciosos y el telón representa al cerro donde las hormigas habían escondido el maíz.*
>
> [A bamboo pole wrapped with banana leaves is used to represent the milpa (cornfield); the Chénchere is the damaging bird which pecks (nibbles) the ears of the green corn; the Tejón is the one who eats the ripe ears; the dancers (Tejoneros) represent the scarecrows; the Payaso kills the damaging animals; the Chichimeco is the dog who reveals where these damaging animals go and the telón (curtain) represents the mountain where the ants have hidden the grains of corn.]

Croda León and Francisco Velasco (2005, 71–72) also discussed the symbols and meaning of the dance. In their view the pecking Chénchere is included in the dance as a reminder of his mythic role in uncovering the hidden storehouse of corn. This corn was then distributed to humankind at a time of widespread famine, so a fiesta followed this great gift, initiating the dance. They further explain regarding some of the characters:

> *El papel del "payaso" representa la dualidad, el bien y el mal, la honestidad y la burla; los "varones", las "damas" y el "cazador" personifican a la humanidad; el "viejo," cubierto con hojas secas de plátano o con un costal o en su defecto con ropa vieja y desgarrada, representa al Diablo. En la danza se observa una fuerte rivalidad entre el hombre y la maldad, que prevalece por siempre. El maíz es sustento no sólo del hombre, sino también de los animales.*
>
> [The role of the clown symbolizes the concept of duality, the good and the bad, honesty and mockery; the male and female characters, including the hunter, represent humankind; the Viejo, wearing dried banana leaves or a sack or old and disreputable clothing, represents the Devil. One can see in the dance the powerful struggle between humankind and the wicked or mischievous (*maldad*) that is eternal. Corn is food not only for humans but also for animals.]

This brief passage is thought provoking. Certainly one can't miss the intention of the authors to underscore the importance of the concept of duality in the understanding of this dance. Equally interesting is the equation of El Viejo with Satan, something we will see again later regarding the Pilatos character in the Negritos dance. This is an excellent example of the ambiguity that one encounters in these dances. At first glance the Dance of the Huehues looks like the simplest of folk dances, but when the available information is collected one feels confused. What does the devil have to do with the gift of corn to humankind by the Spirit of Maíze? Chapter 8 is an effort to sort out these mysteries.

Earlier in this chapter a third level of meaning was described, at least in Huehuetla, Puebla (Lane, *The Tree of Knowledge*: English text nd). The puppets, who supposedly represent Spanish or Mestizos who are living in the woods, are said to be teaching the Totonac Indians in the community how to become Huehues or *Ladinos*, meaning "Indians in the process of acculturation" (Lane, *Notes on the Text of The Tree of Knowledge* nd, 3). But this is an instance of irony and misdirection, as

Lane goes on to explain: "That is, the traditional Totonacs reject *ladinos* for changing their clothes (i.e., adopting a non-Indian identity). Hence the Huehues dance is used as a sanction against improper behavior—as well as an opportunity to 'parody' becoming a Mestizo."

In the Tejonero dances of Veracruz we have encountered yet another stage in the evolution of this dance. The Virgin of Guadalupe has apparently become the patroness of the dancers; her image appears on their hats.

La Danza de los Santiagueros

This dance is a particular example of a class of dances found throughout Mexico that reflect or extend historic events in Spain. In 1491, the forces of the King of Spain successfully defeated the last Moorish stronghold within Spain's borders, completing the "re-conquest" after Spain had been completely or partly occupied by the Moors for a period of 500 years. It was said that the Spanish armies were successful because they were led by Santiago Apóstol, the reincarnation of Saint James the Apostle. On several occasions Spanish soldiers had reported the experience of seeing Santiago mounted on his white horse in the clouds above, urging them to victory. After Cortez established the colony of New Spain (Mexico), theatrical performances were introduced that depicted and glorified the defeat of the Moors, such as *La Danza de los Moros y Cristianos* (the Dance of the Moors and Christians) (Harris 2000).

In other regions of Mexico, for instance in the state of Guerrero, the Moors and sometimes the Christians wear vivid, oversized, wooden masks in these dance performances. In the area addressed in this volume, one sometimes finds the Moors and Christians dance, although neither the Moors nor the Christians wear masks. They do typically wear elaborate costumes. The King of the Moors and the King of the Christians wear crowns and dramatic false beards while a child portraying an angel wears the usual white robe or dress with wings.

Although I have not found this elsewhere in the Sierra, la Danza de los Moros y Cristianos in Hueytamalco, Puebla, does involve other characters that do wear masks. These include *el Diablo Mayor, el Diablo Menor*, and *La Muerte* (major and minor devils along with the figure of death, who wears a skull mask and a skeleton suit). Through a compadre of Carlos Moreno Vásquez, I was able to meet Miguel Ángel Bello Pérez and to obtain a copy of his book about the dance in Hueytamalco (Bello Pérez 2004). Miguel presents the lengthy dialogue between the two opposing sides, along with diagrams of the choreography and dance photos. For his day job Miguel owns and operates a hardware store, but the dance has obviously been his passion. In the course of my research in the Sierra it often happened that I spent days at a time simply traveling from one kindred spirit to another, as occurred on this day.

Next I met the family of Marcelino Santos Castelan of Hueytamalco. They have been strongly active in this dance; they shared dance photos and one of the sons put on his mask and costume, portraying for us a Minor Diablo. We saw a skull mask used by another one of the dancers that was made by Silverio Ochoa Martínez.

Subsequently we met a local carver, Felipe Jiménez Martínez of Llagostera, Puebla. Felipe took us to visit his friend Eusebio Blas Roman, a dancer who lived nearby in Tonalmeyoco, Puebla. Eusebio apparently owns a number of masks for his own use. He had two to show us that had been carved by Felipe, and in short order the men had put on costumes with these masks to demonstrate the full effect. When Eusebio learned that I was writing this book he immediately decided to give me his Diablo mask. He wouldn't allow me to pay him for it because it was damaged, but I was free to make a contribution to the Virgin María in his name. He believed that he had recovered from serious illness through her intercession. I left a contribution at his household shrine to the Virgin.

Other dances developed in the New World that addressed the conquest of the Indians by Cortez, aided by his consort, Malinche. These dances have various names, such as the Dance of the Conquest, the *Archareos* (the archers), and La Danza del Marques, the latter reflecting the title given to Cortez by the King of Spain, the *Marqués del Valle* (Marquis of the valley of Oaxaca). These dances don't seem to be present in the Totonacapán; instead one finds the very popular Dance of the Santiagueros and its variants.

The Santiagueros dance is often described by writers as an offshoot of the Dance of the Moors and Christians. On closer examination, this is not exactly the case; it would seem more accurate to say that the Spanish experience with the defeat of the Moors sensitized the creators of this dance to the prior history and charisma of Saint James the Apostle (Santiago Apóstol), leading them to create another plot that could feature this powerful figure.

In the Santiagueros dance, Santiago Apóstol or *Santiago Caballero* (Santiago on horseback) is portrayed as having taken revenge on the enemies of Christ, following the crucifixion. The dance includes many characters with Roman names, led by Pilate as the arch villain. This entire plot is, of course, an invention, many centuries after the fact, and stands in sharp contrast to the Gospel accounts where Jesus prohibits his disciples from retaliating against his abusers, and even restores a wounded ear (Luke 22:50–51).

The cast of characters includes Santiago, his son Galinche (or Callintsin, etc., apparently invented names for an invented figure), the Santiagueros group of dancers, and a second group, the *Pilatos* (little Pontius Pilates).

Usually Santiago wears a wooden horse at waist level as his identifying feature, along with a characteristic hat or helmet; occasionally he wears a mask. Galinche is never masked.

Depending on local custom, the Santiaguero dancers are sometimes called Santiagos. We will frequently encounter this usage by others, who may even refer to Santiago masks. This is potentially confusing, making it seem that such masks are worn by Santiago Caballero, when this character only occasionally wears a mask. For this reason I will make it a point to write about Santiaguero dancers and masks, and I will reserve the use of "Santiago" to refer to Saint James (the apostle or caballero).

The Santiagueros and Pilatos usually wear masks in our region of interest. Alain Ichon (1973, 394) observed a version of this dance in Pantepec, Puebla, in which all the participants were unmasked except for "*Pilatos, el Presidente, es el único que lleva una máscara; es una representación del Diablo: el rostro negro, viejo y arrugado, un rictus que le descubre los dientes de papel de plata; muy peludo, también con fibras que recubren el sombrero negro de carton.*" [Pontius Pilate, the President, is the only one who wears a mask; it is an image of the Devil: a black face, old and wrinkled, a smirk that reveals foil-covered teeth; thickly covered with hair, along with a black cardboard hat completely covered with fibers.] Ichon includes a small dance photograph (Lámina 22. 2 after 479); the mask has a flowing mustache and a full beard, all apparently made with tufts of animal hair. The hat is covered with thick tufts of sisal. Santiago is wearing his usual horse. As we will see

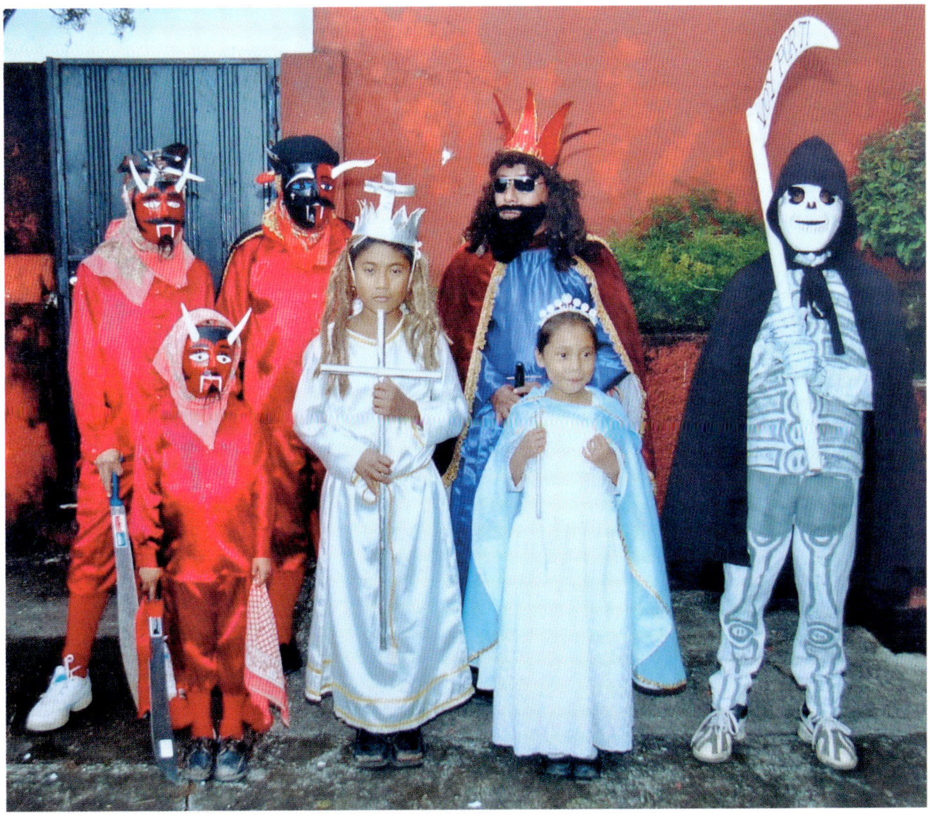

Left: In Hueytamalco, Puebla, the family of Marcelino Santos Castelán shared this photo of characters from la Danza de los Moros y Cristianos. I gather that a number of family members are in this scene, wearing their masks and costumes. Here we see two of the Diablo Mayor figures and one Diablo Menor, along with a crowned Angel, a very young *Reina* (Queen) of the Cristianos with her tiara, La Muerte with his scythe, and one of the Moorish Kings, played by Marcelino himself.

Below left: The son of Marcelino Santos Castelán is wearing his costume and mask to portray the Diablo Menor.

Below center: Felipe Jiménez Martínez of Llagostera, Puebla, is wearing a Diablo mask that he had carved about 10 years ago. It has lost its horns, but still retains the plastic vampire teeth that were added by the mask's owner to enhance that character. Without the horns it vaguely resembles a Santiaguero mask.

Below right: Eusebio Blas Román, a dancer who lives in Tonalmeyoco, Puebla, put on his skull mask and his skeleton coverall to demonstrate how he looked in the Danza de los Moros y Cristianos, in Hueytamalco.

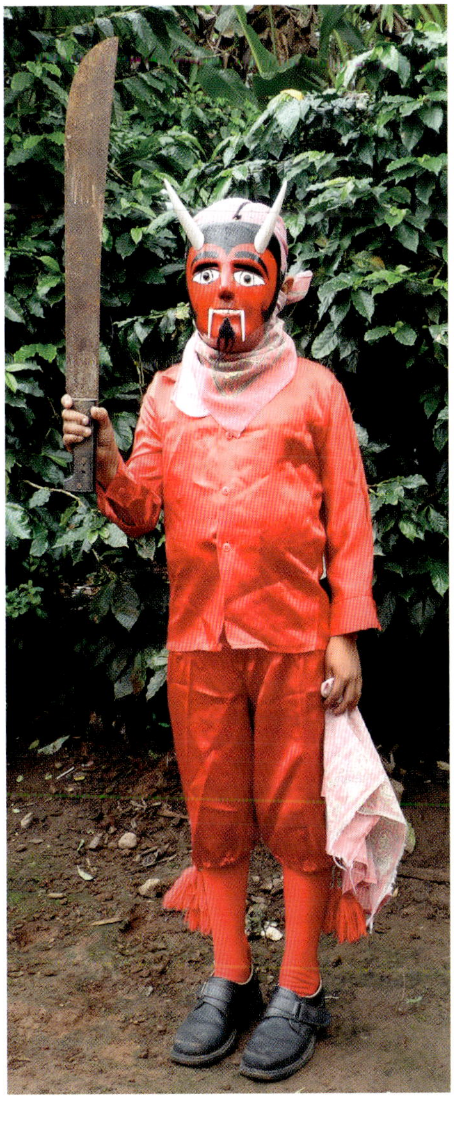

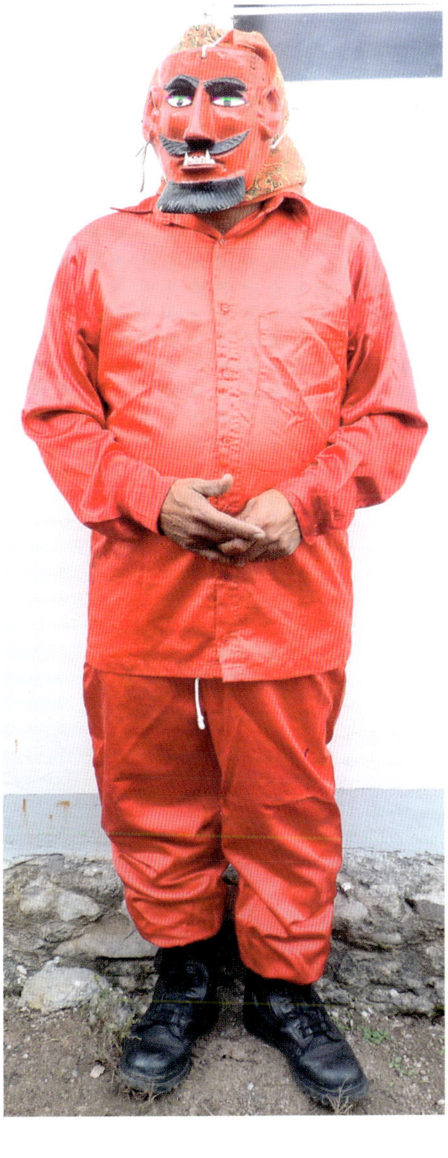

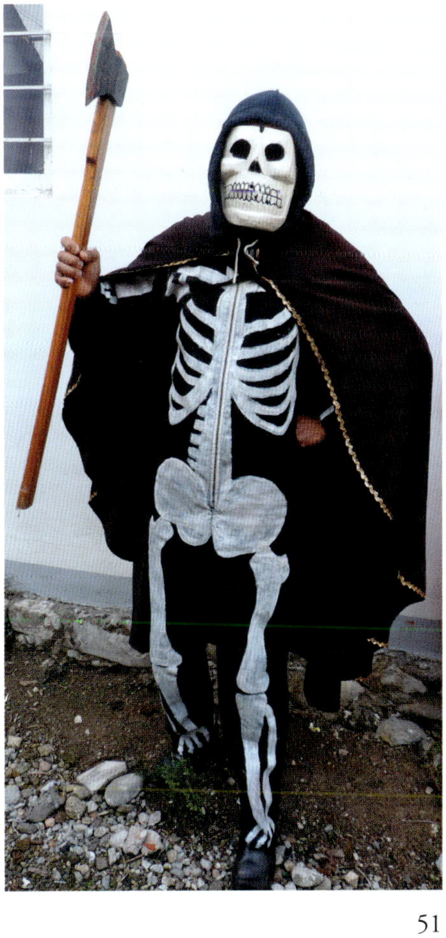

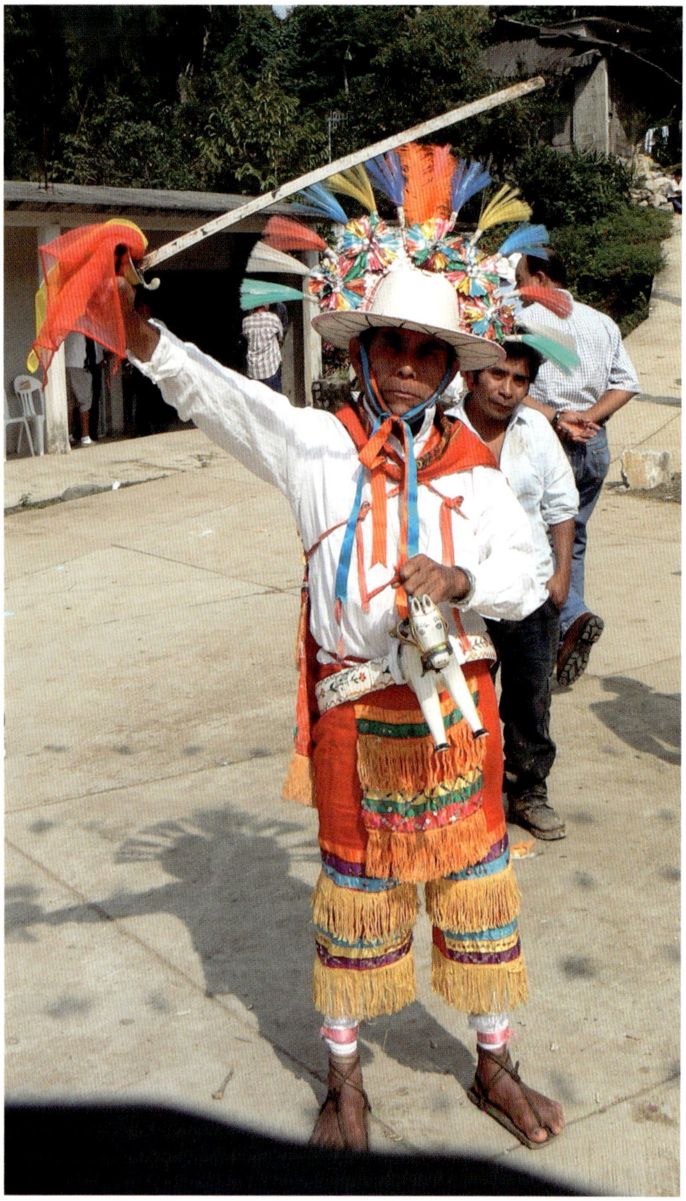

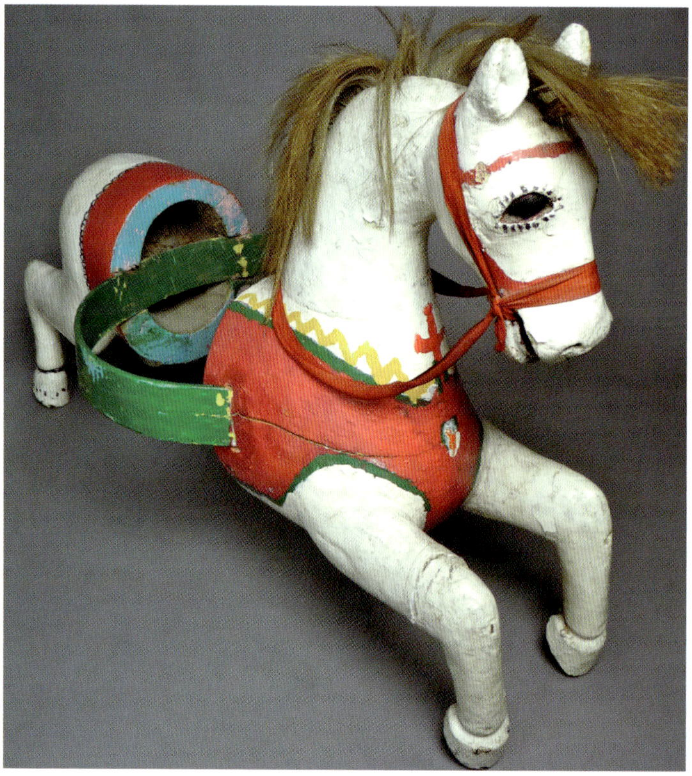

Santiago Apóstol with horse and sword at Cuauhtapanaloyan, Puebla, in December 2008.

This much larger Santiago horse appears to be of the typical style used in Papantla, Veracruz. It too has a hoop-style waist; the hoop is15" in diameter, overall length is 34". Circa 1980. It was allegedly collected with a mask and a helmet that were worn by Santiago with the horse. It is unusual but not unknown for Santiago to wear a mask. *Collection of the author.*

Another small Santiago horse with a hoop waist; the hoop is16" in diameter, overall length is 34". Circa 1980. This one is unusual because it has articulated legs. *Collection of the author.*

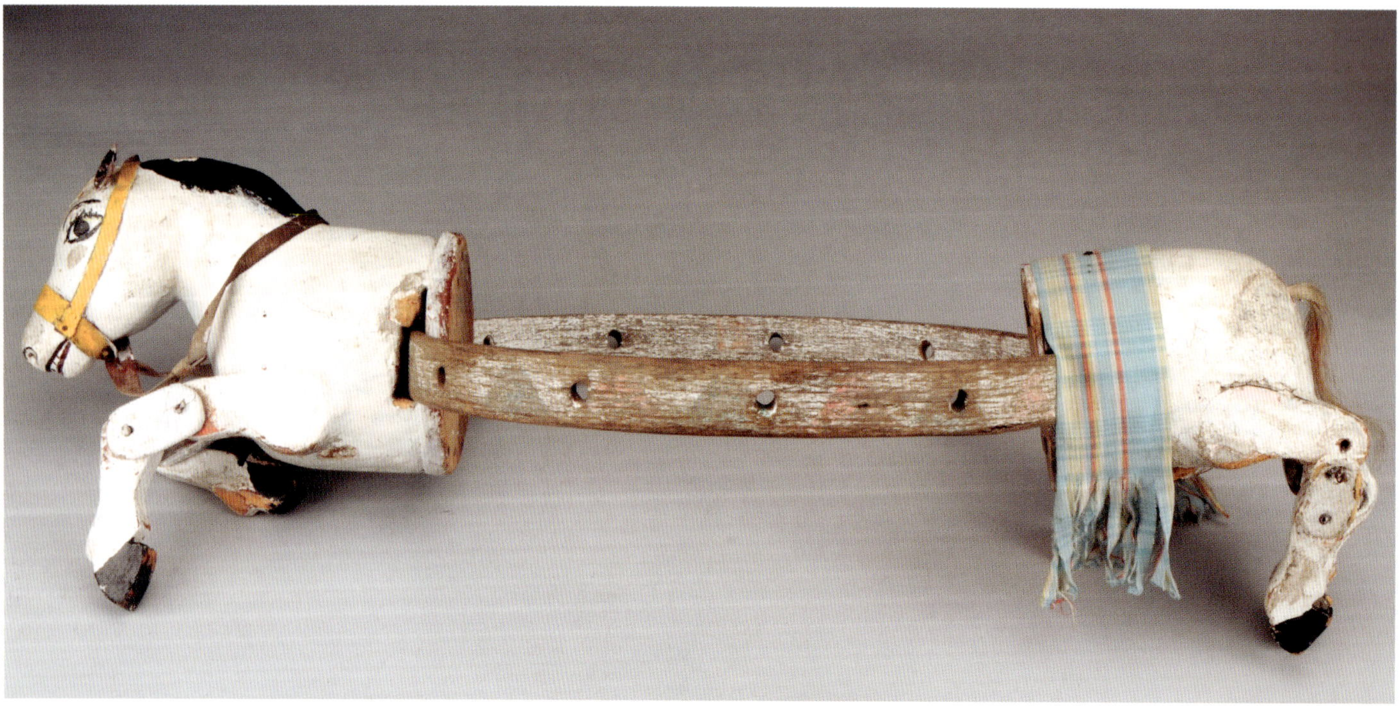

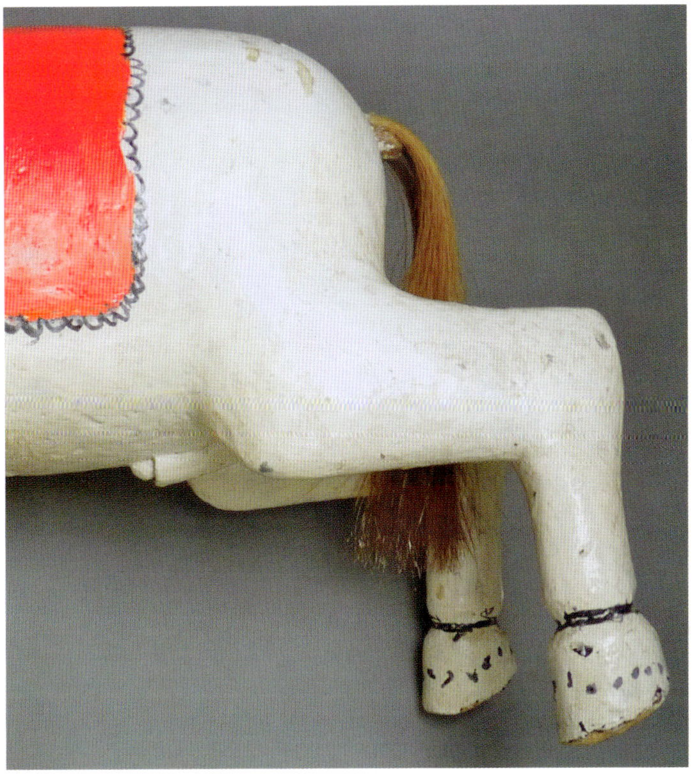

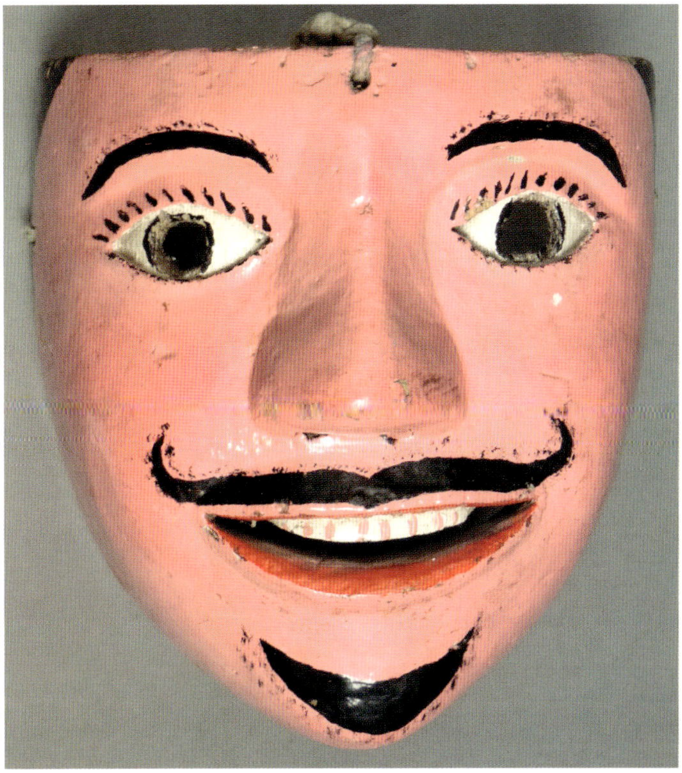

The large Papantla style horse is a stallion.

This Santiago mask was said to have been collected with the horse and helmet; 6½" × 7". Circa 1980. *Collection of the author.*

This Santiago helmet was said to have been collected with this horse and mask; 11" × 12", 8" tall. This helmet is of a classic variant design for Santiago. *Collection of the author.*

This large Santiago horse has a box-type waist; 35" long. Circa 1967. Note the dovetail joints at the corners of the box and the leather halter elements. *Collection of Vernon Kostohryz.*

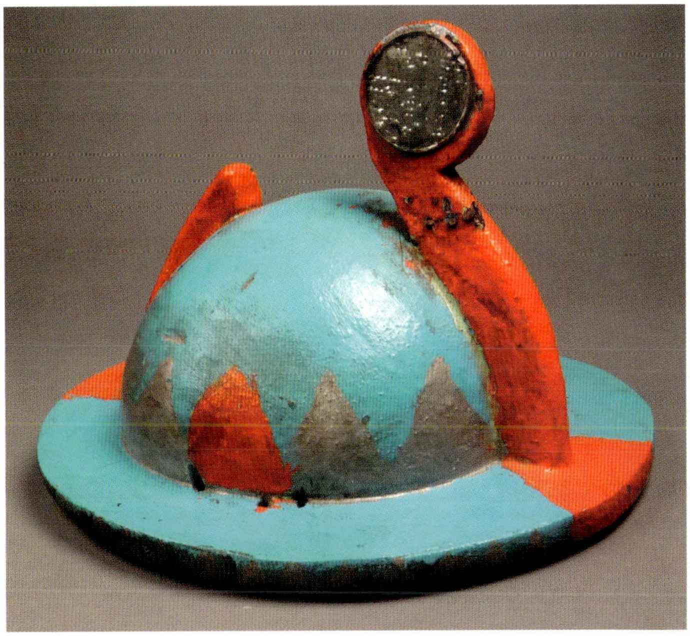

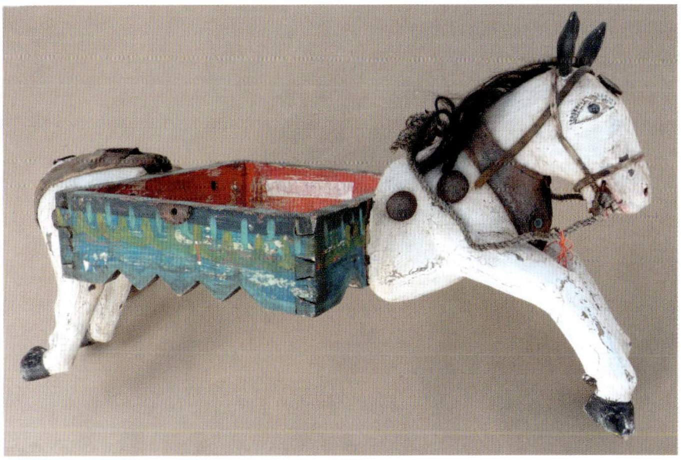

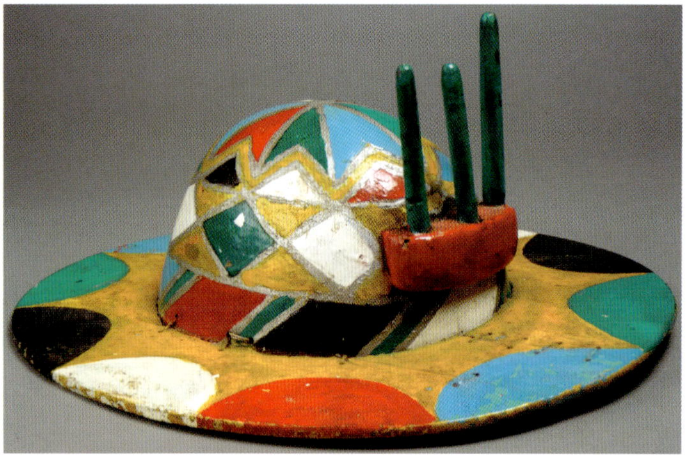

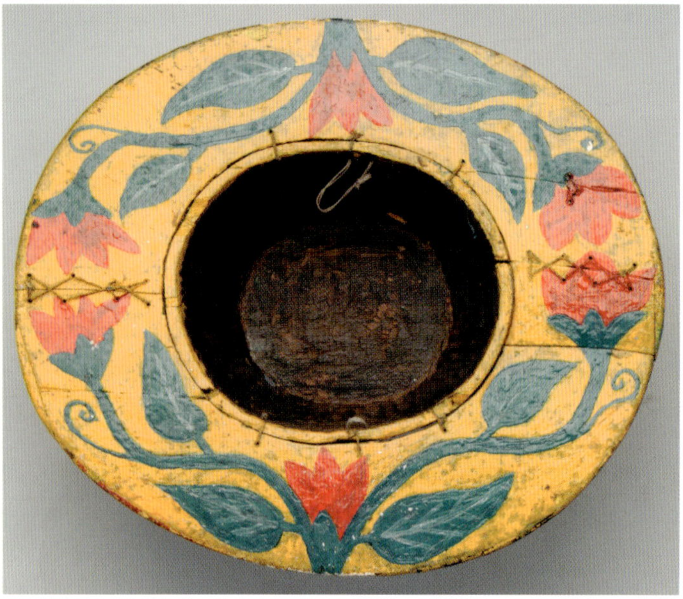

Above: This remarkably decorated, polychrome wooden Santiago helmet was found in Zozocolco de Hidalgo, Veracruz; 11½" × 13½", 4" tall. Circa 1980 or earlier. I don't know the significance of the three posts on the front of the helmet, but this form is otherwise typical of one variety of helmet worn by Santiago. *Collection of the author.*

Below: The underside of the polychrome helmet has an equally beautiful painted design that is completely different from the top.

in the discussion of the Negritos dance, Pilate and the devil are hardly differentiated in this region, and Ichon's description of this mask could be applied to a mask of the devil or to a mask of Pilatos, depending on the community involved.

The Santiaguero dancers have dark red masks, with a cloth border tied under the chin—the *cantunga*, which represents a beard. A Santiaguero wears his mask on his forehead, as if it were the brim of a hat. Behind his head he wears a headdress. A harness around the shoulder or waist carries brass bells, the *cascabeles*. He carries a *chimal*, a small wooden instrument that is said to serve as a ritual shield. Several of the Santiagueros carry banners, for example one of the Virgin of Guadalupe or the flag of Mexico. They wear elaborate red satin costumes and white shirts. They too have Roman names; their leader is Captain Sabario, or simply Sabario.

Leyenaar (1988, 205) reports his impression that only Sabario carries an actual shield in the Santiagueros dance, instead of a chimal. This shield "bears the superimposed image of a golden sun with silver rays." The same writer also describes Sabario's special headdress, "which often hangs down his back" and "is fastened to the back of his head by a cord ... The headdress is an elongated triangle made of a wooden frame covered with glued paper, to which elements such as fiberglass plumes, gold-paper stars, ribbons, and real feathers are attached." A beautiful dance photograph (196–197) includes a view of Sabario's headdress on the second dancer from the left margin. However, I must caution that the photo is mislabeled—"Pilate (left) and Sabarius (right)"—when there is no Pilato in the photo, just Sabario, Santiago with his horse, and three other Santiagueros with morión headdresses. Also note that two of the Santiagueros are wearing their masks on their faces rather than on their foreheads.

The headdress worn by all of the Santiagueros, with the frequent exception of Sabario, is called a *morión*, a *corona*, or simply a *tocado*. The *morión-cabasset* was the traditional steel helmet worn by Spanish soldiers in the 15th century; the headdress worn by the Santiaguero dancers seems to mimic the shape of this helmet. The most traditional method of construction for the morión headdress involves a frame of bamboo splits, covered with tissue paper and decorated with tufts of hair along with a long bundle of feathers extending from the tip. In an alternate construction, a thin board of the appropriate shape is wrapped with shiny paper and decorated.

Toor (1947, photograph 168, after 298) includes a photograph taken by Bodil Christensen prior to 1947 that shows an apparent confrontation between Santiago and a Santiaguero; the Santiaguero is carrying one of these shields, which I will call a "sun shield." This is not clearly Sabario, as the Santiaguero is wearing a morión headdress. When Carlos Moreno Vásquez recently found a sun shield in Olintla, Puebla, and asked which character had carried it, he was told that it had been carried by Callyn, which I took to be a shortened version of Callintsin, the name of Santiago's son.

According to Xochihua Ibarra (2005, 88), the Pilatos group is led by "*un 'presidente' (Pilatos).*" Then there is another character, "*el 'Pilato,' que muchas veces hace el papel de padre de los danzantes*" [Pilato who often plays the role of the father of the dancers]. The author makes an additional point that seems cryptic but interesting: "*El 'presidente' se enfrenta a 'Santiago' y se cubre la cara con una máscara.*" [The President meets Santiago and he covers his face with a mask.] This seems an unusual sequence, to dance unmasked and then to don one's mask when confronting one's enemy. Furthermore, the author makes no reference to mask use by any of the other dancers. This version seems to resemble what Ichon described at Pantepec.

Many other observers, including myself, have attended dances where the members of the Pilatos group do wear masks, which are white or pink. Several of the Pilatos also wear tin crowns as if they represent kings. They carry a sword in one hand and a chimal in the other. The dancer raps his chimal sharply against the flat of his sword, a belligerent gesture of challenge to one's opponent.

In Buena Vista, Puebla, in December 2010, we visited the home of Don Maximo Mateo Corcamo. There, on the family altar, was Santiago's wooden horse, for which Maximo had taken on the duty of providing shelter and care. In front of the horse there were three vessels, which contained corn, water, and salt. Behind the containers there was a small bundle of grass.

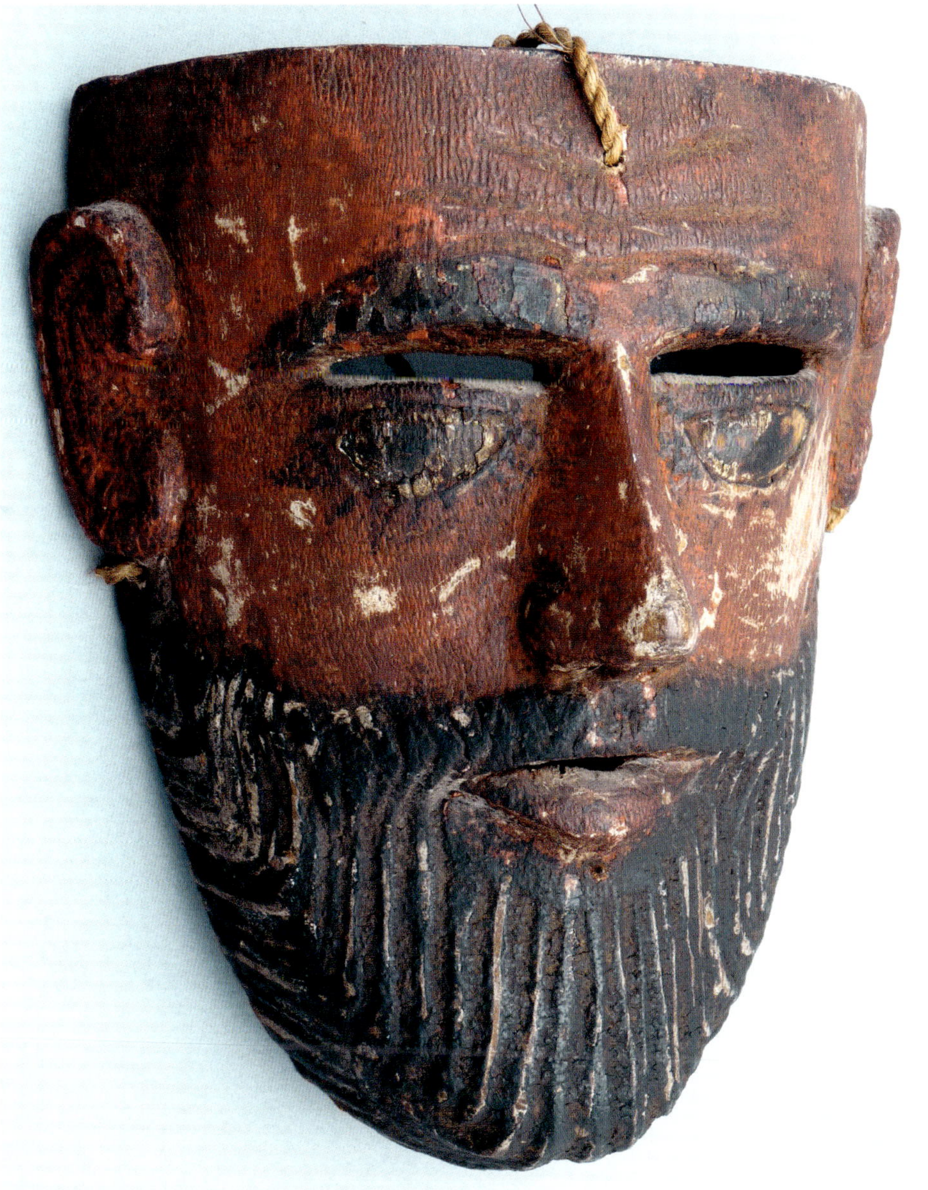

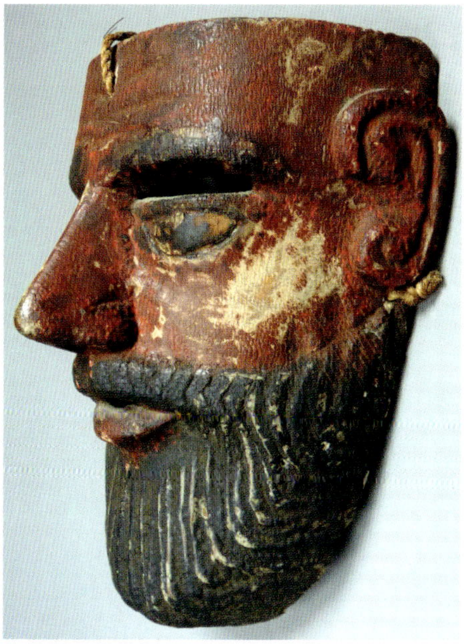

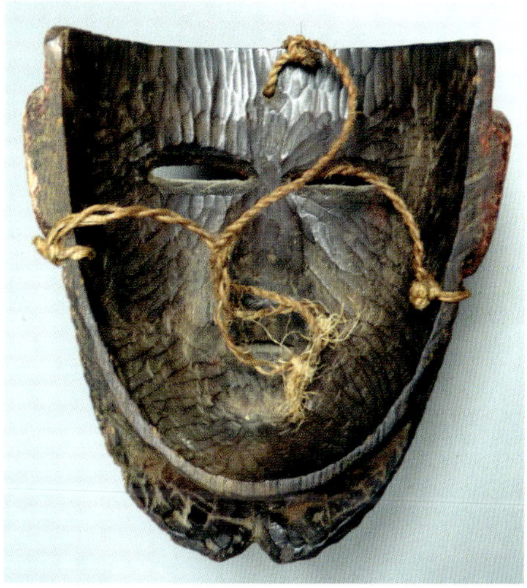

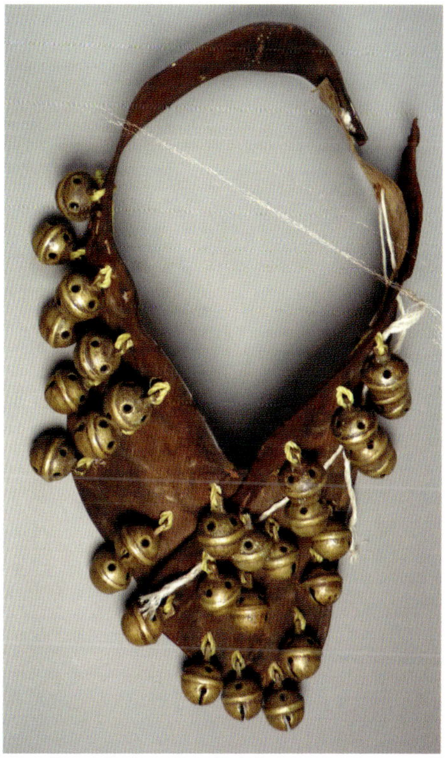

This Santiaguero mask was collected in Mecatlán, Veracruz, in the 1970s. It probably dates to around 1900, based on the paint and the patina on the back. The carver is unknown. *Collection of the author.*

Top right: The side view of the old and nicely carved mask.

Center right: The back of the old Santiaguero mask, which shows marked patina.

Bottom right: A set of cascabeles. This style is worn over one shoulder and under the other arm; sling length is 27". *Collection of the author.*

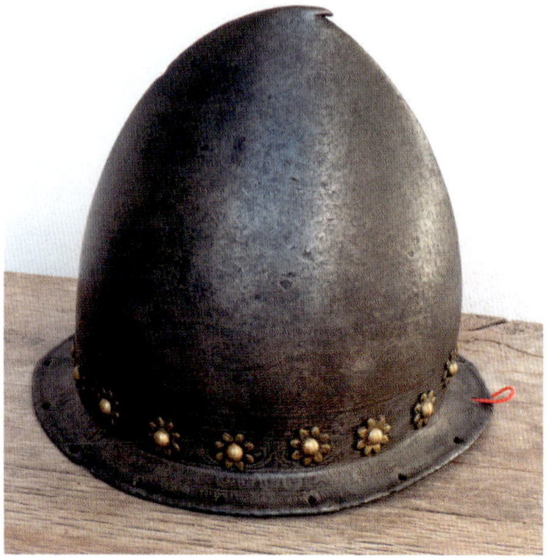

Above: This 16th or 17th century European helmet is one of the types that might have inspired the morión headdress worn by the Santiagueros; 12" tall. *Collection of Vernon Kostohryz.*

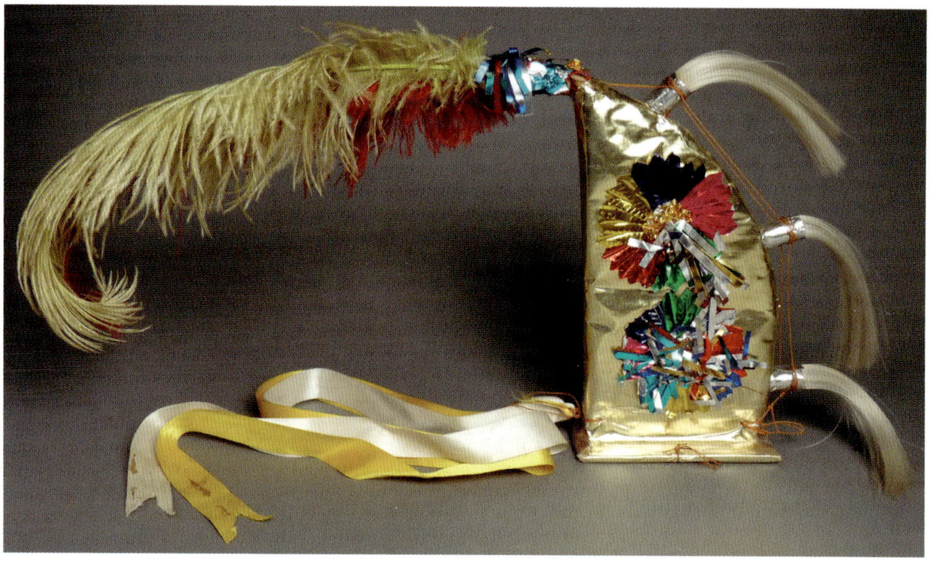

Above right: A morión of the type that is constructed around a thin board; 5" × 10", plus 16" plumes. Circa 2005. This was purchased from a dancer in Cuetzalan, Puebla. *Collection of the author.*

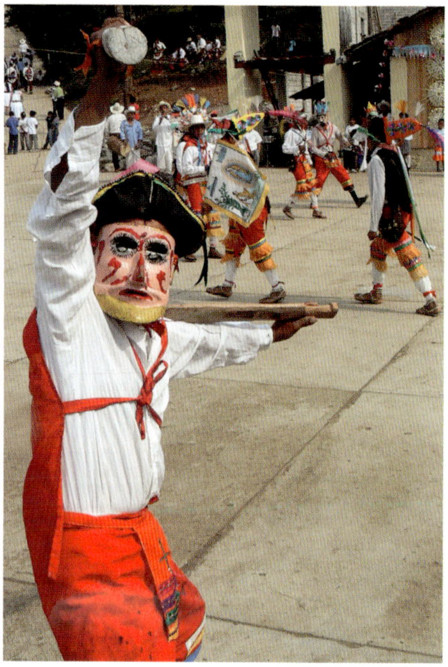

Left: A Pilato dancer at Cuauhtapanaloyan, preparing to strike the flat of his wooden sword with his chimal.

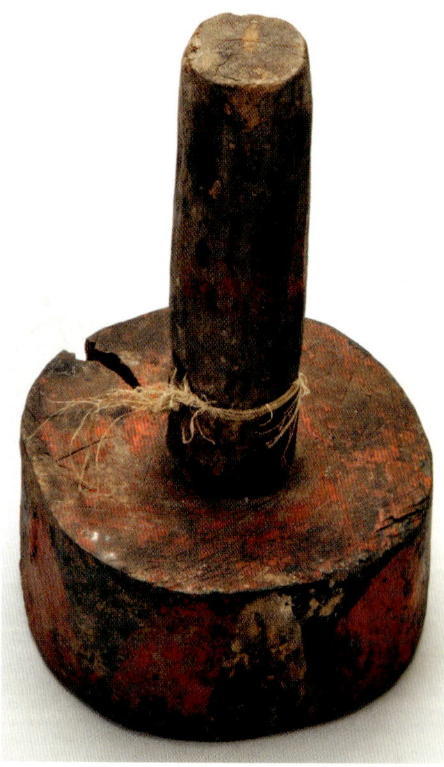

Far left: An old and worn chimal from the state of Puebla; 4½" diameter, 6" long. Circa 1980. *Collection of the author.*

Donald and Dorothy Cordry visited Cuetzalan, Puebla, in 1939 (Furst 1980, xvii); there they learned about Santiago's horse and its care (Cordry and Cordry 1940, 13–15). In that community, the horse is cared for by the dancer who will portray Santiago in the annual fiesta. "During this time he is under obligation to the community to give the horse a bowl of Maíze and a bowl of water each day. It is believed that if this is not done, that if the horse is not treated well, it will run away to another village." The Cordrys explain that the horse can be kept on the family altar or in a special stable made for this purpose. They further report that "We tried to purchase one of these old horses for the Southwest Museum, but it was impossible to do so, as the Indians would not show them to us, and indeed, owing to the reverence which they have for the animals, even denied possessing them." The local carver was even unwilling to make a horse to their order; they had to content themselves with a miniature copy. The Indians seem to treat Santiago's horse as a living being whose status approaches that of a saint, perhaps because of the vital partnership between the horse and Santiago or due to other independent actions, such as in the account that Santiago's horse carried a boy into the sky to become the sun (Stresser-Péan 2009, 443–444).

At Maximo's house a young boy, who is probably Maximo's son, dressed in his costume as Callintsin, the son of Santiago. An older boy dressed as a Santiaguero, another boy dressed as a Pilato, and a neighbor girl, seen later in this chapter, dressed in her costume as a Negrito. Obviously this was another family that generously welcomed the opportunity to share their cultural heritage with us. We might note that the Santiaguero dancer carries a dance wand along with his chimal, a ritual shield. Santiago and Callintsin carry swords. The Pilato carries a sword and a chimal.

Martin Nicolás Francisco, whom we visited in his home in the pueblo of Degaleana, Puebla, in December 2008, rents masks to dance groups. We asked Martin to teach us about the Santiagueros dance, of which at that time we knew very little. To our surprise he brought out a spiral notebook; several pages had the heading, "Relación de los Santiagueros." These notes were carefully written in Náhuatl, apparently copied from some older source to document the characters and the action of the dance. It was exciting to see the continuing tradition of transmission, a process that had been maintained over hundreds of years in some communities. Martin had to study his notes in order to extract from those pages a complete list of characters; in retrospect he was graciously attempting to supply information that was no longer so familiar in some details. Neither Carlos Moreno Vásquez, Vernon Kostohryz, nor I knew enough about the dance to assist Martin in this effort. The main benefit of Martin's teaching was that I realized for the first time that there were two groups of dancers, the Santiagos or Santiagueros (wearing dark red masks) and the Pilatos (wearing either pink or white masks). Until that time I hadn't realized that these two distinctly different groups of masks were in the same dance; I thought they were in two or three different dances.

Martin identified the characters in the Santiagueros group while Carlos took notes. The highlights were that the Santiagueros characters include Alchareo (the General) and five Roman Captains— Sabario, Alveres, Don Antonio, Santorio, and Escribano (the Secretary); of these both Sabario and the General carry flags; Don Antonio wears a *corona* (crown); and the General, Alveres, Don Antonio, and Escribano wear a cantunga on the mask. Martin included Santiago in the Santiagueros group, and he made no mention of Santiago's son.

Then Martin ran down the list of the Pilatos, who wear masks with pink faces in his dance group. They are led by el Presidente (Pilate), and include the Governor, Carifaz (i.e., Joseph Caiaphas, the high priest of the Jewish Temple at the time of the crucifixion), Bartolo, Pilotiso Chocoyotzin (whom he identified as Pilate's son) and two kings. I don't recall any other published reference to the son of Pilate; this is an interesting variation.

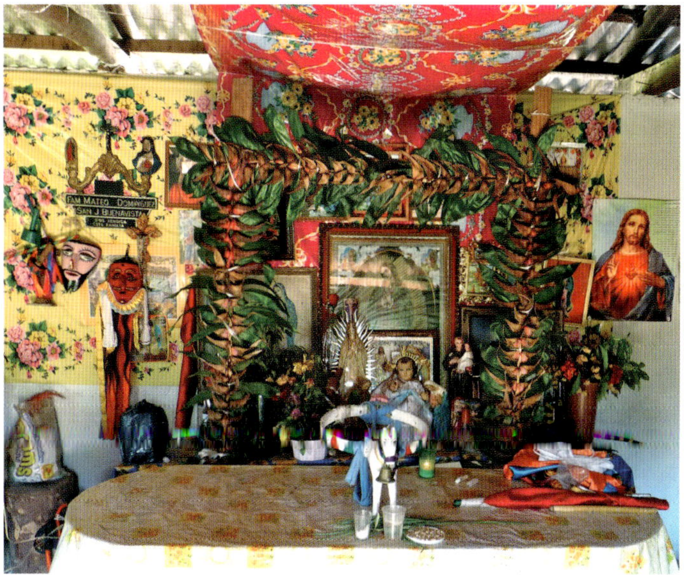

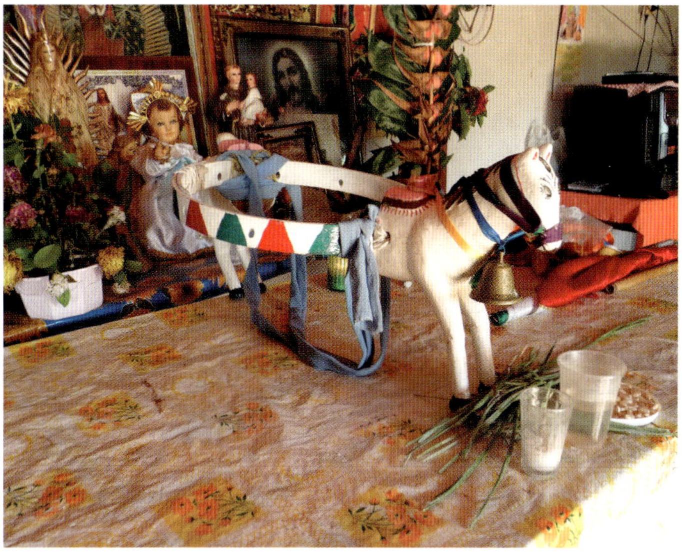

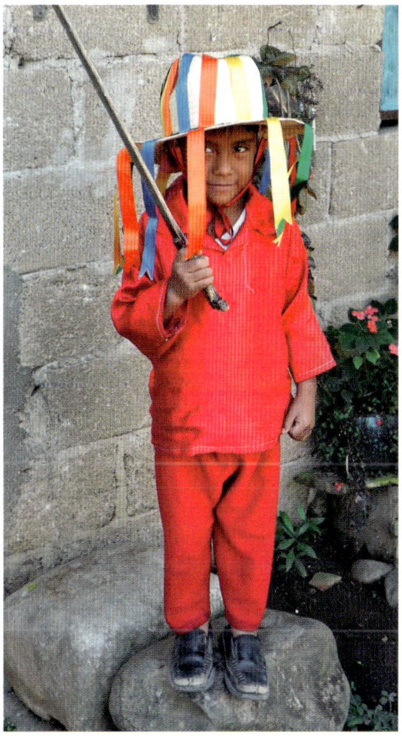

From top:
The table that serves as the family altar has been extended by a second table in front, to make room for the horse. Note how the masks and other dance accessories are stored on or around the altar. At lower left is a bag, which appears to contain a morión headdress.

On the altar table, Santiago's horse has been provided with salt, water, corn, and some grass. Note the heavy old brass bell that is tied to the horse's neck. The hoop for this horse was taken from a wooden drum; that is why there are so many holes in the hoop. Drum hoops are a common source for replacing the original hoop when it fails. The blue cloth straps tied to the hoop are to suspend the horse from the dancer's shoulders.

This handsome boy wears the red satin suit and the hat with ribbons that are traditional in Buena Vista for the character of Callintsin, Santiago's son. He carries a wooden sword for his duty as the protector of Santiago's horse. His expression is a bonus.

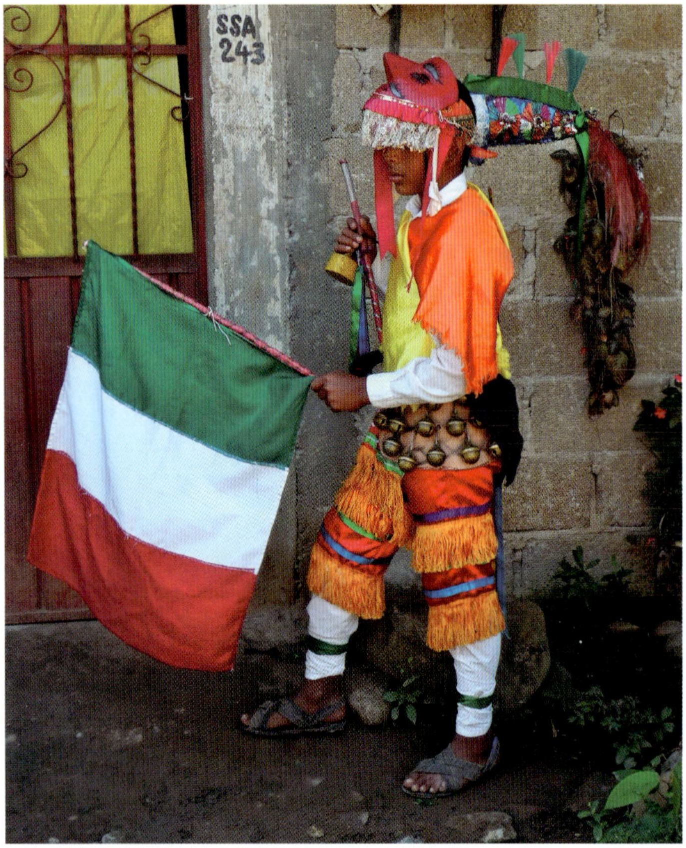

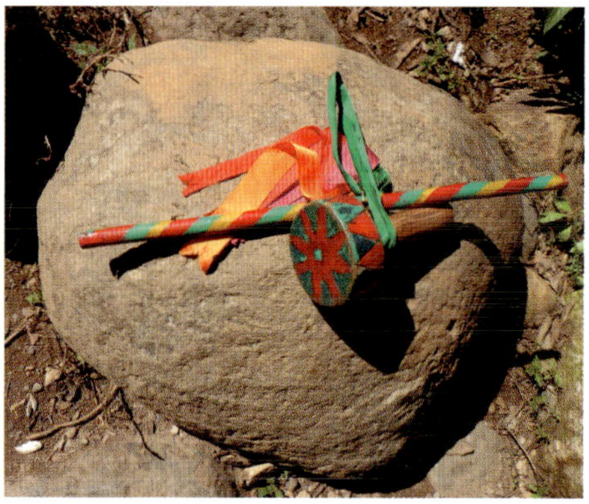

Left: This young man wears the typical costume of a Santiaguero. This includes the mask in the style of this region, the cantunga, the morión headdress, a white shirt under a long black vest and silk or satin scarves tied across his chest, cascabeles around his waist, the typical red satin short trousers with gold fringes over white leggings, and sandals on his feet. He carries a dance wand and a chimal in his right hand; in his left he holds the Mexican flag.

Bottom left: This young man is dressed as a Pilato. He is demonstrating how a Pilato clacks his sword with his chimal. He is wearing a tin crown. Note the flat spot on the chin of his mask, which is a detail seen on the masks of Artemio Zaragoza Zaragoza.

Above: This chimal is beautifully painted and has a very nice patina from long use. The dance wand is also attractive.

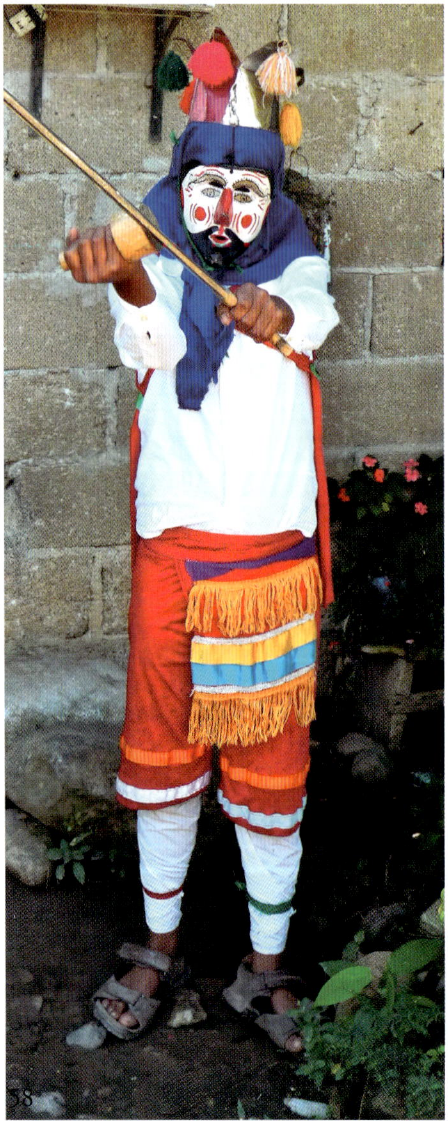

Being a renter of masks, Martin undoubtedly possesses a number of them; apparently most were being rented at the time of our visit. We were thrilled to see two of his favorites, one in a dance photo and the other in his house. Both were clearly carved by a great deceased master from San Antonio Rayón—Narciso Iturbide Charo. The one in the house was very large, with a long, prominent goatee; on the end of the goatee the face of a jaguar was carved and then gilded. Martin told us that he purchased this mask when he was 13 years old; he was 42 at the time of our visit, so he had owned this mask for nearly 30 years and it was already used when he bought it. This was the mask worn by Martin when he played Sabario, he said. Martin reported that when he danced as the General of the Santiagueros he carried the Mexican flag. He showed us a photograph of himself in that role, wearing another fine old mask by Narciso Iturbide Charo, but that one was smaller and lacked the golden jaguar. Such differences undoubtedly connote something about the status of the character portrayed by the mask.

It is a strange fact that the Santiagueros, whose name makes it seem that they are Santiago's allies, actually fail to assist him directly in his battle with the Pilatos. Either Santiago or the Santiagueros challenge the Pilatos; they never do so together. In a Santiagueros dance script quoted by Francis Toor (1947, 350–352) from the state of Morelos, a place that is not very far from our area of study, there is vivid expression of ideas and feelings that make it seem that the Santiagueros are actively in conflict with Santiago. For example. as he leaves Pilatos, apparently to do battle with Santiago, Sabario prays:

> Let the wrath of my burning resolve
> Give off flame
> Leaving Christianity
> In dust and ashes.

In contrast, the names of the Pilatos such as Pontius Pilate, King Herod, or Joseph Caiaphas, clearly demonstrate their status as universal enemies of Christendom.

After repeated clashing of swords, the Pilatos are defeated by Santiago and converted to Christianity. But meanwhile it seems that there was a hidden script. Max Harris explains his discoveries in this regard (Harris 1993, 102–103):

> I had spoken earlier in the day with Sr Pablo Huerta Ramir, who carves and paints masks for several of the troupes in the area. To my surprise, he had said that the *santiagos* represent the sun. This is why, he explained, the face of the mask is red and there are emblems of the sun on the chin, eyes and eyebrows: golden ovals and circles outlined in black and with black rays extending. It also explains why the *santiagos* wear their masks on their foreheads. "They are", he told me, "looking at the sun". There is also an emblem of the sun on the dancer's shield. Although the Yohualichán dancers did not carry shields, a *Santiago* from San Miguel Tzinacapán, whom I had photographed at his home the previous day, did ... The wooden shield, about twelve inches in diameter, is painted sky blue. In its lower half there is a red face, circled by gold and emanating golden rays. Later this dancer was to confirm to me that the *santiagos*, in his words, "son el sol" [are the sun]. At the end of the dance, Sr Huerta added, *Santiago Caballero*, whom he also called "*el rey sol*" [King Sun], would kill "*el rey pilato.*"

Harris (1993, 103) met a Santiaguero who carried such a shield. Thus we have now accumulated four examples of a shield with the sun's image that is carried by one or more of the alleged servants of the sun, whether this might be Callintsin, Sabario, or another Santiaguero. The concrete evidence of these sun shields is strong support for the information collected by Harris regarding the alleged hidden allegiance of the Santiagueros.

Harris continues his inquiry (1993, 103):

> Who then, I asked, are the *pilatos*? Sr Huerta was unclear. In the dance, he explained the sun is challenged by "a less powerful sun", represented by a pink or white mask. The *pilatos* are this less powerful force. Watching the dancers that evening, it dawned on me that the pale face, rosy cheeks and dark beards of the *pilatos'* masks were intended to represent the features of the Spanish conquistadors. My suspicion was confirmed the next day by a spectator who volunteered the observation that the *pilatos* "*son los españoles.*"

In this section about the Santiagueros dance Harris has at least one other important lesson to teach us (1993, 102). On the basis of my observations and reading, I was not aware that the Santiagueros engaged in any direct conflict with the Pilatos; I thought that they left all this to Santiago. However, when Harris made it a point to watch what happened in just one place over a period of two days he observed "a series of stylized clashes between the *santiagos* and the *pilatos*. All

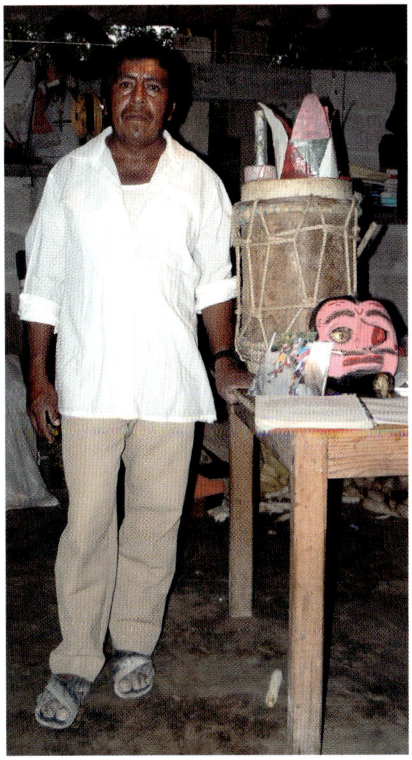

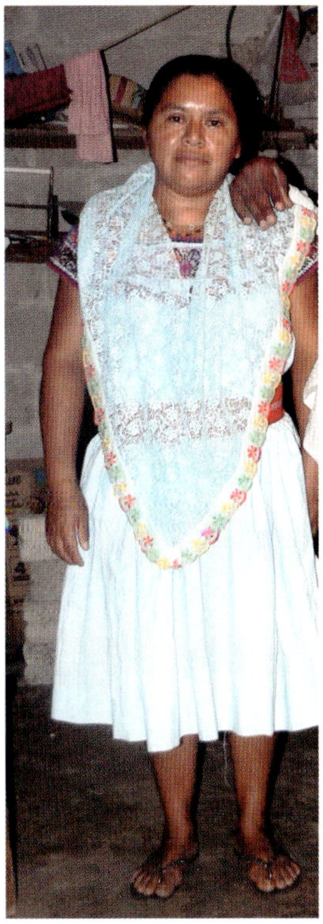

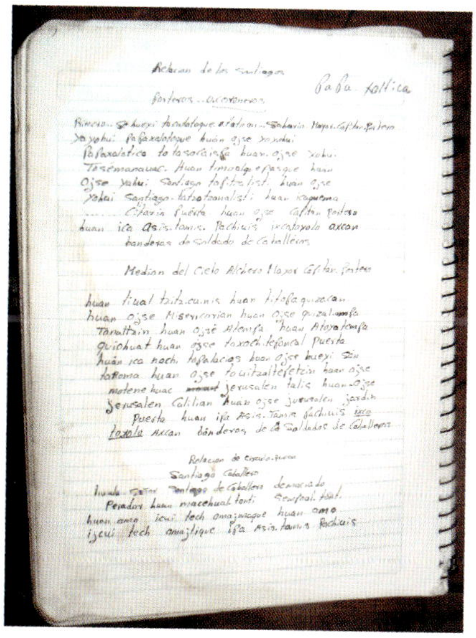

Top left: Martin with dance paraphernalia. His wonderful old mask, carved by Narciso Iturbide Charo, rests on the table beside him, along with a drum, a tin crown for a Pilato King, and a chimal. I can't explain why the mask has a pink face although it was worn by Sabario. In the background we see ears of seed corn from the last harvest, commonly stored in the house to protect them for the next planting.

Top right: Martin's wife, who is standing next to Martin in this picture, has dressed in traditional clothing for my benefit. Her blouse was probably embroidered by hand and her belt was woven on a back strap loom.

Bottom left: A page from Martin's notebook, regarding the "relacion de los Santiagos."

would dance simultaneously, the *pilatos* at one end (away from the altar), the *santiagos* in the middle, and the *caballero* at the other end. Then each of the *santiagos*, designated in turn by the maestro, would challenge the *pilatos*, meeting the proffered sword stroke with a raised fist holding a colored cloth. The *caballero* did not yet approach the *pilatos*, remaining separated from them by the *santiagos* and brandishing his sword in a series of solitary and self-absorbed dance steps."

This pattern continued, Harris observed (1993, 106), until three o'clock in the afternoon of the second day. At that point Santiago began to directly challenge the Pilatos, "ritually threatening them with his sword and walking behind them, drawing his sword across the nape of their necks." Finally Santiago chased the Pilatos into the church and when Harris followed, he discovered that "*el rey pilato*" was lying on the floor as if dead, apparently having been "killed" by Santiago.

To briefly recap, Harris has presented evidence that the Santiagueros may secretly represent the soldiers of the sun, led covertly by Santiago, while the Pilatos may stand for the Spanish or the Mestizos. It seems these latter powers are the ones who must be defeated by Santiago if justice is to be restored.

As mentioned earlier, ambiguity seems to cloak the identity or role of the Santiagueros. In spite of their name they don't stand shoulder to shoulder with Santiago and Callintsin in the fight against Pilate and the Pilatos. They bear the names of Roman captains, as if Pontius Pilate must be their commander. Yet they skirmish with the Pilatos, separately from Santiago. In an old script from a nearby region (Toor 1947, 350–352) Sabario described himself as resolved to leave Christianity in "dust and ashes," as if he and Santiago were the most bitter of enemies. Now in the context of our growing understanding we have the opportunity to re-read Sabario's words in a new light. His allegiance is to the sun, but the sun is Christ, so it is unlikely that Sabario is an enemy of Christianity. However, he is the enemy of the Spanish, who call themselves Christians even as they commit great injustices. Sabario appears to be the enemy of false Christians, of self-labeled Christians who behave otherwise. Thus the dance probably represents a covert indictment of the hypocrisy of the Spanish and a prayer to God to restore justice. The dance ends with the conversion of the false Christians (the Pilatos) to Christianity.

There is a very close variant of the Santiagueros dance called la Danza de los Ormegas or Hormegas. In spoken Spanish the letter "h" is silent, so these two words share the same pronunciation. Neither one occurs in the Spanish dictionary. I am going to assume that these are two variations of the same word, and I will standardize on "Hormega" for a reason that will soon become evident.

Gaona Vega and Acosta Báez (2005, 85–87) describe the dance as a variation of the "danza de los santiagueros." In this dance the Santiaguero dancers are called Hormegas instead; otherwise the cast of characters remains almost entirely unchanged. Sabario leads the Hormegas, assisted by Don Antonio, Santorio, and Akcharrión. Pilatos still leads the Pilatos dancers, and the latter group is still opposed by Santiago and his son Callintsin. The dance includes several characters who seem unfamiliar; these are Tonal Pérez, who is apparently one of the Hormegas, and most mysteriously, el Viejo. The latter will probably turn out be yet another "Pilato" character, although there is no proof of this as yet.

Those authors (Gaona Vega and Acosta Báez 2005, 85–87) report that according to local oral tradition, Pilato had always wanted to kill Jesus, and when he was able to enlist the *Judíos* (Jews) to assist him, he completed the murder. When Santiago heard about Jesus' death, he went after Pilate, trampled him under his stallion's hooves and stabbed him to death with a spear. The Hormegas wear masks that resemble those of the Santiagueros, medium pink with long noses. They wear extremely tall conical caps that are farther extended with upright plumes, instead of the morión headdress worn by the Santiagueros. On the basis of an indistinct photo (87), it is probable that the Hormega dancers wear their masks on their faces and not on their foreheads. This is what one would have expected, because it would be difficult to wear one's mask on the forehead when this very tall cap was in the way.

Several years ago when Carlos Moreno Vásquez, Vernon Kostohryz, and I had combed Ixtepec, Puebla, for masks, we could readily see that the Hormegas dance had once been well established there, because we found at least four or maybe six identical Hormega masks, but just one mask that may have been worn by a Santiaguero. Later I had to consider whether this latter mask might have been worn by a Pilato. Back then we didn't realize that all of the masks in the Hormegas dance were the same shade of red, so we assigned every mask that was dark red to either the Hormegas or the Santiagueros. We also found what was obviously Santiago's hat, and concluded that this too went with the Hormegas dance there. All these things were dusty and neglected, suggesting that the Hormegas dance had not been active there for a number of years.

Recently we had the good fortune to identify an Hormega dance group in Olintla, Puebla. I was permitted to photograph a representative sample of the masks and, subsequently, I was provided with the name of the character that used each mask. Eventually Vernon Kostohryz purchased Santiago's horse, Callyn's sun shield, and one of the Hormega masks from this group while I negotiated to trade for the Pilatos, el Presidente mask. Finally, based on all this data and material we were able to find additional duplicates of some of these masks and in the process to identify the carvers. All this took about one year.

On the Hormega side, I can confirm the impression that the characters in this dance are virtually identical to those in the Santiagueros group, although spellings sometimes vary. We found masks for Sabario, Santorio, and Alberis. On the Pilatos side we discovered that Pilatos, el President had a new name—*el Pilato Malo* (evil or wicked Pilato)—and that his mask was explicitly the mask of a devil, probably Satan. This of course reminds us of Ichon's observations at Pantepec, Puebla, where Pilatos, el Presidente seemed clearly to be the devil. Pilato Malo was assisted by at least two *Ayudantes*, adjutant Pilatos. As will be evident from the photos, Pilato Malo has a human face but the ears of a goat. This mask and several of the Hormega masks were carved by Magno León, a deceased carver who is emerging as one of the greatest masters from this region. These masks are discussed in greater detail in Chapter 6.

As discussed later in the presentation of the Diablo masks that are used in the Miguelitos dance, it is common for a mask that represents the Devil or Satan to have the ears of a goat. Diablo masks from Michoacan or Guerrero demonstrate the same feature. What is different about the Pilato Malo mask is that it is not presented as being the mask of a Diablo; it is said to be the mask of Pontius Pilate. The mask has a finely carved, refined, European face, and not the exaggerated and distorted features of a Diablo mask. It is only when we notice the ears that we realize that we are in the presence of the devil. Rather than being a mask of the devil, this is a mask of *the devil in disguise*. But of course the disguise is transparent; apparently the secret goal of the dance was to reveal that the Spanish behave so badly because their leader is actually Satan himself. Ironically, in the Miguelitos dance, where the mask of the Diablo is so blatantly presented, the character with that mask is much more nuanced, perhaps the secret champion of the Indians, but one can't be sure.

Although the masks for the Hormega characters and the masks for the Pilatos characters are all painted the same dark red color, there is one easy way to tell them apart, and this reflects what we learned earlier from Harris. The Hormega masks have the same painted designs in black and gold or silver and the same golden brows as the Santiaguero masks described by Señor Huerta Ramir, marking them as the agents of the sun, despite the name change. There is, however, no trace of gold or silver decoration on the masks worn by the Pilatos dancers.

As noted earlier, it has proven difficult to determine the meaning of the words *Hormega* or *Ormega* from conventional Spanish dictionaries. The only established word that comes close is *hormiga*, the Spanish word for ant. Ironically, a legend reported by Álvarez Boada (2005, 90–91) to explain the Dance of the Santiagueros seems to supply a possible clue to the understanding of the word *Hormega*. The author describes an apparently anonymous tract or booklet about the life of Santiago Apóstol that was once sold in public markets in the Totonac area of Veracruz: "Vida del Señor Santiago." This was the source of the following legend. Santiago was called by Jesus to become an apostle and he witnessed many miracles during his service in that role. After Christ's death Santiago became a traveling preacher; he went to Spain but later returned to Jerusalem where he continued this ministry. He converted Fileto, a disciple of the magician Hormógenes. The latter was angered by this and directed his band of demons to bind Santiago. They were outmaneuvered by Santiago and became his servants. Hormógenes was subsequently converted to Christianity. This angered the Jews, who asked Herod to condemn Hormógenes to death. Herod agreed and Hormógenes was executed.

In *The Cult of Santiago: Traditions, Myths, and Pilgrimages* (Stone 1927), there is a reference to the *Apostolic History of Abdias*, an early Christian document that may have been the source for the document described by Álvarez Boada. Here are some passages as presented by Stone (115):

> According to this History, which some scholars hold to be little better than romance, St. James was a popular preacher in Jerusalem. In his teaching he was opposed by two magicians, Hermogenes and Philetus … Philetus was won over to the church by St. James, and immediately Hermogenes in anger bound him by magical incantations, and exclaimed: "We will see if James can free you!" The victim of this atrocious spite managed to make known his evil condition to St. James, and St. James sent back his kerchief, and by it Philetus was freed and came to him. Hermogenes, however, was not to be outdone in this wise. He dispatched several demons, probably carefully selected for their courage and skill, and bade them fetch both James and Philetus to him. The demons went their way, but as soon as they got into the presence of the Apostle they began to howl in the air and complain that an angel had bound them with fiery chains. St. James eased them of their pain, and in turn sent them to bring Hermogenes bound to him. They did so.

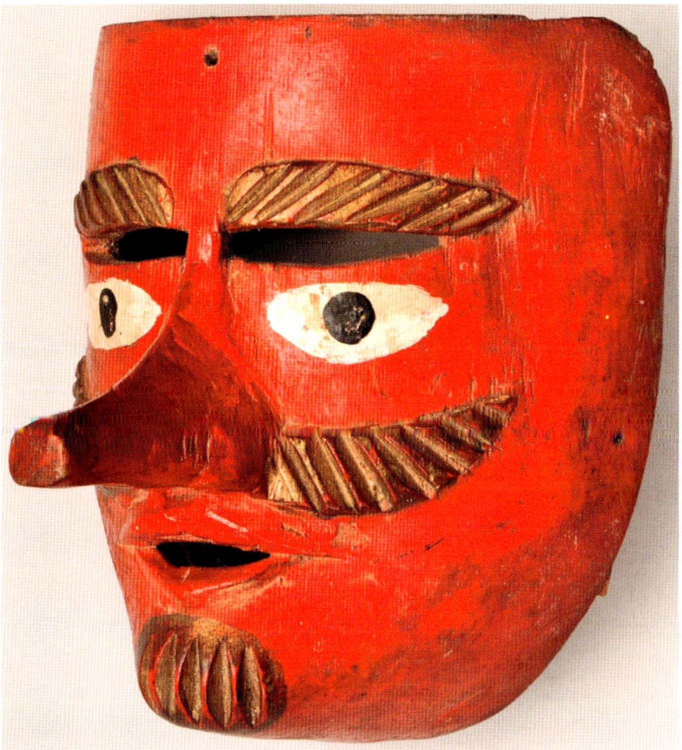

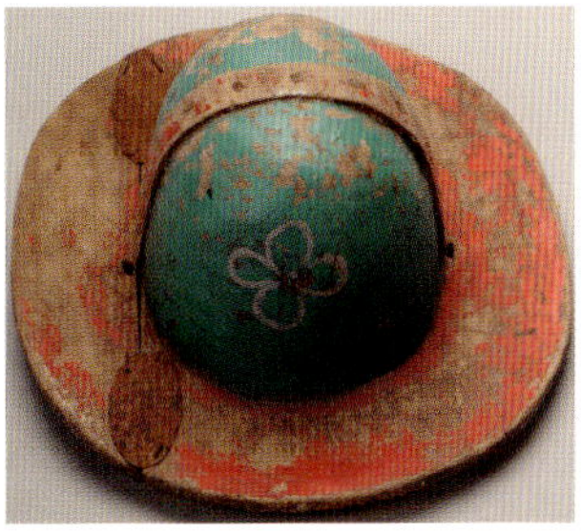

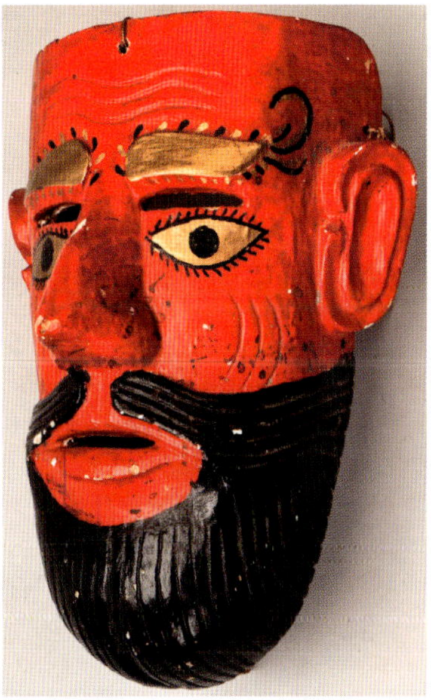

From top:
This is a mask just like the cluster found in Ixtepec, Puebla, in 2007; 5½" × 7". Circa 1980. The carver was Benito Juárez Figueroa. This mask is discussed more fully in Chapter 5. *Collection of the author.*

This is the old wooden Santiago helmet found in Ixtepec in 2007; we assume that it was used in the Hormegas dance there. We wonder whether it was carved by Benito Juárez Figueroa, because he seems to have been the dominant carver in Ixtepec at the time when the Hormegas dance was active; 13" × 15", 5" tall. Circa 1970. *Collection of the author.*

This Santiaguero mask was found in Ixtepec in 2007; 7" × 9½". Circa 1970. It too was carved by Benito Juárez Figueroa, based on the ear design. This mask is discussed more fully in Chapter 5. *Collection of the author.*

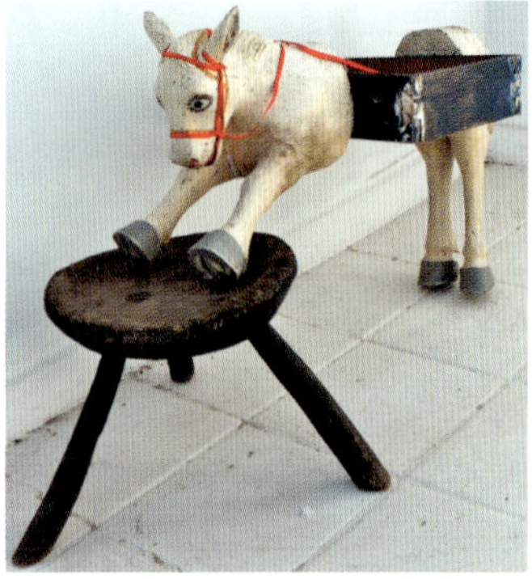

This dance horse for Santiago was part of the collection of the dance group in Olintla; 34" long. Circa 1970. It was carved by Benito Juárez Figueroa. *Collection of Vernon Kostohryz.*

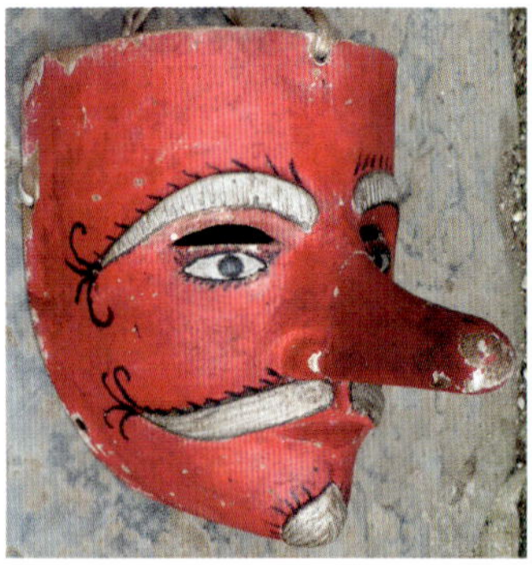

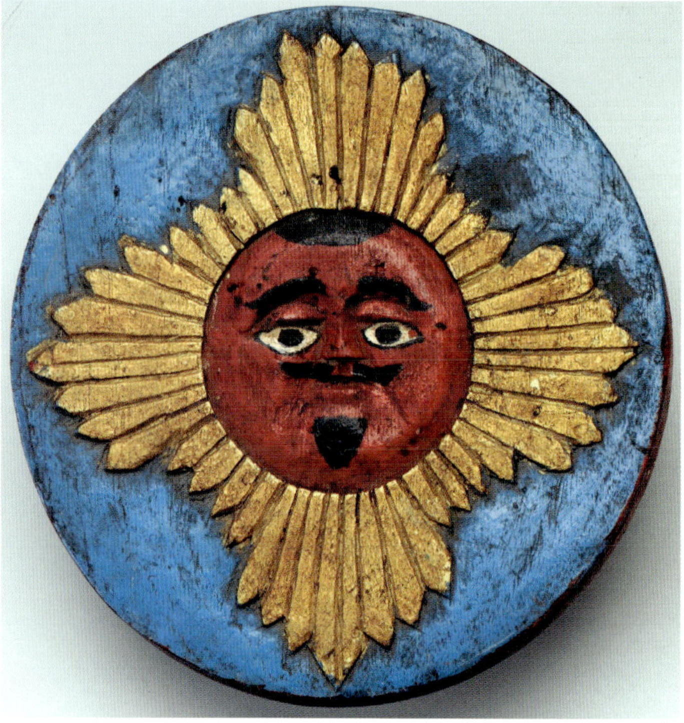

This Hormega mask was worn by the character Alberis. Note the rounded end of the nose; 6" × 7". Circa 1970. The carver was Magno León. *Collection of the dance group.*

This sun shield was also part of the dance at Olintla; 8½" diameter. Circa 1970. It too was carved by Benito Juárez Figueroa. It was said to have been danced by Callyn, which I suppose must be a variation on Callintsin, Santiago's son. *Collection of the author.*

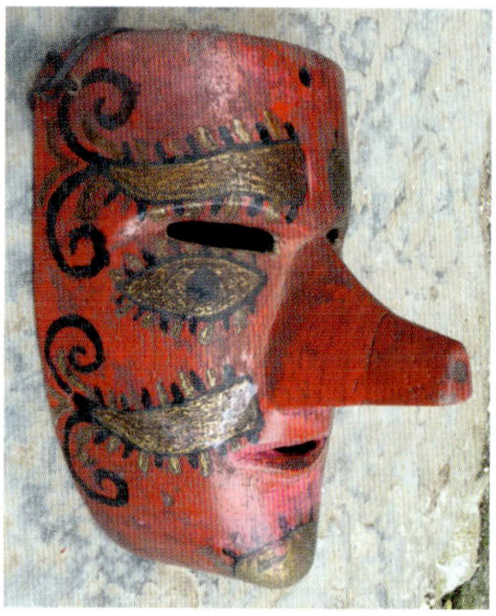

This is one of the Hormega masks from the group in Olintla, Puebla; 6 ¼" × 8". Circa 1970. It was worn by the character Sabario. The carver was Leopoldo Cortez González of Olintla, Puebla. *Collection of Vernon Kostohryz.*

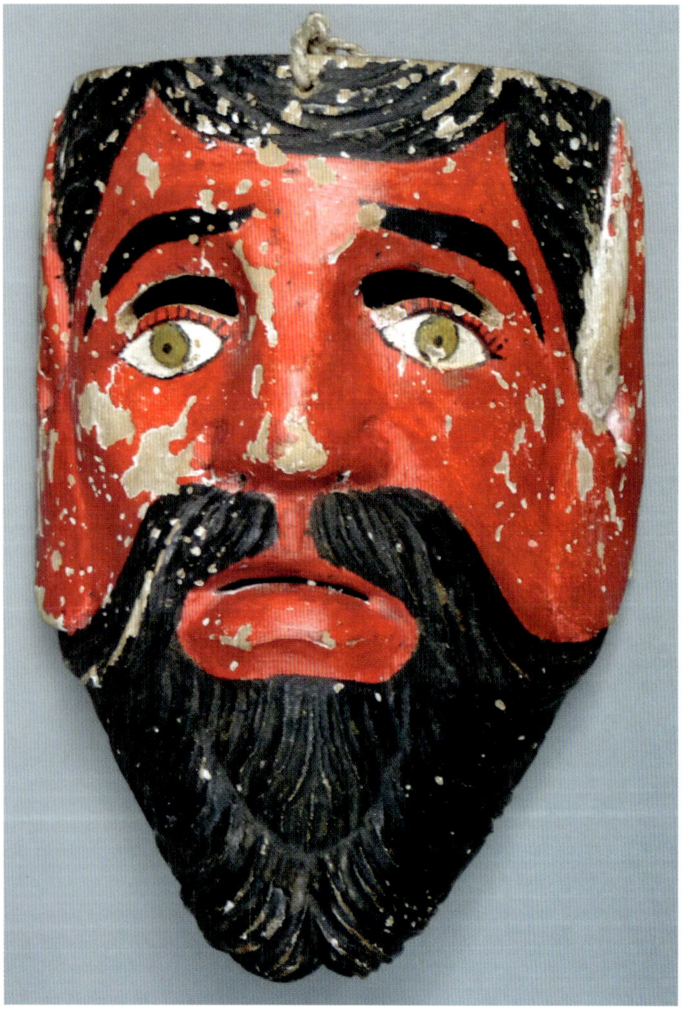

Left: The Pilato Malo mask worn by the Pilatos el Presidente character in Olintla; 7" × 9". Circa 1960. The carver was Magno León. *Collection of the author.*

Below: Seen on the right side of the Pilato Malo mask, the goat's ear extends up to the top border of the mask and down to the top of the curving mustache.

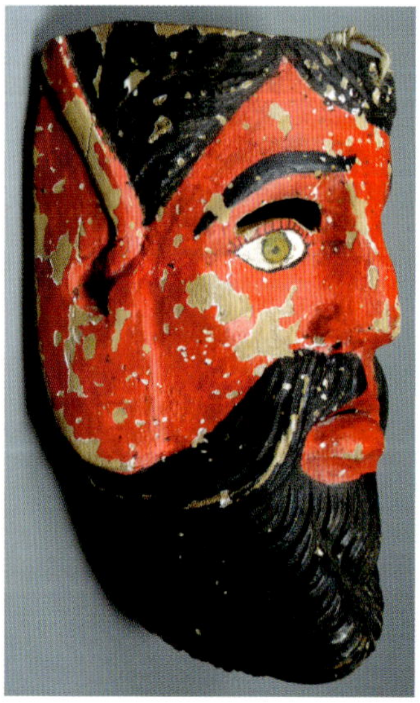

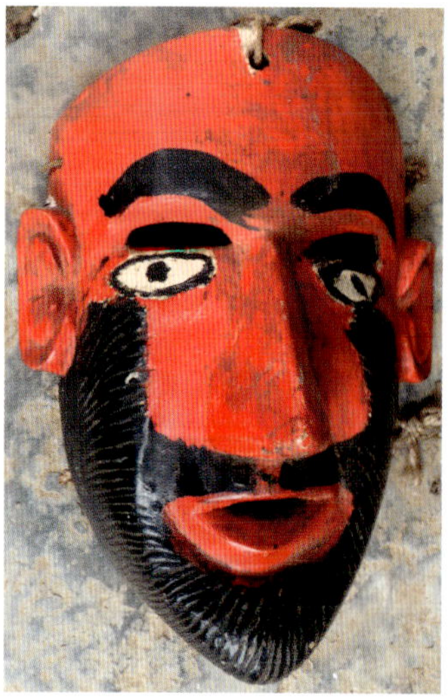

The Ayudante (adjutant Pilato) from the Hormega dance in Olintla. The carver was Leopoldo Cortez González of Olintla, Puebla. *Collection of the author.*

As a result of this experience Hermogenes was also converted to Christianity. This angered the Jews who petitioned Herod to condemn St. James to death. Herod agreed and St. James was beheaded (Stone 1927, 115–116).

We are left to decide what to do with this information. On the one hand, we might wonder whether the "history" reported by Álvarez Boada and then repeated in a slightly different form by Stone has some relevance to the otherwise indecipherable names of this dance—Hormegas or Ormegas. Do the Hormegas depict the demons of Hormógenes/Hermogenes, who in history or legend were the adversaries of Santiago whom he then won over to his side? We don't know the answer to that question. But then there is an interesting follow-up question. If one wanted to more effectively disguise the identity of the soldiers of the sun, instead of giving the game away by calling them Santiagueros or Santiagos, would it be useful to re-label them as demons?

The so-called explanations that one encounters for these dances are frequently of this quality—contradictory, far-fetched, overly simplistic, or too difficult to bother to pursue. As such, they were at one time very effective for their purpose, which was to obscure the underlying plot or theme. One only begins to think in these terms after a prolonged period of confusion.

La Danza de los Toreadores

Stresser-Péan included a description of this dance, which he called the Dance of the Toreros (2009, 346–347):

> This dance holds neither religious value nor indigenous symbolism. It is nonetheless widespread throughout the entire region of study and elsewhere in the rest of Mexico ... it is related to the spectacle of the *jaripeo*, a rodeo type spectacle characteristic of Mexican village festivities, where young Creole and mestizo breeders showed their expertise in taming semi-savage horses and lassoing bulls in their herds.
>
> The Indian Dance of Toreros varies greatly among the region's villages. In its simplest form, all that is needed is the wooden construction of a small bull, its body covered with well-stretched skin and provided with two horns. The man carrying the small bull on his back provides movement, with greater or lesser talent and aggression, often pretending to attack the spectators.

In this description there is no mention of masks. Nor do masks figure in the dance as described by other authors. Francisco Velasco (2005,106–108) makes no mention of masks and includes a dance photo of unmasked dancers with a skin-covered bull like that just described by Stresser-Péan. Francisco Francisco (2005, 109–110) also fails to mention masks, and the photograph accompanying his article also shows the use of such a bull effigy.

However, during my recent visits to Olintla, Puebla, I became aware that the Toreros there assign a dancer wearing a Toro mask to chase other dancers around, in place of the bull effigy.

In a very beautiful book of photographs (González Callado and Cerdeño Lance 2009, 214–215), there are two attractive photos of the Toreadores dancers.

In January 2011, Carlos Moreno Vásquez met a carver, Francisco Hernández Ramos of Hueytlalpan, Puebla, who had made a very appealing example of such a Toro mask, which is shown here.

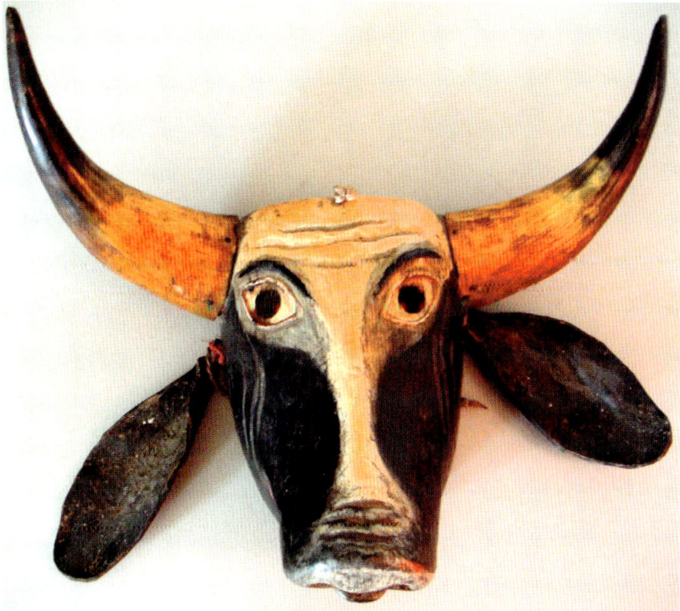

This mask of a bull, Toro, was used in the Dance of the Toreros or Toreadores in Olintla, Puebla; 9" × 11". Circa 1990. *Collection of the author.*

La Danza de los Negros or Negritos

In the Totonac and Nahua areas of the Sierra de Puebla and the contiguous coastal area of Veracruz this dance is very commonly performed, with some variations. It is strongly associated with Papantla and the surrounding villages. According to Acosta Báez (2005, 112–114) there are three versions of the Negritos dance, but the differences mainly involve variation in the costumes of the dancers; the dance and meaning appear to be the same. The Negros Reales of the Sierra wear hats with large prominent feathers of various colors, so that they seem taller than their stature. Another variant, the Negros de la Costa, lacks these feathers and the dancers bend forward, so they appear unnaturally short. Those of the third variety wear yellow instead of black, so they are called *Negros Amarillos* (yellow Negritos).

Aguilera Madero (2005, 117–120) tells us a great deal that is of interest. In the Negritos dance there are three parallel lines of dancers. The foreman or Caporal is the lead dancer for the middle line. Maringuilla, a male dancer dressed as a woman, dances behind the Caporal and her pageboy, Xocoton or Xocotillo, dances behind Maringuilla. Maringuilla carries a wooden serpent. Those leading the other two lines are called *delanteros*, which essentially means lead-men; behind each of the delanteros there are two other Negritos. Then there is El Pilato, a dancer with the appearance of an old man who is described as a clown. The author states that Pilato is known by many names, such as *Padre de la danza* [Father of the dance], *Rey* [king], *Satanás* [Satan], and *Scores*, which has the meaning of *Viejo* [old man]. El Pilato is said to be *el padre de los danzantes* [the father of the dancers] and, more specifically, the Caporal is said to be his eldest son. A photo included with the article, by Aurea Vásquez O., shows what appears to be the Caporal wearing a Negrito mask in the Danza de negritos in Cazuelas, municipio de Papantla, Veracruz.

Madero adds that, in preparation for their use in the dance, there is a blessing ceremony for the wooden serpent and the masks of el Pilato and el Caporal.

The article ends with the remarkable paragraph that I also included in Chapter II, repeated here as an important part of this discussion:

> *Se piensa que todas las danzas se formaron cuando Jesús iba a morir. A cada una de las danzas le dan un representante, así en la de los negritos "Pilato" representó a José, el "caporal" a San Miguel, la "Maringuilla" a la Virgen María y los demás como discípulos y arcángeles de Dios.*
>
> [It is believed that all the dances were formed at the time when Jesus was about to die. To each one of the dances He gave representatives of Himself, thus in the case of the Danza de los Negritos Pilato represents San José, the Caporal corresponds to San Miguel, the Maringuilla to the Virgin Mary, and the rest are thought to represent disciples and archangels of God.] Aguilera Madero (2005, 120)

Acosta Báez (2005, 112–114) adds that Maringuilla carries the serpent in a sack or in a basket. He repeats the same list of alternative names for Pilatos, such as Satanás and el rey. He also confirms that there is a ceremony to bless the serpent and the masks of Pilatos and the Caporal.

García García (2005, 116) tells us more about the Pilato character:

> *Completa este cuadro el "Pilato" ó bufón, especie de espíritu chocarrero que tanto alegra como espanta, critica y gesticula frente a la multitud llevando vestidos viejos y ridículos y el inseparable bastón al que adornan con alguna cabeza de animal disecado. Este "Pilato" lleva una máscara de aspecto horrible, otras veces semeja una eterna sonrisa burlona, los gritos de este personaje forman parte del espectáculo.*
>
> [Completing the scene is El Pilato, a buffoon, a kind of clowning spirit who amuses as much as he frightens with critical remarks and gestures in front of the crowd, wearing old and ridiculous clothing and with his inseparable cane, decorated with some desiccated animal head. This Pilato wears a mask of horrible appearance, or at other times it resembles an eternal mocking smile; the shouts of this personage are a part of the spectacle.]

The description by García García of such expressive el Pilato masks has caused me to search vigorously for concrete examples. Finally I noticed one mask that clearly fits into the category of those displaying the "eternal mocking smile" of this character; I obtained this mask from Jaled Muyaes and Estela Ogazón in January 1998, at a time when I lacked any understanding of what it was. According to my notes at the time of purchase, this was a mask of Pilatos, from San Pedro, a town in the municipio of Papantla, Veracruz. Ironically, I subsequently identified a second probable example in a book by Jaled and Estela (Ogazon 1981, illustration 12, after 23), described as a "Mask of an old man from the state of Veracruz. It is carved of

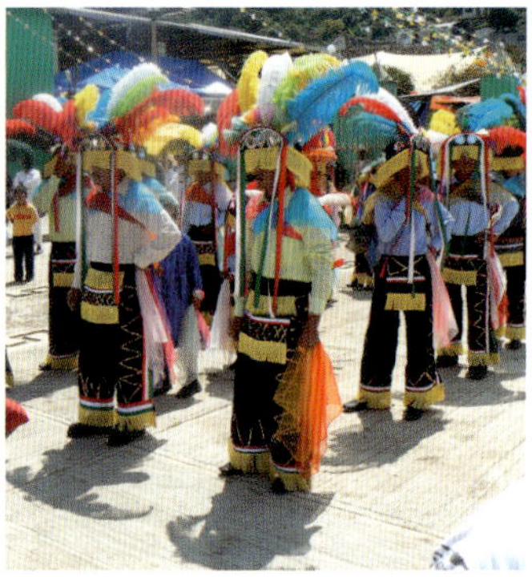

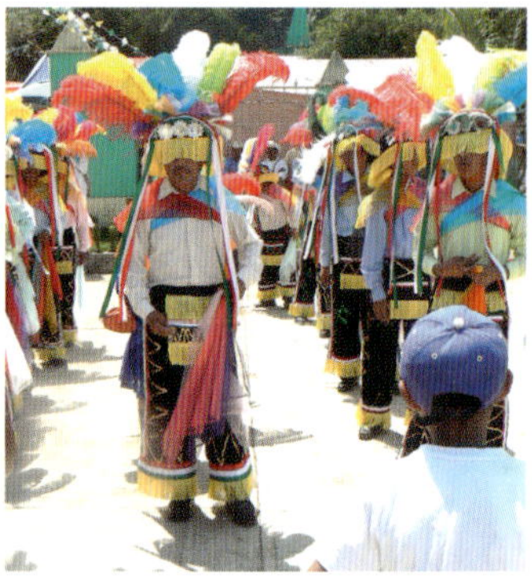

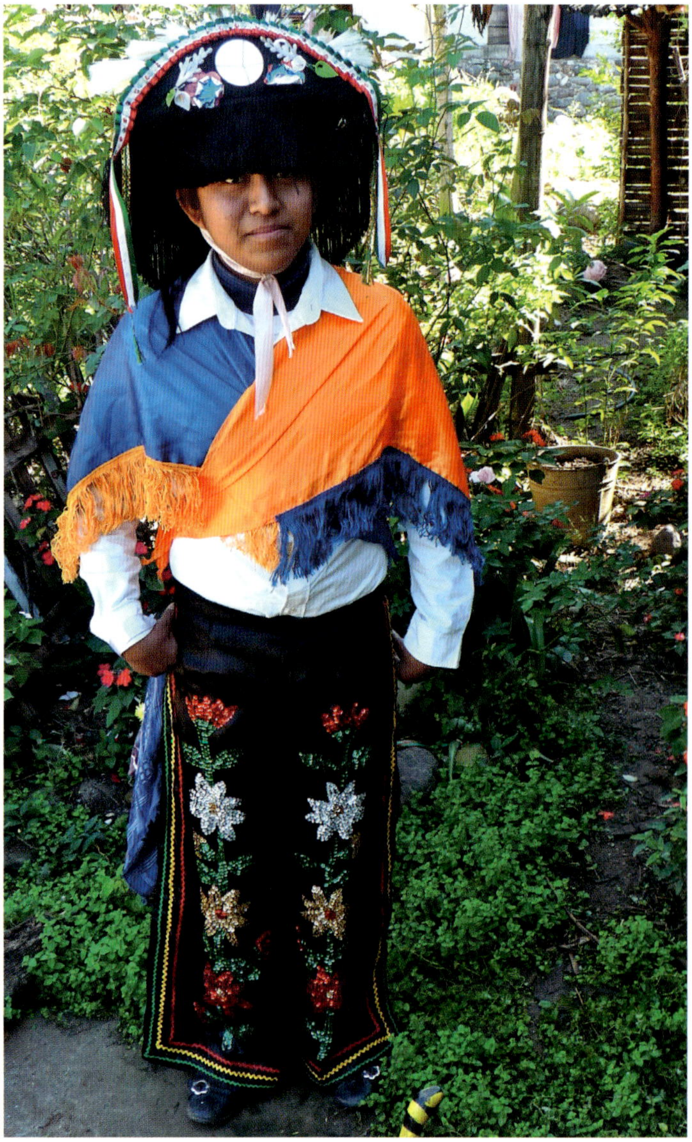

Top left: A view of the Negritos dance at Olintla, Puebla, in March 2010. We see the three columns of dancers and, barely visible, we can glimpse Maringuilla behind the Caporal, who is leading the middle line.

Top right: Still in Olintla, these are the Negros Reales of the Sierra, wearing hats with colored plumes.

Bottom: In Buena Vista, Puebla, at the home of Maximo Mateo Corcamo, an adolescent girl poses in her Negritos costume. A root serpent is at her feet.

wood and has a horsehair beard. Its expression indicates the happiness felt by the old when participating in celebrations." Having owned the Ogazon book for 23 years, I had always taken this description at face value. But recently I looked at the photo with fresh eyes and saw "the eternal mocking smile" of Pilato. This mask is black, with a wrinkled face and a broad smile. Tufts of horsehair sprout from the lower rim of the mask to create a beard.

I have also discovered a single mask that seems sufficiently hideous to fall into that category of being "horrible in appearance" (García García 2005, 116); this was carved by Manuel Antonio Castañeda.

Medina Jiménez (2005, 110–112) provides some background history regarding the Negritos dance:

> *Según la versión que manejan los danzantes en la sierra, esta danza fue creada en el siglo XVI, cuando los esclavos negros traídos a México durante la Colonia fueron bestialmente maltratados, haciéndoles trabajar incansablemente. Se dice que los frailes lucharon para que al menos una vez al año estos esclavos fueran "libres" y se les permitiera divertirse y participar en las fiestas, adornando sus ropas al estilo se su lugar de origen.*
>
> [In the version of the dancers in the Sierra, this dance is said to have been created in the 16th century by black slaves brought to Mexico during colonial times, where they were grossly mistreated and forced to work without any respite. The padres fought for the slaves to have freedom once a year at least, and they were permitted to take part in the fiestas, dressed in costumes in the style of their country of origin.]

Jiménez notes (111–112) that because the slaves were still chained together when they danced, this essentially limited them to certain movements. We could add that certain movements, such as stamping the feet, would create a dramatic sound and rhythm due to the clanking of the chains.

The same author also provides one version of the plot of the dance. The setting is a sugar cane plantation where a foreman, El Caporal or Don Juan, supervises eight farm workers. A woman named María or Maringuilla also works there. A dramatic mystery unfolds.

> *Un día en las labores cotidianas de la hacienda la "Maringuilla" llevaba el almuerzo a los peones, de pronto uno de estos, asustado al ver una enorme serpiente que lo atacaba, gritó y pidió auxilio a sus compañeros, que luego dieron parte al señor amo, por lo que este de inmediato ordenó a la "Maringuilla" que fuera a cerciorarse para ver si en realidad existía dicho animal, pero el resultado fue una negativa. Esta situación se repetía una y otra vez, hasta que un día el caporal se dispuso a ir al lugar de los hechos para ver lo que occuría en realidad; de pronto se topó con la serpiente que de inmediato avanzó sobre él clavándole sus filosos colmillos en una pierna.*

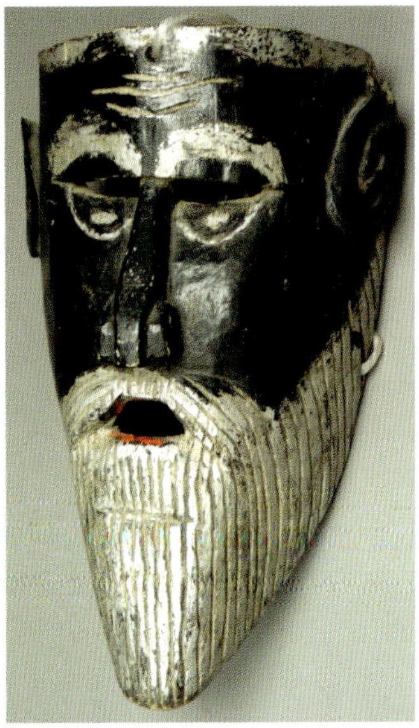

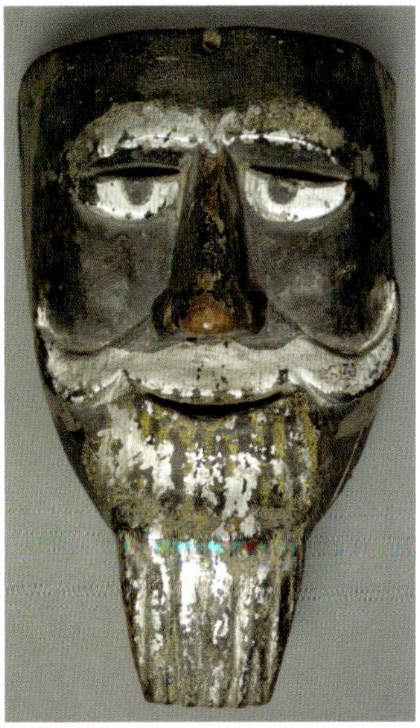

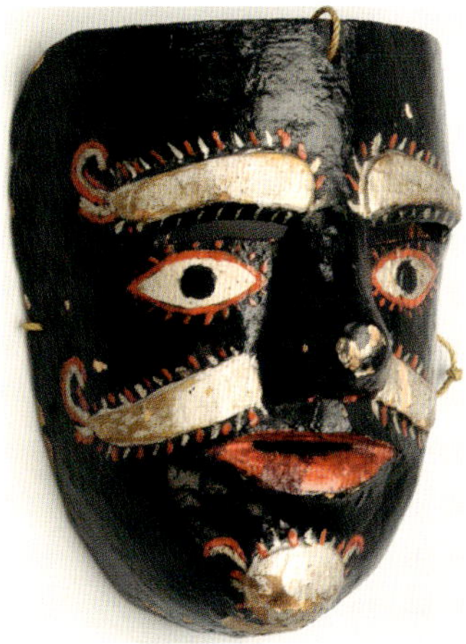

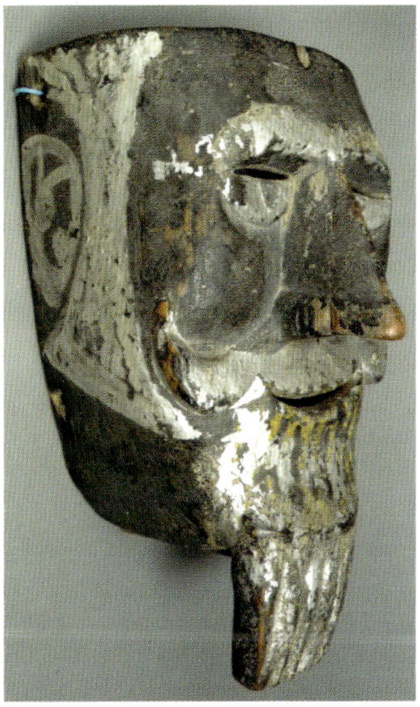

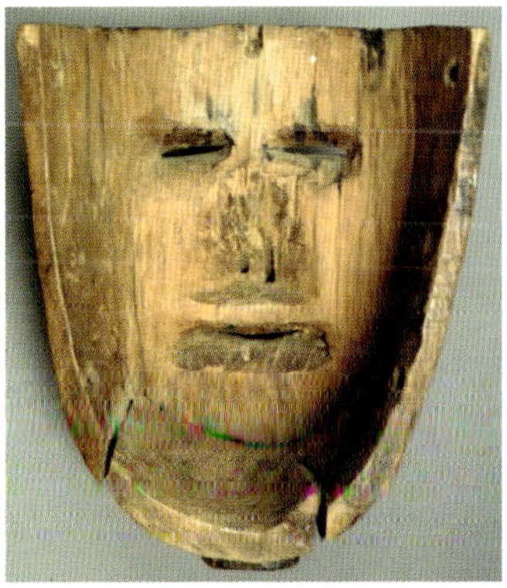

Top left: This Caporal mask was identified by its owner as one worn by the Jefe de los Negritos. The owner also had an articulated snake for the Negritos dance. This mask was found in El Espinal, Veracruz. Another Caporal mask will be presented regarding the work of Benito Juárez Figueroa in Chapter 6. *Collection of the author.*

Bottom left: This is a Negrito mask from Olintla in the style of Benito Juárez Figueroa; 6¼" x 7½", Circa 1980. Probably it was originally worn by the Caporal. It was purchased from the director of the dance in Olintla in December 2010. *Collection of the author.*

Top right: This Pilatos mask is from San Pedro/Papantla; 7" x 10". Circa 1970. It has a prominent smile and a very well carved mustache. I believe that this was worn by the Pilatos character in the Negritos dance. Such a mask could also be used in the dance of el Matarachín. *Collection of the author.*

Center right: The side view of the Pilatos mask.

Bottom right: From behind one can see that this mask required a repair to the back of the chin.

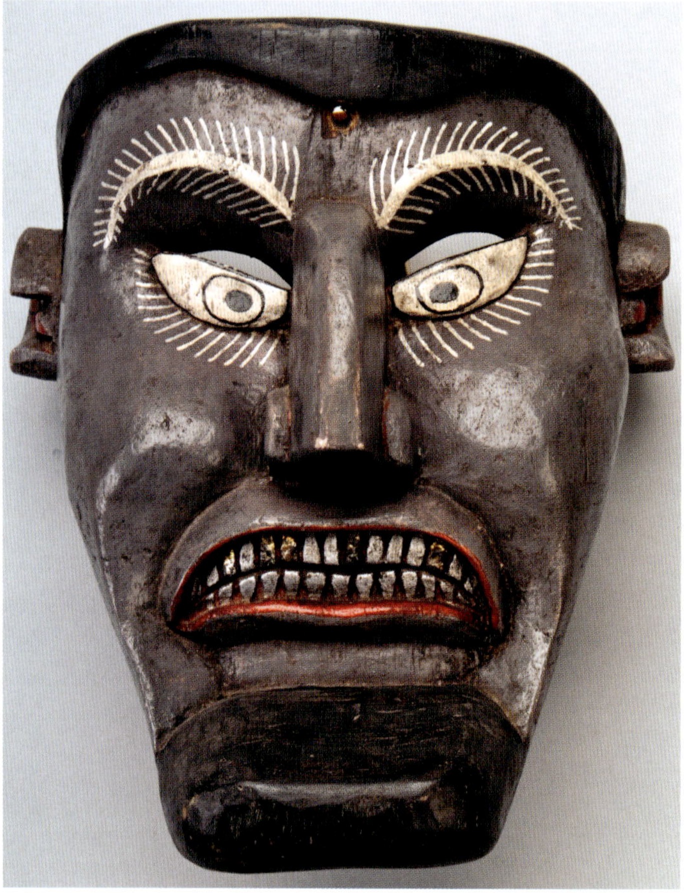

This is a mask carved by Manuel Antonio Castañeda that seems sufficiently "horrible in appearance" to depict Pilatos; and otherwise one would have to call it a Viejo (or demon), as in the dance of the Matarachín. It is discussed more fully in Chapter 6; 8½" × 9". Circa 1980. *Collection of the author.*

> [One day during the daily work of the hacienda Maringuilla brought lunch to the workers, when suddenly one of them, terrified, saw an enormous snake attacking him. He cried for help from his companions, who called for help from Don Juan, who ordered Maringuilla to go see if there was a real snake—there was not. This situation repeated itself again and again, after which one day the Caporal went to see what was happening. He met up with the snake. The snake attacked, digging his fangs into the Caporal's leg.]

Jiménez explains that a healing ritual followed and the Caporal recovered. These events inspired the invention of the Negritos dance. Subsequently the Totonacs had adopted this slaves' dance for their own use.

Aguilera Madero (2005, 121–123) believes that, although the Totonacs may have initially copied a dance of African slaves, they subsequently revised it to suit their own purposes, and this "*proceso de sincretismo*" (syncretic process) has continued or expanded over the years. He examines the costumes worn by the Negritos dancers of the Gulf coast. Their costume is black and they wear mirrors on their hats; these elements remind Madero of symbols related to Tezcatlipoca. Yellow fringes on the costumes of the Negritos may symbolize the sun, he thinks. The serpent makes one think of Quetzalcoatl. Seeing such clues, says the author, "*Se vislumbra una versión de la danza aún más antigua, la que se inclina al origen precortesiano y nos refiere la imposición de rituales propiciatorios de origen nahoa generados en funcíon de la expansion de este grupo a partir de las guerra's floridas.*" [One glimpses a version of an older dance, which suggests the preconquest origin and the imposition of propitiatory rituals of Nahua origin following the wars of conquest.] That is, Madero is considering the possibility that the Negritos dance might represent an older dance that has been maintained in a disguised form.

In the Negritos dance the dancers step vigorously in a *zapateado* style, like tap dancing. This establishes a heavy and exciting rhythm, which is one reason that the Negritos dance has been growing in appeal in recent decades, according to Stresser-Péan (2009, 341).

The Negritos may also include a traditional maypole dance as part of their performance (see photos).

In the Negritos dance, the Caporal and the Pilato or Pilatos character frequently wear masks in some of the villages in Veracruz. However, this is just the beginning of the story.

Arizpe Schlosser and Kandt (1972, 11) described their visit in the late 1960s to Olintla, Puebla, a place they described as "*inaccesible excepto a caballo*" [inaccessible except by horse]. In a brief discussion of their observation of the Negritos dance there is no mention of mask use (57–63), but they did include a dance photo (58) in which at least one of the dancers is wearing a Negritos mask. In a second photo (60) they showed the maypole dance in an unnamed place, performed by six apparently unmasked Negrito dancers, assisted by Maringuilla and two masked characters wearing ordinary clothing, such as would be worn by Mestizos.

Leyenaar (1988, 195–201) discussed the Negritos dance in the area around Cuetzalan, Puebla. He stated that only the two clowns associated with the dance wore masks. He included a dance photo (206) of Negritos dancers engaged in the maypole performance at San Andrés Tzicuilan, Puebla, in 1969, which was clearly taken on the same occasion as the maypole photo included by Arizpe Schlosser and Kandt (1972, 60) above. There we see "two buffoons and Malinche." The clowns are wearing Caucasian masks that resemble those of the Huehues or Tejoneros; again Malinche and a Negrito in this scene were unmasked.

In 2007, I collected a Caucasian mask with a "whistling" mouth near San Antonio Rayón, Puebla. The seller stated that the mask was used in the maypole dance by the Negritos dancers in San Antonio Rayón.

When I observed the Negritos dance in Huehuetla, Puebla, in December 2006, the Negritos did not wear masks, but there were two clowns associated with the Negritos group and they wore Negrito masks. Looking at these masks now, after years of investigation, I am surprised to note that both masks demonstrate one of the typical styles of Benito Juárez Figueroa.

In March 2010, I observed the Negritos dance in Olintla. I had been told that there was at least one Negrito dancer in Olintla who wore a mask in the dance. However, when I observed the Negritos dance, none of the Negritos wore masks.

I returned to Olintla in December 2010 and observed the Negritos dance again. This time there were two dancers wearing Negrito masks, but neither one was a lead dancer. Later in the day when I saw the dance again, none of the dancers wore a mask. Much later, the manager of the Negritos dance spontaneously offered to sell me one of those masks. He said that he had been thinking about selling it for some time. It was clear to me that the use of masks in the Negrito dance at

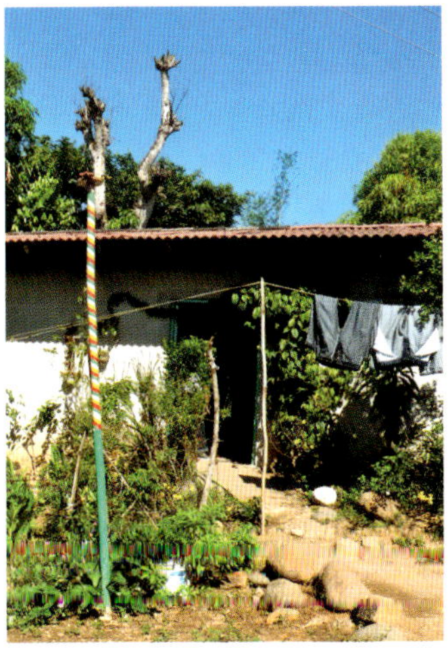

The maypole for the Negritos dance, standing in the front yard of Maximo Mateo Corcamo in Buena Vista, Puebla.

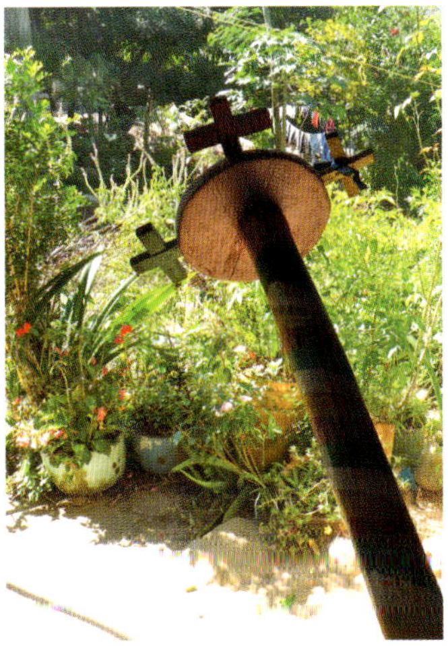

A closer view of the maypole at Buena Vista, showing three of the four crosses at the top.

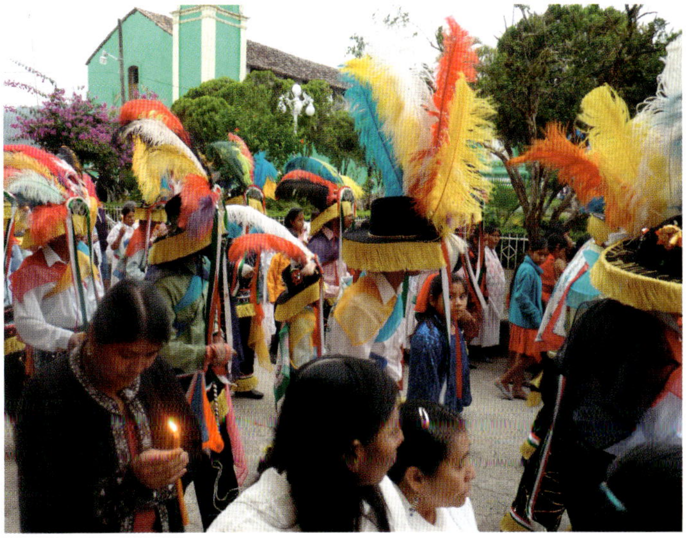

In Olintla, in December 2010 I saw two Negrito dancers wearing masks. Here is one of those masked dancers. He is wearing a green shirt and is walking next to the woman in the foreground who is carrying a candle. He is not a lead dancer, nor is he dressed as a ragged old man, so he is neither the Caporal nor Pilatos. To the viewer's right you can see Maringuilla, in this case portrayed by a young girl, looking directly at the camera; she is wearing a jacket with blue sequins.

Olintla had gone out of fashion. Meanwhile this was another mask that was typical of the work of Benito Juárez Figueroa.

Mauldin (1999, 36) includes a photo of Negritos dancing in Olintla that was apparently taken by Ruth Lechuga in about 1980. It showed a "masked clown and other unmasked dancers, including a young man dressed as Malinche and wearing sunglasses and hat." On the same page she illustrates a Negritos mask that was collected in the area of Papantla in about 1975 by Jaled Muyaes and Estela Ogazón. She also includes a photo of a rather distinctive Negrito mask from Cuetzalan, Puebla, with ears carved in low relief, which was apparently collected by Donald Cordry in about 1950.

As mentioned earlier, Donald Cordry and his wife, Dorothy, had initially traveled to Cuetzalan, Puebla, in 1939 (Furst, 1988, xvii). The Cordrys (1968, 225) described travel conditions at that time: "To reach Cuetzalan in 1939, one went from the city of Puebla northward to Zaragoza by train, and by road to Zacapoaxtla, and from thence by horse." They (Cordry and Cordry 1940, 16) observed the Negritos dance there but make no mention of any Negritos masks. They did collect a "painted wooden snake" that had been carried by Maringuilla in the Negritos dance there. It was just 7 inches long and it was painted silver. They included a vivid drawing of the snake's head (1940, 17)

In the Museo Nacional de Antropología in Mexico City (Palacios Sánchez 1992, 220) there is a Negritos mask that was apparently collected in Olintla in 1964 (inventario #68236). This mask is quite similar to the one I purchased in Olintla. In fact, if one compares all of the Negritos masks that were either photographed in Olintla or collected there, along with the masks worn by the clowns in Huehuetla, they all seem by the same hand, and I feel confident that they were all carved by Benito Juárez Figueroa. We see that he was one of the principal mask makers for a rather broad region, over the course of many years. In the same museum there are two other notable Negrito masks, one from Papantla, Veracruz (inventario #35236), and the other from La Lagunilla, Veracruz (inventario #34944).

Victor José Moya Rubio (1986, 114) includes a dance photo (plate 136) from Papantla, Veracruz, which shows a costumed Negrito dancer wearing a black-faced mask. In the accompanying text (127–128) he states that *"El Caporal de la danza es el único que usa máscara."* [The leader of the dance is the only one to wear a mask.]

Cerdeño Lance (González Callado and Cerdeño Lance 2009, 219–223) includes several photos of masked Negritos dancers, but without any captions. They appear to be dancing in Zozocolco de Hidalgo, Veracruz.

In a review of observations of this dance by other writers, there were several instances where Negrito masks were not observed at all. For example, Fergusson (1934, 174) observed the Negritos dance in Coxquihui, Veracruz, in September 1933, after riding two days on horseback from Zacapoaxtla, Puebla (160–161). She does not describe any mask use by the dancers. In contrast she made it a point to describe masks in other dances (172–173, 186–187). Frances Toor (1947) discussed the Negritos dance in Papantla, Veracruz, in 1945, where there were two clowns with painted faces, while Maringuilla wore a "rose-colored mask." The Negritos were apparently unmasked (354–356 and plate 158).

I also visited Xonalpú, a village near Huehuetla, Puebla, in December 2010. There, none of the Negrito dancers wore masks, and when we inquired about this we were told that some of the Negritos dancers did wear masks in the past, but that this was no longer the practice.

As noted previously, a serpent plays a prominent role in the Negritos dance. Stresser-Péan (2009, 340) includes two drawings, one of a "hinged serpent" (articulated serpent), the other of a "root serpent," both used in Tepetzintla, Puebla. He explains that Maringuilla carries the small, articulated serpent in a cloth or container, then "releases" it at the appropriate time in the dance. Subsequently there is a part of the dance when the dancers pretend to kill the snake, dancing around it and pretending to strike at it. For this part a larger snake carved from a twisted root is substituted for the small, articulated one. Stresser-Péan says that this is because the smaller snake is viewed as more vulnerable to potential damage.

There are two of the articulated serpents in the collection of the Museo Nacional de Antropología (Palacios Sánchez 1992, 215), both collected in 1964. I have collected two more that were found in Zozocolco de Guerrero, Veracruz. More recently I purchased another that was made by Andrés Juárez García of Xonalpú, Puebla.

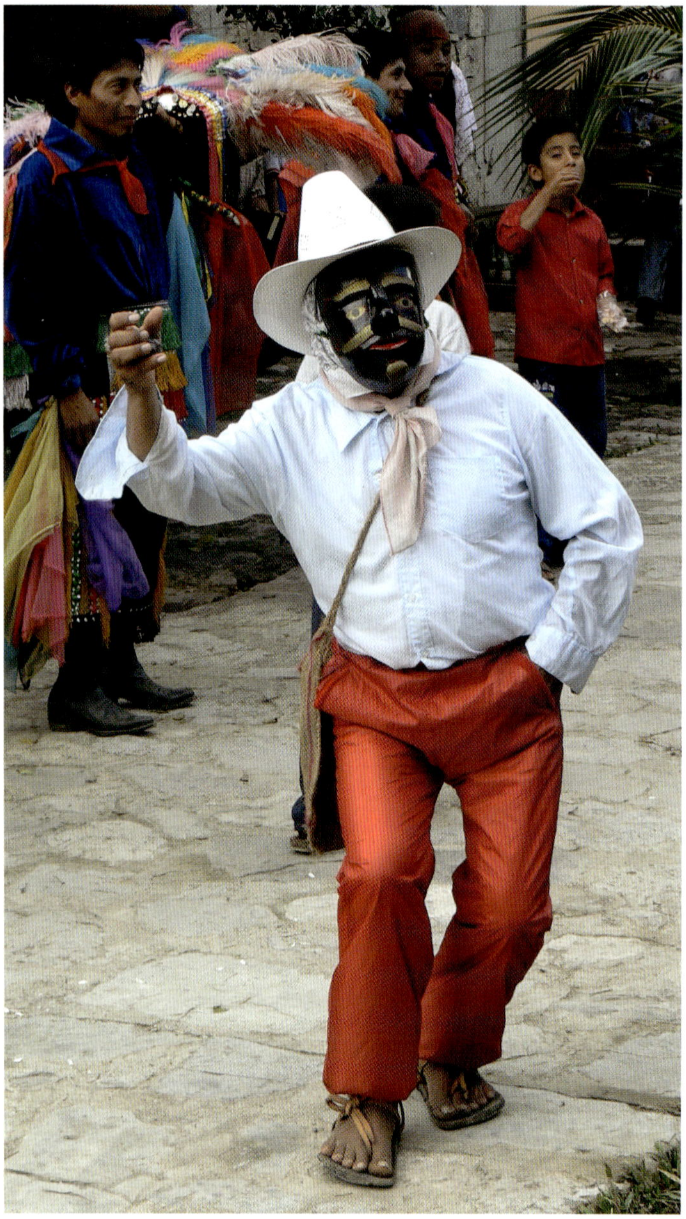

I have seen a number of the root-type snakes in Buena Vista, Puebla. When I visited Guadalupe Ortiz González there, I saw those that he was making. On a later visit to Maximo Mateo Corcamo, I saw the one currently in use by the community dance group, which is remarkable. In a previous photo this serpent was on the ground in front of the adolescent girl dressed as a Negrito. This snake was kept on the back of the family altar, with the horse up front. You can see the tail of the snake protruding on the viewer's right, in the photo of the altar below.

From this large quantity of data regarding the use of masks in the Negritos dance, it is evident, above all, that mask use in this dance is not highly predictable for at least two reasons: communities differ widely in their pattern of mask use in the dance and prior patterns of dance use appear to be fading. Generally it can be said that it is not unusual for there to be no masks in this dance, and that, when there are masks, the most likely wearer will be the Caporal and the next most likely will be a clown or clowns. Pilatos is said to be a clown so he may or may not wear a mask due to that role. However, Pilatos is no ordinary clown.

I have been impressed that the dance seems so mysterious, that there appears to be much more to this dance than the available information can explain. I am a strong believer in the theory of Aguilera Madero (2005, 122–123) that a syncretic process has resulted in the maintenance of an older dance in disguise, or alternatively that older dance elements have provided the foundation for an evolving dance.

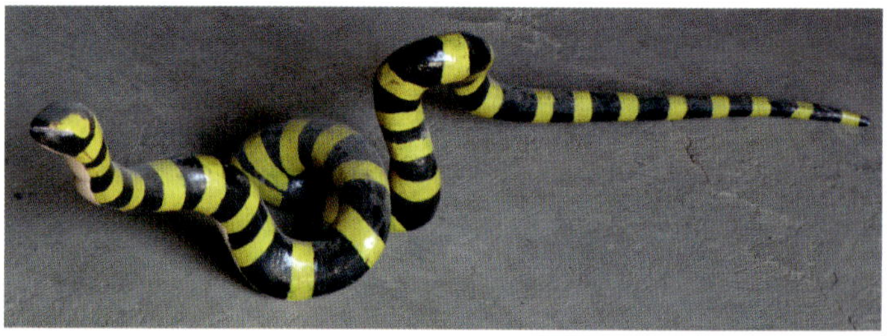

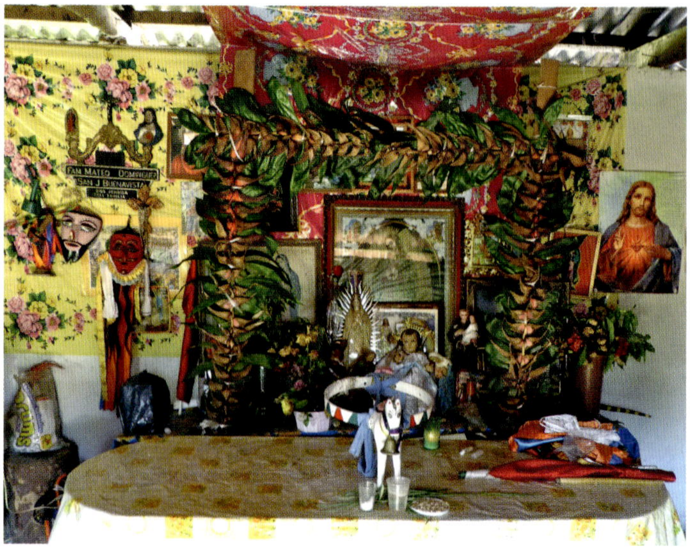

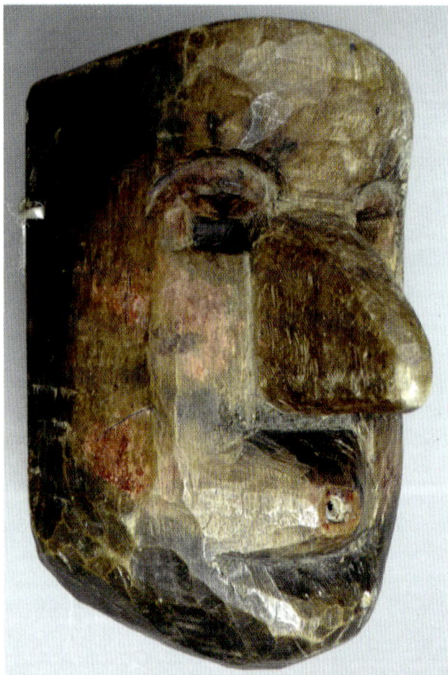

Above: This Negrito Payaso is one of a pair of Negrito clowns seen in Huehuetla, Puebla, in December 2006. They were clearly associated with the Negrito dancers. In the background you can see one of those dancers holding his feathered hat. The Negrito dancers themselves did not wear masks.

Left: A Payaso mask, with "whistling" mouth, used in the Negritos dance in San Antonio Rayón, Puebla; 6½" × 9". Circa 1970. *Collection of the author.*

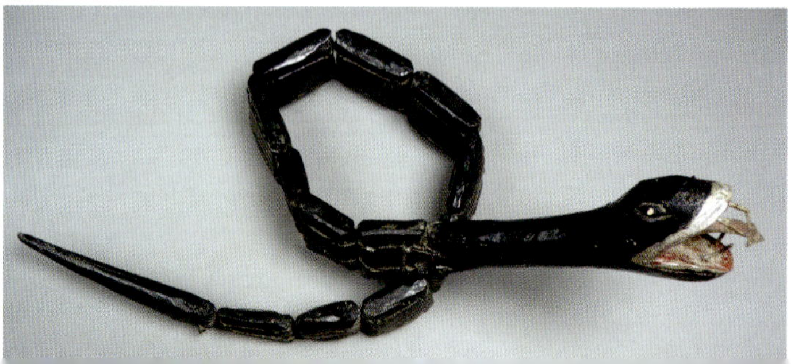

Danza de los Miguelitos or Migueles

San Miguel (Saint Michael), one of the archangels according to the Spanish Catholic tradition, may or may not be directly portrayed in this dance, but his surrogates, the Miguelitos (or Migueles), occupy center stage in his absence. These dancers are unmasked, but otherwise dressed as angel warriors, with wooden helmets and wings of wood or tin, along with costumes that seem medieval or even Roman in style. Each Miguelito carries a sword and a cross. The Miguelitos oppose *el Diablo* (the devil), who usually wears a vivid horned mask.

Medina Jiménez (2005, 92–93) described a legend regarding the interaction between Jesus, San Miguel, and el Diablo. The devil once ruled the world; every seven years he killed all the living humans for food. Jesus confronted the devil about his conduct on earth. In frustration the devil moved to Heaven: "*Decía que era el único dios y rey de los hombres, que gobernaría tanto en el cielo como en la tierra y que viviría para hacer el mal.*" [There he said that he was the only god, and that he was the king of men, who would govern in Heaven as well as on earth and that he would live in order to do evil.] San Miguel was sent to Heaven to battle with Satan; this led to renewed negotiations between Satan and Jesus:

> *Jesús le dijo al Diablo: "...No tienes porqué hacer tanta maldad a los humanos, ellos deben vivir mucho tiempo, pero tú los dejas vivir sólo siete años." El Diablo contestó: "...Está bien, pero me corresponden la mitad de los hombres." Y Jesús aceptó ese convenio con la advertencia de que sólo tenía que vivir en la tierra. Las gentes hacen maldades aquí en la tierra porque aquí está ese dios de la maldad.*
>
> [Jesus said to the devil: "You have no reason to do such evil to human beings. They should live a long time but you only let them live seven years." The devil responded: "OK, I will take only half of the people." Jesus accepted this arrangement with the warning that Satan had to live only on earth. People do evil things here on earth because the god of evil is here.]

Acosta Báez and Gaona Vega (2005, 94–102) observed that this dance seemed to be rapidly disappearing twenty years ago. They provided a sample of the dialogue, with comments. The dance is particularly interesting because, although on one level the devil is cast as the villain, on another level he appears to be the spokesman against a pattern of injustice and exploitation by the Spanish. For example, the devil complains that he has given his beautiful daughters to San Miguel, only to see them starved and mistreated.

Opposite, top right: A wooden snake carved from a tree root. This is the one currently being used in the Negritos dance in Buena Vista, Puebla. *Photo courtesy of Maximo Mateo Corcamo.*

Opposite, center right: The Negritos root snake is kept on the back of the family altar, with the horse up front. The tail of the snake can be seen protruding at the right.

Opposite, bottom right: This articulated snake is one of an older pair discovered by Carlos Moreno Vásquez in Zozocolco de Guerrero, Veracruz; 36" long. *Collection of the author.*

Acosta Báez and Gaona Vega (2005, 94–102) point out that the Totonac idea of the devil diverges from the Christian view, in that the devil is perceived as one agent in a duality and thus important for his contribution towards the creation of balance. This is in contrast to a more conventional Christian view, where the devil is seen as entirely bad, versus Jesus or Christianity as entirely good. Neither the devil nor his counterparts, Jesus and San Miguel in this case, are perceived as having a monopoly on virtue, nor is either free to rule independently. Rather, "*uno no existe sin el otro y los dos son necesarios para sustentar, de manera dinámica, el equilibrio del universo mismo*" [one cannot exist without the other and both are necessary to sustain in a dynamic manner the balance of the universe itself]. The authors say that from the Totonac perspective the existence of Jesus makes sense only with reference to the devil. Each is viewed as having the same strength or will as the other; inevitably they will share power equally over the world and humanity.

The performance alternates between the exchange of bellicose speeches by San Miguel (or a Miguelito) and the devil, and combat; ultimately San Miguel or a Miguelito is the victor. Along the way each appeals to the crowd, saying such things as "My opponent is a lying devil, please help me to defeat him." When the devil utters such lines it may seem particularly ironic (Acosta Báez and Gaona Vega 2005, 94–102).

At the end of the dance, the player who portrayed the devil places that mask on the ground, then he publicly prays to Jesus, to forgive his portrayal of disloyalty and to restore their usual relationship (Acosta Báez and Gaona Vega 2005, 94–102):

> *Ya te voy a guardar de nuevo,*
> *no vayas a creer que nada más te jugué,*
> *no quiero que me hagas soñar,*
> *por eso te estoy hablando,*
> *y cuando te vuelva a necesitar,*
> *te volveré a tomar de tu lugar.*
> [I am going to keep you again,
> you are not going to believe that I never played against you,
> I don't want you to cause me dreams,
> for this reason I am speaking to you,
> so that when I may need you again,
> you will return to take your usual place.]

On December 8, 2010, as Carlos Moreno Vásquez and I were driving towards Zozocolco de Hidalgo, Veracruz, on the day of the Fiesta of the *Purísima Concepción* (the Immaculate Conception of Mary), we came upon a troupe of Miguelitos by the road. They welcomed our interest and readily permitted me to take photographs for this book. We visited their chapel, decorated for this holiday. Later we saw them dancing in front of the church in Zozocolco. We did not see the devil, who must have joined them later.

Stresser-Péan (2009, 516) reports that "The Feast of the Immaculate Conception of the Virgin Mary has lost its former importance because it was too close to December 12, the major feast day of Our Lady of Guadalupe." That is, the fiesta for Guadalupe has eclipsed that of the Virgin of Concepción in some communities. There is an advantage in this for someone who is interested in these dances, as some can be seen on one day and others on another day in adjacent towns.

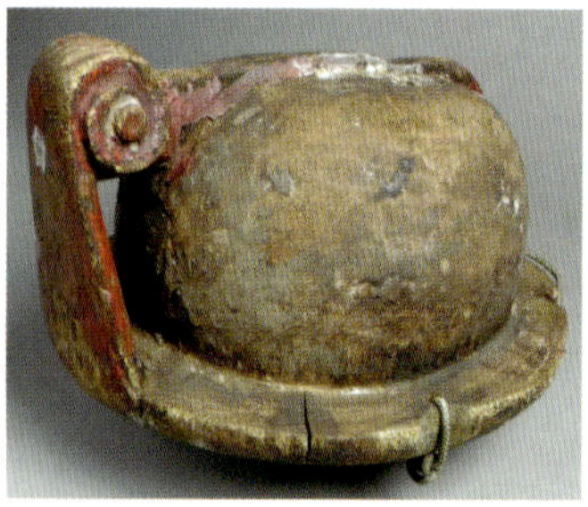

This is an old and worn helmet of the style worn by the Miguelito dancers in the past; brim 9½" × 10½", 5" tall. Circa 1970. It is elaborately carved. *Collection of the author.*

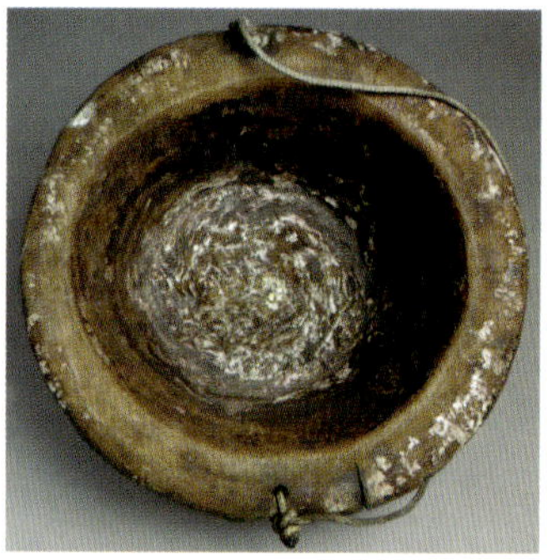

The bottom view of the very old Miguelito helmet.

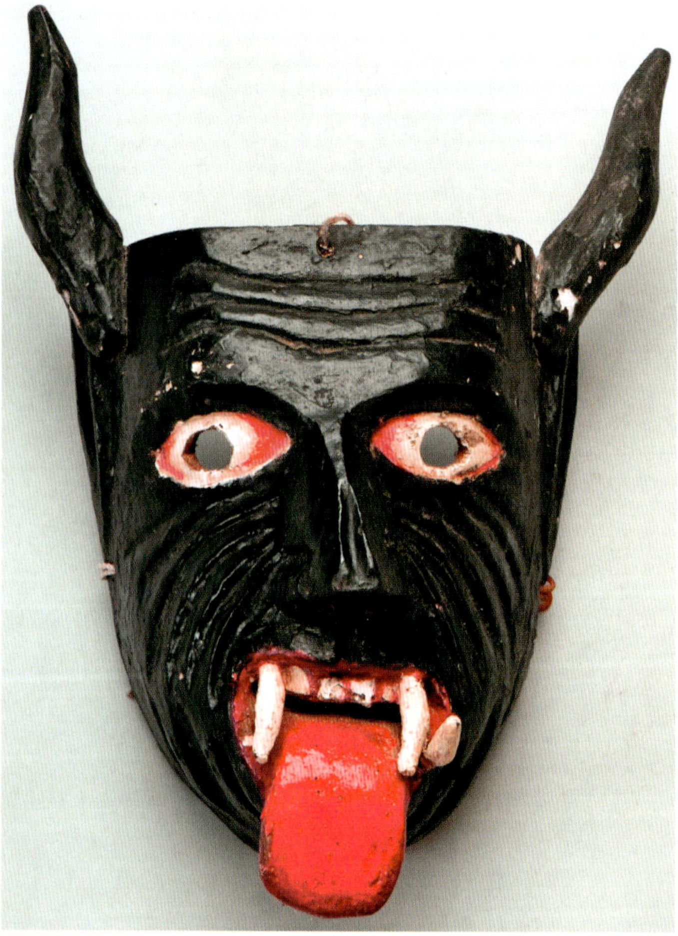

A Diablo mask found in Zapotitlán, Puebla, and typical of the masks used in the Migueles dance; 9" × 10½". Circa 1980. *Collection of the author.*

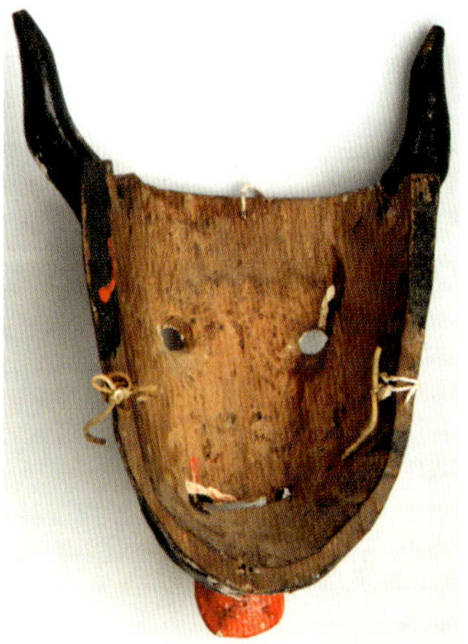

The back view of the devil mask. The patina is very nice.

It has become a doctrinal belief in the Roman Catholic church that the Virgin Mary must have been born without original sin for her to have been a pure enough vessel to have given birth to Christ. Historically the Virgin of Concepción has been depicted as one of the most radiant and important images of Mary. (http://en.wikipedia.org/wiki/Immaculate_Conception)

In an old photo of the dance (Acosta Báez and Gaona Vega 2005, 94), there is the Diablo of the San Miguelitos dance, standing in front of the same church at Zozocolco, with no Miguelitos. That Diablo is carrying a pitchfork. This is a monochrome photo, but I believe that the Diablo is wearing a red jumpsuit and a red devil's mask with horns. Diablo masks seem to come in two colors, red and black. Based on photos and Diablos that I have seen, a Diablo wears either a black mask with a black suit or a red mask with a suit of that color. I do have a Diablo mask that is red, grey, and black; I don't know what color of costume would be preferred for that one.

Todos Santos

This holiday and that of Carnaval represent traditions that were introduced by the Spanish, based on European practices, but yet they apparently provided a vehicle for the Indians of Mexico to maintain some of their own prior beliefs and practices, particularly regarding the dead.

In medieval Spain, two special days were dedicated to the memory of those who had died. November 1, All Saints Day, was for the memory of the Saints while November 2, All Souls Day, was for all the rest who had died. In Mexico these names and dates were apparently adjusted by early Indian converts to Christianity. The name *Todos Santos* (All Saints) was retained, but functionally November 1 was rededicated to the memory of all who had died, not just to the Saints. So one sees *Todos Santos* translated as All Saints or as All Souls Day. In Mexico there persists the widespread belief that the souls of those who died have the opportunity to visit their home communities for 24 hours each year, on the occasion of Todos Santos. In the area of the Huasteca, just north of the Sierra de Puebla, the fiesta of All Saints/All Souls is named for its pre-Hispanic version, *El Xantolo* (Ogazon 1981, 86–87). Masks used for the occasion in that area have been called Xantolo masks. As we shall see later, other names are used for the masks and dances of Todos Santos, outside of the Huasteca.

All Souls was combined with All Saints on November 1, but then the celebration was expanded again, so that there was a new allocation

Opposite, top: Miguelitos dancers from just outside of Zozocolco de Hidalgo, Veracruz. Note the wings of the dancer on the right, made with metal salvaged from corrugated metal cans for stiffness and strength.

Opposite: bottom left: Details of the costume of one of the Miguelitos. The helmet is decorated with plastic flowers. In his right hand he carries a sword, in his left hand a cross.

Opposite: bottom right: The Miguelitos are dancing in a chapel just outside of Zozocolco de Hidalgo. Notice that the young men dance with vigor but the older gentleman dances with polished grace.

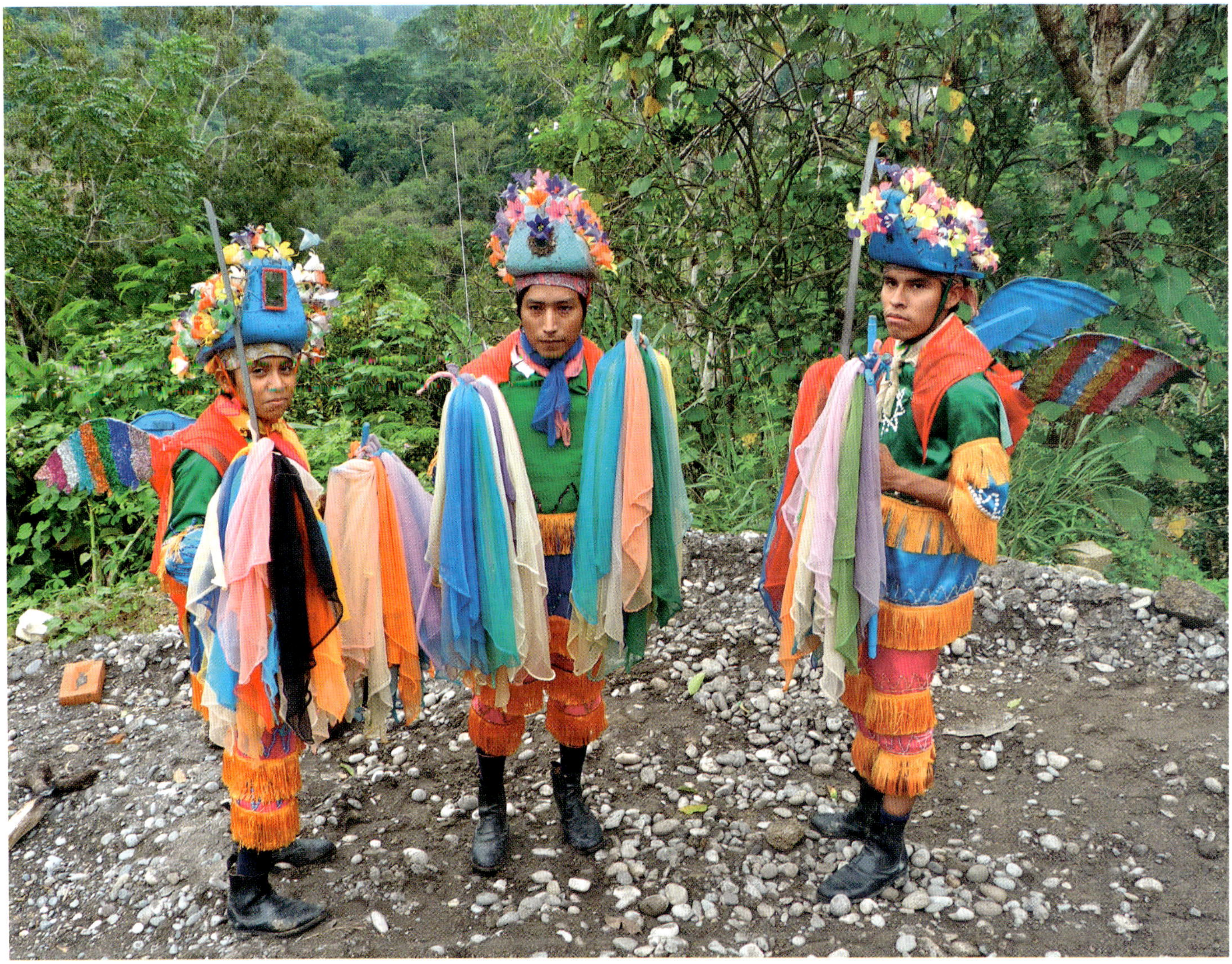

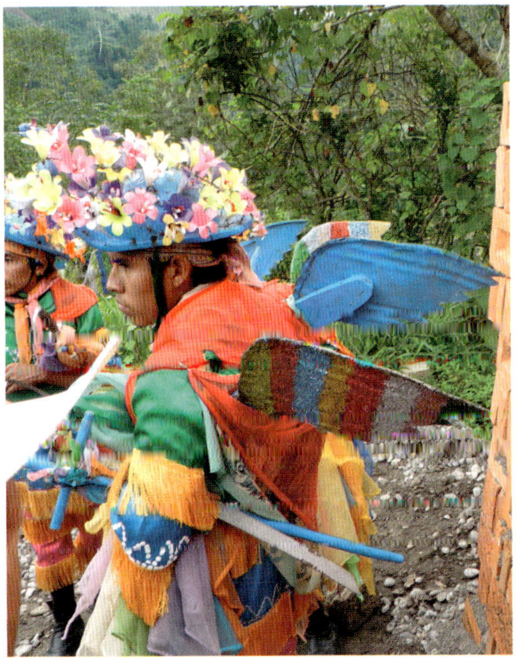

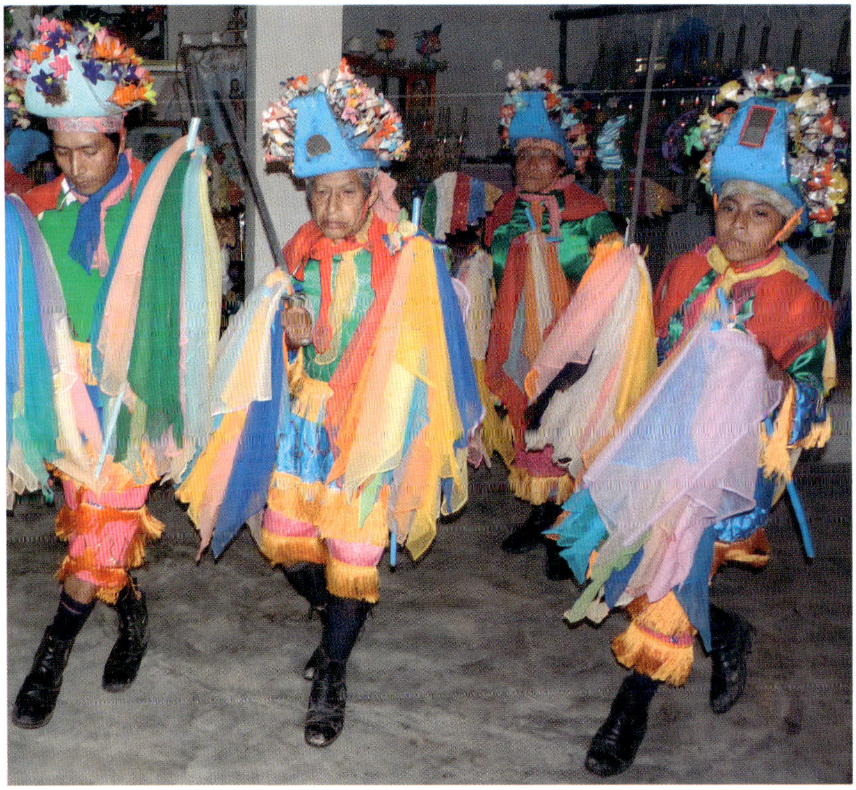

of the days. At Cuetzalan, Puebla, the souls of those who died in accidents visit on October 28; on October 29 one welcomes the souls of those who died a violent death. On October 30 the souls of unbaptized children are received, and at noon on October 31 the visitation of the souls of baptized children begins. The souls of adults who died a natural death are thought to arrive on November 1. All are expected to visit for 24 hours and then depart. To mark their departure, a ceremony is held at the cemetery on November 2, the graves are decorated with flowers and there are prayers (Andrade 2001, 24–27).

I have identified just one masked dance that can occur during the period of Todos Santos or somewhat later, essentially extending the holiday, in the villages around Papantla, Veracruz. This is the Dance of El Matarachín. Croda León reports that the dancers are referred to as Viejos or Huehues (2005, 149–152).

Here let us recall that there are two kinds of Huehues. There are Huehues who would otherwise be called Tejoneros (as in the Dance of the Huehues or Chéncheres); they seem to represent, among other things, the ancient spirits of the trees and the forested mountains. It is *not* said that they represent the dead. The other Huehues, also called Viejos or Viejitos, explicitly portray the dead. These characters dance during Todos Santos and Carnaval in the Huasteca, where they are sometimes called Xantolos. In the Totonac area of Veracruz, the Viejos dance as characters in the Matarachín dance. It is far less clear whether they also dance in Carnaval (or Mardi Gras). To add to the confusion, there are also Viejos, Viejas, and Viejitos in other Mexican dances, for instance in the Viejitos dance in Michoacan.

Regarding the Huehue characters in the Dance of the Matarachín, Croda León (2005. 149–152) provides this description:

> *Los huehues son la personificación de los difuntos, son los antepasados, las ánimas que vagan por las calles y bailan ante los altares de las casas del pueblo proporcionando un poco de diversión a cambio de un óvolo que consiste en comida, bebida o dinero.*
>
> [The Huehues are the personification of the deceased, they are the ancestors, the souls that wander the streets and dance before the altars of the town, providing a little diversion in exchange for offerings that consist of food, drink, or money.]

He provides a long list of characters that are depicted by the dancers, noting that some seem ordinary and others fantastic. These include *el diablo* [the devil], *la muerte* [death], *el brujo* [wizard], as well as a soldier, a foreman, a doctor, a professor, an herbalist, an athlete, and the Matarachín.

Croda León (2005, 149–152) reports that the dance occurs at the time of Todos Santos and that there is a follow-up performance beginning on the *octava*, meaning on the eigth day. This phase lasts for three days and ends with an unmasked visit to the cemetery where they dance tracing the shape of a cross. Only at the very end of this phase does the Matarachín dancer appear and perform.

The Matarachín is most easily described in terms of the process that prepares him to perform in this role. A slender and, it is hoped, flexible young man lies on his back on the ground, his arms extended above his head. He is wrapped with a blanket that is tied in place with a rope, leaving only his hands and his feet exposed. Then one mask is tied to his hands, another to his feet. He is said to resemble a *gusano*, a two-headed worm. If he bends sharply at the waist, for instance by doing a sit-up, the two masks will clack together, nose to nose. The mark of a skillful dancer is his ability to rapidly alternate between extending and bending his body, so that the masks repeatedly tap and separate. Having explained all this, Croda León (2005,149–152) ends by stating that the Matarachín demonstrates the principle of duality.

Williams García (2005, 148–149) traveled to a place near Paso de Valencia, Veracruz, in the mid-1980s to witness the Matarachín performance. His account is similar to that of Croda León.

Hernández Vázquez (2005, 130–131) provides a myth about the origin of this dance. A rebellious daughter became pregnant out of marriage, so her parents threw her out of the house. She gave birth to her son in the open and in total darkness. He was born with two heads. His parents initiated a dance for his healing and he became normal.

The author (Hernández Vázquez 2005, 130–131) describes the cast of characters. *El turco* (a reference to a Turk or Moor) is the foreman. He is dressed in black and wears a black mask. There is a *bebé* (infant); he is the two-headed worm. The infant's father is named Matarachín and his mother, Úrsula. There are Viejos who wear masks and hats with horns.

Hernández Vázquez makes some interesting further points:

> *Esta danza únicamente actúa fuera de la casa durante el período que corresponde a las posadas, de diez de la noche a una de la mañana, aproximadamente. Se considera que es una danza del mal, que representa todo lo malo. En ella también pudiera estarse representando a Tezcatlipoca, el dios todopoderoso, multiforme y ubicuo, dios negro del cielo nocturno, patorno de los hechiceros y los malvados.*
>
> [This dance only takes place outside the house and during the period from ten at night to one o'clock in the morning, approximately. It is considered to be a dance of evil, which represents all that is bad. Alternatively it could be representing Tezcatlipoca, the all-powerful, multiform and ubiquitous god, black god of the night sky, patron of wizards and evildoers] (2005, 130–131).

Hernández Vázquez echoes the other authors by referring to the principle of duality (2005, 130–131):

> *En la danza del Matarachín se encierra el principio de la dualidad, del bien y del mal, del día y la noche, posibles reminiscencias de la concepción mesoamerican acerca de la existencia de un dios luminoso, Quetzalcóatl, y uno de la oscuridad, Tezcatlipoca.*
>
> [In the Dance of the Matarachín the principle of duality is embedded, of good and evil, the day and the night, possibly reminiscent of the Mesoamerican concept about the existence of a luminous god, Quetzalcóatl, and a dark one, Tezcatlipoca.]

From this account, it seems that the Dance of the Matarachín occurs in apposition to the celebration of Christmas. In the latter, one celebrates a baby of light and perfection, in the other an infant of darkness and deformity. There appears to be a duality between these two babies. It is this contrast that causes Hernández Vázquez to recall the classic Mexican beliefs regarding the duality between those two great gods. We know already that Quetzalcóatl, under the name of el Niño, has become identified with Christ and the sun in the Totonacapán. Now we encounter the idea of a balancing force, Tezcatlipoca and Satan.

In March 2010, Vernon Kostohryz, Carlos Moreno Vásquez, and I visited José González Hernández. We asked him to link masks he had made to specific dances. He identified several of his masks that he said were Viejitos or Huehues for the Matarachín dance.

On another occasion, Carlos Moreno Vásquez and I drove on to the small community of Colonia del Valle, Puebla; Carlos had heard of a carver there. The mask maker was not at home but his family brought out masks and costumes. I purchased three Huehue masks that they said were used during a dance at Todos Santos and represented the dead. These were evidently masks for the Matarachín dance.

The next day we had the privilege of visiting Señor Leonardo Carcamo Palomino in his home on the outskirts of Zozocolco de Hidalgo, Veracruz. Leonardo is the leader of a dance group there. The masks and headdresses were very dramatic and unusual. At the time of the visit I found them so unfamiliar that I was uncertain about the identity of the dance. They did not include masks for the "gusano" character. Leonardo told us that all of the characters were *Reyes malos* (evil kings). Leonardo, his son Isias Carcamo Pérez, and our guide, Alejandro Segura Fernández, put on some of these masks and headdresses for us. Several days later we discovered a book by González Callado and Cerdeño Lance (2009, 224–227) that included several photos of this group in the section about the Danza del Matarachín, but without any captions. The mask with the pointed ears can be seen (227) in the back row, obscured by a snake but wearing the identical headdress.

Las Danzas de Carnaval

In contrast to Todos Santos there is Carnaval (Carnival or Mardi Gras). We must begin by considering two apparent truths, which have the possibility of contradicting or negating one another. On the one hand, there is the historic observation in Mexico that Todos Santos (All Saints/All Souls Day) and Carnaval form two elements of one general ceremonial perspective, one that assumes and celebrates the visitation of the souls of the dead among those who are still alive. From this perspective all Carnaval performances can be viewed as possible portrayals of the dead.

Furthermore, in some areas of Mexico there has been the belief that the souls of those who died by violent means may become the tools of the devil, returning to trouble the living, and that these visits would occur at the time of Carnaval, and not at Todos Santos (Stresser-Péan 2009, 343–346).

On the other hand, Carnaval is never the same from one town to the next; rather, its persistent performance results from local themes and interests, which will reflect some unique combination of tradition and innovation. While there are many publications available that explain the persistence of belief among Mexicans that the dead visit

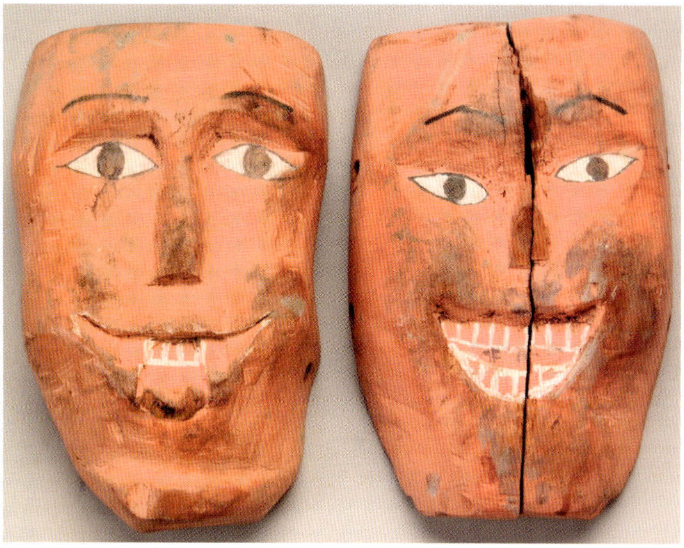

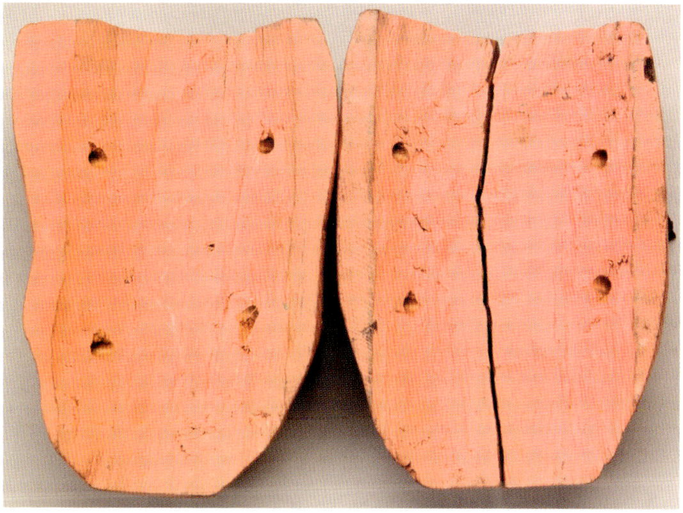

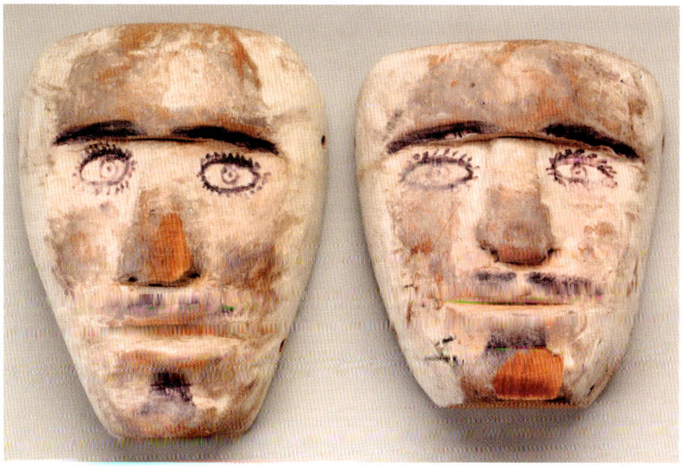

From top:

This set of masks for the Matarachín character was purchased from the dance leader in El Espinal, Veracruz; 6½" × 9". Circa 1994; the masks had been danced for 15 years and were retired in 2009 when one of them split in half. *Collection of the author.*

The back view of the Matarachín masks. They are not worn on the face, so one doesn't observe the usual patina.

This pair of masks for the Matarachín character was carved in 2009 to replace a broken set; 6" × 9". They were danced for one year in El Espinal, Veracruz, and collected in March 2010. The backs are unremarkable. *Collection of the author.*

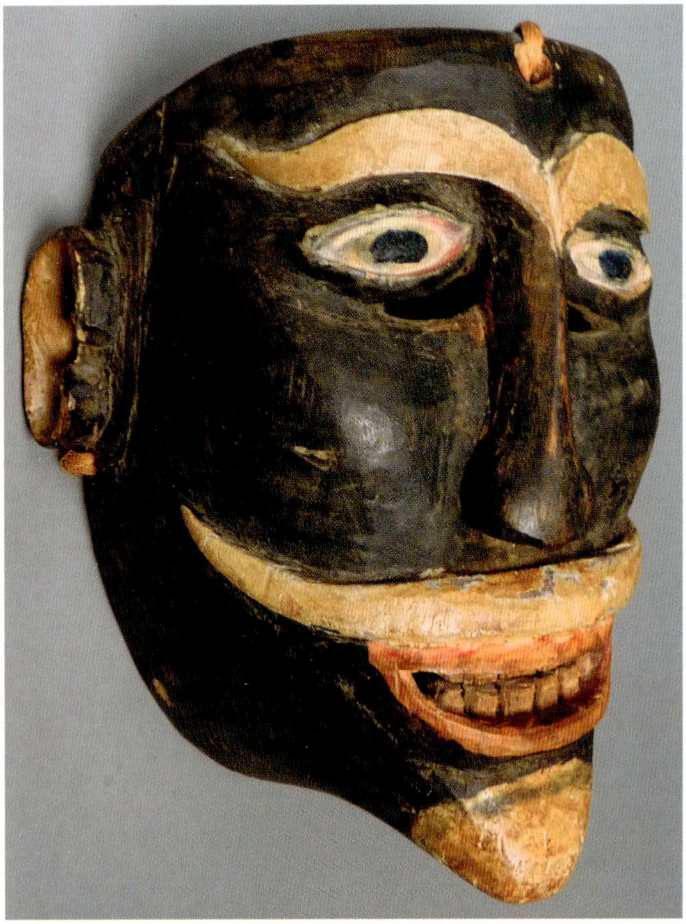

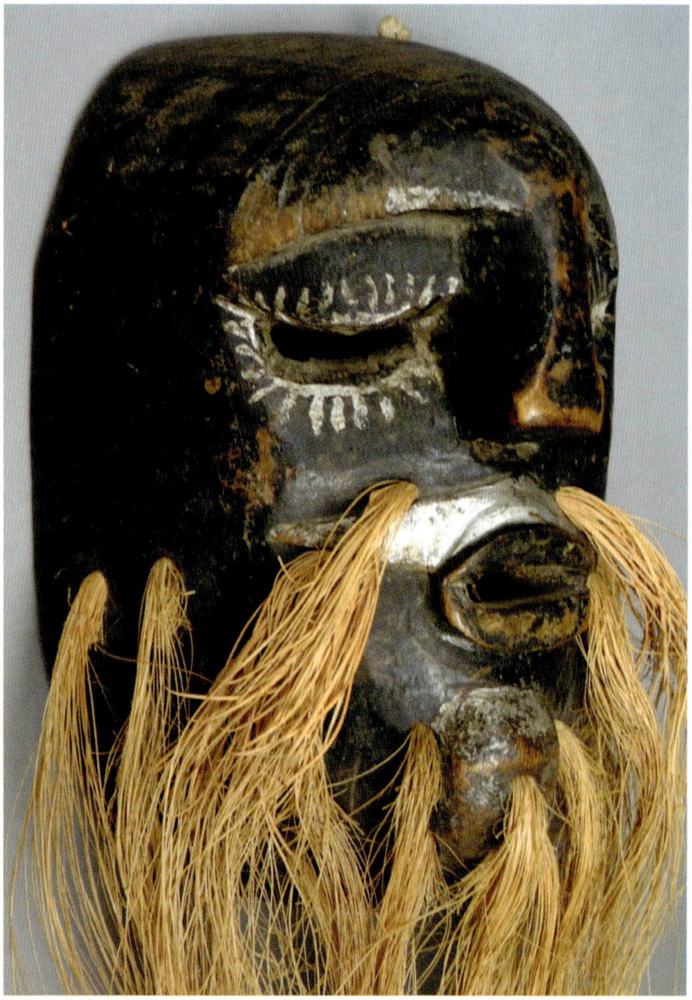

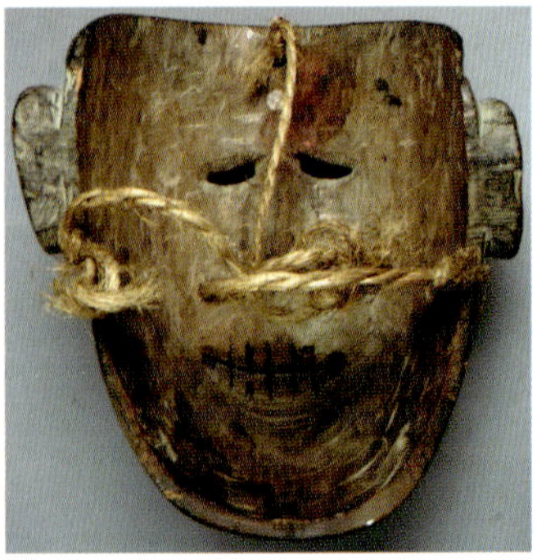

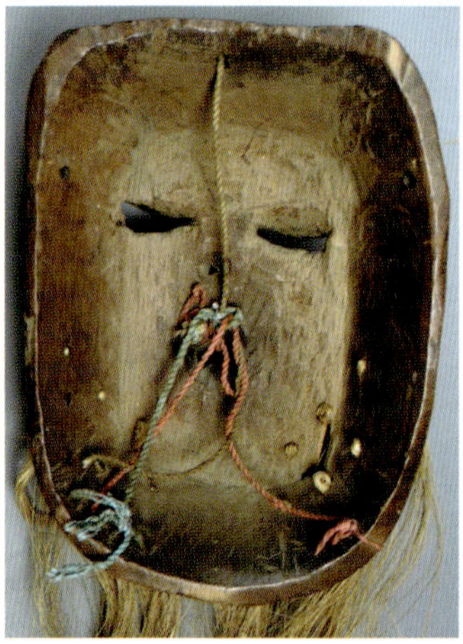

Top left: This mask was labeled as a Xantolo, from Paso de Valencia, Veracruz; 8½" × 9". Circa 1970. As noted earlier, Xantolos are from the Huasteca, not from the Sierra. But if this name is to indicate usage during Todos Santos, then it is a Huehue or Viejo from the Danza de los Matarachín, a dance that has a documented history in Paso de Valencia. In that dance or in another, this is another mask with the expression we might associate with the Pilatos character, who does appear in the Matarachín dance. *Collection of the author.*

Bottom left: The back view of the Huehue or Viejo mask shows good patina.

Top right: This mask was purchased from Jaled Muyaes and Estela Ogazon in 1997; 6½" × 9". Circa 1970. The label provided very limited information—Huehue, Veracruz. This mask would be a likely participant in the Matarachín dance as one of the Huehues or Viejos. The hooded eyes make one think of the dead; the mouth does not make one think of Pilato. With the tubular mouth and the knob chin, this is a beautiful old mask. *Collection of the author.*

Bottom right: The view of the back of the Huehue or Viejo mask. It has great patina.

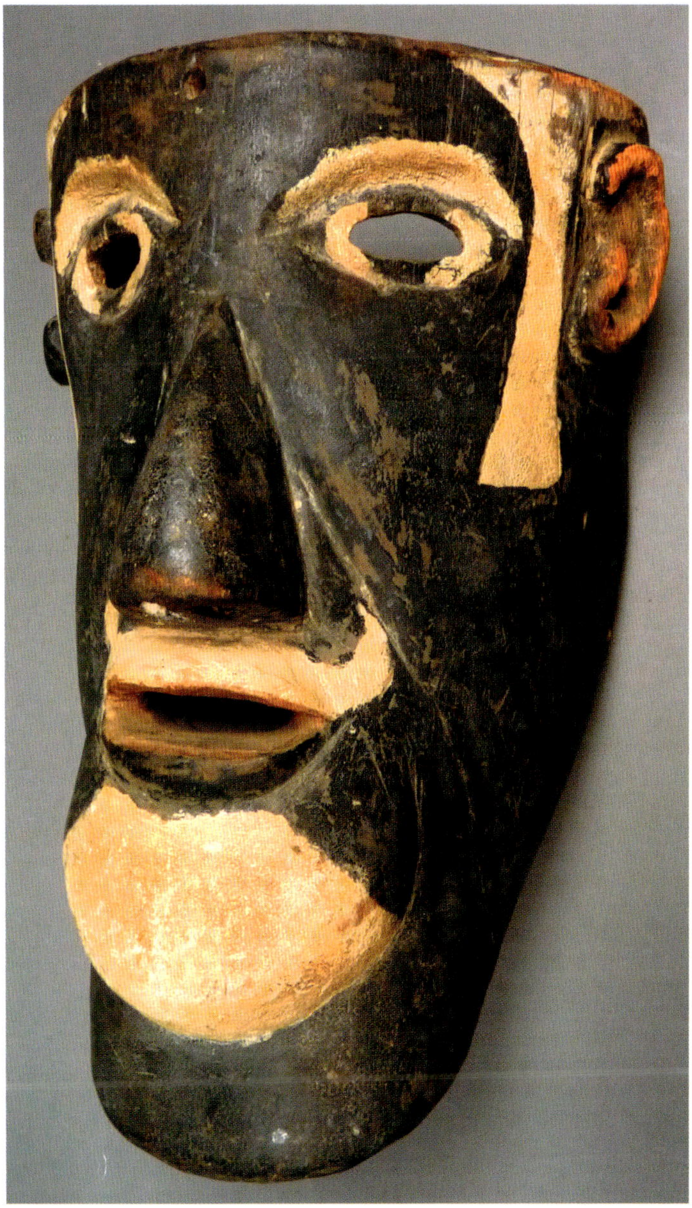

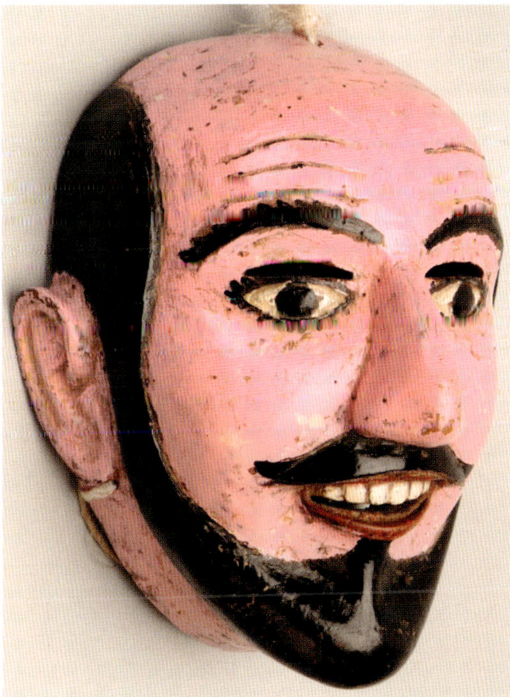

each year on Todos Santos, it is not as clear whether such visits are consistently a central focus of Carnaval in the Sierra de Puebla area.

In the Totonacapán, the Carnaval dancers wander through the village, rather than centering their performance on the church or the village plaza. They go from house to house, performing and begging for money, not unlike the Matarachín dancers. The devil is frequently prominent as the leader of the Carnaval troupe; he is not described as sinister or menacing, but rather as a buffoon, dressed in ragged clothes, not unlike the Pilatos/Satanás character in the Danza de los Negritos.

Ontiveros Peña (2005, 152–153) wrote about *Carnaval en Solteros de Juan Rosas*, in Veracruz. The inhabitants of this town are mainly Nahuas along with some Totonacs. The celebration lasts for the four days before Ash Wednesday. On the Friday evening before the fiesta begins there is a special ceremony that honors el Diablo, "*a quien se le dedica la celebración*" (to whom the celebration is dedicated). The masks that will be worn during the fiesta are arranged in one or two rows, face up on the ground. Each mask is provided with a plate of food and a cup of coffee. All this is supervised by a *curandero* (a healer), "*quien da la comer a las máscaras y le reza al 'rey de carnaval' (el diablo) con el fin de que no se moleste y permita a todos jugar felizmente durante la fiesta*" [who offers food to the masks and prays to the "King of the Carnival" (the devil) in order that he is not offended and so he will allow all to participate happily during the celebration].

Ontiveros Peña (2005, 153–156) describes an interaction between a devil character and the masks:

> *Cuando todo está servido, el curandero ordena al "Diablo"—ya con el disfraz, al igual que algunos "viejos" y "damas"—que brinque siete veces por encima de las máscaras, mientras los músicos tocan el "son del Diablo," Con el cumplimiento de este rito, absolutamente todos los participantes quedan protegidos de algún posible incidente.*
>
> [When every mask has been served, the healer directs the "Devil"—already in costume—to jump seven times over the masks, while the musicians play the "song of the Devil." It is believed that through this rite the participants will be protected from some possible accident.]

A photograph of the devil jumping over the masks is included in the article; one can see that the masks depict humans of various races.

On the following morning, Ontiveros Peña continues, the Diablo gathers and leads a crowd of dancers through the streets, singing and dancing (2005, 154, 156). Peña includes two photos of the *Carnavaleros* (masked revelers) in action. They are wearing old clothes and unremarkable human-faced masks.

In another article, Francisco Velasco (2005, 157–160) describes the celebration of Carnival in an Otomí community. The performance may appear to be playful, but it has a serious purpose:

Top left:
This mask was found in La Union, Veracruz, in a private collection, it may well have come from some other town. It was said to be a Brujo or witch; 7½" × 11". Circa 1970. There is a Brujo character in the Matarachín Dance. *Collection of the author.*

Bottom left:
This is the finest mask that I have seen by José González Hernández; 7½" × 8¾". Circa 1980. It is a Viejito for the Matarachín dance. *Collection of the author.*

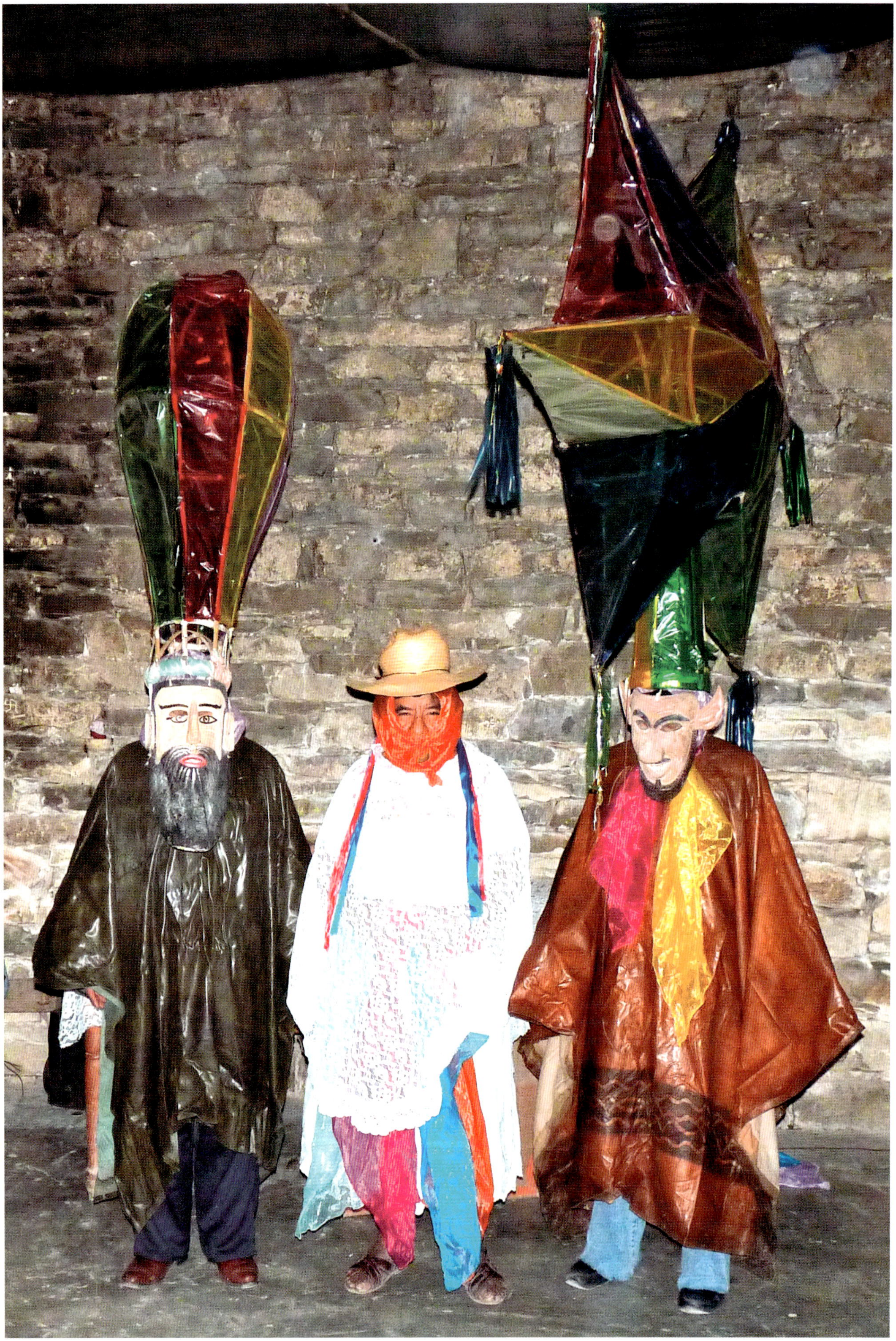

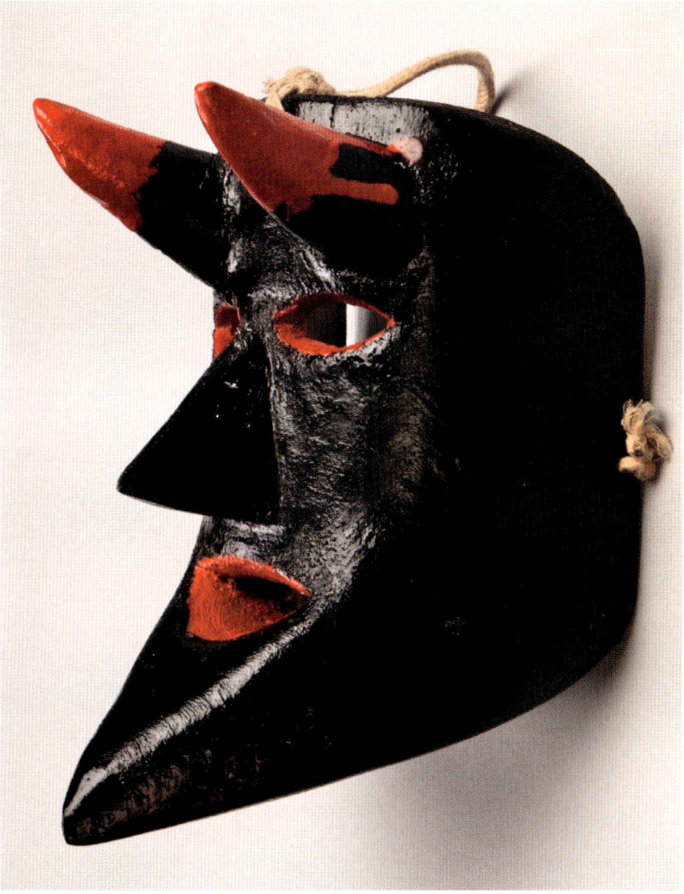

This Diablo, or devil, mask from Colonia del Valle, Puebla, is used during Todos Santos and represents a dead person; 6" × 8". Circa 2008. *Collection of the author.*

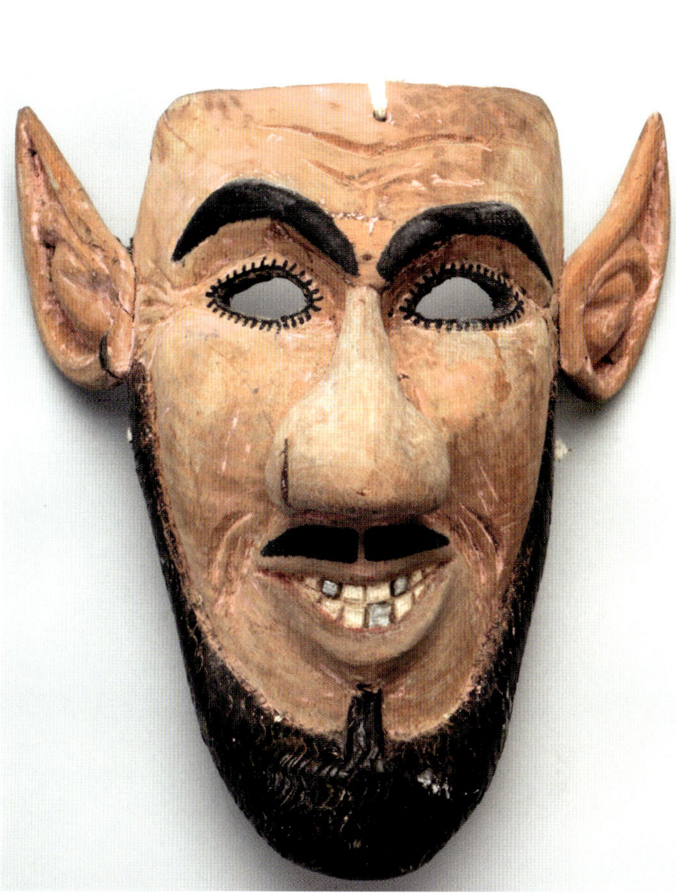

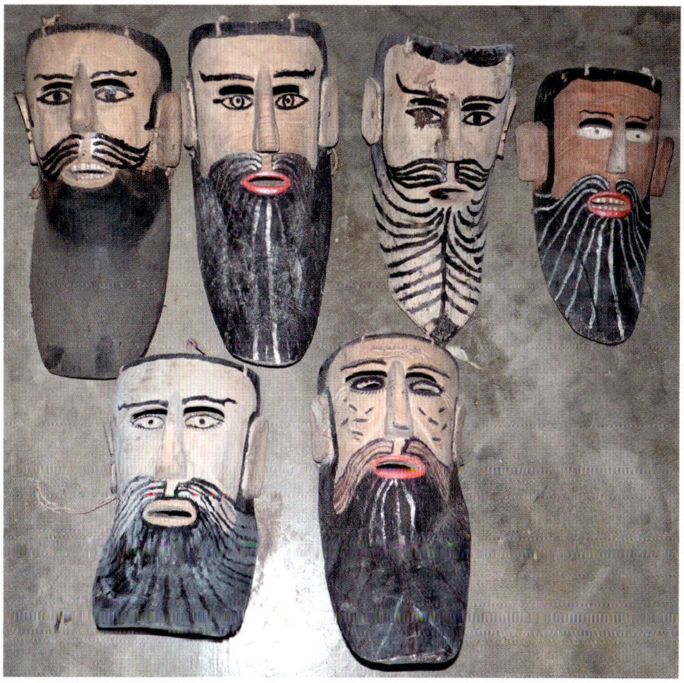

Opposite page:
Leonardo Carcamo Palomino on the left, his son Isias on the right, and their friend Alejandro Segura in the middle, dressed as Malinche. These headdresses are remarkably tall but very light in weight. These characters are Reyes Malos, "evil kings," and the masks are from Zozocolco.

Top: This mask from Zozocolco is one of the evil kings; 10" × 10". Circa 1990. He is obviously a Diablo, based on his ears. *Collection of the author.*

Bottom: A selection of Reyes Malos masks from Zozocolco for the dance. The carver is said to be from Pasando El Puente Anayal, Veracruz.

Sino una oportunidad para agradecer y manifestarse alegres ante los patrones de la naturaleza. Los otomíes piensan que desde tiempos remotos han existido dos patrones en la humanidad y que éstos siempre han estado en disputa para reinar en este mundo, son Dios y el Diablo. Por ello durante la celebración del carnaval se respeta y se ofrenda a estos patrones.

[It is an opportunity to be thankful and to pronounce themselves glad before the landlords of nature. The Otomíes think that from remote times there have existed two landlords of humanity and that these have always been in dispute to reign in this world; these are God and the Devil. During the celebration of Carnival respect and offerings to these landlords are given.]

Velasco continues to broaden his explanation of the Otomí worldview (Francisco Velasco2005, 157–160):

En Carnaval se debe de ofrendar a los patrones pues se considera que el hombre está dotado de dos poderes y que si los valorara no confundiría las cosas y viviría en armonia consigo mismo.

[During Carnaval one presents offerings to both masters because it is thought that a man is endowed with two powers and that if he valued them he would not be confused and he would live in harmony with himself.]

Francisco Velasco reports that the dance includes viejo characters who wear masks, and there are also unmasked Diablos (2005, 158–160). He includes a photo of the dancers, who look very much like male and female Tejoneros.

Eva Hernández Orea (2005, 161–163) has documented the available history about the Carnaval en Cuyuxquihui, Veracruz, at a time when this was no longer being performed. On the one hand, the author describes activities that seem playful. Some dancers constructed a male bull, a female cow, and a mule from reeds. Then the animals were carried on the backs of dancers, to create the pantomime that they were living. On the last day they hacked the reed bulls apart with machetes and pretended to sell the meat. On the other hand, the dancers are described as being careful to follow purification rites at the beginning and again at the end of the fiesta, as if they had been engaged in some serious interaction with dangerous powers or spirits, although the author's description does not reveal such exposure.

Hernández Orea (2005, 161–163) does include a description of one character of particular interest—el viejo, whom she says is Pilatos. He wears ragged clothing and the mask of an old man. He plays the clown. It is not indicated whether any of the other dancers wear masks.

Sara Méndez García (2005,164–167) has written about Carnival in the town of Ojite de Matamoros, in the municipio of Coxquihui, Veracruz. A photograph shows a male and a female dancer, both with veiled faces; Méndez García makes no mention of masks. The dance depicts a competition between *el marqués* (the Marquis, a possible reference to Cortez, whose title was el Marqués del Valle) and an Indian, *el apache,* for the love of a woman, la Malinche or la dama. Malinche conspires with the apache to kill the marqués, and el Diablo carries the body to the door of the church. There is a large cast of supporting characters, including priests, doctors, mice, mummies, and la Llorona (a character from Mexican folklore, the "crying woman").

Méndez García (2005,164) includes an interesting myth:

Para explicar el posible origen de esta danza, se cuenta que, cuando Jesús estuvo en peligo se crearon muchas danzas con el propósito de despistar a sus enemigos. El "Diablo," con sus engaños y piruetas lograba distraer a los enemigos de Jesús, los "judíos."

[To explain a possible origin of the dance it is said that when Jesus was in danger, many dances were created with the intent of putting his enemies off the trail. The "devil" with his tricks and turns managed to distract the enemies of Jesus, the "Jews."]

Finally, Aguilera Madero and Márquez Hernández (2005, 168–169) write about Carnaval en Joloapan. The participants wear old clothes along with a variety of masks—of "*catrines, payasos o diablos, … algunos usan máscaras de animal.*" *Catrines* connotes Tejonero-style masks of handsome men and beautiful women. The dancers also use masks of clowns, devils, and animals. The dance includes the character Pilatos, wearing ragged old clothes. His mask is always either red or black. He carries a small wooden horse that he pretends to ride. He constantly clowns or begs for money. Children bait him, he chases them, and they run away, shrieking.

These references suggest that a great variety of masks can be used for Carnaval. It is clear that the masks for this dance are commonly borrowed from other dances, either without any alteration or repainted and/or embellished. From the few dance photos that are available, one can see that most of the masks are rather conventional in design, depicting Caucasian men and women. They are likely to have been borrowed from the Dance of the Huehues or Tejoneros. From the description and photos of the masks used in the Matarachín dance, it will be obvious that those would be highly suitable to wear during Carnaval. Likewise, the Viejo and Pilatos masks used in such dances as the Santiagueros, the Voladores, the Huehues, and the Negritos would all be compatible with the ambiguous Carnaval characters. La Muerte from the Moros y Cristianos dance would certainly be welcomed in this dance, as would devils from that dance or from Los Migueles.

I have occasionally encountered masks that were acknowledged to have been used in Carnaval, and others that have the appearance of having been altered for that dance. I purchased a very old Tejonero mask in March 2010, immediately after it had been returned to the owner following use in Carnaval. This mask had clearly been carved by Benito Juárez Figueroa. An old Huehue mask, with classic features of masks by Daniel Ramos Ramos of Nanacatlán, Puebla, was found decorated with colored yarn, as if for Carnaval. An old Tejonero mask with an articulated jaw was originally carved by Don Lillo and subsequently embellished with hair by someone else, apparently for Carnaval. My Carnaval Ghoul, a remarkable old mask, which depicts a ghoul or some such character, was said to have been danced in Carnaval for more than 50 years in Zapotitlán, Puebla. The carver was Magno León of Hueytlalpan, Puebla. These masks are described in Chapter 6, shown under their respective carver.

La Danza de Lakapíjkuyu

Ygnacia Hernández Vázquez (2005, 132–133) provides us with some information about this masked dance found in Totonac areas of Veracruz. It is performed during the Christmas season in conjunction with the Posadas. In that latter tradition unmasked singers go from house to house in the late evening hours, asking if anyone will take in Saint Joseph and the Virgin Mary, prior to the birth of Jesus. While the Posada singers circulate, the Lakapíjkuyu dancers perform only within the church or within private homes, in front of the Saints on the house altar. There are two lines of dancers, all men. They dance to the music of a violin. In one row the dancers wear black-faced masks and men's clothing; in the other row they wear women's garments and their faces are hidden by veils. A dance photo at the end of the text shows two lines of Lakapijkuyu dancers in Coxquihui, Veracruz, the men wearing the typical dance boots of this region and Negrito masks. The "women" (men dressed as women) wear white lacy dresses, shawls, and head coverings; the outline of a cowboy hat is visible under the scarf, which drapes over the crown and brim of the hat to form a long, full veil. In Spanish the dancers are referred to as *Varones* (gentlemen).

The author (Ygnacia Hernández Vázquez 2005, 132–133) explains that the name of the Lakapíjkuyu dance comes from two Totonac words, *lakán*, which means face, and *pijkuyu*, referring to the black-feathered garrapatera or piskuyu bird. The black mask of the dancers is said to represent the face of this bird. The dancers represent those who came to honor the newborn baby Jesus, particularly the pijkuyu birds. According to a legend, these birds sheltered the baby Jesus from the dust and wind by spreading their wings over his face and body.

Hernández Vázquez (2005, 132) recounts a legend:

> *Cuentan que antes de que naciera Jesús, todo estaban en completa oscuridad y cuando él nació, entonces amanecié. Una de los aves que se acercaron para adorlarlo y bailarle fue precisamente el "ave garrapatera," pues ésta presintió que aquel niño iba a gobernar el mundo; de ahí surgió la danza.*
>
> [A legend describes a time when the world was dark. When Jesus was born the sun abruptly rose for the first time. The garrapatera birds had a vision that this child would govern the world, so they came to pay their respects.]

Gaona Vega and Juárez Hernández (2005, 134–139), wrote about the Dance of the Lakapíjkuyu in the municipio (county) of Coxquihui, Veracruz. Their description of the dance is much like that of Hernández Vázquez, except that they describe three rows of dancers, with male characters on the outside rows, while the middle row of dancers are dressed as females with veiled faces. They elaborated on the legends associated with this dance.

> *Antes del nacimiento de Jesucristo, la gente nacía y vivía en la oscuridad, cuando Él nació apareció en el cielo un lucero que iluminó todo e 'hizo aclarar.' En esa época hacía mucho frié y por esta razón el niño lloraba mucho; al darse cuenta de esto, los ancianos y los animales como el oso, el tlacuache, los piskuyus (aves garrapateras) se alegraron infinitamente por habérseles dado la luz; presintiendo que el que había nacido iba a 'mandar' en el mundo, ellos se le acercaron y bailaron para que dejara de llorar. Los piskuyus llevaron sonajas y con las alas extendidas protegieron al niño del polvo; el tlacuache fue en busca de una brasa para que se calentara el niño, trajo la brasa enredada en la cola, por ello desde entonces la tiene quemada.*
>
> [Until the birth of Jesus, the world was dark, but at the moment of His birth an extremely bright star appeared. There were people and animals who apparently understood that the light was a gift from this newborn baby, so they gathered around him. The animals included the *Oso* (bear), the *tlacuache* (opossum) and the *piskuyus* (garrapatera birds). They danced for Jesus and he immediately stopped crying. The piskuyu birds spread their wings over the infant to protect him from the dust and wind, and the opossum brought a live coal for warmth, which he carried wrapped in his tail. This burned him, and that is why the opossum's tail is bare.] (2005, 135).

A variation on this legend provides a more complicated story (Gaona Vega and Juárez Hernández 2005, 135):

> *Cuando nació el niño Jesús estabo oscuro y sólo un lucero empezó a alumbrar intensamente, las personas se admiraron y se acercaron disfrazadas de animales, algunos iban con la finalidad de adorar al niño, le bailaron y cantaron, otros se acercaron para robarlo y matarlo, pero antes de lograr su propósito amaneció totalmente, por lo que amanecieron disfrazados y como castigo fueron convertidos para siempre en los animales que representaban y se fueron a refugiar en el monte. A los que pitaron con flautas se les quedó el pico largo, los que tenían máscaras se les quedó el pico corto y los que iban disfrazados de 'viejos' fueron convertidos en guajolotes.*
>
> [When the baby Jesus was born, it was dark and a single bright star began to burn intensely, the people admired it and came near, dressed as animals. Some went with the goal of admiring the child by dancing and singing to him. Others came near Jesus with the goal of robbing and killing him but before they could do so, the sun rose completely and those who were dressed as animals were punished by being turned into the animals that they represented forever, and they went to find refuge in the mountains. Those who were playing flutes ended up with big beaks and those with masks of viejos were turned into turkeys.]

The myths don't clearly explain what happened in this process, but it seems that some visitors were admitted to proximity with the baby and others were not, based on their intentions. The Lakapíjkuyu dancers represent those who were admitted. Those who were not admitted were somehow defined as outsiders and transformed into animals, and then they went to find refuge in the mountains. They are said to be represented by the viejos in the Lakakgolo dance, which also includes the Oso. Apparently the Matarachín was at one time included in the Lakakgolo dance, although now he has his own separate dance (Gaona Vega and Juárez Hernández 2005, 135).

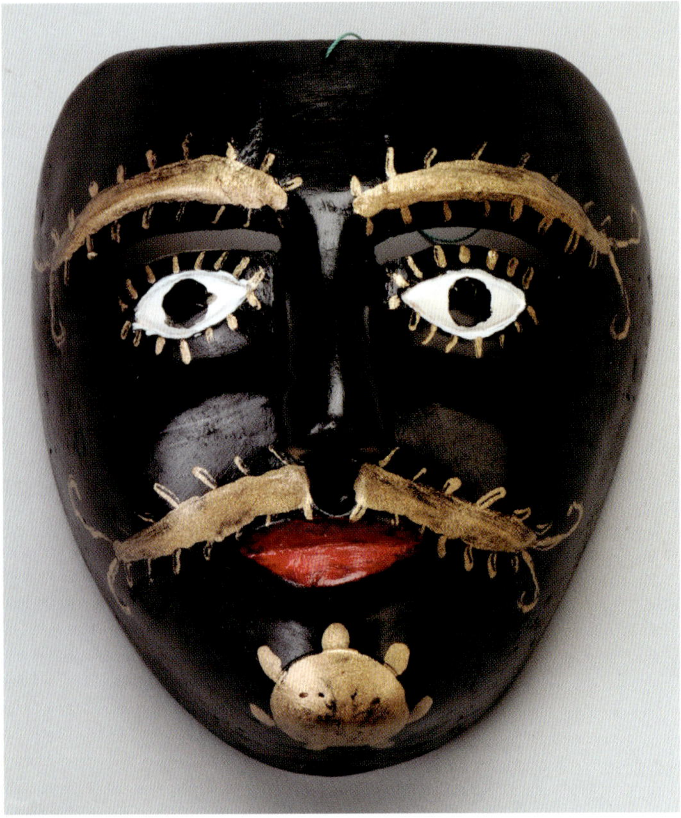

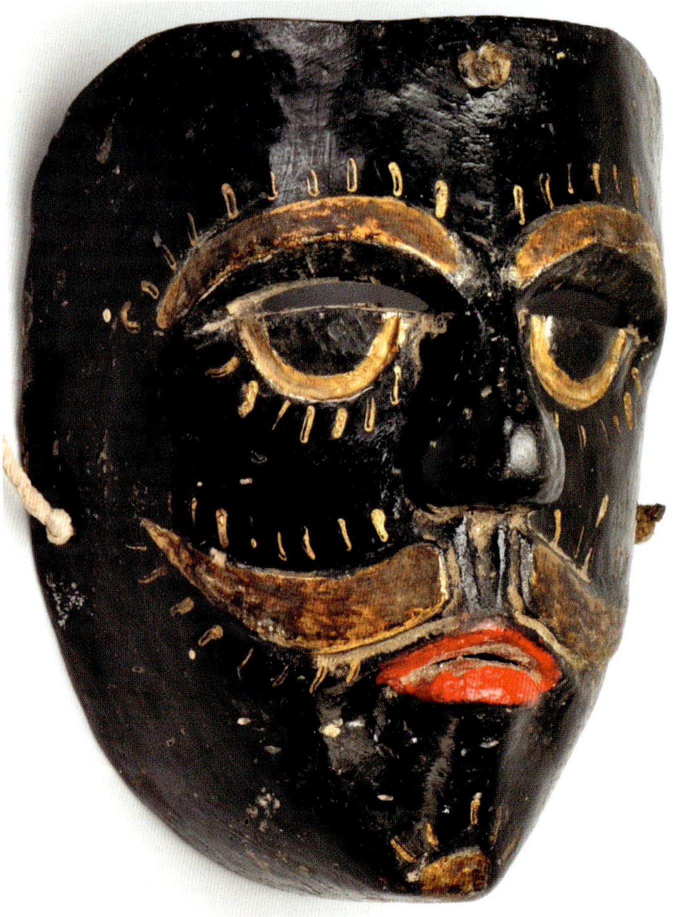

La Danza de Lakakgolo or los Viejos

Sara Méndez García (2005, 140) has written the only published account that I have been able to discover on the Danza de Lakakgolo, also called the Dance of the Viejos. She begins by providing a list of names. The Totonac name for the dance is *lakakgolo*; she reports that this is translated as *cara de viejo* in Spanish (face of the old one). The dance has a second name, *lakakiwi* in Totonac, or *cara de palo* in Spanish, meaning face of the pole or tree. Then the author reports that the dueño of this dance is Kiwíkgolo, in Spanish *palo viejo* (old pole). This personage is said to be the *viejo del monte* (the old one of the forest).

In Huehuetla, Lane was told that the puppets and masks in the Huehues dance were made of "living wood" (*Notes on the Text of The Tree of Knowledge* nd). Now we may have been introduced to the master of the living wood in the belief system of the Totonacs. Kiwíkgolo is the supreme tree spirit, a tree with the face of an old man. As such he is the host of the *monte*, which was said to be the refuge for those creatures who were expelled from the presence of the infant Jesus in the description of the Lakapijkuyu dance.

So these myths begin to converge, revealing two parallel worlds, the world of natural spirits and the world of Christianity. Given these two worlds, it seems, two dances were needed to glorify Christ. The Christian worshippers are represented in the Lakapíjkuyu dance, while the worshippers from the natural world appear in the Lakakgolo dance. Allegedly evil elements from the natural world have been segregated in the Matarachín dance.

This dance is extremely unusual and interesting. One of the characters, in the myths and in this dance, is El Oso, the bear. In all of Mexico, this is the only dance known to me where there is an explicitly defined character that wears the mask of a bear. Other characters in this dance include *El Charro* (the cowboy), an old couple, *El Anciano* and *La Anciana*, *El Policía* (the policeman), a soldier, and a group of *Civiles* (federal police) carrying wooden rifles (Mendez García 2005, 140).

Top: This Negrito mask, carved by Don Lillo, a maskmaker in Coxquihui, is of the style worn by the male dancers in the Lakapíjkuyu dance; 6 ¼" × 7". Circa 2006. *Collection of the author.*

Bottom: This is a Negrito mask carved by José González Galindo of Coxquihui, for the Lakapíjkuyu dance; 5½" × 6½". Circa 1980. It is old and worn, with a beautiful patina. *Collection of the author.*

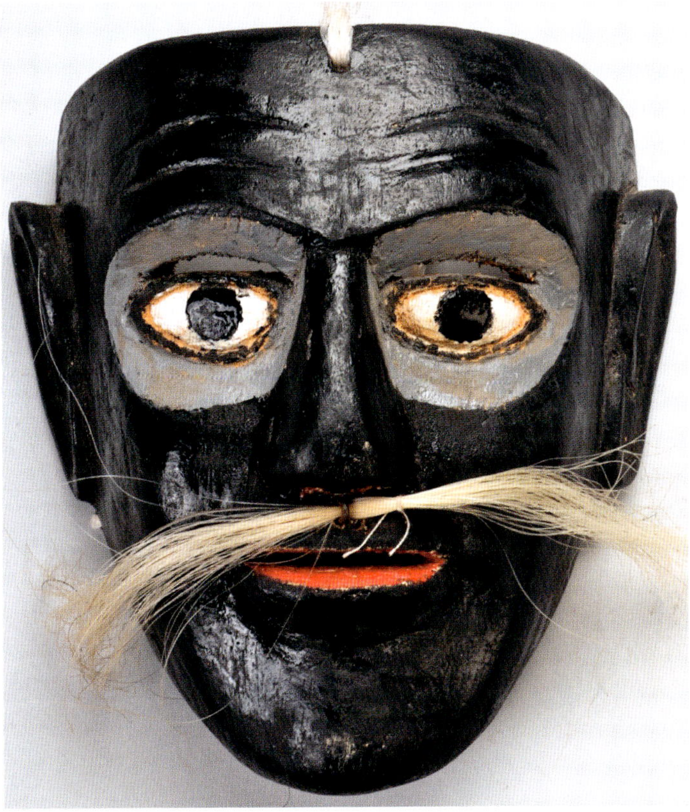

This black-faced Viejo mask was carved by José González Hernández for the Lakakgolo dance; 7½" × 7". Circa 2000. *Collection of the author.*

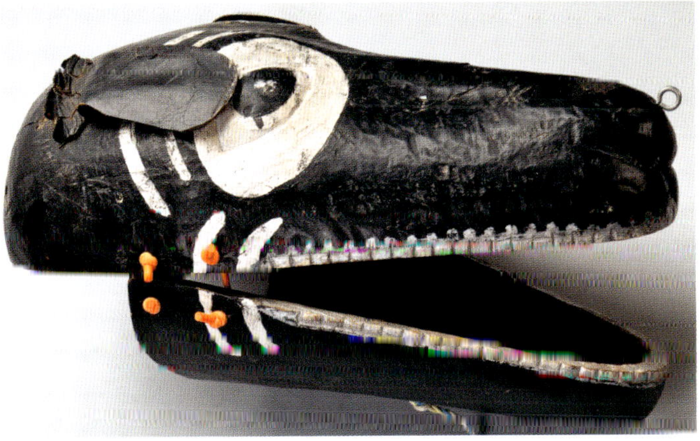

This black *Oso* (bear) mask was carved by José González Hernández for the Lakakgolo dance; 11" × 19". Circa 1990. *Collection of the author.*

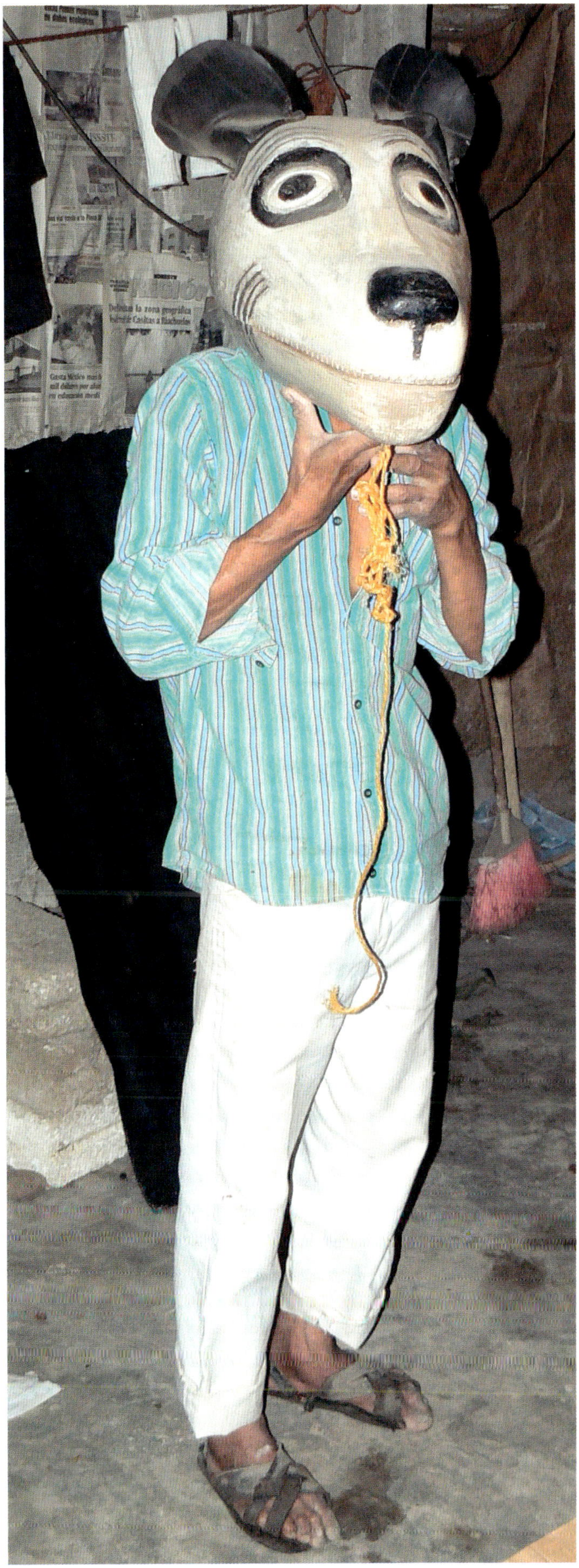

José González Hernández modeling his Oso mask in December 2008.

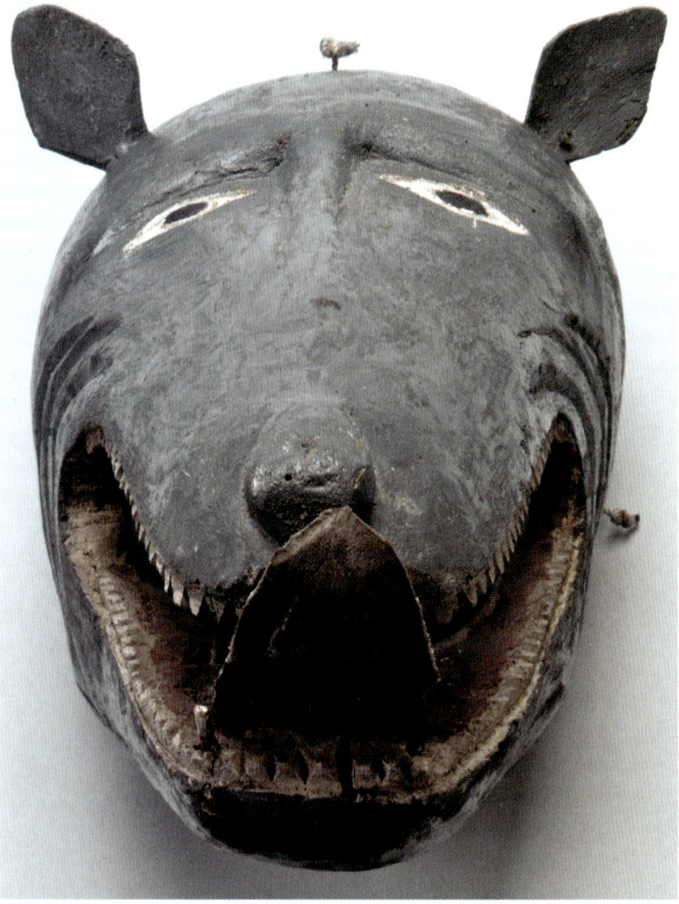

Left: This Oso mask was reportedly from Comunidad Morelos, but not carved by José González Hernández; 8" × 9", 15" long. Circa 1990. *Collection of the author.*

Below: The side view of the bear by an unknown carver.

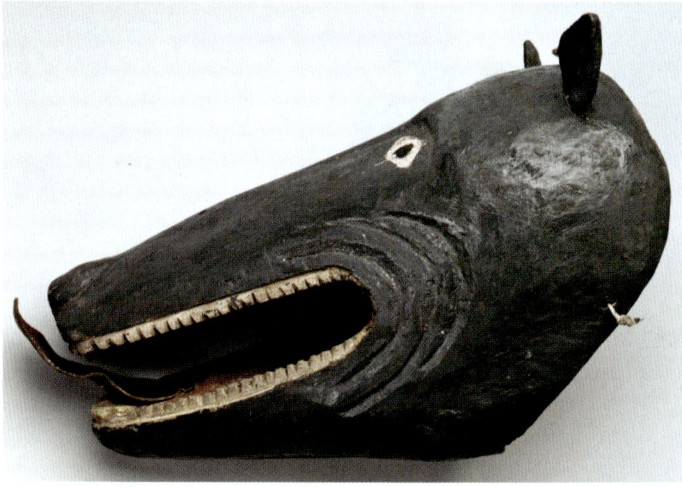

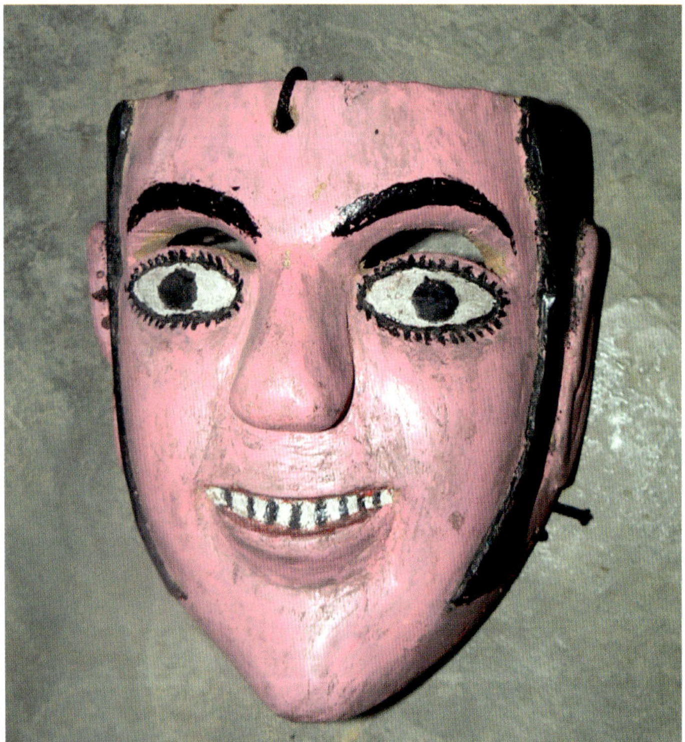

This pink Viejo mask was carved by José González Hernández for the Lakakgolo dance. *Collection of* José *González Hernández.*

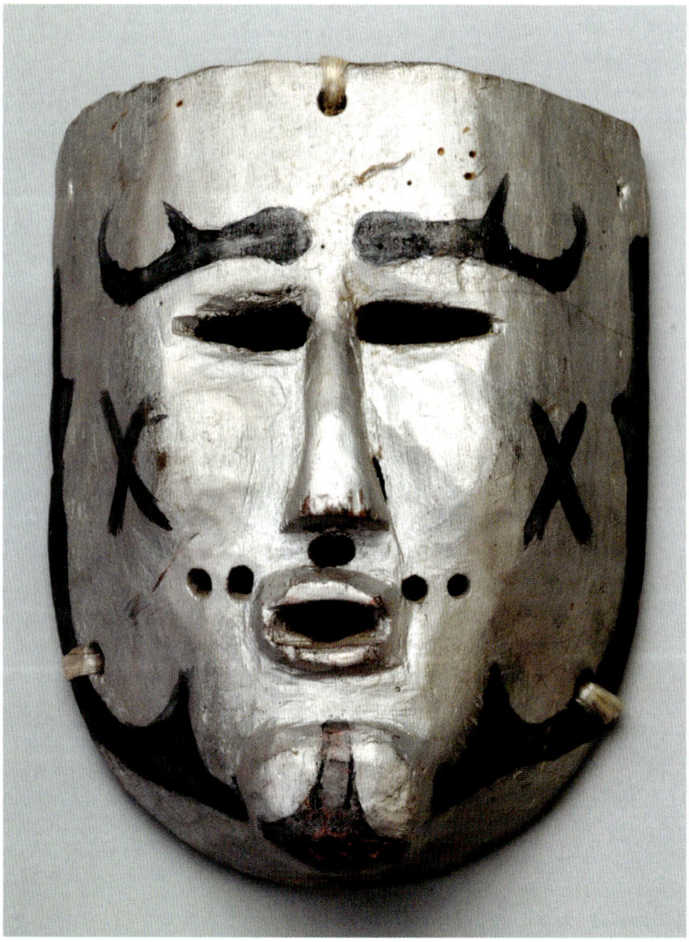

This Viejo mask danced with the Oso mask in the Lakakgolo dance; 6" × 7". Circa 1990. *Collection of the author.*

Chapter 5

The Process of Looking at Masks

There are many ways to look at a mask. During actual use in the community of origin, a mask may not even be perceived by the traditional audience as an independent object; rather, it contributes to the overall appearance of the dancer who wears the mask as part of his costume. In that case a mask may emerge as a separate entity only when the dancer removes it from his face. In North America, separated from the cultural context that created a particular mask, we usually encounter a mask as an isolated artistic creation. Then we may choose to view this mask either as a whole or as a collection of elements. These two perspectives tend to emphasize different qualities that a mask may possess.

When looking at a mask as an integrated whole, it seems most important to note that a mask can possess a level of charisma that is not due so much to the details of the carving, but results from such things as the overall size or shape, or from the creative use of color, either to emphasize the shape of the mask or to project a quality or pattern that has little to do with its shape. For example, in Chapter 6 we will see Pilato masks from the area of Cuetzalan, Puebla, that are not finely carved or carefully painted, yet the blocks of color applied to these masks seem to be the medium of expression that defines the character of the wearer. Furthermore, the effectiveness of such a mask may derive more from its visibility from a distance, across a crowded plaza, and less from the details of the mask's actual features. Another example involves masks used to represent the dead, or more particularly the souls of those dead who are perceived as potentially menacing. Such masks are often painted blue or green, and it may be that these colors are reserved for such characters, to differentiate them from more positive entities, whether spirits, saints, or others considered to be still alive. Individual tastes vary, and there will certainly be readers who prefer these masks that draw their visual power from the overall gestalt of the design.

It also seems pertinent to examine the masks from this region in greater detail, as a collection of design elements. This approach is useful if one is attempting to characterize a mask in terms of its possible place of origin, authenticity, and degree of use, or trying to attribute the mask to a specific carver. This manner of looking lets one better appreciate a mask if certain details emerge into focus as particularly artistic. Such an approach also allows a more accurate estimate of the age of a mask, as this should fall within the lifetime of the identified carver.

Such analysis is necessary for Mexican dance masks because it has been so common, over recent decades, for masks to be collected in the field by pickers or dealers without careful documentation. A vast floating body of anonymous masks has resulted and these have been sold to tourists, collectors, and museums all over the world, without provenance or with some limited labeling of uncertain reliability. Subsequent re-labeling of these masks has ranged from minimal to whimsical or fantastic; signs of neglect (damage and grime) have been interpreted as evidence of great age. I have often had the experience of encountering masks by some of the greatest Mexican master carvers in the holdings of some important museum, but finding them labeled with only the name of the Mexican state of probable origin.

Various factors have conspired to prevent careful identification and labeling of masks at the time of collection. The most obvious cause has been that the picker was unaware that such information was important. A more surprising problem has been that many of the dancers who used these masks were not particularly concerned about the identity of the maker. Some dancers appear to view masks as interchangeable tools; others have favorite masks, but, even then, may or may not actually know the name of the carver. Masks are frequently taken to a local carver to be repainted, which can create the impression that the person who repainted the mask was also the original carver, when this was not the case. The likeliest scenario is that a dancer will accurately identify the town of origin of a mask and credit it to a familiar carver from that town, when it was actually carved at an earlier time by another carver.

To establish a reliable correlation between carvers and their masks, we have found it most helpful to question the individual carvers or members of their respective families. With the exception of those who have reached senescence, carvers are usually able to recognize their own work. They may be able to identify current users of their masks in their community. Often they can also recognize the work of an earlier local carver, particularly if that carver served as a mentor. Family members may retain masks that were carved by a deceased father or grandfather, and sometimes they can supply old photographs of masks made by their relative, even dance photos. It has sometimes seemed useful to purchase new, undanced masks directly from the carver in order to document his or her style most directly. It has been helpful to identify the various places where a particular carver has been in residence, as this should correlate with a scattering of communities where his masks have figured prominently in dances.

Despite their uncertain reliability, the dancers themselves have been another important source of information. Their attributions may provide information that can be verified or doubted following further inquiry. Indeed, the report of the mask owner may identify a carver who was previously unknown to us, and then we could interview the mask maker or his family directly. A person living in the community who buys and sells masks can be a wonderful source of information that can then be further researched.

One can find a wide variety of mask forms in the universe of Mexican masking and in this specific region. Many Mexican mask collectors are initially engaged by masks of animals, particularly those of jaguars, monkeys, or dogs because these can be so dramatic. Or they may be interested in human-faced masks that are particularly amusing or grotesque, such as devils or clowns. Some do also appreciate masks of humans that are handsome, beautiful, or subtly whimsical in appearance, or they may later develop a taste for such masks.

Although all of these types can be found in our area of interest, certain ones predominate while others are rare. The Sierra de Puebla is one of only a few regions in Mexico where mask carvers as a group seem to focus on the creation of human-faced masks that are handsome or beautiful. We find this also in neighboring Tlaxcala, and, at a greater distance, in Chiapas and Michoacan. In part this preference undoubtedly reflects the fact that a number of the best mascareros were or are also santeros, carvers of saints. Apparently these carvers carry the aesthetic standard of the saints' faces over to their masks. Indeed it seems that many of the very best masks from the Sierra de Puebla depict an idealized human face. For those who appreciate such things, the masks of this area present an unusual experience or opportunity to see or collect such masks. It happens that my discussion of mask features and identification will focus on Santiaguero or Hormega masks, but we will see that the carver's interest in the beauty of the human face will even be expressed in such masks as these. We will see this emphasis again when we look at the puppets of this region.

There is yet another reason to develop an eye for the details of masks, because there has been, since the latter 20th century, an outpouring of invented or falsely aged masks in Mexico, politely referred to as "decoratives" (Lechuga 1988, 218–241). As this problem came into focus, it became apparent that, to a significant degree, the masks in many public and private Mexican collections were not what they were said to be (Jacobson and Fritz 1985, 11–15). The identification of genuinely good masks on the basis of positive features then becomes increasingly important.

In the Sierra de Puebla, I have not perceived a major outpouring of invented masks that were meant to appeal to collectors; I have seen masks that were innovative, but created or altered for use by traditional dancers. I have noticed that carvers in other areas of Mexico, particularly in the state of Guerrero, will sometimes imitate the masks of surrounding regions. For example, false copies of traditional Juanegro masks from northern Veracruz have become suddenly common. I haven't yet seen imitations of masks from the Sierra de Puebla, but such counterfeiting would not be unexpected.

The alteration of traditional masks to make them seem more desirable—false aging techniques—is another problem. Usually this involves two practices, abrasion or damage to the face of the mask and staining of the back. The decorative masks from Guerrero that were produced in the 1970s and later usually show the use of both these techniques. The backs of such masks were literally black with "age." More recently such false aging has used subtler staining that is less obvious and more difficult to identify as such.

Not all treatments of the backs of masks are meant to deceive. There are communities that make it a practice to treat the backs of masks with some coating such as paint or varnish in order to better protect the mask against the threat of boring insects. Such infestation can destroy a mask in just a few months. The well-known Catrine masks from Tlaxcala are almost invariably painted blue on the back for some reason. Parachico masks from Chiapa de Corzo Chiapas are frequently painted or varnished on the back. Curpite masks from Michoacan are often coated with some sort of varnish also. Other masks have received chemical treatment in order to eliminate such an infestation. A common solution has been to dip the entire mask in kerosene for a few days to kill the insects, then hang the mask to dry; the odor gradually dissipates over a period of years. Such masks have a glazed appearance on the back that never goes away; this glaze does imitate the patina of long and heavy use by a dancer. At least these masks may carry clues to their histories, the holes left by the boring insects on the face and back along with the faint odor of some petroleum product.

I suspect that there are individuals in the Sierra de Puebla who alter traditional masks with the hope of making them seem more appealing to collectors. In particular, I sometimes see masks that appear to have greater darkening on the face and back than I would have expected. I am left to wonder about such masks, but of course it is possible that their appearance resulted from having been very heavily danced and/or neglected. So I would offer the following advice: choose masks to collect that are appealing to you on the basis of design and condition, rather than primarily on the basis of the apparent age.

The rating system below should be of some assistance. By using it, a mask will emerge with a certain identified level of quality. When you are considering the purchase of a Mexican mask, focus on the mask as a whole, as a collection of elements that contribute to the determination of its quality. As I said earlier, the patina should not become the primary measure; if anything it should be one of the last reasons to choose a particular mask. It is likely to be more satisfying over time to collect masks that are intact and well carved versus masks that may seem ancient. But if a mask appeals to you because it has all of these elements, then go for it. I will show you many of those too.

A Rating System

Having given considerable thought to the question of just what contributes to quality and value in a mask, I have developed an arbitrary system that permits a mask to receive from one to six stars, based on five quality indicators. Such a system will sharpen one's ability to examine a mask in a comprehensive way. The age of the object will not enter into the rating, leaving one to bring this into play as an additional dimension as this seems appropriate. Likewise the rating system will not distinguish between carvers, although the best masks by the very best carvers will surely be more desirable than those by other carvers.

1. One star (*) is granted to any mask or object for which the likely carver can be identified as one of the listed carvers in this book, based on specific individual characteristics of style (range—one star or none).
2. One star (*) is given if the condition of the mask is good. Such a mask may have a stable crack, a split that has been repaired in a stable fashion (laced, wired, or glued) or a small broken area along part of the rim, but prominent broken areas or obviously unstable cracks would negate this star. Obvious structural damage from old infestation by boring insects or due to dry rot would be another reason to withhold this star. If a mask is in obviously poor condition, the rating ends with that conclusion (range—one star or none).
3. One star (*) is assigned for the apparent artistic merit of the mask or for the quality of the carving, if this is judged to be good. To begin with, such a mask should have been carefully carved. Then this should be a mask whose face is attractive, comical, or otherwise charismatic. For truly exceptional artistry one might grant 1½ stars. Here are examples of such masks: one that portrays the beauty of a saint; a particularly delightful mask of a clown; or a mask of a negative character that effectively projects evil, malice, or depravity in a delightful way. A mask of mediocre artistry, effective in a dance but with carving that was not carefully detailed, is denied a star (range—1½ stars, one star, or none).
4. One star or ½ star (*) can be assigned for excellent patina on the face of a mask or puppet, and up to one star for evidence of darkening or wear on the back. If the painted surface of the mask or other object has some degree of wear,

then this is worth ½ star; profound wear is worth one star. On the other hand, new or peeling paint receives no credit towards this category. On the back or on the hidden areas (for example, in the case of puppets) one might observe some darkening or what I call "sweat varnish" to grant ½ star, and for extreme darkening one awards a full star. Thus if the mask has fresh paint, and good patina on the back, it rates ½ star. If the finish on the face is obviously very old and beautifully worn, and the back likewise, up to two stars can be assigned (range—from two stars down to none).

5. One star (*) is assigned for a mask that is rare and 1½ stars for extreme rarity. Obviously this assessment is based on personal experience. Generally speaking, there are several categories of masks that are rare, such as fine examples by a long deceased master (1½ stars), examples by a recently deceased master carver (from one to 1½ stars), and unusually fine early examples by a living carver (from one to 1½ stars). Then there are isolated masks or puppet sets that stand out because Vernon Kostohryz and I have never seen another like it (1 ½ stars). Rarity is assessed only for an object that has at least 3½ stars from the other categories; it is meaningless to rate the rarity of examples of average quality (range—1½, 1, and 0 stars).

I will apply this rating system to most of the illustrated objects in the rest of book, listing the five data elements that would permit one to rate the mask, along with the rating. The goal of this system will be to distinguish the average good mask (two or three stars) from those that are less remarkable and from those that are more exceptional (four, five, and five plus stars). In the discussion that follows of a number of masks carved by Benito Juárez, a slightly expanded reporting of the rating system will be offered for each mask or object. I will rate the masks and puppets in chapters 6 and 7 by the same criteria but more concisely.

Assessment Based on the Elements of Design

I first learned to approach a mask as a collection of design elements from my friend Tom Kolaz, who had been studying Yoeme (Yaqui) and Yoreme (Mayo) Pascola masks for a number of years. Tom noticed that such features as the rim decoration, the carving of the back, the manner of attachment of the hair, and various other elements were often highly characteristic of a particular carver. If one profiled a mask in this way and compared the findings to those of other masks, it was likely the maker could be reliably identified. Tom himself was building on the work of James Griffith, who attempted to simultaneously analyze and classify a sample of Mayo Pascola masks back in the 1960s (Griffith 1967).

When I met Vernon Kostohryz, he explained that he had also been teaching himself to look at masks in this way. He was particularly impressed that the manner of carving the ears on a mask in this region was highly individualized, so much so that the ear design was often as good as a signature. It is a fact that there is a highly unusual emphasis on including ears on masks in this area, compared to most other parts of Mexico, where masks more commonly lack ears.

Over several years, Vernon and I entered into an intense dialogue about the various design elements that seemed useful to examine for the masks of this region. I'll list the most useful from our perspective:

1. The manner of carving of the hair. I should note that masks from this region often have a carefully carved hairline in relief, although a painted hairline is not uncommon as an alternative.
2. Whether there are carved wrinkles across the forehead.
3. Whether the arch over the eyes is carefully sculpted.
4. Whether the eyes are indicated by paint alone, by minimal incising, or by very careful three-dimensional carving.
5. The manner of carving slits or other shapes, in the area of the eyes, to permit the wearer to see. I will call these vision slits.
6. The shaping of the ears.
7. The nose can be carved in a very simple manner or more elaborately, and a carver may give his noses a characteristic shape or size.
8. The same can be said about the carving of the mouth. The shape of the mouth can be distinctive.
9. As one might have expected from the items above, the mustache on a male mask is frequently also carved in relief, and a particular carver will shape the mustache in a characteristic way.
10. One opportunity for a masterful carver to animate a mask is to sculpt the shape and planes of the face around the necessary elements—the eyes, nose, and mouth. For example, there may be a subtle groove carved vertically between the bottom of the nose and the upper lip, or there may be a soft rim around the mouth.
11. Some carvers characteristically carve a flat spot on the chin.
12. Occasionally one encounters a carver who makes it a point to introduce asymmetry in his masks.
13. The manner of painting a mask can be distinctive, although one must hasten to add that there seems to be a fairly generic approach to painted features for many carvers. Due to this, however, the artistic alternative designs really stand out.
14. The condition of the paint can tell something about age, although the tendency to frequently repaint masks in order to freshen their appearance will negate this analysis.
15. The back of a mask can also be highly characteristic for a particular carver. There is a regional generic design, where the back is smoothly carved in a soft curve. Some carvers create a more box-like contour, or they take special pains to hollow the back to grant space around the eyes, nose, or mouth, maybe with a shelf at the level of the chin. Many smooth the marks from the chisel, but some do this more and some less.
16. Of course the other aspect that one examines closely on the back is the pattern of staining or darkening of the wood, which is suggestive of age or the degree of use, although such judgments tend to be highly subjective.

All this is based on the observation that many of the carvers in this region do follow a consistent approach. Perhaps they always use the same model or a limited repertoire of models for their carving, and if they vary this the change process is often gradual and subtle. However, there are apparently some carvers who vary their approach more freely, perhaps in response to a customer's request, or because the carver is so inventive, thereby confounding our ability to identify a consistent profile.

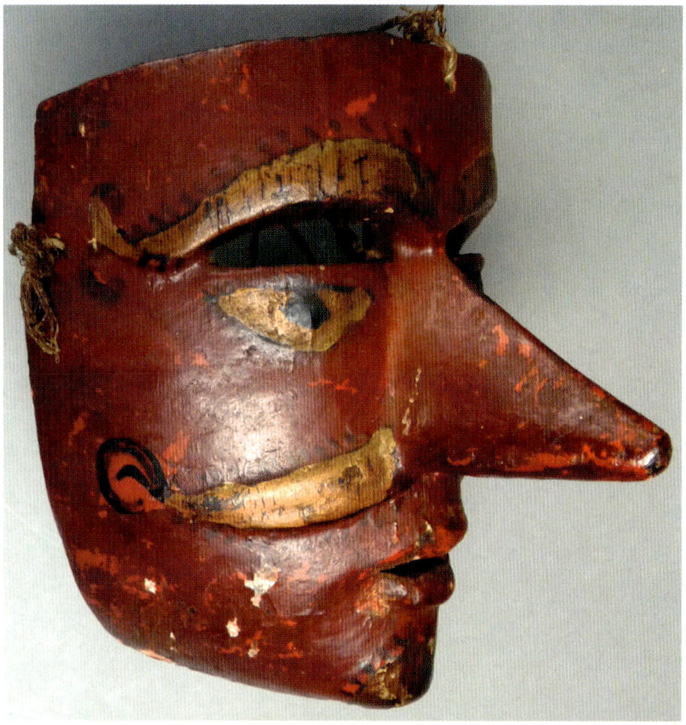

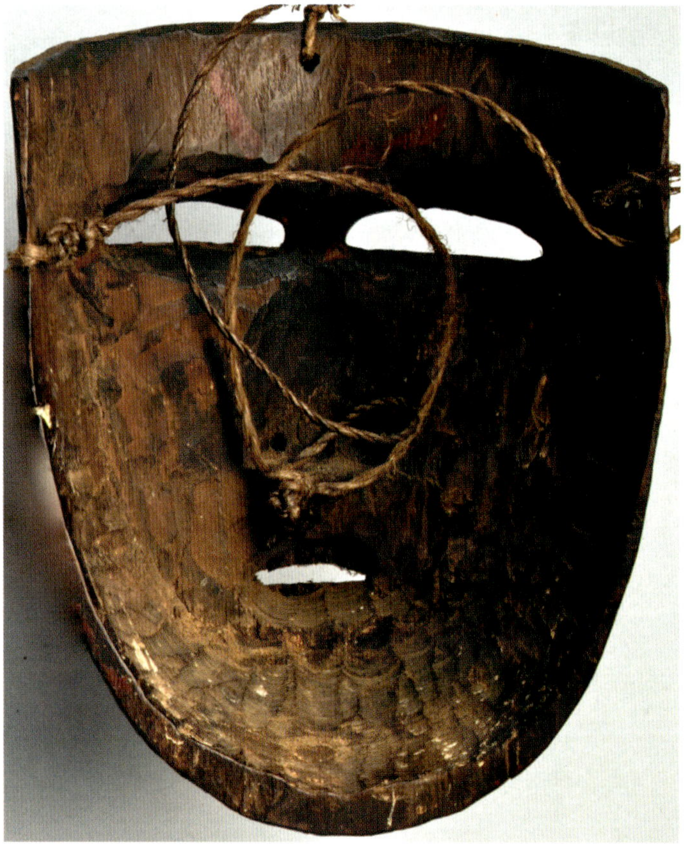

Top: Hormega Mask #1. This very old Hormega mask by Benito Juárez Figueroa has slightly flaking paint; the mask has been repainted maroon over a lighter red. The brows and mustache are carved in low relief. The eyes are also lightly carved; 5½" × 7". Mid-20th century or earlier. Rating: known carver (1*), excellent overall condition (1*), well carved (1*), unstable paint (½*) with extreme patina (1*), and rare (1*), *****½. *Collection of the author.*

Bottom: Hormega Mask #1. On the back, a space is hollowed with vertical chisel marks to accommodate the nose, the edges of the vision slits are beveled, and the mouth is pierced to aid breathing. All these details are consistent with the work of Benito Juárez.

Putting It All Together

By way of illustration, let us consider masks by one of the great master carvers of this region—Benito Juárez Figueroa. Here we will look at a series of four of his Hormega masks (these are essentially Santiaguero mask variants bearing an alternative local name) along with one Santiaguero mask proper, one Negrito mask, and then a bonus photo.

The first two masks that follow demonstrate marked or extreme patina on their backs, and the next three show moderate or above-average patina. This is what genuine patina looks like, staining of the wood along the sides and bottom of the back where the mask meets the face, versus less darkening on the back proper due to much less skin contact there. Even greater or more generalized staining is possible, depending on the quantity of sweat and whether the dancer does or does not wipe the back of the mask with a cloth after use. However, patina like that on these examples is what one would like to see, adequate and obviously genuine at the same time.

Now we are going to examine these masks according to the list of 16 elements described earlier. But before I begin, I'll remind you that Benito began carving by the time he was a young adult and he lived to the age of 84 at the time of his death in 1994. His style gradually changed over this long period of time, and this will be readily apparent from the mask observations to follow. The following points correspond to the examination steps listed previously.

- His Hormega masks have no indication of a hairline (although his Huehue masks, shown in Chapter 6 in the section about Benito, do have carefully carved hairlines).
- His Hormega masks never have any indication of wrinkles across the forehead, but we do see this feature on the Santiaguero mask.
- There is no arch over the eyes; rather, this area is flat in the vertical dimension (and again, the opposite is true for his Huehue masks).
- The management of the eyes evolved over time, it seems. The masks that appear to be older have more carving of the eyes; his later masks have eyes that are simply painted. This variability of the eyes is true across all his mask types.
- The vision slits are simply carved, and are always found above the eyes.
- His Hormega masks never have ears, but his Santiaguero and Huehue masks do.
- The nose on his Hormega masks is invariably quite long, tapered, and usually flat on the bottom surface. The more recent masks have a dramatic narrowing towards the tip. The end of the nose is usually flat.
- The lower lip has a very graceful shape that is more pronounced in the newer masks. Many of the older masks have a beautiful sweeping curve around the mouth, which is highly distinctive but difficult to describe in words. See particularly Hormega masks #2 and #3.
- The mustache is only painted on some older masks, in which case the brows and goatee are painted as well. On the more recent masks the mustache, brows, and goatee are all carved in relief and usually also grooved. So we see that the management of these features seems to clearly demarcate his older masks from those with a newer design.

- There is a finely carved groove vertically between the bottom of the nose and the upper lip in all but the earliest examples.
- The chin is normally shaped, and an oval goatee is invariably painted or carved. The carved goatee is grooved, like the mustache and brows.
- His masks are intended to be symmetrical.
- The swirling lines painted at the ends of the mustache are highly characteristic of this carver, not only on this type of mask but on other characters as well, such as his Negrito masks. I have the impression that this feature is found only on his earlier masks.
- On several of these masks the paint is demonstrably worn, but the more modern examples have been repainted in the course of their use.
- The design of the backs of these masks is somewhat variable; there is often a hollow for the nose. The chisel marks are partially smoothed, in most cases.
- Comparing the backs of this series of masks, one sees that the masks that appear to be the oldest, in terms of their design, are also the ones with the darkest staining of the back.

This exercise demonstrates that the masks of a particular carver will be recognizable in terms of certain rather characteristic features, while other aspects may be too generic to help with the identification process. For Benito Juárez Figueroa, we began by confronting the observation that his style has apparently evolved over the 70-plus years that he was actively carving, so we see early and later examples. The tapered slender nose on his Hormega masks is highly suggestive of his hand over time. His older masks are easily recognized due to the painting style, with those elaborate swirling decorations that he employed across several mask types. The more recent masks are difficult to miss, when one sees this characteristic relief carving and grooving of the brows, mustache, and chin, along with the sculptural management of the lower lip and the grooved space between the nose and the upper lip.

In Chapter 6, as we consider the work of other carvers, we will see that different combinations of features will seem more prominent, depending on the carver.

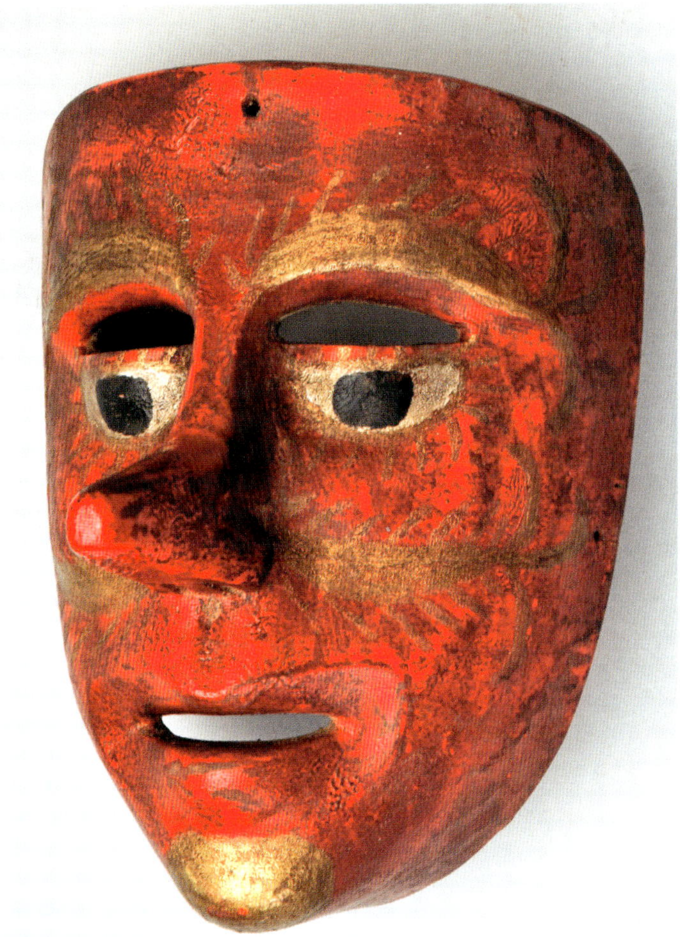

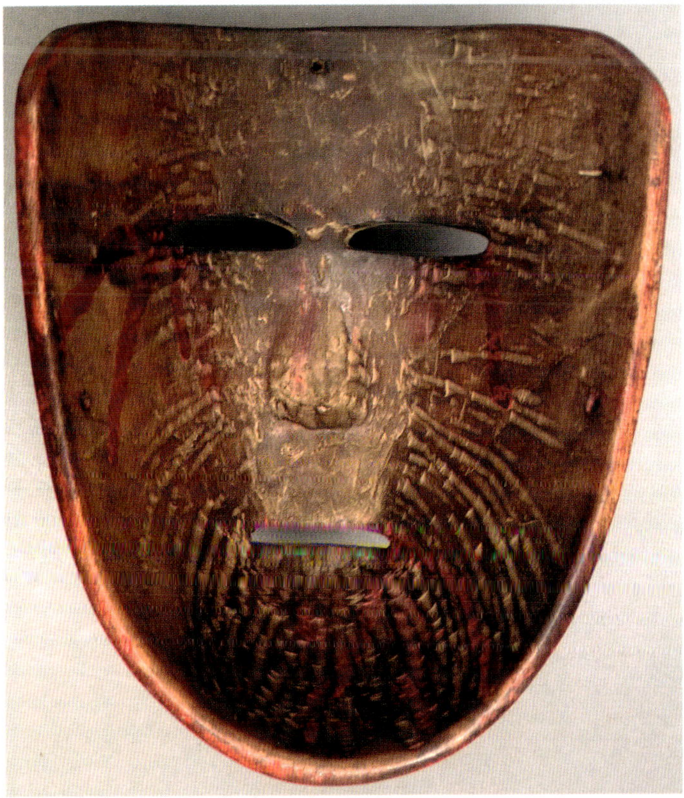

Top: Hormega Mask #2. On this mask by Benito, neither the brows nor the mustache are carved in relief, but the carving around the mouth is very beautifully done, and the ornamented painting style is also more prominent; 5¾" × 7". Mid-20th century. Rating: known carver (1*), excellent condition (1*), well carved (1*), excellent paint (1*) with excellent patina (1*), and rare (1*), ******. *Collection of the author.*

Bottom: Hormega Mask #2. The back is quite similar to that of the previous mask but smoother. Both this mask and the one before demonstrate extreme patina on the back.

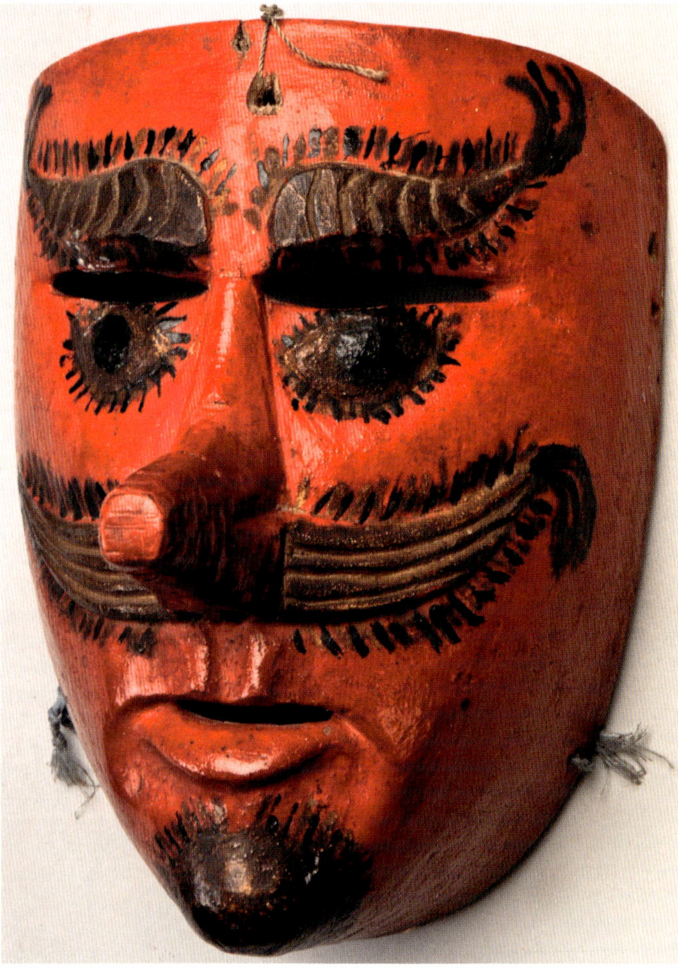

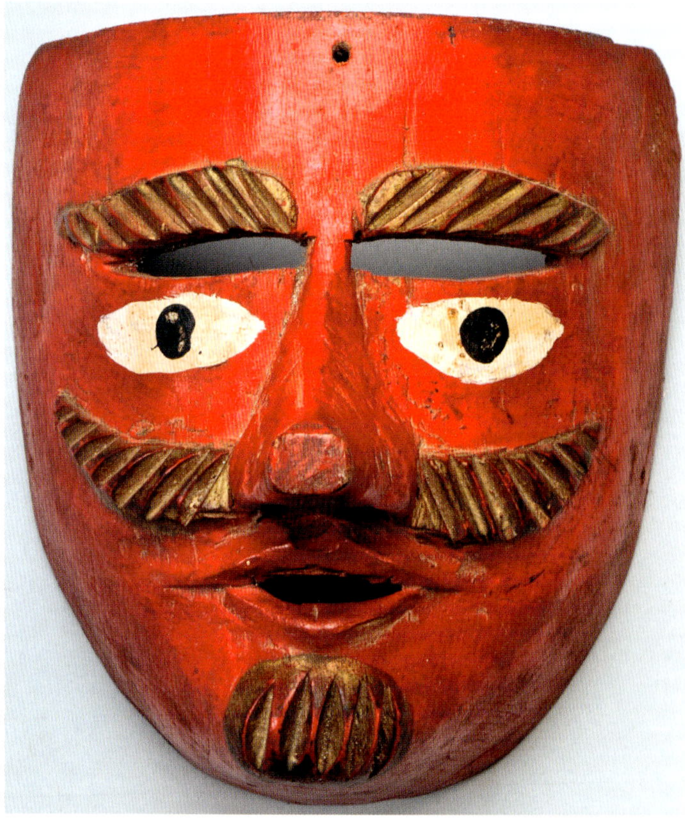

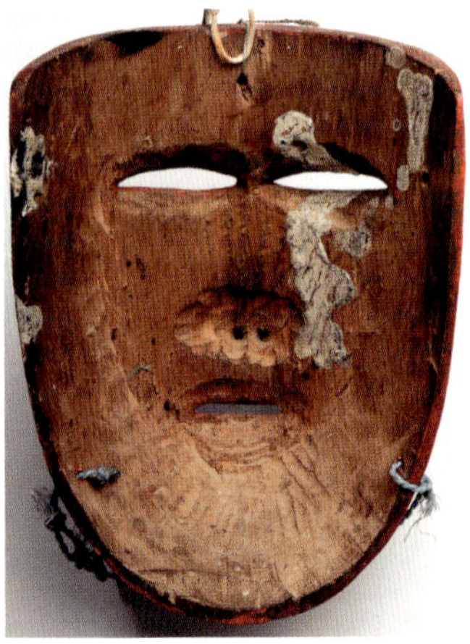

Above: Hormega Mask #3. This Hormega mask by Benito has the relief carving of the brows and mustache and these elements are grooved for an enhanced decorative effect. The eyes are distinctly carved, and the handling of the mouth is once again very nicely done; 5½" × 7½". Mid-20th century. Rating: known carver (1*), excellent condition (1*), very well carved (1½*), excellent paint (1*) with above-average patina (½*), and rare (1*), ******. *Collection of the author.*

Left: Hormega Mask #3. Looking at the back, we see that this is a more recent mask than the other two and done with a little less care. We begin to see how a carver's style can vary within a certain range of possibilities. This mask and the next both demonstrate moderate wear on the back.

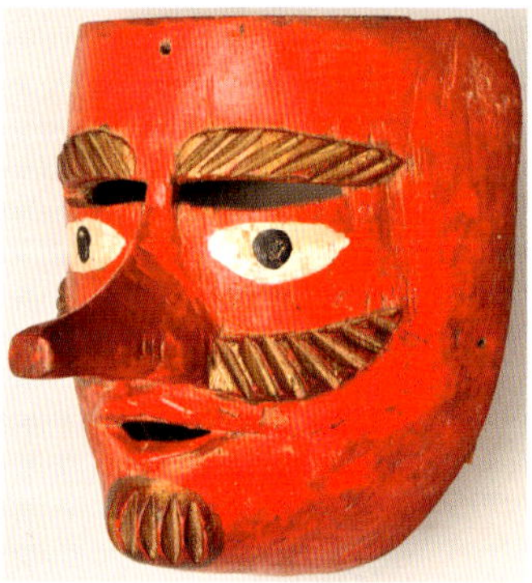

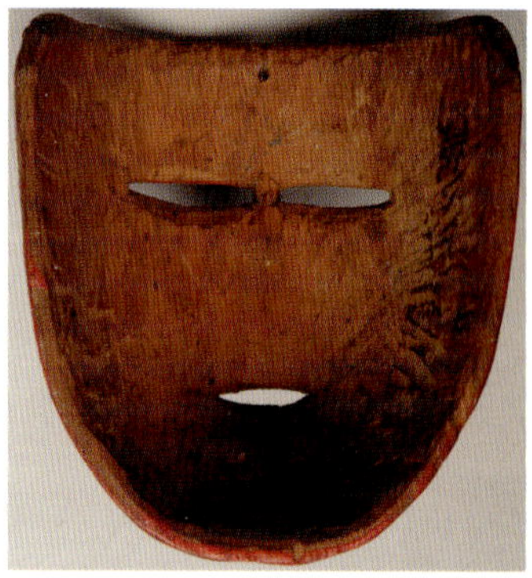

Top: Hormega Mask #4. Looking for masks in Ixtepec, Puebla, we were offered half a dozen of this design, ranging from broken to intact. The carver has really simplified his approach in this version, but the relief-carved and, then, grooved brows, mustache, and goatee give the mask flair; 6" × 6¾". Circa 1970. Rating: known carver (1*), excellent overall condition (1*), well carved (1*), excellent paint (1*) with moderate patina (½*), and rare (1*), *****½. *Collection of the author.*

Bottom left: Hormega Mask #4. From the side this mask is simple but effective in design.

Bottom right: Hormega Mask #4. The back is typical for this carver except that there is no hollow for the nose. I have seen this lack in other later masks by this carver.

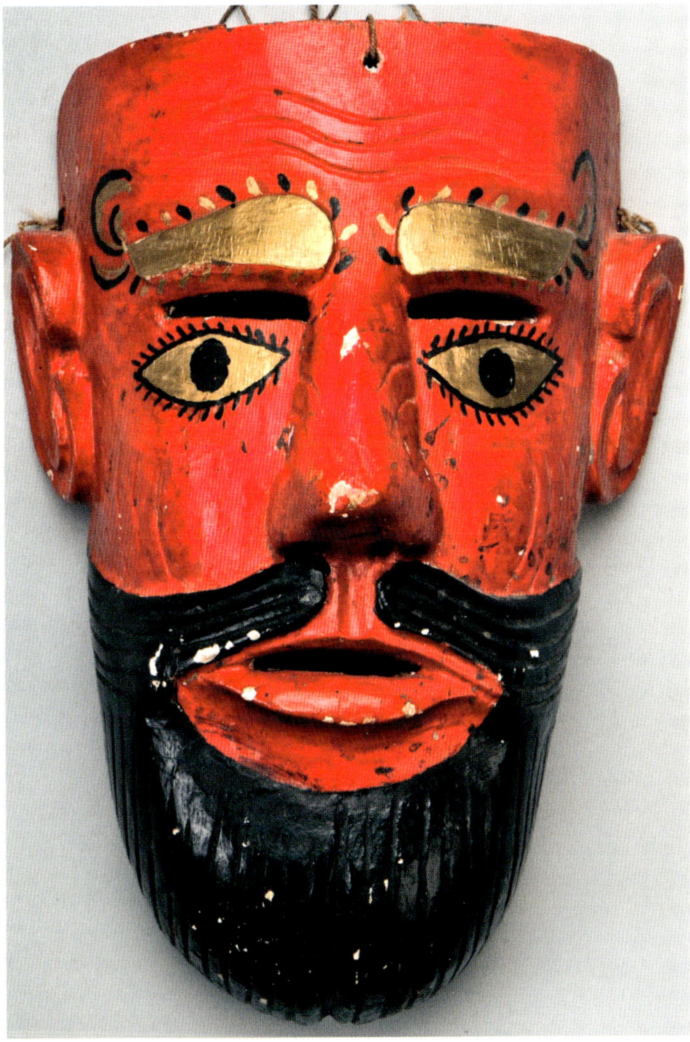

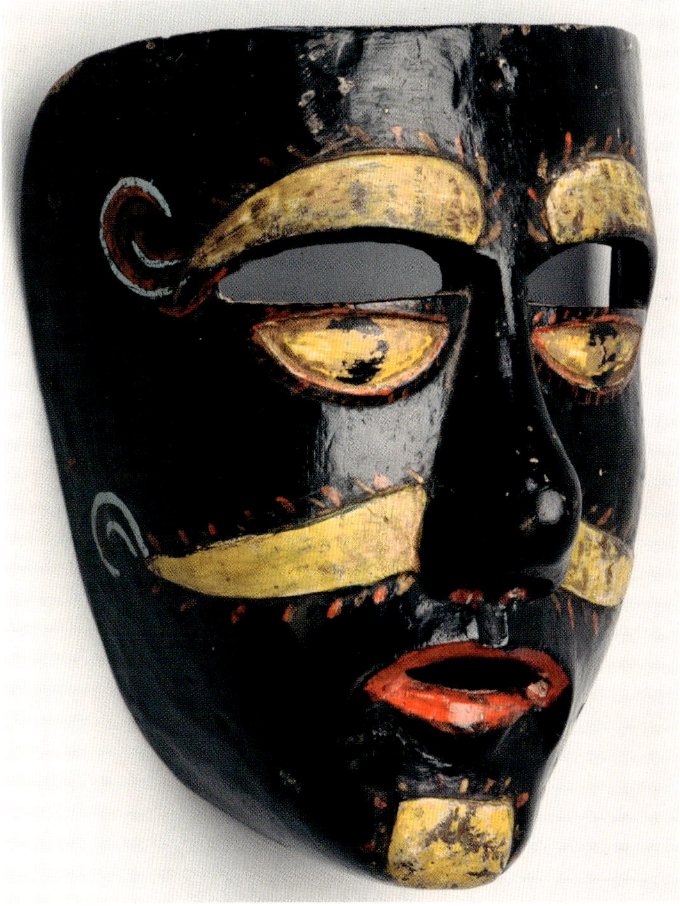

This elaborately carved Negrito mask by Benito Juárez Figueroa is discussed more fully in Chapter 6. This view is included to demonstrate features that span various mask characters. The brows, mustache, and goatee are all carved in low relief. The eyes are very finely carved, likewise the mouth. This is a masterpiece. Paradoxically, it is also lopsided or asymmetrical; 5½" × 6½". Mid-20th century or earlier. Rating: known carver (1*), excellent condition (1*), very well carved (1½*), excellent paint (1*) with marked patina (1*), and very rare (1½*), *******. *Collection of the author.*

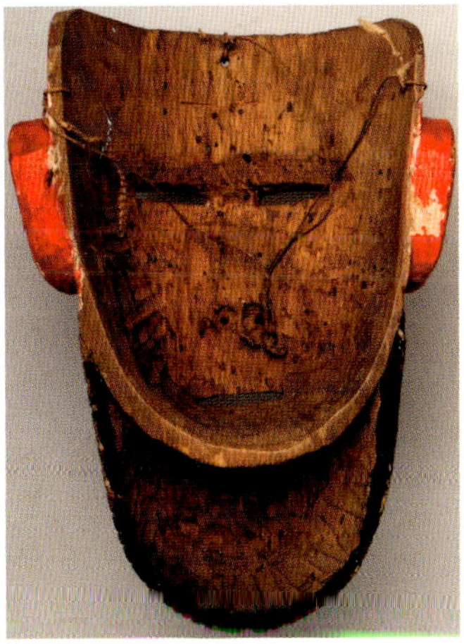

Above: Santiaguero Mask. When Benito Juárez Figueroa carved this Santiaguero mask, he included the ear design that he almost always used on Huehue or Tejonero masks, the design he inherited from his father and grandfather and refined. The eyebrows are carved in low relief and there are wavy lines across the forehead. This is a magnificent mask; 7" × 9½". Circa 1970. Rating: known carver (1*), excellent overall condition (1*), very well carved (1½*), excellent paint (1*) with moderate patina (½*), and rare (1½*), ******½. *Collection of the author.*

Left: Santiaguero Mask. The back is typical for this carver. More generally, the hollowing of the beard is a feature of this area by various carvers. The patina is moderate.

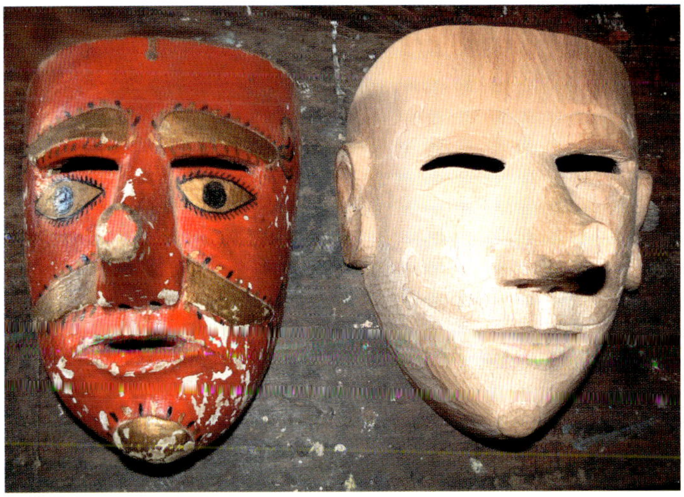

Roberto Villegas has been commissioned to make a set of eight Santiaguero masks. For a model, he is using an old Hormega mask that he owns, which was carved by his friend Benito Juárez. This mask is much like the first three in the series above, but not exactly the same as any of them; mid-20th century. He has elected to add his own typical ear design. He is substituting relief carving for the painted lines at the ends of the brows and mustache, and he is carving the eyes as he always does, even though the mask he is copying had only painted eyes. One master is copying another's design and then making it his own.

Chapter 6

Mascareros of the Sierra de Puebla

A Word about Names

In Mexico an individual has a given name (first name) followed by the father's surname (last name) and then frequently the mother's surname as well. So for example there is José González Galindo. We can refer to him by his full name or we can call him José González, the short form. We would not properly refer to him as José Galindo or simply Galindo. But among the carvers included in this book there are three who could be addressed as José González. These are José González Diaz; his father, José González Galindo; and the unrelated José González Hernández. Furthermore, there are a number of carvers who share the same father's surname, such as "Juárez." In any part of the book where the discussion is obviously about just one carver, he will be referred to initially by his full name and thereafter by either the short form or simply by his first name or nickname. Sometimes, in order to refer to a feature of a carver's work in an unambiguous way, his full name will need to used in the first occurrence, and subsequently his father's surname or his initials—e.g., "a de Aquino Type 2 ear" or "the JGG-style mouth design." Only when it is absolutely necessary to avoid confusion will a carver be repeatedly referred to by his full name. The carvers will be discussed in alphabetical order, arranged according to the father's surname. That is, Manuel Aldana Valencia will come before Manuel Antonio Castañeda.

Manuel Aldana Valencia (Don Lillo)

Manuel Aldana Valencia, better known in his community as "Don Lillo," was born on May 9, 1933, so he is currently in his late 70s. He lives in Coxquihui, Veracruz. He creates masks, puppets, and also various household items from wood.

He is a lovely gentleman, invariably friendly, generous, and easy to talk to. When we visited him, Vernon and Carlos would draw him out about various local dances, and Don Lillo seemed very knowledgeable. For example, they were talking about the task of finding good wood for the carving of masks, and somehow their conversation turned to discussion of the indigenous (in this case Totonac) perspective, whereupon Don Lillo related to Vernon the following belief in Spanish, which Vernon has translated for us: "When one wishes to enter the forest, it is considered necessary to ask permission of the trees, as they are the sentinels."

You may recall that Stresser-Péan described such ideas, saying that the Nahua and Totonac peoples of the Sierra de Puebla have always believed that everything has a soul or spirit, including the trees, the animals, and the mountains themselves.

Don Lillo is a prolific carver; whenever I visited his workshop there were a number of completed masks, ready for sale and use. The masks of this carver are clearly well liked and heavily used in the community, because they are nicely carved, comfortably finished, and rather inexpensive. Don Lillo seems to have decided, long ago, to produce good masks that were affordable, rather than striving for a level of perfectionism that would raise the cost. There is a disarming simplicity to his masks that makes it easy to overlook the fact that he carves them so well. Yet he is a talented carver, and sometimes this comes into sharper focus, for instance in several sets of puppets for the Tejoneros dance.

Occasionally one encounters masks of Don Lillo that seem mysterious and anomalous. Carlos found several masks in Zozocolco de Hidalgo, Veracruz, that all shared an unusual feature—the masks had been modified so that the jaws were able to open and close. According to Ernesto Bernabé Sánchez, he and his father had modified the masks of other carvers in this fashion. Indeed, there was a similar mask from the group that had the typical ear design of Antonio Bernabé Mora, but copied the classic Don Lillo rectangular dished ear. Apparently Antonio and Ernesto performed the jaw operation on a group of masks that were made by various carvers. As part of this effort, the masks were also fitted with mustaches and goatees made of horse tail or some such fur.

Puppet sets by Don Lillo are discussed in Chapter 7.

In summary, Don Lillo is one of a small number of living master carvers in this region.

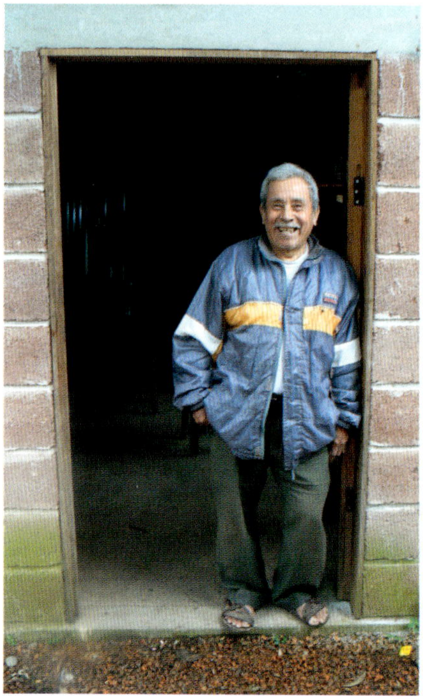

Manuel Aldana Valencia, whose nickname is "Don Lillo," standing in the doorway of his workshop in Coxquihui, Veracruz. This photo was taken in March 2010. He removed his new eyeglasses for this photo.

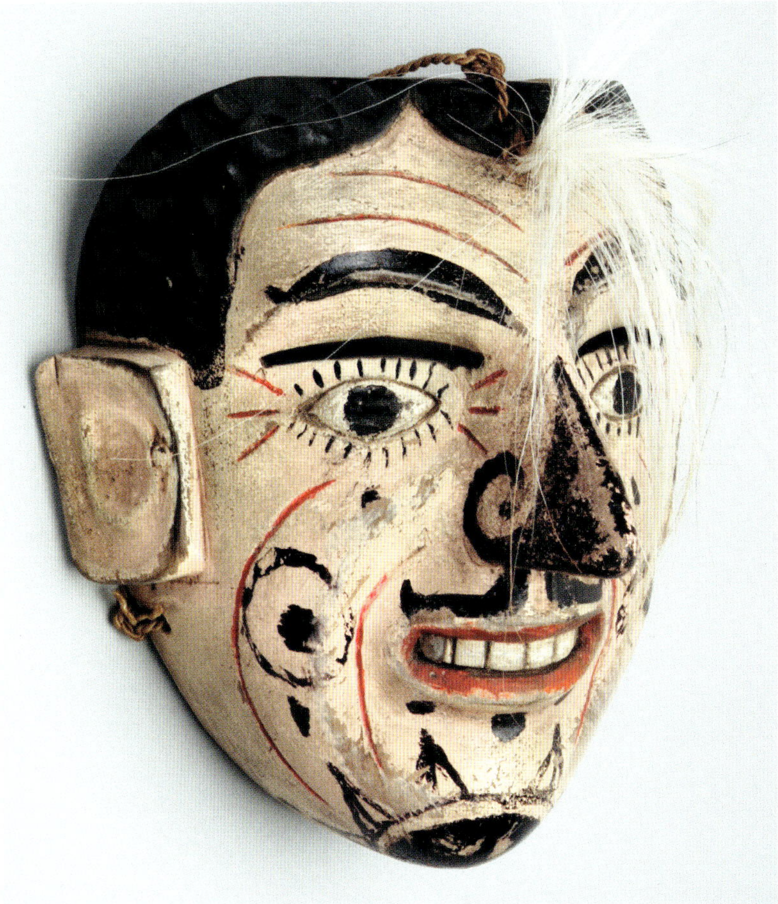

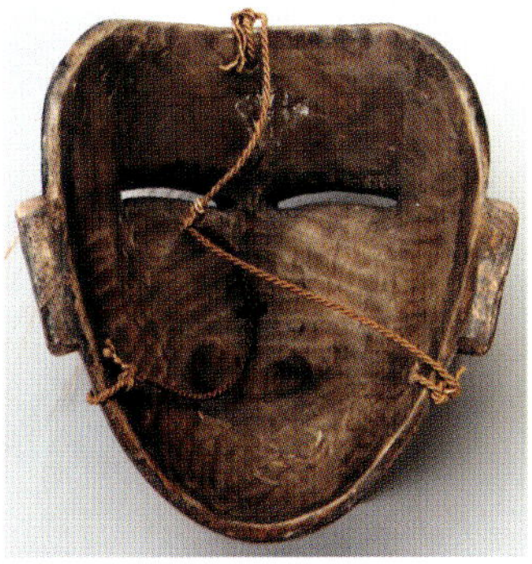

Left: A Payaso mask for the dance of the Tejoneros. This is Don Lillo's typical design for a clown mask; 7" × 7". Circa 1980. Note the simple, rectangular, dished ear and the sun-like decoration on the chin. These ears are attached by glue and a wooden peg. The area of the hair has been chiseled to create some texture. The eyes are nicely carved. The painted surface of this mask is quite old, on close inspection. Rating: known carver, good condition, very well carved, excellent patina, and rare, ******. *Collection of the author.*

Above: The back is very dark from age or use.

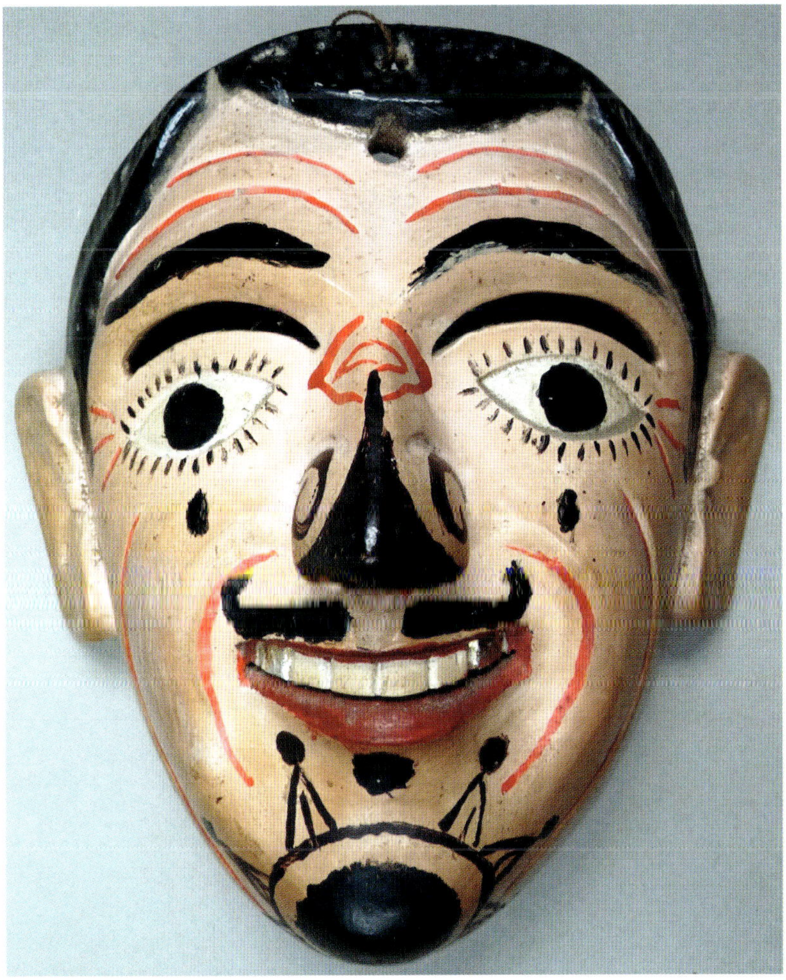

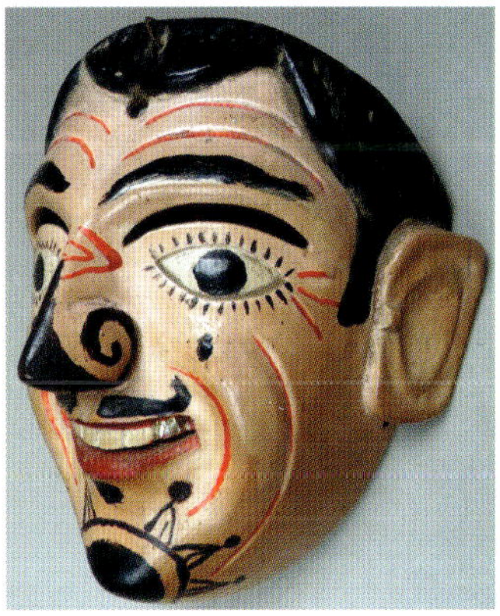

Left: This is another classic Payaso mask by Don Lillo; 7" × 7". Circa 1964. It is even more finely carved than the last, but it has newer paint and the patina is not quite so dark. It is quite elegant. Again the hair is grooved, but more carefully carved. Rating: known carver, excellent condition, very well carved, nice patina, and rare, ******. *Collection of Vernon Kostohryz.*

Above: From the side view, we see that the ear is more finely carved than Don Lillo's usual practice. There is no evidence of a peg. From this angle the mouth is very graceful. From the back (not shown), the blocks for the ears were glued onto the main block without pegs. The back is very thinly carved.

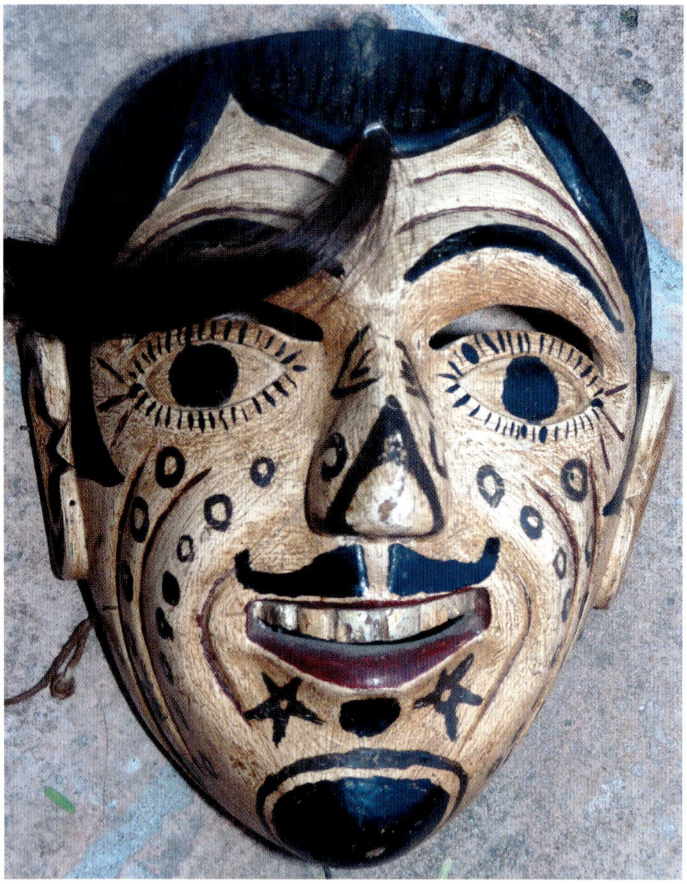

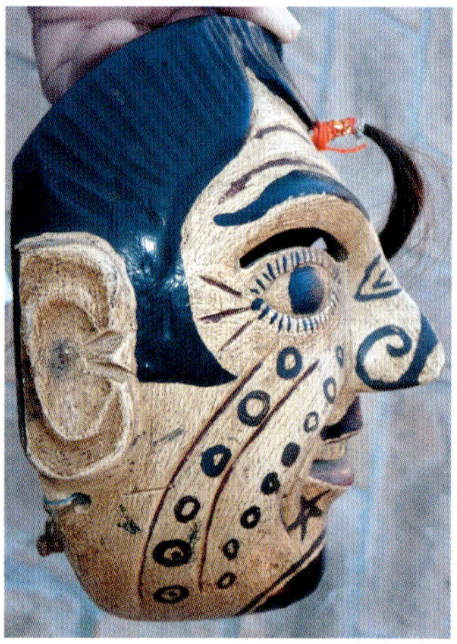

Far left: Here is a third example of a very nicely carved Payaso mask by Don Lillo; 7" × 7". Circa 1980. It is very similar to the last one; it even has the same grooved hair. The paint is older of course. Rating: known carver, excellent condition, well carved, good patina, and rare, ******. *Collection of Bill LeVasseur.*

Left: The side view, revealing again what appear to be particularly fine ears. The step at the back of the ear suggests that the blocks for the ears were also glued on the main block for this mask, again just as for the other two Payasos.

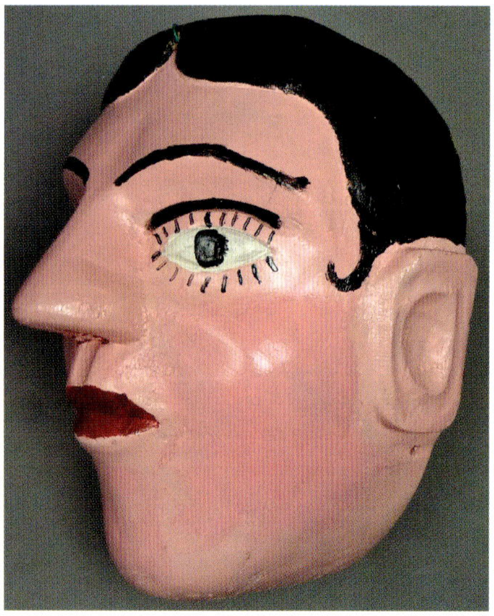

A new, undanced mask of a female Tejonero, purchased from Don Lillo in December 2007; 6" × 7½". Rating: known carver, good condition, well carved, undanced, and not rare, ***. *Collection of the author.*

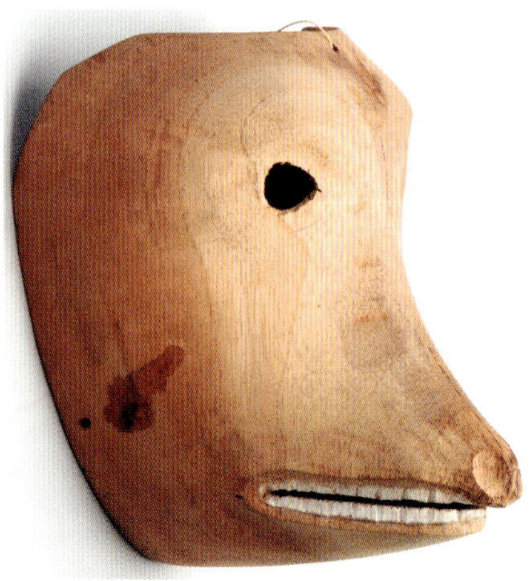

A Perro mask that was purchased from the carver in March 2010, prior to completion; 6½" × 7". It lacks paint and ears and of course it was never danced. Rating: known carver, good condition, very well carved, never finished, and not rare, **. *Collection of the author.*

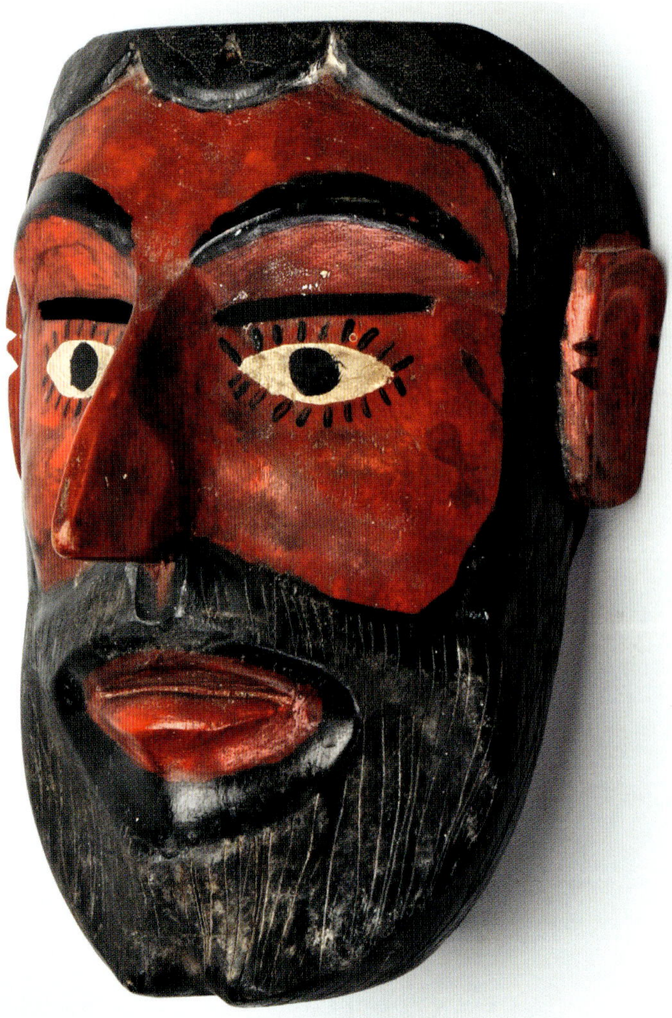

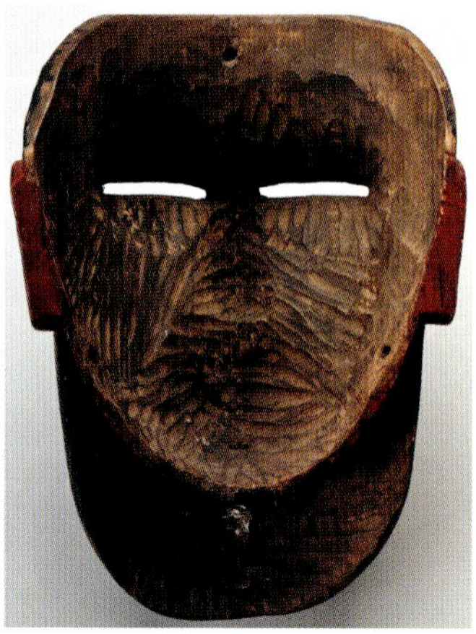

Above: A nicely carved Santiaguero mask by Don Lillo, which resembles a Viejo mask (Lakakgolo dance) that was seen in his shop, although this one is much older and more finely carved; 7" × 10". Circa 1980. Rating: known carver, good condition, very well carved, excellent patina, and rare, ******. *Collection of the author.*

Left: The back view reveals dark patina.

Manuel Antonio Castañeda

Manuel Antonio Castañeda was born on September 24, 1928; he was 81 years old at the time of this writing and had stopped carving masks at least 5 or maybe 10 years earlier. He lives on the outskirts of San Antonio Rayón, Puebla. Vernon Kostohryz, Carlos Moreno Vásquez, and I had separately or together attempted to meet Manuel on numerous occasions over a period of five years, but he was invariably away from home, working in his distant cornfield. To our great pleasure, we finally succeeded in finding him at home in March 2010. He informed us that he taught himself how to carve dance masks, and that he did not learn the craft from a relative.

We have identified a group of masks that were certainly carved by Manuel, as these were purchased directly from the family or from his neighbor. We have encountered a few additional masks in a somewhat different style that were being used within the community around San Antonio Rayón, apparently during Carnaval. We have no idea whether additional masks will emerge but we certainly hope so, because the examples known to us seem brilliant in their design and execution, marvelously sculptural and inventive, carefully carved, and often very nicely painted. His masks have an exaggerated, inflated quality, so I think of him as the Fernando Botero of Sierra mask makers.

I am puzzled that we have found so few masks by this carver. It is a fact that the community of Rayón was supplied for many years with masks by another great local master, Narciso Iturbide Charo (to follow), and it is unclear where Manuel's masks might have fit in. Manuel was equally talented in our view, but his style was somewhat different from that of Narciso.

In summary, I view Manuel Antonio Castañeda as one of a very small number of superlative living master carvers from this region. His masks demonstrate a fresh originality combined with excellent detailed carving technique.

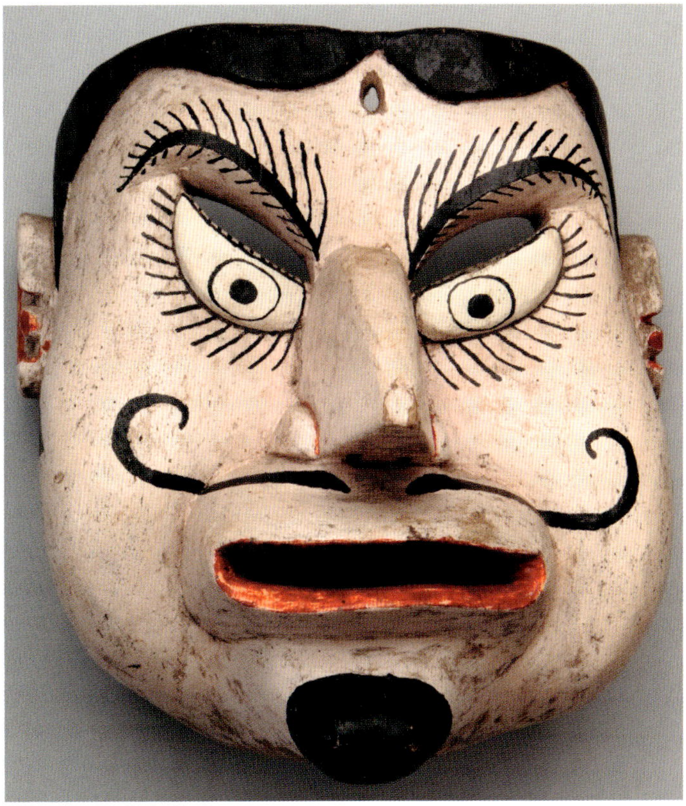

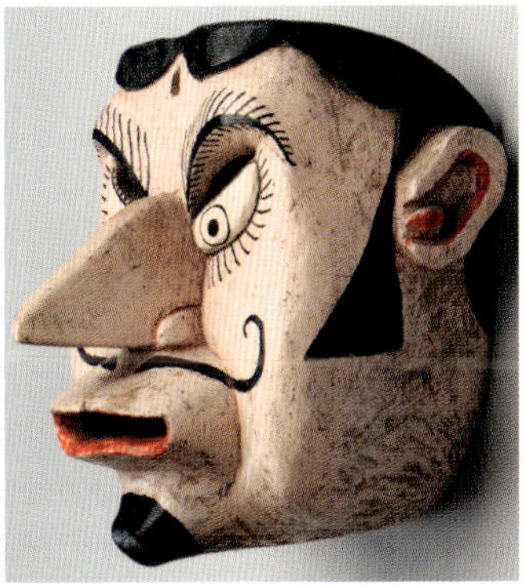

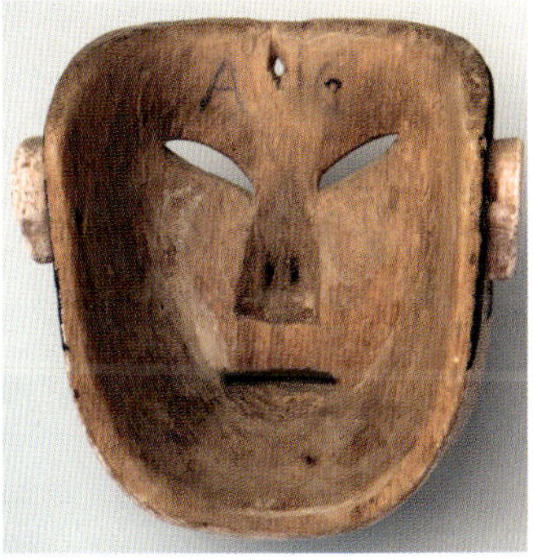

Top: This boldly carved Pilato mask exemplifies Manuel Antonio Castañeda's ability to project a novel vision onto a traditional form. The features are so exaggerated, the face so inflated, as if Manuel were the Fernando Botero of Mexican mask carvers; 8" × 8". Circa 1980. Rating: known carver, good condition, remarkable design, excellent paint with good patina on the back, and rare, ******. *Collection of the author.*

Bottom left: A side view of this mask, showing the typical ear design and a remarkable profile.

Bottom right: The back of this mask.

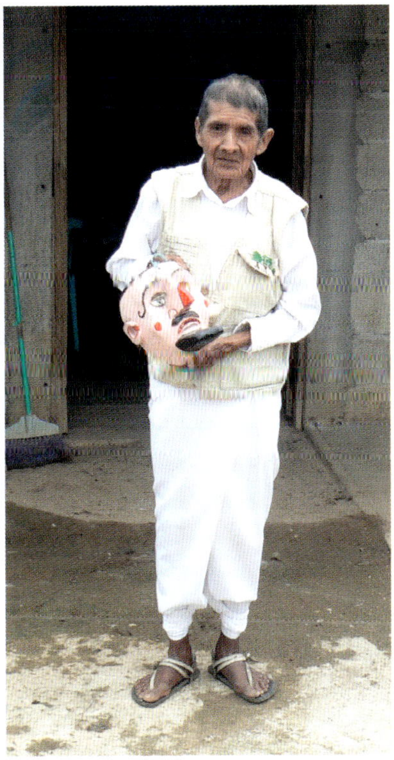

Manuel Antonio Castañeda standing in front of the doorway of his home in March 2010. He is holding an undanced Pilato mask that he had made about five or ten years earlier.

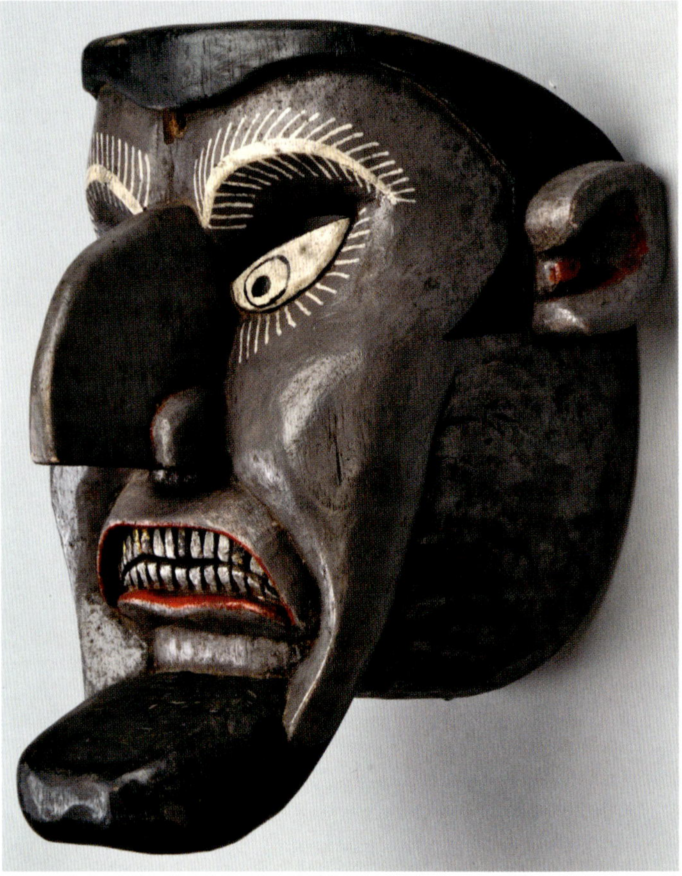

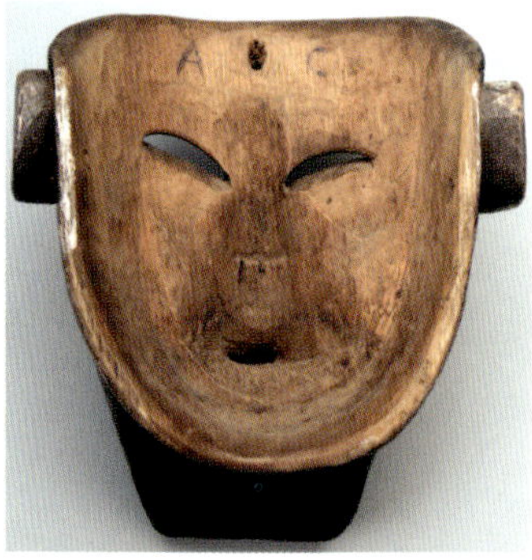

Far left: This appears to be a mask of El Pilato, demonstrating the version "of horrible appearance," as described by García García (2005, 116) for the danza de los Negritos; 8½" × 9". Circa 1980. This mask is unmistakably by the same hand and equally dramatic as the one that came before it. The front view was presented in Chapter 4 (page 66). Rating: known carver, good condition, remarkable design, excellent paint with good patina on the back, and rare, ******. *Collection of the author.*

Upper right: The back of this mask, obviously identical to that of the inflated Pilato mask shown previously.

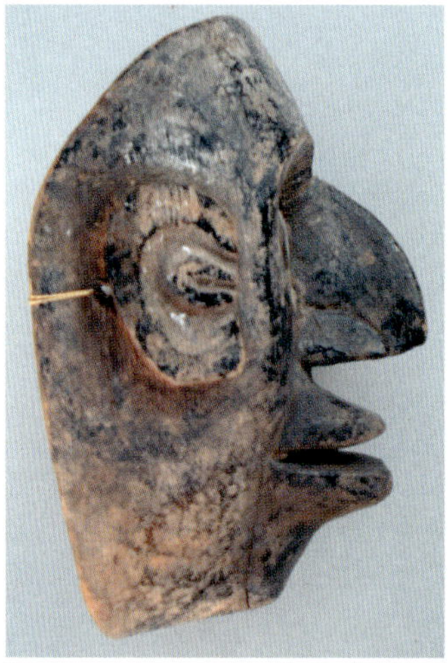

Left: This Negrito mask also demonstrates Manuel's tendency to inflate a traditional form for dramatic effect. Circa 1980. Rating: known carver, good condition, remarkable design, highly worn paint with good patina on the back, and rare, ******. *Collection of Joris Miller, who provided this photo.*

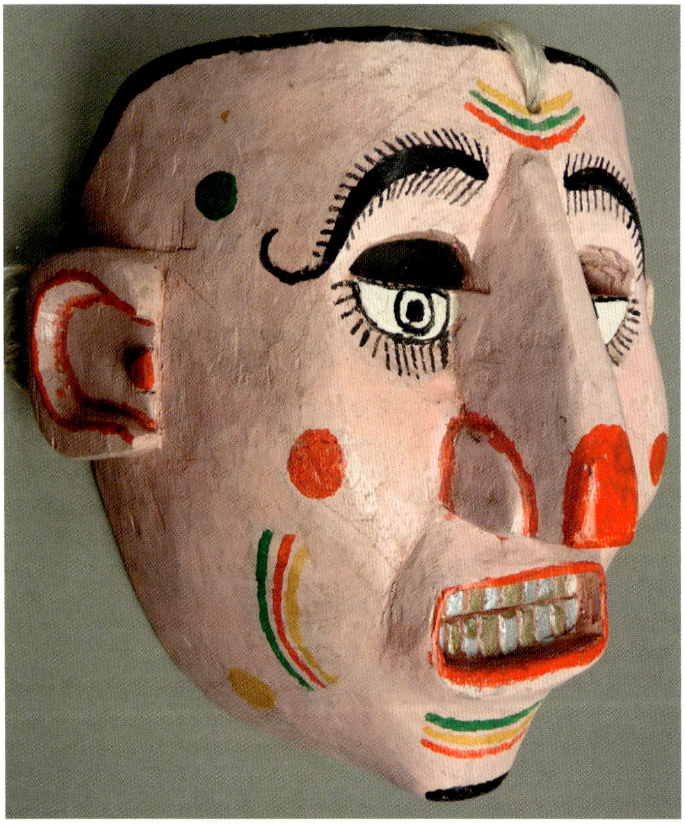

This undanced mask was one the last masks carved by Señor Castañeda; 8" × 9". Circa 2000. It may be a Pilato, but the rainbow decorations suggest that it is a Payaso. Rating: known carver, good condition, well carved, no patina (and uncommon or rare), ***. *Former collection of Vernon Kostohryz.*

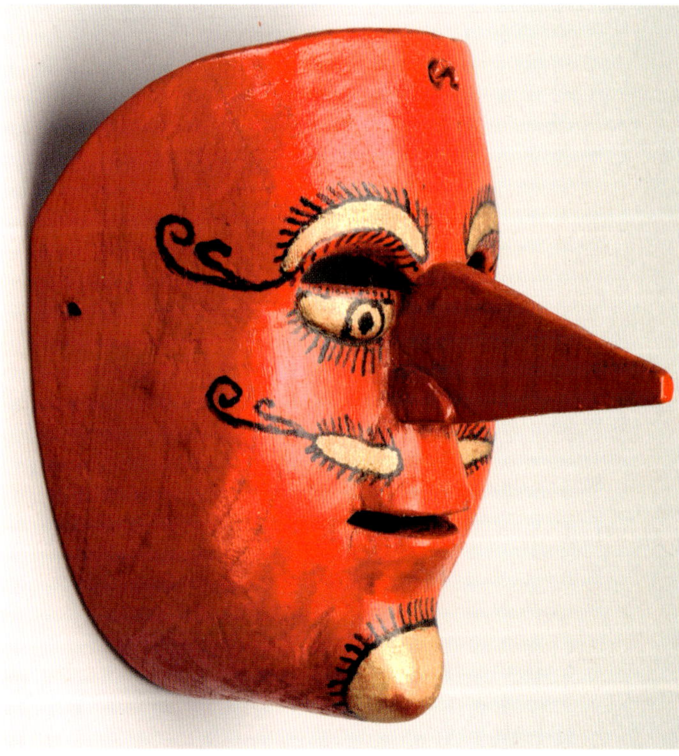

This undanced Santiaguero mask by Manuel may facilitate the identification of his danced masks. This mask simultaneously conforms to the local norm for the character and yet demonstrates many typical features for this carver, although in a more muted form; 6½" × 8". Perhaps this is because there would be a group of Santiaguero characters whose masks should be uniform, along with one or two leading Santiagueros such as General Sabario, who might wear more dramatic variants, as seen with the Sabario mask of Martin Nicholás Francisco that was carved by Narciso Iturbide Charo. Circa 2000. Rating: known carver, good condition, well carved, no patina (and rarity unknown), ***. *Collection of the author.*

Francisco de Aquino

Francisco de Aquino was born on June 20, 1928, and died on January 24, 2003, at the age of 74. He lived in Xochitlán de Vicente Suárez, Puebla. Francisco was an excellent carver, and it seems that his masks were widely used. His widow provided us with some old photos of his work, which demonstrate a variety of characters. I have seen his masks of Huehues, Perros, Payasos, and Santiagueros, while the photos also indicate that he carved saints.

Francisco's style seems to have varied over the course of his long career, but the faces of his human-faced masks were highly attractive and distinctive throughout, just as we might have expected from a santero.

Francisco was definitely one of those Sierra carvers whose masks demonstrate several stereotyped ear designs. The most striking of these ears, which I have called de Aquino Type 1, are extremely thick and complex, with characteristic furrows on the leading edge. Many other of Francisco's huehue masks of Caucasian human faces and clowns have a less dramatic but more or less formulaic ear design that I will call Type 2. These ears are not abnormally thick and the front edge may have a single valley, but the consistency in design is seen from the side, as with the ear designs of most other carvers. I include a single example of a mask with a very simple ear design, where the feature that points to de Aquino as the carver involves a highly stylized hairdo.

This leads me to discuss a generic problem that one encounters with some mask carvers, that of inconsistency. The masks of a particular carver may demonstrate visible variation, not in the design per se but in the detailed execution of this design. One mask will be very precisely carved while another will seem sloppy by comparison, as if this is a carver who has "good days and bad days." One is left to wonder whether the less well-carved masks are truly the work of the same carver. In the case of Francisco De Aquino, one encounters masks that appear to have crudely carved versions of the Type 2 ear, and I have gone back and forth in my thinking as to whether these masks should also be attributed to this carver.

Recently Carlos Moreno Vásquez discovered a dramatic Santiaguero mask that was attributed to de Aquino by the owner; this had double vision slits and was reportedly used by Voladores in Xochitlán, Puebla. A very attractive old Jaguar mask was also said to have been worn by a Volador; this one had more normal eyes.

In summary, then, I am suggesting that there are at least three versions of the De Aquino ear: the primitive, muted Type 2 ear on the very early mask with the distinctive hairstyle, and then there are Types 1 and 2 that are represented by numerous examples for each style. More generally I would note that Francisco's masks are very well carved, with precise, thin walls, so that they are strong yet rather light in weight.

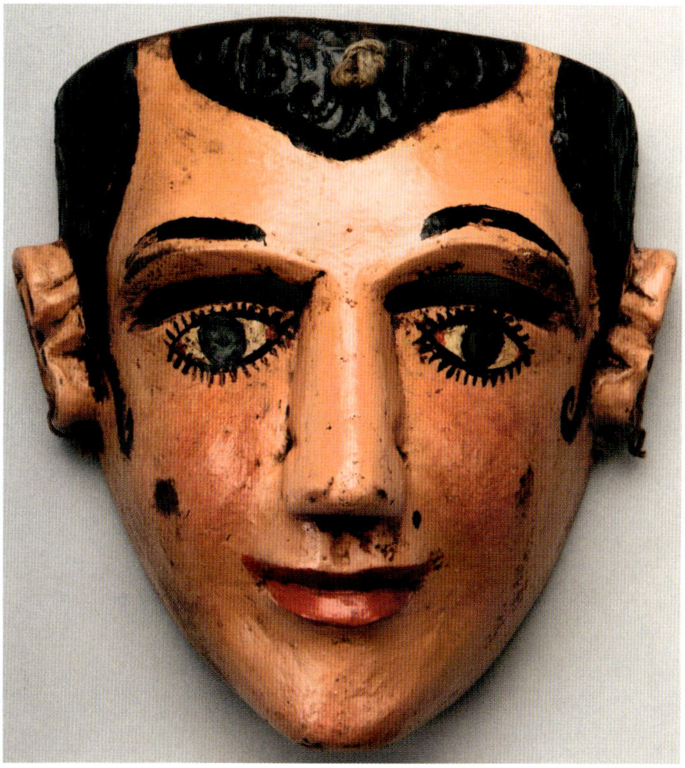

Above: This female Huehue mask with red painted back demonstrates a remarkably complex ear design seen on some of Francisco de Aquino's Huehue masks, which I call the de Aquino Type 1 ear; 6½" × 7". These ears are relief-carved, they are twice the thickness of the ears of most other carvers, and there is an emphasis on the skin folds along the leading edge of the ear. These ears are so unlike those of any other carver that they are certainly the equivalent of a signature, when present. Circa 1970. Rating: known carver, good condition, excellent design, good paint and patina on the back, and rare in this condition, ******. *Collection of the author.*

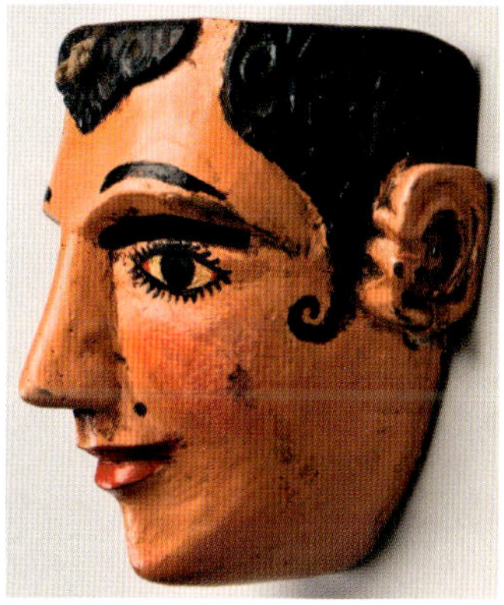

Right. Side view of this mask to better show the De Aquino Type 1 ear design.

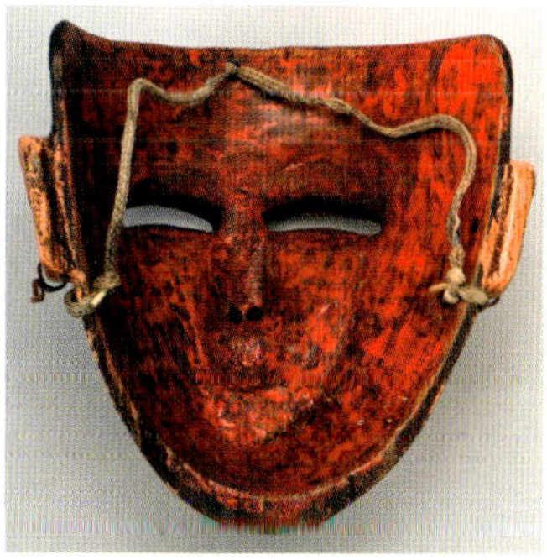

Bottom right: The back of this mask is painted red.

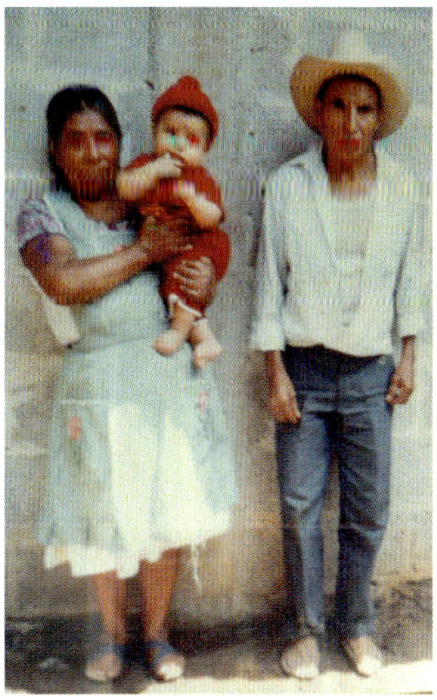

Francisco de Aquino and his wife. A copy of an old family photo. *Photo courtesy of the wife of Francisco de Aquino.*

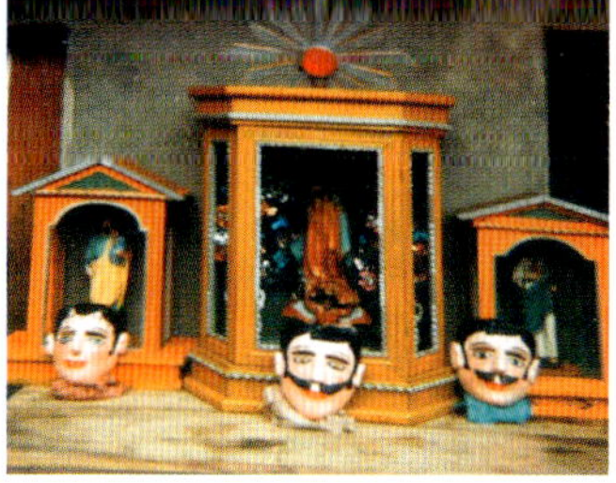

This photo provided by the family demonstrates two interesting points. We see that Francisco was a carver of saints. In the foreground there are three Huehue masks that demonstrate a trait that seems really striking, the sharp shaping of the hair over the forehead. The family no longer owns these masks, but we were able to find an apparent example elsewhere, which is attributed to this carver on the basis of the carving style. *Photo courtesy of the de Aquino family.*

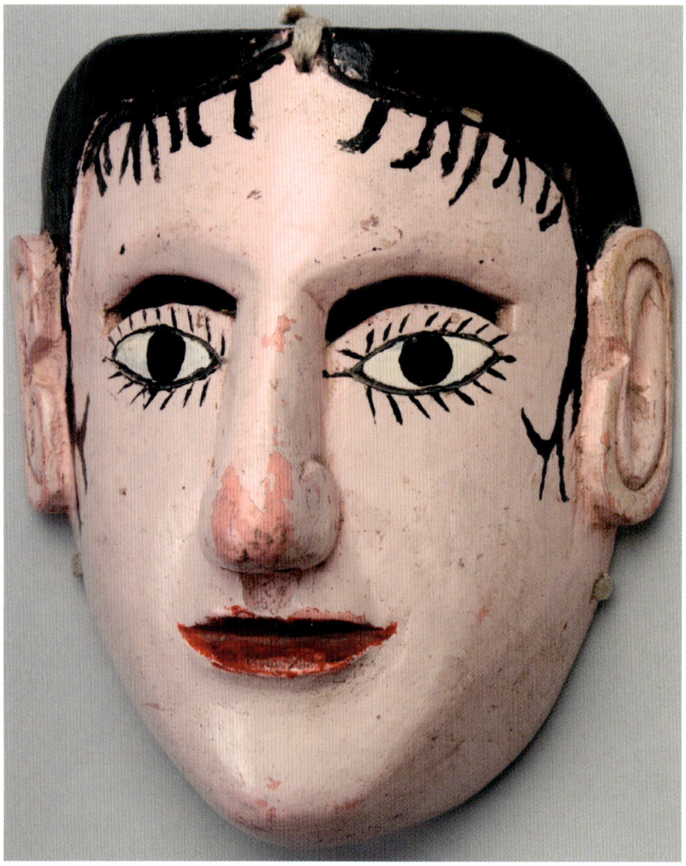

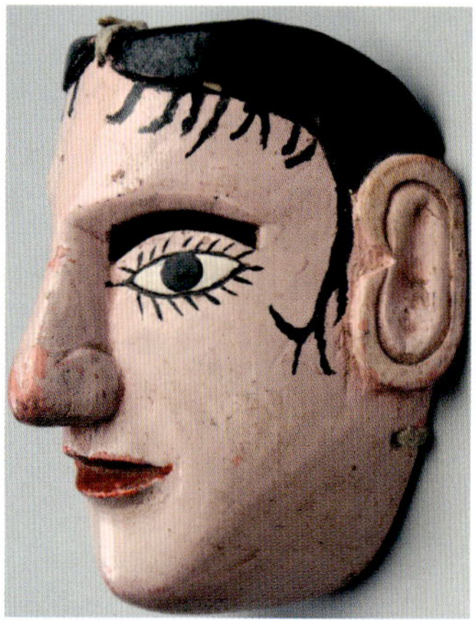

Left: This female Huehue mask was carved long ago by Francisco de Aquino; 6¼" × 6¾". Circa 1980. She has a pretty face in spite of the flaking paint on her nose. Notice that the midline part in her hair extends all the way to the top edge of the mask; this is often a marker for this carver's masks. The mask has Type 2 ears. The black strands of hair framing the face tell us that the mask has been repainted by Ernesto Bernabé Mora; it is not uncommon to see his hand on the older masks of other carvers. Rating: known carver, good condition, excellent design, moderate paint but with excellent patina on the back, and rare, *****½. *Collection of the author.*

Upper right: The side view demonstrates the Type 2 ear design.

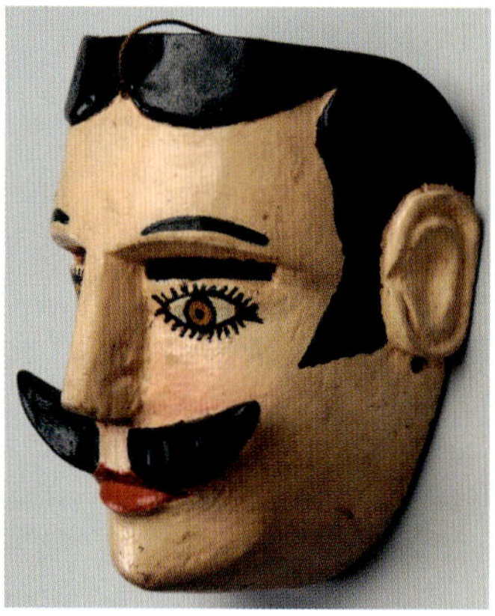

This is a typical male Huehue mask by Francisco de Aquino, with a prominent relief-carved mustache; 7" × 8". Circa 1980. Note the Type 2 ear design. The characteristic feature of this style is the C-shaped groove that lies just inside the outer wall of the ear and which narrows at each tip of the groove. Rating: known carver, good condition, excellent design, good paint and patina on the back, and rare in this condition, *****. *Collection of the author.*

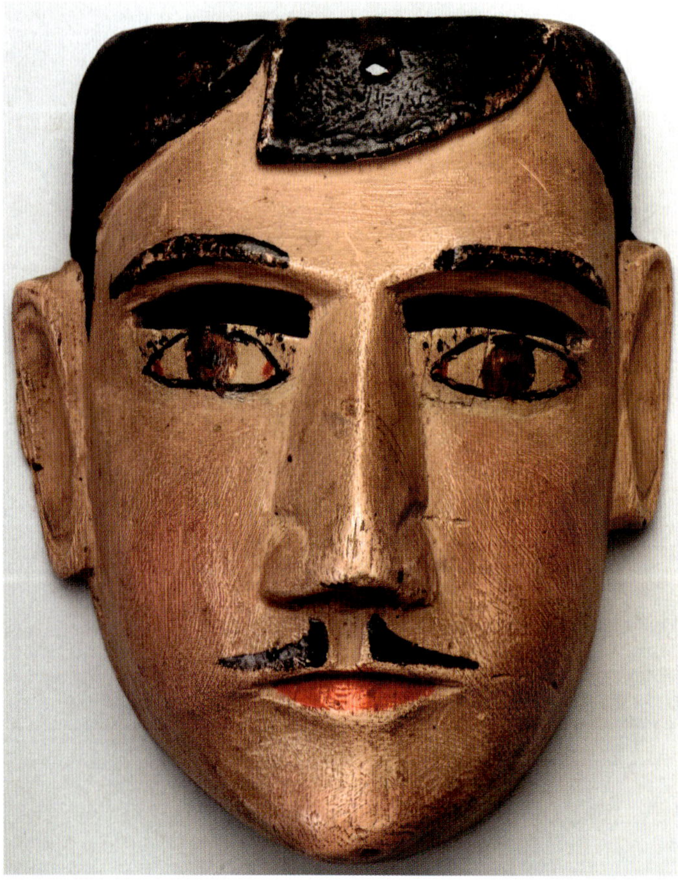

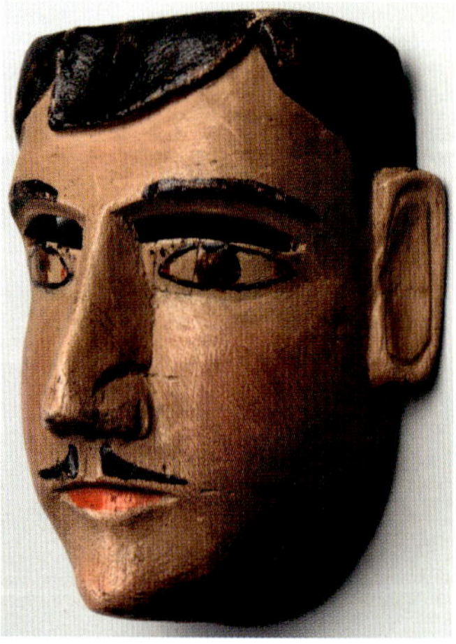

Left: This child's Huehue mask clearly resembles those with sharply defined hairlines in the old family photo; 5¾" × 6¾". Circa 1950. It is a bit of a stretch to describe the ears on this mask as fitting into the Type 2 category; maybe they demonstrate the transition between Types 1 and 2? It has a thin C-shaped groove in the right place (Type 2) along with two rudimentary valleys along the front edge (suggestive of Type 1). At any rate there are no features that are markedly discordant with the usual de Aquino ear designs. Rating: known carver, good condition, striking design, good paint and patina on the back, and very rare, ******+. *Collection of the author.*

Above: In the side view of this mask, there is a feature that is very characteristic of de Aquino's masks, the curving shadow that one sees on the side of the chin. It seems that de Aquino always carved the chin with this contour.

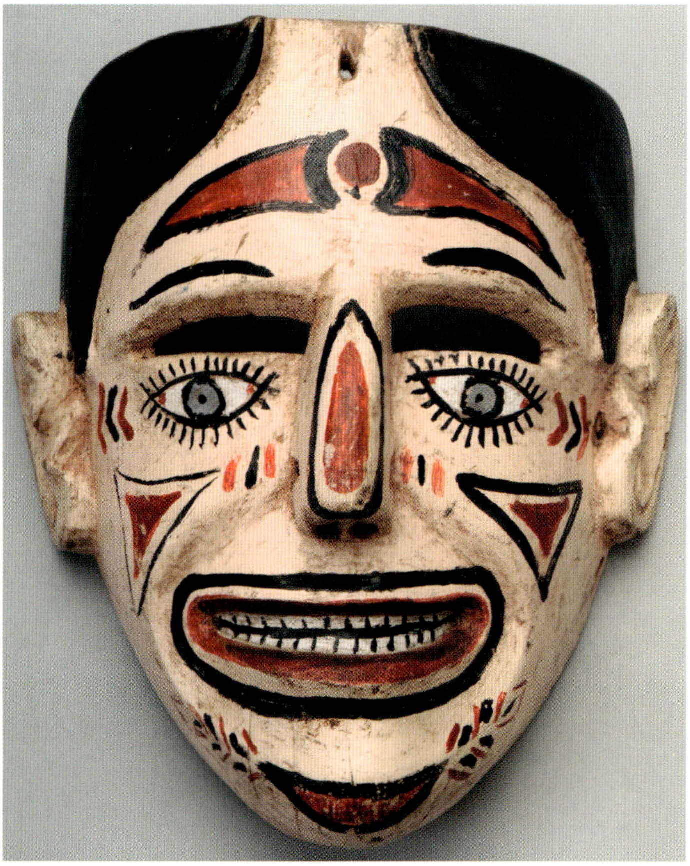

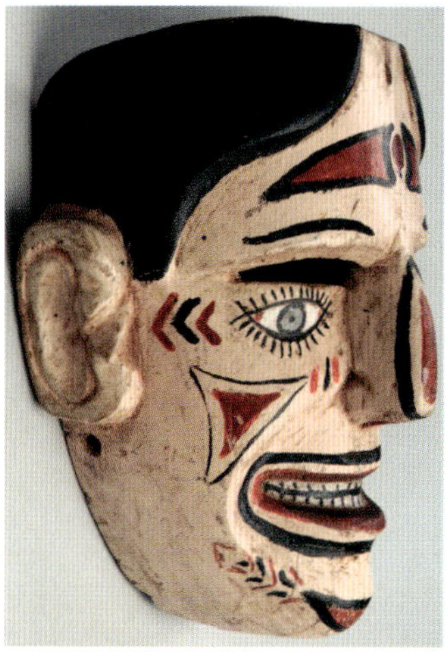

Far left: This is a very typical Payaso mask by de Aquino, a design that his family members have recognized as his and which has a very typical Type 1 ear; 7¼" × 7½". Circa 1980. Rating: known carver, good condition, excellent design, good paint and patina on the back, and rare, ******. *Collection of the author.*

Left: The side view of this mask, demonstrating the Type 1 ear design.

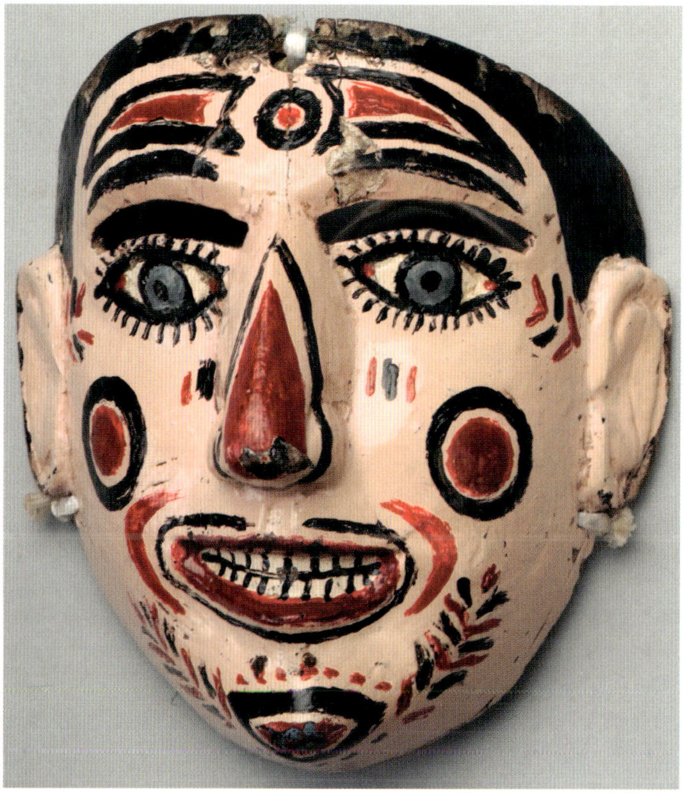

On this child's Payaso mask, the paint and carving style match the adult Payaso, but the ear is of the Type 2 design; 6" × 6". Rating: known carver, good condition, good design, good paint with extreme patina on the back, and extremely rare in the child version, ******+. *Collection of the author.*

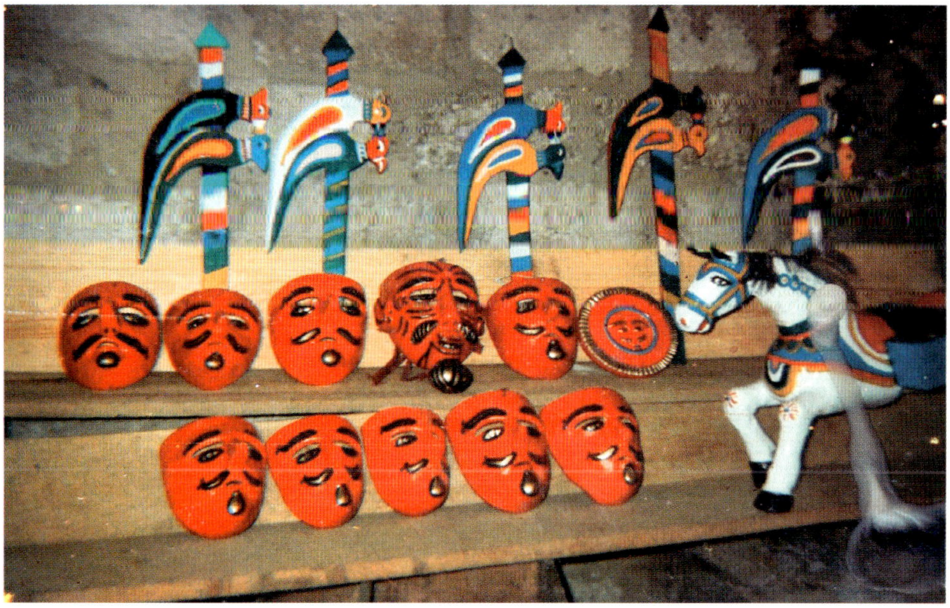

An extremely interesting old family photo that shows a set of Santiaguero masks carved by Francisco de Aquino. The mask with relief-carved mustache and goatee was apparently meant to be worn by General Sabario. Sabario's sun shield, a hoop-style dance horse for Santiago Apóstol, and ceremonial lances are also in the picture. *Photo courtesy of the family of Francisco de Aquino.*

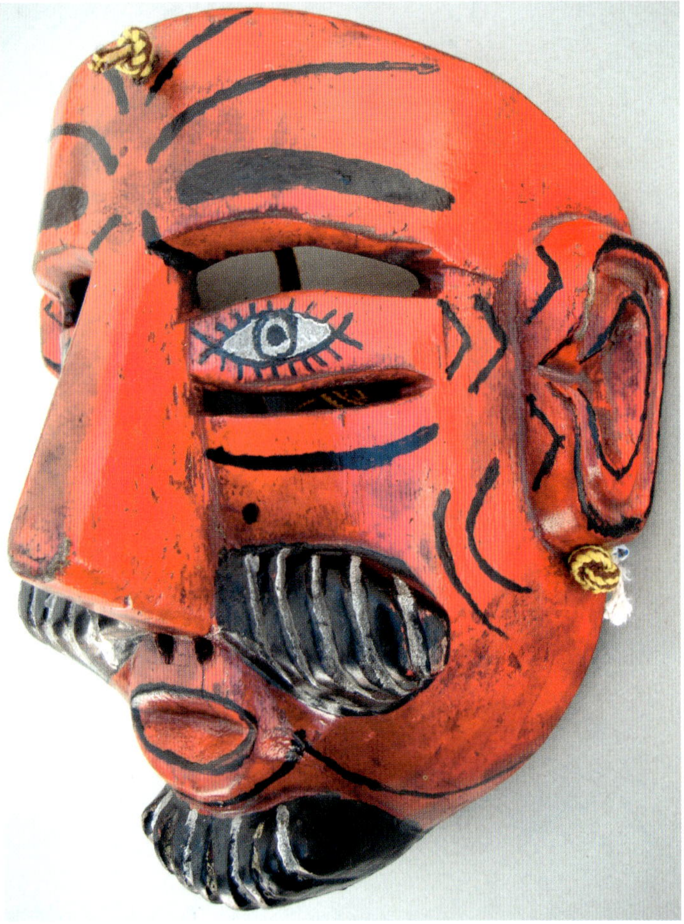

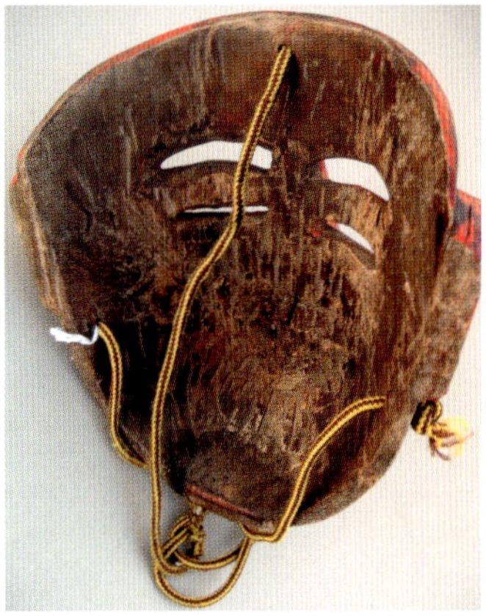

Left: This mask has vision slits above and below the painted eyes. The mask has Type 2 ears, but they are marked as if to be carved in the Type 1 style. Circa 1980. There is no doubt that de Aquino was the carver. The mask was reportedly worn by a Volador. Rating: known carver, good condition, excellent design, good patina on both front and back, and rare, ******. *Collection of Vernon Kostohryz, who supplied the photos of this mask.*

Above: The back of this mask is heavily worn.

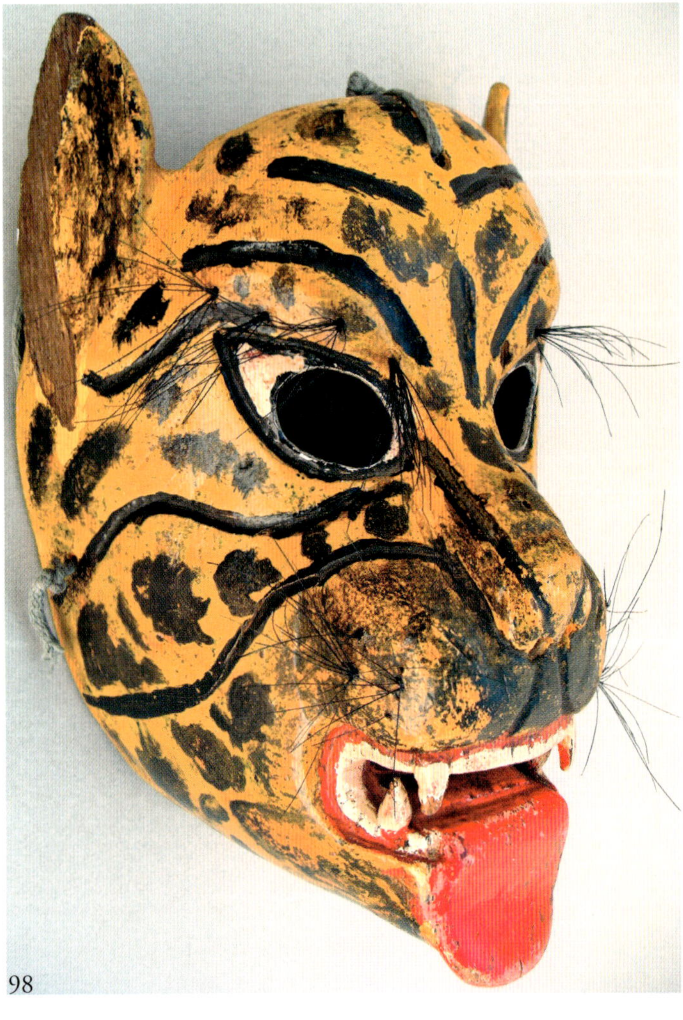

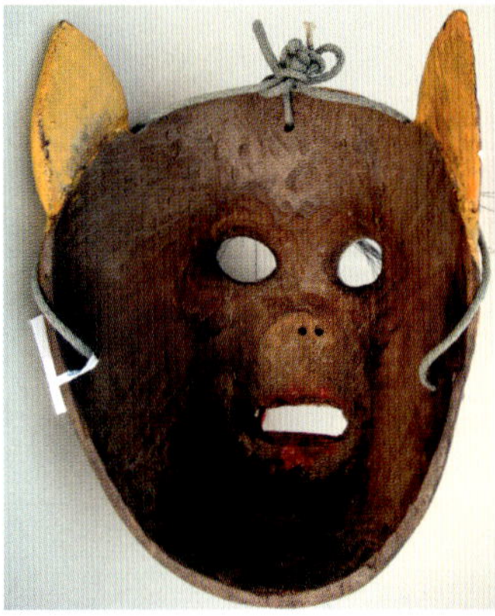

Left: This jaguar is obviously a striking mask. It was reportedly worn by a Volador. Rating: known carver, good condition, excellent design, good patina on both front and back, and rare, ******. *Former collection of Vernon Kostohryz, who supplied the photos of this mask.*

Above: The back of this mask is heavily worn.

Antonio Bernabé Mora and Ernesto Bernabé Sánchez

Antonio Bernabé Mora was born on June 13, 1905, and died on January 26, 1980. He lived in Zozocolco de Hidalgo, Veracruz. He was an excellent carver, and we have found a number of danced masks that we can identify as his from his distinctive ear design. All of these have been masks for the Tejoneros dance—male and female Tejoneros along with Payasos. Among these Payaso masks we have seen one that was clearly a copy of a very well known mask from this community that was widely admired although no one seemed to remember the name of the original carver. Recently we identified the original as the work of Mateo Luna Vásquez, better known as Luis de Luna.

Ernesto Bernabé Sánchez, the son of Antonio Bernabé Mora, was born on December 7, 1961; he continues to live in the house where his parents had lived in Zozocolco de Hidalgo, Veracruz. Ernesto is also an excellent carver of Tejonero masks. I do not believe that he has developed his own style; generally he seems to copy older masks of other carvers, such as those of his father and of Luis de Luna. He has a second career; he sings and plays in a band that he describes on his business card as the "Trio Huasteco-Los Caimanes." When I visited Ernesto in December 2010, he gave me a CD of his band, and I am pleased to report that they play and sing very well. For those who don't know, Huasteca music is very lively and engaging; an important feature is that the lead singer will often use a falsetto voice to exciting effect. A well-known example of Huasteca music is "La Bamba."

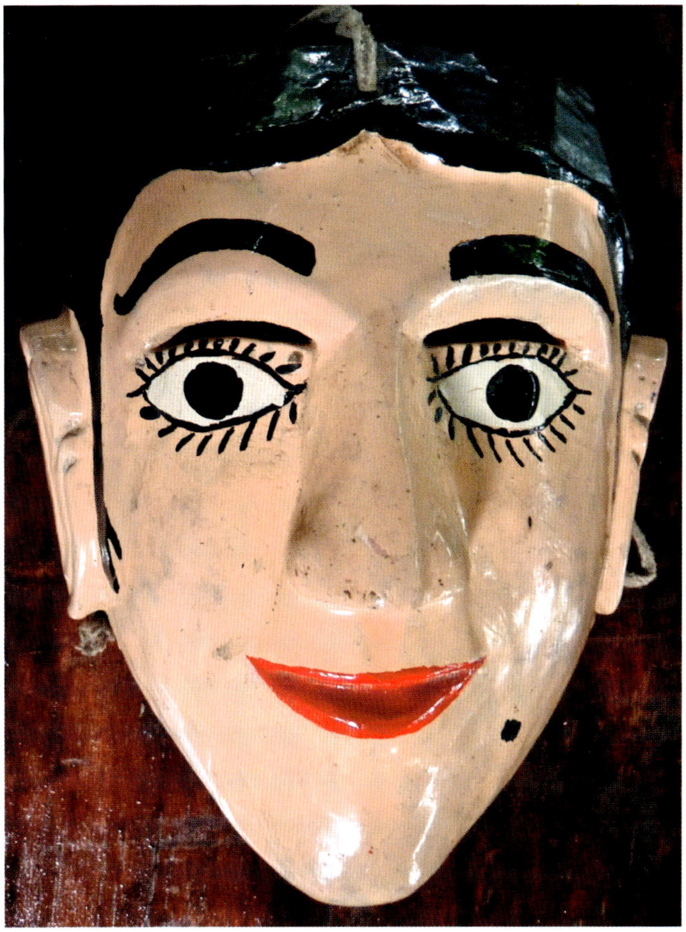

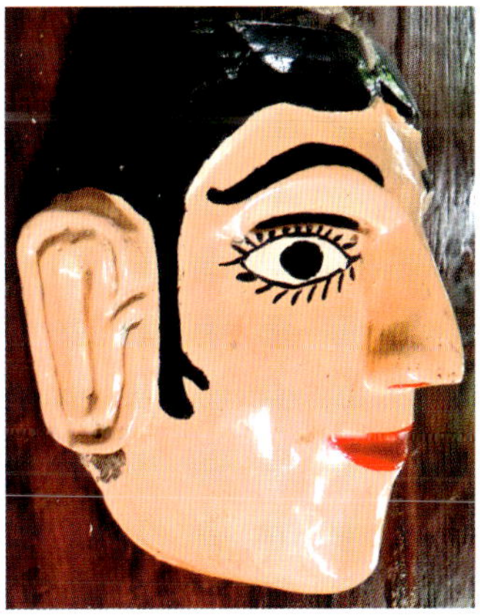

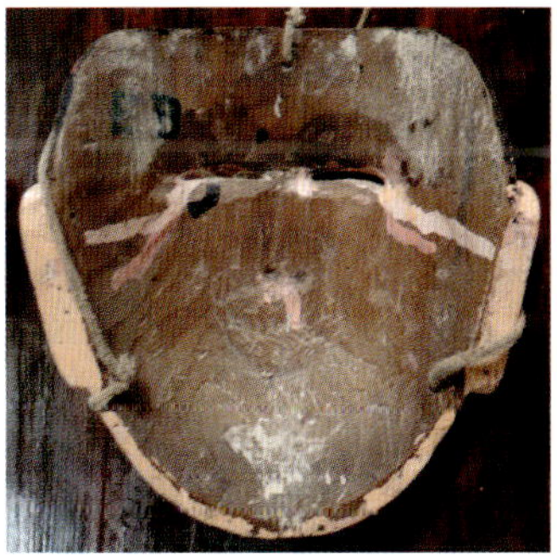

Top: An old female Tejonero mask carved by Antonio Bernabé Mora; 6½" × 7". Circa 1970. Rating: known carver, excellent condition, very well carved, repainted but good patina on back, and rare, ******. *Collection of the family, subsequently sold.*

Above left: A view to show the right ear design.

Above right: The back of this old mask, dark and worn.

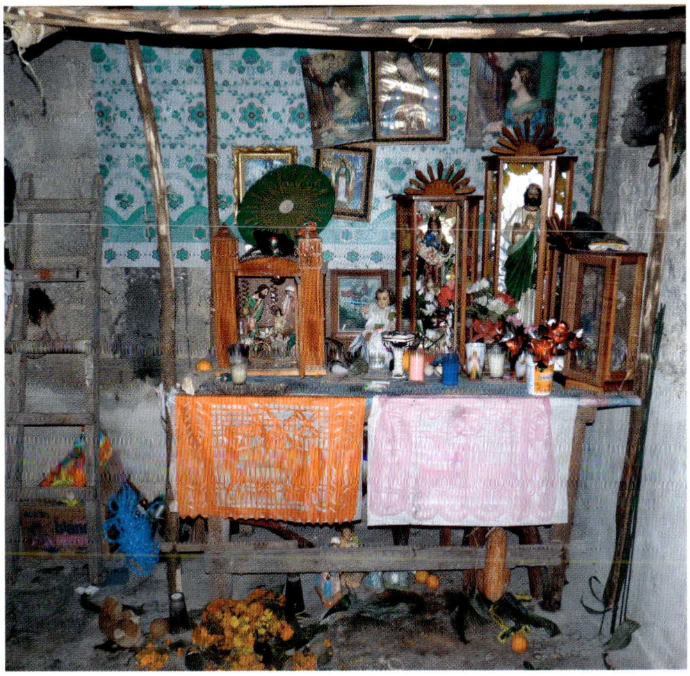

A photograph of a family altar in the home of Ernesto Bernabé Mora, *Courtesy of Ernesto Bernabé Sánchez. Photo by Carlos Moreno Vásquez.*

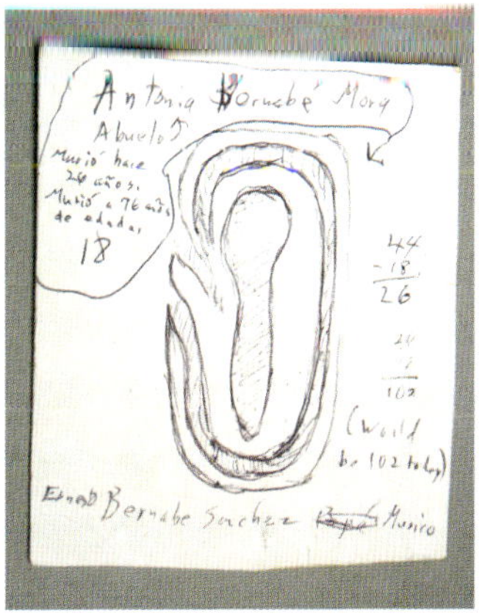

A drawing by the grandson of Antonio Bernabé Mora to document the ear design on an old Tejonero female mask in the family's possession that was carved by Antonio.

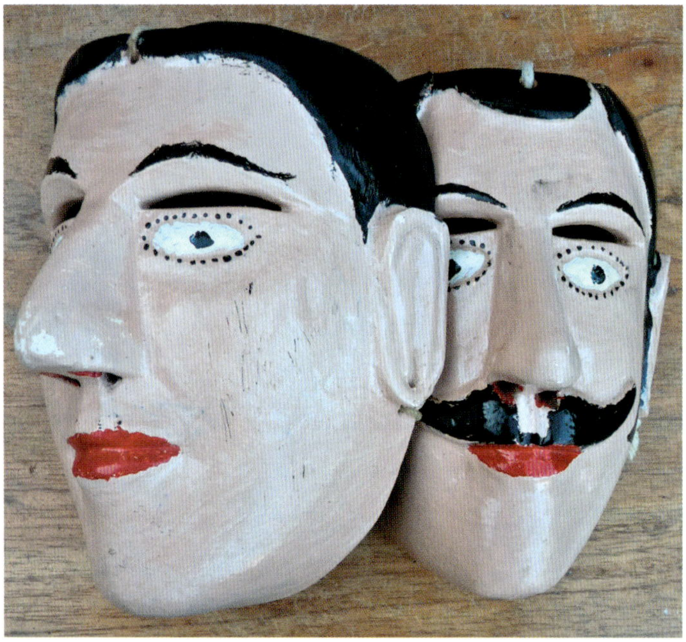

A pair of Tejonero masks from a dance group in Sabanas de Xalostoc. Circa 1970. One glance at the ears and one immediately knows the carver. *Courtesy of the dance group.*

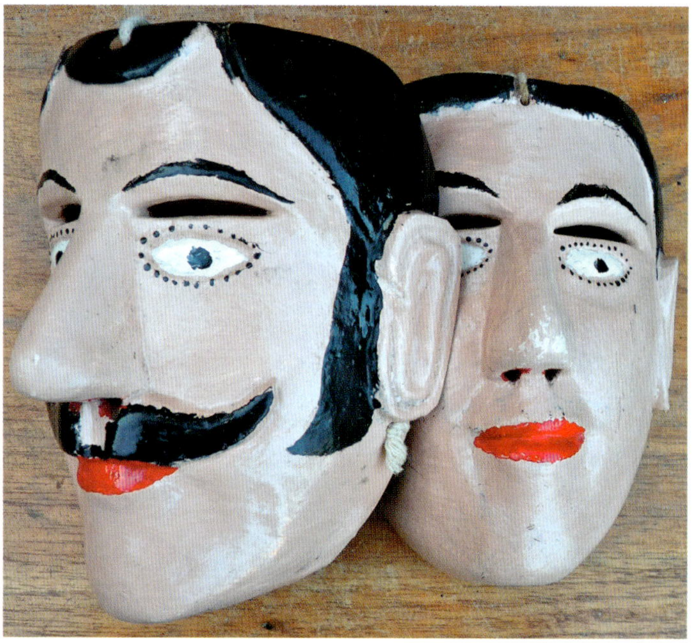

Another view of this couple. The ear on the male matches the drawing; that of the female does not. The backs showed moderate wear.

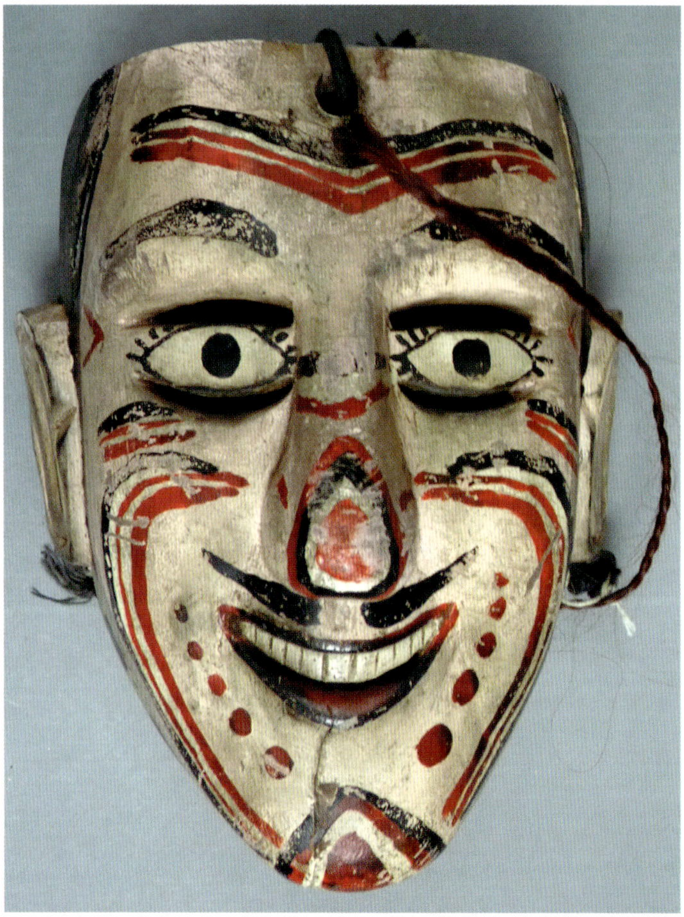

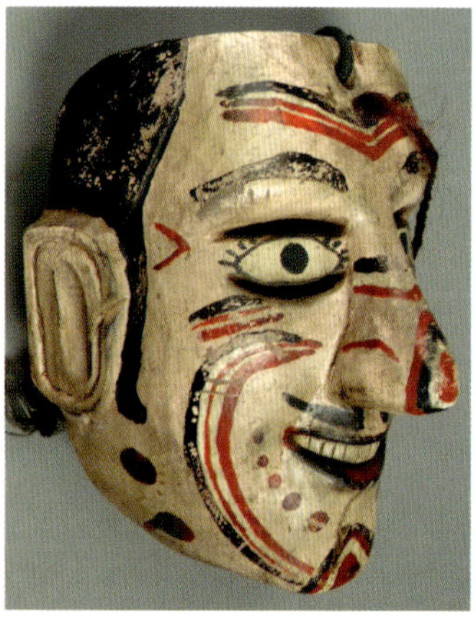

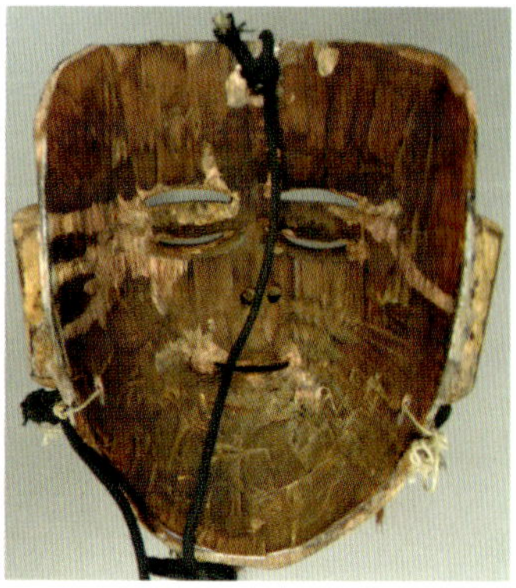

Left: A Tejonero Payaso mask carved by Antonio Bernabé Mora; 6½" × 8". Circa 1960. Note the double vision slits, above and below the painted (not relief-carved) eyes as if used by the Volador troupe from Zozocolco. This mask is obviously modeled on a locally famous mask carved by Luis de Luna. That mask is shown in a later section about Luis de Luna. Rating: known carver, excellent condition, very well carved, good patina, and rare, ******. *Collection of the author.*

Above left: The ear design is clearly that of Antonio Bernabé Mora.

Above right: The back shows darker patina. Otherwise it looks a little different from the rest due to the double vision slits.

Ernesto has told Vernon Kostohryz that his father would alter the masks of other carvers, converting them to masks with articulated jaws. Ernesto acknowledged to me that he has continued this practice. More specifically, he said that he was the one who converted the pair of Tragedy and Comedy masks that were originally carved by Silverio Ochoa. In this book you will have the opportunity to see a number of masks that were apparently converted by either Ernesto or Antonio, and these are very cleverly done. There are Sierra carvers who will occasionally carve a mask with an articulated jaw as an original feature; these include José González Galindo, Andrés Juárez García, Luis de Luna, and Roberto Villegas Santiago. I don't know how it happens that Ernesto makes these alterations; at least two possibilities come to mind. Perhaps dancers bring their masks to Ernesto, specifically requesting certain changes such as repainting or creating an articulated jaw. The other possibility is that Ernesto, who travels widely as a musician, may pick up interesting masks along the way, which he then alters and resells.

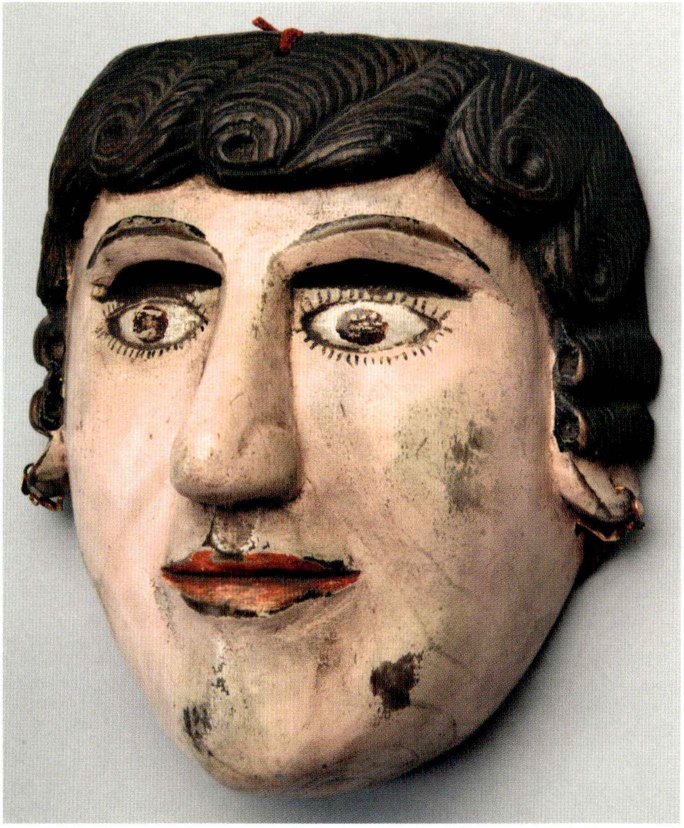

Above: A female Tejonero mask carved by Ernesto Bernabé Sánchez; 6¾" × 7½". Circa 2000. It has a beautiful face. The curly hair is unusual, but Vernon Kostohryz has observed Ernesto carving masks of this design. The mask does have an unusual wear pattern. For this reason I like the mask, but I take the patina with a grain of salt. Rating: known carver, good condition, well carved, questionable patina, and probably not rare, ***. *Collection of the author.*

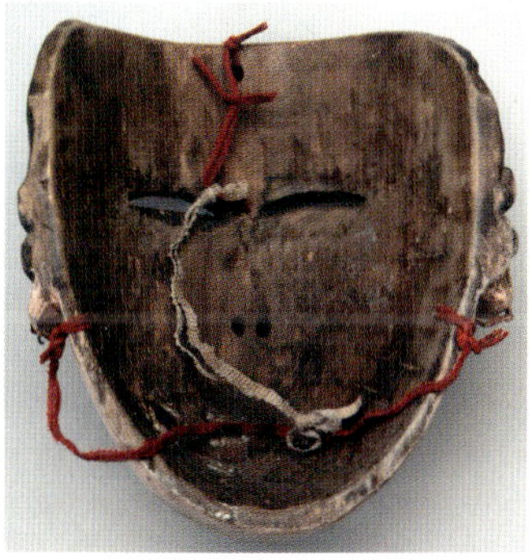

Right: The back of this mask. It appears to have good wear, but I question this because of the wear pattern on the face.

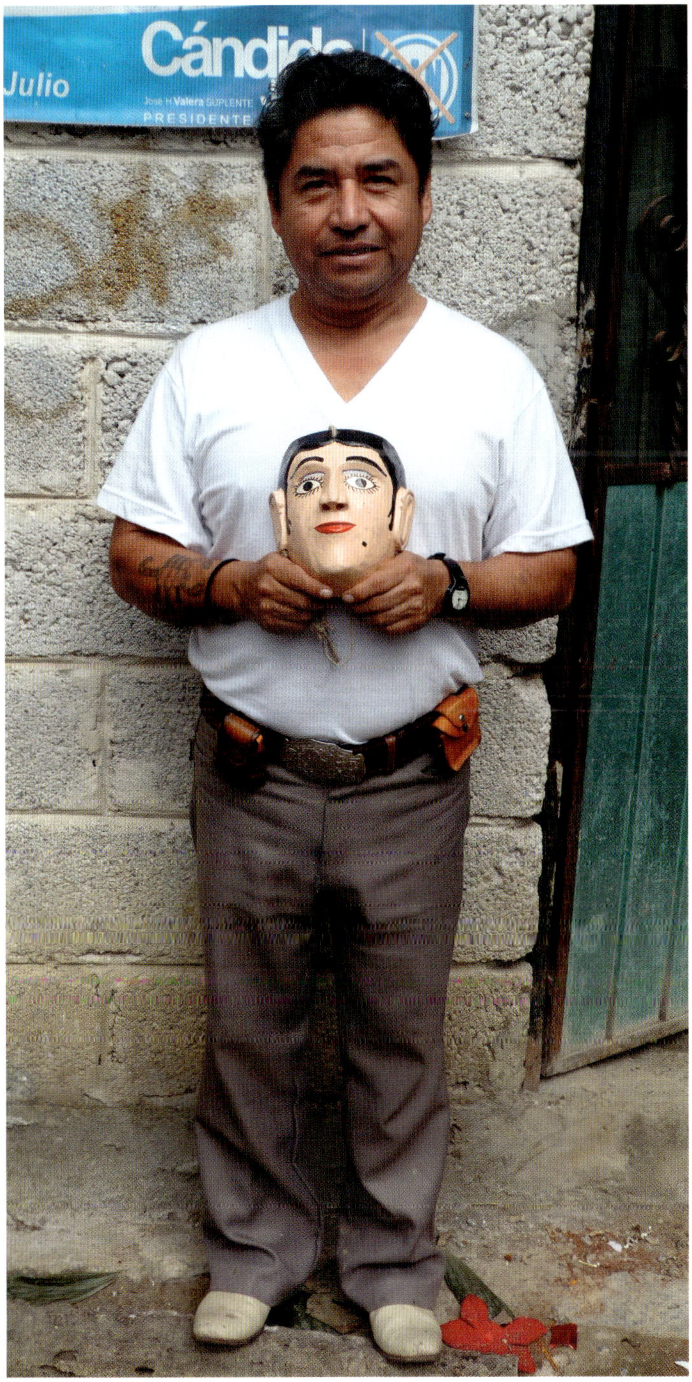

Ernesto Bernabé Sánchez holding the old female mask carved by his father Antonio.

Lorenzo Ciriaco García (El Kalimán) and Leonel Lecona

Lorenzo Ciriaco García was born on October 8, 1951, and died due to complications of diabetes on November 25, 2006. He lived in Huehuetla, Puebla, a Totonac community. As a young man he was handsome and muscular; this caused his friends to compare him to a popular character from Mexican radio serials and comic books—El Kalimán—and so Lorenzo acquired this nickname. Lorenzo (hereafter I will call him "Kalimán") was a very talented carver of masks for the Huehues dance. I had been told about Kalimán by Vernon Kostohryz, so I visited his community in December 2006 and learned then that the carver had just died. I visited his childhood friend there, Leonel Lecona, who shared with me a DVD in which Kalimán was shown dancing as a Huehue. Leonel also appeared in this film as Manuel, a young Mestizo man who was interviewed about his knowledge of the Huehues dance. The film, which was made by Bruce "Pacho" Lane (2005), is called *The Tree of Knowledge* and is still available in the DVD format.

I intended to revisit Leonel Lecona; in fact, I went back to see him in December 2007, but he was not at home. He died in 2010, before I could follow up with him. I would like to include here a mask that was carved by Leonel at the age of 16, because I have no doubt that Leonel wore this mask in the Huehues dance in the company of Kalimán, back in the 1960s. Vernon purchased the mask from Leonel in about 2006. Leonel had scraped the paint off of one side of the mask, meaning to repaint it, and then he never got around to doing so.

I did also visit Kalimán's widow and children during that trip in 2006; they allowed me to photograph some old photos of Kalimán, along with his tools and a number of his masks and puppets that they had kept. In the years that followed I eventually purchased the male Huehue mask and the puppets from the family.

From his teen years Kalimán was a dancer and a mask carver. His Huehue masks are very nicely carved and quite attractive. I have included masks of Huehue men and women, payasos, and a blue *Perro* (dog). In Chapter 7 we will look at two sets of Huehue puppets by Kalimán. As you will see, the ears on his human-faced masks are very gracefully carved and come in at least three different designs. On his Huehue masks, we see a beautiful ear design, which I will call Kalimán Type 1. On his Payaso masks, Kalimán used at least two other ear designs. The Type 2 design bears some resemblance to that of De Aquino but seems more elegant.

Puppets are used in the Huehues or Tejoneros dance. Kalimán's puppets are distinctive for very detailed carving, including hats on the male puppets that are carved from the original woodblock. I will discuss Kalimán's puppets in Chapter 7.

In summary, Kalimán was the master carver for his community in the late 20th century. His masks have a distinct personal style, and I find them quite attractive.

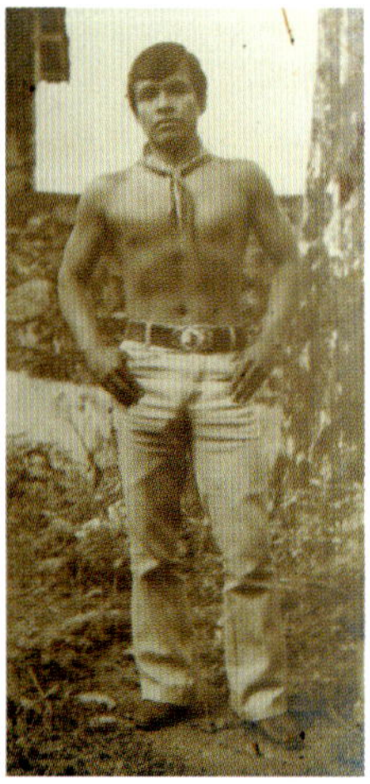

"El Kalimán," Lorenzo Ciriaco García as a young man. This photo was copied from a family photo. *Courtesy of Lorenzo's wife.*

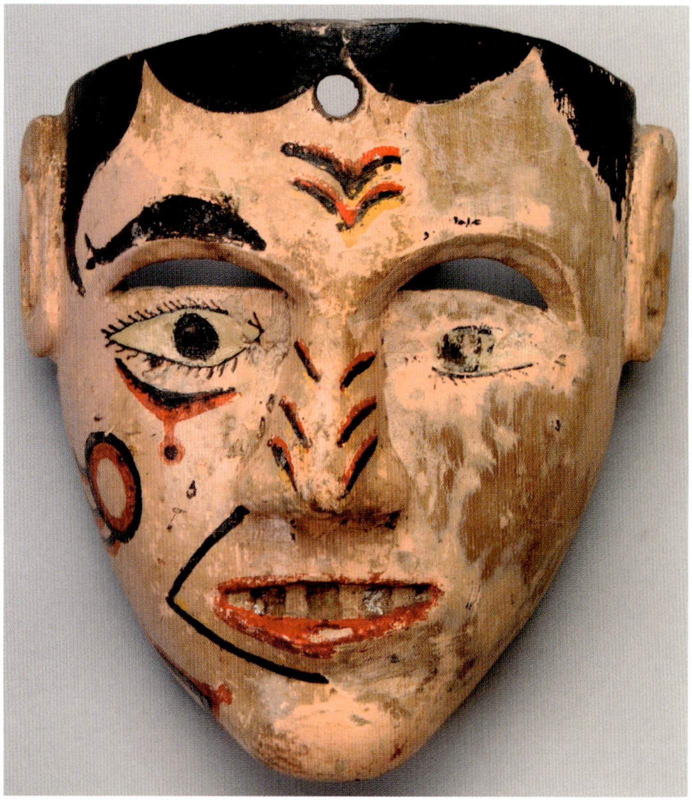

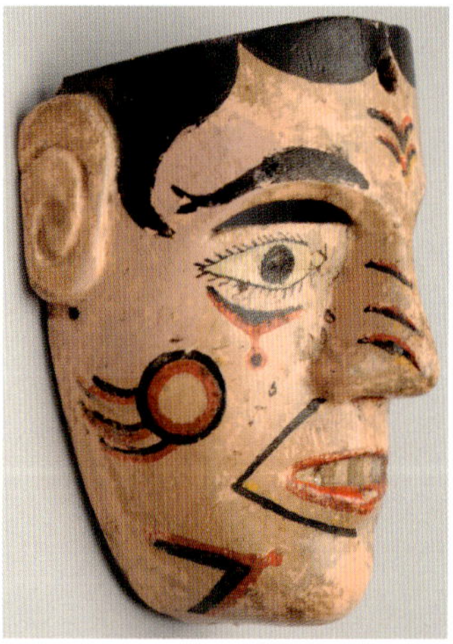

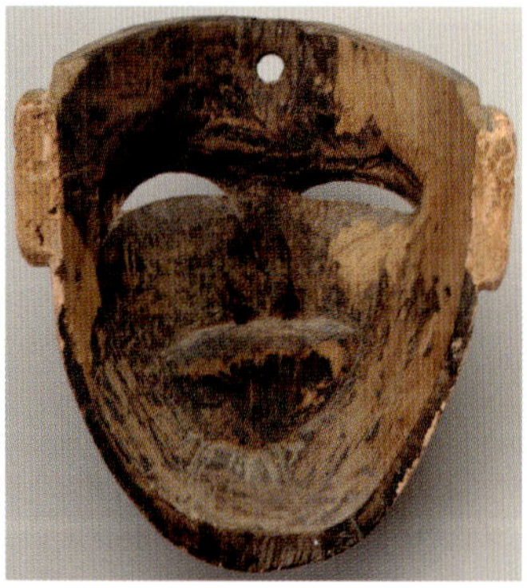

Above: This Huehue mask was carved by Leonel Lecona when he was 16 years old; 6½" × 7½". He subsequently danced with this mask alongside his friend Kalimán. Leonel later scraped off the paint on one side, meaning to repaint the mask, one half at a time. He never did repaint the mask and sold it to Vernon Kostohryz in about 2005, more than 40 years after he had made it. Rating: known carver, excellent condition, well carved, good patina, and rare, *****. *Collection of the author.*

Center left: The view from the left side provides a clear picture of the original paint. Leonel had developed his own ear design. There is a nicely carved arch over the eye. It has a clown's mouth to match the painted decorations on the face.

Left: The back is carefully carved; there is a small hollow for the nose and a shelf under the chin, something like the back of a mask by Benito Juárez. At some time, parts of the back were scraped; usually this is done to adjust the mask to a new wearer's face. The contrast between the stained and scraped areas provides a nice picture of what 40-plus years of exposure and use can look like.

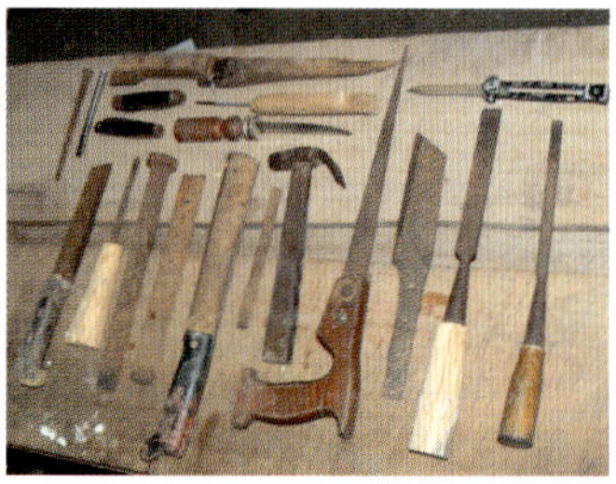

Kalimán's tools in his house, December 2006. *Courtesy of Lorenzo's wife.*

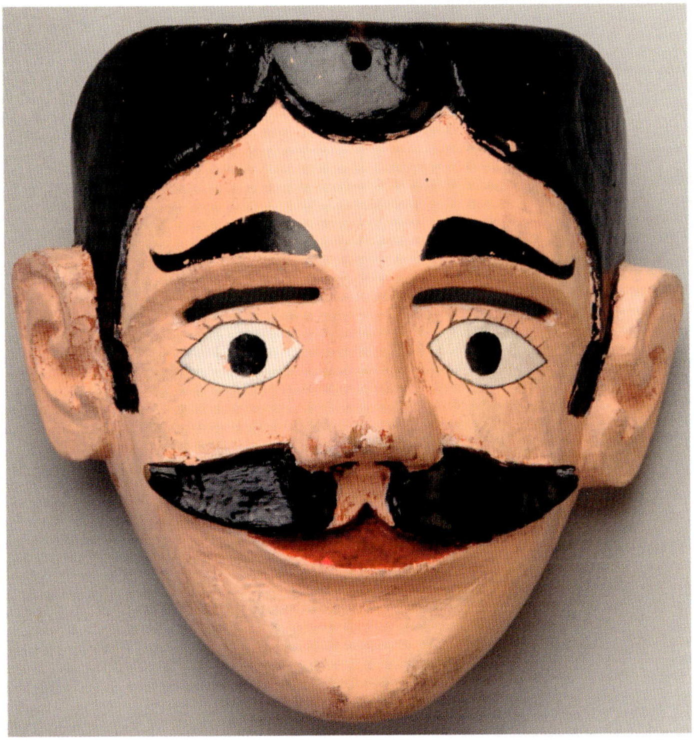

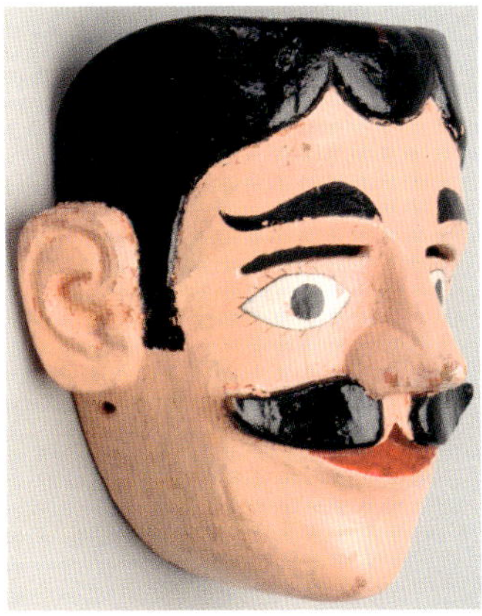

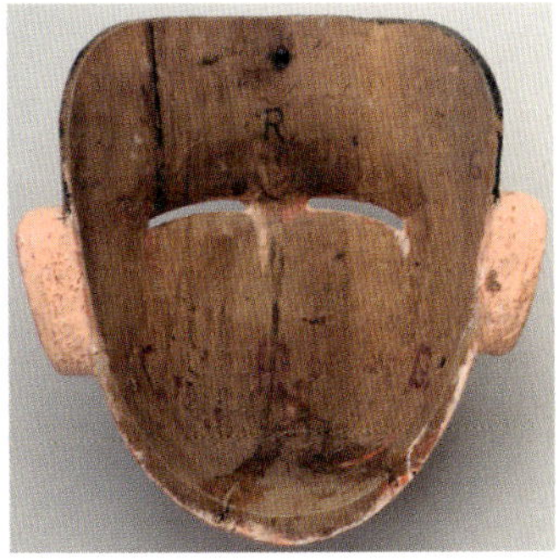

Left: A male Huehue mask purchased from Kalimán's family several years after his death; 7¼" × 7¼". Circa 1970. This is nicely made, with a relief-carved hairline. The shape of the mouth is distinctive. Rating: known carver, excellent condition, well carved, good patina, and rare, ******. *Collection of the author.*

Above left: The side view of this mask reveals a very attractive ear design, which he may have used only on his Huehue masks. I am calling this the Kalimán Type 1 ear.

Above right: The back of this mask demonstrates a very simple, clean design.

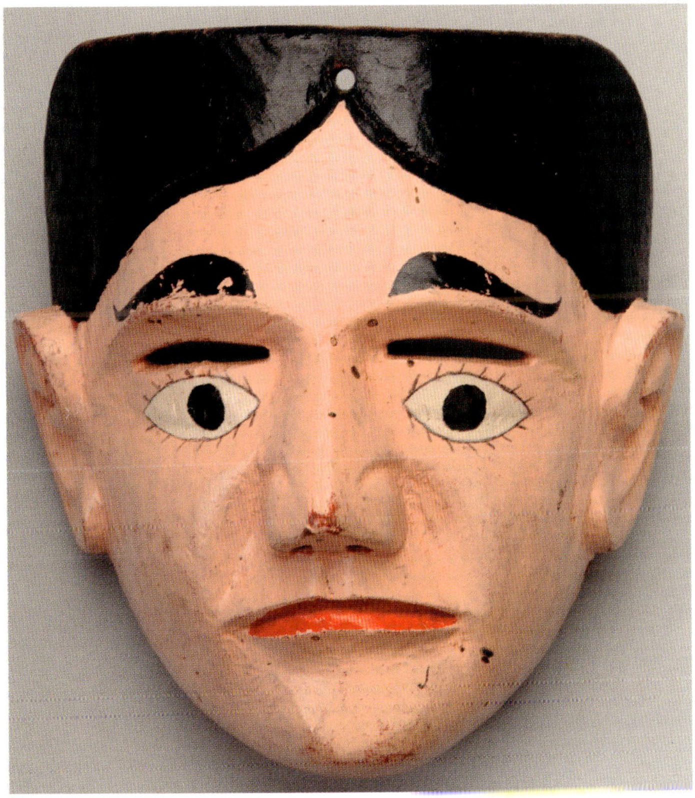

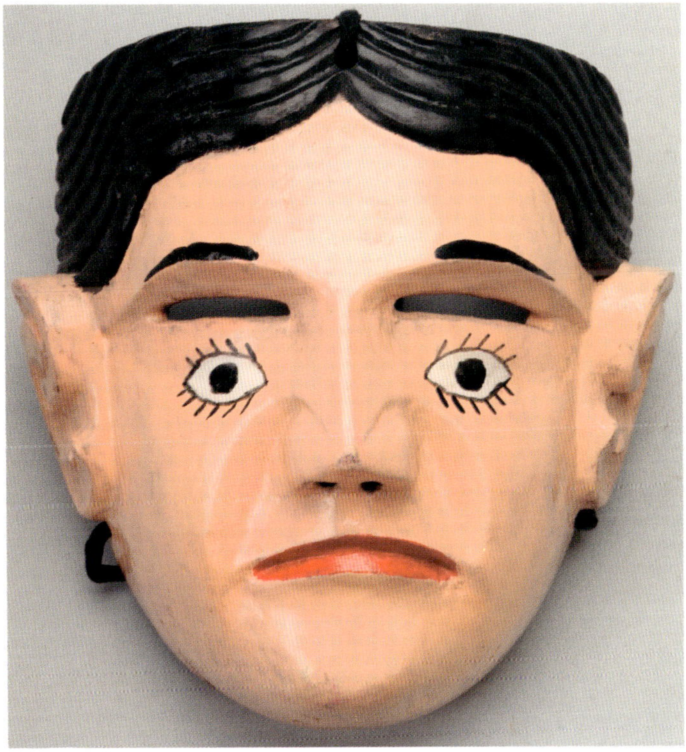

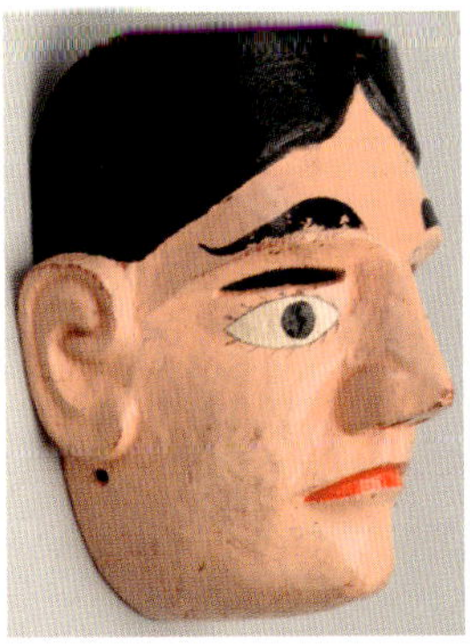

Above: A female Huehue mask purchased by Vernon Kostohryz from a dance group in Huehuetla, Puebla, in 2005; 7½" × 6¾". Circa 1970. The overall quality of the carving is rather evident in this view. On this female mask is the same dramatic hollowing of the face that can be seen on a mask by José González Galindo; apparently this expression was taken from the face of some saint. Rating: known carver, excellent condition, well carved, good patina, and rare, ******. *Collection of the author.*

Left: The side view of this female Huehue mask reveals a very clear picture of Kalimán's Type 1 ear design.

A second female Huehue mask by Kalimán that was purchased by the author from Andrés Juárez García in 2010; 7" × 7". Circa 1980. This mask also shows the hollowed design above the mouth. The hair is grooved; otherwise this mask is much like the previous one. Rating: known carver, excellent condition, well carved, good patina, and rare, ******. *Collection of the author.*

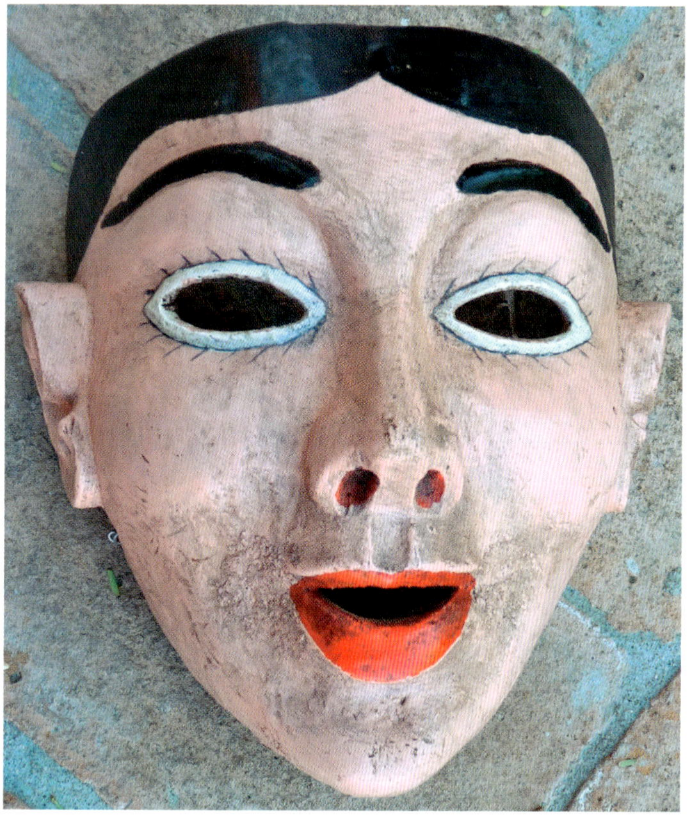

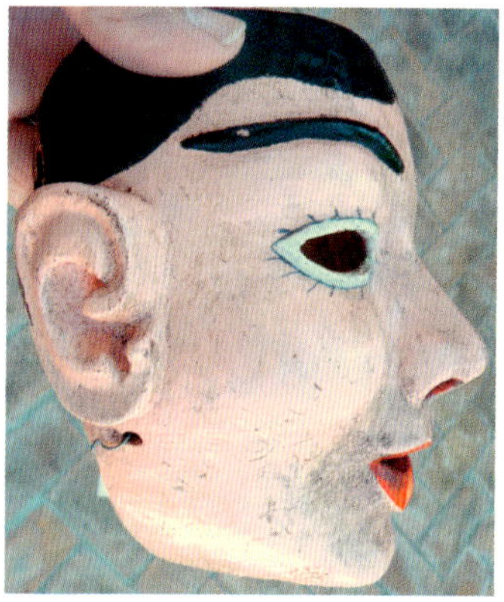

Left: This is a highly attractive, but initially mysterious, mask; 7½" × 7". Circa 1980. Then one notices that this mask has the ear design of Kalimán's Huehue masks. The painted lines around the eyes are like those on Kalimán's Payasos. None of the other design elements fit very well. In fact, it was attributed to Kalimán by the seller. The open mouth suggests that this is a female clown. Notice that the upper lip is finely carved but poorly repainted. This is a rare example of a female Huehue Payaso by Kalimán. Rating: known carver, excellent condition, very well carved, excellent patina, and extremely rare, ******. *Collection of Bill LeVasseur.*

Above: The profile view of this mask shows the beautiful Kalimán Type 1 ear design that was found on one male and two female Huehue masks by Kalimán. Otherwise we see a wonderful animated face, clearly the work of a master carver.

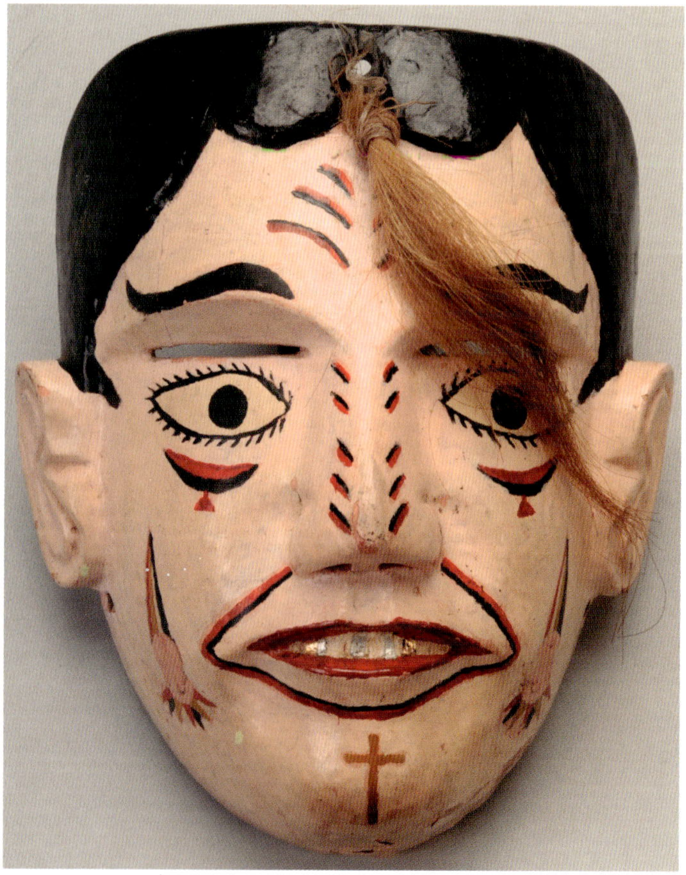

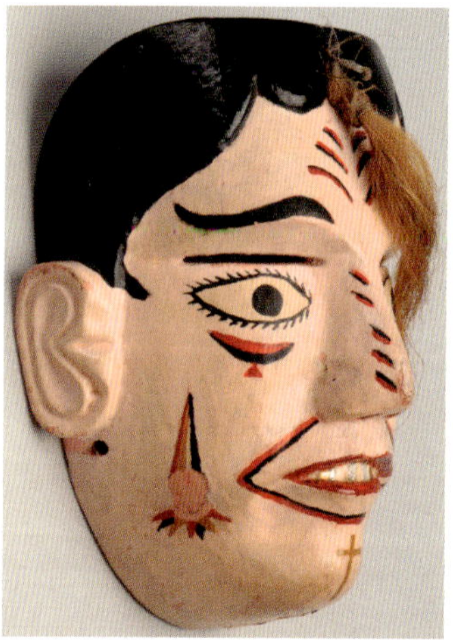

Left: A Payaso mask purchased from a dance group in Huehuetla, Puebla, in 2005; 6½" × 7½". Circa 1970. Note the cross on the chin and the painting of a clown on the cheek. We see that the ear design on the carver's Payaso masks differs from that on the Huehue masks. I am calling this the Type 2 ear design. Rating: known carver, excellent condition, well carved, good patina, and rare, ******. *Collection of the author.*

Above: The side view of this Payaso mask from Huehuetla. The Type 2 ear design is rather striking.

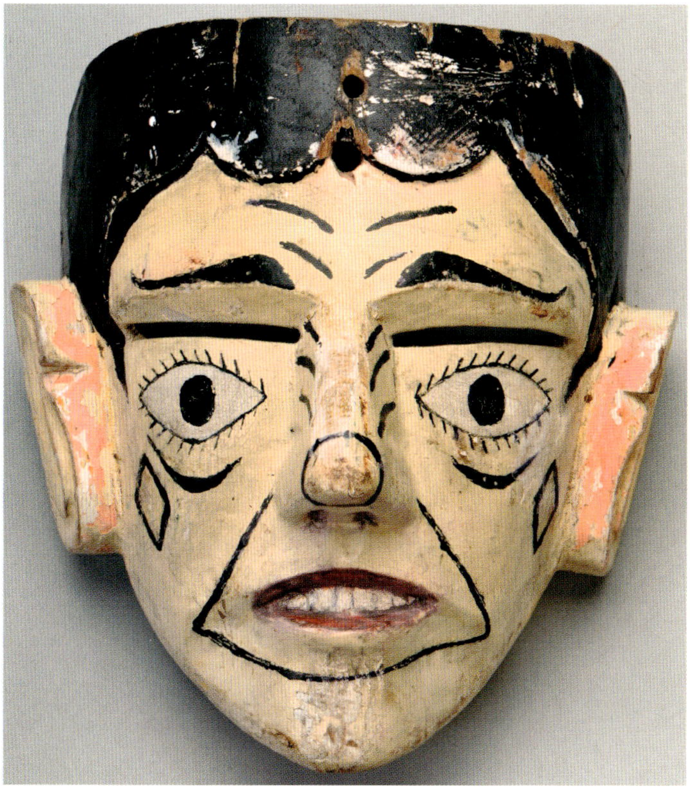

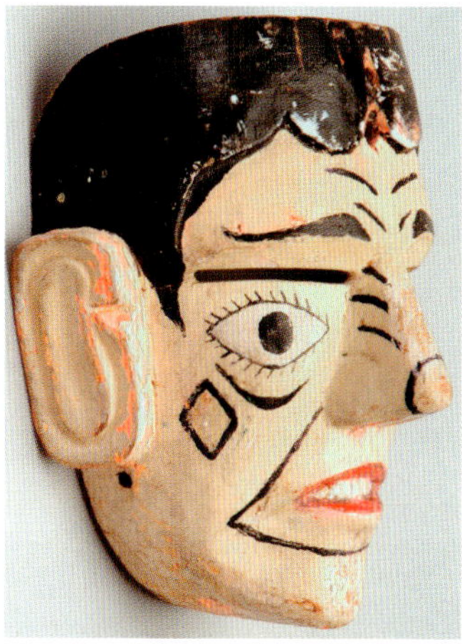

Far left: Another Payaso mask found in Hueytlalpan, Puebla, in 2009, said to be at least 30 years old, and with obvious stylistic details to suggest that it, too, is the work of Kalimán; 7" × 7". Circa 1980. Rating: known carver, excellent condition, well carved, good patina, and rare, ******. *Collection of the author.*

Left: The side view of the Payaso mask from Hueytlalpan, demonstrating a variant of the Type 2 ear.

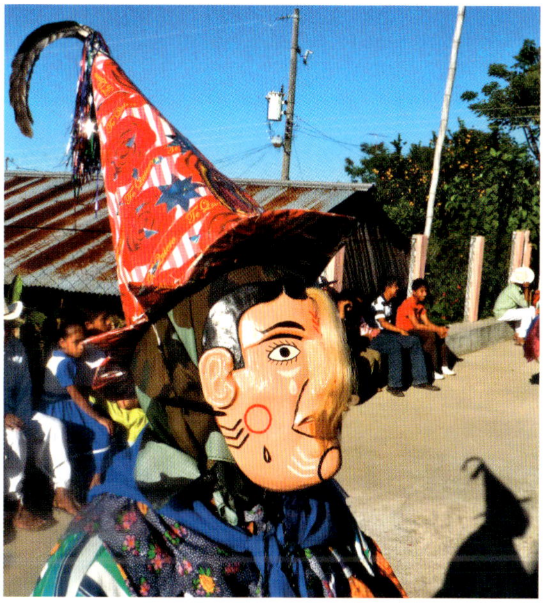

In this dance photo from Xonalpú, Puebla, taken in December 2010 we see yet another ear design by Kalimán. Vernon Kostohryz had collected another mask with this design that was definitely attributed to this carver, but there is no photo. Rating: known carver, excellent condition, well carved, good patina, and rare, ******. *Collection of dance group.*

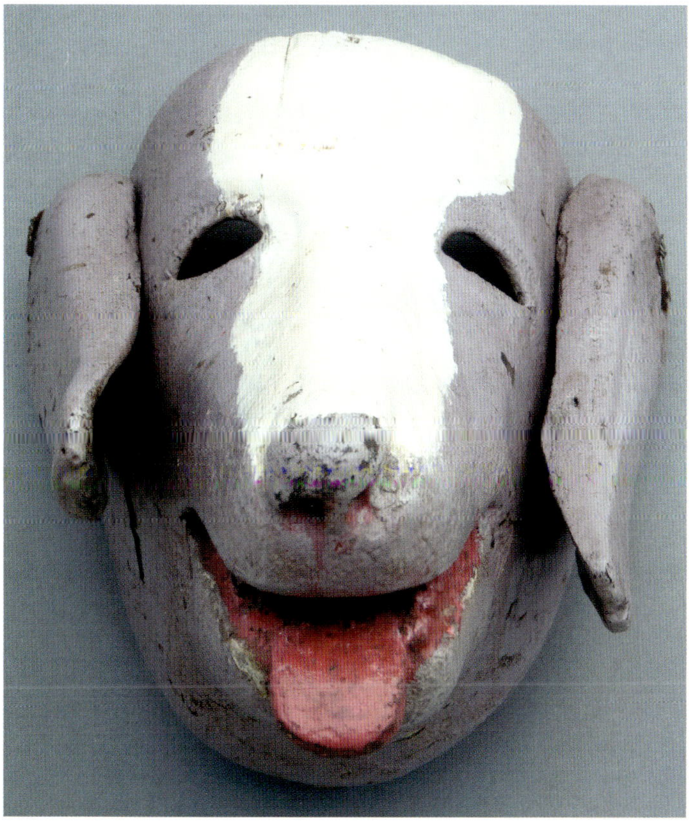

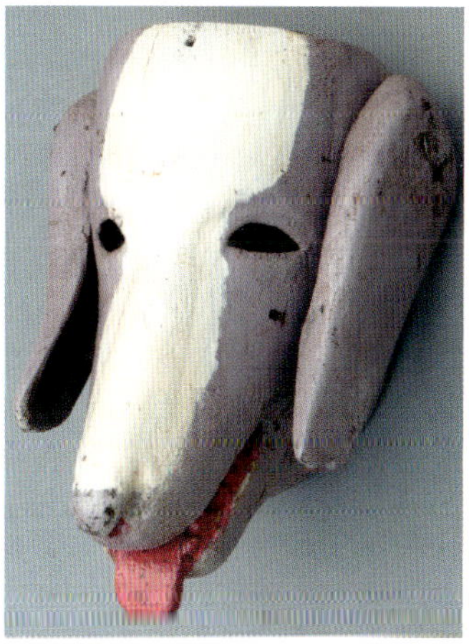

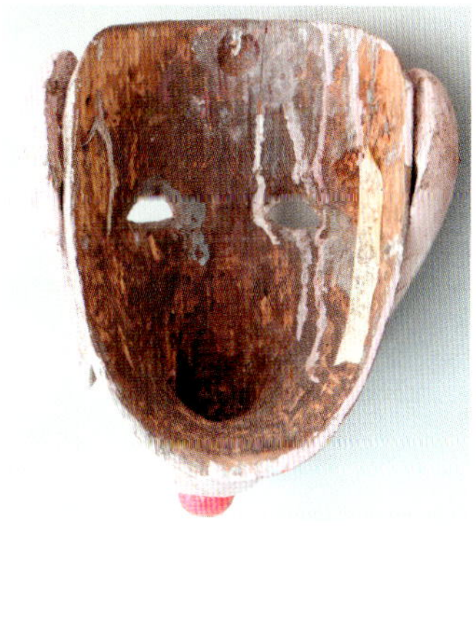

Left: This Perro mask from the Huehues dance was found in Tuzamapan, Puebla, with a group of Huehue masks carved by Roberto Villegas Santiago. Circa 1980. Vernon Kostohryz showed the mask to Roberto, who informed him that it was carved by Kalimán. It is painted purple, and this paint has good patina, although chipped paint reveals that the mask was previously black. Rating: known carver, excellent condition, well-carved, great patina, and rare, ******. *Collection of James Annis.*

Above left: From this angle one can see that the ears are hollow on the inside surface, an elegant touch. There are carved teeth on the lower lip.

Above right: The patina on the back of the dog mask is quite dark, indicating long and heavy use.

Leopoldo Cortez González (Polo)

"Polo" Cortez lived and worked in Olintla, Puebla. We have recently seen a number of his masks, for the Hormegas dance, in Olintla and in surrounding towns. As yet we don't know when he was born and when he died. He was clearly an excellent and interesting carver.

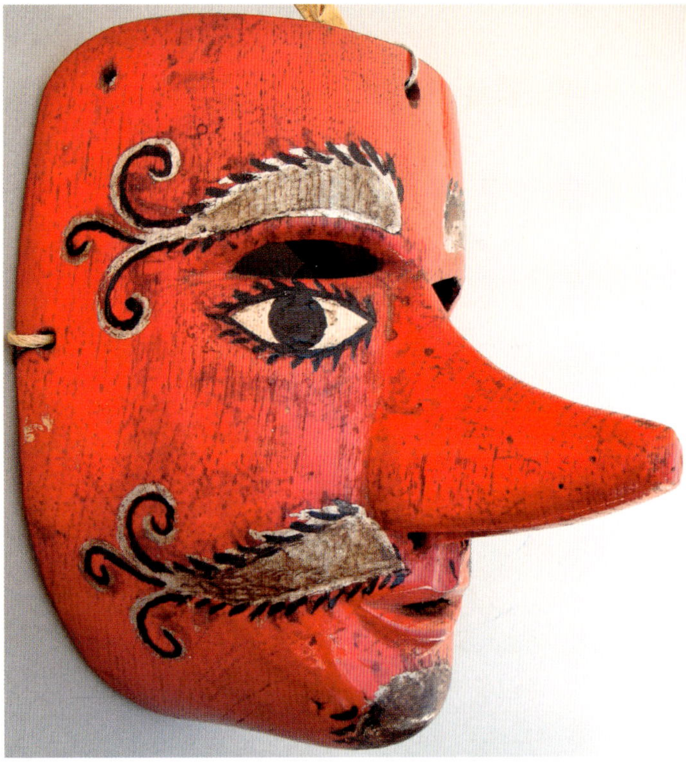

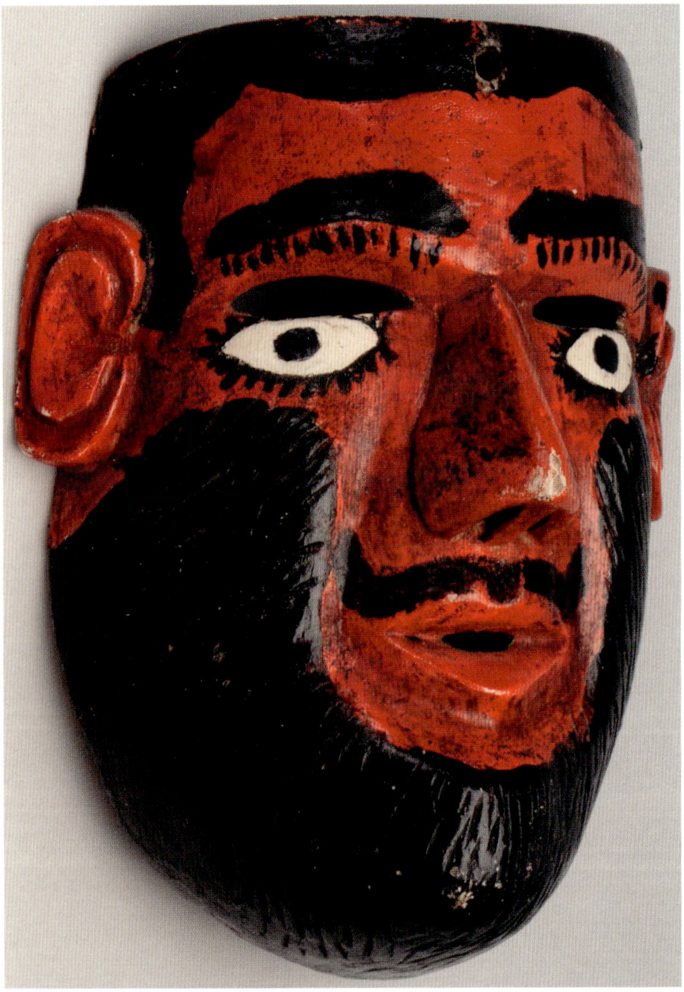

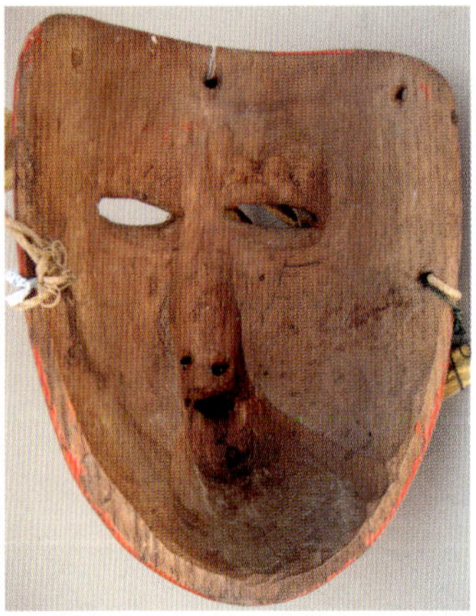

Above: Carlos Moreno Vásquez purchased this Hormega mask from a dance group in Olintla, Puebla; 6½" × 8". Circa 1960. It is instructive to notice various small details that distinguish these Hormega masks by Polo from others by Benito Juárez Figueroa and Magno León. These include the rake, shape, and point of extension of the nose, the shaping of the mouth, and details of the painting. Rating: known carver, excellent condition, well carved, good patina, and rare, ******. *Collection of Vernon Kostohryz, who supplied these photos.*

Left: The back of this mask from Olintla, demonstrating again the distinctive way that Polo shapes the backs of his masks.

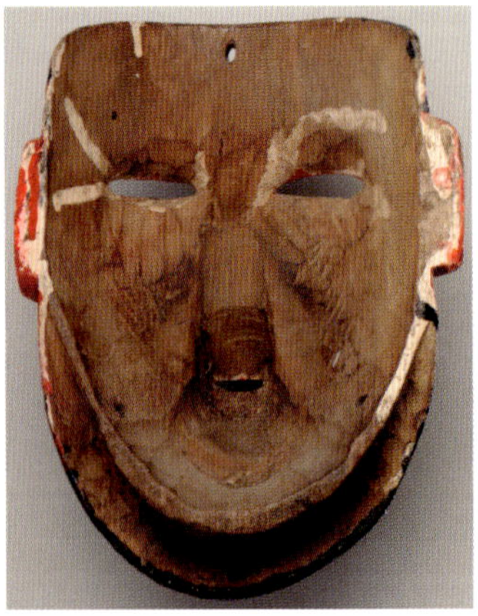

Above: Vernon Kostohryz purchased this Ayudante Pilato mask in Vicente Guerrero, Puebla, in 2006; 6½" × 8". Circa 1970. In 2010 we found a pair of identical masks that were a part of the Hormegas dance in Olintla, Puebla; they were Pilato characters, adjutants to Pilatos el Presidente. At the very end of 2010, Carlos Moreno Vásquez was finally provided with the name of the carver, Polo González. Rating: known carver, excellent condition, well carved, good patina, and rare, ******. *Collection of the author.*

Left: The back of this mask shows a configuration that seems to be typical for this carver. Particularly distinctive is the scooped-out channel across the chin, connecting to a hollow area that extends from the back of the nose down to the mouth. Mateo Vega also uses this design; further research by Vernon and Carlos will establish whether they are two separate carvers versus the possibility that we might have one carver but two names. There is a hollow beard below the chin of the mask. The mask has excellent wear and seems fairly old.

Alejandro Dominguez

Alejandro Dominguez lives and carves in Xochimilco, Puebla. I have seen several very fine Santiaguero masks by this carver and also a Santiago horse that he may have carved. I believe that he is quite talented.

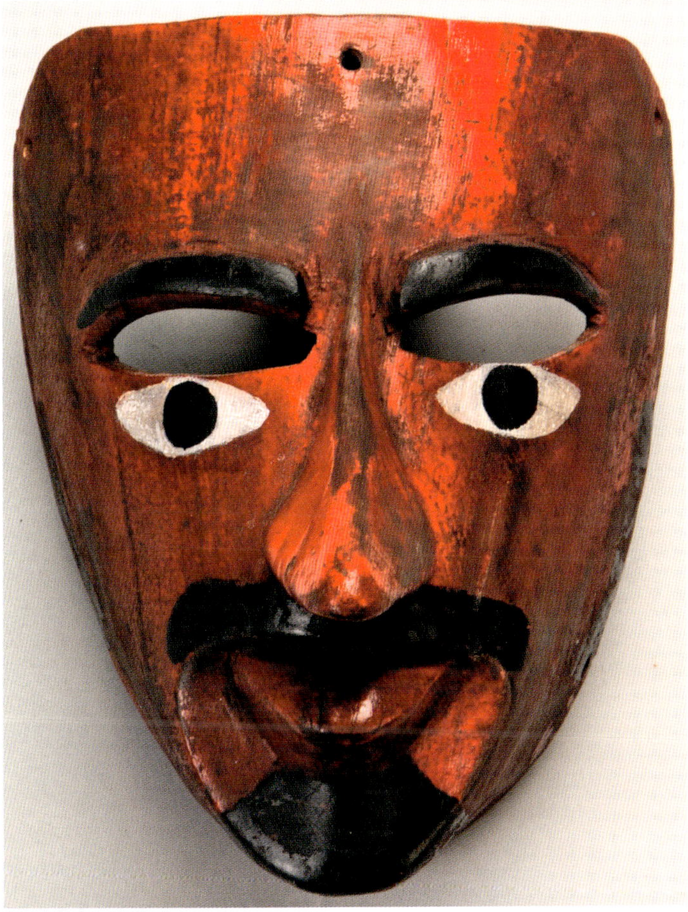

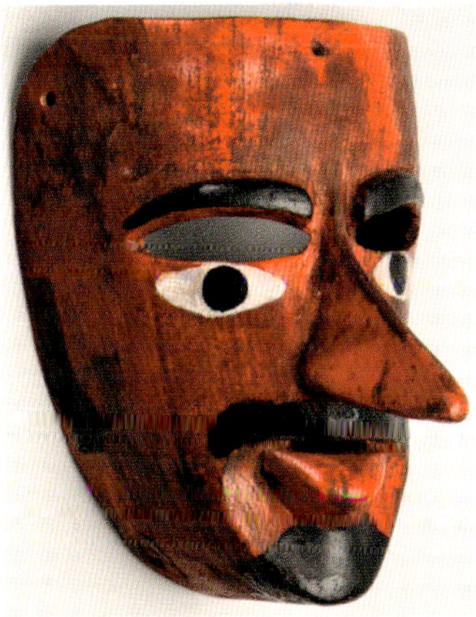

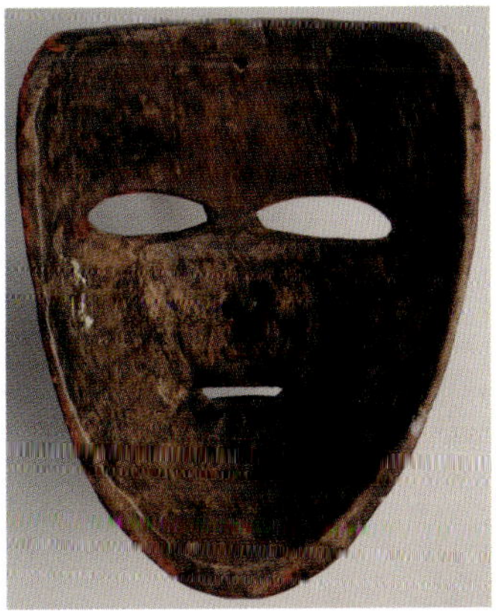

Top: This graceful Santiaguero mask was found by Vernon Kostohryz in Xochimilco, Puebla; 6¼" × 7 ¾". Circa 1980. Subsequently we have seen a dance set of identical masks, complete with morión headdresses, but we were not permitted to publish photos of that group. Rating: known carver, excellent condition, well carved, good patina, and possibly rare, *****. *Collection of the author.*

Bottom left: The side view of this handsome mask.

Bottom right: The back of this mask has dark patina.

Simón Fernando García (Don Simón)

Simón Fernando García was 67 years of age when I visited him on December 12, 2007. He lives in Comunidad Tuncuhuini, in the municipio of Coxquihui, Veracruz.

One approaches Simón's house from a distant road, by following a trail across a beautiful meadow. On one side of the trail there is a very tall hill, which seems to stand in isolation from any others, as if it could be an unexcavated pyramid. Whether it is a pyramid or not is unknown to me (see photos at the end of Chapter 1).

I found Don Simón to be a clever and artistic craftsman who appeared to do many things well. Several of those things seemed unusually interesting.

Like many of the mascareros in this region, Simón had carved a puppet set, and these were charming. As usual, the puppets lived in their own wooden box, but Don Simón had chosen to decorate the box with painted images of Tejoneros holding colored handkerchiefs.

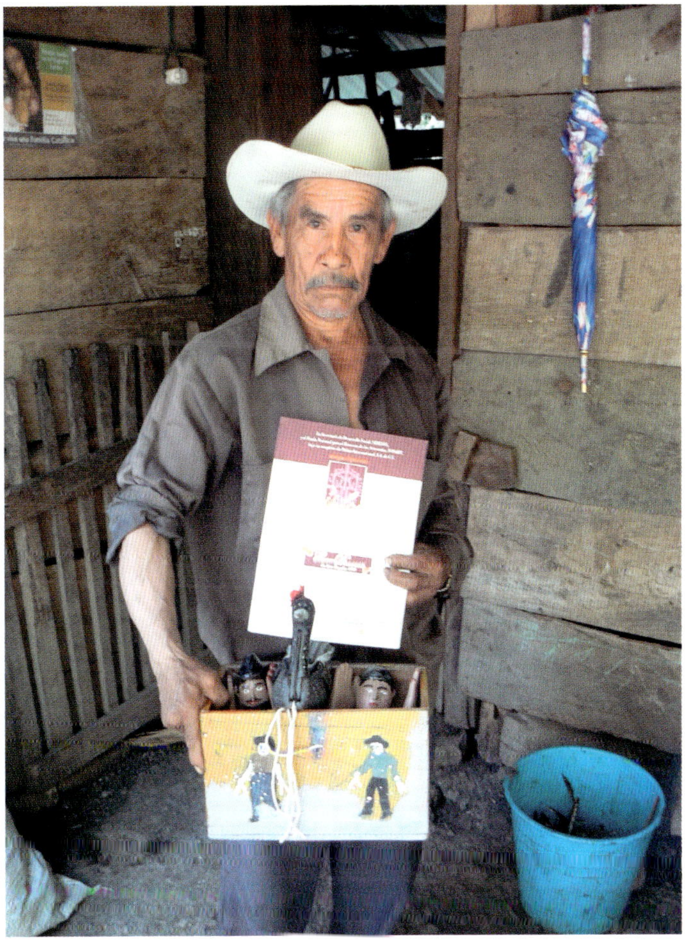

When we visited Don Simón in December 2007, he was a gracious host. Here he is showing his puppet set peering from their box. In his other hand he holds a certificate from a government agency that identifies him as a cultural artist. Behind him one sees a wooden gate that serves very well as a door in this coastal climate; it keeps the farm animals out of the house.

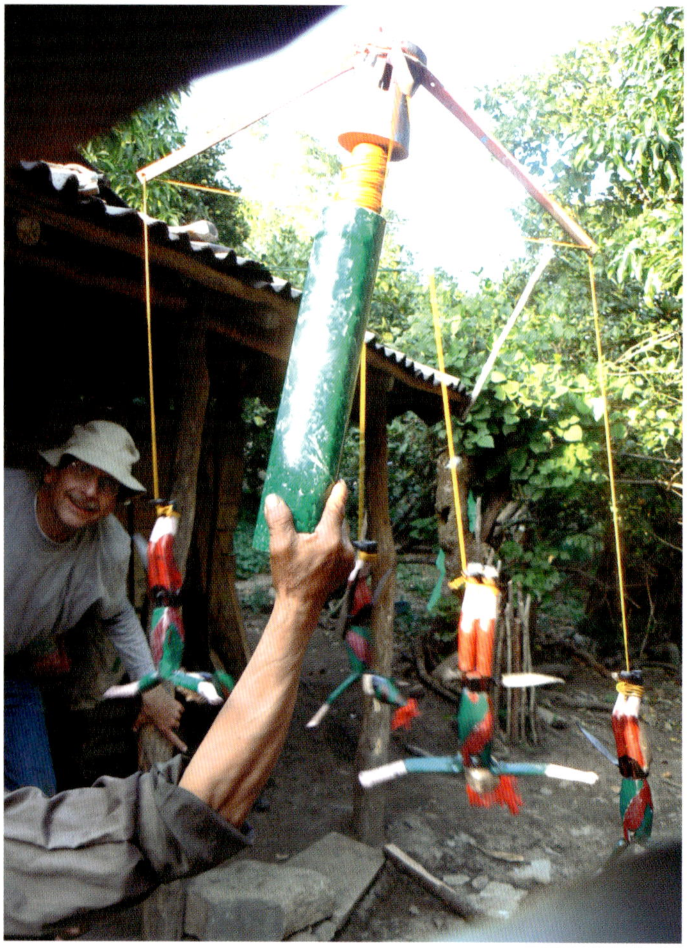

Don Simón demonstrating his Voladores device to Vernon Kostohryz in December 2007.

Don Simón, who is quite a showman, brought out and assembled a miniature Volador pole, complete with unwinding ropes (made of heavy string), diagonal arms to mimic the effect of the Voladores platform, and miniature flyers, who looked like little elves. Simón explained that this apparatus was carried on a tall pole during a procession, and that it had served in this capacity for about eight years. We were so dazzled by this presentation that we hastened to acquire the setup from its maker, but forgot to ask additional questions, including questions about the meaning of the procession.

Vernon had previously collected a Payaso mask by this carver, and I also acquired a male and female Huehue mask pair that Don Simón had carved and which he was in the process of refinishing. Several years later we discovered several of his Huehue masks that were being used in Sabanas de Xalostoc, Veracruz.

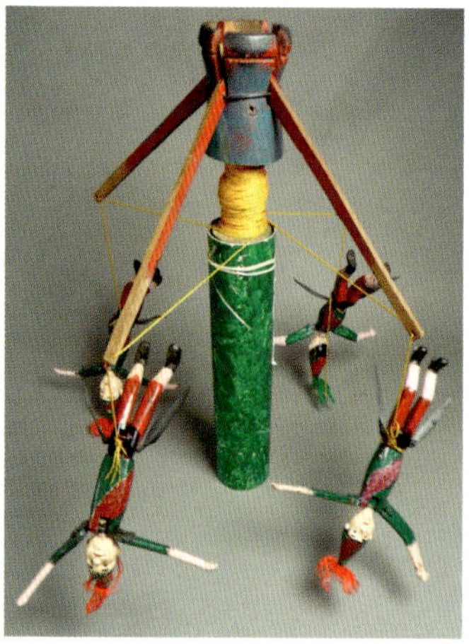

The contraption set up in a studio setting. The diameter from the tip of one arm to that of the opposite arm is 21". Rating: known carver, excellent condition, well carved and creative, unremarkable patina, and possibly rare, ****. *Collection of the author.*

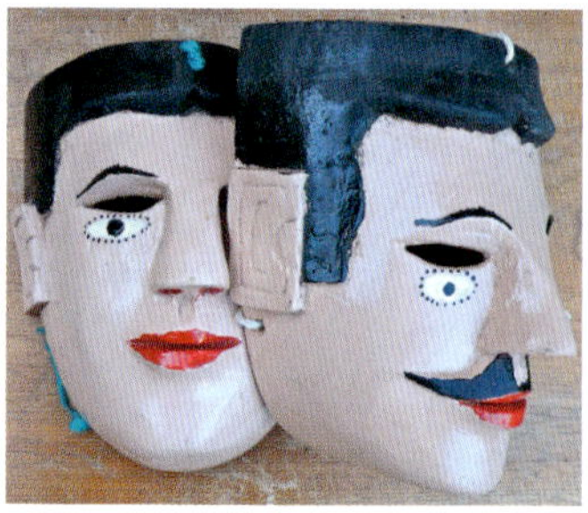

A Tejonero couple by Don Simón, late 20th century. The masks demonstrate the normal Tejonero form with closed mouths. Note the geometric quality of the ear design. Rating: known carver, excellent condition, well carved, normal patina, and not rare, ****. *Collection of the dance group, Sabanas de Xalostoc, Veracruz.*

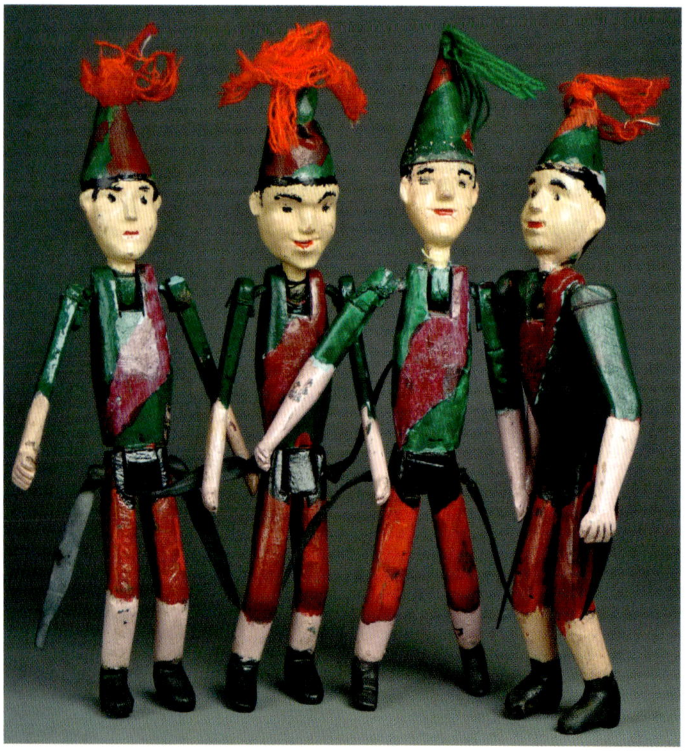

The four Volador dolls, 10" tall including their caps.

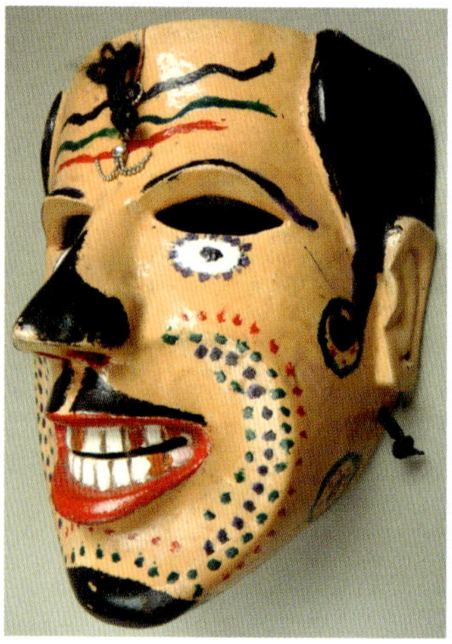

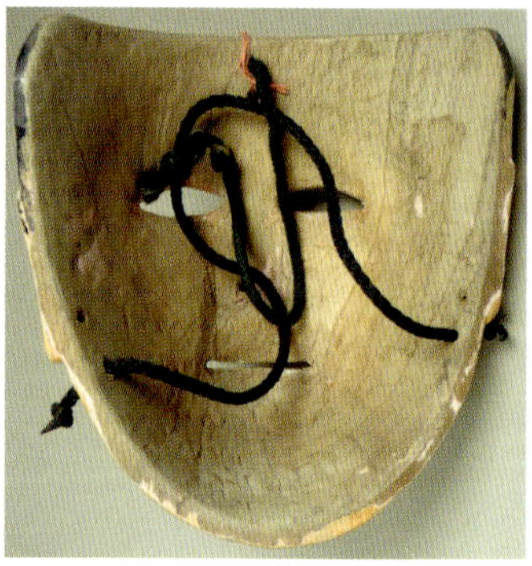

Above left: A male Payaso mask, with its typical toothy grin, from the dance of the Tejoneros, carved by Don Simón; 6" × 7". Circa 1990. The features of this mask are nicely shaped and painted. The ear design used by Don Simón is geometric rather than naturalistic. Rating: known carver, excellent condition, well carved, normal patina, and probably not rare, ****. *Collection of Vernon Kostohryz.*

Above right: The back of the mask is rather plain. Although not visible from these photos, there are two holes in the forehead of this mask; one at the top is for the attachment of the string and another just below is for the tuft of hair that one usually finds on a Payaso mask.

Celestino Gaona Luna

Celestino Gaona Luna was born in 1897 and died in 1975. He was a carver in Coxquihui, Veracruz. Recently Carlos Moreno Vásquez purchased a very well carved Tejonero mask by him from the carver's son. In this way we became aware of him for the first time.

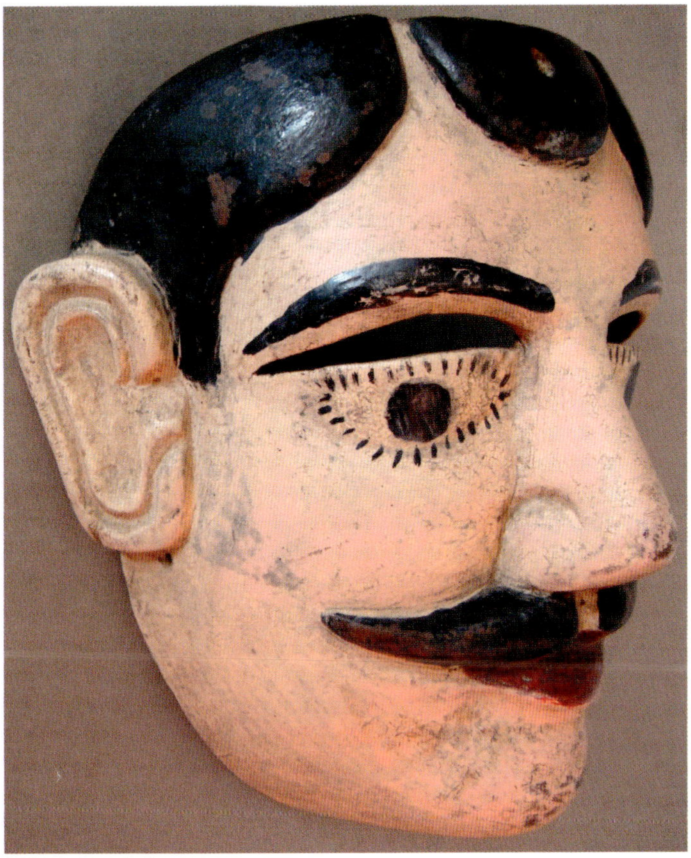

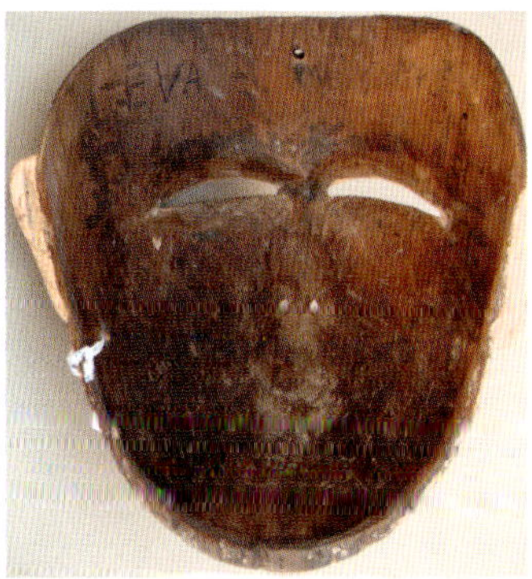

Top: According to the history provided by the son of the carver, this beautiful male Tejonero mask by Celestino is about 90 years old; 6¾" × 7". Circa 1920. The ear design is particularly distinctive. Rating: known carver, excellent condition, very well carved, excellent patina, and rare, ******. *Collection of Vernon Kostohryz, who supplied the photos of this mask.*

Bottom: The back of this mask shows extreme wear/great patina.

José Gonzáles Galindo and José González Diaz

José González Galindo was born on August 31, 1935. He lives in Coxquihui, Veracruz, where he operates a small grocery store. He carves masks and saints in a workshop behind the store. In contrast to some carvers who have taken pains to develop an individual style, José appears to be more of a generalist, someone who feels free to use any model that his customer might request, and for whom the carving of saints seems nearly as important as the carving of masks. Indeed, he told me that there are several full-sized saints in the Coxquihui church that he had carved. I can report that they were very well carved. A number of smaller saints were displayed in his store; these were adequately carved but fell below the quality of those in the church. I have included some of these.

José's Tejonero masks frequently appear to be modeled on those of Benito Juárez, but also on those of Manuel Pérez and probably others, I have seen Payaso masks by José that were modeled on the clown masks of Don Lillo. I have seen a Santiago horse and a Sun shield from the Santiagueros dance that were reportedly carved by José but were clearly modeled on examples by Benito Juárez. Nevertheless, after one has seen a number of carvings by José González Galindo it becomes more apparent that he usually adds his own stylistic details to these objects, so that often one can see at a glance that they are his, and not the product of the carver who provided the model. In this way one gradually discovers the depth of his skills and sees that he is so adept at borrowing the work of other masters from prior generations. Some of his interpretations were so excellent that I struggled for years to decide whether they were by this carver or by the carver of the model. Only recently, as I built up a study collection of really good examples of José's work, have I come to appreciate the degree of his skills. One way to think of this carver is to notice that almost every other excellent carver known to him has at one time or another provided a model for José to use. This leads one to repetitive experiences of being taken by surprise and then saying to oneself, fooled again. The most unexpected example of this was a Viejo or Pilato mask that I saw on a masked dancer in Huehuetla, Puebla, in 2006. In 2010 one of the members of that Voladores group informed Carlos Moreno Vásquez that this was yet another mask by José González Galindo. It greatly resembles a similar mask in this book that was carved by Roberto Villegas Santiago.

Some of José's Perro masks for the Tejoneros dance have the appearance of black panthers; others look more like dogs. In general the Perro masks of this border region (Puebla/Veracruz) tend to be more catlike than canine. They may resemble jaguars but usually they are called Perros.

All these masks are rather attractive, and one finds them in common use in the Coxquihui area and far beyond. I have seen a number of Negrito masks carved by José for use in the Lakapfjkuyu dance. These have probably been modeled on those of Benito Juárez, but although more simple in form, they are very beautiful.

In December 2010, Carlos Moreno Vásquez and I visited the family of Amalia Luna Gaona in Coxquihui, Veracruz. There we found an older dance horse of the type that is worn by Santiago Apóstol in the Santiagueros dance, along with two wooden crosses to be carried by Santiago, a Santiaguero mask, and the wooden shield carried by Captain Sabario in that dance. All these things were said to have been carved by José González Galindo. This is the only dance horse known to me that has been attributed to José, so I was very pleased to see it.

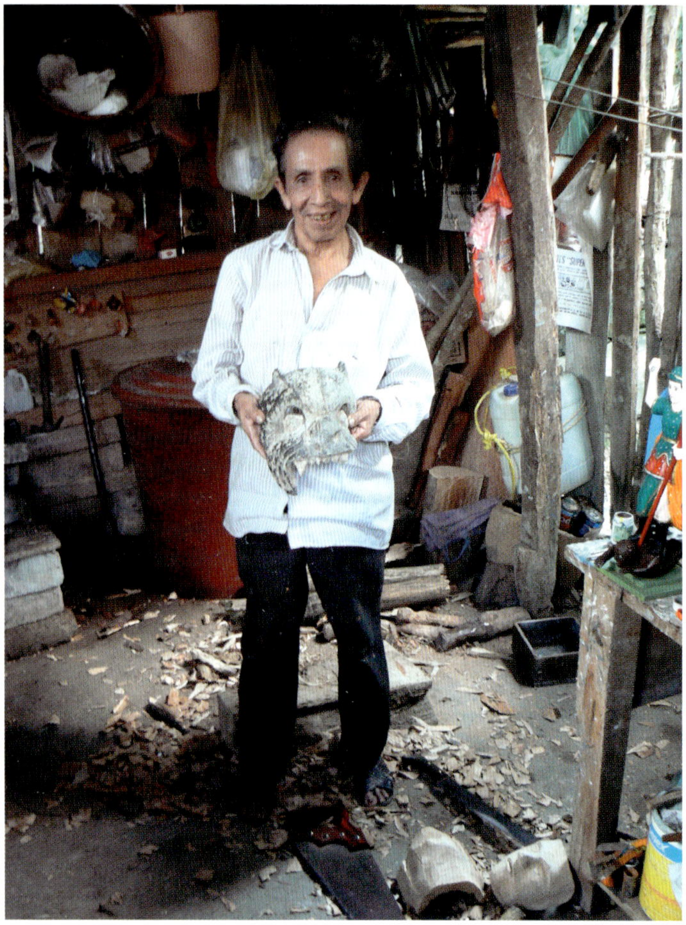

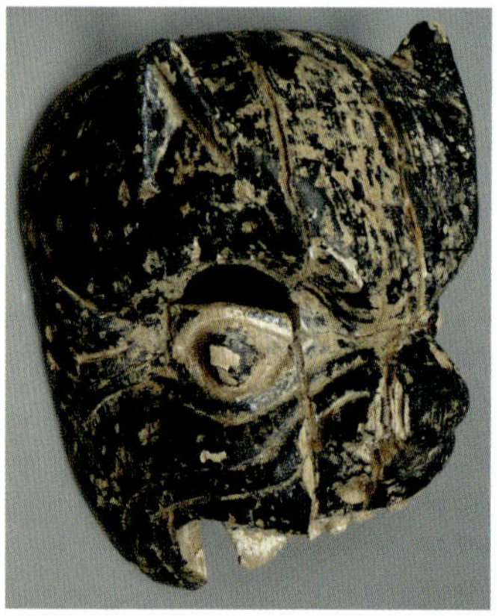

Far left: José González Galindo standing in his workshop in December 2006. He is holding a damaged *Perro* (dog) mask from the Danza de los Tejoneros. On a table to the viewer's right there is a Santo of San Miguel Archangel; at his feet are masks that are only partly carved.

Left: The damaged Perro mask fragment in the previous photo; 8" × 10". I don't know whether Don José was the carver of this mask, but clearly he kept it as a model. One can see that the mask was very well carved; it must have been beautiful when it was intact. Not rated. *Collection of the author.*

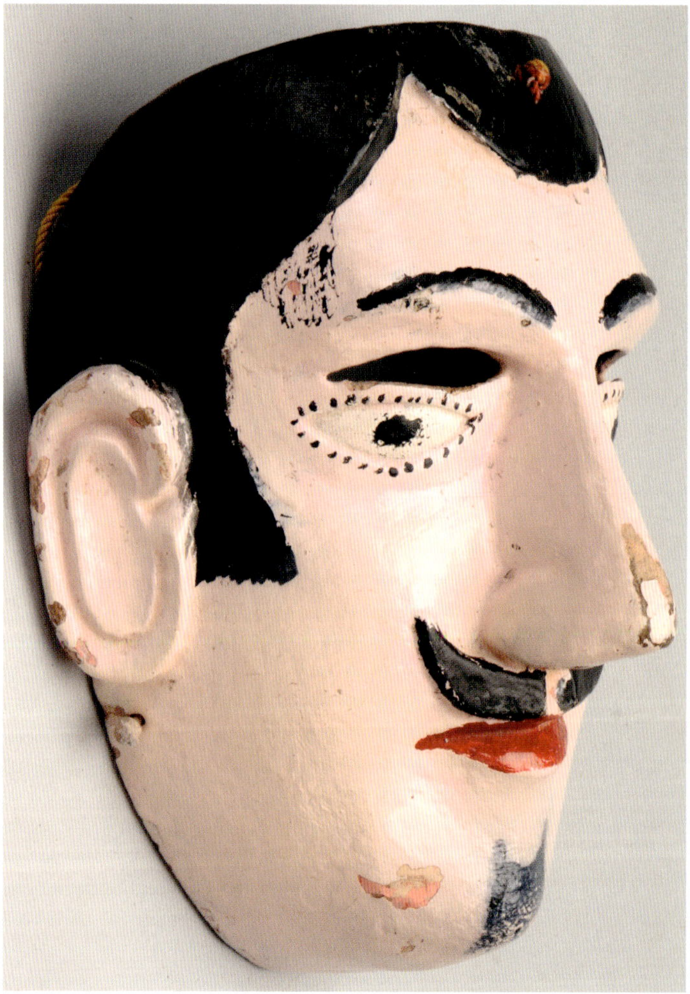

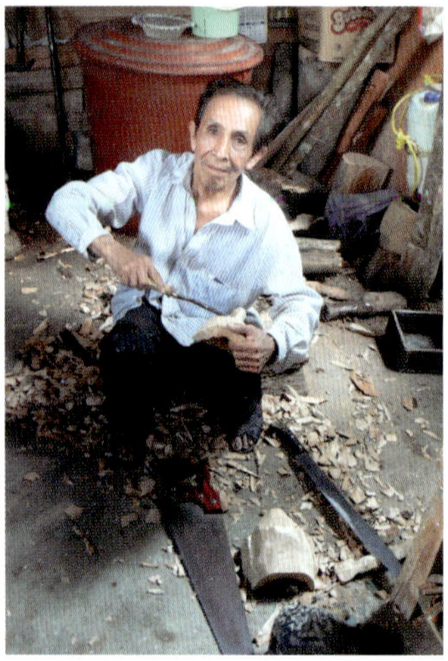

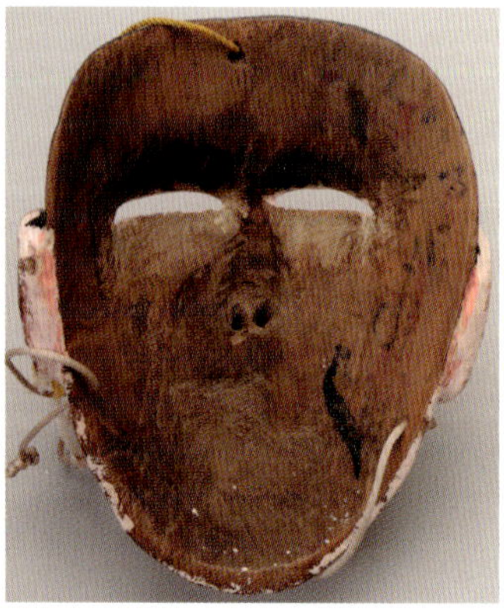

Above: This male Tejonero mask and a female to appear later were collected in Sabanas de Xalostoc, Veracruz, in December 2007; 6½" × 7½". Circa 1980. The seller said that they were carved by José González Galindo. This is a good example of a body of masks carved by José that seem to be modeled on the masks of Benito Juárez. However, José was much more likely than Benito to carve the eyes in relief; usually they look just like this. The ear design resembles that of Benito Juárez, but it has been simplified by José. One often sees him carve this ear design. Rating: known carver, good condition, well carved, worn paint on the face with good patina on the back, and rarity unknown, ****. *Collection of the author.*

Above left: The back of this mask shows considerable wear. There is some variation in the way José carves the backs of his masks; this one is very simply carved and quite smooth. This back would never be confused with one carved by Benito Juárez.

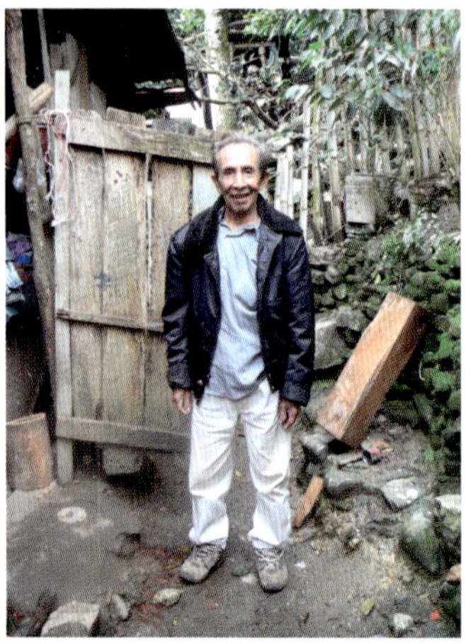

Top left: José demonstrated the carving of a mask in December 2006. Here he is either squatting or sitting on a low stool. Whenever I would ask a carver to demonstrate his manner of carving, this proved to be the preferred position. Note the machete, used to rough carve a mask, and the wooden mallet next to José's left elbow, used to strike the head of the chisel during the carving.

Left: The carver standing outside his workshop in March 2010.

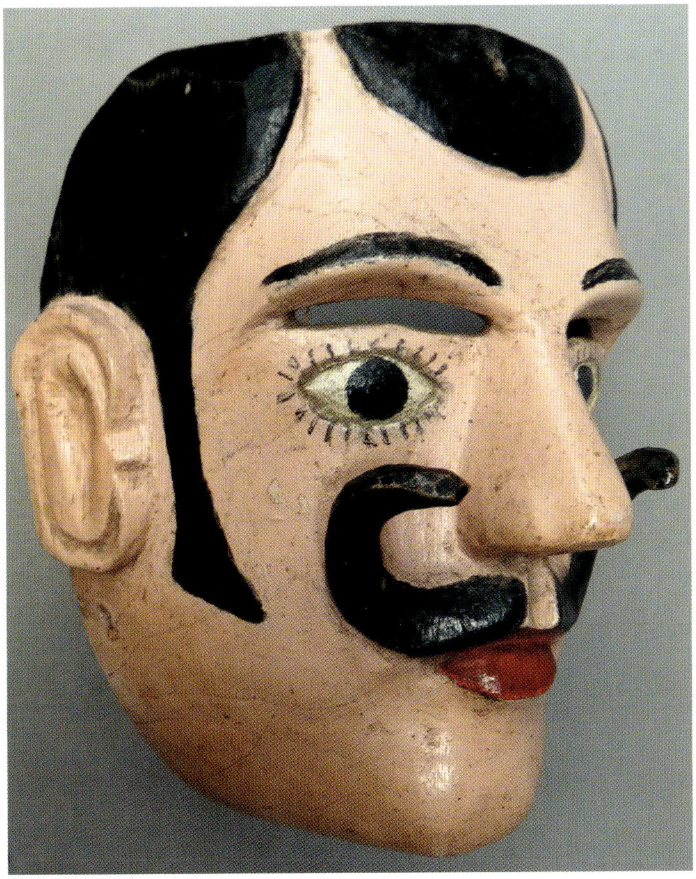

This male Tejonero mask was purchased from Manuel Aristeo Gómez, a friendly, elderly gentleman in Coxquihui, Veracruz; 6¼" × 7". Circa 1980. Due to age and associated infirmity he is generally confined to bed, so he can no longer dance. He reported that he obtained this mask and the next directly from José González Galindo, 30 years earlier, and that he had danced these masks for many years. We see a mask that has been modeled on one by Manuel Pérez; the elaborate mustache is the indicator of this. You will observe a similar mask in the section about Manuel Pérez in this chapter. There is another ear design on this mask, one that I particularly associate with José González Galindo. You will see this design again on several masks that follow; let's call it Galindo Type 1. Rating: known carver, good condition, very well carved, good paint on the face with moderate patina on the back, and rare in this form and condition, *****. *Collection of the author.*

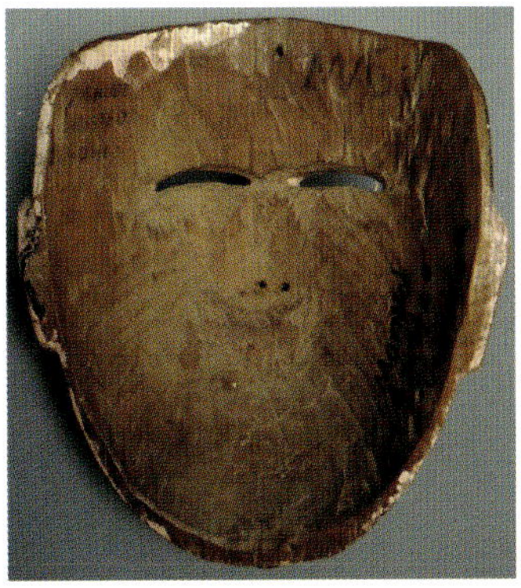

On the back we see moderate wear. A recess has been carved for the nose; notice that this was so successful in providing space for the nose that this area has little patina.

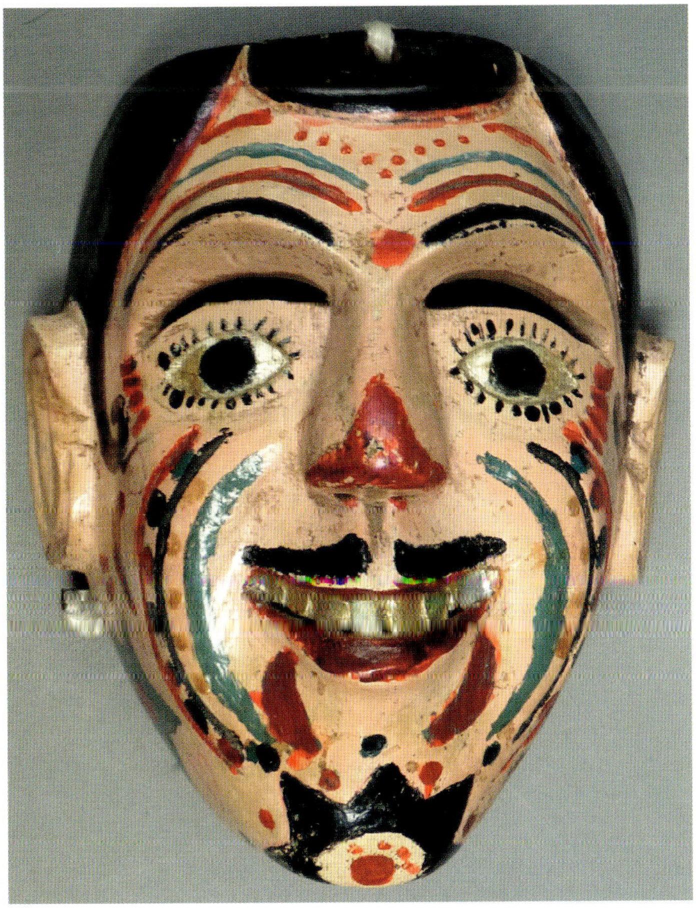

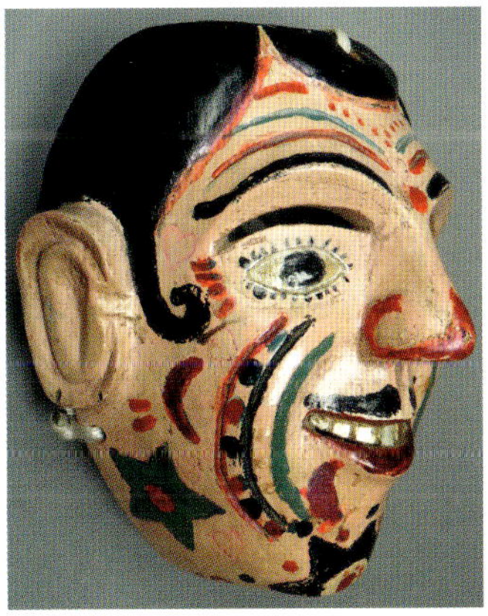

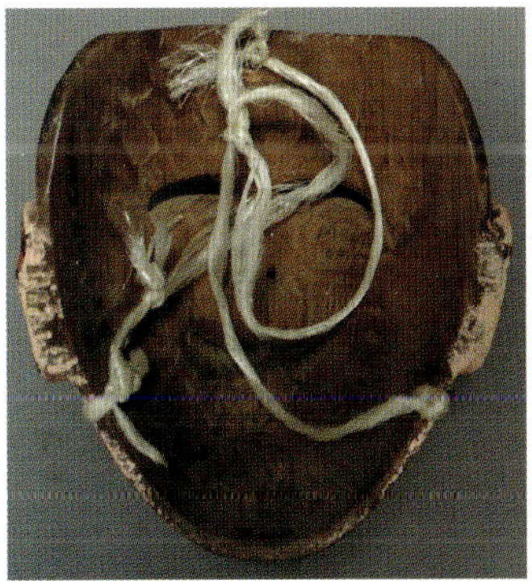

Left: The second mask from the gentleman in Coxquihui, Veracruz; 6½" × 7". Circa 1980. Here we see a Payaso that appears to have been modeled on a design I associate with Don Lillo (Manuel Aldana Valencia). You have seen several of those masks earlier in the section about him. This mask is attractive and vividly decorated. Rating: known carver, good condition, well carved, beautiful old worn paint on the face with excellent patina on the back, and rare in this form and condition, *****. *Collection of the author.*

Above left: The side view reveals this ear design that marks some of José's masks.

Above right: The back view. The patina is better than in the photograph.

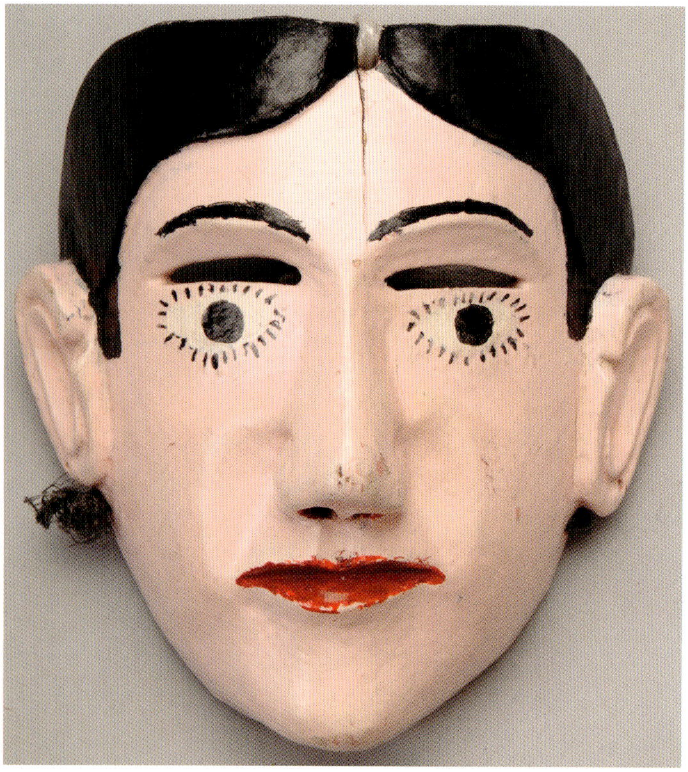

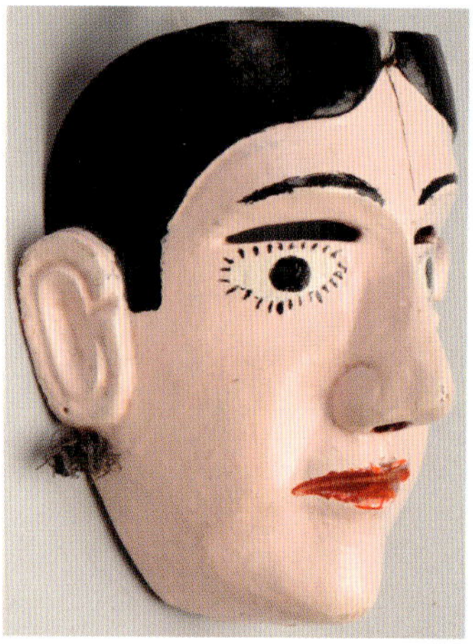

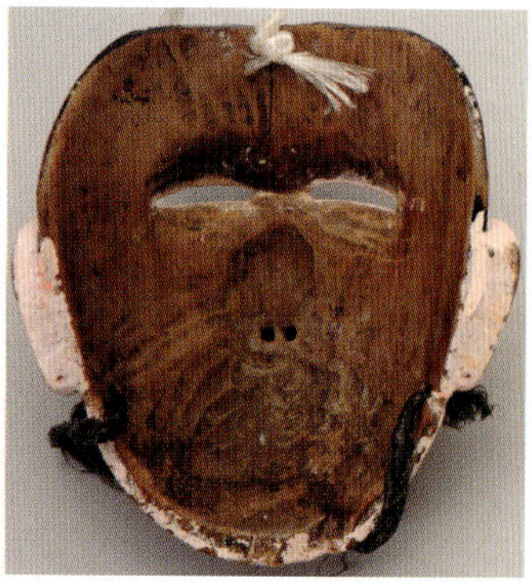

Left: A female mask that was collected in Sabanas de Xalostoc, Veracruz, along with the male mask shown earlier, in December 2007; 6½" × 7". Circa 1980. This mask is interesting due to the dramatic hollowing of the face above the mouth. This mask is very nicely shaped. Rating: known carver, good condition, well carved, very good patina, and rarity unknown, ****½. *Collection of the author.*

Above left: The side of this mask. We see another ear based on the design of Benito Juárez.

Above right: Notice the beautiful patina on the back of this mask. There is a hollow carved for the nose, but there is no shelf at chin level.

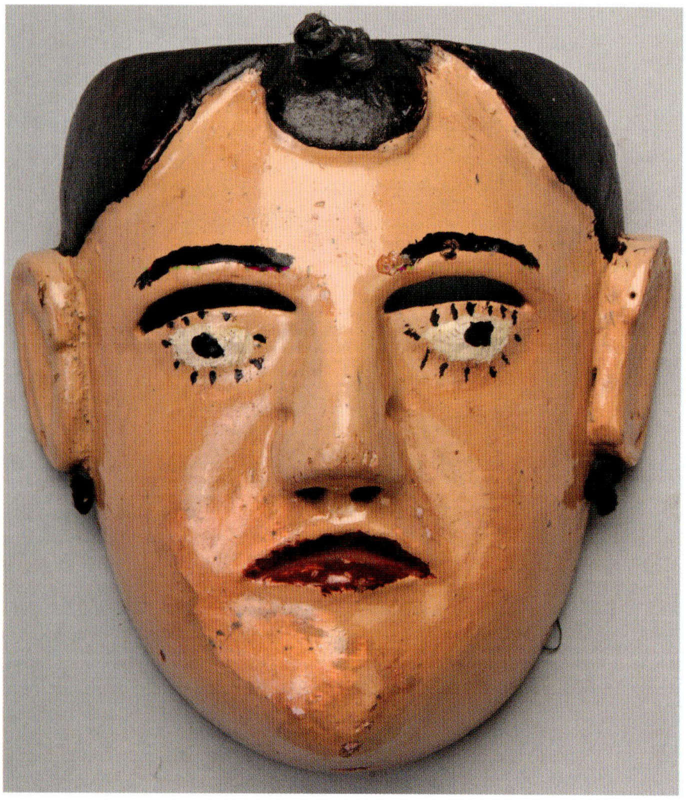

This mask had always been a mystery; 6" × 6". Circa 1970. The face is well carved, the back demonstrates marked patina, but the hairline is odd. The major barrier to the identification of the carver resulted from applied ears of a nondescript design. This mask would have to remain forever anonymous but for the combination of hollow cheeks and a sweet mouth, permitting me to see the hand of José González Galindo. Comparing this mask to the previous female, their great resemblance is evident; the noses are also identical. Ironically, this one is older. Rating: known carver, excellent condition, well carved, excellent patina, and of unknown rarity, *****. *Collection of the author.*

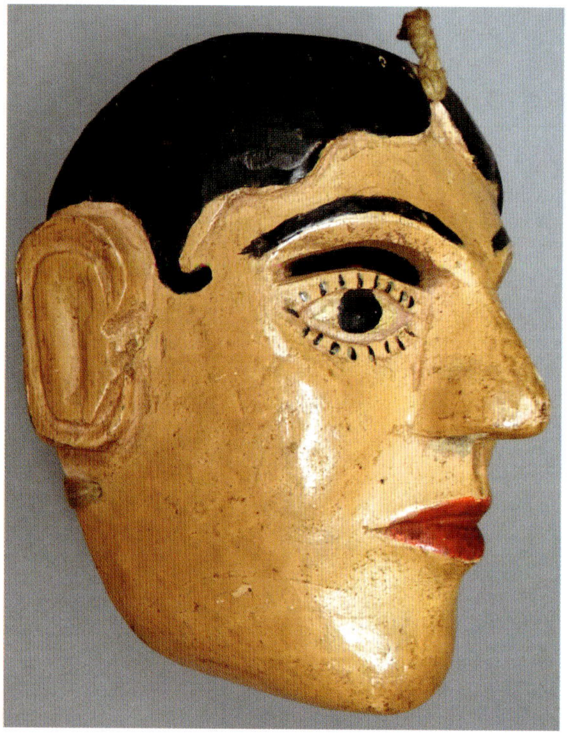

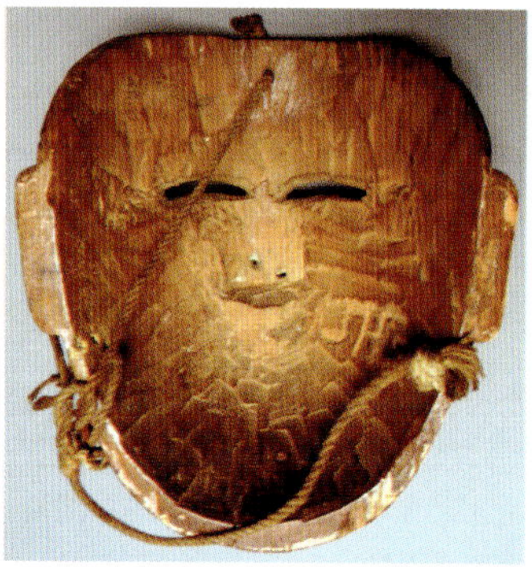

Above: This attractive female mask has an elaborate hairline; 6½" × 7". Circa 1980. There are relief-carved eyes in this carver's style. Observe the Galindo Type 1 ear design. Rating: known carver, good condition, well carved, beautiful worn paint on the face with dramatic patina on the back, rarity unknown, *****. *Collection of the author.*

Left: On the back we see beautiful old patina.

Nearby we met Don Mateo Espinosa Pérez, who said that he was 108 years old. He showed us an old Diablo mask that he had owned for 60 years, carved by José González Galindo.

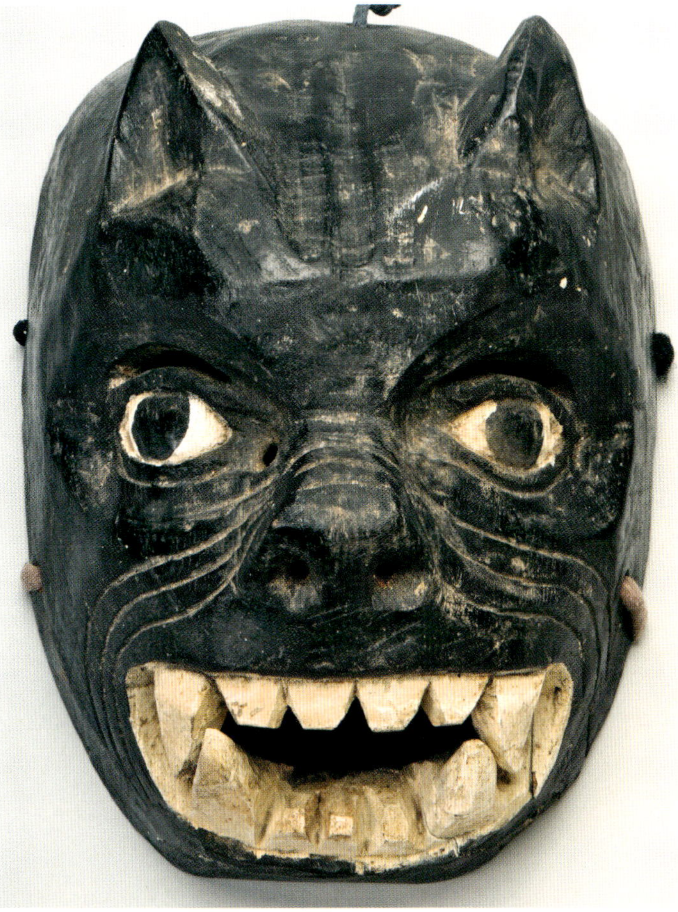

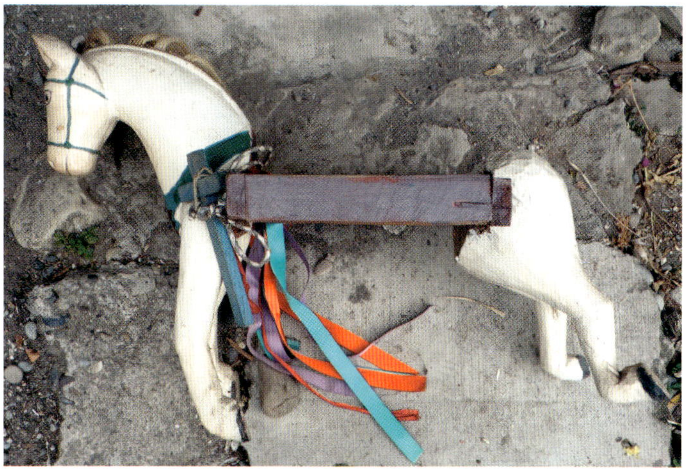

The Santiago's horse owned by Amalia Luna Gaona; length 36". Circa 1980. The front and rear halves of the horse are well carved, but the parts are connected in a manner that suggests a history of damage and informal repairs. The small wooden cross that Santiago carries in his hand is hanging on the frame. One very typical feature of this horse is the construction of the mane using bundles of horsehair that are inserted in a line of holes on the neck. Rating: known carver, the major elements are in good condition (the frame or hoop could be easily restored), well carved, good patina, and rare, ******. *Collection of the family.*

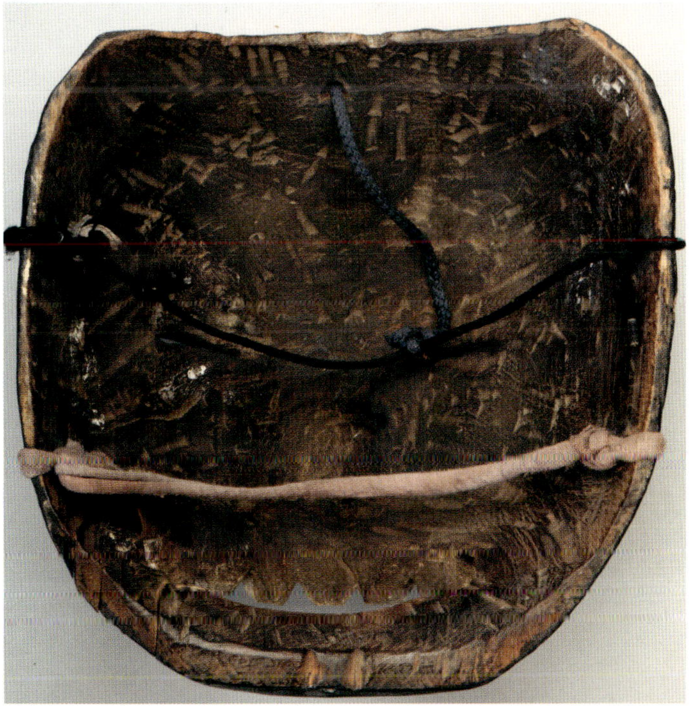

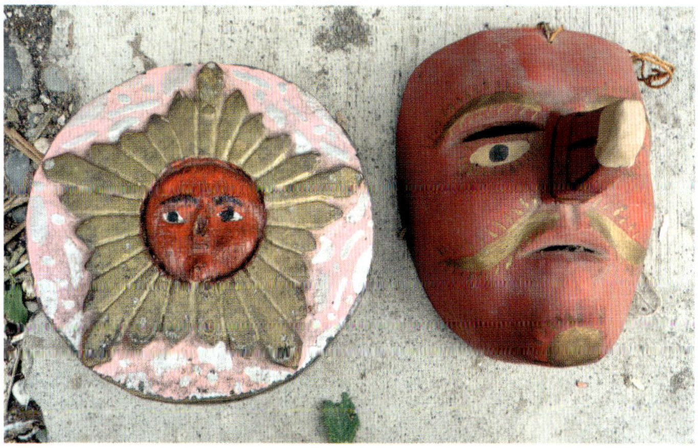

Top: A black Perro mask by José González Galindo, apparently modeled on the damaged fragment you saw earlier; 8" × 10". Circa 1990. In comparison to that mask, this one is intact after being danced for a number of years. Rating: known carver, good condition, well carved, good patina, and rarity unknown, ****. *Collection of the author.*

Bottom: The back view of the Perro mask demonstrates apparent artificial darkening. This does not look like normal patina.

A Santiaguero mask along with the shield that is carried by Captain Sabario as the leader of the Santiagueros, both from the household of Amalia Luna Gaona. The design of the shield resembles that of a shield carved by Benito Juárez for the Hormegas dance (see Chapter 4). It is attractive, worn, and very rare. The Santiaguero mask appears to be modeled on the design used by Don Lillo (Manuel Aldana Valencia).

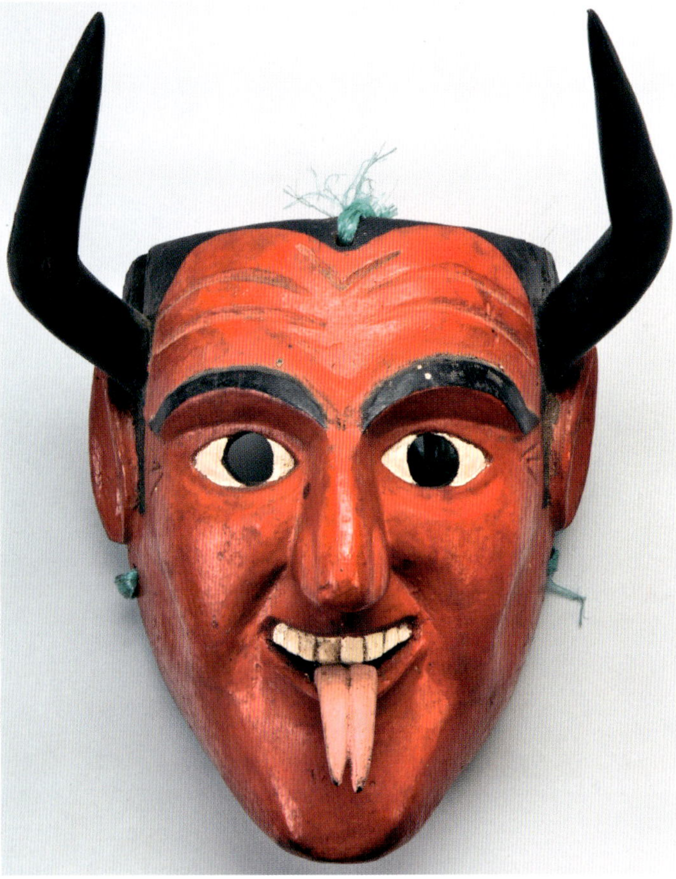

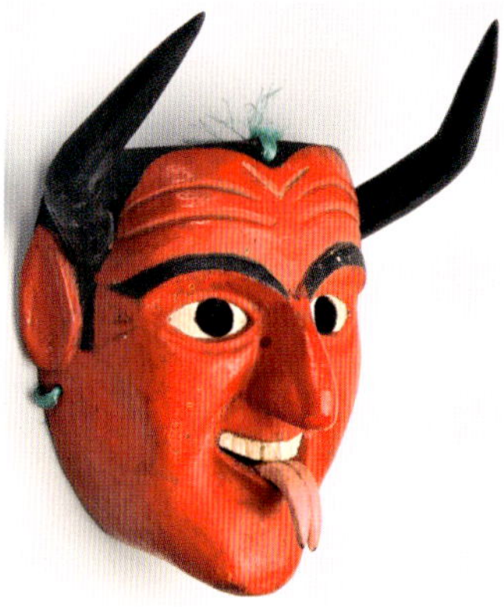

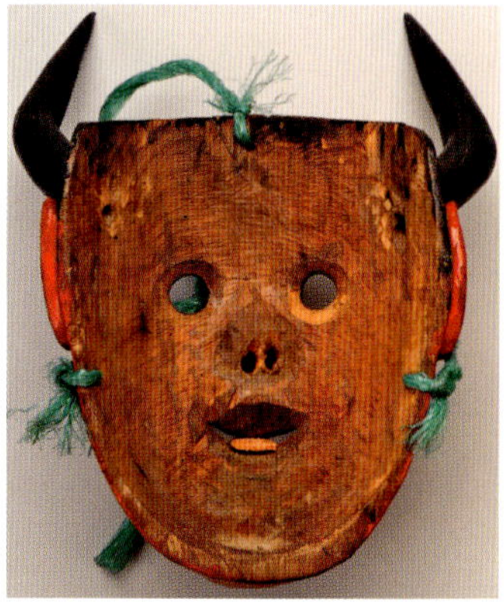

Left: An old Diablo mask; 8" × 10". Circa 1950. The former owner, Don Mateo Espinosa Pérez, stated that this mask was carved by José González Galindo, 60 years earlier. Rating: known carver, excellent condition, well carved, good patina, and rare, ******. *Collection of the author.*

Above left: The side view of this mask, showing the hollow cheek of the devil's face as created by José.

Above right: The back of this mask with less dark patina than expected, given the dancer's history. Some dancers routinely wipe the sweat from the mask, reducing the accumulation of patina.

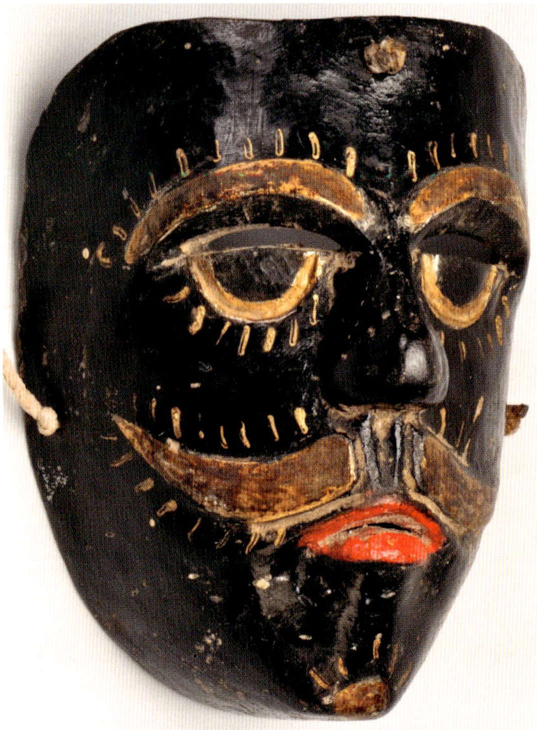

Above: The Lakapijkuyu Dance, which is performed just before Christmas, and only in the area around Coxquihui, Veracruz, has male and female characters, but only the males wear masks. Those dressed as females are veiled instead. This beautiful old mask is an example of those worn by the male characters; 5½" × 6½". Circa 1980. Although it looks like a Negrito mask, it is said to symbolically represent the face of one of the piskuyo birds that, in local legend, comforted and shielded the infant Jesus when he lay in the manger. Rating: known carver, excellent condition, well carved, good patina, and uncommon, *****. *Collection of the author.*

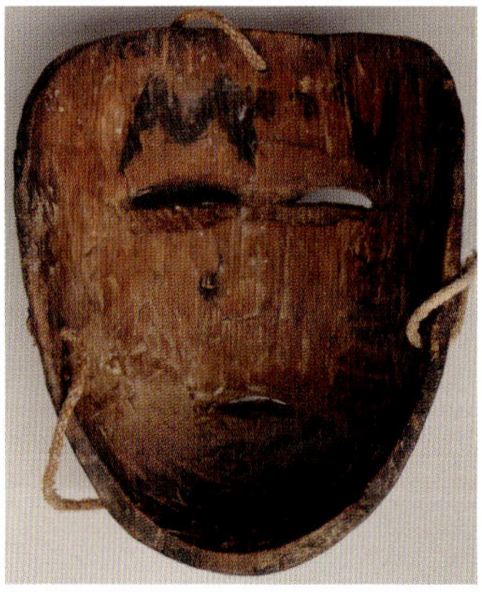

Right: The back of this mask has very nice patina.

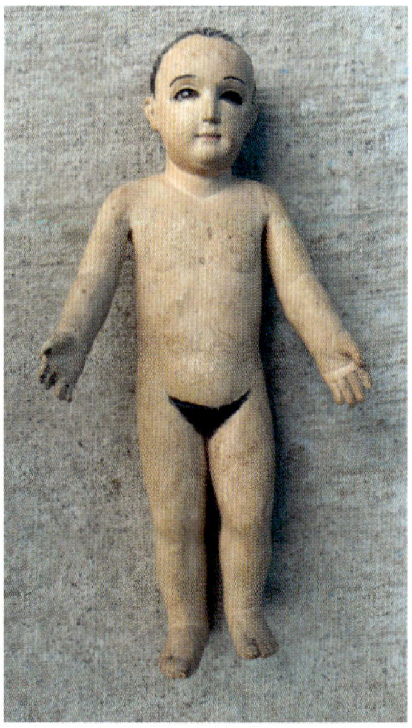

Left: A Santo Niño figure of the infant Jesus that was carved by José González Galindo many years ago and which remains a part of the carver's home altar; 14". Circa 1970. A carving like this, where José has carefully made an object for his own use, provides the best demonstration of his great talent. Unrated.

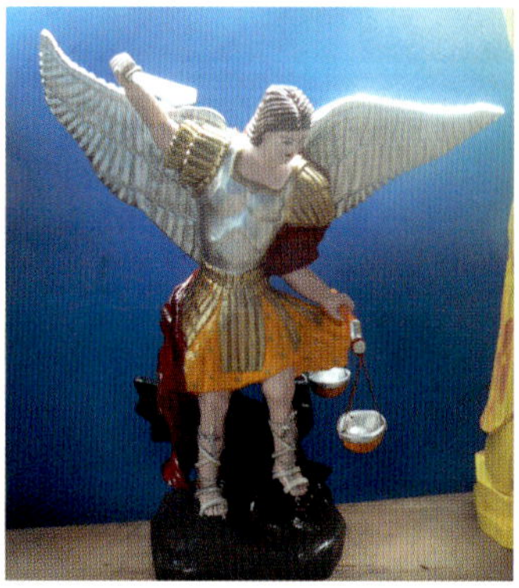

A carved Santo representing San Miguel Archangel, carved by José González Galindo. This Santo is dramatically different from the one glimpsed in an earlier photo and was recently carved. As you can see, it is very attractive. *Collection of José González Galindo.*

Visiting Coxquihui recently, I met José González Diaz, who is the son of José González Galindo. He too has been carving very nice Tejonero masks. Like his father, José González Diaz is also carving from a number of models. Some of his Tejonero masks have very remarkable ears, and I have obtained an older mask by an unknown carver that would appear to be the model for those ears. Yet other Tejonero masks by José González Diaz have a different ear. Anyway I am very impressed by the carving skills that this young man is demonstrating. He is also carving saints.

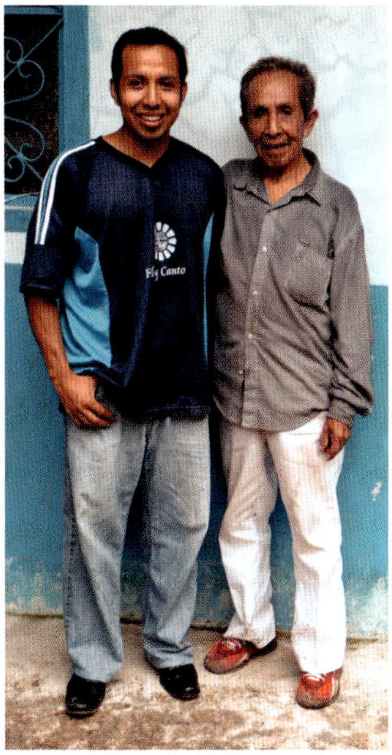

José González Galindo and his son, José González Diaz, outside their home in December 2010.

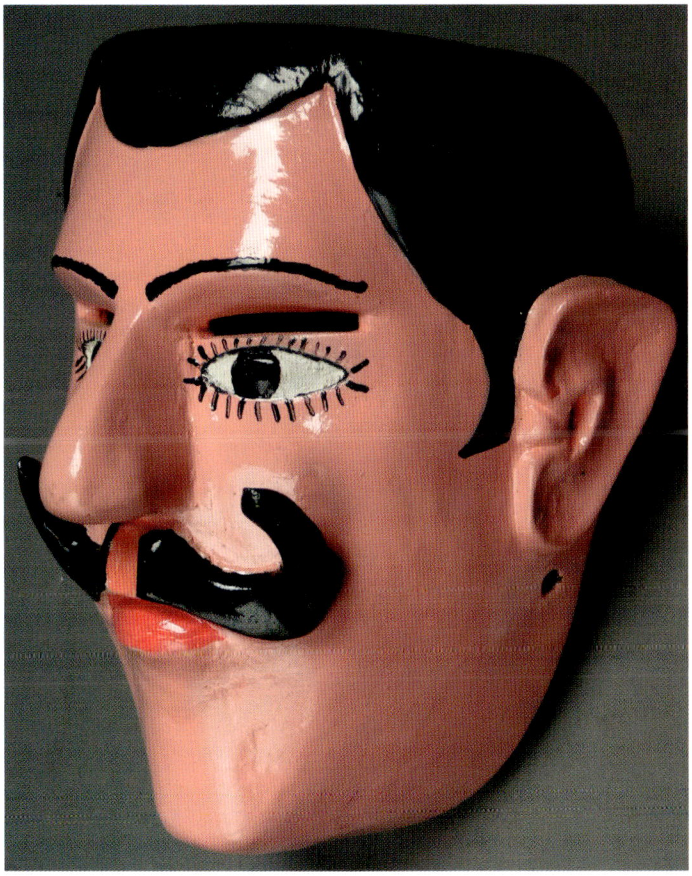

A mask by José González Diaz. It is very well carved; 6 3/8" × 7". 2010. Note the elaborate ear design. Rating: known carver, good condition, well carved, undanced, and not rare, ***. *Collection of the author.*

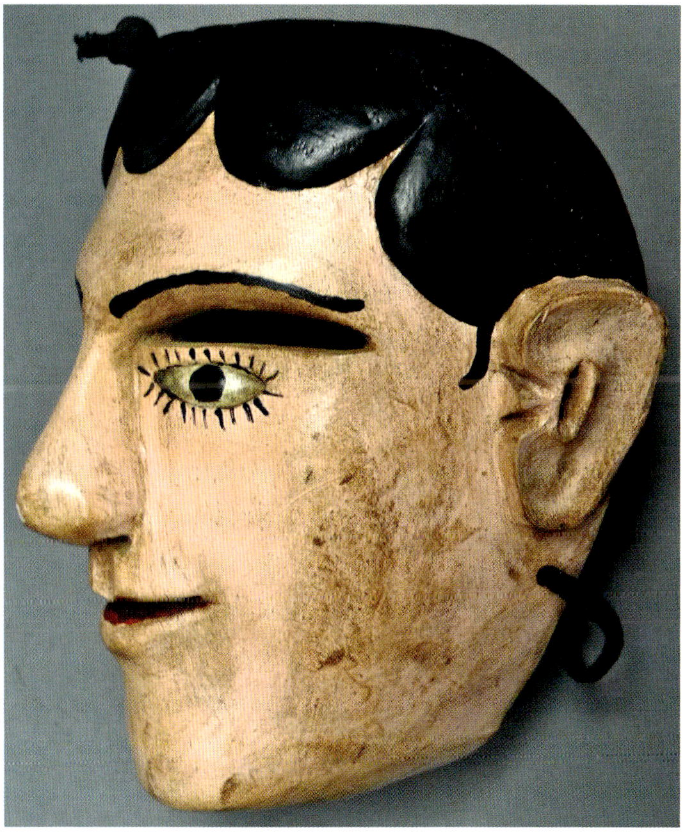

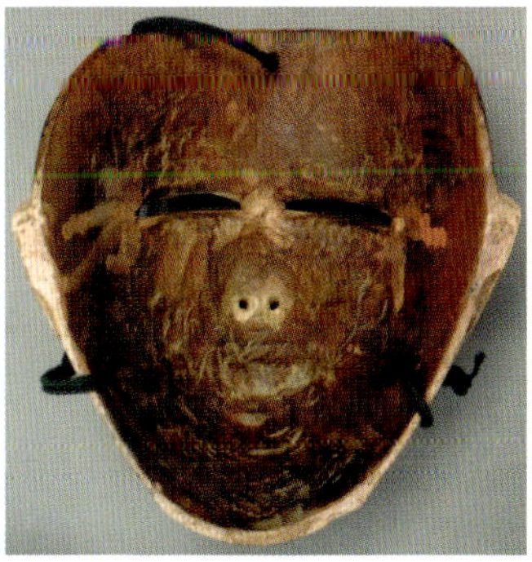

Above: A mask by an as yet unidentified carver; 6" × 6 ¼". Circa 1980. José González Diaz is currently carving masks with this ear design. I doubt that he has been carving long enough to have carved this mask. It does seem likely that a mask by this carver has served as a model for the elaborate ears on his new masks. Rating: unknown carver, good condition, well carved, good patina, and rarity unknown, ****. *Collection of the author.*

Left: The back view.

José González Hernández

José González Hernández was born on April 8, 1951. He lives in Comunidad Morelos, in the Municipio of Coxquihui, Veracruz.

José has produced a number of exciting, beautiful, and interesting masks. These can be very well carved. At his best, he appears to be a wonderful master carver, among the most talented we have seen in this region. However, he will sometimes carve to a lower standard; his work is uneven. I wouldn't have mentioned this, but for the fact that I am willing to praise his best work so highly. When we visited him in March of 2010, he had carved two new Oso (bear) masks for the Lakakgolo Dance, both exceptional.

The human-faced masks carved by José González Hernández for the Lakakgolo dance resemble the viejito masks that he carves for the Danza del Matarachín. However, they differ in scale; the viejito masks are about 1" larger than those masks made to dance with the Oso. The viejito masks would also be highly appropriate for Carnaval, as they depict demonios, who represent the dead.

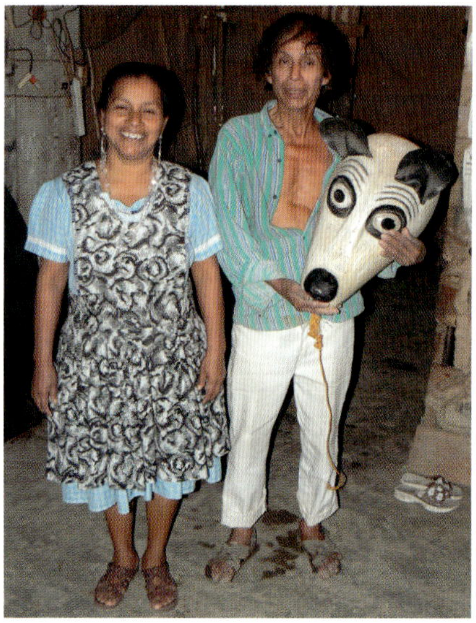

José Gonzales Hernández and his wife in their house in December 2008. José is holding a white *Oso* (bear) mask used in the Lakakgolo dance. Rating: known carver, excellent condition, very well carved, normal patina, and not rare, ****. *Collection of Vernon Kostohryz. Courtesy of José González Hernández.*

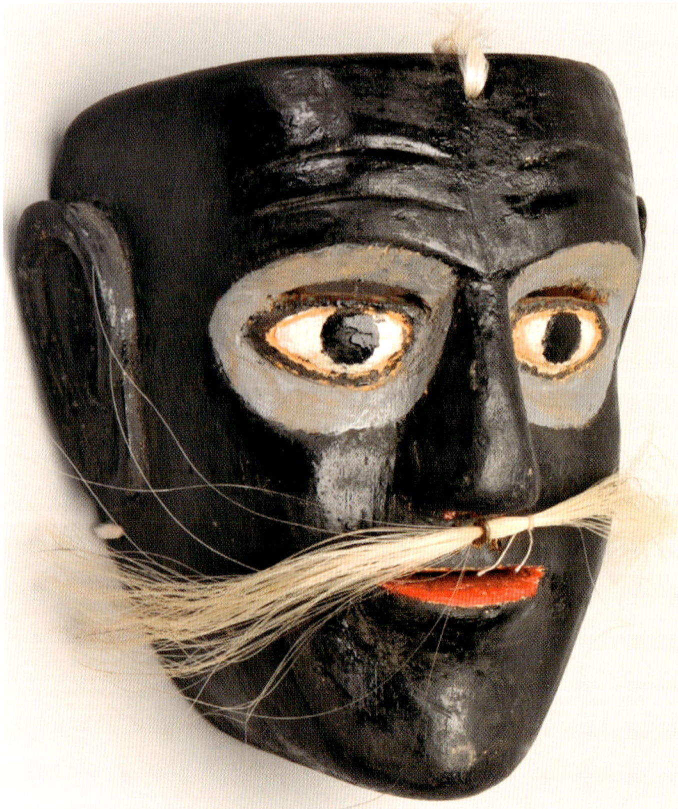

A black Viejo mask that dances with the Oso mask in the Lakakgolo dance; 7½" × 7½". Circa 2000. Average carving and mild wear. Purchased from the carver in March 2010. (Frontal view on page 81.) Rating: known carver, excellent condition, average carving, mild patina, and not rare, ***. *Collection of the author.*

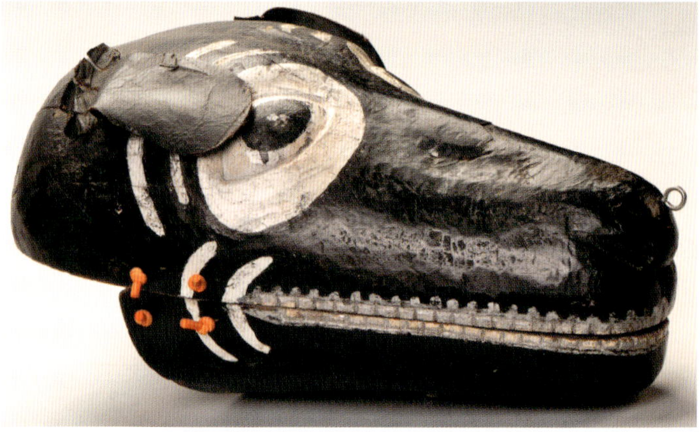

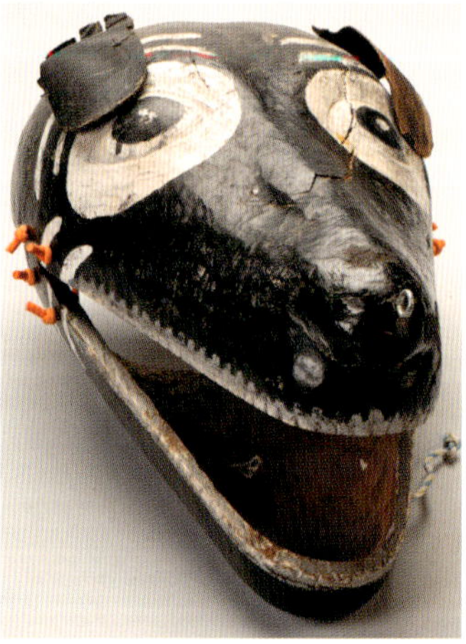

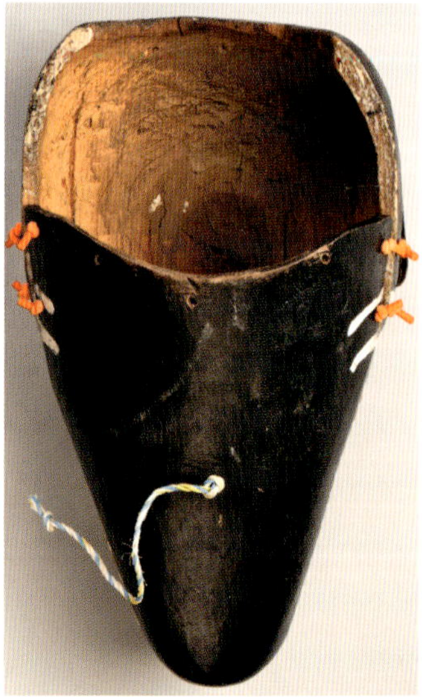

Top: An Oso mask of a black bear purchased from the carver in 2005. Note the ring in the nose for another dancer to lead the bear with a rope. The jaw opens and closes if the wearer pulls on a string under the lower jaw; 11" × 19". Circa 1990. Rating: known carver, excellent condition, very well carved, good patina, and not rare, *****. *Collection of the author.*

Above left: The frontal view of the black Oso mask with the jaw open.

Above right: A view of the black Oso mask from underneath, with the cord to clack the jaw.

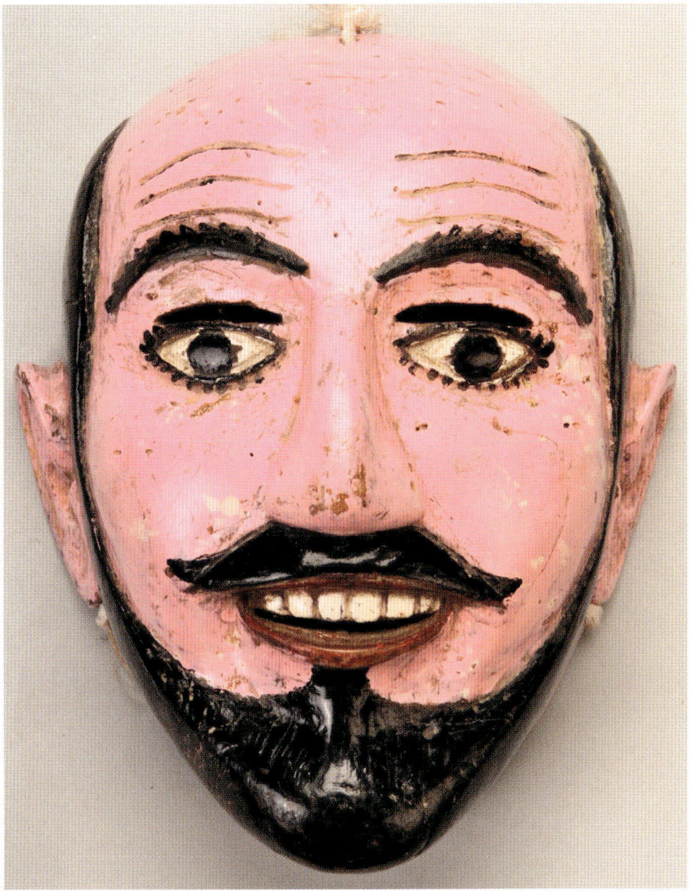

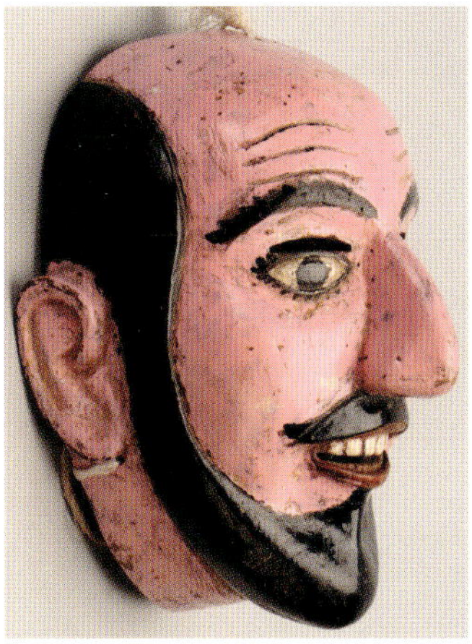

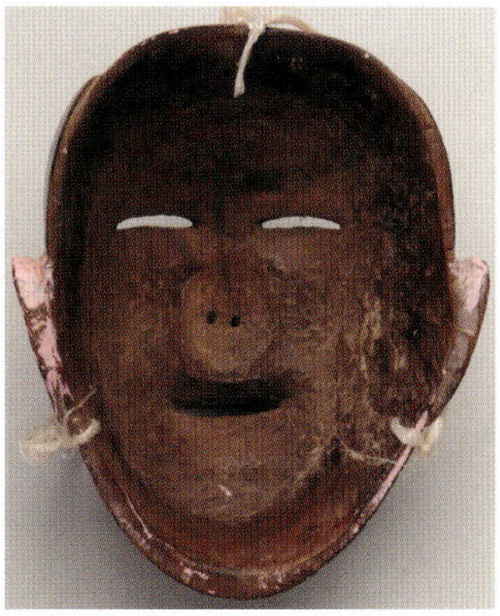

Left: A bearded pink-faced viejito for the Dance of El Matarachín or for Carnaval, purchased from carver in 2005; 7½" × 8¾". Circa 1980. This mask is very finely carved. Rating: known carver, excellent condition, very well carved, excellent patina, and rare with this age and quality, ******. *Collection of the author.*

Above left: The side view showing more details of the carving and the ear design.

Above right: The beautiful old worn back of this mask.

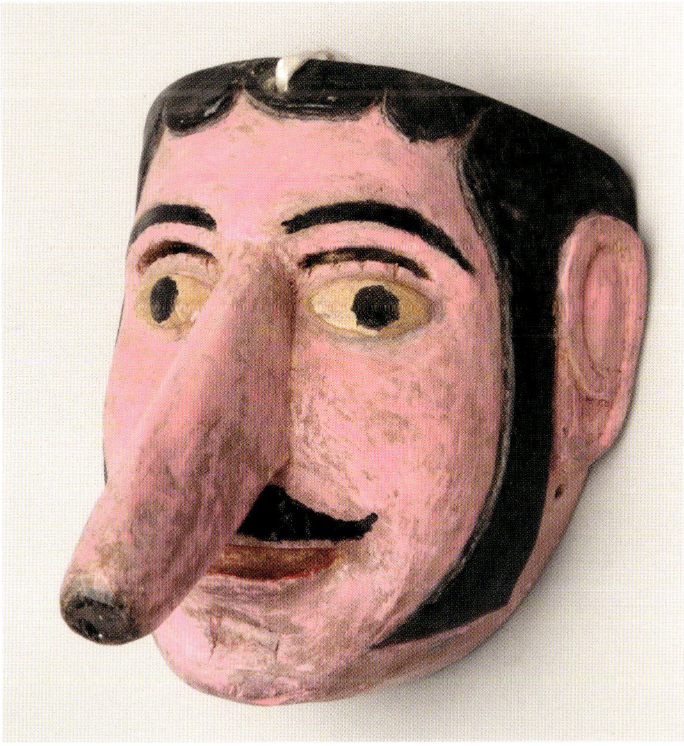

Another Viejito by José González Hernández for the Dance of El Matarachín or for Carnaval, purchased from carver in 2008; 6¾" × 7". Circa 1990. Rating: known carver, excellent condition, novel design but average carving, mild patina, and not rare, ***½. *Collection of the author.*

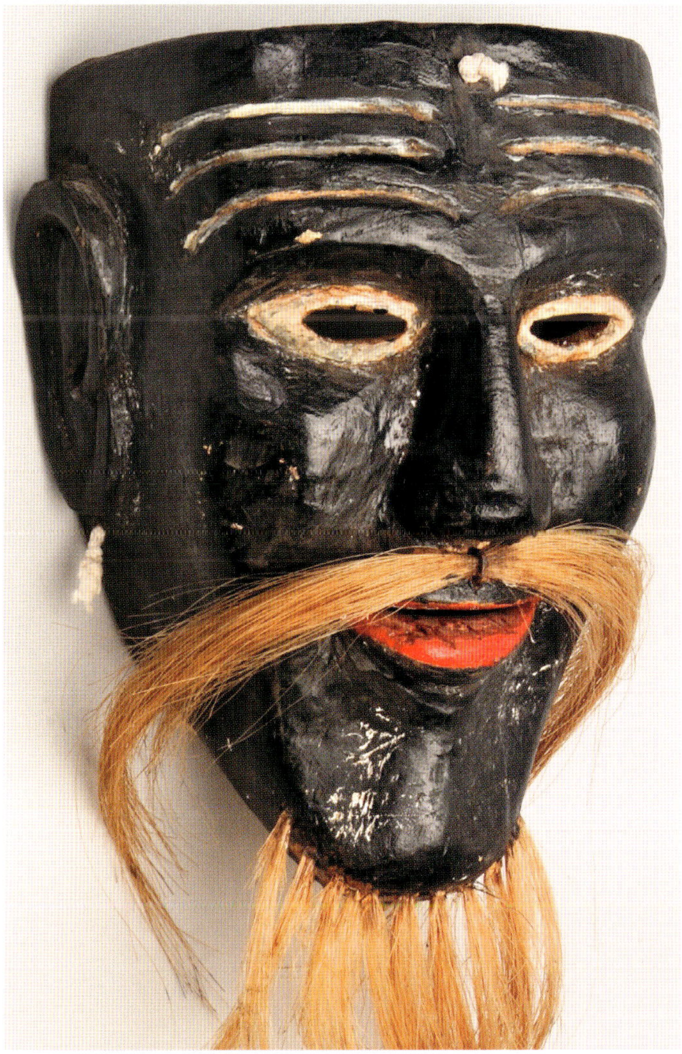

Viejito Lorenzo for the Dance of El Matarachín or for Carnaval, purchased from carver in 2005; 7½" × 9" plus beard. Circa 1980. Although less finely carved, this mask still has age and charisma. Rating: known carver, excellent condition, well carved, great patina, and not rare, *****. *Collection of the author.*

Germán Guerrero

Germán Guerrero lives in Tuzamapan, Puebla, but recently he has been working in Mexico City. Germán is not actually a carver of masks. Rather he constructs and decorates wooden boxes that are meant to contain and protect the puppets that are used in the Huehues or Tejoneros dance. For several years we were aware that there was an artist in this area who was making such boxes; only in the last year did we discover his identity. In this section I'll simply show the front panel of the first box of his that we discovered. In the chapter on Puppets I'll show the entire box.

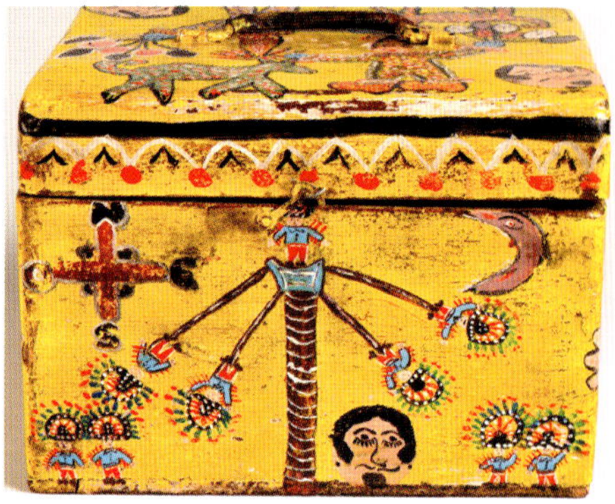

This was the first painted box by Germán that came to our attention; 8" × 10" × 10" deep. Circa 1990.

Miguel Hernández

Miguel Hernández apparently lived in the area of Ahuacatlán, Puebla. He is said to have died about 40 years ago. Vernon learned of this carver through a single mask, which he subsequently chose to have repainted because the old paint was in such bad condition. He had another old mask repainted at the same time. To our surprise the two masks looked suddenly similar to one another, although there is some difference in the ears. The carving of the backs of the two masks is fairly similar, to reinforce the idea that they might both be by the same carver.

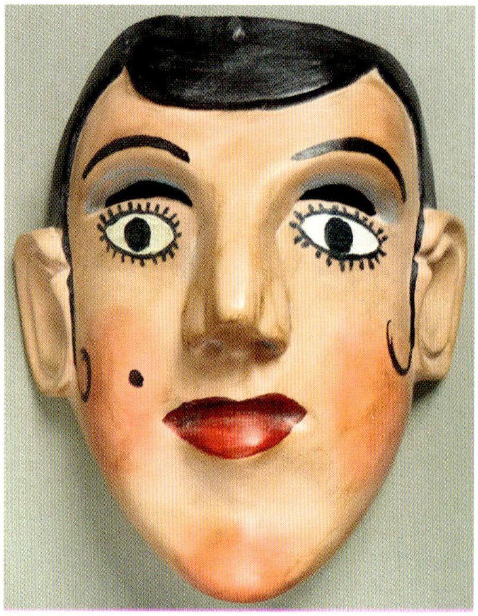

This is a female Huehue mask by Miguel Hernández; 6½" × 7¼". Circa 1960. It is well carved. It has been newly repainted. Rating: known carver, excellent condition, well carved, newly painted with mild patina on back, and unknown rarity, ***½. *Collection of Vernon Kostohryz.*

Francisco Hernández Ramos

Francisco Hernández Ramos lives in Hueytlalpan, Puebla. We discovered him just as the book was being completed; so far we have seen only one mask that was definitely carved by Francisco, a *Toro* (bull) for the Danza de los Toreadores. He seems friendly and we look forward to learning more about him and his masks.

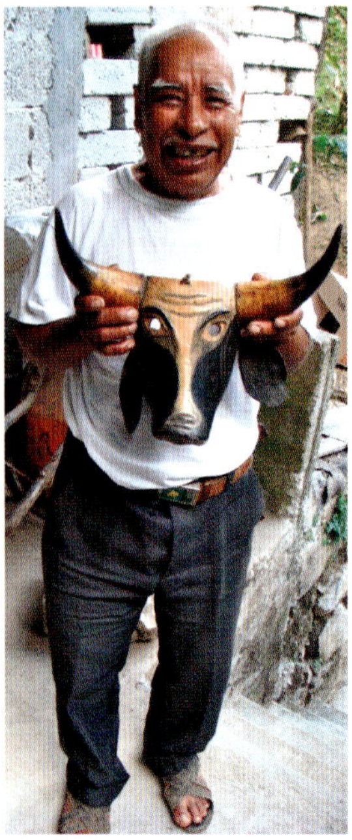

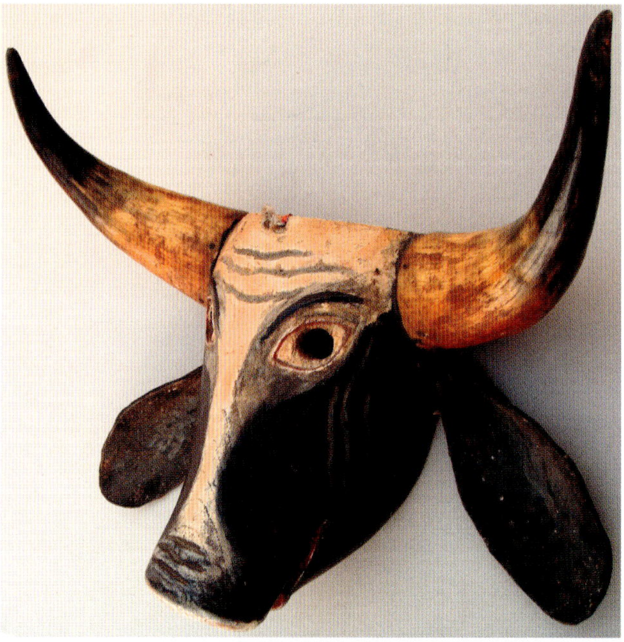

Far left: Francisco Hernández Ramos holding his Toro mask. *Photo by Vernon Kostohryz.*

Left: A Toro mask for the dance of the Toreros or Toreadores, carved by Francisco Hernández Ramos; 9" × 11". Circa 1990. Rating: known carver, excellent condition, well carved, excellent patina, and rarity unknown, ****. *Collection of the author. Photo by Vernon Kostohryz.*

Pablo Huerta Mora

Pablo Huerta Mora, the brother of Pedro Huerta Mora, was born on June 29, 1927. He continues to live in Cuetzalan, Puebla. Pablo was undoubtedly a competent carver in his younger years. Leyenaar (1988, 209) shows a Santiaguero mask that was carved by Pablo; this mask had been worn by General Sabario in the dance, and was subsequently collected in 1977. It is currently in the Rijksmuseum vor Volkenkunde in Leiden, Netherlands. In Pablo's home in Cuetzalan there are some older danced masks. Unfortunately, Pablo states that he does not remember who carved these older masks. I'm of the opinion that some of them were carved by Pablo.

There are also some masks that were more recently carved, possibly by Pablo, but if so these were probably carved at a time when his skills had begun to wane, because they are not as well carved. I don't believe that these recent masks should be taken to reflect his prior level of carving. Fortunately, this ambiguity about Pablo's masks was recently lessened when I purchased a Pilatos mask on eBay and then learned from the seller that it had apparently been identified as the work of Pablo at the time of initial purchase, in 1999. This mask has features like those on the masks of Pablo's brother Pedro, but it seems less sharply detailed. I have long wondered whether the two brothers had a relative who served as their teacher.

In any event, I have concluded that Pablo was a competent carver whose masks were widely used in his community in the past.

When Max Harris visited Cuetzalan in 1988, he spoke with Pablo Huerta Ramir, who is the son of Pablo Huerta Mora. Harris states that Pablo Huerta Ramir was carving and painting dance masks at that time. More recently when Carlos met with him, Señor Huerta Ramir denied that he was still carving. It was Pablo Huerta Ramir who told Harris that the Santiaguero dancers are secretly the soldiers of the sun (Harris 1993, 102–103).

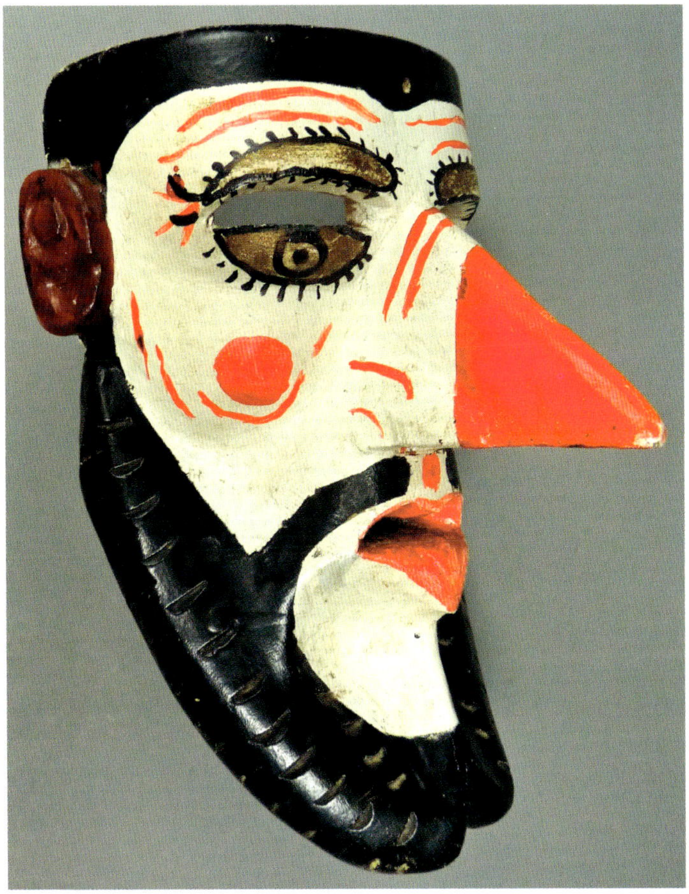

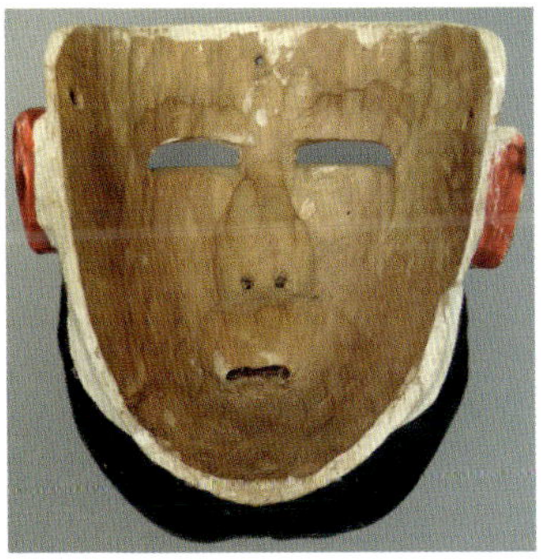

Top: A Pilato mask purchased on eBay™ in 2011; 7" × 9". Circa 1995. The seller had purchased this mask from a dance group in Cuetzalan, Puebla, in about 1999. At that time he was informed that the mask had been danced for four years and that Pablo Huerta Mora was the carver. Subsequently he met Pablo. This mask is well carved and it would be quite effective in a dance performance. The mouth has the shape like those on the masks of Pedro Huerta Mora, but this example is more informally carved. We see an entirely different ear design, compared to the masks of Pedro Huerta Mora; this one is less abstract, more realistic. Rating: known carver, excellent condition, well carved, good patina, and rarity unknown, ****. *Collection of the author.*

Above left: The back shows a level of wear that is consistent with the history.

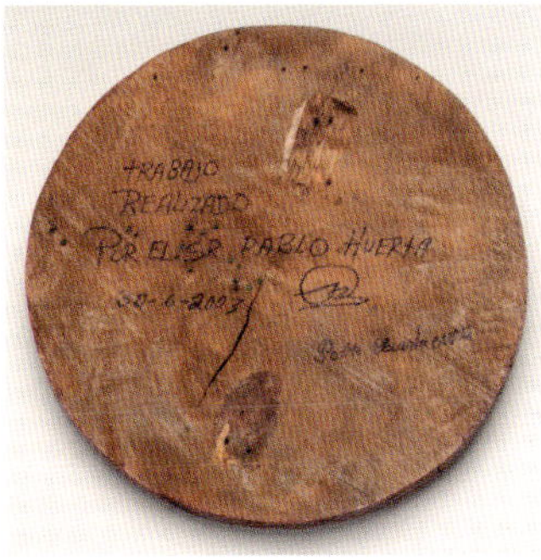

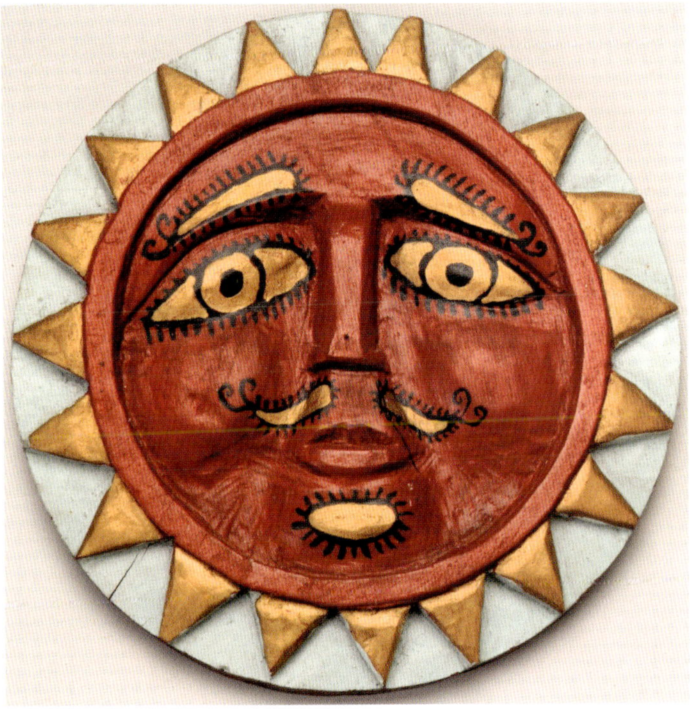

Left: A sun shield; 9" × 9". It was purchased in 2008 from the carver; on the back it is signed by Pablo Huerta Mora and dated June 30, 2003. Rating: known carver, excellent condition, well carved, undanced, and rarity unknown, ***. *Collection of the author.*

Above: The back of the shield, signed and dated.

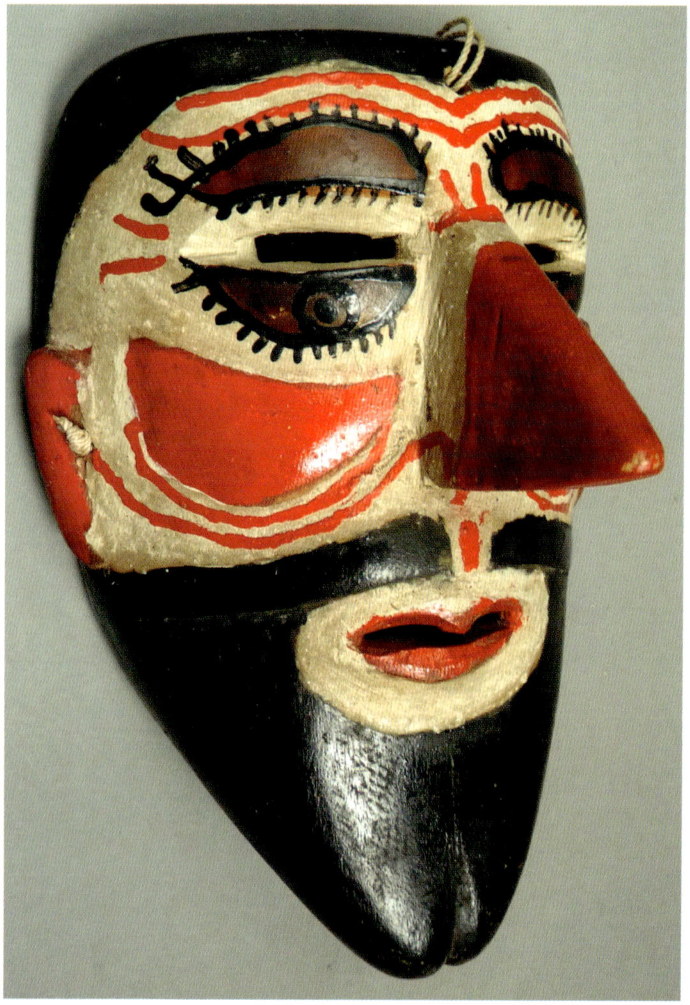

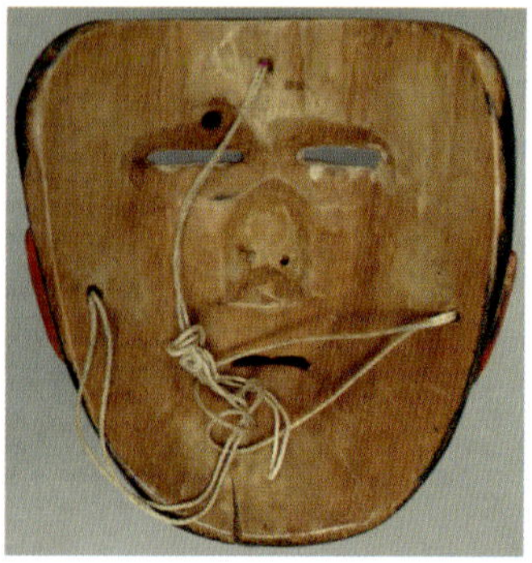

Above: This Pilato mask was collected in Cuetzalan, Puebla, in 2007; 7½" × 9½". Circa 1980. This is probably another mask by Pablo Huerta Mora, based on comparison with the previous mask. As usual with the masks of this carver and his brother, we find such variation in the ear designs that they provide little guidance. This mask is undoubtedly by one of these two brothers and in the style of Cuetzalan. Rating: known carver(s), excellent condition, very well carved, excellent patina, and rarity unknown, ****. *Collection of the author.*

Left: The back is nicely carved with good patina.

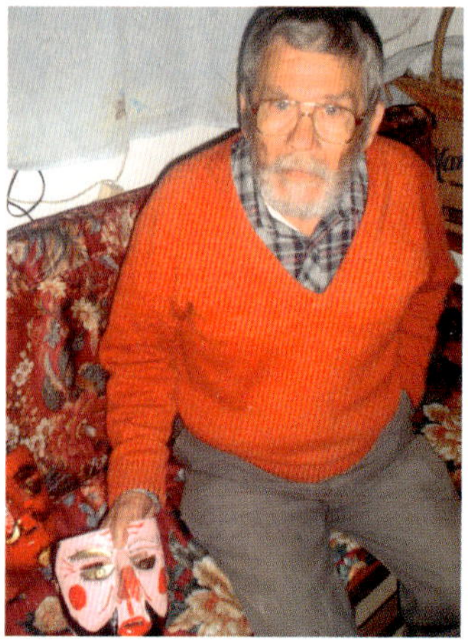

A photo of Pablo Huerta Mora was taken in 2008. He holds a recent mask in his hand. *Photo by Carlos Moreno Vásquez.*

Pedro Huerta Mora

Pedro Huerta Mora was born on December 17, 1918, and died on December 17, 2007. He lived in Cuetzalan, Puebla. I initially visited his workshop in the year prior to his death, and although I met his son at that time, I never met Pedro himself. At that time we obtained several undanced masks from his son that were carved by Pedro.

These were rather remarkable carvings, and on the basis of these masks we were subsequently able to identify a number of heavily danced examples that we found in the community or in other collections. Having found this body of masks by Pedro, I am confident that he was a highly gifted carver, apparently one of the best of the Cuetzalan carvers during the middle years of the 20th century.

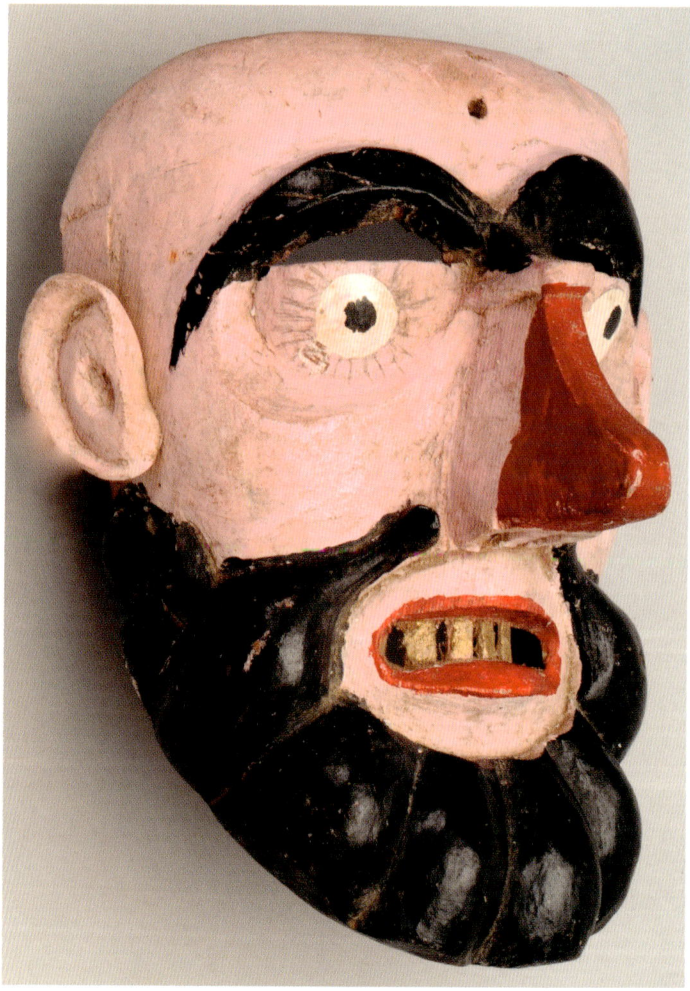

An undanced, eccentric Pilato mask that was apparently never finished; 8" × 9½". Circa 2000. The mask was obtained from the carver's son in the year prior to Pedro's death. The carving on this mask is quite bold, the features exaggerated, the effect memorable. Notice the extremely unusual design of the nose. There is an applied ear, and the paint around the eye is merely sketched in. The back, not shown, was only roughly carved. Rating: known carver, excellent condition, extremely vivid carving, undanced, and rare, ****½. *Collection of the author.*

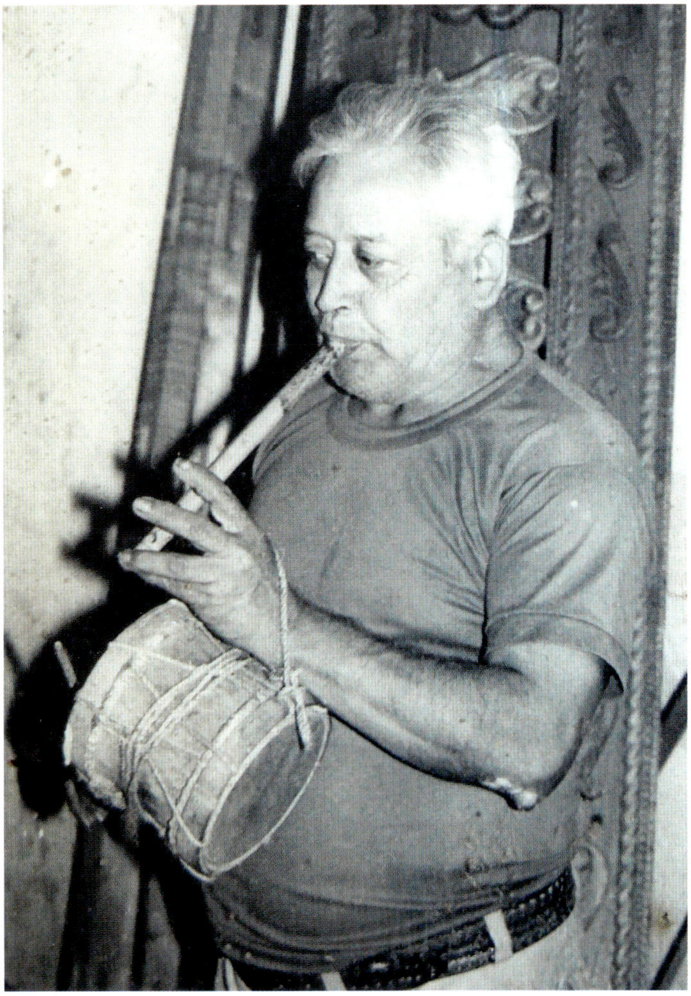

A copy of a family photo of Pedro Huerta Mora playing the flute. *Photo included with the permission of Pedro's son.*

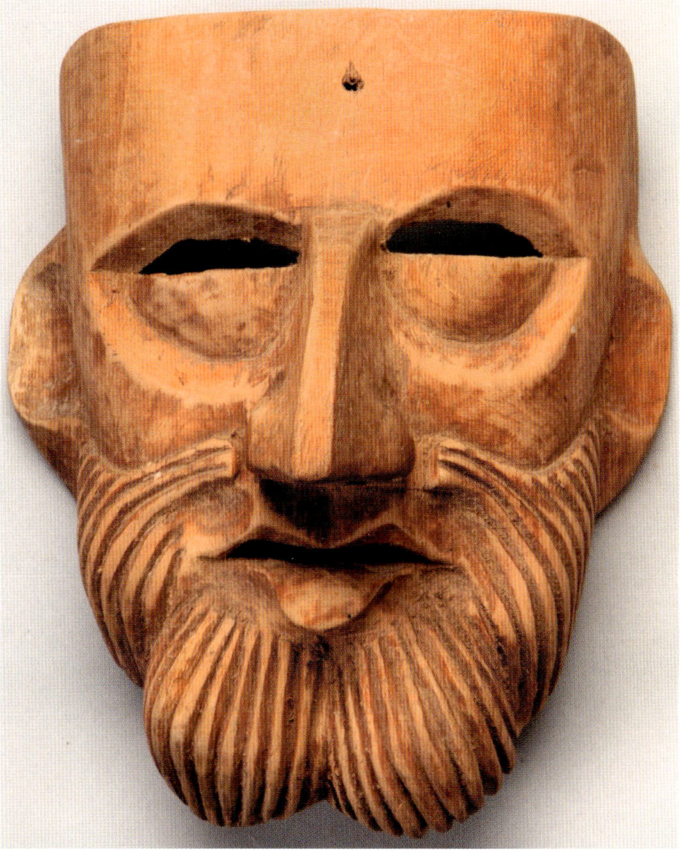

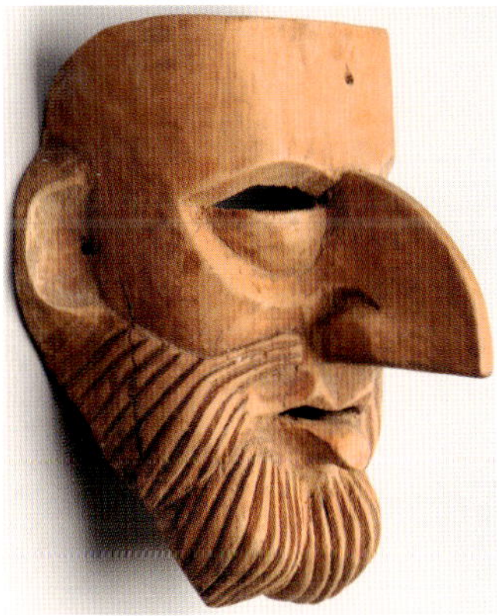

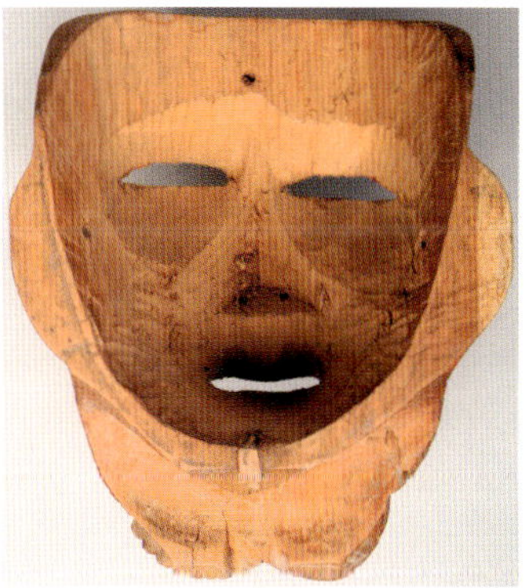

Top: Another undanced Pilato mask that was carefully carved but never painted; 7½" × 8½". Circa 2000. It was also obtained from the carver's son in the year prior to Pedro's death. Many of the features of this mask, such as the prominent nose, the carefully grooved beard, the simple ears, and the curled lower lip will be seen in several heavily danced masks that follow. Rating: known carver, excellent condition, very well carved, unpainted and undanced, and rare, ****½. *Collection of the author.*

Above left: A side view. Look how the plane from the corner of the eye sweeps around to terminate in the side of the nose above the curve of the nostril. This is extraordinary carving.

Above right: Even the back of this mask is carved in a complex fashion.

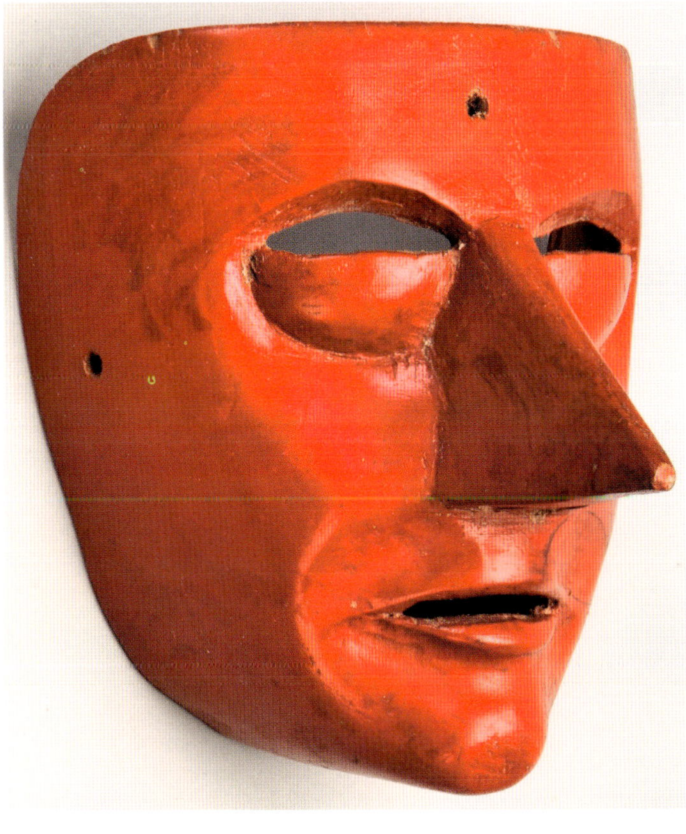

We purchased this undanced Santiaguero mask from the carver's son in December 2007, after Pedro's death; 6¼" × 6¾". Circa 2000. From this angle many beautiful details of the carving are visible. Rating: known carver, excellent condition, very well carved, undanced, and rarity unknown, ***½. *Collection of the author.*

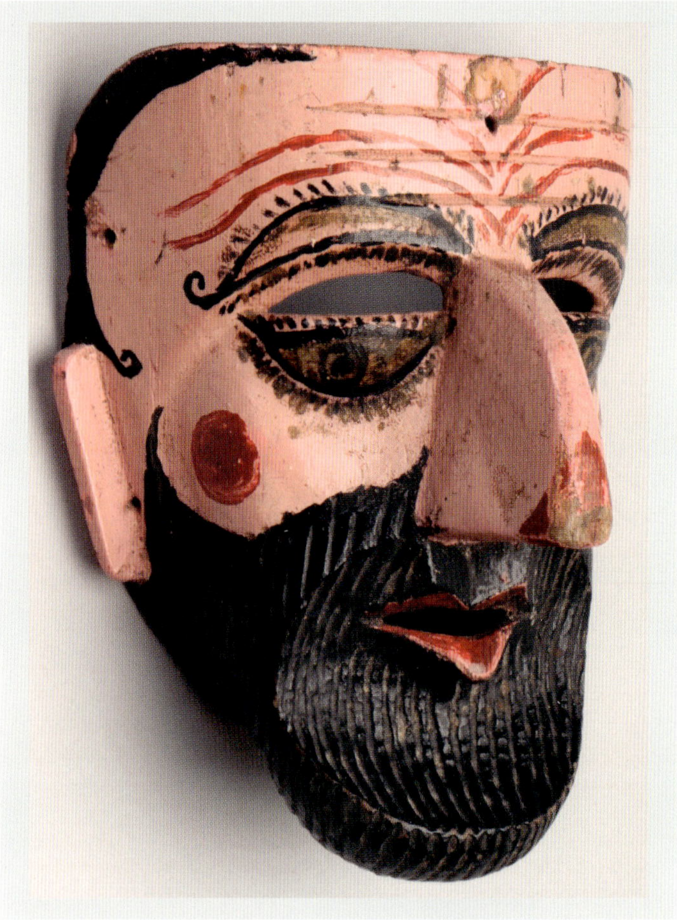

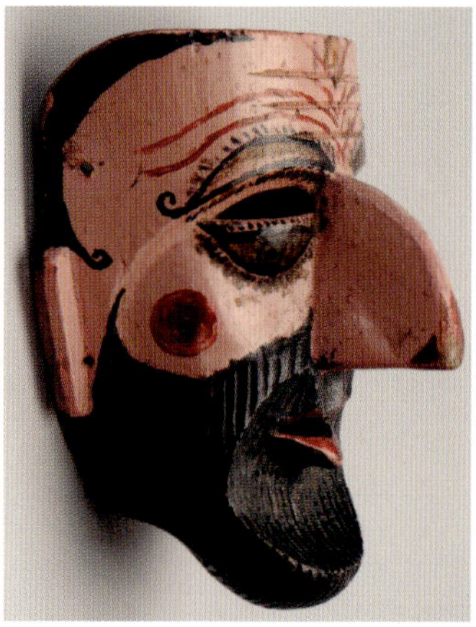

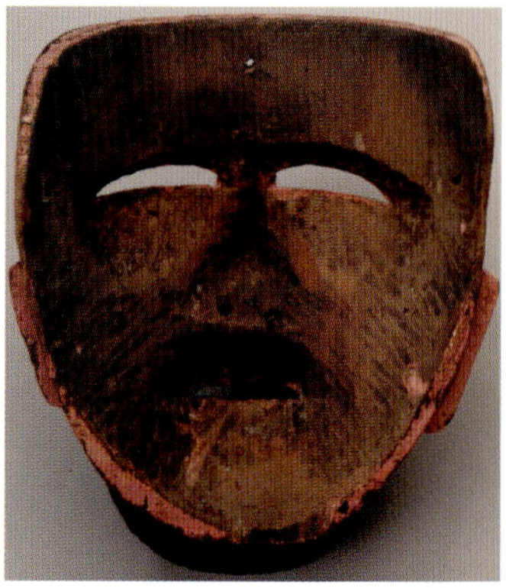

Left: A wonderful older and heavily used Pilato mask, probably the best that I have seen by this carver; 6¾" × 8". Circa 1960. It shares many of the features of the unpainted mask above; however, these features are a little more sharply defined here, as if we are seeing a greater level of proficiency from a time when the carver was at his peak. The manner of carving of the grooved beard and lips is majestic, the work of a great master. From this angle the mask demonstrates another feature that deserves attention. Pedro carefully carves curving margins where different planes of the face meet, such as the arc that swings down from the corner of the eye to the beard. Rating: known carver, excellent condition, extremely well carved, excellent patina, and rare, *******. *Collection of the author.*

Above left: In this profile view we notice the dished contour of the beard and the very simply shaped ears. The lower lip pouts dramatically.

Above right: The back is nicely carved and demonstrates a wonderful patina.

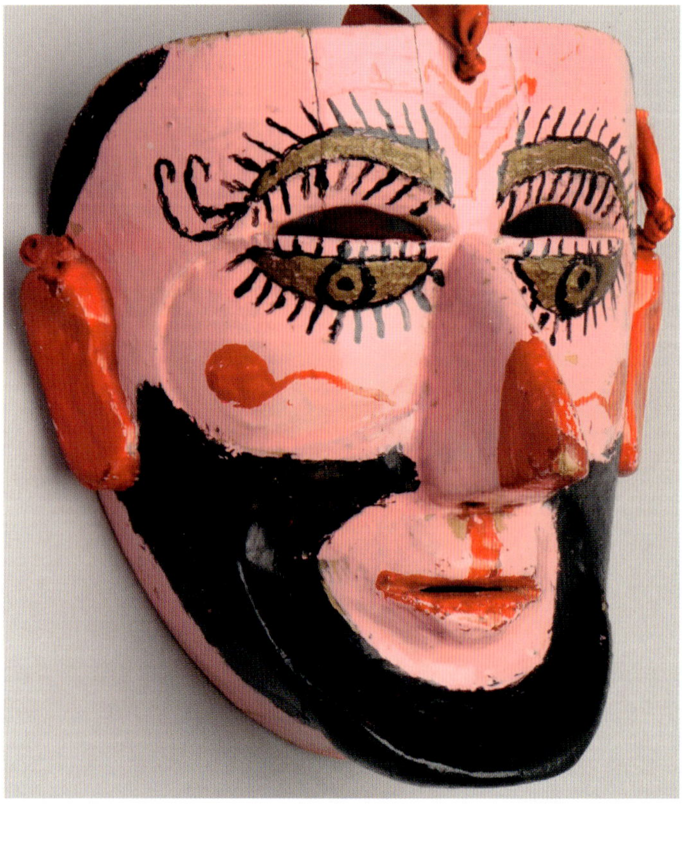

This Pilato mask is attributed to Pedro Huerta Mora on the basis of the carved contour lines along with the prominent nose; 6½" × 7". Circa 1980. There is a lot of variety in the ears of this carver, so they are of little help, compared to other more obvious shared features. Rating: known carver, excellent condition, very well carved, good patina, and rare, ******. *Collection of the author.*

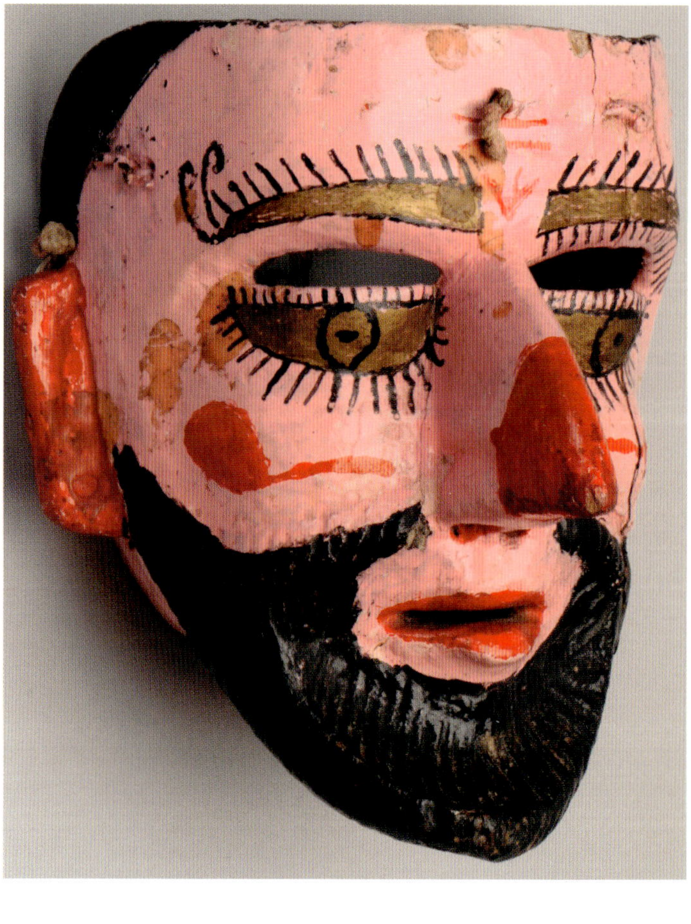

This old cracked mask is very similar to the adjacent masks. Note the contour line around the cheek and the finely grooved beard; 7 ¼" × 8". Circa 1970. Rating: known carver, old repairs, very well carved, good patina, and rare, ******. *Collection of the author.*

Narciso Iturbide Charo

Narciso Iturbide Charo was born on August 6, 1921, and died on March 18, 1996. He lived and carved in San Antonio Rayón, Puebla. According to Manuel Antonio Castañeda, who knew him well, Narciso was self-taught.

When I first began to collect Mexican dance masks in 1987, I had the good fortune to acquire some remarkable Santiaguero masks from Puebla, lyrical in design and oversized. Twenty years later, when I was working closely with Vernon Kostohryz to sort out the carvers and their styles, I realized that my masks had been carved by a deceased master carver whose identity had only recently been discovered by Vernon Kostohryz and Carlos Moreno Vásquez**.** This was, of course, Narciso Iturbide Charo.

I'll explain the identification part of the story later; for now I'll just note that Narciso's masks all demonstrated elements of a very distinctive and easily recognized style. I could see those elements in the masks I had collected so much earlier, masks that had in fact been collected from the area immediately surrounding Narciso's home in San Antonio Rayón.

It was exciting enough to be able to identify the carver of the old set of oversized masks, but then the story became even more interesting, as I realized that Narciso was the only logical candidate to have carved a truly remarkable group of masks from rural Puebla, the "three-faced Moros." All those masks had been scouted out by pickers in the mid-1980s. Vernon and the pickers who worked with him had never seen any of these three-faced masks or even knew that they existed.

As has been so often the case, the identification of Narciso emerged within a broader inquiry. The son-in-law of one carver (Manuel Antonio Castañeda) was the son of Narciso, so finding one led to finding the other. One of Narciso's sons had retained a group of his father's masks that really made the linkage concretely clear. Much later we discovered that Manuel Antonio Castañeda had also preserved an oversized Pilato mask by Narciso (to follow). He knew him, of course, and Señor Antonio Castañeda was even able to confirm our theory that Narciso was the carver of the three-faced masks.

At this point there will be readers who are asking themselves, what are these three-faced masks, these so-called three-faced Moros? Briefly, these are the only examples known to me of Mexican masks with three separate faces that are clearly not decorative or false. I'll tell the little that was known or remembered by Robin and Barbara Cleaver, who discovered these masks in the early 1980s (personal communications, 1988 and 2010). In about 1984 Robin Cleaver visited a folk art dealer in the city of Puebla, and he saw this dealer stripping the "ugly pink paint" from a remarkable helmet mask, a mask with three faces, set at 90 degrees to one another like a three-sided box, with one side open. This had the worn back of an old, heavily danced mask. Robin purchased the mask, and thinking that it looked like a Santiaguero, he had it repainted as such.

Subsequently, having learned the source of this mask, Robin and his wife, Barbara, joined with Jaled Muyaes and Estela Ogazon of Mexico City to send a picker to the identified area, armed with Barbara Cleaver's camera and instructions to collect as many of these masks as possible.

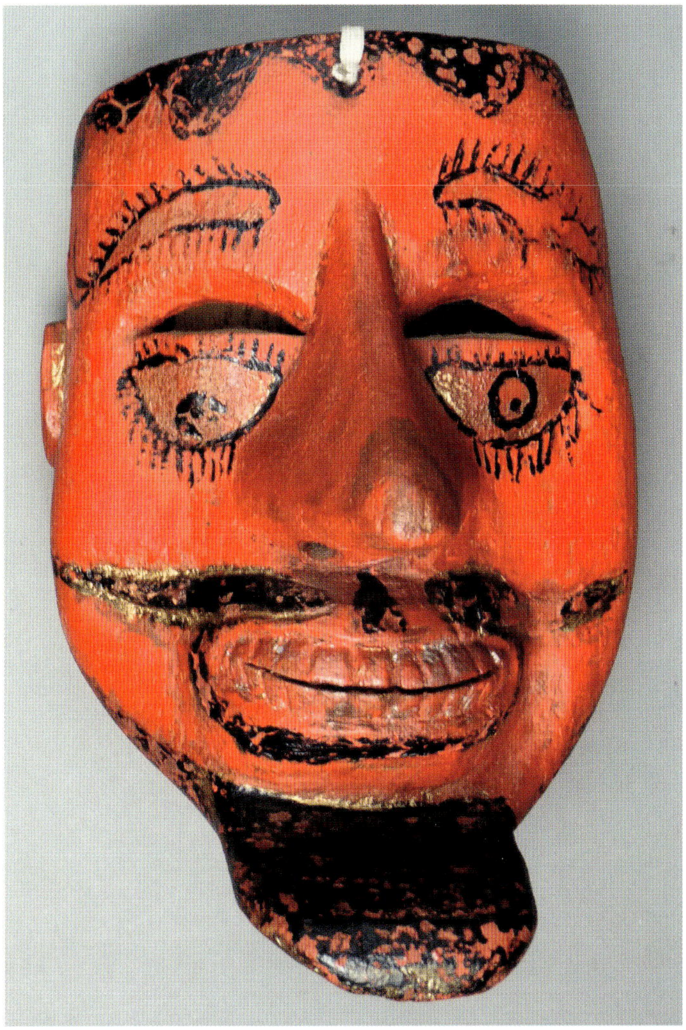

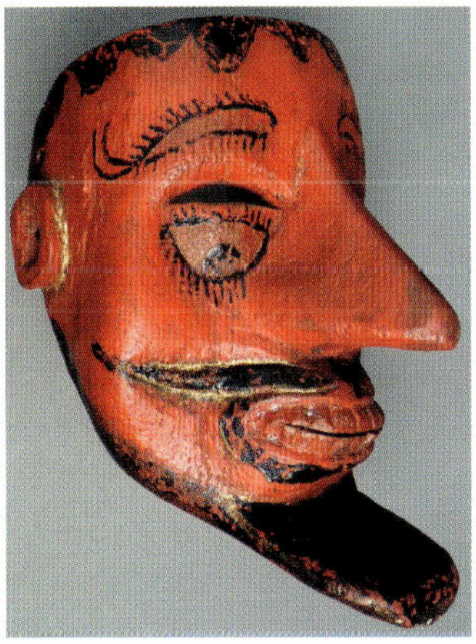

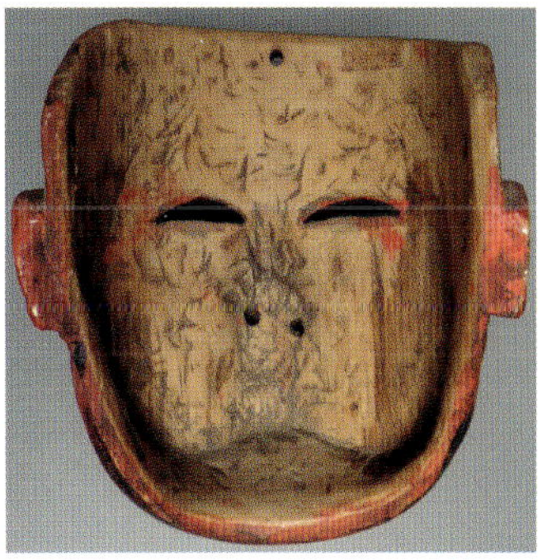

Top: This oversized Santiaguero mask was collected in Ayotoxco de Guerrero, Puebla, by Jaled Muyaes and Estela Ogazon; 7½" × 11½". Circa 1970. The toothy leer is particularly striking. The big goatee, extending forward in parallel to the dramatic nose, is a nice touch. Rating: known carver, good condition, remarkable design, excellent paint with good patina on the back, and rare, *******. *Collection of the author.*

Bottom left: In the side view we see the typical ear design of Narciso, rectangular with a central depression. The dynamic and sublime nature of the carving is obvious from this view.

Bottom right: The back of this large mask shows good evidence of wear.

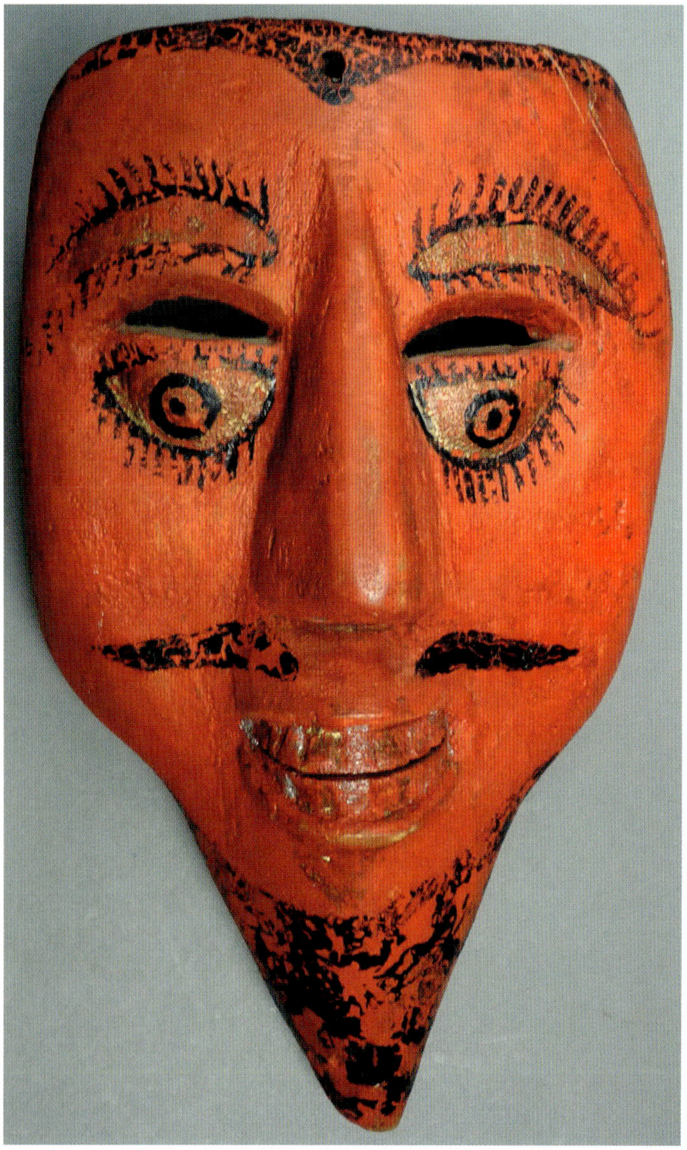

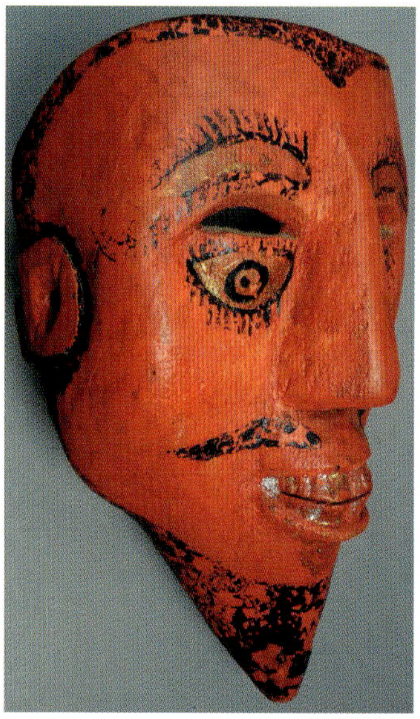

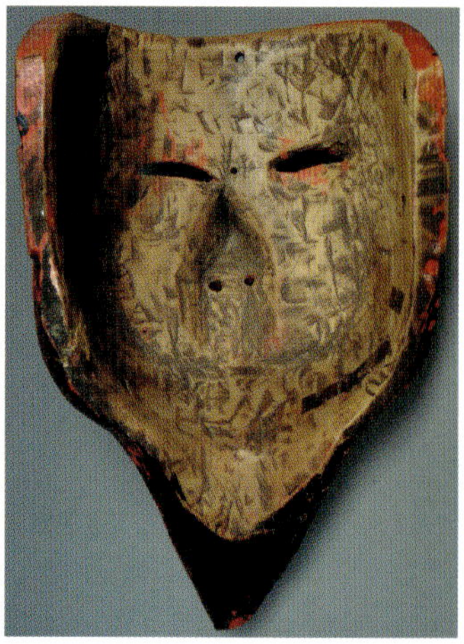

Left: A second example of the oversized Santiaguero masks collected in Ayotoxco de Guerrero, Puebla, by Jaled Muyaes and Estela Ogazon; 8½" × 13½". Circa 1970. This mask has a triangular goatee that extends downward. We see again the toothy leer. Rating: known carver, good condition, remarkable design, excellent paint with good patina on the back, and rare, ******. *Collection of the author.*

Above left: The side view of this mask, showing the rectangular or D-shaped ear.

Above right: The back of this mask shows good wear.

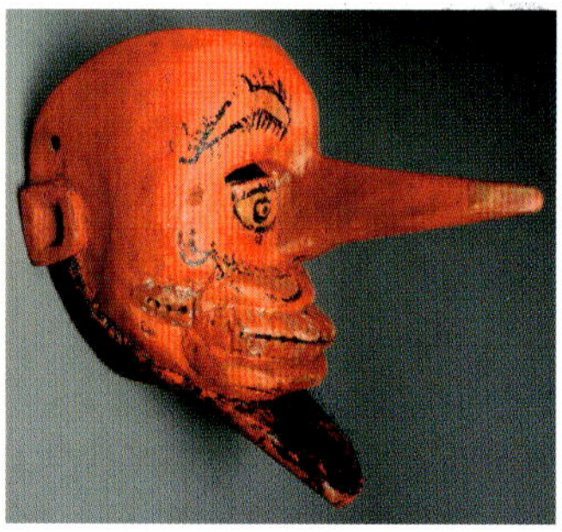

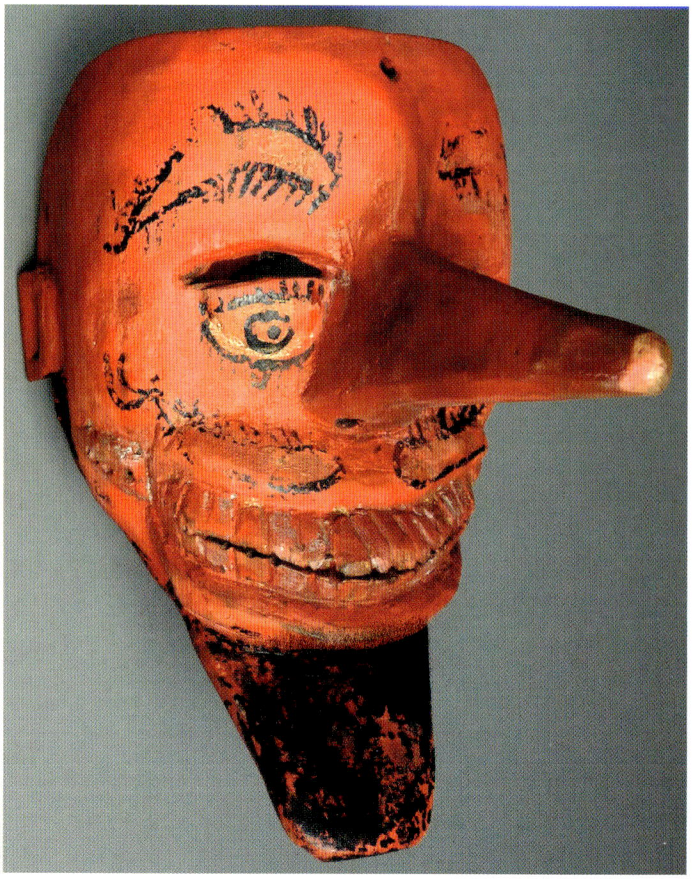

Right: This large Santiaguero mask originally had a normal-sized nose like that above, but later it was elongated by the addition of another piece of wood; 7½" × 12". This one was collected in San Antonio Rayón, Puebla, by Jaled Muyaes and Estela Ogazon. Rating: known carver, good condition, remarkable design, excellent paint with good patina on the back, and rare, ******. *Collection of the author.*

Above: From the side view, the teeth are particularly impressive on this mask. The holes in the area of the mustache suggest that there might have been tufts of hair.

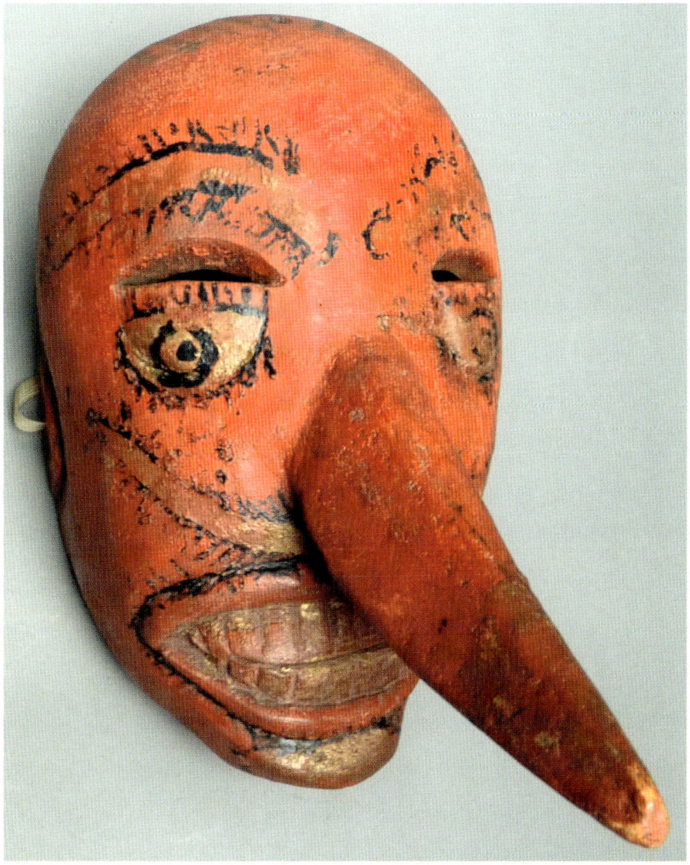

An oversized Santiaguero mask that was intentionally carved from a log with an attached branch, permitting a very long and slightly curving nose, along with the characteristic prominent teeth; 7" × 12". Collected in Tenampulco, Puebla, by Jaled Muyaes and Estela Ogazon. Rating: known carver, good condition, remarkable design, excellent paint with good patina on the back, and rare, *******. *Collection of the author.*

The first fruit of all this was a dance photograph, taken in some town in the Sierra de Puebla, showing three dancers wearing these three-faced masks, along with crowns, headdresses, and the typical costume elements found in the Santiagueros dance. The camera reportedly jammed after the first photo, so there were no additional images. It was learned that the three faces were meant to represent Herod, Pontius Pilate, and Joseph Caiaphas, the high priest of the Jewish temple at the time of the crucifixion.

The runner collected a group of maybe 15 or 16 additional three-faced masks from this area, which was described as isolated and remote, only reachable by mule or on foot along a trail. Some of these masks were subsequently sold to collectors, but the name of the town was explicitly kept secret, because the possibility remained for a second expedition. I purchased several of these masks, including the index specimen that had been repainted.

More than 20 years later, in the context of my identification of Narciso as the probable carver, I asked the Cleavers to break the code on the site of collection. As it turned out the name had been forgotten, but inside one mask was written a name—Tecpancingo. Inside a second mask, in fact the one on the middle dancer in the dance photograph, was the name of another town—Paso del Jardín. These are small towns that lie several miles outside of San Antonio Rayón, Puebla, the town where Narciso Iturbide Charo lived. Which one of these towns was the one in the dance photo, I wondered?

In March 2010, I visited these towns with Vernon Kostohryz and Carlos Moreno Vásquez. By then both towns were connected by passable roads to San Antonio Rayón, and that town was easily reached by paved roads from a number of cities in Puebla. What we were told in each of those outlying towns was that the dance photo was of the central plaza of San Antonio Rayón itself, but that some of the dancers may have come into that center from these other towns, which would explain the labeling. Apparently dancing with three-faced masks was not continued after the initial collection in the mid-1980s, although Narciso lived for another 10 or 12 years afterwards, an interval when replacement masks might have been carved.

Looking at the old dance photo in March 2010. Manuel Antonio Castañeda confirmed that the place was San Antonio Rayón. He said that the dancer on the left was Pilatos (in English, Pontius Pilate), who, we must assume, was appearing in his usual position as the identified villain, while Manuel called the one in the center Akcharrión. This latter name, which is also spelled as Accharreón, Ekcharrión, etc., shows up in various written accounts of the character list in the Hormegas and Santiagueros dances. Alain Ichon, describing the Santiagueros dance in Pantepec, Puebla, identified Ekcharión as one of *los capitanes Romanos* (Roman captains) in the dance, along with Sevario (or Sabario) and Herodes (1973, 395).

In a follow-up interview with Carlos Moreno Vásquez in August 2010, Manuel provided some interesting further details. The name of the dance that used the three-faced masks was La Danza de los Pilatos y Santiagueros. The dance included Santiago, wearing his usual wooden horse. A boy played the part of Santiago's son; it was his job to protect the horse from harm. Not only did Narciso carve all of the three-faced masks and the horse for Santiago, he also wore one of his three-faced masks in the dance. Antonio felt almost certain that the middle figure in the dance photo was Narciso himself, based on the particular mask design and other costume details. Of course Antonio was asked whether he had also participated in the dance? He replied that he was the flute player for the occasion in the photograph and more generally for that dance. It seems that there were Pilatos and Santiagueros dancers, all wearing the same three-faced masks. Señor Castañeda said that there was also a single Pilato who had no other name.

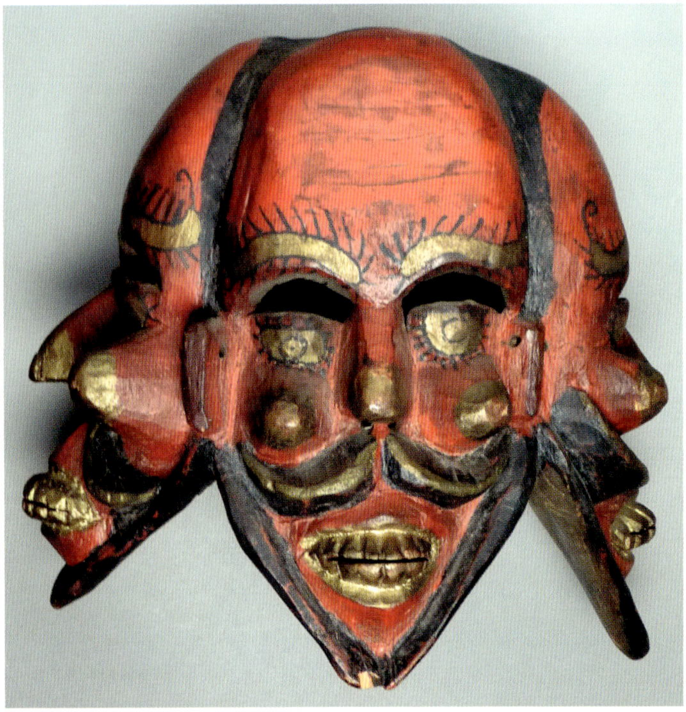

Above: This is the three-faced index mask discovered in Puebla by Robin Cleaver in about 1984; 13" × 12". Circa 1970. We see a face in the center flanked by faces oriented to the two sides. At the corners there are ear-like tabs. The holes in the tabs provide points for the attachment of the *cantunga*, a ruffled cloth accessory beard. Virtually all the features are carved in relief. Particularly strange are the conical cheeks. The prominent teeth are certainly familiar to us from the oversized Santiaguero masks above. Rating: known carver, good condition, remarkable design, excellent paint with good patina on the back, and very rare, *******+. *Collection of the author.*

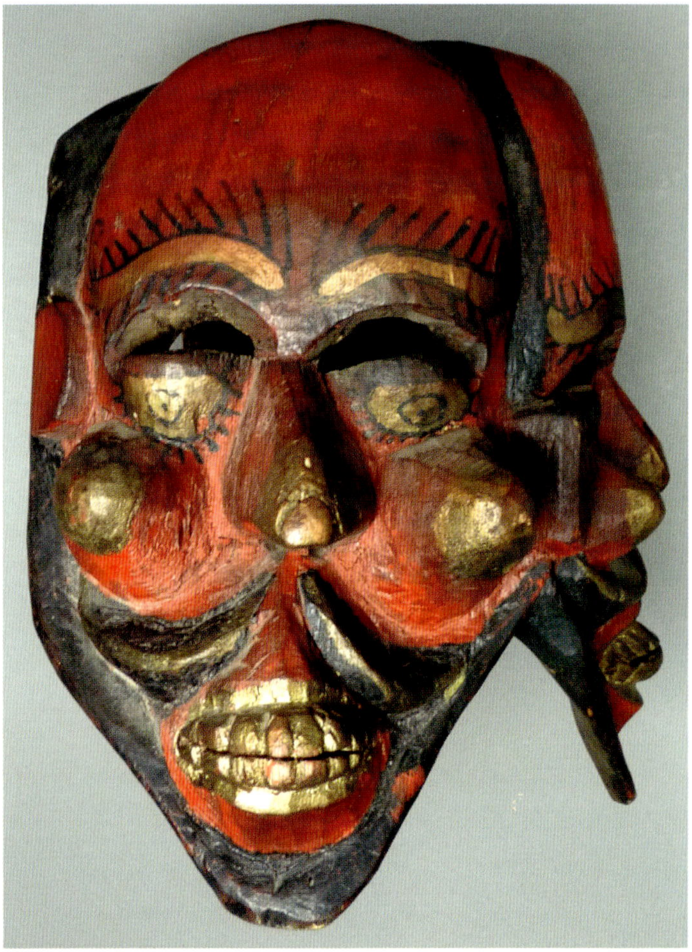

Right: The face on the right side of the mask. The vision slits on the sides must be there for an artistic purpose; I doubt that they serve any practical function.

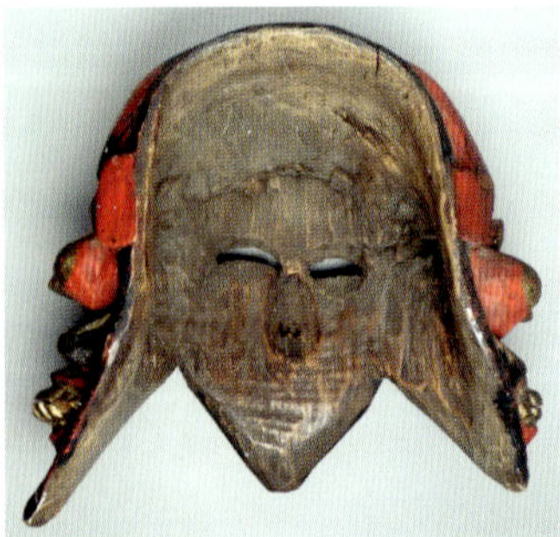

The view of the back. The age and wear will be obvious.

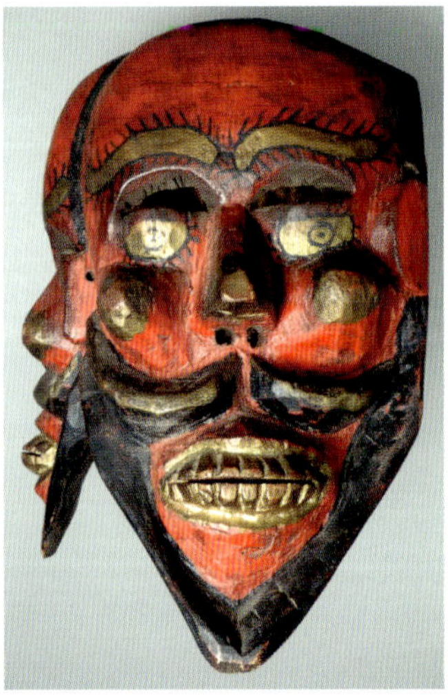

The face on the left side of the mask.

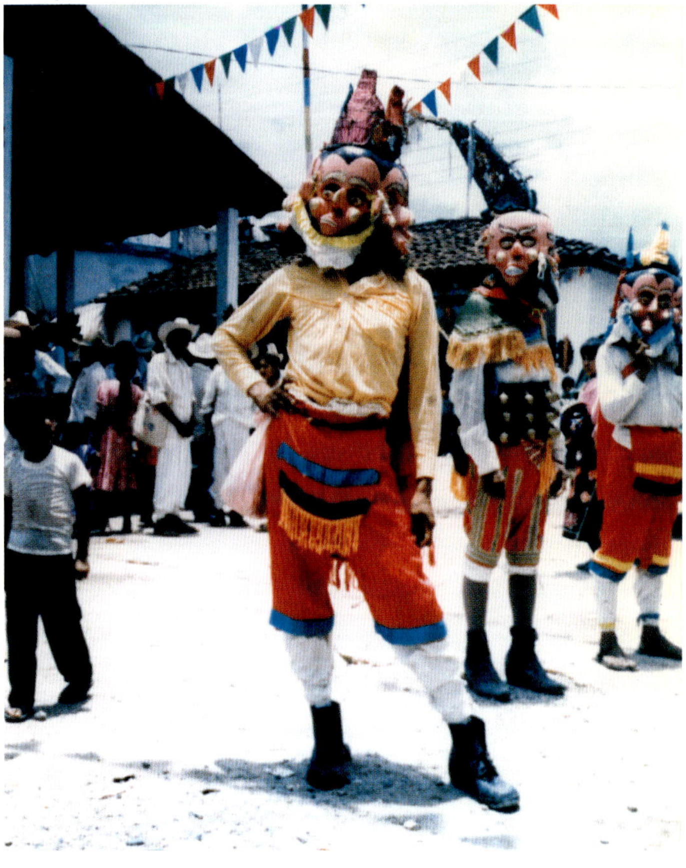

This is the only dance photograph known to me that documents the performance of the Santiagueros dance with three-faced masks. This photo was taken in about 1984 in a then-unnamed town in the Sierra de Puebla. The dancers on the left and right are clearly Pilatos characters, as they are wearing crowns. The middle dancer is wearing the classic morión headdress of a Santiaguero. *Photo courtesy of Robin and Barbara Cleaver.*

The photos document more of the three-faced masks that were collected at that time.

Meanwhile in about 2005 Vernon Kostohryz and Carlos Moreno Vásquez began finding more normal-sized Santiaguero masks in the area around San Antonio Rayón, Puebla. Eventually they were introduced to one of Narciso's sons, who had retained some of his father's masks, which he later permitted me to photograph. These family masks were all similar in style and scale to the others that were recently collected; it was at that point that a positive identification of Narciso as the carver of this style of mask became clear.

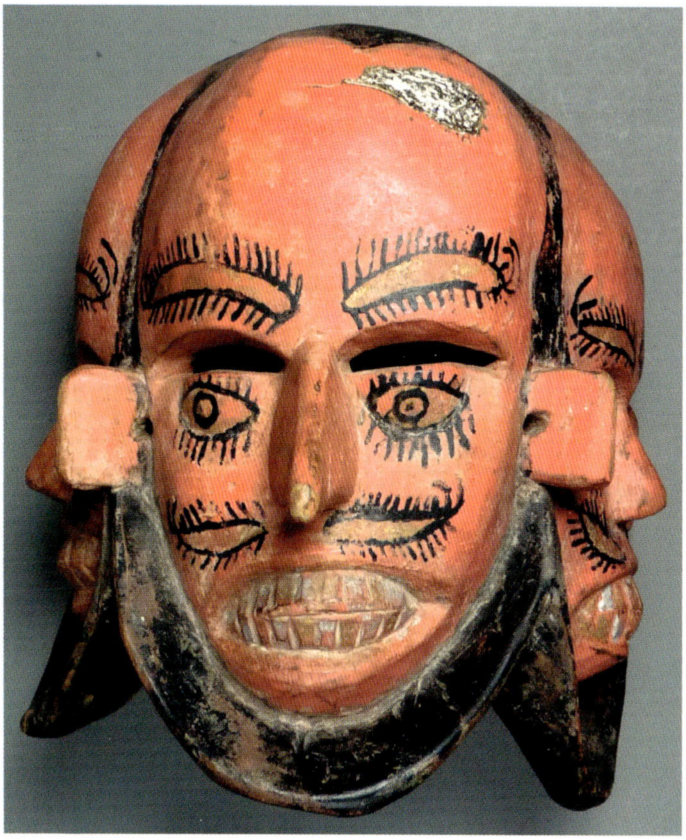

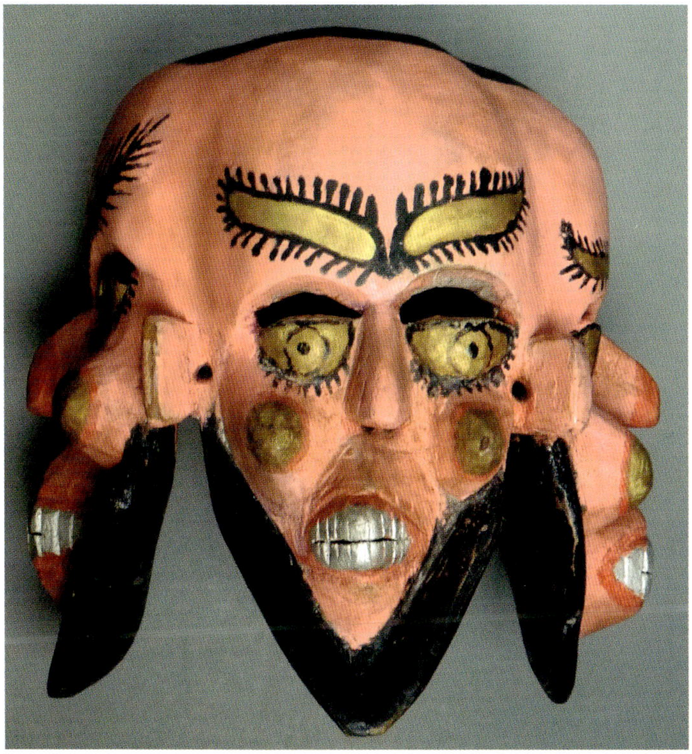

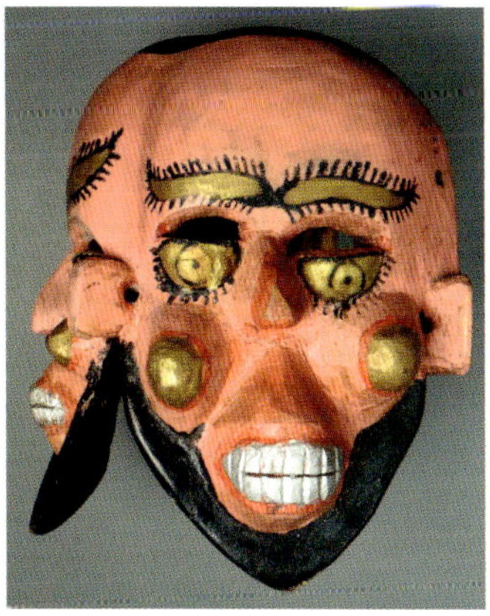

Above: Here is the Akcharrión mask that appears on the middle figure in the dance photo; 10½" × 11". Circa 1970. We see again the general design that we found on the index mask, including the conical cheeks and the tabs for the cantunga, but not the relief-carved mustaches. On the back, in pencil is written "Paso del Jardín." Rating: known carver, good condition, remarkable design, excellent paint with good patina on the back, and rare, *******. *Collection of the author.*

Left: The mask as seen from the viewer's right, showing the left corner. We see the front of the mask from the side.

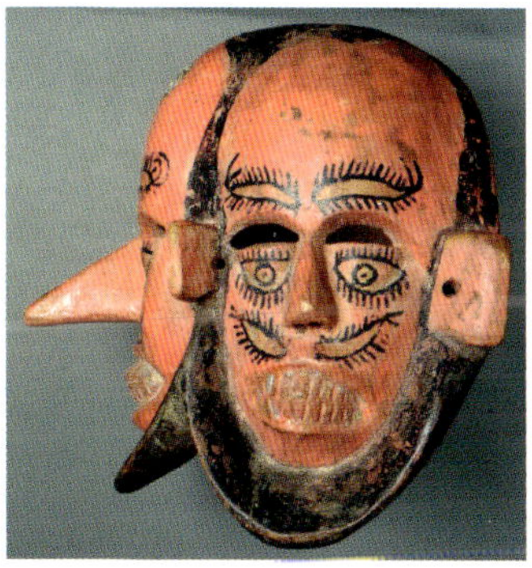

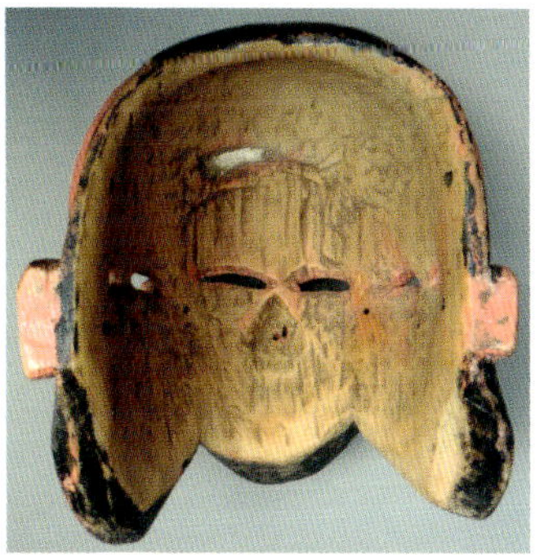

Above: Here is another example of the three-faced masks that were collected together in the mid-1980s; 10" × 13". Circa 1970. This one has a long nose on the central face. It lacks conical cheeks and the mustaches are painted, not carved. On the brow a hole in the wood was repaired with plaster. Rating: known carver, good condition, remarkable design, excellent paint with good patina on the back, and rare, *******. *Collection of the author.*

Left, above: Here the face on the left is revealed, and one sees the long nose of the central mask in profile. A very attractive aspect of this mask is that the beards of the three faces are so elegantly integrated.

Left, below: The back of this mask; the plaster patch is visible on the inside as well.

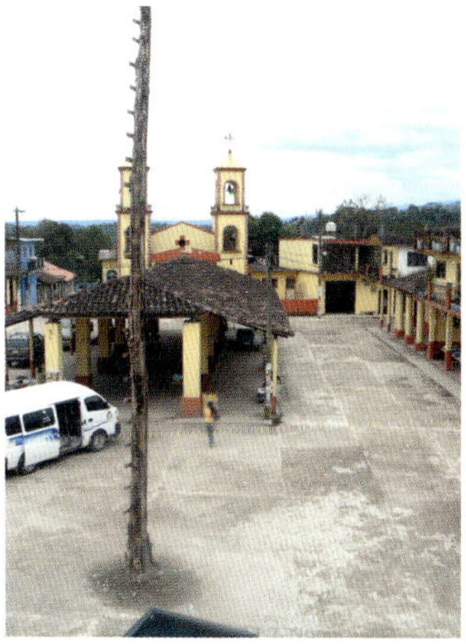

A photograph of the Plaza in San Antonio Rayón, taken in March 2010 from the balcony of the town hall building. In the foreground one can see the pole for the Voladores. Behind that pole is the open-sided building that ordinarily serves to shelter market venders. The corner of the market building, which we see in the center of this photo, is also visible in the old dance photo, immediately to the viewer's left of the three costumed dancers.

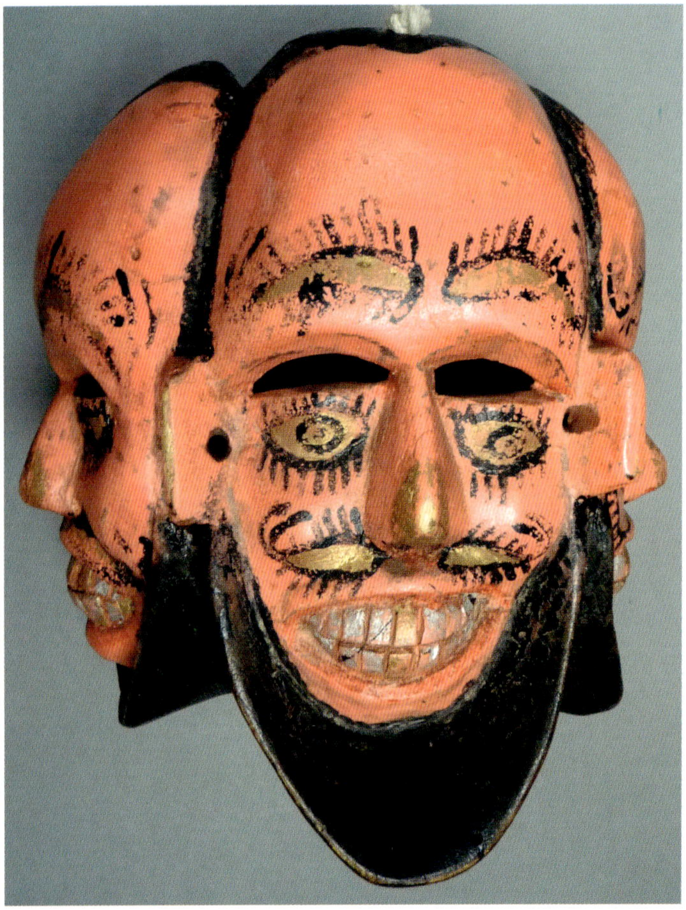

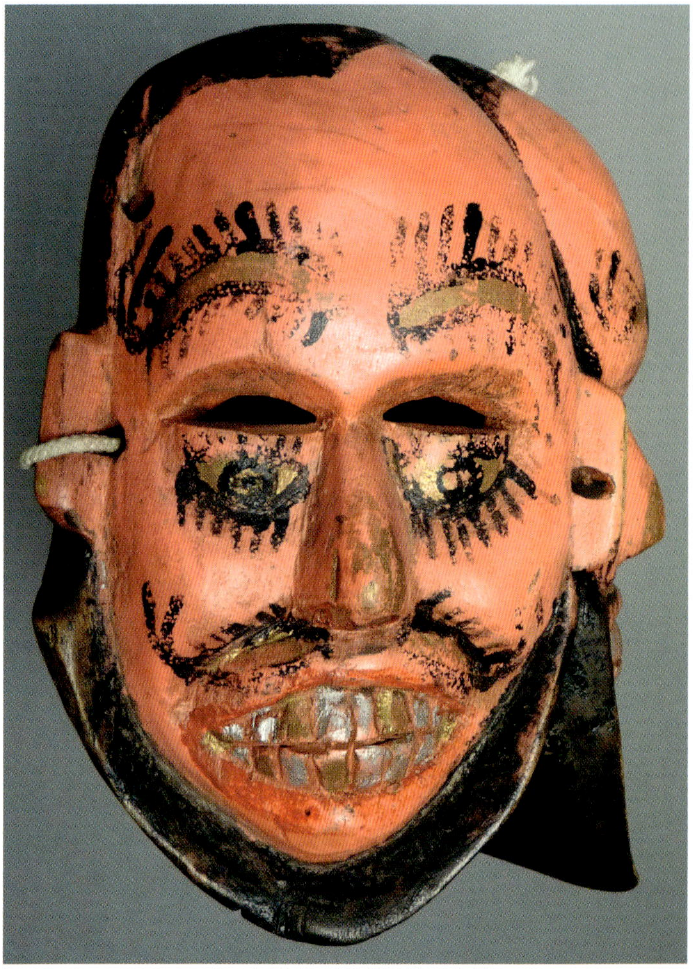

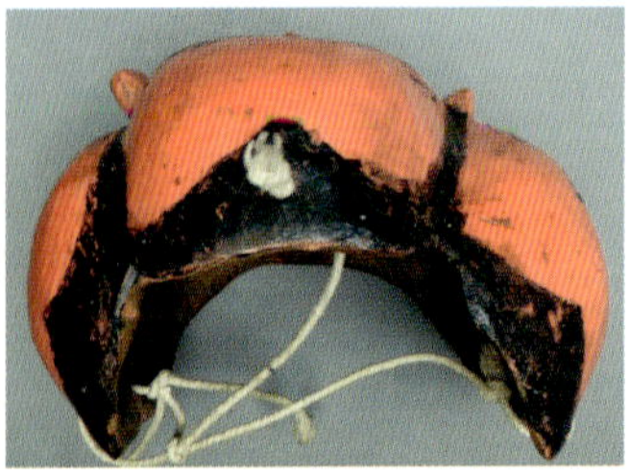

Above: A smaller three-faced mask that may have been carved for a child; 9" × 11". Circa 1970. Rating: known carver, good condition, remarkable design, excellent paint with good patina on the back, and rare, *******. *Collection of the author.*

Above right: The view of the right side of the child's mask.

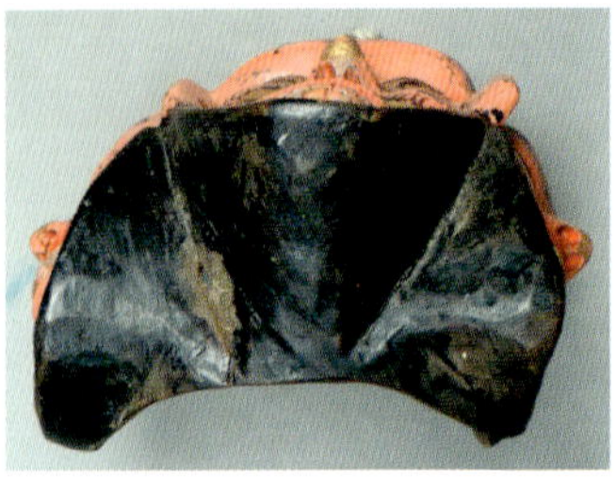

Left, above: The view of the child's mask from above.

Left, center: The view of the child's mask from below.

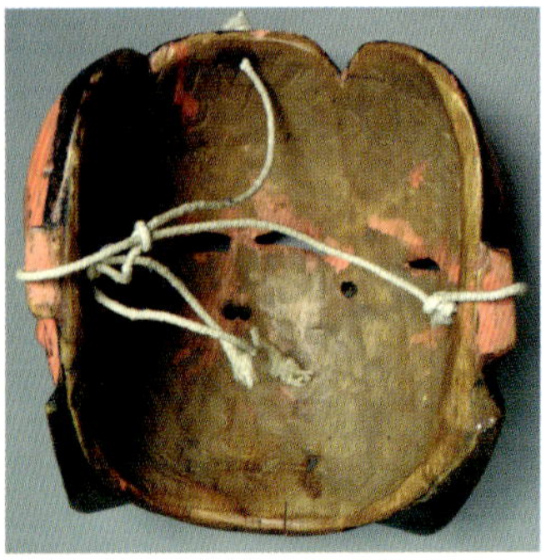

Left, below: The back of the child's three-faced mask.

The masks that Vernon and Carlos found, seen here, closely resembled those in the possession of Narciso's son. Unfortunately, that gentleman has taken a job at a distance from San Antonio Rayón, so we have been unable to meet with him to obtain his permission to include photographs of the masks in his collection.

In summary, as you will surely notice from the photos, Narciso was a remarkable carver whose masks tend to be dramatic. Perhaps we should think of Narciso Iturbide Charo and Manuel Antonio Castañeda as constituting the "San Antonio Rayón School" of mask carving, exemplified by dramatic exaggerated features.

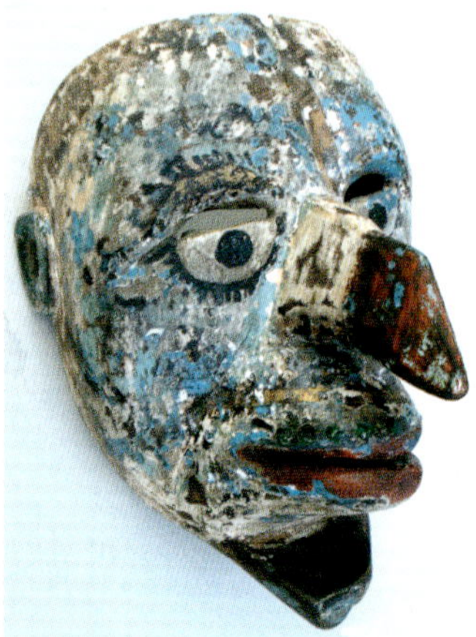

Here is another dramatic mask by Narciso that has been repainted for Carnaval. Rating: known carver, good condition, remarkable design, marginal paint with good patina on the back, and rare, *****. *Collection of Joris Miller.*

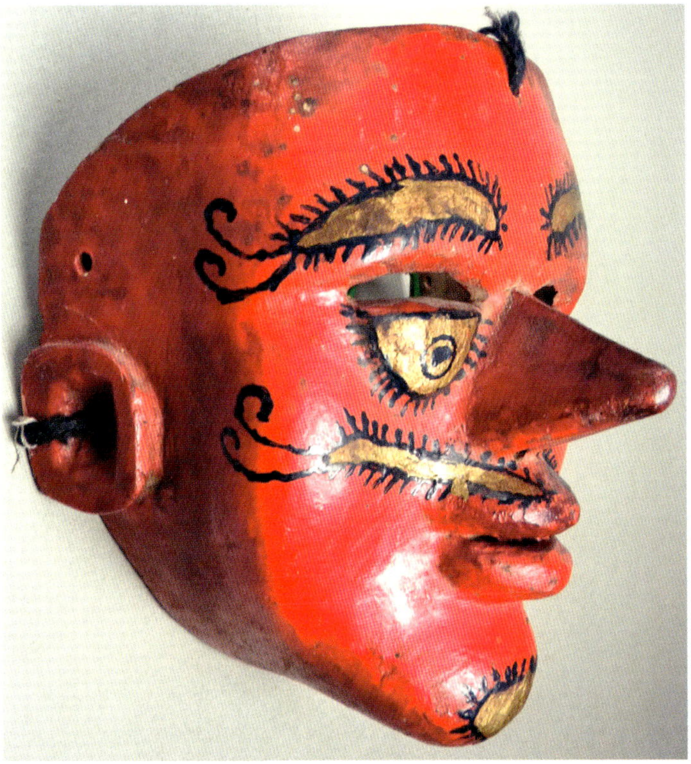

This is a good example of the moderate-sized and less dramatic Santiaguero masks of this carver; 6¾" × 7". Circa 1980. This one was collected in the area of San Antonio Rayón. Rating: known carver, good condition, well carved, good paint with good patina on the back, and rare, *****. *Collection of Vernon Kostohryz.*

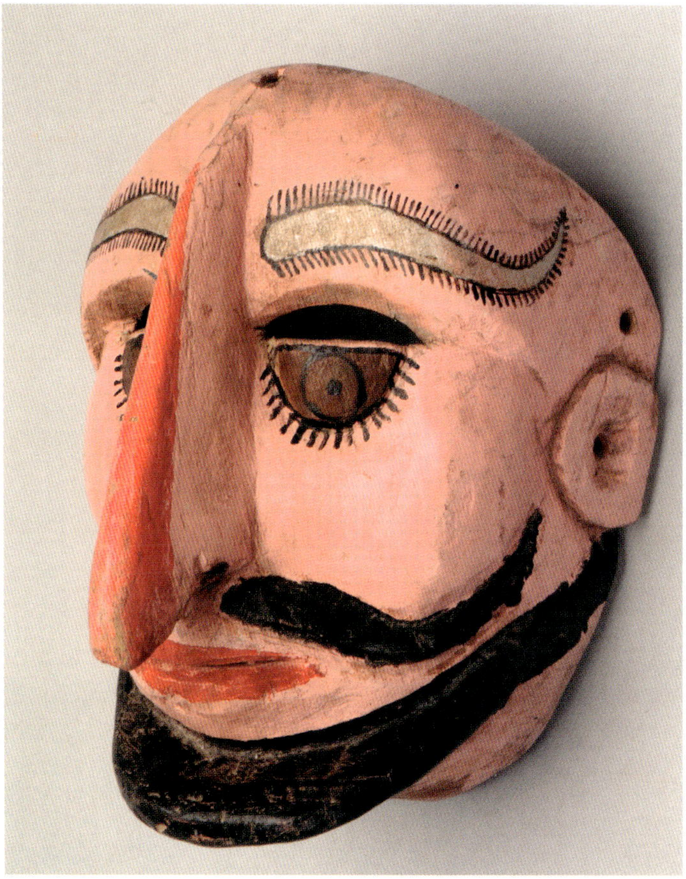

This oversized Pilato mask was formerly owned by Manuel Antonio Castañeda but carved by Narciso. Generally this mask is rather different from all the rest, except for the typical ear design; 8" × 12". Rating: known carver, good condition, well carved, good patina, and rare, *****. *Collection of the author.*

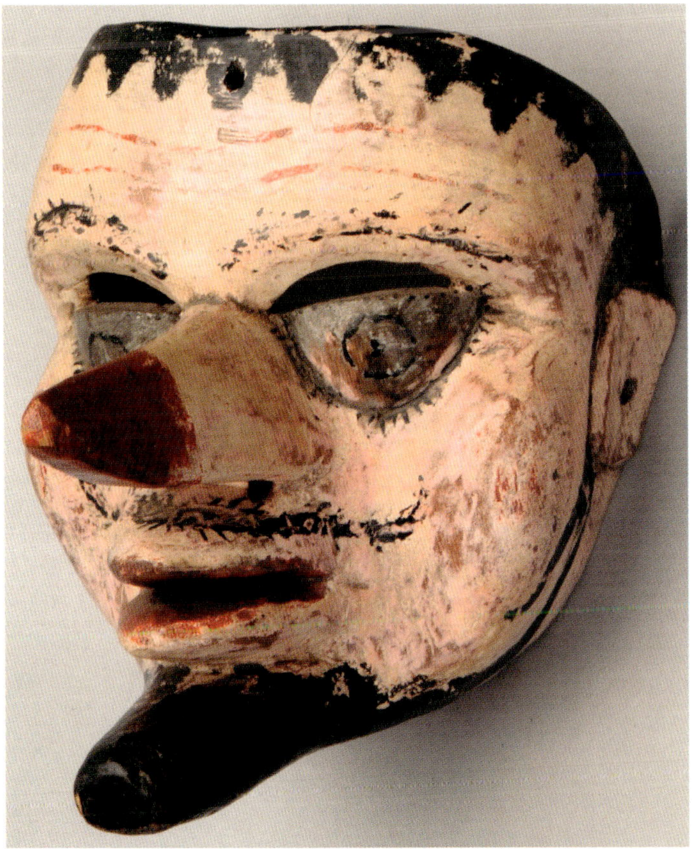

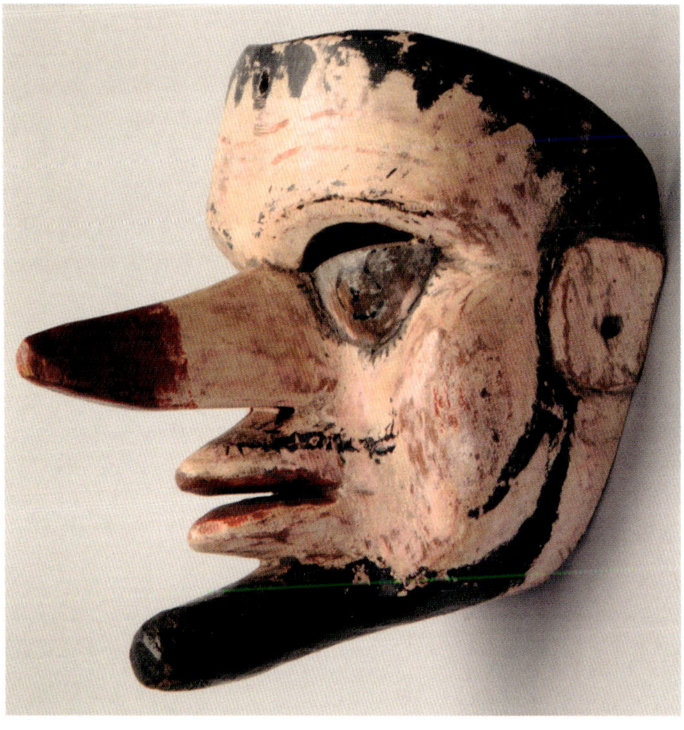

Left: This normally sized Pilato mask was collected in San Antonio Rayón; 6¾" × 9". Circa 1970. In form it much resembles the Santiaguero masks. Rating: known carver, good condition, well carved, great patina, and rare, ******. *Collection of the author.*

Above: The mask has a dramatic profile.

Felipe Jiménez Martínez

Felipe Jiménez Martínez lives in Llagostera, Puebla. In Chapter 4 you may have seen Felipe and his friend Eusebio Blas Roman wearing two of his masks for the Danza de los Moros y Cristianos dance. Here are those masks shown in greater detail.

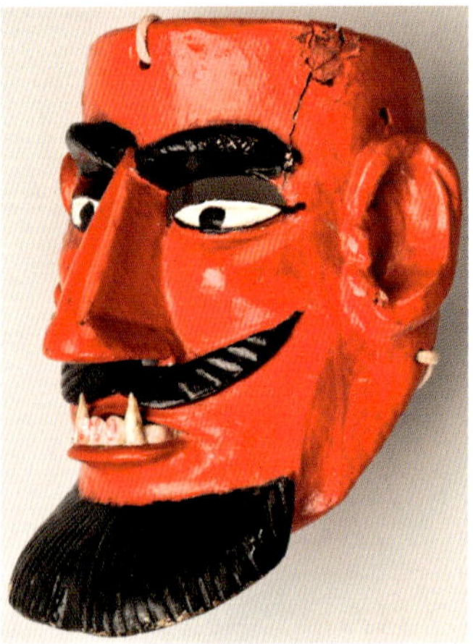

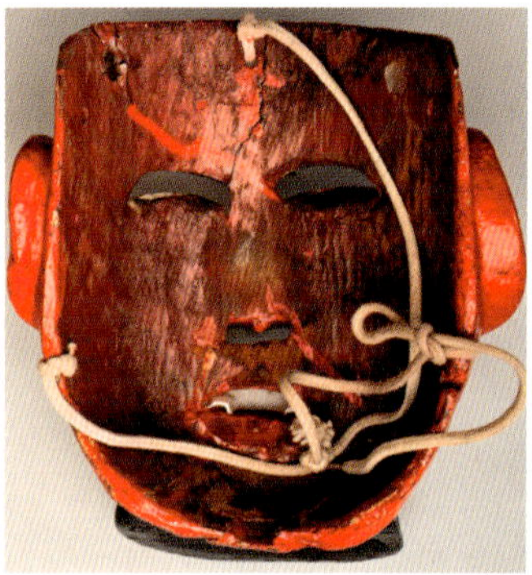

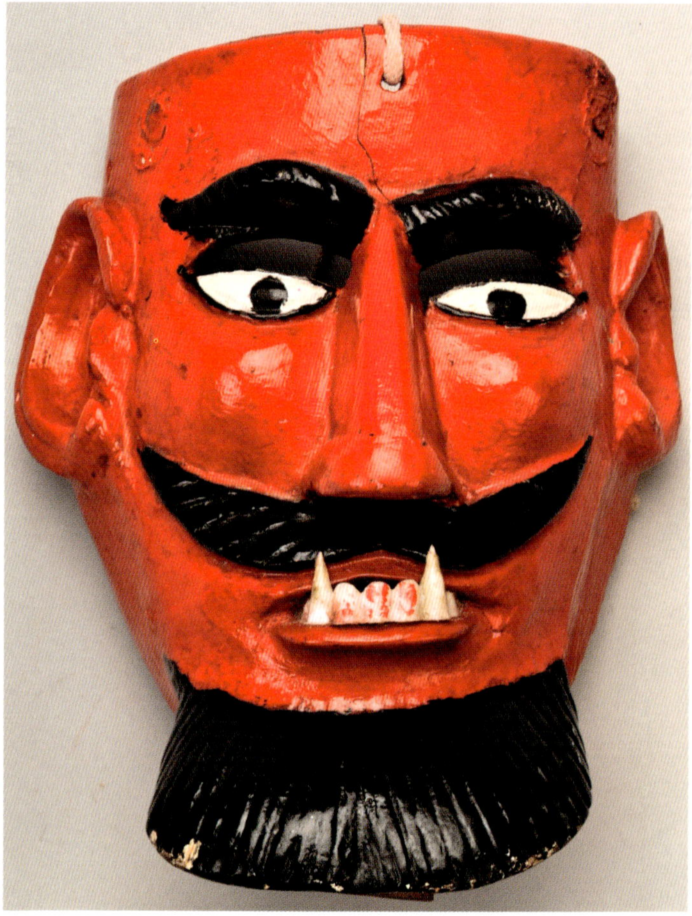

Right: A mask of the devil for the dance of the Moros y Cristianos; 7½" × 9". Circa 1990. It is very nicely carved, with brows and mustache in relief, a flared goatee, and elaborate ears. It has lost its horns. Plastic toy vampire teeth have been added with good effect. Rating: known carver, good condition except lost horns, well carved, nice paint with marked patina on the back, and rarity unknown, ****. *Collection of the author.*

Above left: The side view. It is well carved. *Above Right:* The back shows marked wear.

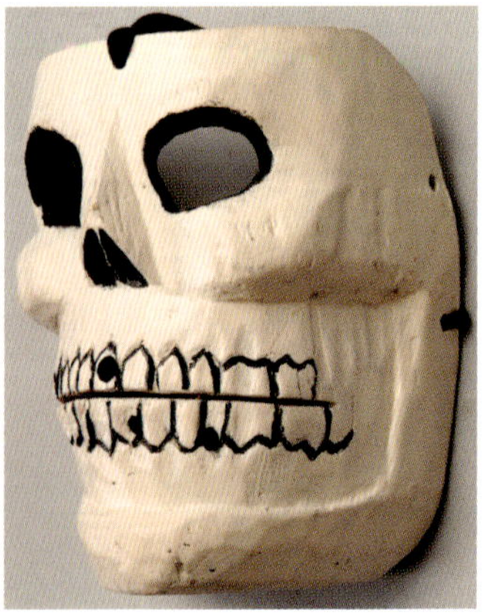

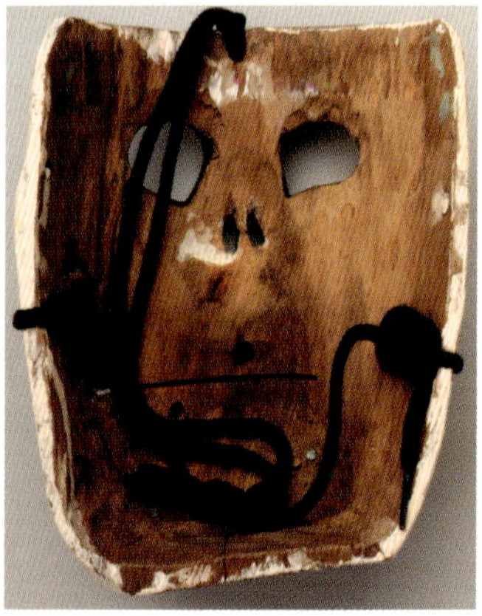

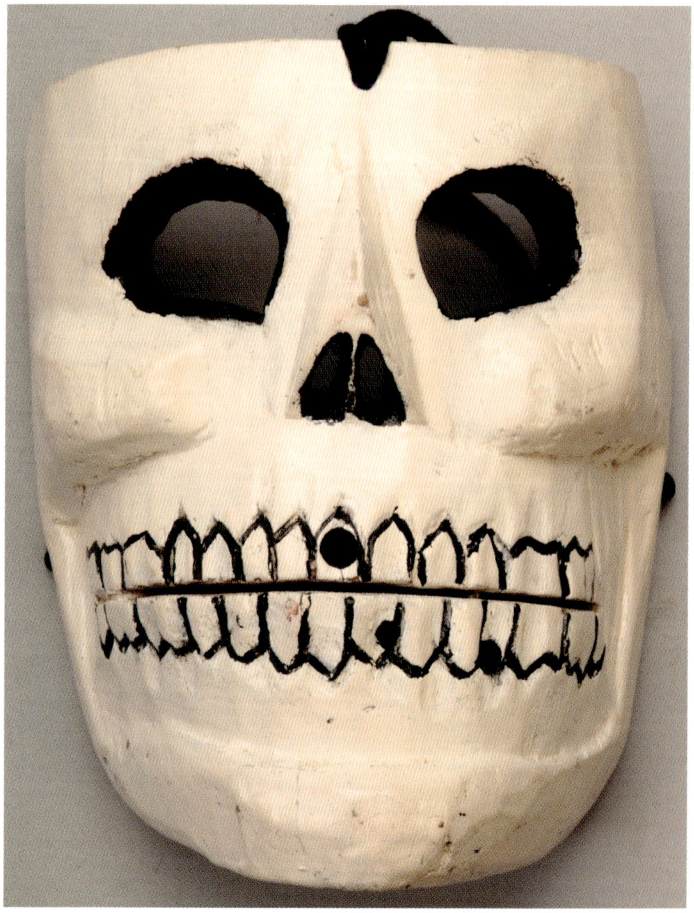

Right: This is an effective skull mask; 6¼" × 7½". Rating: known carver, good condition, well carved, vividly repainted with marked patina on the back, and rarity unknown, ****. *Collection of the author.*

Above left: The side view. *Above Right:* This back shows moderate wear.

Miguel Juan Marquez

Miguel Juan Marquez was born in 1952. He lives in África Vieja, a very small and isolated community in the municipio of San Felipe Tepatlán, Puebla. He is a santero and a carver of masks. Carlos has been told by informants in nearby towns that Miguel's work is highly regarded in this region. I too would say that he is an excellent carver; I find his masks nicely carved and quite charming. Thus far we have seen several Huehue masks, two Payaso masks, one Perro, and a set of puppets, all for the Huehue dance.

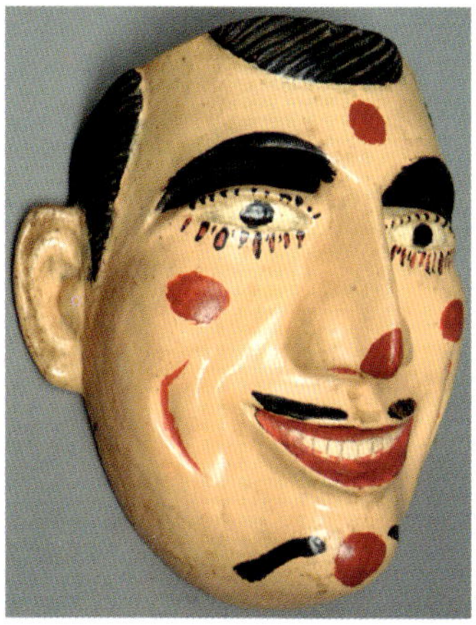

The side view provides a slightly better view of the ear.

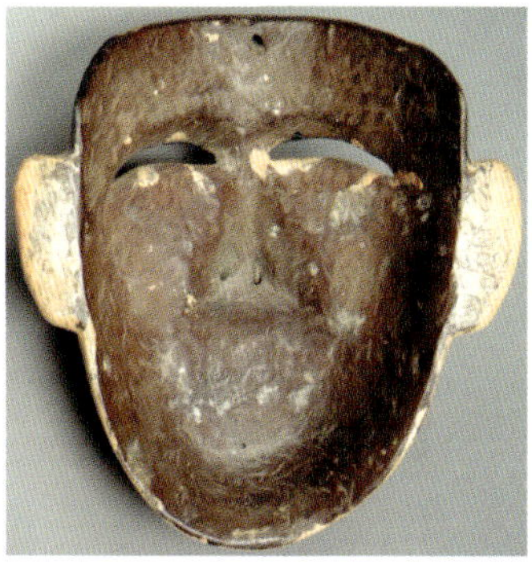

The back has great patina.

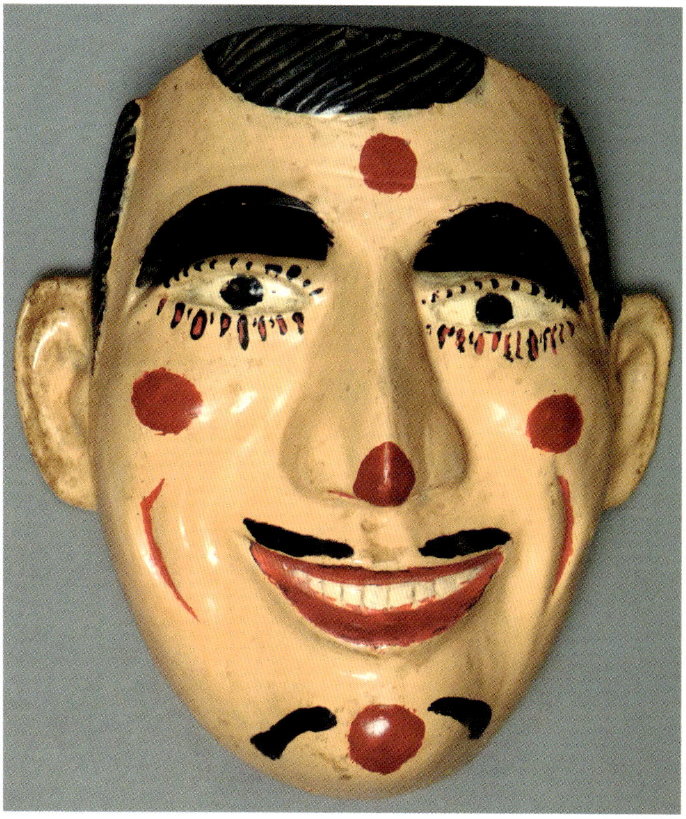

This is a Payaso mask by Miguel Juan Marquez; 7¾" × 8½". Circa 1980. It is an elegant mask, very well carved from walnut wood and nicely painted. Rating: known carver, excellent condition, very well carved, good patina, and rare, ******. *Collection of the author.*

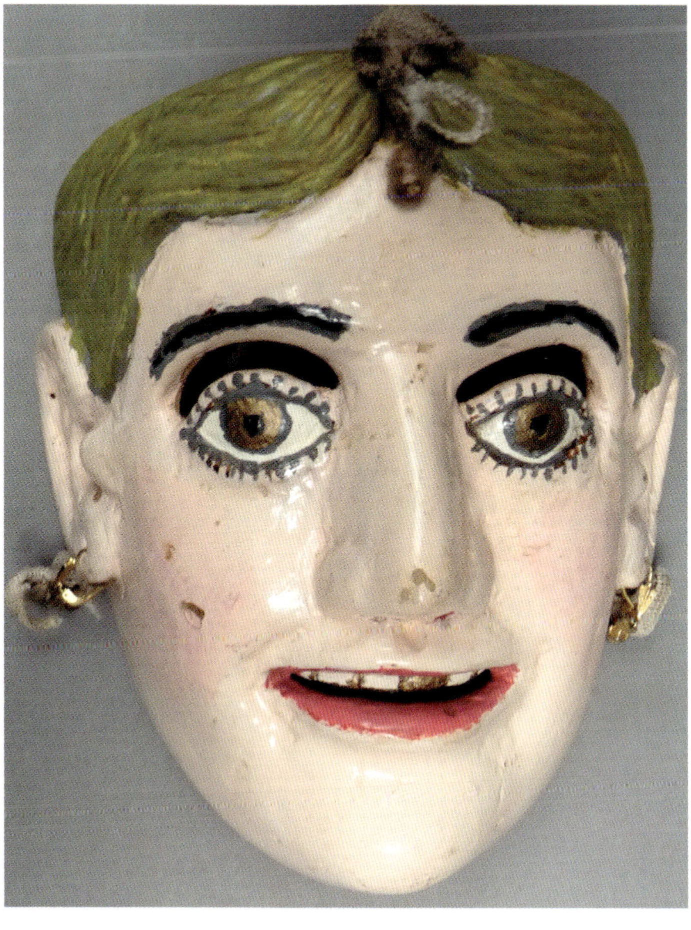

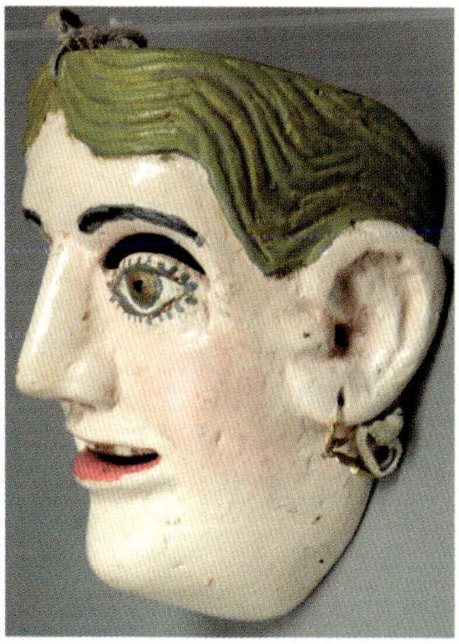

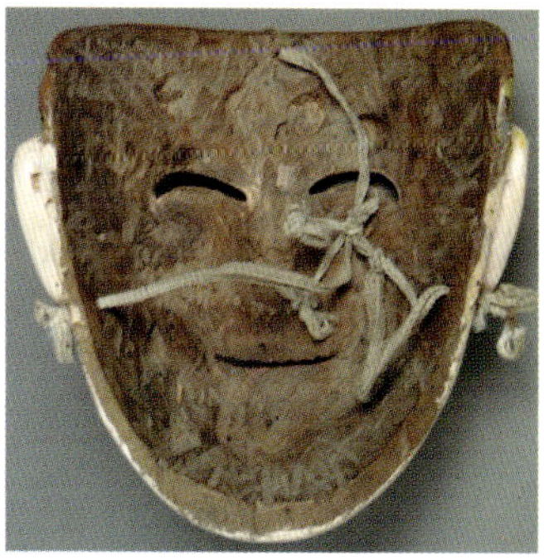

Left: This female Payaso mask was nicknamed "La Gringa" by the carver, due to her yellow hair; 6¾" × 7½". Circa 1980. It is well carved and projects a lot of personality. Rating: known carver, excellent condition, very well carved, good patina, and possibly rare, *****. *Collection of the author.*

Above left: The side view shows the beautiful car design as well as the nice carving around the mouth.

Above right: The carver used a hand auger drill to hollow the back, and then he scraped the wood with broken glass to smooth it. You can still see a few of the drill holes. The patina is moderate.

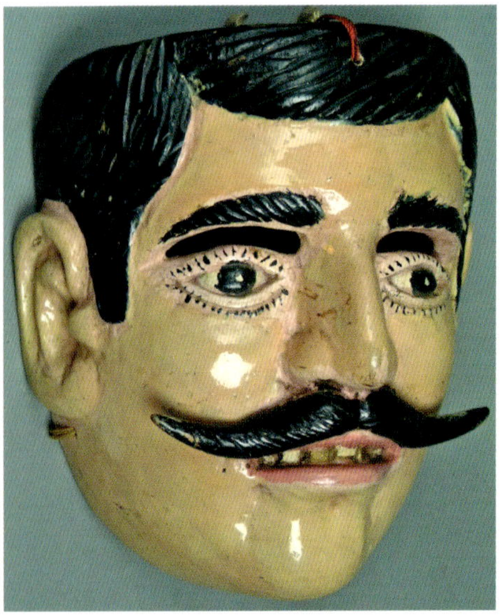

This male Huehue mask, by Miguel Juan Marquez, is very well carved: 6¾" × 7½". Circa 1980. Rating: known carver, excellent condition, very well carved, good patina, and possibly rare, *****. *Collection of the author.*

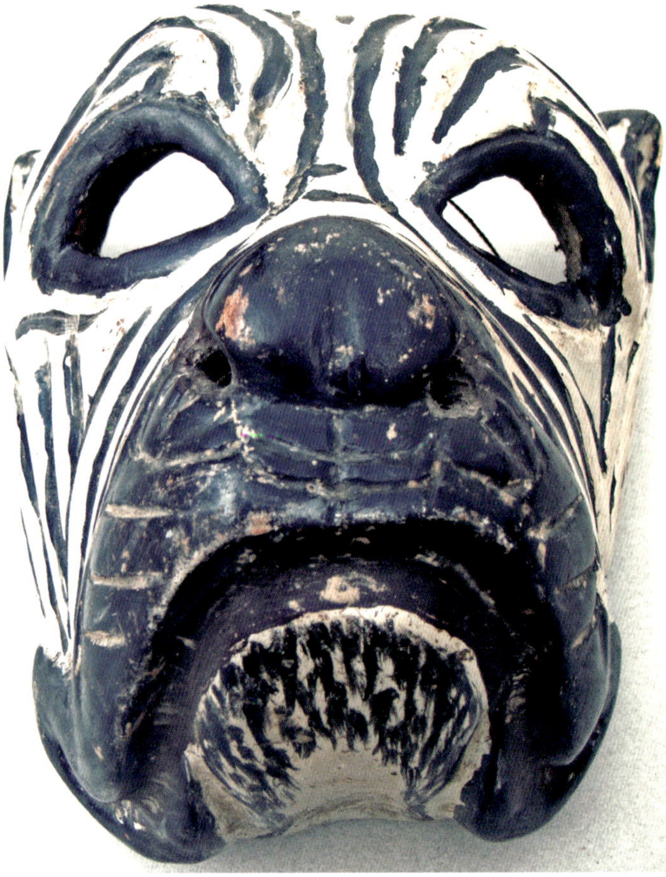

A Perro mask by Miguel Juan Marquez. Like the Payaso, this mask has great style; 8" × 7½". Circa 1980. Rating: known carver, excellent condition, very well carved, good patina, and unusual, *****. *Collection of Vernon Kostohryz, photos courtesy of Vernon.*

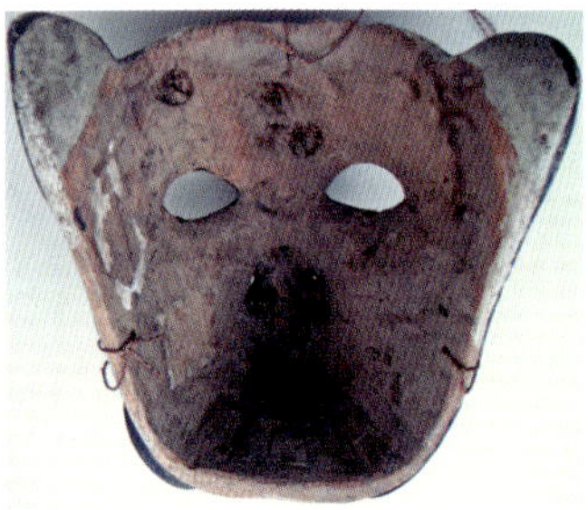

Right: The back of this mask still shows the marks of the auger bit used to hollow the mask.

Benito Juárez Figueroa, Jose Juárez, José Juárez García, and Alina Juárez Pérez

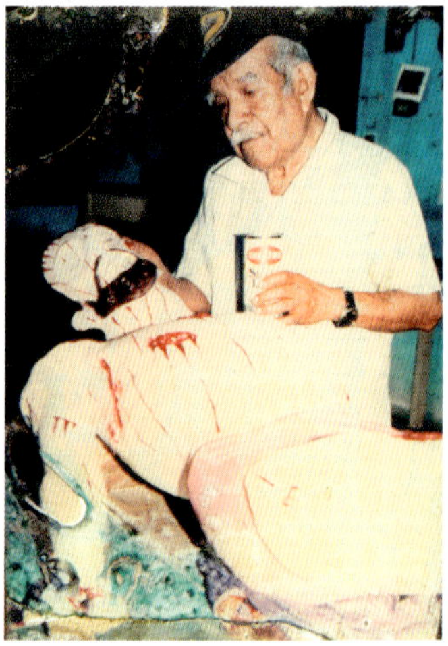

In this copy from a family photograph, Benito Juárez Figueroa is painting his completed carving of a wooden saint, probably Christ. *I thank Alina Juárez Pérez for permission to copy this photo of her father, along with carvings in her collection.*

Benito Juárez Figueroa was born in Nanacatlán, Puebla, on February 14, 1910. He began carving there as an adolescent. He married at the age of 20, moving to Ixtepec, Puebla, where he lived with his wife until he reached 60 years of age. He then moved to Filomeno Mata, Veracruz, but moved back to Ixtepec at 73 years and died there at 85, on June 24, 1994. Both his father (José Juárez García of Nanacatlán) and his paternal grandfather (José Juárez) were also mascareros. It seems that Benito was a prolific carver, and one still finds occasional fine examples of his masks in the area around Ixtepec and in the area of Filomeno Mata as well. He was apparently also a very accomplished carver of saints. In our region of study, Benito would appear to have been one of the greatest master carvers of the middle decades of the twentieth century.

I obtained one very early mask by Benito from his daughter, Alina. She allowed me to photograph masks that were in her possession that were carved by Benito, his father, and his grandfather. Comparing these masks, I got the impression that when Benito was a young man he attempted to develop his own style, independent of those of his grandfather and father. However, it also seems that Benito later adopted his father's style, perhaps upon his father's death? That is, his early mask has a very beautiful ear design that is substantially different from that of his father and grandfather. His later masks seem to build on the ear designs found on his father's and grandfather's masks.

In the photo that follows of the back of this early Tejonero mask from Alina's collection, we begin to see elements that we will come to recognize as enduring markers for Benito's style of carving the backs of masks: There is a depression for the wearer's nose, carved out with vertical chisel strokes; there is more or less of a shelf at the chin level; in general, the chisel strokes on the back of the mask are softened but not smoothed over, and they were allowed to remain showing.

Benito's father was José Juárez García, of Nanacatlán, Puebla. We lack specific dates, but based on what we have learned from Alina Juárez Pérez, we believe that he was born c. 1875 and died c. 1925. I can offer photos of a mask that was attributed to him by his granddaughter Alina. This was very well carved, and I believe that this mask shares features with similar anonymous examples, persuading me to attribute these other masks to this carver. Briefly, the ears typically carved by José Juárez García are quite different from those used by Benito Juárez. They are different in a more subtle way from those carved by Benito's grandfather, José Juárez. The carving of the chin area is also different for each of these carvers, although this is easier to see than to describe. The chin on a mask by José Juárez García tends to be oval or roughly square while that of José Juárez is more knob-shaped. The backs of their masks also are more simply carved than those of Benito. It is hoped that this will be clearer in the photos.

Benito's paternal grandfather was José Juárez. Again we lack specific dates to define his life; we suppose that he was born in about 1850 and died early in the 20th century. I was privileged to photograph a child's mask definitely carved by him that was in the possession of Alina Juárez Pérez. Then on the basis of those photos I was able to identify and purchase a second, nearly identical example that was adult-sized in Tuxtla, Puebla, a village that lies between Ixtepec and Nanacatlán. Subsequently I found several more masks that were probably his work as well.

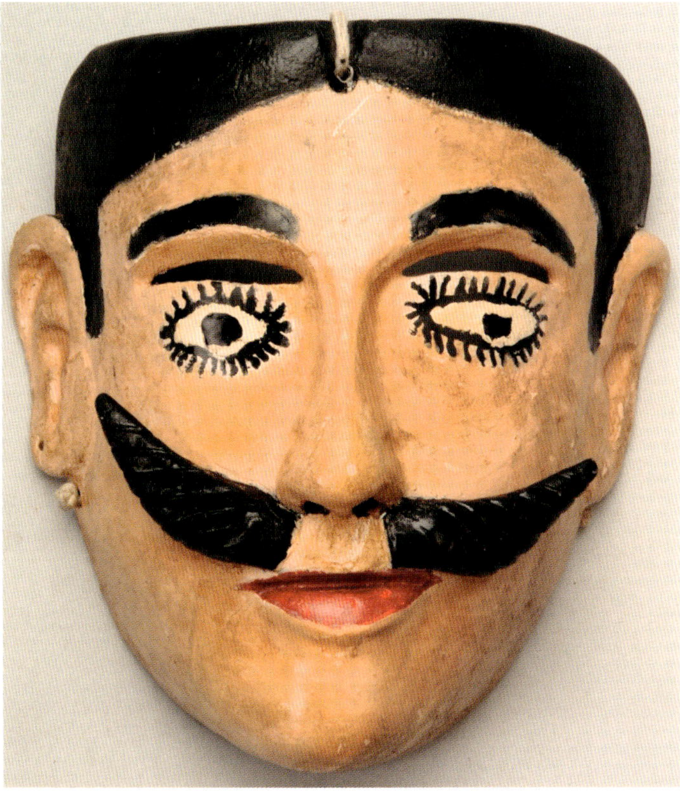

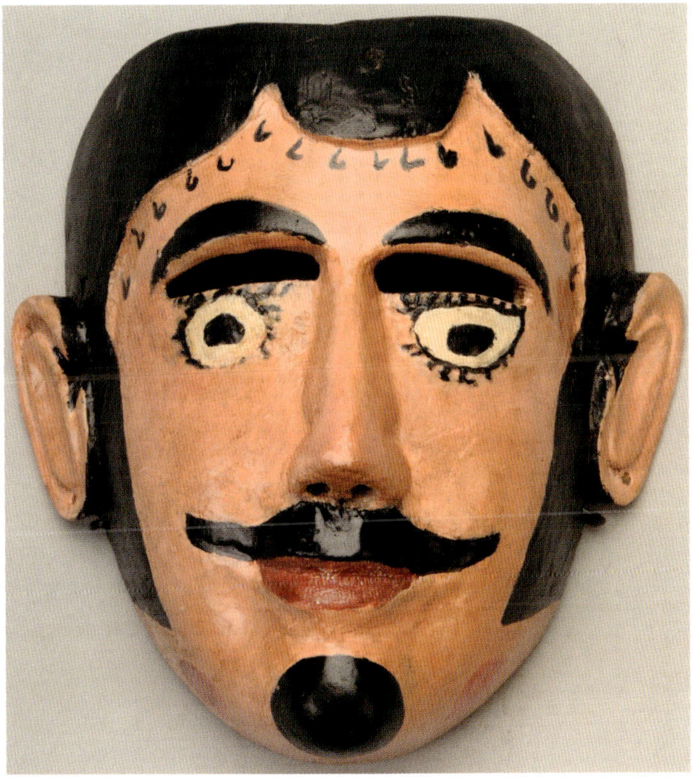

Above; This mask was a puzzle, but gradually the hand of José Juárez can be recognized, as the ears closely resemble his design, as does the nose, the knobbed chin, and the general shape of the back; 6½" × 7". Circa 1880. The hairline is oddly severe in shape. This is a Huehue mask of ambiguous gender, with sideburns carved in low relief and extended by paint, ears pierced for earrings, and a mustache carved in very low relief, then amplified by paint. There are pink circles on both sides of the chin—what do they signify? There is a painted goatee that is not associated with any relief carving in that area. I can only speculate that this was originally a male, was converted to a female for a time, and then converted back to a male by exaggerated painted features. Little feminine curls linger across the brow. Rating: known carver, good condition, well carved, recently repainted but with good patina on the back, and very rare, ******. *Collection of the author.*

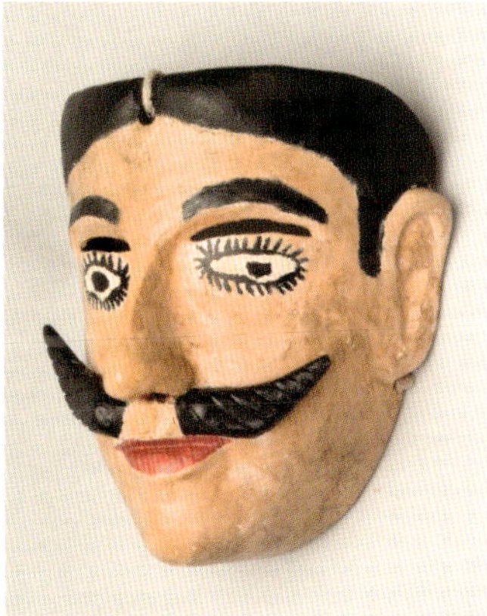

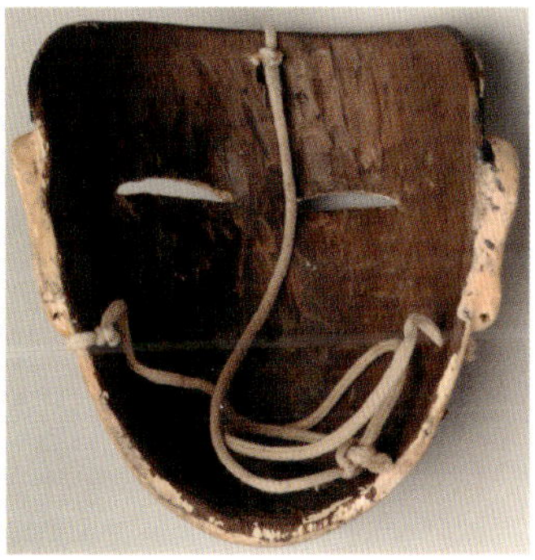

Top: The Tejonero or Huehue mask in Benito's earliest style, which the author purchased from the carver's daughter, Alina Juárez Pérez; 6½" × 7". Circa 1930. The mustache is attached by nails. Rating: known carver, good condition, well carved, worn paint with good patina on the back, and very rare, ******. *Collection of the author.*

Above left: On the side view, note the beautiful simple design of the ear. Although not obvious from this view, both ears are pierced for earrings, confirming my suspicion that this was originally a female mask, converted to a male with a nailed-on mustache.

Above right: The back of this very early mask by Benito. Like many others, this mask was at one time painted white and at another time pink. The age and wear on this mask can be seen clearly from this view.

Right: This Huehue mask was reported by Alina Juárez Pérez to have been carved by her paternal grandfather, the father of Benito—José Juárez García; 6½" × 7". Circa 1900. The family had repainted a female Huehue mask to be a male by the addition of a painted mustache, but it was not very convincing. This mask has the beautiful face that we associate with the santero tradition. Rating: known carver, good condition, well carved, recently repainted but with good patina on the back, and very rare, ******. *Collection of Vernon Kostohryz, who has had it repainted to be a female.*

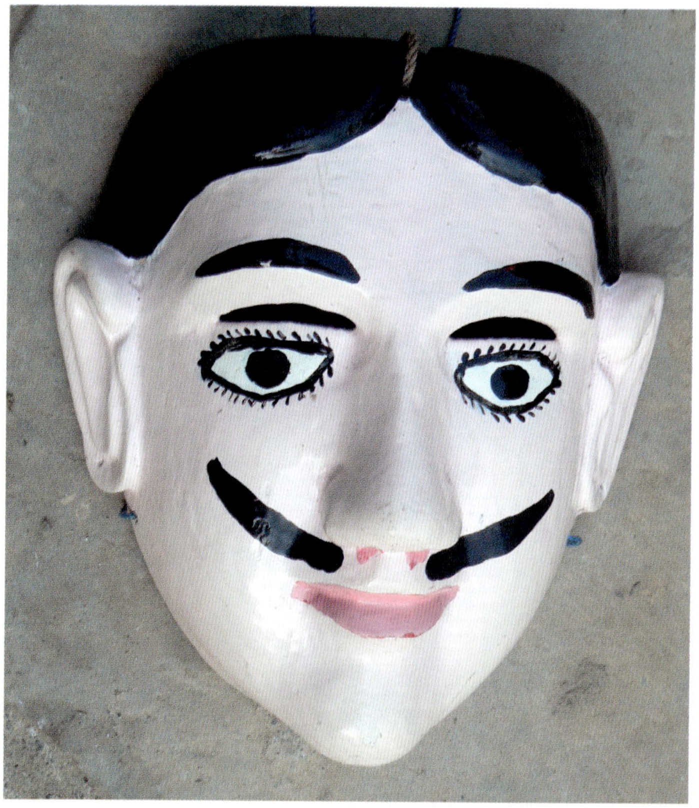

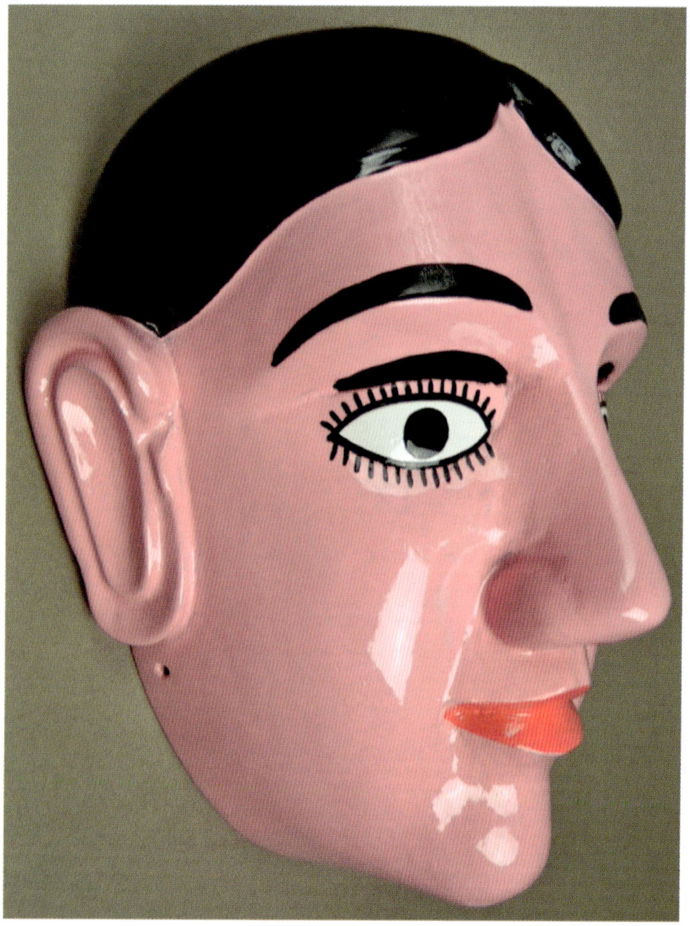

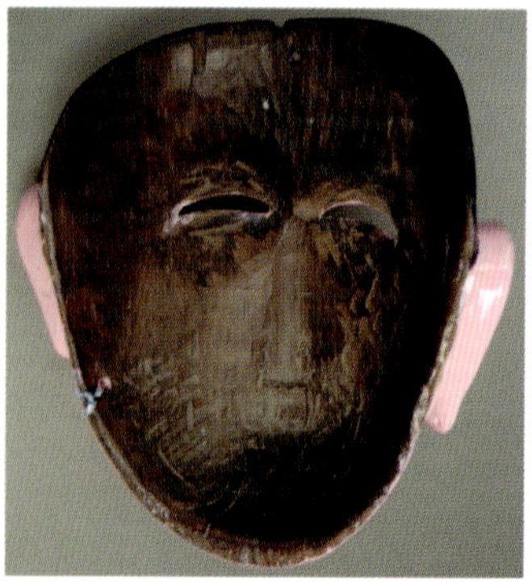

Above: The side view of the mask above, after being freshly repainted as a female, demonstrates the typical relief-carved hairline for a female Huehue mask in the Juárez tradition. The ear is very beautifully carved, but the hole for an earring has been painted over. You will see that this graceful ear design is unlike the one seen on Benito's early masks and also softer than the ear Benito typically carved for most of his career.

Left: The back of this mask. We see again very soft contours along with a tiny shelf at chin level.

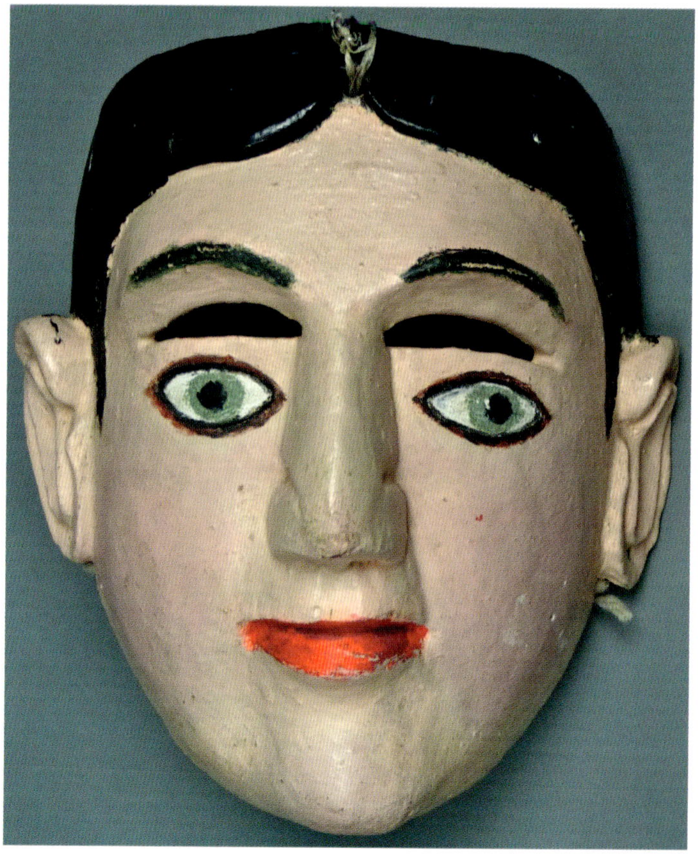

Right: This female Huehue mask is attributed to José Juárez García; 6½" × 7¼". Circa 1900. Comparing this photo and the front view of the mask above, reveals that both the ears and the lower portions of the two faces are virtually the same. Also they have identical hairlines. It is difficult to imagine that they were not carved by the same hand. Yet there are minor differences; for instance, the eyes are carved in relief on this mask but not on the one above. Vernon Kostohryz and I agree to attribute this mask to José Juárez García. Rating: known carver, good condition, well carved, with good patina on the face versus marked patina on the back, and very rare, *******. *Collection of the author.*

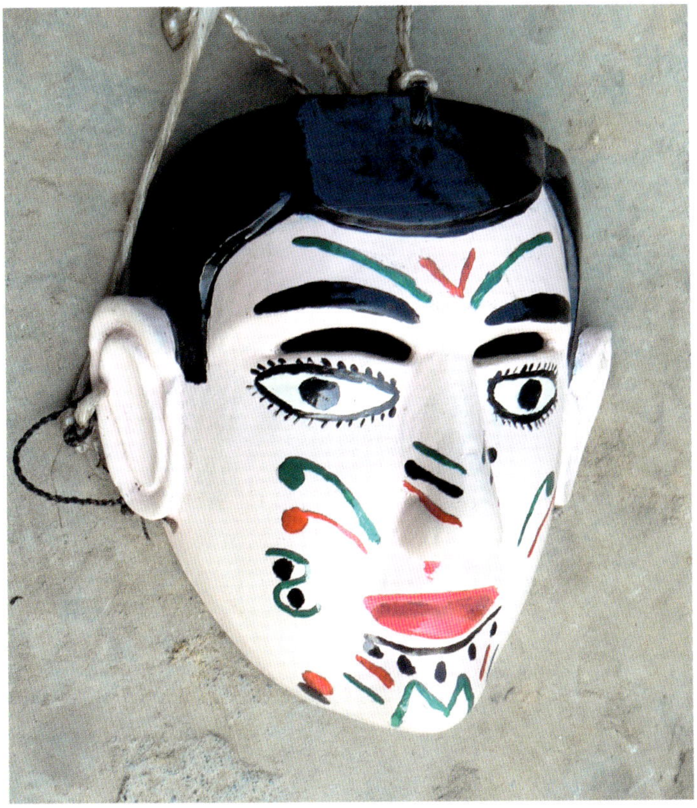

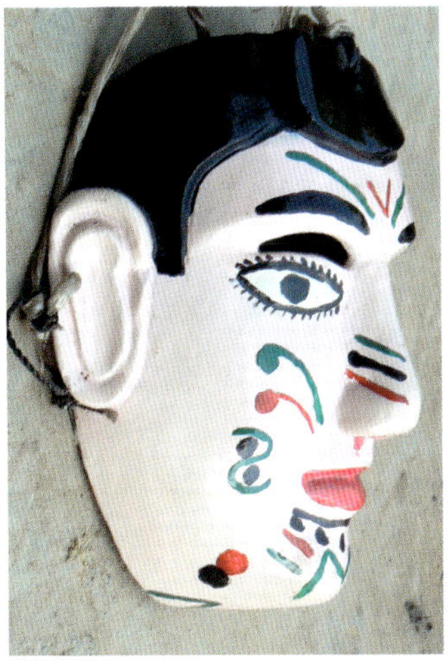

The side view to show the ear design from another angle.

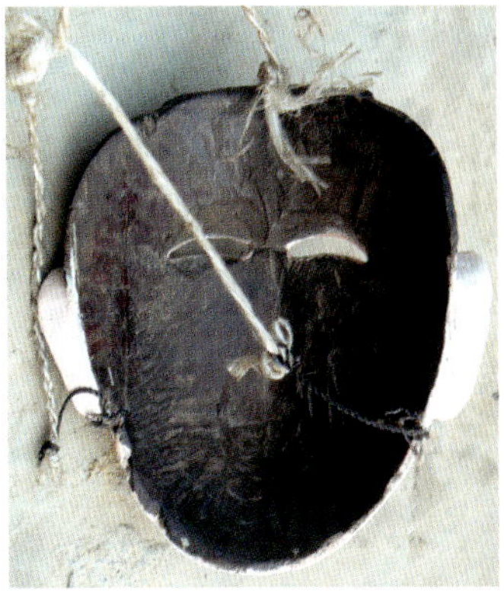

The back of the mask by José Juárez. The patina is very dark. The carving of the back is again quite simple, lacking the typical features on the back of a mask carved by Benito Juárez.

This Huehue mask was reported by Alina Juárez Pérez to have been carved by her great-grandfather, the grandfather of Benito Juárez; his name was José Juárez. The ear design on this mask is rather similar to that of the masks of his son, yet just a little different; they are very different compared to the design that Benito Juárez used on most of his masks. The manner of carving the hair on this mask is highly stylized and different from that of Benito's father and Benito's as well; 6" × 6". Circa 1880. Here we see another conversion of a male Huehue mask to that of a Payaso. This mask is slightly smaller than usual; it is a boy's mask. Rating: known carver, good condition, well carved, fresh paint with good patina on the back, and very rare, ******. *Collection of Vernon Kostohryz, who has had it repainted to be a male Huehue.*

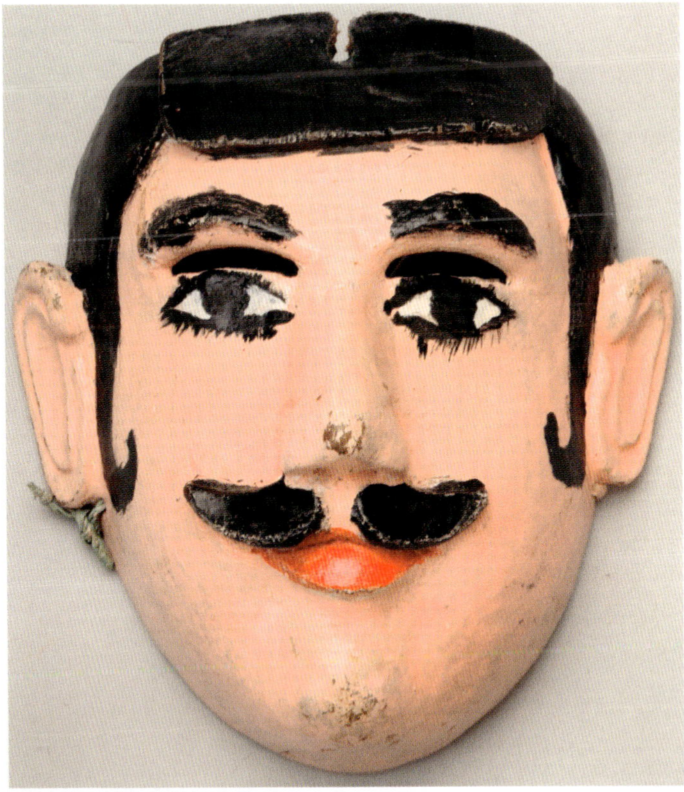

On the basis of my photo of the mask above, Vernon Kostohryz and I were subsequently able to identify and obtain another mask by José Juárez, in Tuxtla, Puebla. This one has both the identical hairstyle and ear design, but it was made for an adult; 6½" × 7". Circa 1880. Rating: known carver, good condition, well carved, with good patina on the face versus marked patina on the back, and very rare, *******. *Collection of the author.*

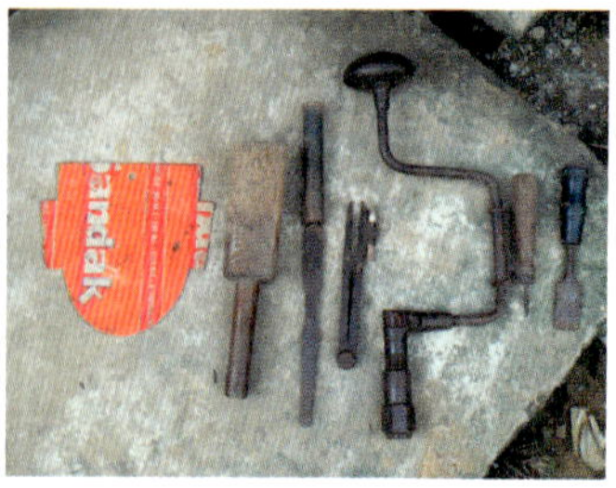

Above: The set of tools that belonged to José Juárez García and were used by Alina when she began carving masks.

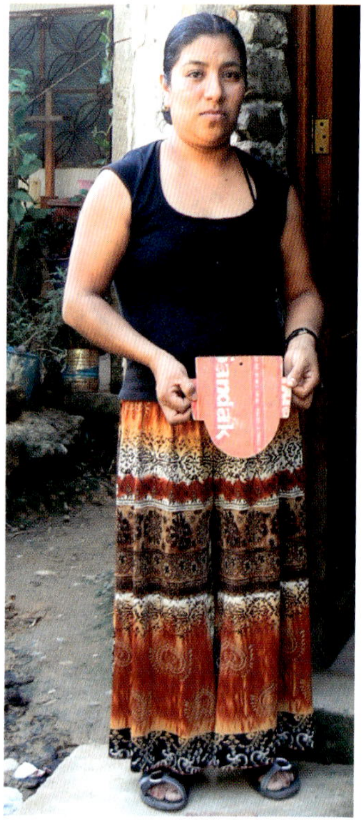

Right: Here is a recent photo of Alina Juárez Pérez, holding a paper pattern that her father made for her when she was 15 years old, to prepare the wooden block from which one would subsequently carve a mask. *These photos of Alina, her tools, and her masks all appear with her permission.*

Benito's daughter, Alina Juárez Pérez, was born on October 14, 1973, and she lives with her husband in Filomeno Mata, Veracruz. With her father's support, she too began carving masks at about the age of 15 years. I have seen only a few of her masks, one of which was carved when she was quite young, and so I lack a clear idea of the range or depth of her carving. It does seem to me that mask carving has never been such a central preoccupation for her, compared to that of her father, as she was otherwise busily engaged in the roles of wife and mother. I would think that she is still developing her mature style as a carver, and that her greatest work in this area is yet to come.

In this book you will see masks by Benito Juárez that portray various characters, including Hormegas and Santiagueros, Huehues or Tejoneros, Negritos, and one Perro (dog) that would have been part of the Huehues dance.

I used a series of masks by Benito in Chapter 5 to illustrate elements of style and also the process of evolution that apparently develops in some carvers. As you will have seen in that chapter, Benito consistently utilized many distinctive stylistic elements in the carving of his masks, and although these shifted and changed over time, there was sufficient overlap on most of his masks to permit one little doubt about the identity of the carver.

Earlier I described a very early mask by Benito that had an elegant ear design, one that marked a major departure from the design used on masks carved by Benito's father and grandfather. I have discovered two other very old masks that appear to have a similar ear design; I believe that they were also carved by Benito.

One of these, an old Negrito with a beard, is interesting on so many different levels. Vernon Kostohryz purchased this mask in Zozocolco de Hidalgo, Veracruz, from Chucho Arroyo, who said that he bought it from a friend who was the actual wearer. It has been provided with a second set of vision slits, under the painted eyes, apparently for use by the Voladores. One is tempted to speculate that the "friend" whose mask this had been was actually one of Chucho's sisters, and that the carver of the new slits was Luis de Luna. In a prior life, this very old mask had been used in the Negritos dance; it was said to be the *Jefe de los Negritos*, the chief. The ears on this mask resemble those of the earliest masks by Benito Juárez, and on the back we see Benito's characteristic hollow for the nose. Also the mask has carved wrinkles across the forehead that are quite familiar from a few other Benito Juárez masks.

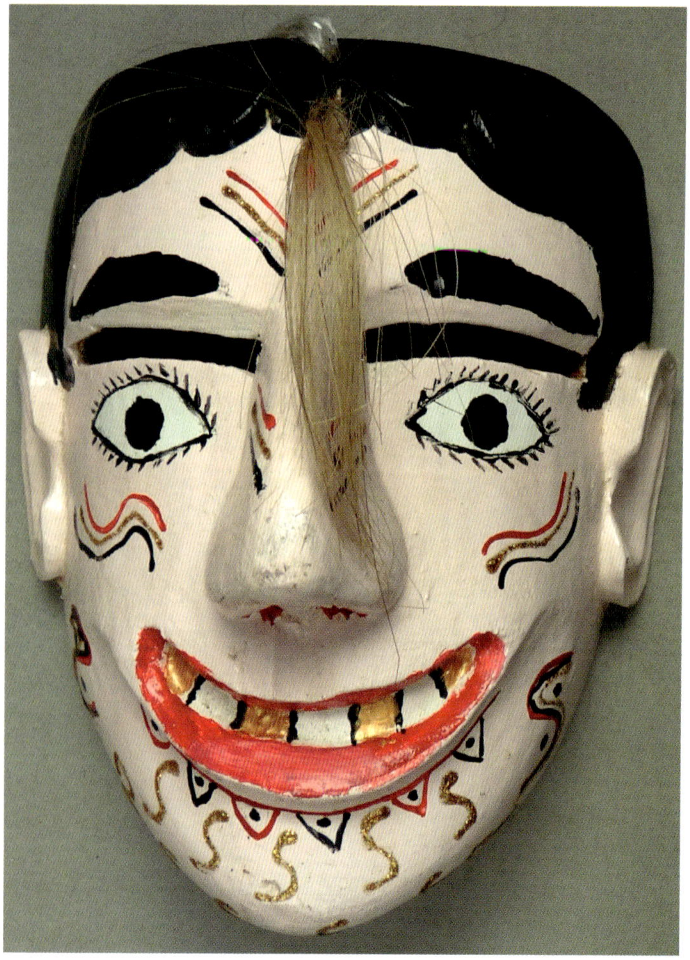

A Payaso Huehue mask by Alina Juárez Pérez, apparently carved in recent years; 6½" × 7". Circa 2000. She seems to have developed a style of her own. Rating: known carver, good condition, well carved, undanced or with little obvious patina, and rarity unknown, ***. *Collection of Vernon Kostohryz.*

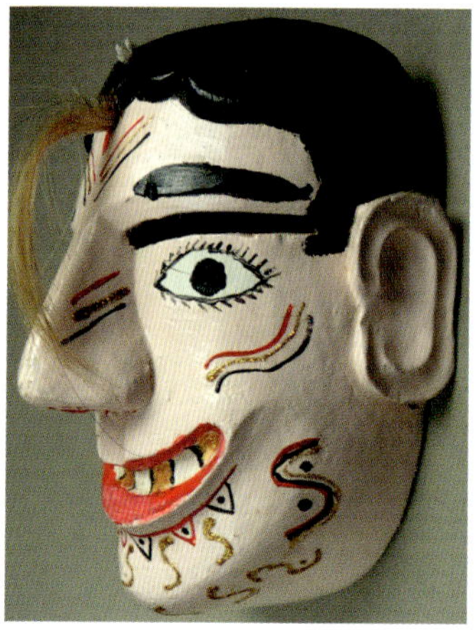

The side view showing the ear design.

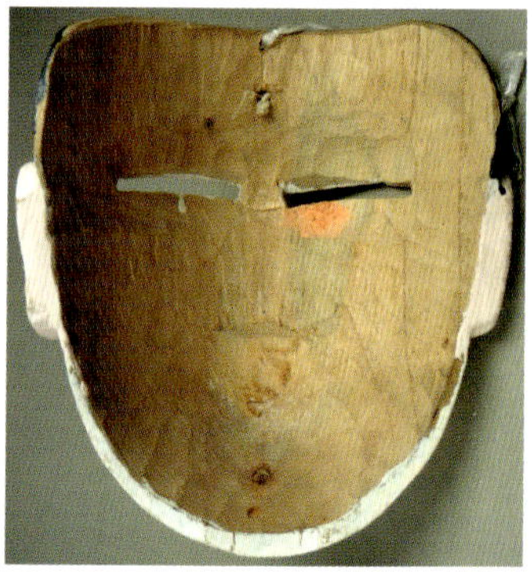

The back is nicely finished, and Alina has carved a hollow to accommodate the wearer's nose.

The other mask that appears to have Benito's very early ear design is a female Huehue that was painted with white enamel.

The most distinctive feature of the majority of Benito's masks was his execution of the ear design that had apparently originated with his grandfather (if not earlier) and which was then refined by Benito into something more modern. We have many well-documented examples to demonstrate Benito's mastery during the phase of his career after he adopted this element. A more variable element was the hollow area to accommodate the wearer's nose on the back of the mask, usually carved with thin vertical chisel marks.

Sometimes Benito would carefully carve the eyes on the face of the mask, but more typically he would simply paint the eyes, as on most of the masks that follow.

Benito would carefully shape some areas of the mask, such as the arch of the brows, the groove above the mouth and the planes of the area around the mouth. On some masks he carved a subtle flat or hollow spot over the top of the nasal ridge and between the brows. He had a particular painting style that is also easily recognized. The net result of all this is that his masks have a simple grandeur.

When I visited Olintla, Puebla, a village that is not very far from Ixtepec, I found older masks there that seemed absolutely typical of Benito's work, along with much newer-seeming masks that were either the work of Benito or they were very competent copies. Benito's son lived in Ixtepec until his recent move to Mexico City and it may be that he had continued his father's traditional style, although I have not been able to confirm or deny this as yet. I can say that I also saw in Olintla masks that were apparently modeled on Benito's style but which were clearly the work of a different carver.

Benito's older male Huehue or Tejonero masks typically have relief-carved mustaches. That is, the mustache was carved in place from the same block of wood that was otherwise shaped to make the rest of the mask. In contrast, some newer male Huehue or Tejonero masks with features typical of Benito may have applied mustaches that are nailed or glued on. In one photo that follows of three masks, you will see that the mask in the center has the relief-carved style of mustache while those flanking have applied mustaches.

I have wondered whether the masks with applied mustaches were female masks, which were later converted to males, because a male Huehue mask almost invariably has a mustache; if a male mask was intended one would expect the carver to have included the mustache in the initial carving process. Having had the experience of examining so many masks by Benito, we noticed that the carving of the hair provides a clear indication of the initial gender of the mask. The raised hairline on Benito's Huehue or Tejonero masks stops at the top of the ear for a female and extends down to mid-ear for a male. Using this clue, I have seen that it has been common for a mask with a female hairline (and pierced earlobes) to be converted to a male by the addition of a painted or applied mustache.

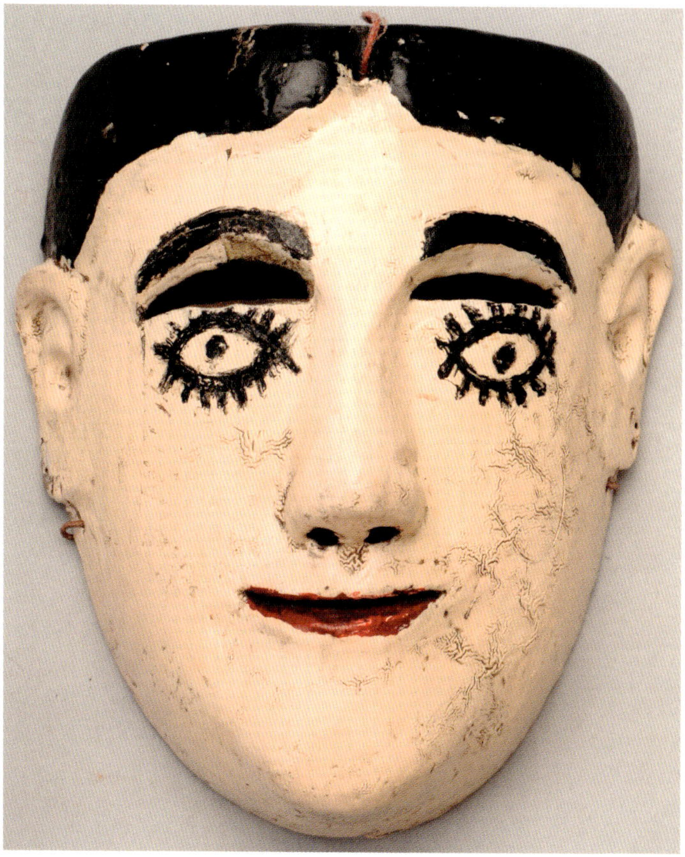

This female Tejonero mask was found in the area of Coxquihui, Veracruz; 6" × 6¾". Circa 1930. She is well carved; the ear is particularly beautiful. The mask is attributed to Benito Juárez because of the resemblance of the ears and the carving of the back to those features on the early Benito mask from Alina's collection. When Vernon Kostohryz purchased this mask, it appeared to be covered with brown varnish. He washed the mask with soap and water; to his surprise it turned suddenly white. We have since observed that this stark white complexion is not unusual on older masks that remained in the collection of the Juárez family. Rating: known carver, good condition, well carved, old crinkled paint on the face but with dramatic patina on the back, and very rare, ******. *Collection of the author.*

But then we discovered a new twist. It seems that this style of mustache, so handsome and dramatic, had at some point become desirable for itself, so that male Huehue masks were being deliberately carved with these attached mustaches instead of the ones in low relief. Among the masks that Vernon Kostohryz collected recently in Olintla, there were two Huehue masks of moderate age and with the typical features of Benito Juárez that had both these sweeping mustaches and the male hairline; clearly they were deliberately constructed in this form.

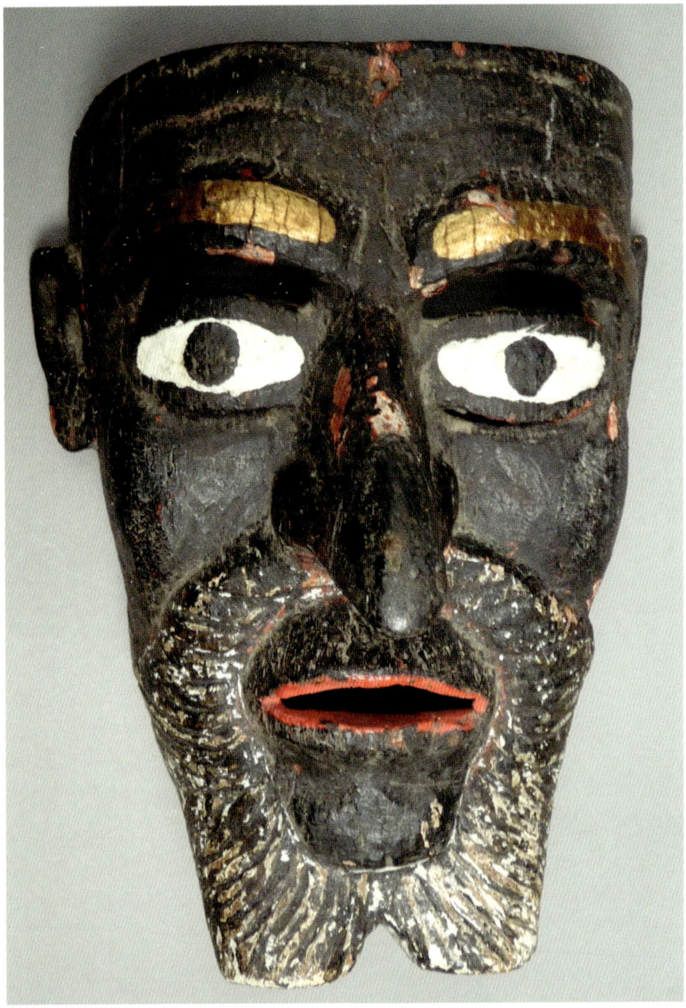

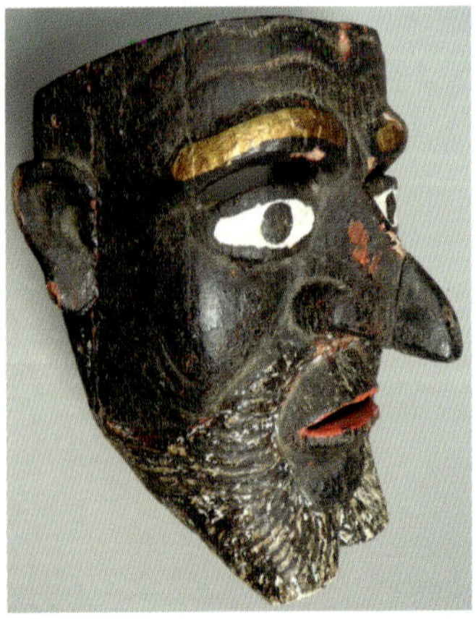

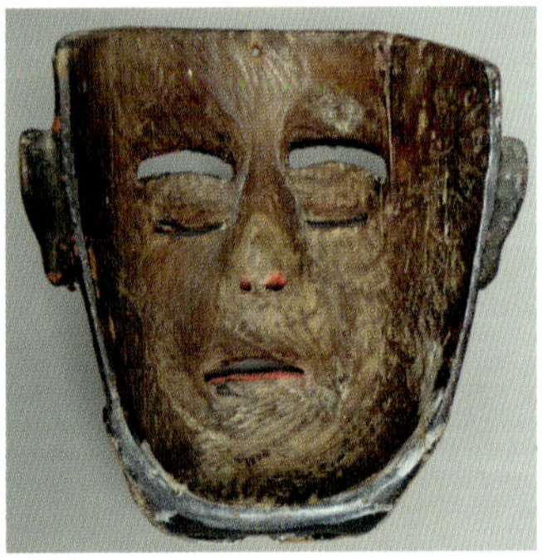

Top: Another very old mask that seems to have the early Benito Juárez ear design; 7¼" × 9". Circa 1930. It was said by its owner to represent the Jefé de los Negritos in the Negritos dance. Viewed from an angle, this mask has a dramatic design, with mustache and beard surrounding the protruding mouth. The tip of the nose was broken off and has been re-attached. There may be a prior layer of red paint under the black, as if this were once a Santiaguero mask. In Chapter 5 there is a Santiaguero mask of this general design by Benito, obviously carved later in his career. Rating: known carver, good condition, remarkable design, excellent patina on the front and back, and very rare, *******. *Collection of the author.*

Above left: The mask has a particularly remarkable profile, obviously reflecting the talent of one of the great master carvers of the mid-20th century. In Chapter 4 we looked at this mask as an example of masks modified for use by Voladores, with double vision slits.

Above right: The impressively ancient, worn back of this Negrito mask. The double vision slits are most easily seen from the back.

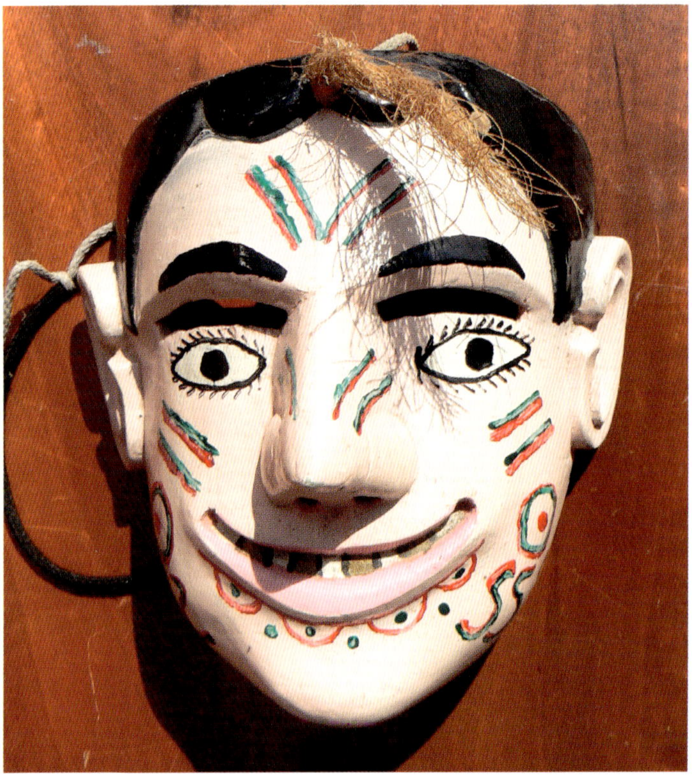

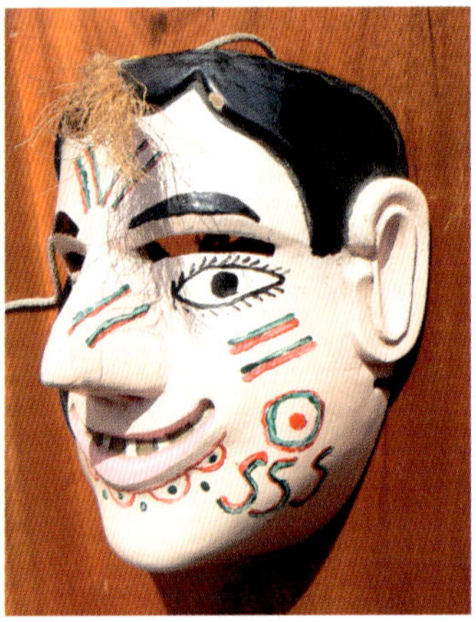

Above: This Payaso mask by Benito Juárez served as the partner to a Payaso carved by his daughter Alina, in the collection of the former neighbors in Filomeno Mata. Circa 1980. The ears are strongly carved; the relief-carved sideburn ends at the middle of the ear. Rating: known carver, good condition, well carved, recently repainted but with good patina on the back, and very rare, ******. *Private collection in Filomeno Mata, Veracruz.*

Left: The side view to show Benito's classic ear design.

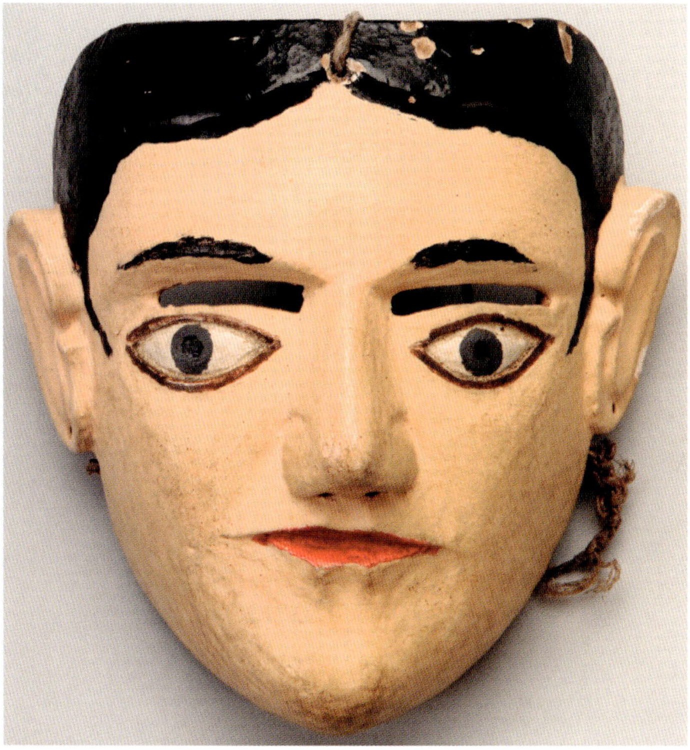

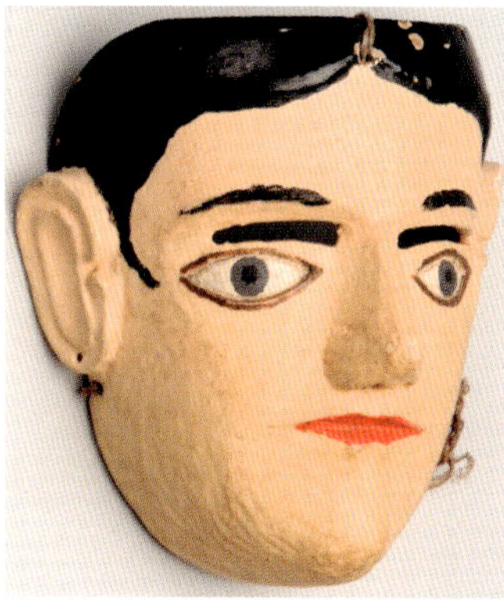

The side of this old female mask. The ears are of course typical, and they are pierced for earrings.

This female Huehue was found in Atlequisayan, Puebla, an isolated mountain town that is reached by a road from Ixtepec, Puebla; 6½" × 7". Circa 1970. The mask has many features that are typical of Benito's style, including the ears, nose, and mouth. The eyes have been carefully carved, as we find on only a minority of Benito's masks. She has a flat spot over the bridge of the nose, another uncommon feature that can also be seen on the more typical female mask that directly follows. There is a vertical groove over the mouth that is classic for this carver. I have no doubt that this mask is by Benito, and I particularly like it because it is unusually well carved. The paint is stable but looks almost bumpy from age and layering. Rating: known carver, good condition, remarkable design, excellent patina on the front and back, and very rare, *******. *Collection of the author.*

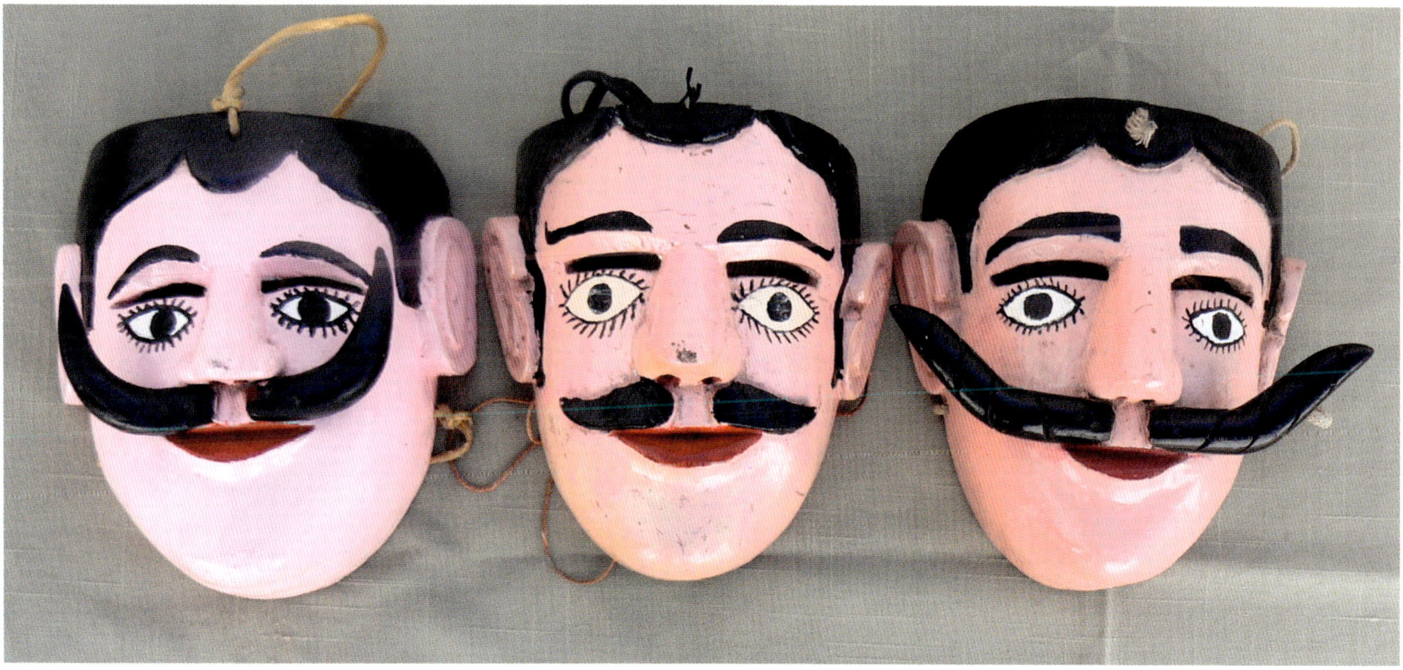

The Huehue mask in the center is a classic Benito Huehue mask, carved to his usual high standard. This was collected in Zozocolco de Hidalgo, Veracruz. Flanking this mask are two masks that were collected in Olintla, Puebla. The mask on the right is probably by Benito, but of the type with an applied (attached) mustache. Comparing this to the mask in the center, there are subtle differences that may simply mean they were carved at different stages in Benito's career. On the left is a mask that imitates Benito's style, but, on comparison, the differences are obvious. The angle of attachment of the ears to the face and the detailing of the ears themselves are enough to tell the viewer that this mask was not carved by Benito. On the other hand, although the applied mustache varies from the one on the opposite side, this difference is not significant. This looks like a mask by Francisco Tino. *Collection of Vernon Kostohryz.*

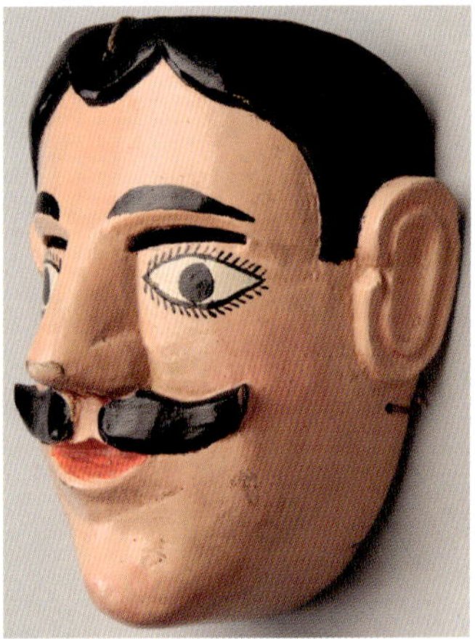

Right: A Tejonero or Huehue male mask carved by Benito; 6¼" × 7". Circa 1960. This one always depicted a male; the mustache is carved from the same block as the mask itself, not added on. Rating: known carver, good condition, well carved, good patina, and rare, ******. *Collection of the author.*

Above: This mask demonstrates once again the typical Benito ear design, and the relief-carved sideburns extend to the middle of the ears.

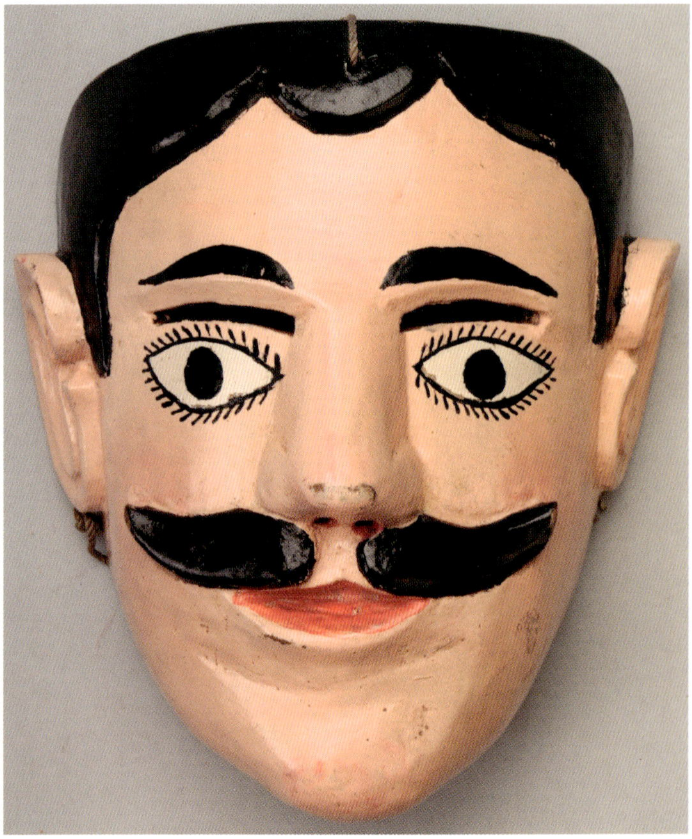

I'll end the presentation of the work of Benito Juárez by showing some other forms, including an example of a Perro (dog) mask and a series of additional Negrito masks.

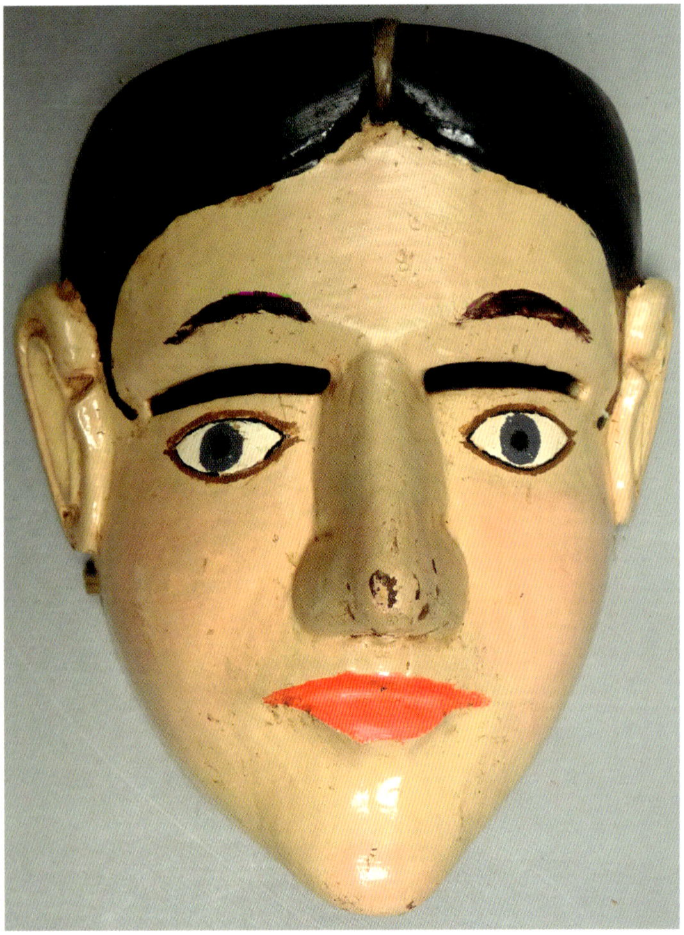

This lovely female Huehue mask was found in Ixtepec, Puebla; 7" × 7¾". Circa 1960. The dancer had died; we obtained the mask from his daughter. This mask has a flat spot carved on her forehead, there is a groove above her mouth, and the eyes are painted without being carved. That is to say, this mask is entirely typical of Benito's work. Rating: known carver, good condition, good design and carving, excellent patina on the front and back, and very rare, ******. *Collection of the author.*

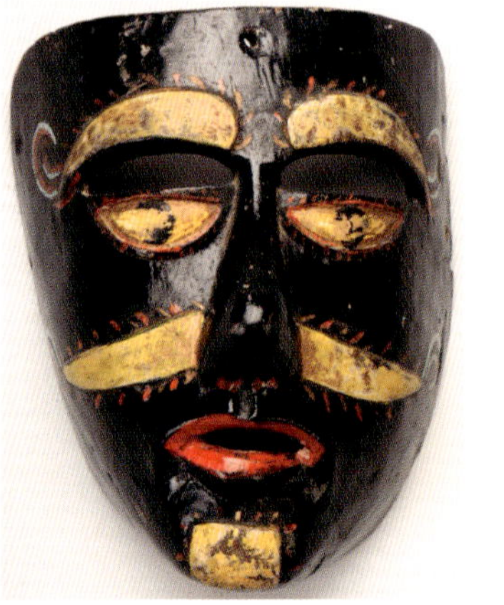

This beautiful old Negrito mask by Benito Juárez was obtained directly from the carver's daughter, Alina Juárez Pérez; 5¼" × 6½". Circa 1940 or earlier. This mask was shown in Chapter 5 as well. In contrast to the previous old Negrito, this mask has rather formal relief-carved brows, mustache, and goatee. The eyes are beautifully carved. Rating: known carver, good condition, very well carved, beautiful paint on the face with dramatic patina on the back, and very rare, *******. *Collection of the author.*

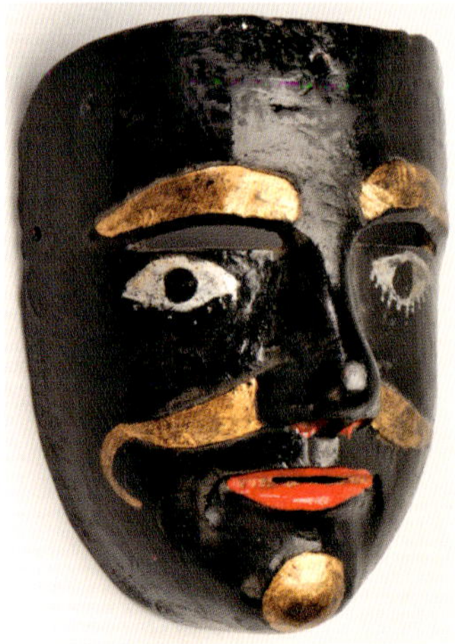

Another beautiful old Negrito has been repainted, such that the relief-carved mustache has been given a new twist on the ends; 5¼" × 6¾". Circa 1940. The brows and goatee are carved in relief, but the eyes are simply painted. Rating: known carver, good condition, very well carved, beautiful paint on the face with dramatic patina on the back, and very rare, ******. *Collection of the author.*

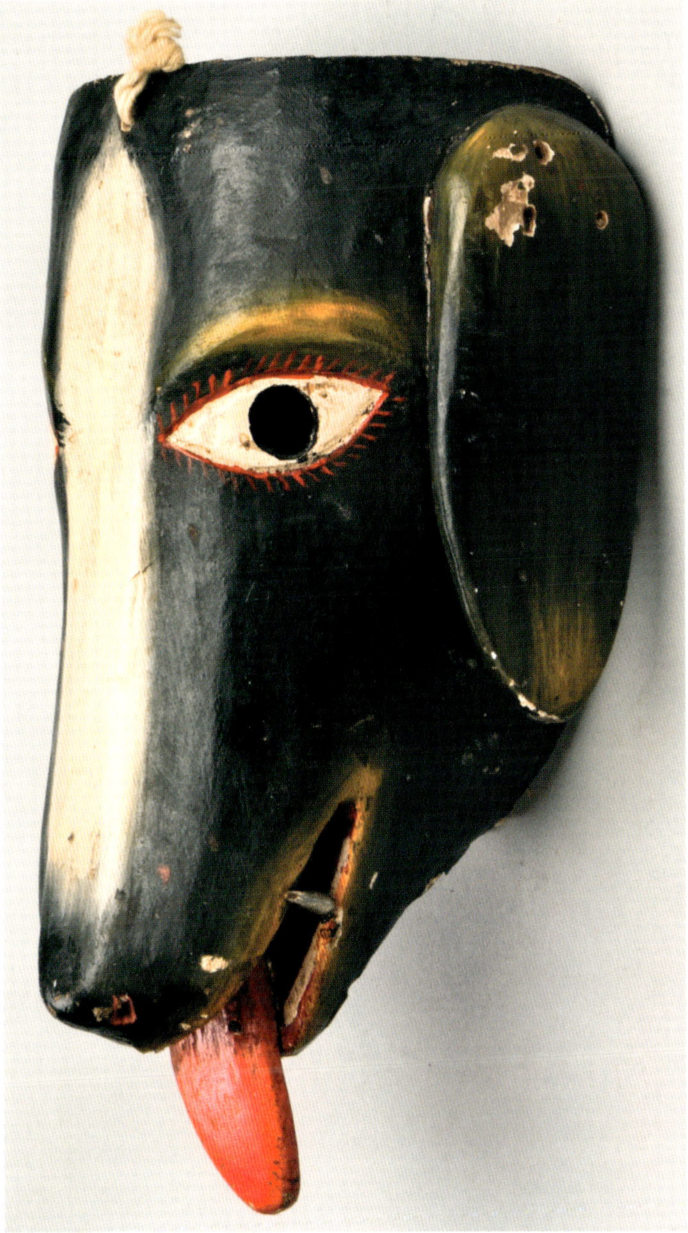

A *Perro* (dog) mask used in the Huehue or Tejonero dance that was carved by Benito; 7" × 11". Circa 1960. Rating: known carver, good condition, well carved, good patina, and very rare, ******. *Collection of the author.*

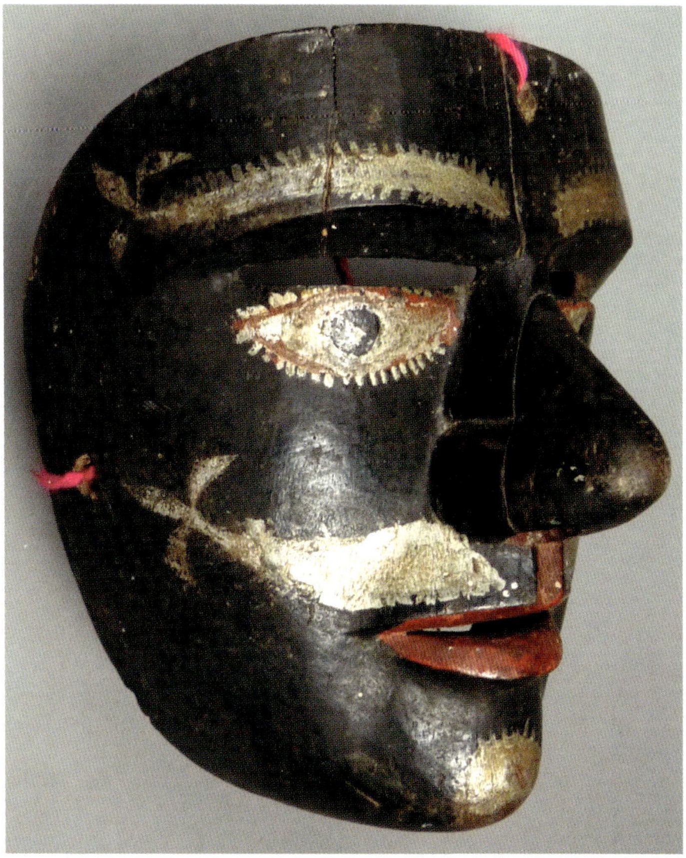

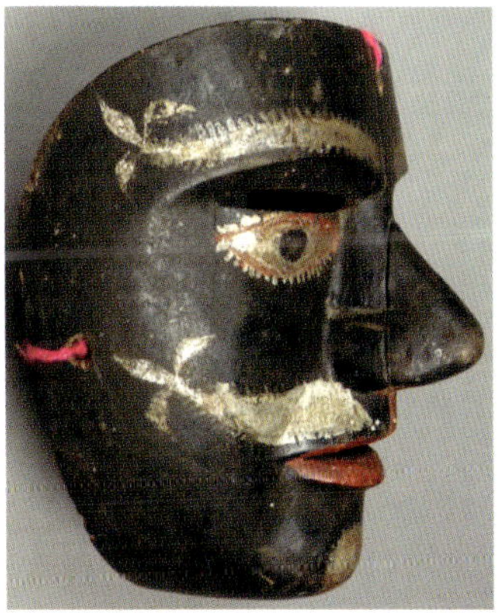

Above: This old Negrito mask for the Negritos dance is magnificent; 5¾" × 6½". Circa 1960. In this frontal view, one sees quite clearly how Benito has sculpted the arch of the brows; where the arches meet he has created that small flat spot that we have seen on some of his Huehue/Tejonero masks. The rather prominent nose is very well carved; it has apparently broken off and been re-glued. There is the usual vertical groove above the upper lip. The lips are gracefully carved. Rating: known carver, good condition, well carved, beautiful old worn paint on the face with dramatic patina on the back, and very rare, ******. *Collection of the author.*

Left: On this angle view, the outstanding feature is the ornamental quality of the silver paint.

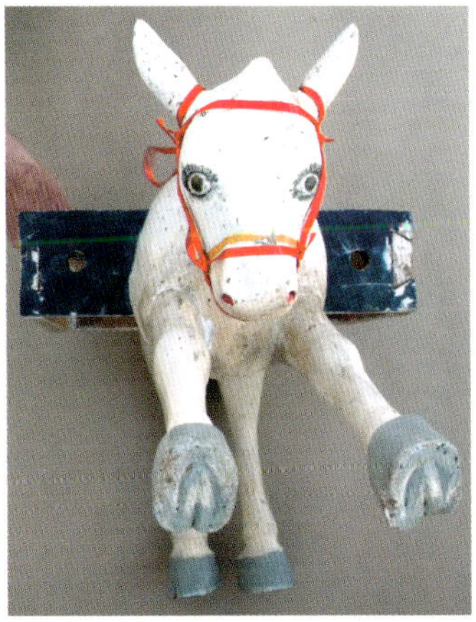

A dance horse for the Hormegas dance that was found in Olintla, Puebla; length 34". Circa 1970. It was reportedly carved by Benito Juárez. It has an unusual posture, with extended front legs while the hind legs are upright and straight. The mane and the detachable tail are both finely carved to create the illusion of hair. The box-type waist is dovetailed. Rating: known carver, excellent condition, very well carved, good patina, and extremely rare, *******+. *Collection of Vernon Kostohryz.*

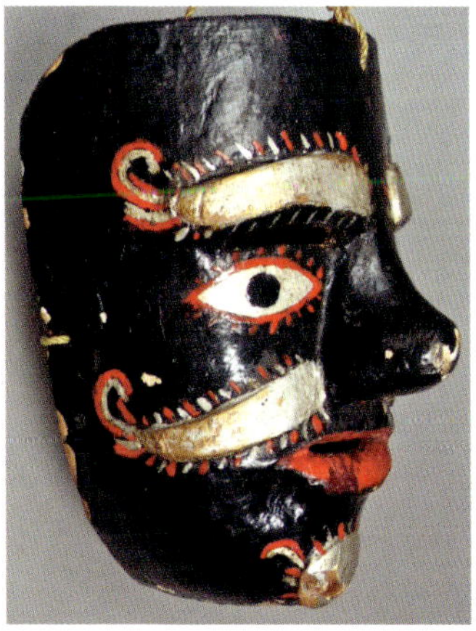

I saw this mask dance in Olintla, Puebla, on December 12, 2010. But later I saw that the dancer had chosen to dance without a mask. I literally saw the tradition ending, and then I was offered the opportunity to buy this mask; 5½" × 7". Circa 1980. It is a classic Benito Negrito. Rating: known carver, good condition, very well carved, slightly unstable paint on the face with good patina on the back, and very rare, ******. *Collection of the author.*

Andrés Juárez García and Pedro Juárez García

Andrés Juárez García was born on May 10, 1971. He lives in Xonalpú, Puebla, a small mountain town just outside of Huehuetla, Puebla. Andrés is the leader of a Huehues dance group, and I had actually seen this group dance in Huehuetla on December 12, 2006, not knowing that they came from another town. Most of the members of the dance group wear very effective masks that were carved by Andrés; I included some Huehues dance photos in Chapter 4 that showed the masks of Andrés in action. His masks are distinctive and somewhat nontraditional in that they show a strong tendency to caricature. This quality makes them immediately recognizable. I saw puppets perform with this dance group; Andrés had carved the very attractive male and female puppets, and his father had made the wonderful Chénchere.

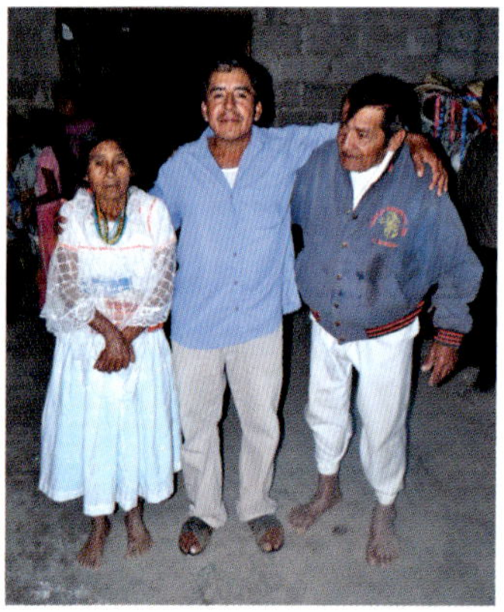

Andrés is flanked by his mother and his father. Both parents are wearing traditional clothes, although Pedro's baseball jacket makes this less apparent.

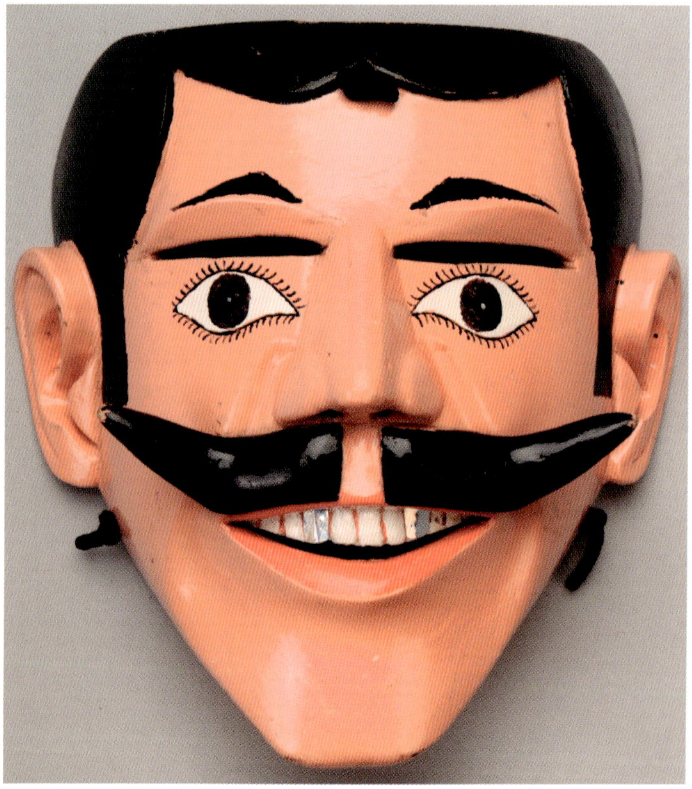

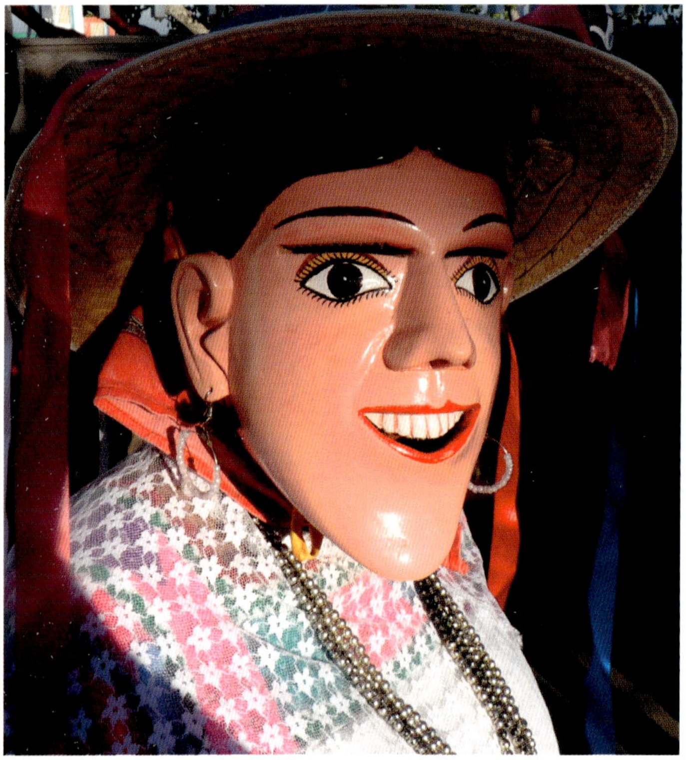

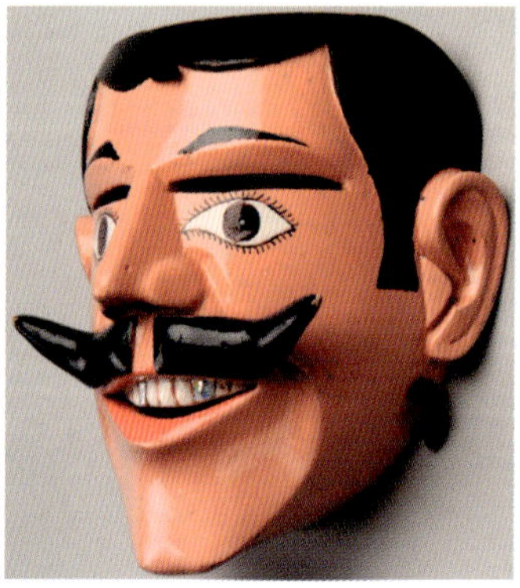

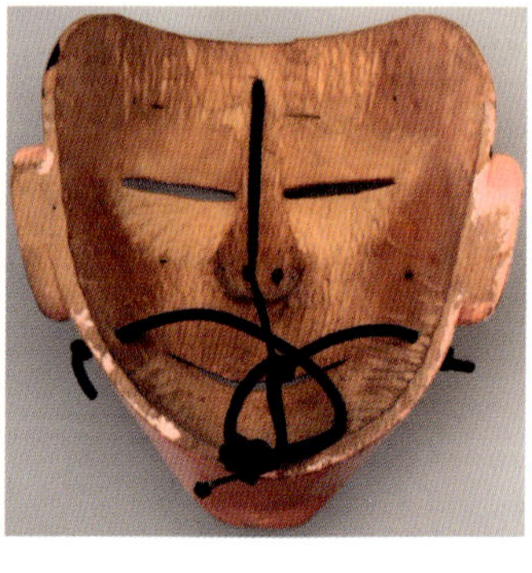

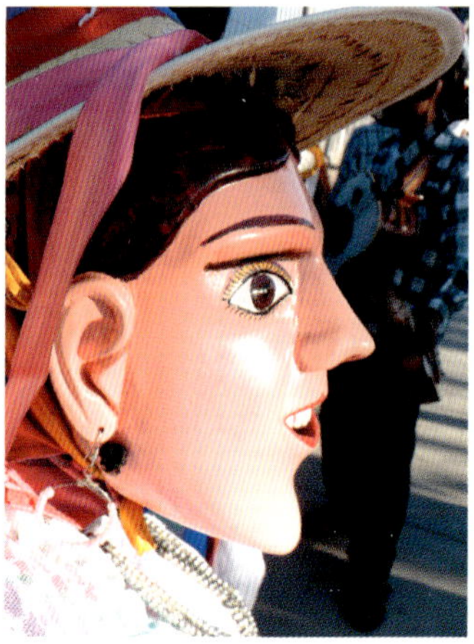

Above: This female Huehue mask was also carved by Andrés Juárez García. Circa 2006. One sees again his distinctive design skills. Ironically the hollowing of the cheeks is not used on this mask. Rating: known carver, excellent condition, very well carved, normal patina, and not rare, ****. *Former collection of Andrés Juárez García, who granted permission for these dance photographs.*

Right: The side view of this mask, which provides a clear view of this carver's ear design.

Top: This male Huehue mask by Andrés Juárez García has dramatic exaggerated features that demonstrate the considerable talent of this carver; 7½" × 7". Circa 2006. The hollowing of the cheeks above the mustache greatly resembles such a design feature on the older female Huehue masks of Kalimán. Rating: known carver, excellent condition, very well carved, normal patina, and not rare, ****. *Collection of the author.*

Above left: The side view reveals the distinctive ear design of this carver.

Above right: The back of this mask.

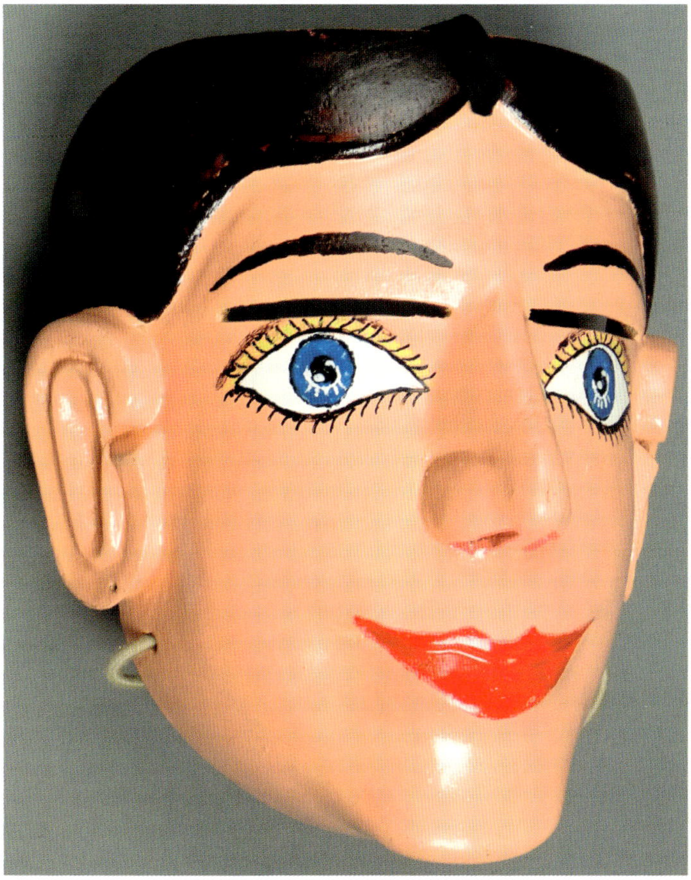

This mask by Andrés has the same face as the female puppet by this carver in Chapter 7; 6½" × 7½". Circa 2006. Andrés has carved her ears modeled on those of Benito Juárez, but the other features don't resemble those of Benito. Rating: known carver, excellent condition, well carved, normal patina, and not rare, ****. *Collection of the author.*

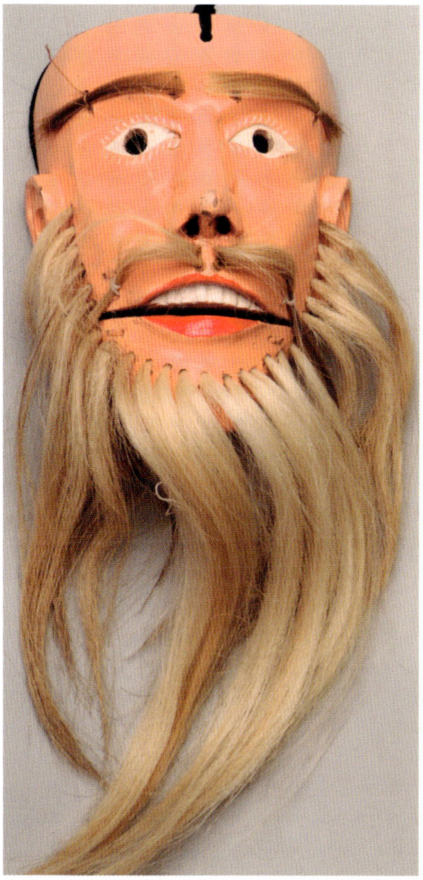

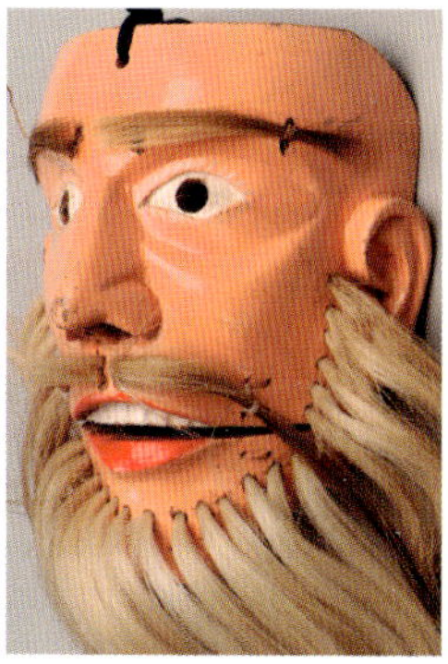

Left: This Viejo mask by Andrés Juárez García could have been used in either the Huehues dance or the Voladores dance in the area of Huehuetla, Puebla; 6¾" × 8". Circa 2006. It has an articulated jaw that was part of the original design. Rating: known carver, excellent condition, very well carved, normal patina, and not rare, **** ½. *Collection of the author.*

Above: From an angle one can see that the jaw is articulated.

Pedro Juárez García is the father of Andrés Juárez García. He was born on May 3, 1941. He and his wife also live in Xonalpú, Puebla.

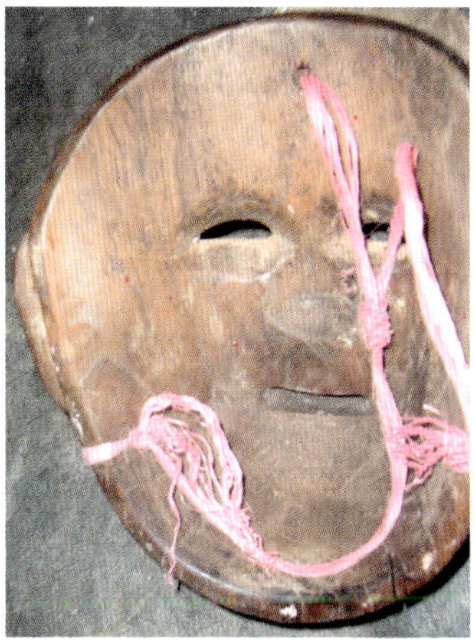

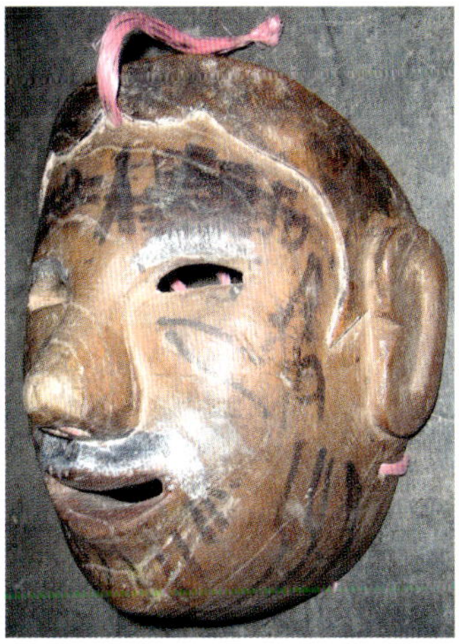

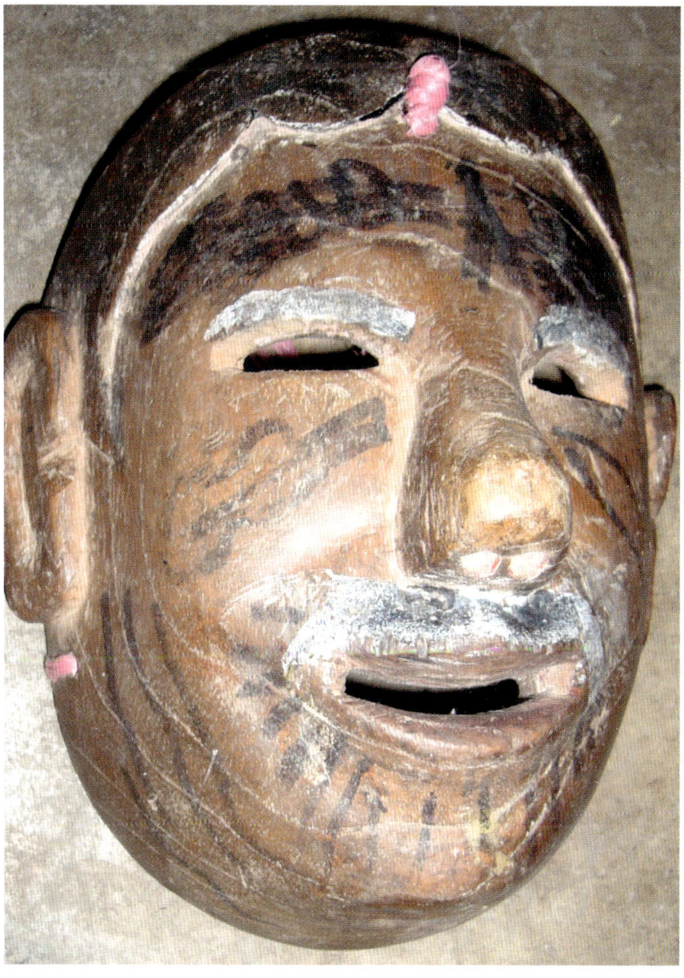

Right: This is a Huehue mask that was carved By Pedro Juárez García, about 45 years ago; 7" × 8¼". *Photos courtesy Carlos Moreno Vásquez.*

Above left: A view of the back. It looks old, with excellent patina.

Above right: A side view of this mask by Pedro, showing his ear design.

Magno León

Magno León has recently come to our attention as the carver of several remarkable masks. He was born in Jicalapa, Puebla, on March 12, 1914. He was married and later he lived in Hueytlalpan, Puebla, with his second, common-law wife. He died on April 11, 1997, at the age of 83. In March 2010, we had discovered a superlative Carnaval Zombie mask in Zapotitlán, Puebla. Later Carlos Moreno Vásquez returned to this area and discovered that Magno was the carver of the Zombie mask. Pursuing the name led to further masks. These are equally striking, although some are much more formal in their design. On the basis of these masks, we have concluded that Magno was surely one of the greatest master carvers in this region during the early 20th century; we have now seen a number of his beautiful Saints and related carvings. I have seen three Hormega masks in Olintla that also appear to be his work.

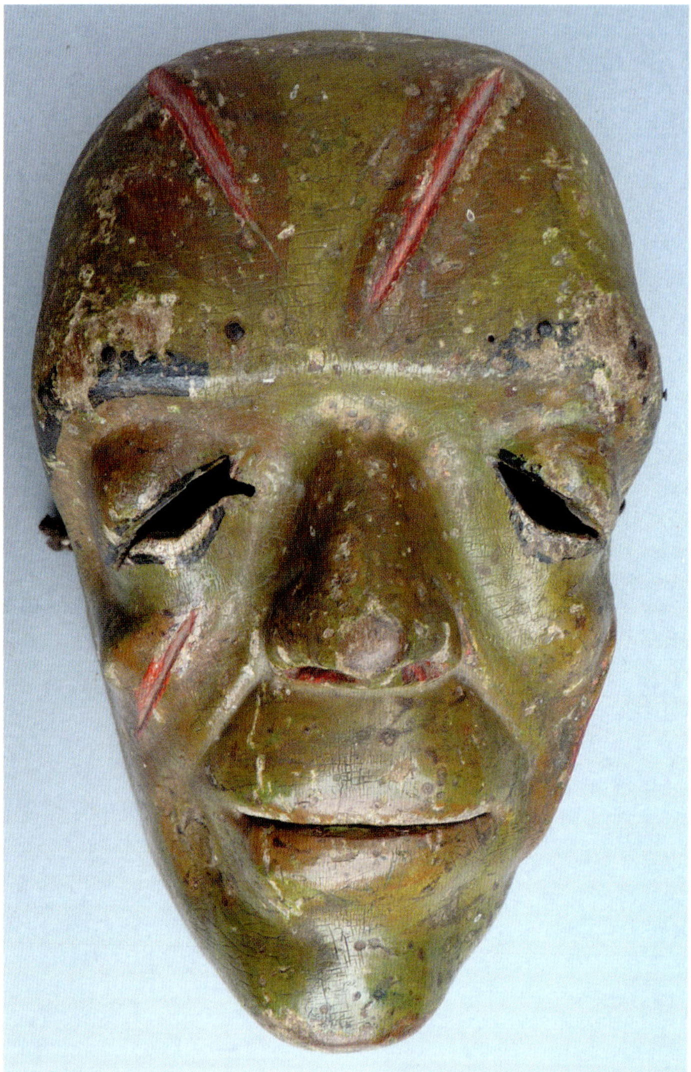

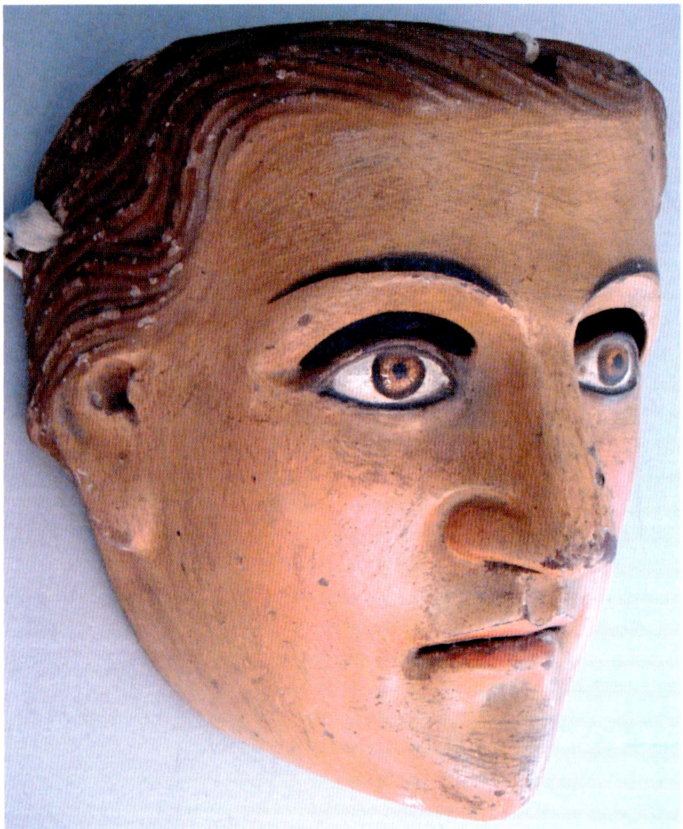

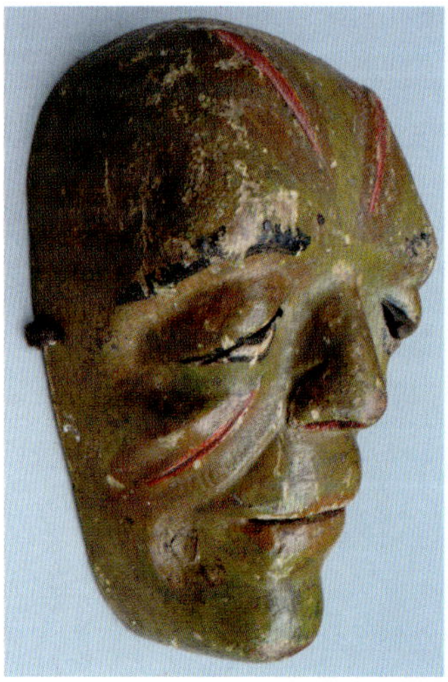

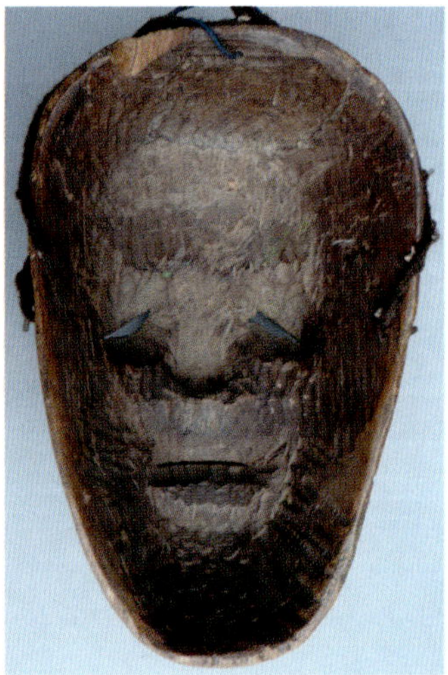

Above: This remarkably beautiful female Huehue was also carved by Magno; 6" × 7". Circa 1950. Here is a clear view of the lower ear, carved as if emerging from the carved hair. Rating: known carver, excellent condition, sublimely carved, great patina, and extremely rare, *******. *Collection of Vernon Kostohryz, who supplied these photos.*

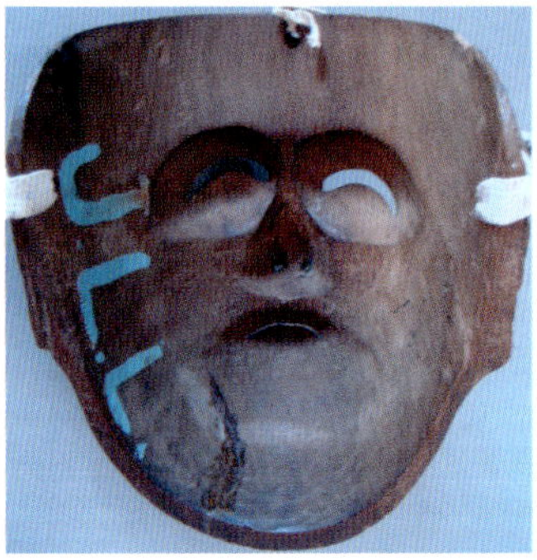

Right: The back of this mask is as exquisitely carved as the front. Note the precise carving around the vision slits, the hollow for the nose, and the large separate hollow space for the mouth. This is Magno's signature back, and the back of the male mask that follows looks exactly the same.

Top: In March 2010, we discovered this remarkable mask in Zapotitlán, Puebla; we have never seen another one like it; 6½" × 10". Circa 1960; it was reportedly used for Carnaval over a period of 50 years. The carver was the late Magno León. Rating: known carver, excellent condition, remarkable design, wonderful patina, and extremely rare, *******. *Collection of the author.*

Above left: The side view of this mask showing the strange hooded eyes.

Above right: The back demonstrates a marker for this carver—the careful hollowing around the vision slits, for the nose, and for the mouth. This pattern will be more apparent in the adjacent mask.

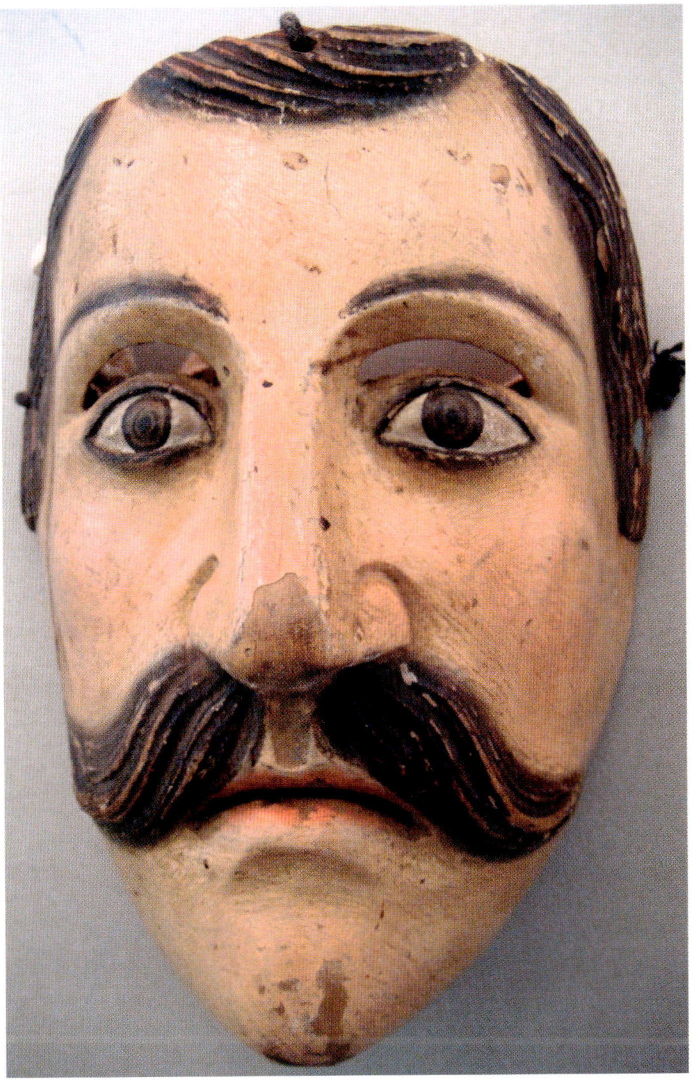

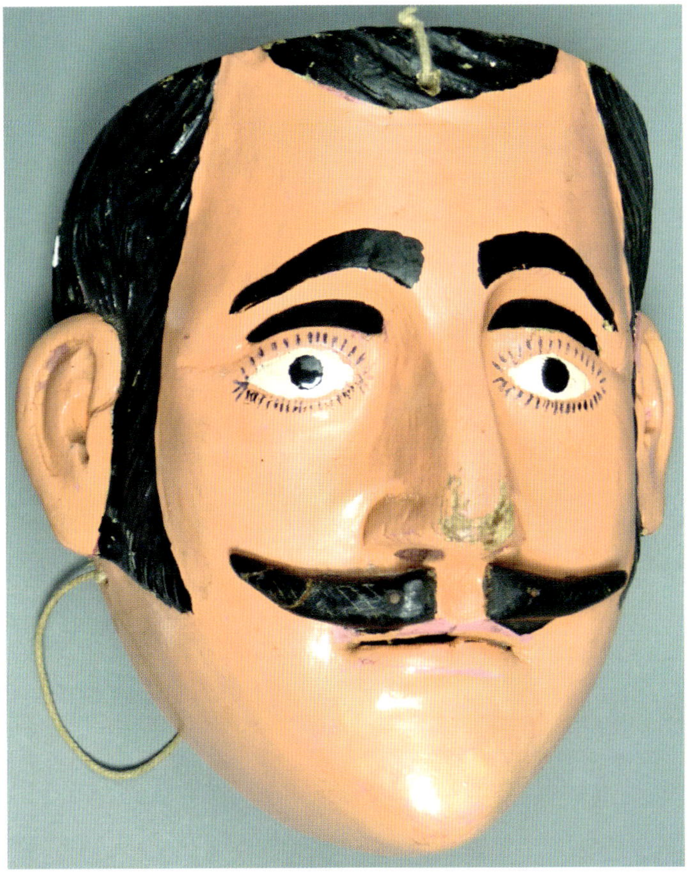

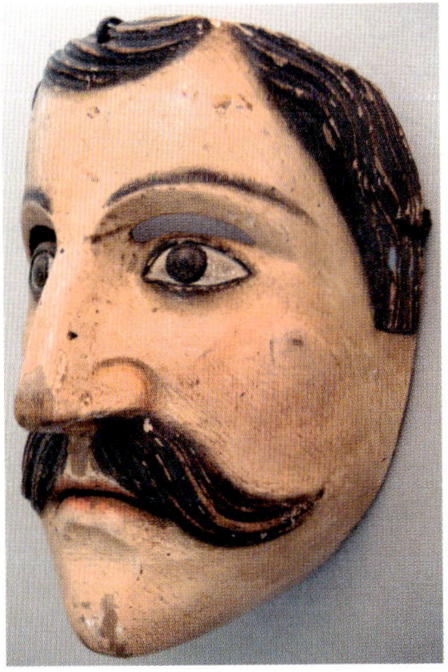

Above: This male Huehue mask was among a recently discovered trove of works by Magno León; 6¼" × 7½". Circa 1950. It, too, is very finely carved. It lacks ears, which is unusual for this region. Rating: known carver, excellent condition, very well carved, good patina, and rare, *******. *Collection of Vernon Kostohryz, who supplied these photos.*

Left: From the side, this mask lacks ears.

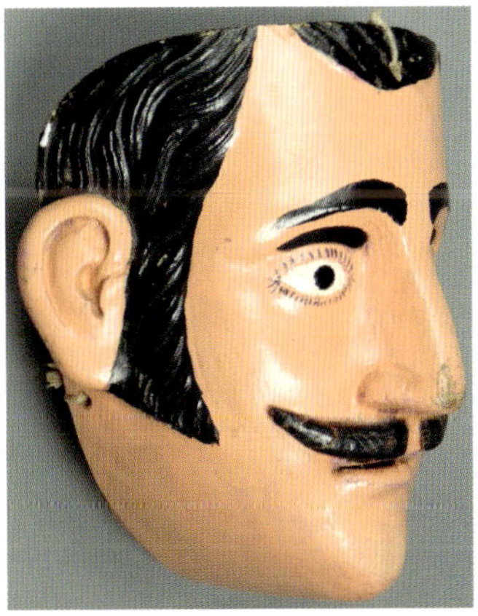

Above: This Huehue mask by Magno was purchased from his family; 7" × 7½". On this example we see the full ear. There are remarkable relief-carved sideburns. He has an applied mustache, far less elegant than the mustache on the previous male Huehue. But since this mask was collected from the family, we may assume that Magno was the one who added the mustache. Rating: known carver, excellent condition, very well carved, good patina, and rare, *******. *Collection of the author.*

Left: From the side, a better view of Magno's beautiful stylized ear design. The way that he carves the hair on his masks is particularly fine.

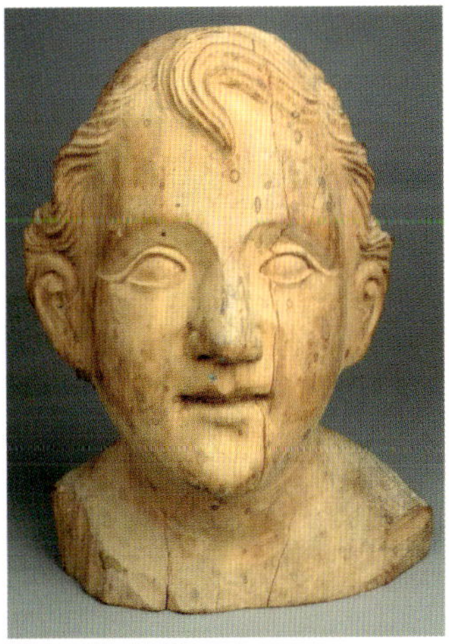

A small carved head of a Saint, one of a group of religious carvings that were also purchased from the family; width of head 5", 7" tall. Circa 1960. It will be immediately obvious that Magno used the same carving style for saints and masks. Unrated. *Collection of the author.*

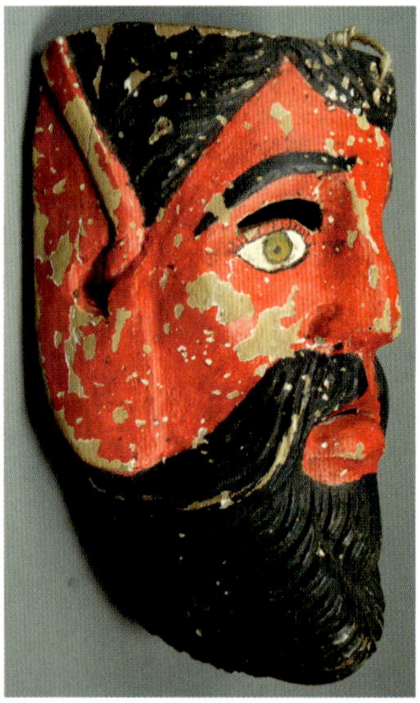

Here again is the evil Pilate, a very rare and wonderful character who happens to represent Satan in disguise; 7" × 9". Circa 1960. From the side one sees the very long goat ear that reveals the character's secret identity. The paint has flaked as a consequence of insect deposits; these deposits are also visible on the back. The paint requires restoration. Rating: known carver, excellent structural condition, very well carved, mixed patina, and rare, *******. *Collection of the author.*

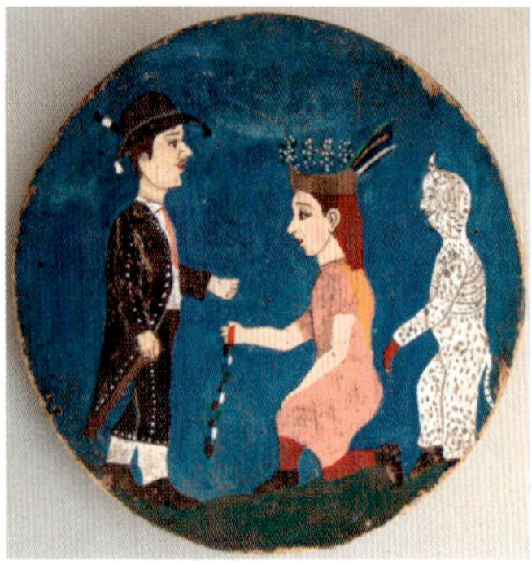

A painted shield for the dance of the Moros y Españoles (Cristianos), carried by one of the Españoles; 8½" in diameter. Circa 1960. Obtained from Magno's family, this was probably carried in the dance by Magno himself. Rating: known carver, excellent condition, very nicely decorated, good patina, and extremely rare, *******. *Collection of Vernon Kostohryz.*

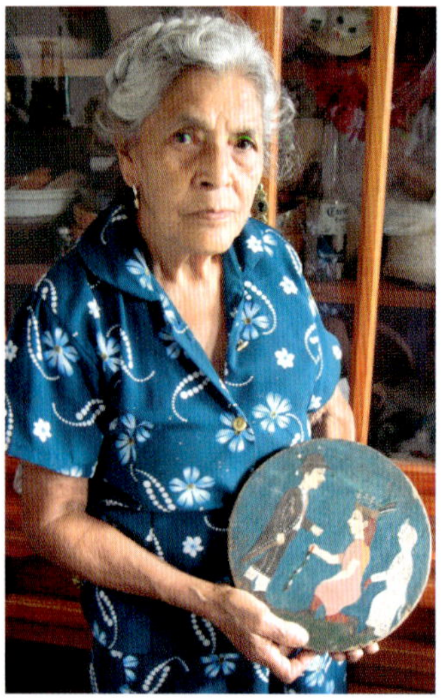

The widow of Magno Léon is holding the shield, in March 2011. *Photo by Carlos Moreno Vásquez, courtesy of the widow.*

José Lopez Gaona

I know of José Lopez Gaona of Filomeno Mata Veracruz as the carver of one interesting mask. Undoubtedly he has carved others that I have never seen. I really like this one.

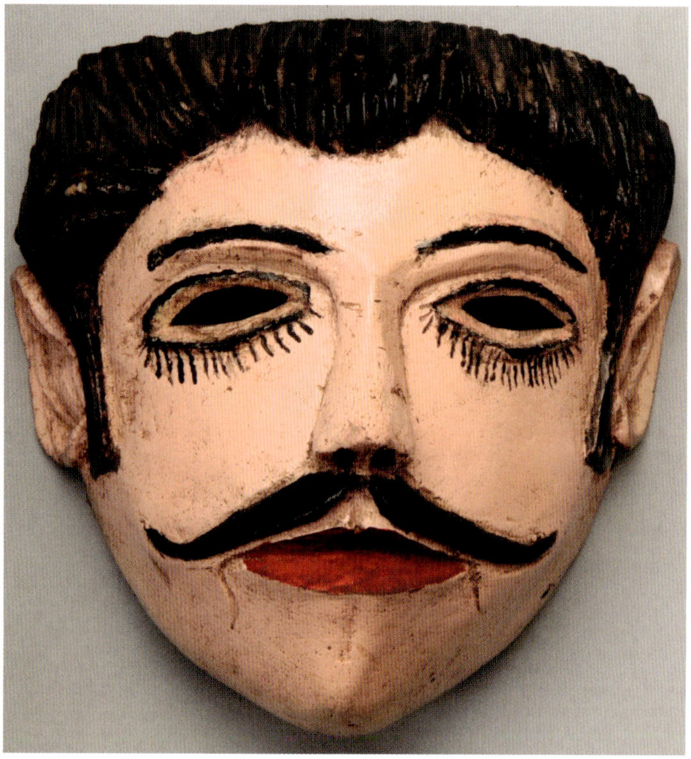

Above: Note the very carefully relief-carved hair and mustache on this Tejonero mask; 6¾" × 6¾". Circa 2000. The rim surrounding the opening of the eye is also carved in relief. Rating: known carver, excellent condition, well carved, good patina, not rare, ****. *Collection of the author.*

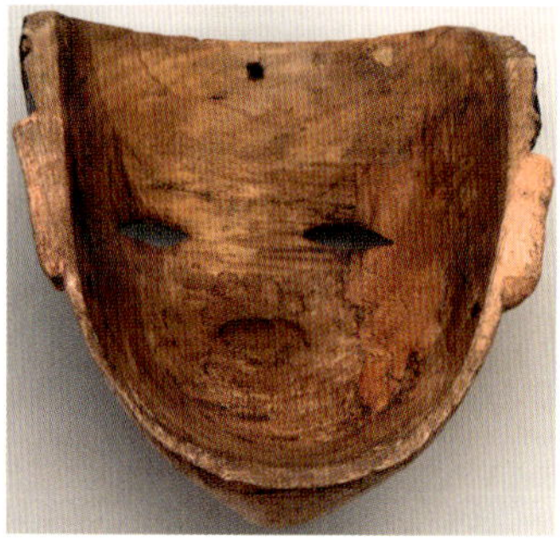

Right: The back of the mask is very simple. It seems to have a protective coating.

Mateo Luna Vásquez (Luis De Luna)

Mateo Luna Vásquez, who was known in his community only by the nickname "Luis de Luna," was born on December 23, 1953, and he died at too young an age, on May 14, 2008, of liver disease. He lived and worked in Zozocolco de Hidalgo, Veracruz.

When I met Luis at his home, in December of 2006, he was identified as someone who carved masks, but it didn't seem that he was particularly well thought of for this, and my visit to Luis was incidental and brief. Fortunately I did manage to take his photograph, holding a recently carved mask.

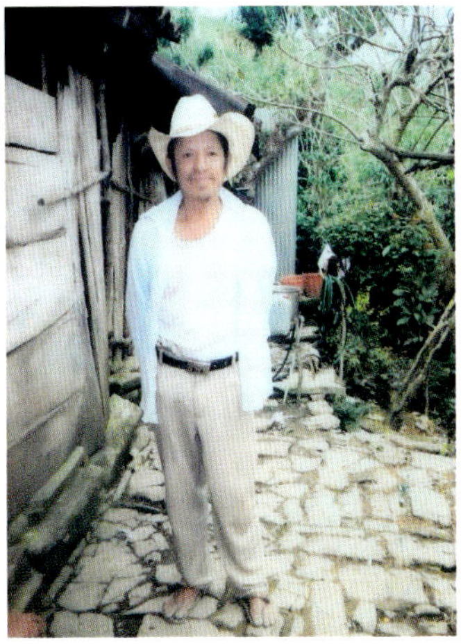

Mateo Luna Vázquez, who was more commonly called Luis de Luna, in a family photo. *Photos of Luis de Luna are included with the permission of his wife.*

By this time Vernon had purchased a mask from Jesus "Chucho" Arroyo that was famous within the Zozocolco community, considered to be a masterpiece. No one seemed to remember who had carved this mask; apparently it had been carved many decades earlier and was used by Chucho to conceal the introduction of female Voladores (i.e., Voladoras), beginning in 1972, as noted in the description of that dance.

Meanwhile we encountered the expected stream of additional interesting masks without provenance, so we were engaged in our usual process of investigation, checking out this name and then that one in terms of carving styles.

Suddenly a number of trails came together, more than a year after my meeting with Luis, and we realized with a sense of shock that Luis de Luna was the carver of the Chucho Arroyo mask and of various additional masks of nearly equal quality. It was strange to realize that a carver could continue to live in his home community and yet his past work would no longer be linked to his name, apparently a consequence of his own decline in activity. We made plans to visit Luis again, but learned that he had already died.

Since then we have made a vigorous search for other examples of Luis's work, and it does indeed seem that he was a great master carver in his community in past years. His masks combine excellent carving technique with what one might call a "sculptor's eye." This is particularly true for his Payaso masks.

In hindsight, it might seem that our search for the carver of the Chucho Arroyo mask would have been easier had we focused on the clue of the double vision slits. After all, there was Luis de Luna holding his mask with that feature in December of 2006. But back then we could already see that there had been more than one carver who made such masks, and we were attempting to identify each one. Since then all this has come into much sharper focus. It seems likely that Luis was the mascarero enlisted by Chucho Arroyo to add second vision slits to existing masks and to carve new masks with this feature. I would speculate that the famously well carved Payaso mask was commissioned by Chucho for his own use, and that this explains why Luis took such pains to carve what appears to be one of his finest masks. But then when the mask was so admired in the community, both Luis and Antonio Bernabé Mora made copies, Luis using his standard ear design and Antonio likewise using his. In the end, it was the ears rather than the eyes that brought the story into focus, and subtle differences in the carving of the face clearly link Luis's copies, and not those of Antonio, to the Chucho mask. Subsequently we have identified several other masks by Luis which were apparently commissioned, causing Luis to go beyond his usual designs, and this has become yet another factor for us to consider when we attempt to assign a carver to a particular mask.

In 2006, Vernon found a set of eight masks for the Tejoneros dance, four men and four women, which proved to be the work of Luis de Luna. Photos from masks in that set follow, along with a Viejo or Payaso mask that was also carved by Luis and used in his community. As we began to accumulate examples of his work, we became increasingly impressed by the talent that Luis de Luna had demonstrated at the height of his skills. In summary, Luis de Luna was a highly respected carver in the past.

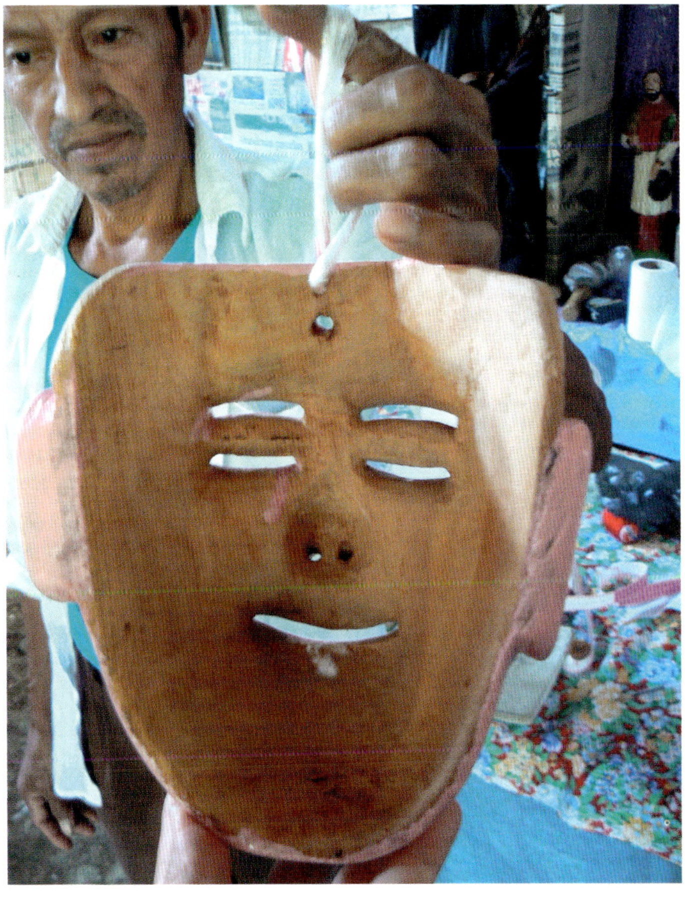

Luis de Luna in his home in Zozocolco de Hidalgo in December 2006 holding up a recently made mask.

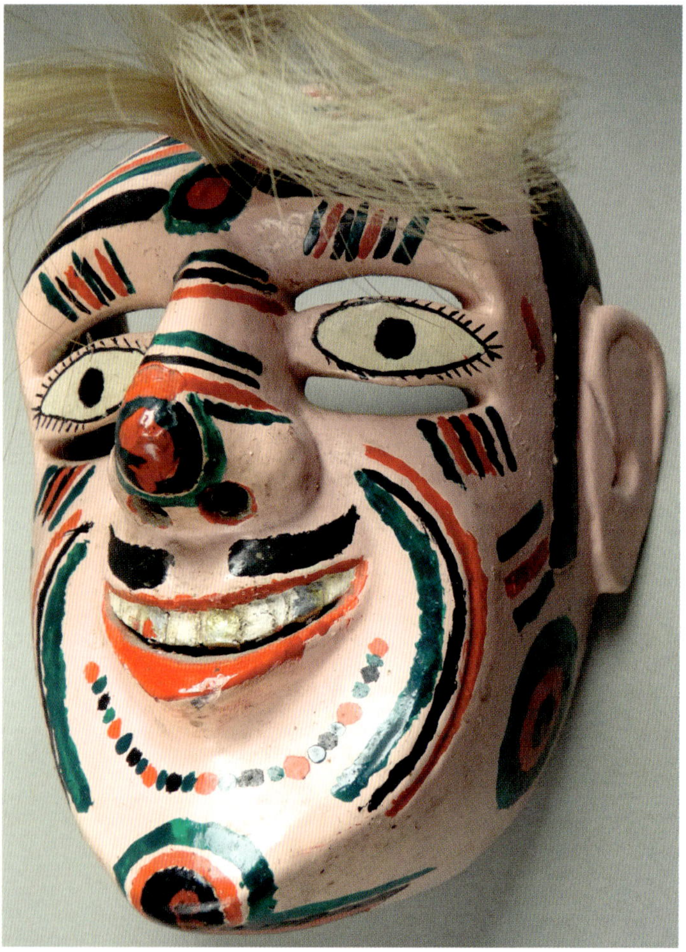

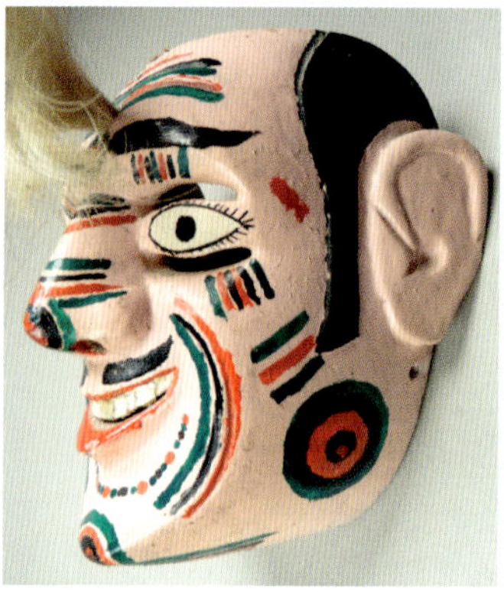

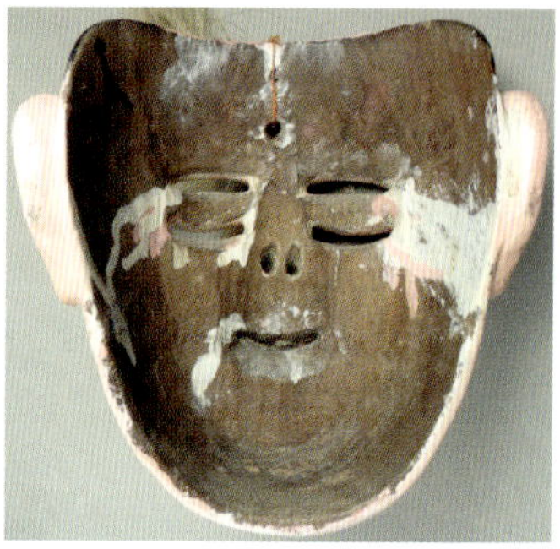

Left: The favorite mask of Jesus "Chucho" Arroyo, of Zozocolco de Hidalgo, Veracruz; 7" × 7". Circa 1975. Like the mask held by Luis de Luna in the photo on page 147, this mask has vision slits above and below the painted eyes. Rating: known carver, good condition, very well carved, excellent patina, and rare, ******+. *Collection of Vernon Kostohryz.*

Above left: A side view of this mask, showing the fine modeling around the mouth and the carefully carved ear.

Above right: A view of the back of this mask. Jesus Arroyo has marked his combined initials with a marker, "JA." One reason that the mask is so highly admired is that the walls are very thinly carved, yet the mask is strong and stable.

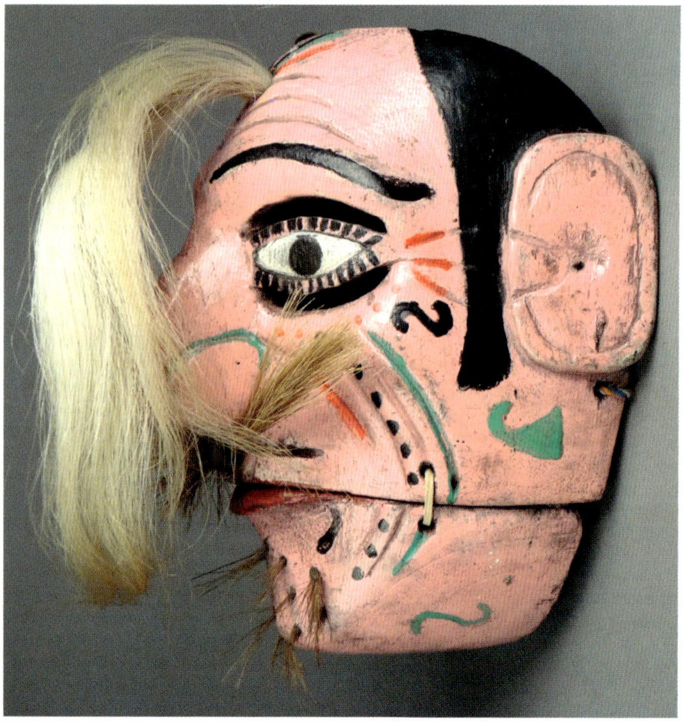

The side view of a Payaso mask for the dance of the Tejoneros, carved by Luis; 6½" × 7½". Circa 1960. It has an articulated jaw that flaps during the dance. This is a wonderful mask. Rating: known carver, good condition, remarkably carved, extreme patina, and very rare, *******. *Collection of the author.*

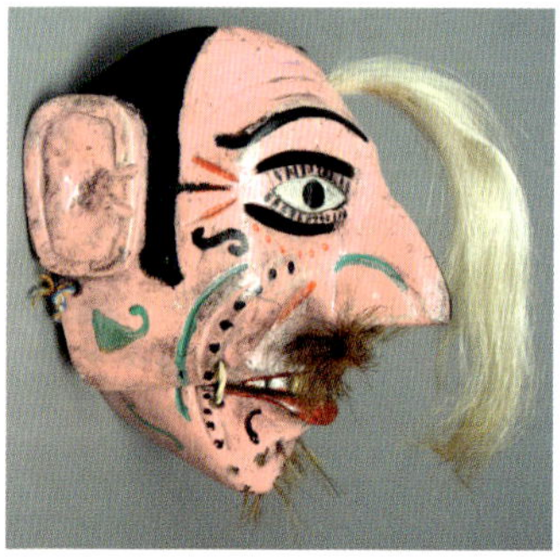

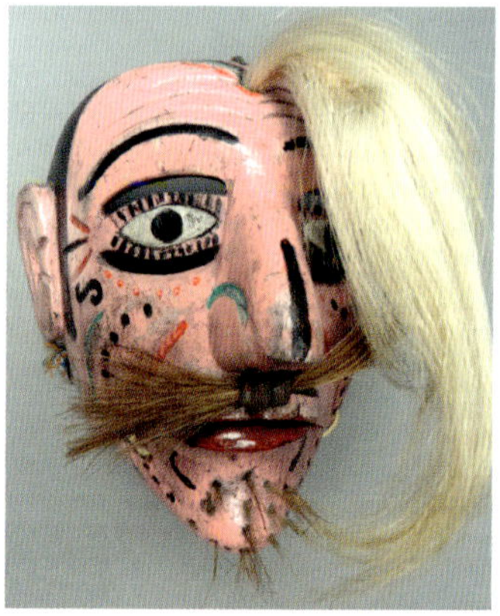

Above: Another view from the side with the mouth slightly open.

Above right: The front view with closed mouth.

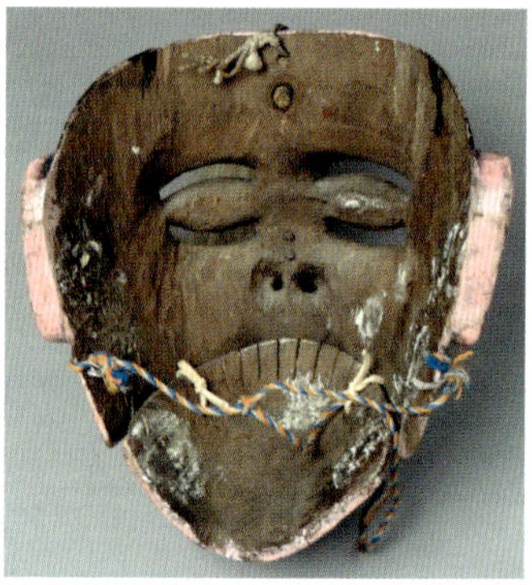

Right: The back of this mask. The patina is extreme. The carving of the upper teeth suggests that the articulated jaw was an original feature of the mask, a design detail provided by Luis de Luna. The manner of carving of the articulated jaw is quite unlike what has been seen on other masks that were altered by Ernesto Bernabé Sánchez.

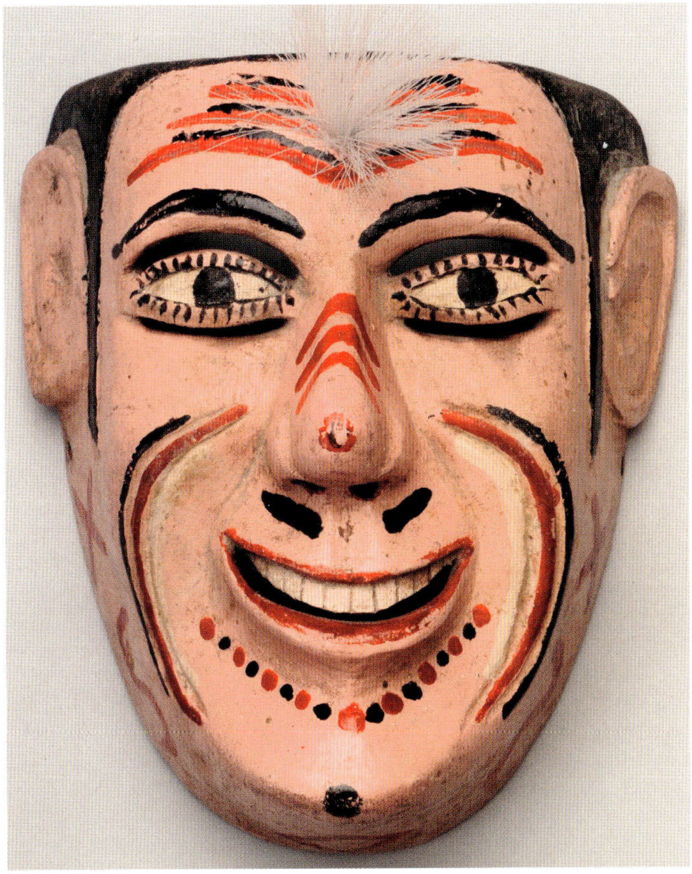

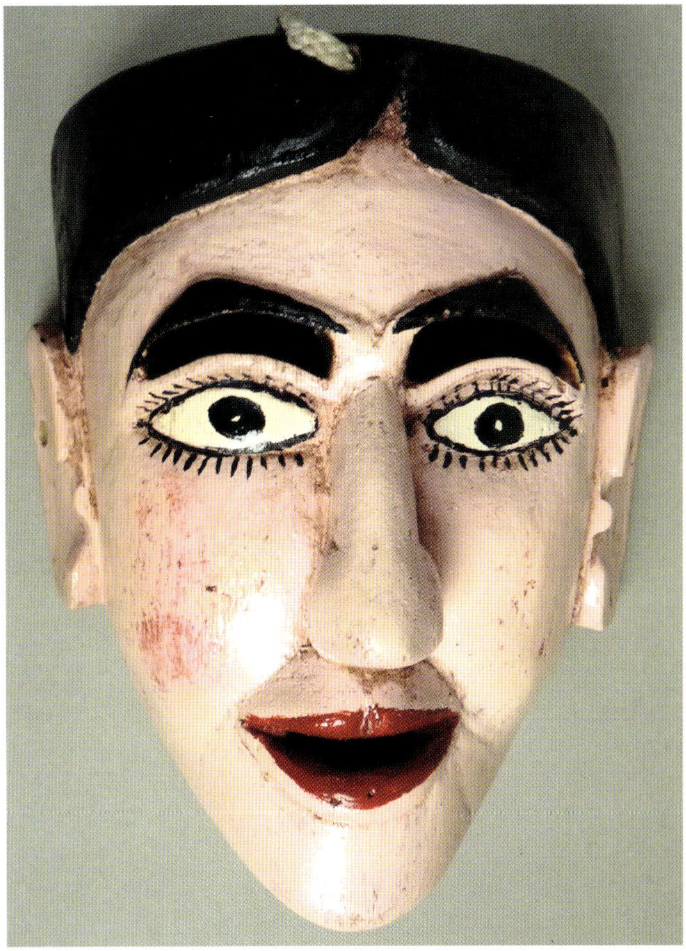

Above: A duplicate of the Chucho Arroyo Payaso mask that was made by Luis de Luna for Chucho Arroyo's brother and subsequently obtained from that owner; 6¾" × 7½". Circa 1975. Rating: known carver, good condition, very well carved, excellent patina, and rare, ******. *Collection of the author.*

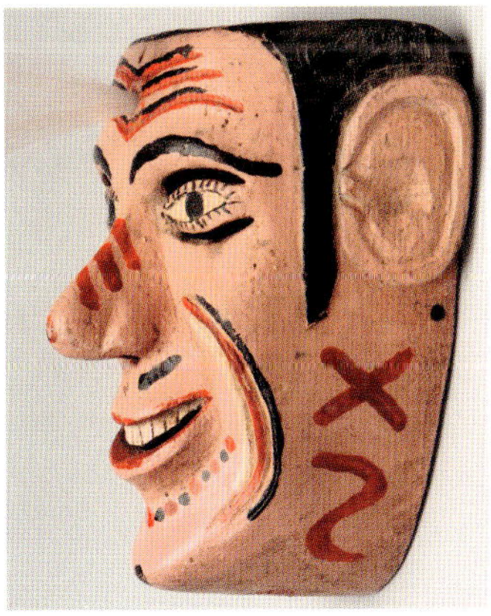

Right: A side view of the copy. Note that this mask demonstrates the usual ear design used by Luis de Luna. The Chucho Arroyo mask had a more elaborate ear design that was an enhanced version of this one. On this view one can see the very fine carving of the lower face, which is very similar to the carving on the Chucho Arroyo mask.

Above: Another female Tejonero mask with a different style; 6¾" × 7". Circa 1985. Note particularly the way that her relief-carved eyes are hooded, tucked under a curving shelf. This mask is a minor masterpiece. Rating: known carver, good condition, very well carved, marked patina, and rare, ******. *Collection of Vernon Kostohryz.*

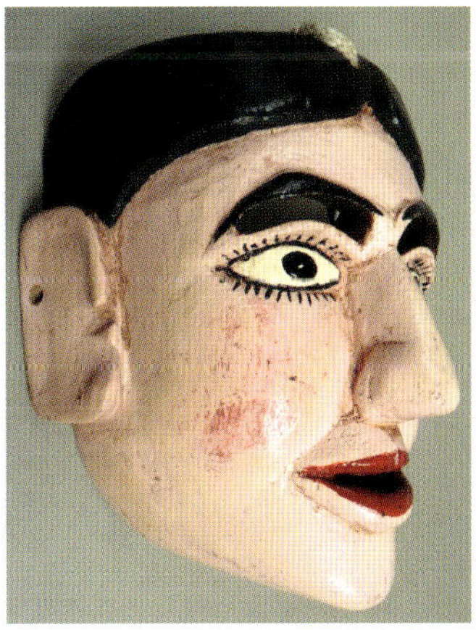

Right: The view of this mask from an angle, which provides another perspective on the carving of the eyes. Also note how nicely the right ear is carved.

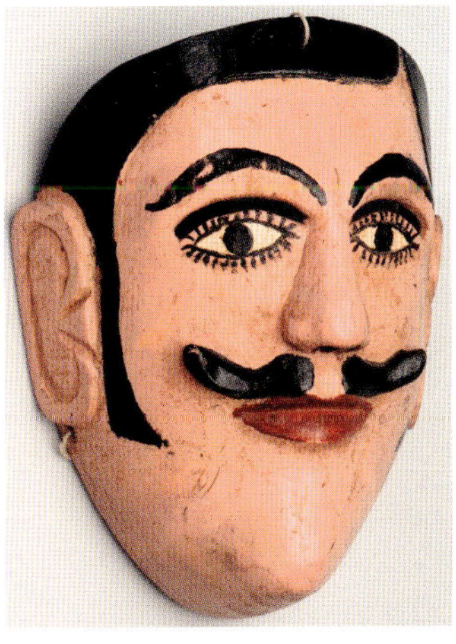

The male Tejonero mask from a pair; 6¼" × 7¾". Circa 1985. He has an interesting relief-carved mustache. His left ear lacks the central depression that is present on most of Luis's masks. Rating: known carver, good condition, very well carved, good patina, and rare, *****½. *Collection of the author.*

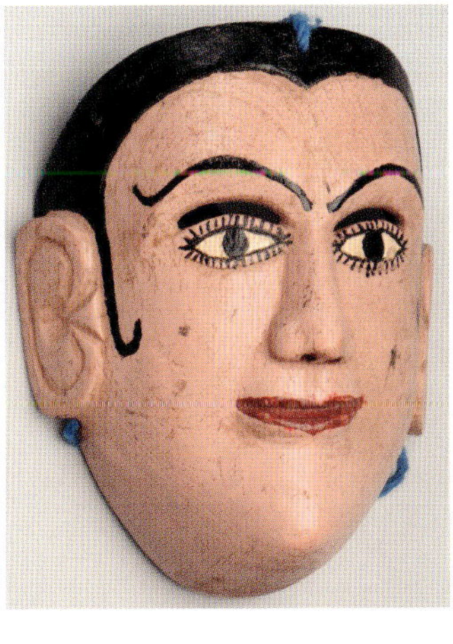

The female Tejonero mask from this pair; 6¼" × 7¼". Circa 1985. Her right ear demonstrates Luis de Luna's usual ear design. Rating: known carver, good condition, very well carved, good patina, and rare, *****½. *Collection of the author.*

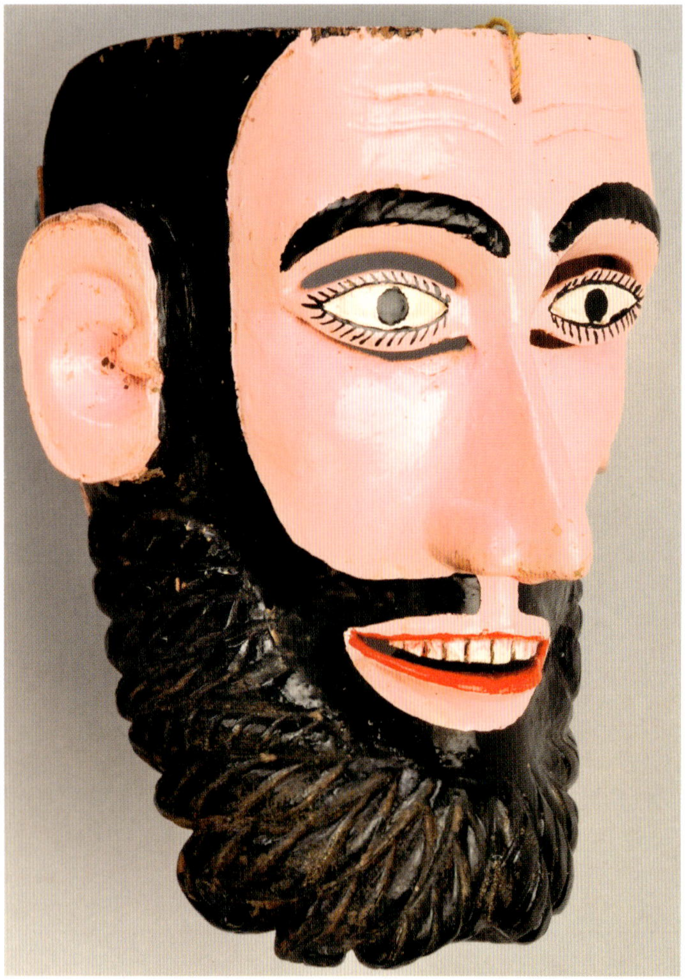

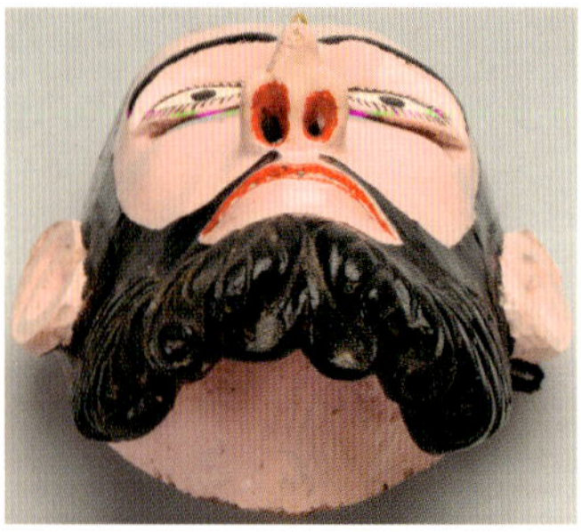

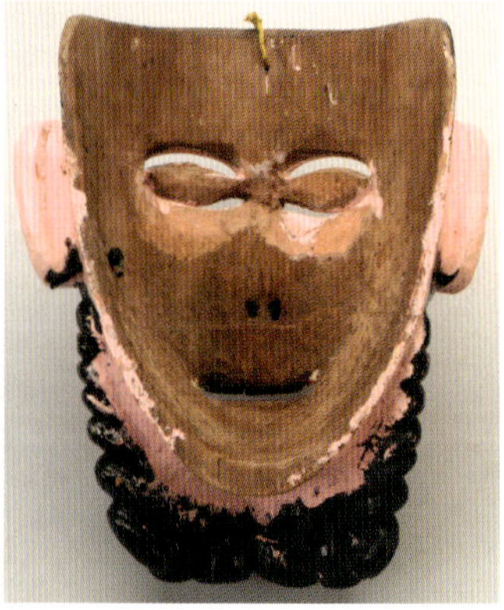

Top: A Pilato mask for the Dance of the Santiagueros; 8½" × 10". Circa 1975. This mask has beautiful ears, which diverge from the carver's usual model. The beard is very well carved. I feel certain that this mask is so beautiful because it was made to special order for some customer. We have learned that the face of this mask was modeled on a carved wooden image of San José in the church in Zozocolco de Hidalgo, Veracruz. This church is less than one block away from the house where Luis was living until his death. Rating: known carver, good condition, very well carved, excellent patina, and extremely rare, *******. *Collection of the author.*

Above left: A view of the mask from below, to show again the carving of the beard.

Above right: The back of this mask has very dark patina. There are double vision slits.

Manuel Mariano Santos

Manuel Mariano Santos lives in Mexcalcuautla, Puebla. I know of him as the carver of a very nice Negrito mask that Vernon and Carlos discovered several years ago. This is another one of those carvers who seems quite talented.

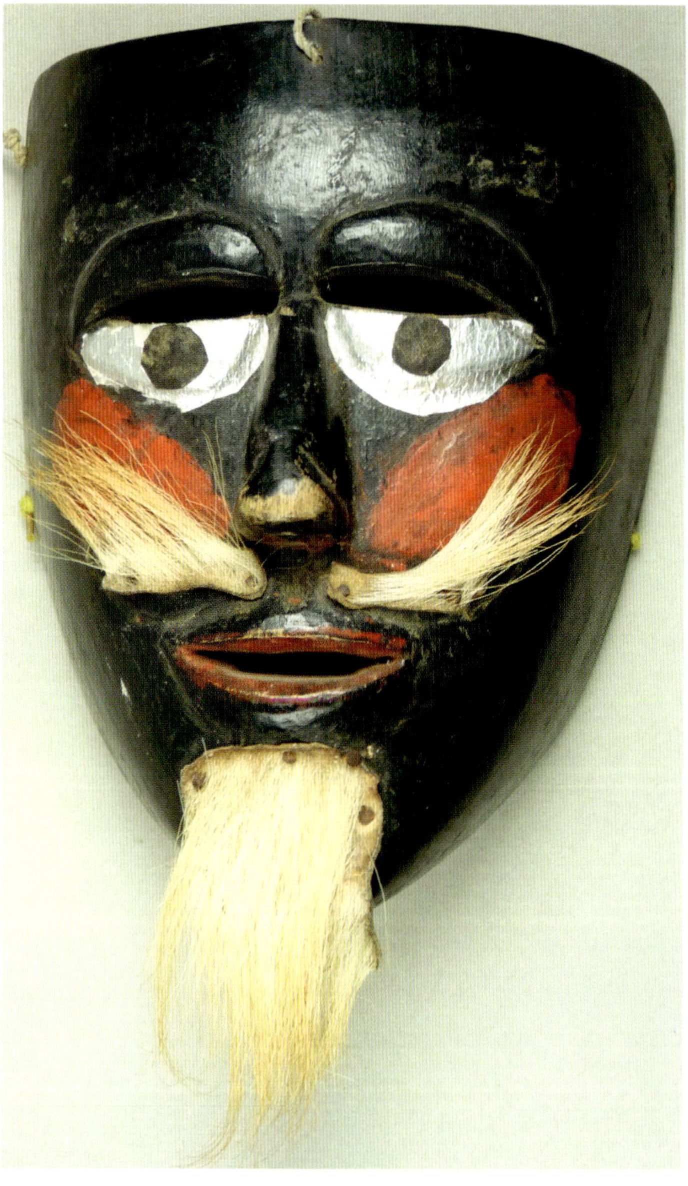

This beautiful mask has relief-carved brows and great patina; 6" × 7". Circa 1985. The mustache and beard are of applied fur. Rating: known carver, good condition, well carved, rough paint, and possibly rare, ****. *Collection of Vernon Kostohryz.*

Marcelino Nuñez Vázquez

Marcelino Nuñez Vázquez was born in 1923. He lives in San Juan Ozelonacaxtla, Puebla. His main occupation has been the construction of furniture. Long ago, he carved an exceptional mask of a Viejo, a design that could have been used in either the Voladores or the Huehues dance. He carved this mask for his own use, and I don't know whether he carved any others. He was clearly a talented carver as a young man when that mask was made.

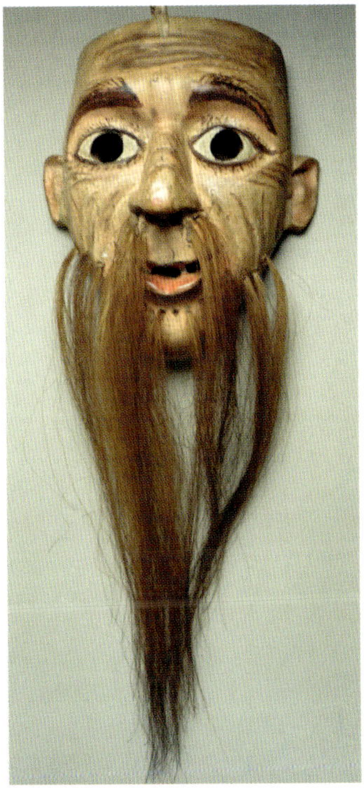

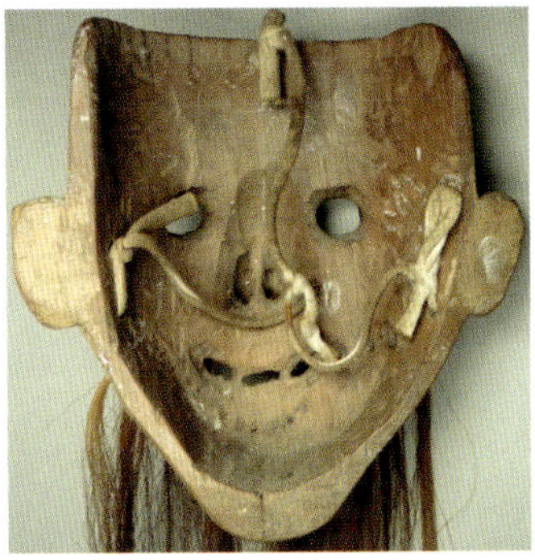

Above left: This is an attractive mask of the Viejo or Pilato character that can dance in the Voladores or the Huehues dance; 9" × 9½" plus beard. Circa 1955, it was reportedly 50 years old when Vernon found it five years ago. Rating: known carver, good condition, well carved, great patina, and rare, ****. *Collection of Vernon Kostohryz.*

Above right: The back is well carved with good patina.

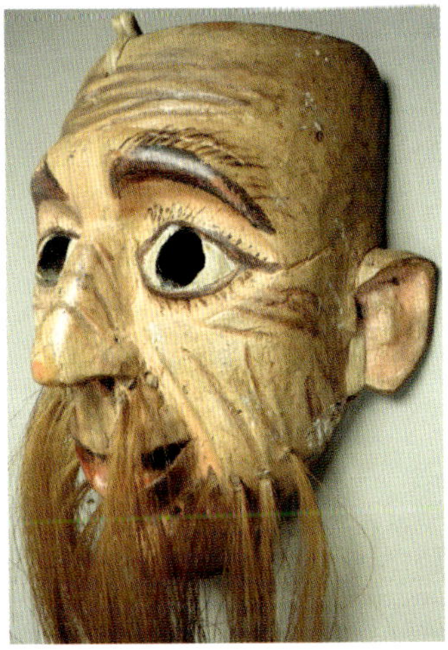

Below left: The mask has a jolly face, and the large ears are nicely shaped.

Silverio Ochoa Martínez

Silverio Ochoa Martínez was born on June 20, 1944. He is another of the mascareros who appears to be younger than his age. He lives in San Juan Xiutetelco, Puebla. Silverio learned to carve masks from an older carver in his community, Mariano Lopez, who died about 20 years ago, at about the age of 80. In the mask photos that follow, the last will be of a mask by Mariano Lopez.

Silverio is an excellent mask maker. His masks are well designed, very carefully carved and finished, and beautifully painted. When a customer brings back a danced mask to be repainted, Silverio carefully removes the old finish in order to provide a clean base for the new coat. Silverio has long specialized in one specific design, which can be painted pink or black in complexion. The backs of his masks are also carefully smoothed. In the photos that follow, I will primarily include examples of his classic design.

Silverio has stated that Mariano Lopez taught him a particular technique that he often uses in his masks, to drill the hole for the forehead string or strap diagonally through the top of the mask's rim to the inside of the back, so that the knotted end of the string doesn't mar the appearance of the front of the forehead. This is in contrast to virtually every other mask in Mexico (except for those from the north, which lack a forehead strap), in which the forehead strap ends with a prominent knot or loop in the middle of the forehead.

When we visited Silverio in 2008, I saw that he was also carving what appeared to be Pilato masks, but different than his usual style. Silverio explained that this type was used in the nearby village of Atempan, Puebla. They resemble a similar mask that I have found in Cuetzalan, carved by Pedro Huerta Mora, so they seem traditional and appropriate for this region.

In contrast to the previous time, when I visited Silverio in March 2010, I was surprised to see that he was carving some forms that were new to him, copies of masks that appeared to be from the state of Michoacan, even a copy of a classic type from Guatemala, black-faced with an elaborately carved gilded headdress. I suppose that I shouldn't have been so surprised; Ruth Lechuga (1988, 215–243) pointed out that carvers in the state of Guerrero had routinely produced traditional masks for local dancers to use alongside made-for-sale masks in other designs. Now we are encountering this in Puebla.

When I visited Silverio again in December 2010, he was carving the traditional designs as before. The Guatemalan Vaquero mask was not in evidence, but there was one mask that looked like something from the northwest coast tradition. Silverio called this a pirate mask; he said it was a design that he had invented.

During that visit I showed Silverio a pair of oversized masks that Carlos Moreno Vásquez had found elsewhere. Silverio said that the two represented Tragedy and Comedy; he had carved them for use in Carnaval. He denied that he had made the masks to have movable jaws. Later when I visited Ernesto Bernabé Sánchez, in Zozocolco de Hidalgo, Veracruz, that carver acknowledged that he had converted the masks to be articulated, and he had embellished the design by painting the black vine-like hair that frames both faces.

Subsequently I commissioned Silverio to make a copy of the Pilato Malo mask by Magno León, because the owner of the original was willing to trade for a group of new masks but he was unwilling to simply sell that mask. Working from a photo, Silverio made a terrific copy.

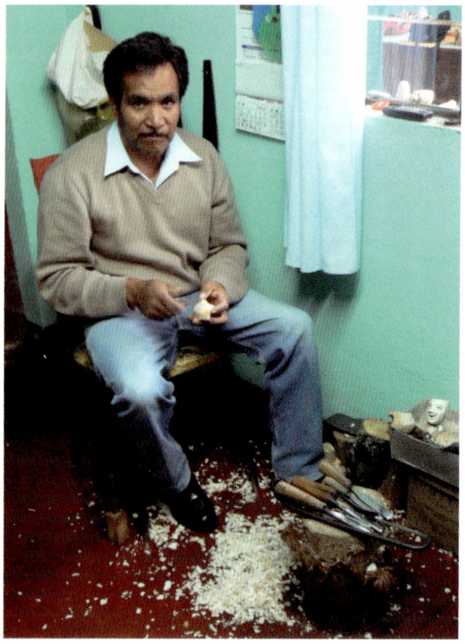

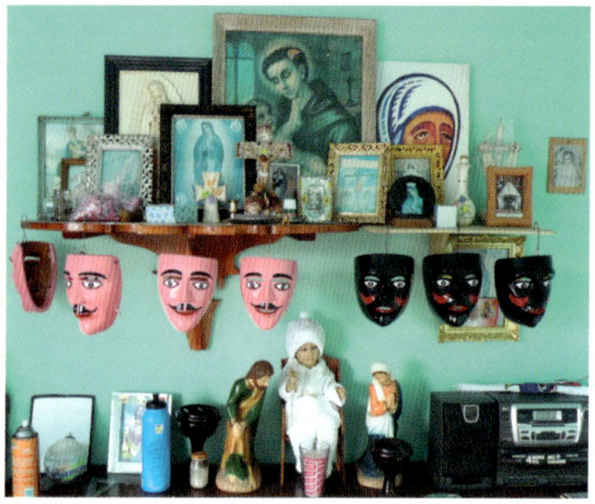

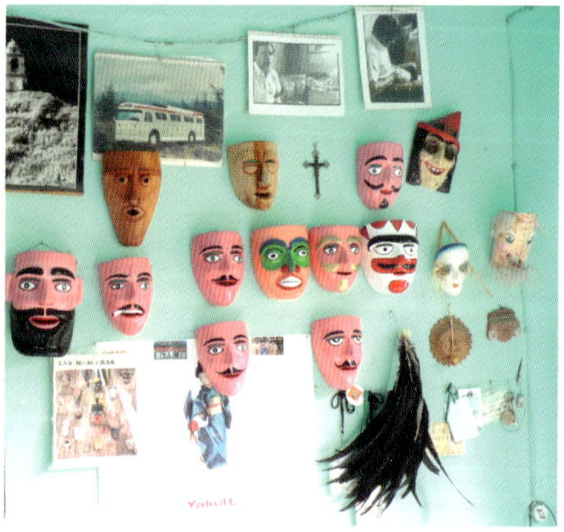

Top: Silverio Ochoa Martínez carving in his workshop in December 2007. He is working on a miniature mask; he sells these in pairs as handicraft items. *All photos of Silverio and his masks are included with the permission of the carver.*

Center: The altar in Silverio's house, with completed masks, in December 2010.

Bottom: The wall opposite the altar displays a variety of completed masks and two old photographs of Silverio. The mask with the green around the eyes was said to represent a pirate.

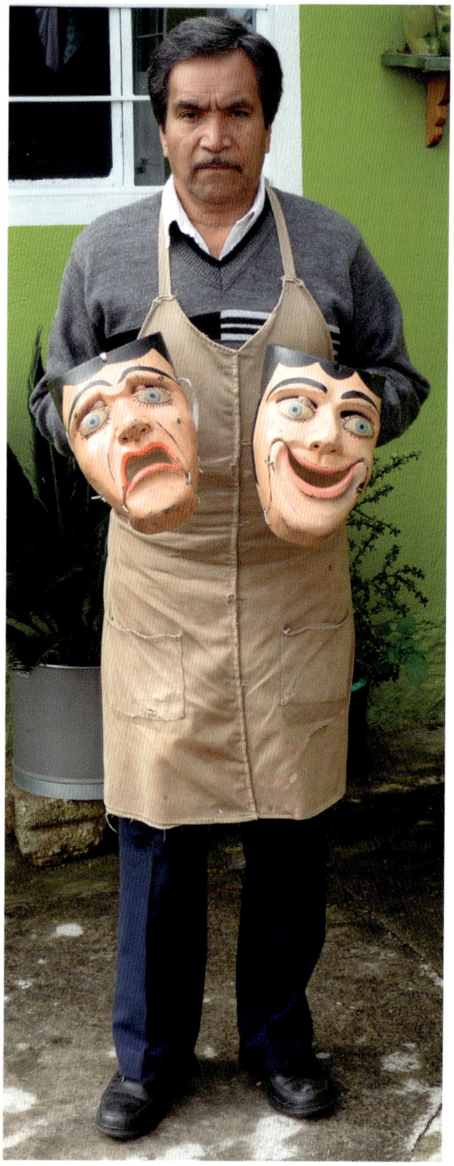

Silverio holding a pair of oversized Tragedy and Comedy masks in December 2010. He stated that he made these for use in the dances of Carnaval.

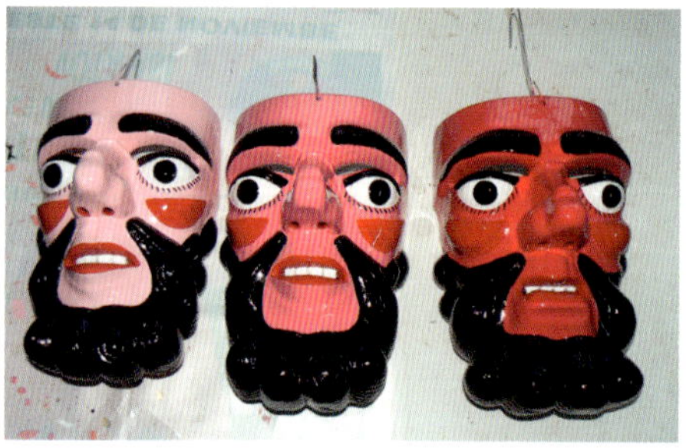

Three undanced Pilato masks in the style of Atempan, Puebla, photographed in Silverio's workshop in December 2008. Rating: known carver, excellent condition, very well carved, undanced, and not rare, ***. *Collection of the carver.*

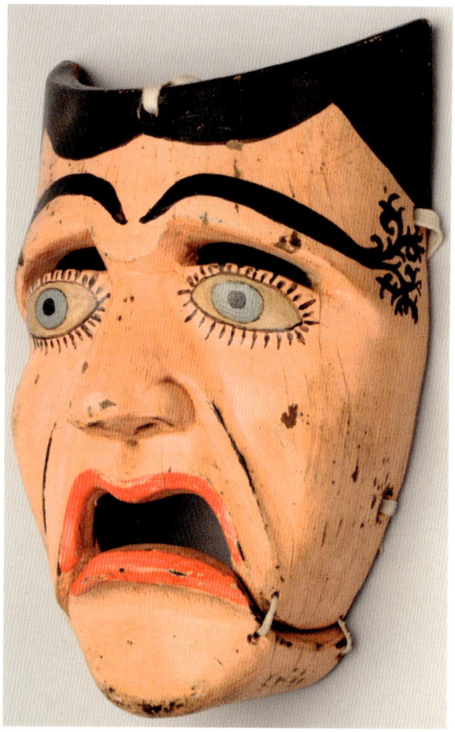

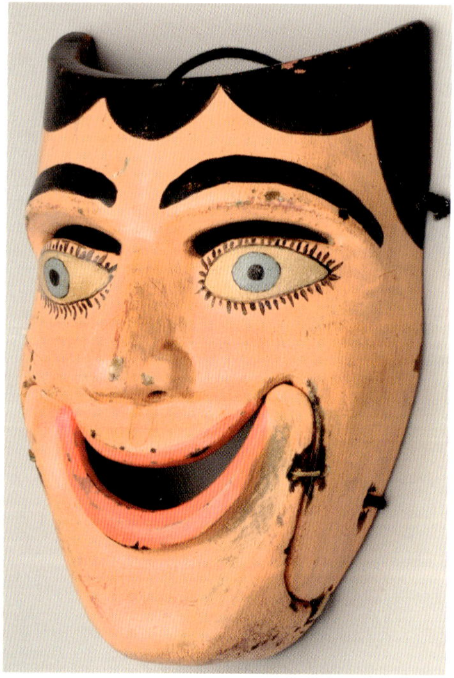

Top: The oversized Tragedy mask by Silverio; 7½" × 11½". Circa 2005. Note the clever manner with which Ernesto Bernabé Sánchez has created the articulated jaw. Rating: known carver, excellent condition, very well carved, good patina, and unusual, ****. *Collection of the author.*

Bottom: The oversized Comedy mask by Silverio; 7½" × 11". For a smiling face, Ernesto had to cut out the jaw in another shape. Rating: known carver, excellent condition, very well carved, good patina, and unusual, ****. *Collection of the author.*

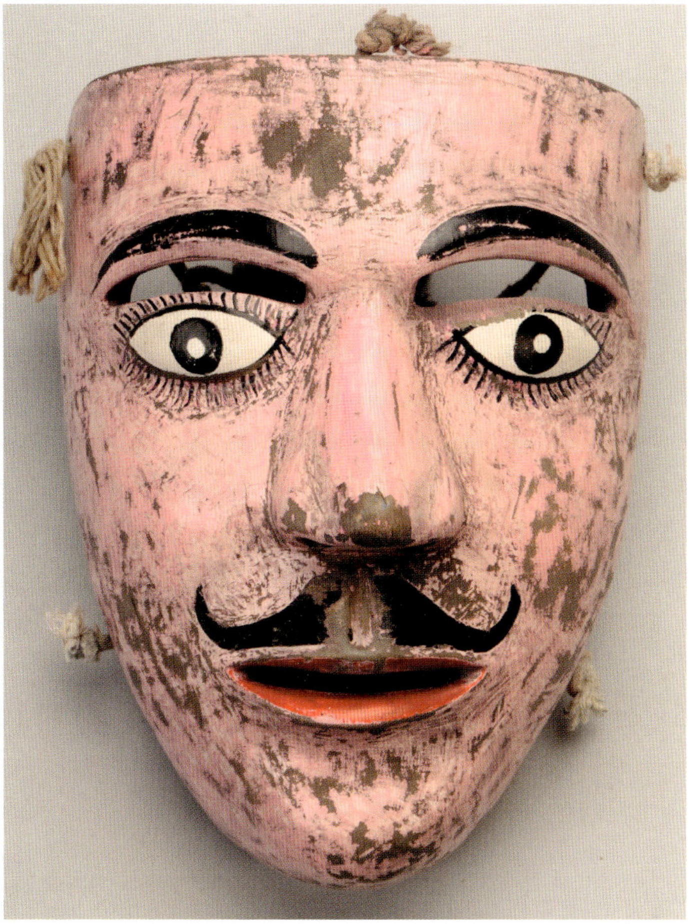

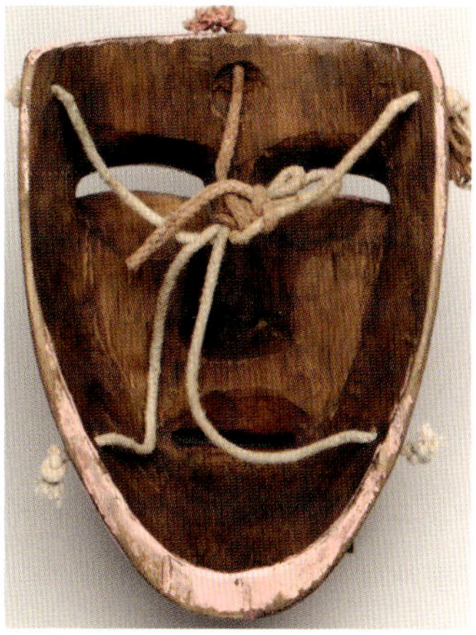

Left: A typical Pilato mask by Silverio Ochoa Martínez, beautifully carved; 5½" × 6½". Circa 1990. This one is very worn. Note the knot visible at the top of the forehead. Silverio's masks lack ears, in contrast to the majority of masks from this region. Rating: known carver, excellent condition, very well carved, good patina, and not rare, ****. *Collection of the author.*

Above: From the back, one can see that the forehead strap is drilled diagonally from the top edge to the back, not front to back as is so usual throughout Mexico.

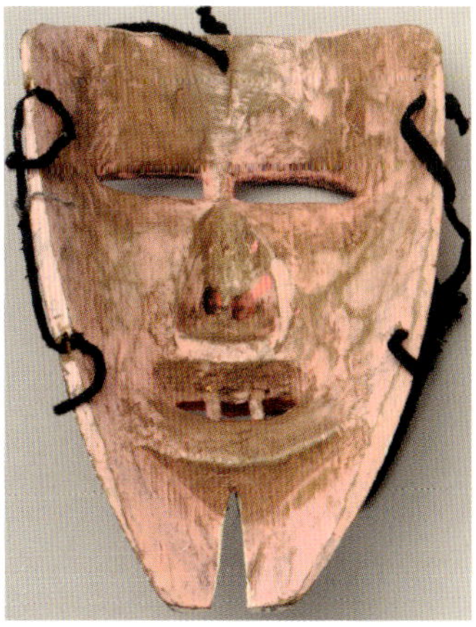

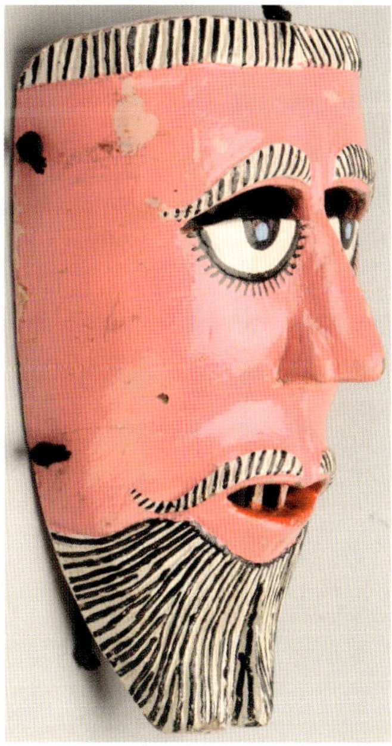

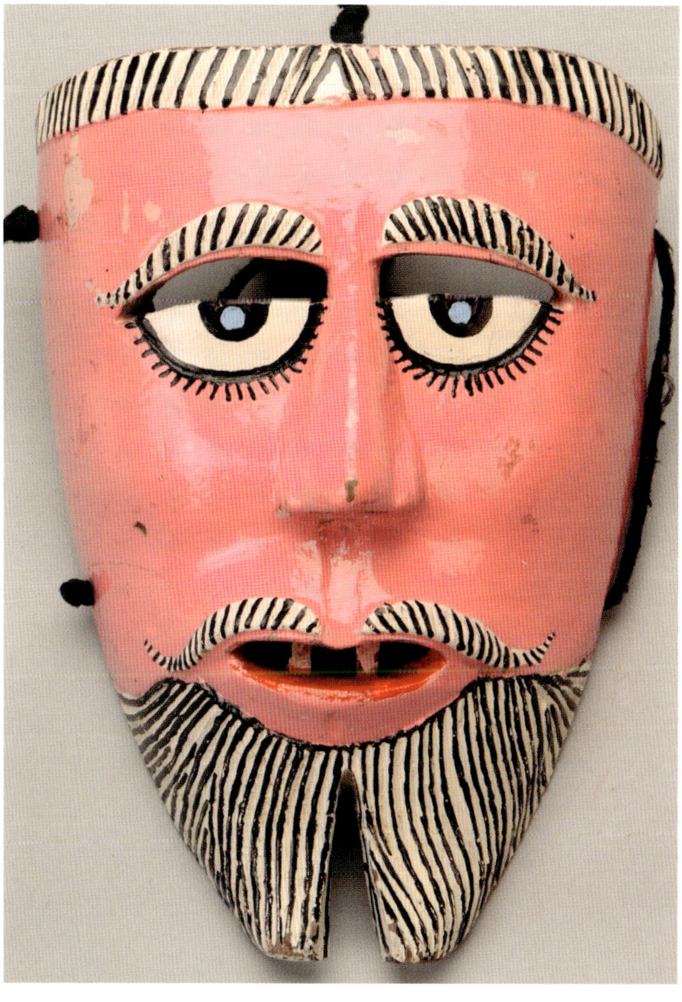

Right: A mask by Mariano Lopez that demonstrates his management of the forehead strap in the same manner as described by his pupil, Silverio; 7" × 10". Circa 1980. The design of this mask is distinctly different from other carvers in this region. Rating: known carver, excellent condition, very well carved, good patina, and rare, *****. *Collection of the author.*

Above left: The back view.

Above right: The side view.

Guadalupe Ortiz González

We met Guadalupe Ortiz González at his home in Buena Vista, Puebla. In his younger days he was active as a dancer in the Negritos dance. He still carves wooden snakes for that dance, using branches and roots, one of which is shown. You will see a large and beautiful Chénchere by this carver in Chapter 7.

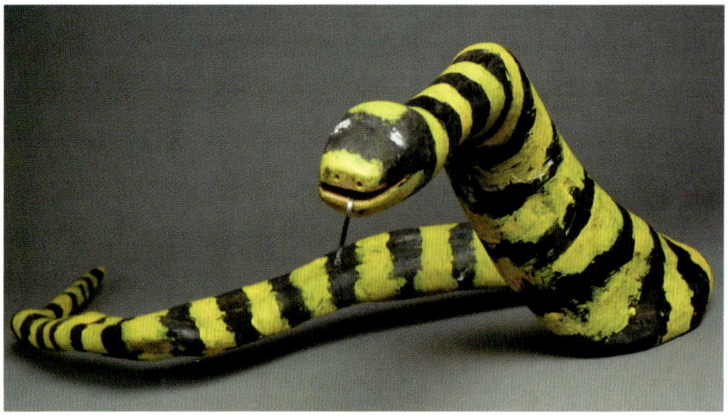

This root serpent for the Negritos dance measures 29" from tail to nose, and 50" in actual length. Circa 2006. Rating: known carver, excellent condition, well carved, undanced, and not rare, ***. *Collection of the author.*

Don Manuel Pérez

Don Manuel Pérez apparently lived and carved in the area of Coxquihui, Veracruz. He taught Don Lillo to carve; Manuel Pérez had learned from Benito Juárez Figueroa. Don Lillo has repeatedly attributed four old masks to Manuel Pérez.

At first glance, one is most aware of the individuality of each of these masks. The ears share some common qualities, as do the backs. Of course, the first two male Tejonero masks seem obviously similar. Also it is easy to see a resemblance between those masks and the masks of Manuel's teacher, Benito Juárez Figueroa.

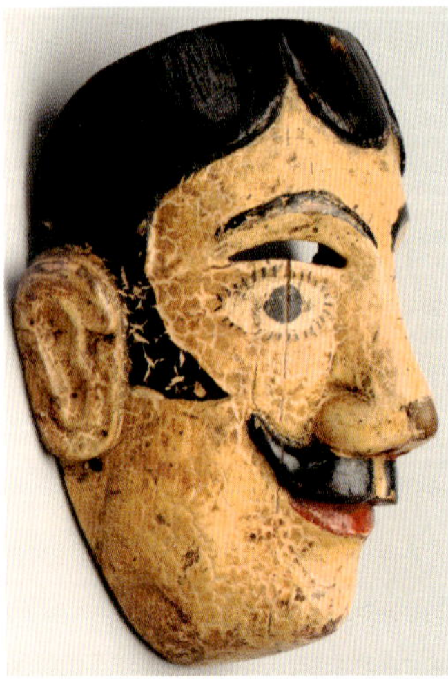

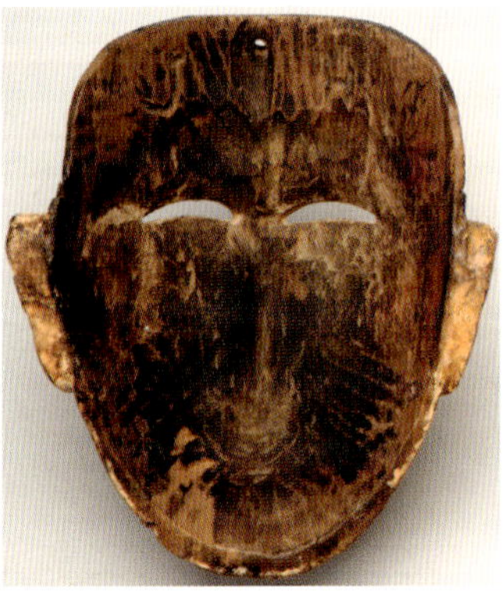

Above left: The design of the ear appears to be a variation on that of Benito Juárez. The big difference is that the front notch occurs higher on the ear.

Above right: The back of this mask is well carved and very worn.

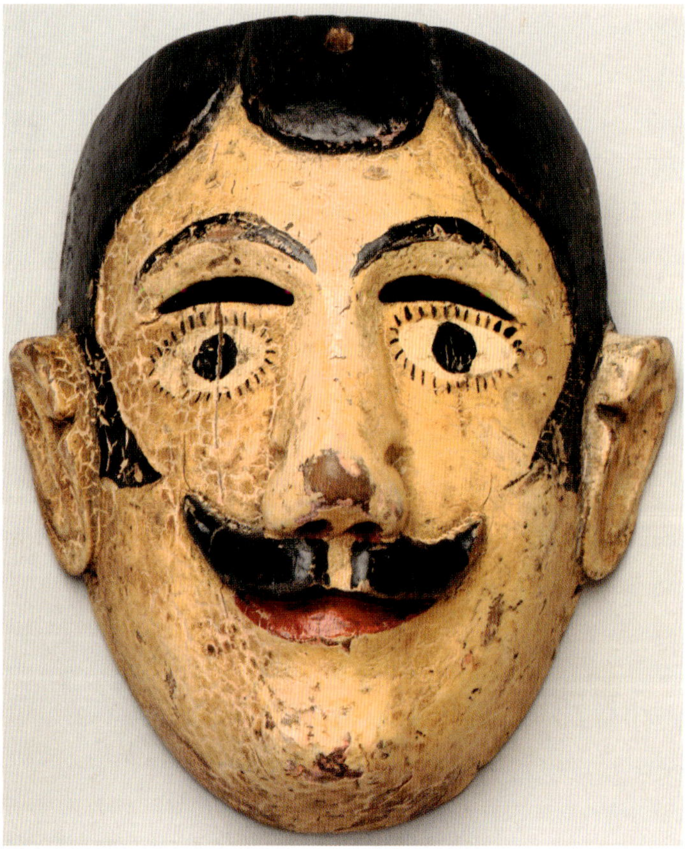

This very old and beautiful Tejonero mask by Manuel Pérez is well carved and has a complex ear design; 6½" × 7½". Circa 1940. The eyes are painted and not carved. Rating: known carver, excellent condition, very well carved, marked patina, and very rare in this condition, *******. *Collection of the author.*

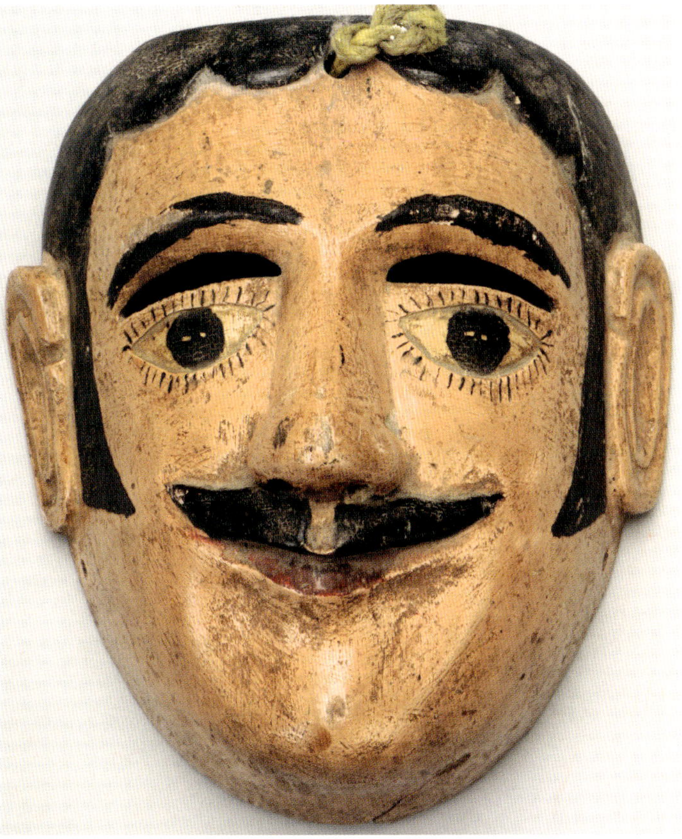

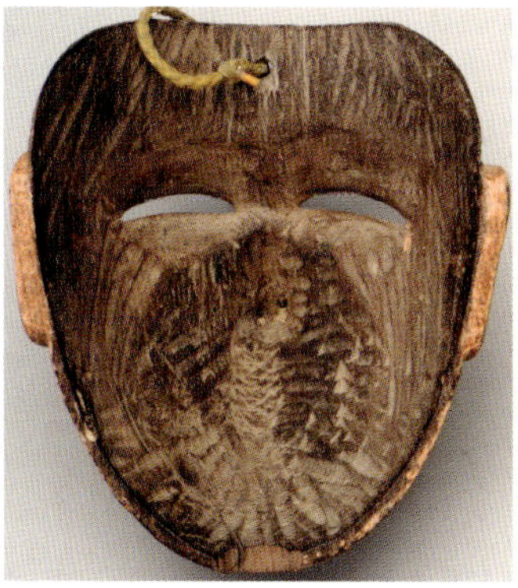

Left: Another equally well carved mask by Manuel Pérez; 6¼" × 7". Circa 1940. The ear design is similar although more refined. The left and right eyes each appear to have two pupils, an odd and unusual detail. The eyes are carved and painted. In some ways this mask is even more beautiful than the first. Rating: known carver, excellent condition, very well carved, marked patina on the back, and very rare, *******. *Collection of the author.*

Above: The back of this one also shows remarkable wear.

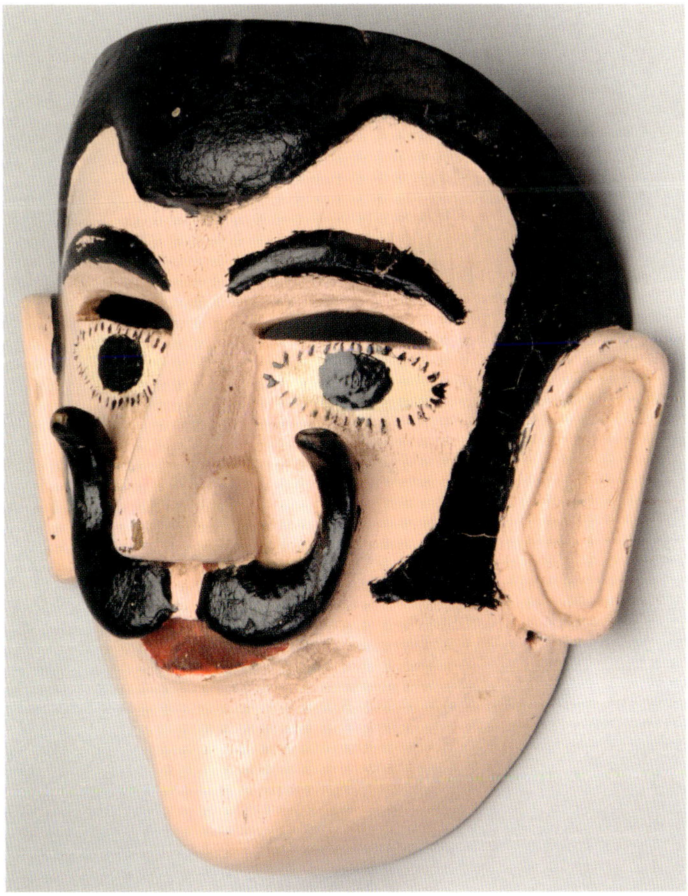

This elevated curling mustache is charming; 6½" × 7½". Circa 1940. The eyes are painted and not carved. The ear design on this mask is unusual and different, with two notches. Rating: known carver, excellent condition, very well carved, excellent patina, and rare, ******. *Collection of the author.*

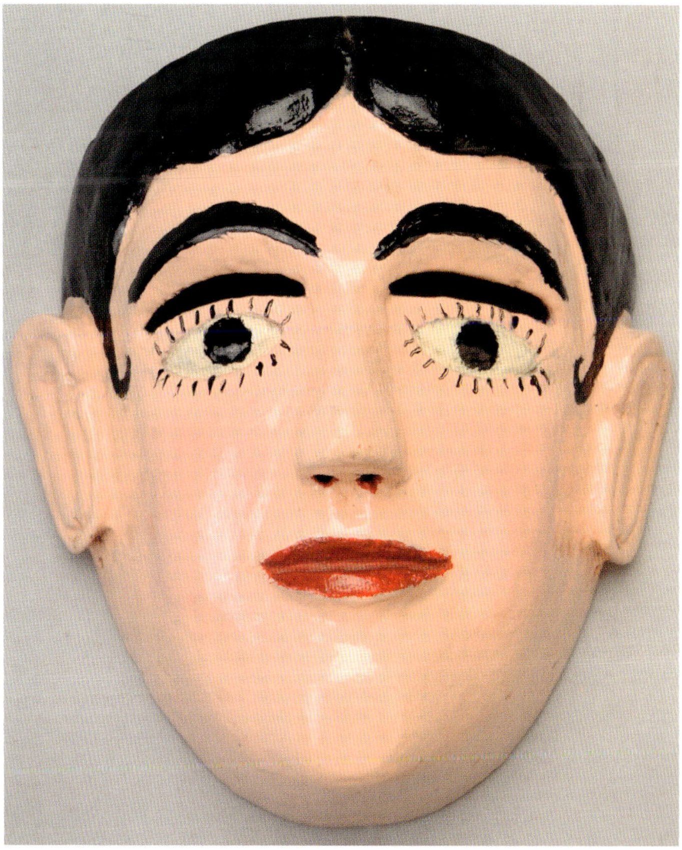

A female Tejonero mask by Manuel Pérez with fresh paint; 6½" × 7½". Circa 1940. The carved eyes look very similar to those of the mask above. Rating: known carver, excellent condition, very well carved, good patina, and rare, *****½. *Collection of the author.*

Odilón Pérez Salgado and Odilón Pérez Ciriaco

Odilón Pérez Salgado was born on July 5, 1941. He lives in Xochitlán de Vicente Suárez, Puebla. We have visited him on several occasions in the past five years, and he has shown us a series of very well carved diablo masks for use in the Migueles dance. For a period of years, he kept one heavily danced mask that we have always coveted; then he abruptly sold it to someone else. Later we learned that Odilón had promised to dance as a Diablo for a period of several years and so he kept the mask until he had completed his *manda* (promise). I have another heavily danced example in my collection that he acknowledges as his work. In December 2008 I purchased an unpainted and undanced Diablo from Odilón, to better document his style. I don't believe that I have ever seen any other characters that he has carved. In summary then, his diablo masks are very good, and I view him as an excellent mascarero.

Odilón Pérez Ciriaco, the son of Odilón Pérez Salgado, lives with his parents. He also appears to be an excellent carver, on the basis of a pair of Perro or Tigre masks.

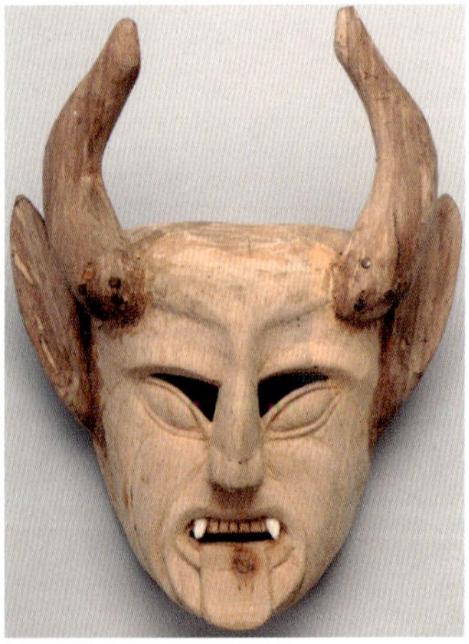

An unpainted and undanced Diablo carved by Odilón Pérez Salgado; 7½" × 13". 2008. This was purchased from the carver in December 2008. The lack of paint permits one to see the very nice details of the carving, such as the relief-carved eyes and the vision slits. Note the plastic fangs, yet another marker for the Diablo character. Rating: known carver, excellent condition, very well carved, no wear or patina, and not rare in this form, ***. *Collection of the author.*

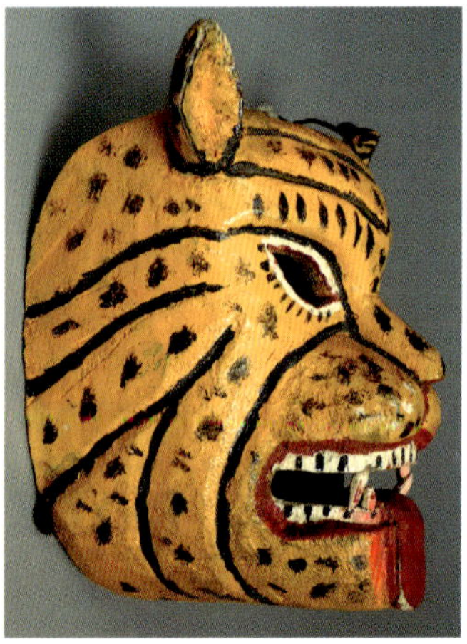

This Tigre mask was carved by Odilón Pérez Ciriaco and danced in the dance of the Voladores; 6¼" × 7½". Vernon Kostohryz and Carlos Moreno Vásquez saw it danced in Zacapoaxtla in December 2008. I subsequently purchased it from the carver. Rating: known carver, excellent condition, well carved, normal patina, and unusual but probably not rare, ****. *Collection of the author.*

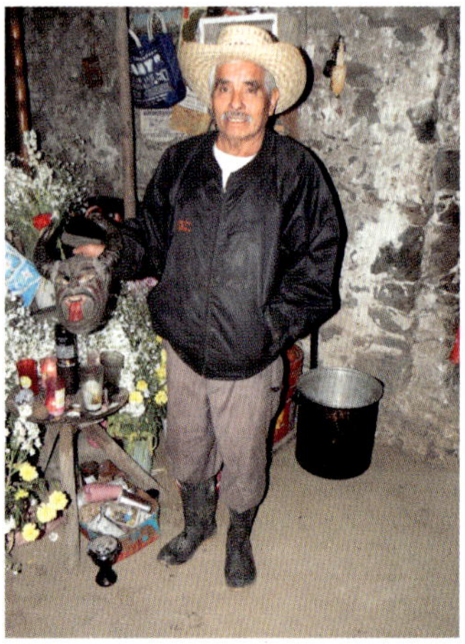

Odilón Pérez Salgado holding his favorite Diablo mask in December 2008. *Photo included with the permission of Odilón Pérez Salgado.*

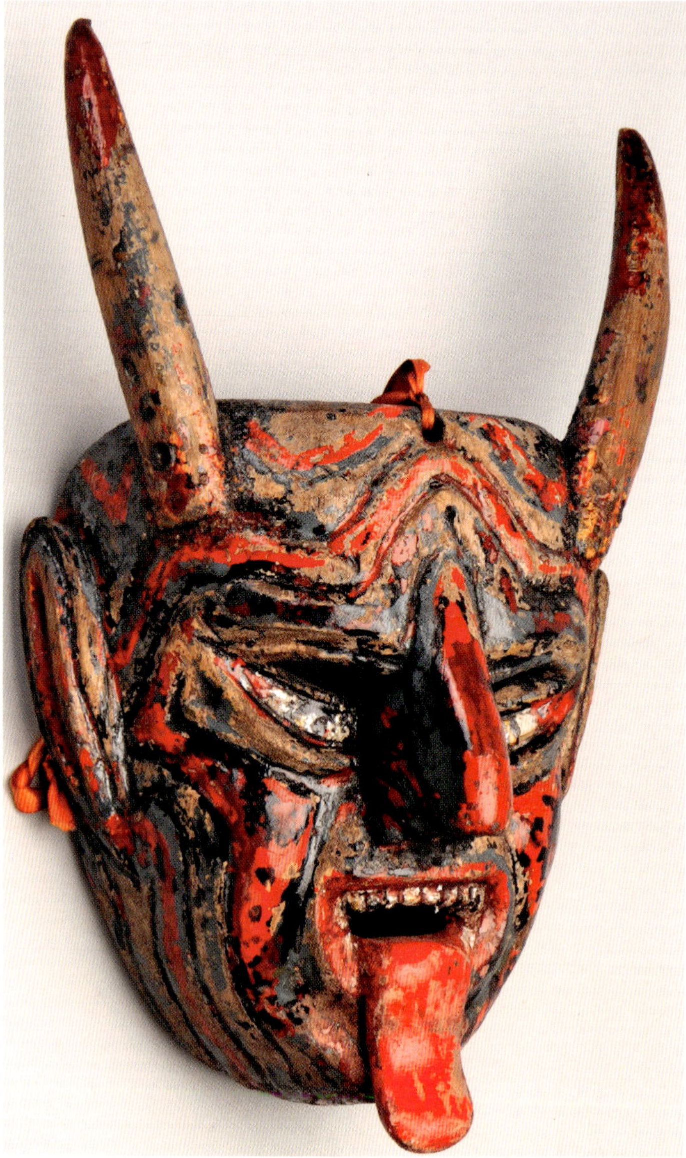

Above: An old and heavily worn Diablo mask that was carved by Odilón Pérez Salgado; 9" × 12". Circa 1980. Note how the Devil is usually depicted with goat's ears. A human-faced mask, with or without horns but with such ears, is likely to represent the devil. Rating: known carver, excellent condition, well carved, excellent patina, and rarity unknown, ****. *Collection of the author.*

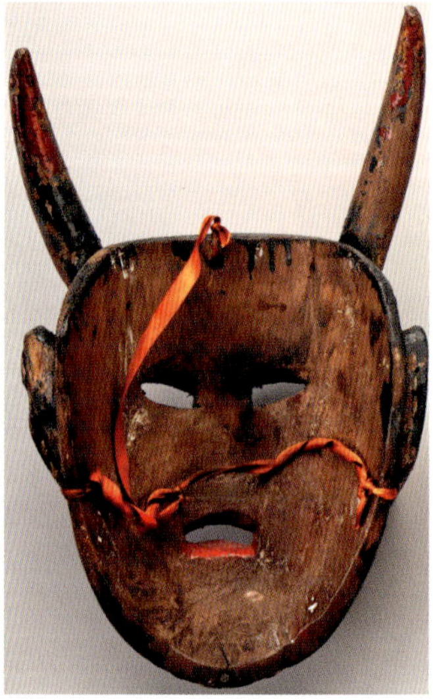

Left: The back shows heavy use.

Pedro Ramirez

Pedro Ramirez is a carver who lives in Caxhuacan, Puebla. I have not had the opportunity to meet him, but I do have one of his masks, and Vernon Kostohryz has several more. He appears to be an excellent carver.

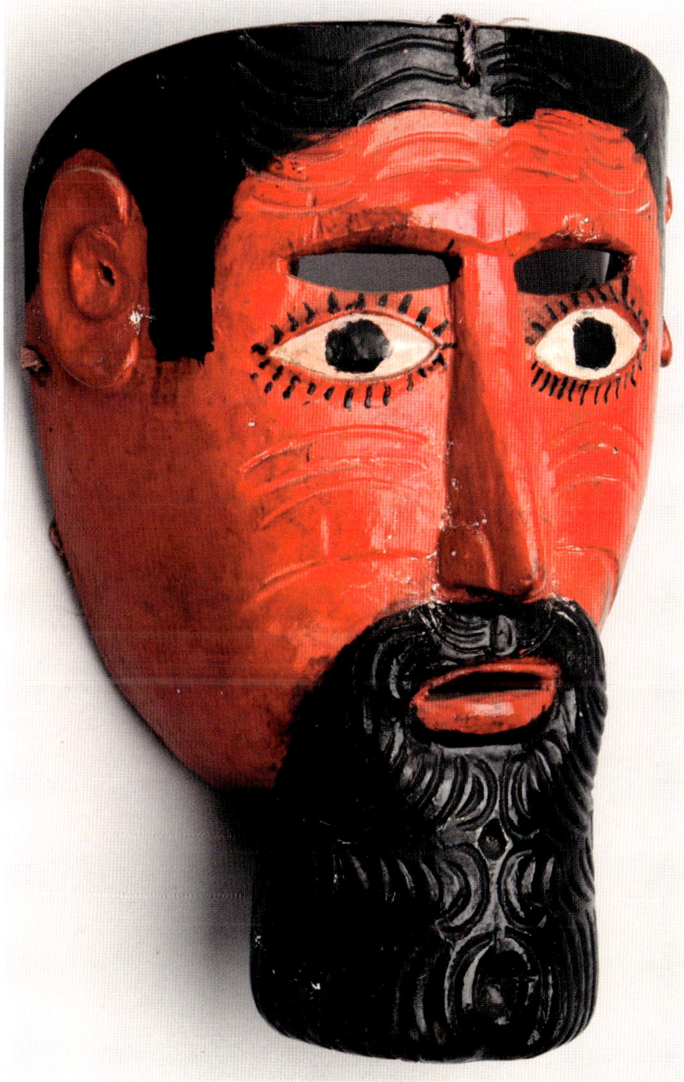

Above: This Santiaguero mask by Pedro Ramirez is nicely carved and the ears are particularly distinctive; 6½" × 9½". Circa 2000. The eyes are carved in relief. There is an unusual beard. Rating: known carver, excellent condition, very well carved, good patina, and rarity unknown, ****. *Collection of the author.*

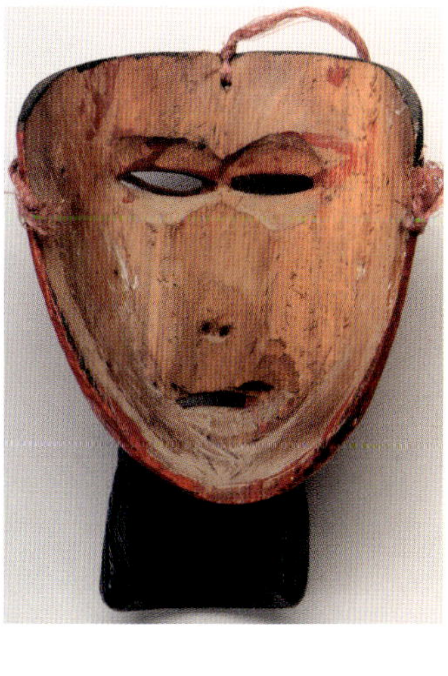

Right: The back is nicely carved and shows normal wear.

Felix Ramos and Daniel Ramos Ramos

Felix Ramos, who was born in 1920, was a prominent carver in Nanacatlán, Puebla, until his recent death in about 2008. According to Cora Govers, based on her fieldwork in Nanacatlán during the period from 1989 through 1998, Don Felix "comes from a family of shamans and is the informal leader of the village. He owns some coffee land but earns most of his income as a carpenter and carver of ritual wooden objects such as masks and religious statues for the whole region. He is also a widely known healer… Though he is very much respected he also faces accusations of *brujería*" (Govers 2006, 282–283).

Brujería means witchcraft, which was often perceived as a probable cause of illness. Those who heal illness are vulnerable to the accusation that they may also cause illness. To learn more on the subjects of healing and perceptions about witchcraft in rural Mexico, see "Sickness and Social Relations" (Abrams and Rubel 1967, 335–356).

We are aware of only a few masks that were allegedly carved by Felix Ramos; surely there are others. We know that there are carved saints by Felix in the community, and I have seen Daniel Ramos Ramos in the process of repainting one of his father's saints.

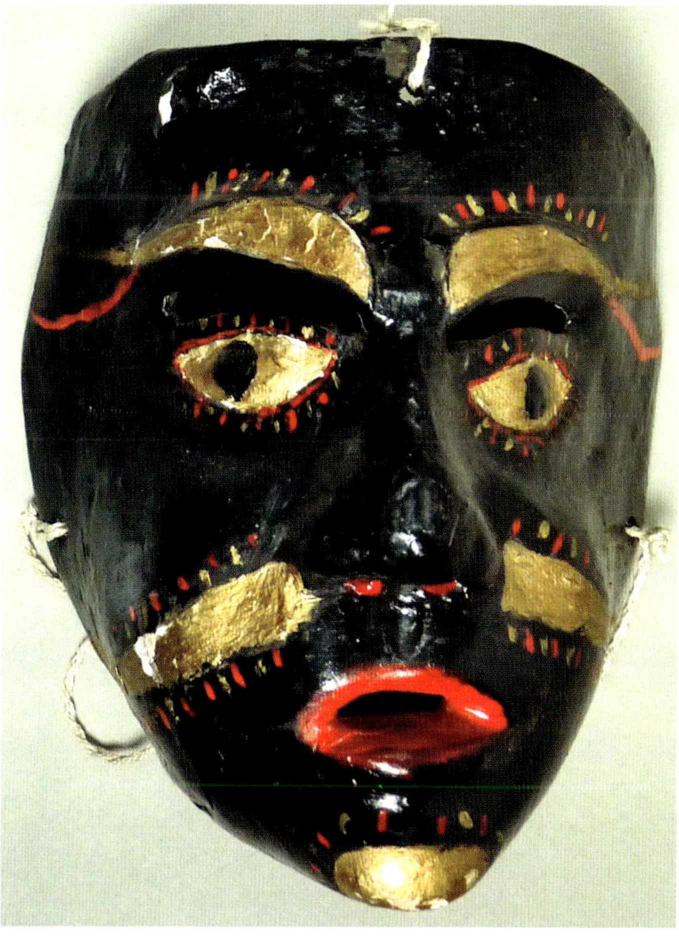

A Negrito mask carved by Felix Ramos; 5¾" × 7½". Circa 1980. It appears to be modeled on the Negrito masks of Benito Juárez Figueroa, although it is more simply carved. For example, none of the features are carved in relief. Rating: known carver, good condition, adequately carved, good patina, and probably rare, ****. *Collection of Vernon Kostohryz.*

Daniel Ramos Ramos lives in Nanacatlán, Puebla. His date of birth is July 21, 1941. Daniel is one of those carvers who demonstrate a very distinctive style. Even though the level of precision and detailing in his carving has gradually fallen off as he has grown older, his masks still retain a characteristic expression that makes them easy to recognize. You will notice that his masks demonstrate a number of phases; for a time we doubted that they were all by the same carver. Yet they remain interesting and vivid. Only the most recent example seems to fall below his usual standard.

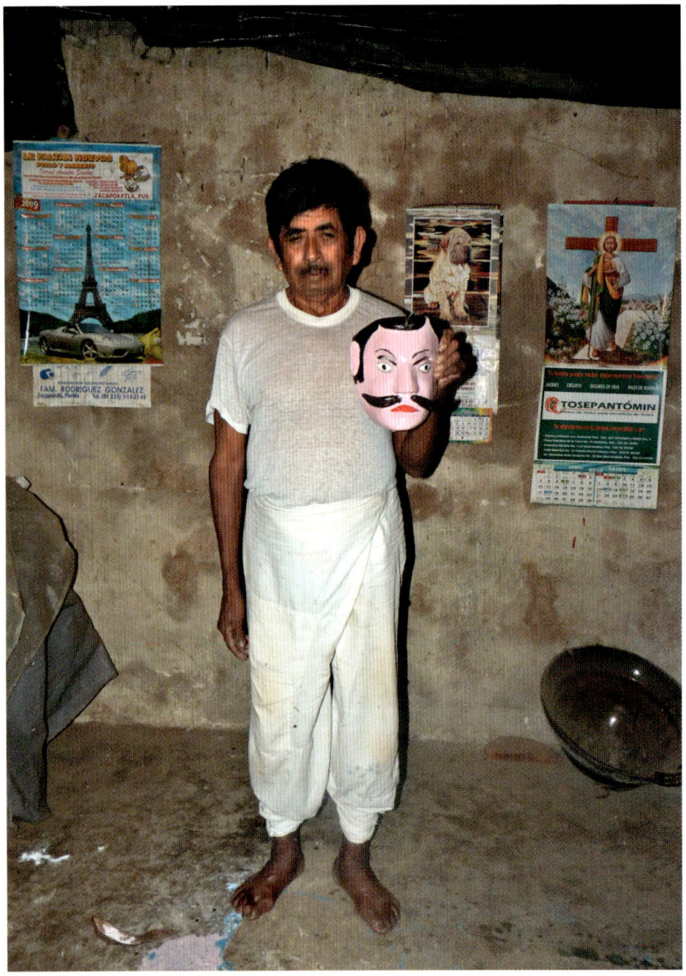

A photo of Daniel Ramos Ramos taken in December 2010. He is holding a recent mask. The calendars on the wall lend an international flavor to Daniel's comfortable but very simple Mexican house. *Photo included with the permission of Daniel Ramos Ramos.*

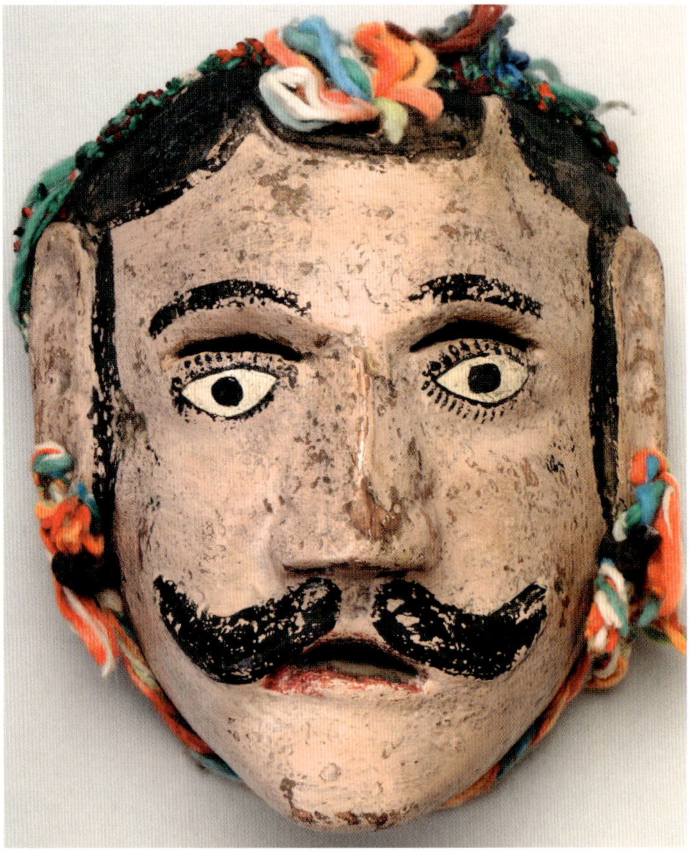

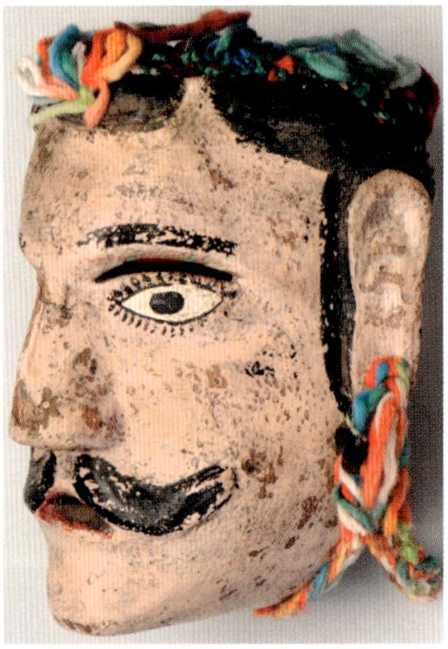

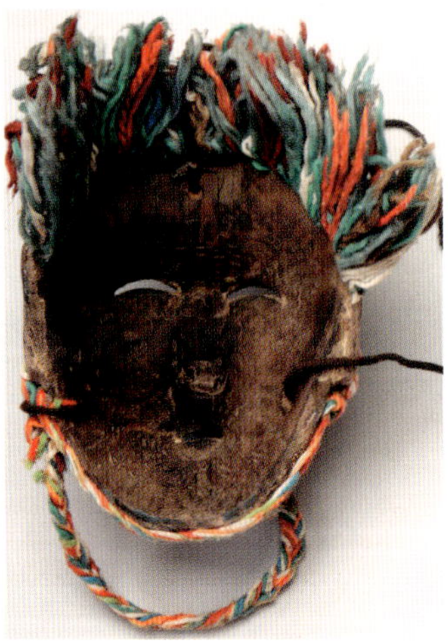

Above: This nicely carved older Pilato mask was made by Daniel Ramos Ramos of Nanacatlán, Puebla; 7 ½" × 8 ½". Circa 1960. The mustache is carved in low relief, but the eyes are only painted. The paint on the face is worn. Colored yarn has been braided around the edge, apparently to decorate the mask for re-use in Carnaval. This is an example of his early masks. Rating: known carver, good condition, well carved, good patina, and rare in this older design, *****. *Collection of the author.*

Center left: From the side view, one can see that the ear design used by Daniel on this mask is unusually long and somewhat complicated. There are five hollow spaces in a vertical row; the central one is round, and the rest are shaped like quarter moons. I will call this the Ramos early ear form, because what we shall see on his later masks are various forms that appear to reflect simplification of this form or evolution away from this level of complexity.

Bottom left: The back is well carved and extremely dark from age or use.

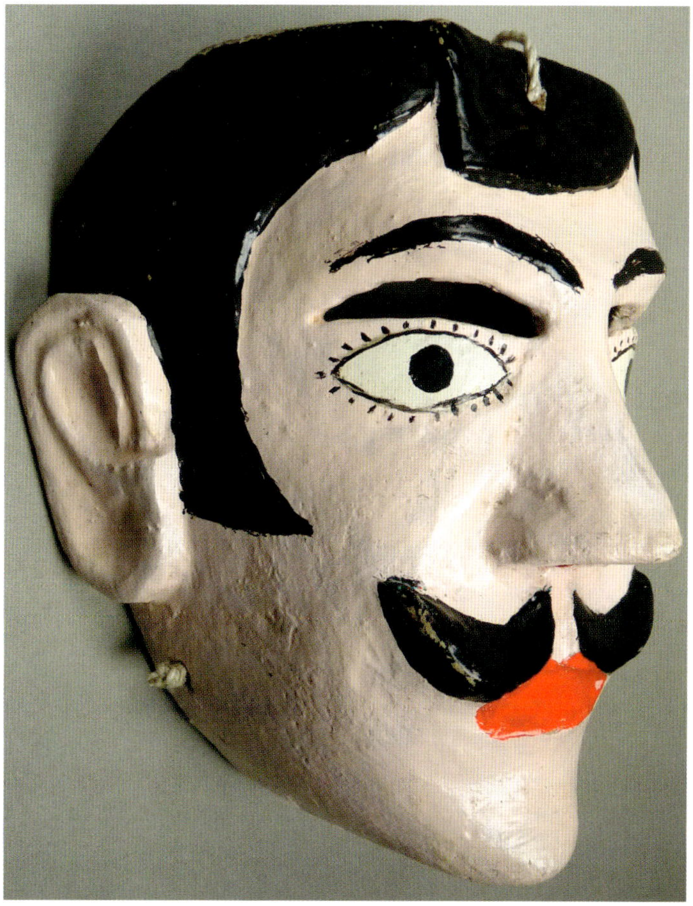

This male Huehue mask and the two Huehues that follow have been acknowledged by Daniel as his work. They are so different from the early design that they were initially thought to be by a different carver such as Francisco Tino. Yet one can see a resemblance in the facial expressions. This mask is well carved and expressive; 7" × 7". Circa 2000. Rating: known carver, excellent condition, well carved, normal patina, and probably not rare, ****. *Collection of Vernon Kostohryz.*

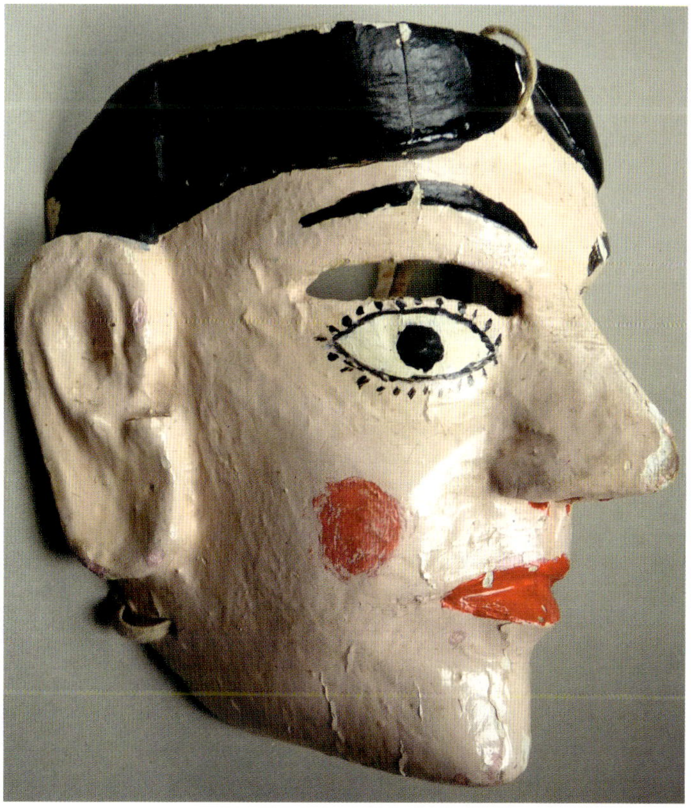

A female Huehue mask from this series; 7" × 7". Circa 2000. Rating: known carver, excellent condition, well carved, normal patina, and probably not rare, ****. *Collection of Vernon Kostohryz.*

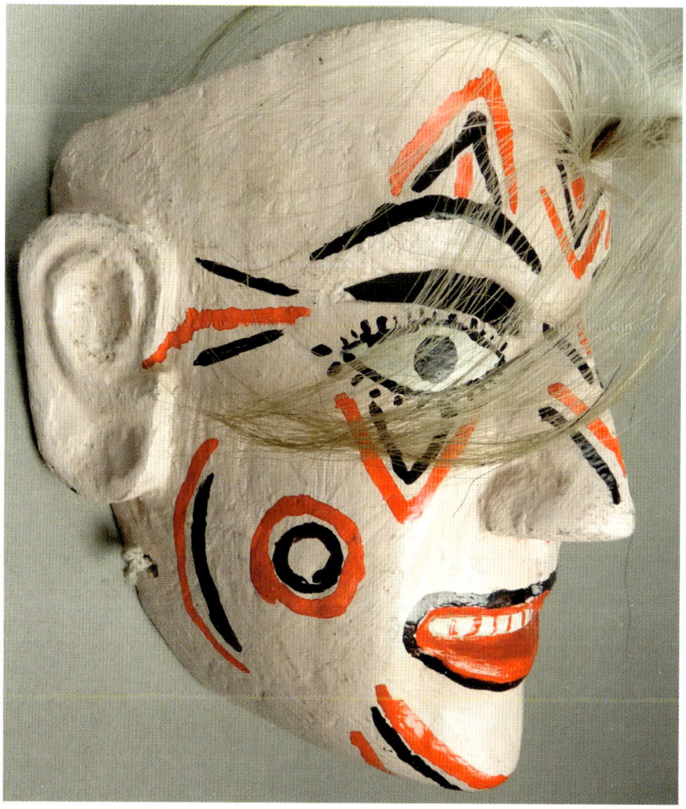

A Payaso from the Huehues dance, also carved by Daniel; 7" × 7". Circa 2000. Rating: known carver, excellent condition, well carved, normal patina, and probably not rare, ****. *Collection of Vernon Kostohryz.*

Arturo Salazar

Arturo Salazar, of Xochitlán de Vicente Suárez, Puebla, was born on January 8, 1985. I visited him in 2008. The masks that he was carving at that time seemed unremarkable, but I did purchase a lively small carving of Santiago Apóstol from him that has continued to impress me as the work of a talented carver. Recently Vernon Kostohryz found an older mask by Arturo that has some flair. I would like to see others by this carver that were so imaginative.

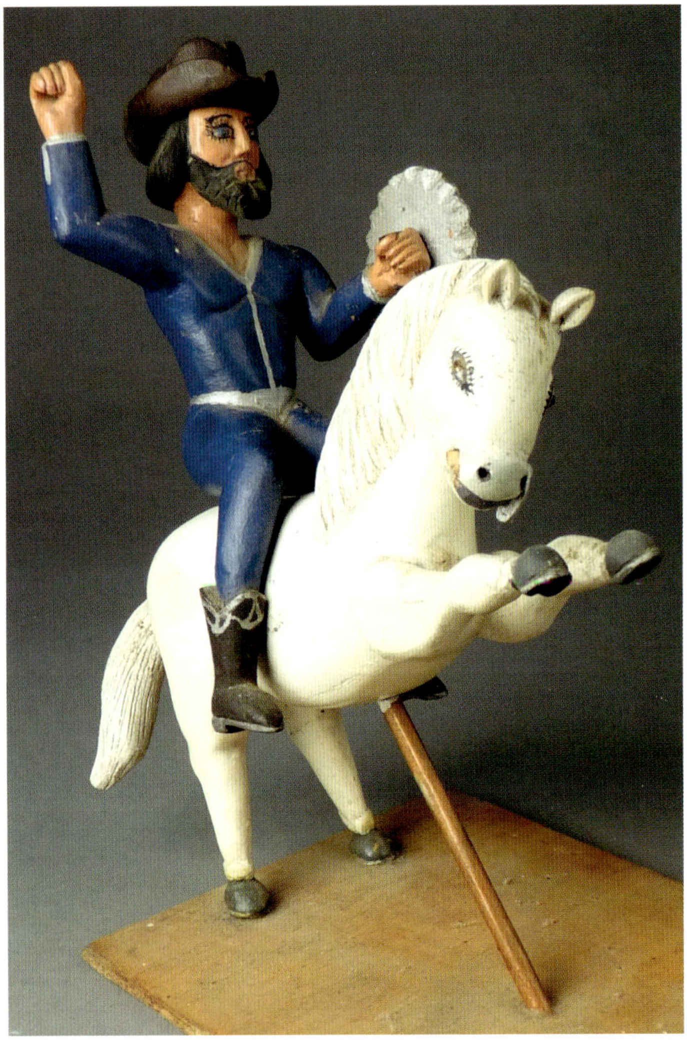

This vigorous carving of Santiago on his horse is small; the horse is 7" long and 6" tall, as is the Santiago figure. Unrated. *Collection of the author.*

Teodoro Tacuepián Galvan

Teodoro Tacuepián Galvan, whom we shall call Don Teodoro, was born on July 14, 1911. After seeing his masks in common use for a number of years, Vernon finally met this carver on December 31, 2005. Teodoro lives in Tatoxca, very near Zacapoaxtla, Puebla. He only began carving masks when he was 63 years old, and now he is just 100 years of age. It is evident that Don Teodoro has been a highly prolific carver in the interim, and one encounters his masks at great distances from his home.

It is Vernon's impression that the masks of this carver have become popular with merchants who make a practice of buying undanced examples very cheaply and then artificially aging the masks in an effort to make them seem more valuable or desirable. In contrast, it may be that some of these apparently "doctored" masks have been repainted by their owners for use in Carnaval. So, with regret, he advises us to evaluate these masks very carefully, if we are tempted to buy them.

One is likely to feel tempted, because Don Teodoro's masks are vividly carved. One commonly sees Negritos, male and female Huehue masks, and Pilatos masks from the Santiagueros dance—human faces wearing crowns that are carved as part of the mask. His Huehue masks can be quite attractive; I regret having only one good example to include here.

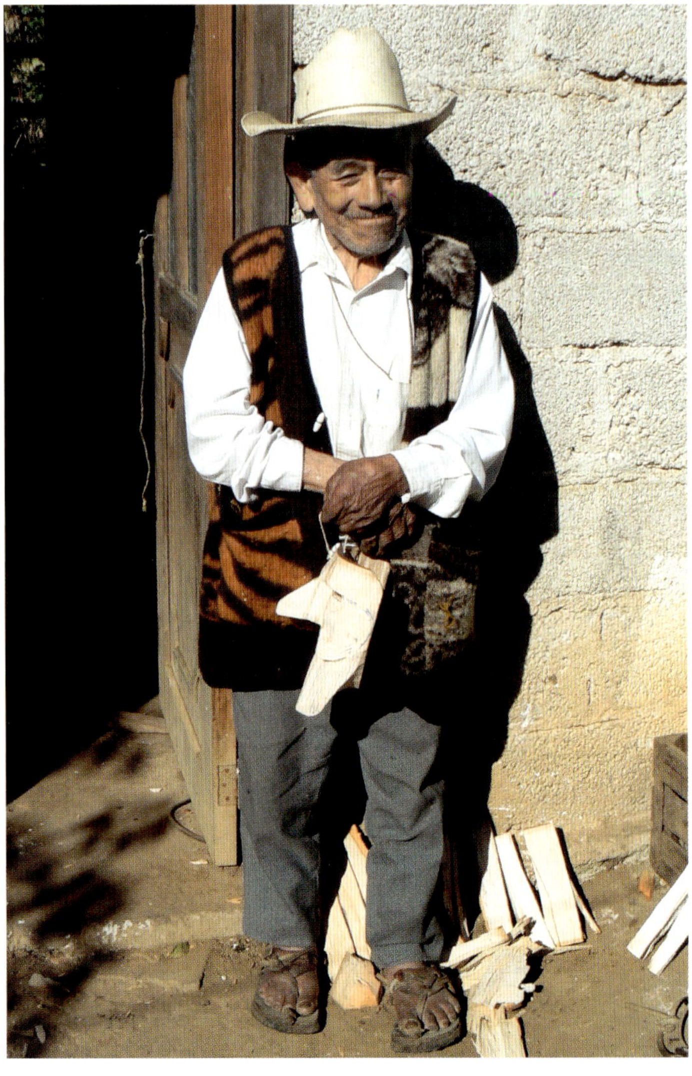

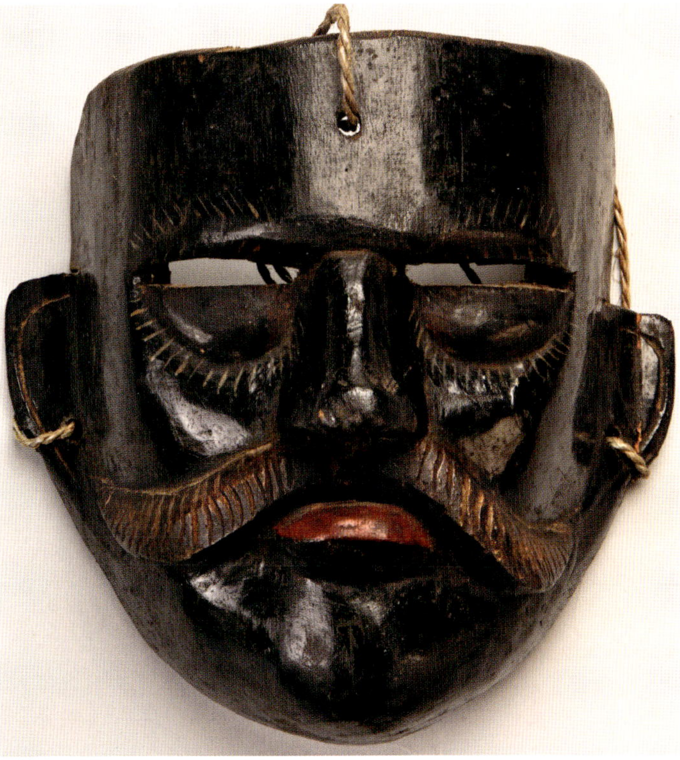

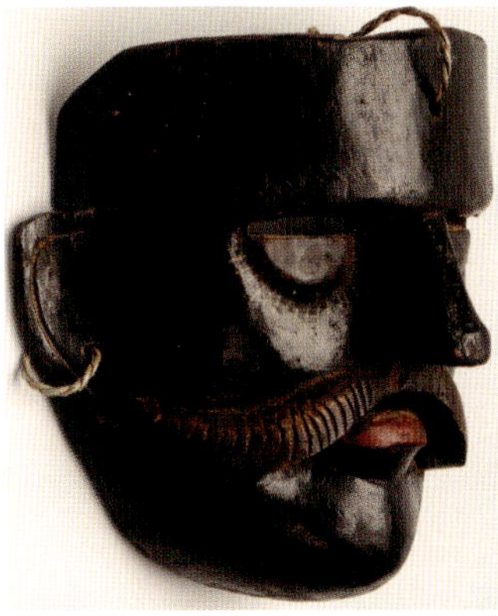

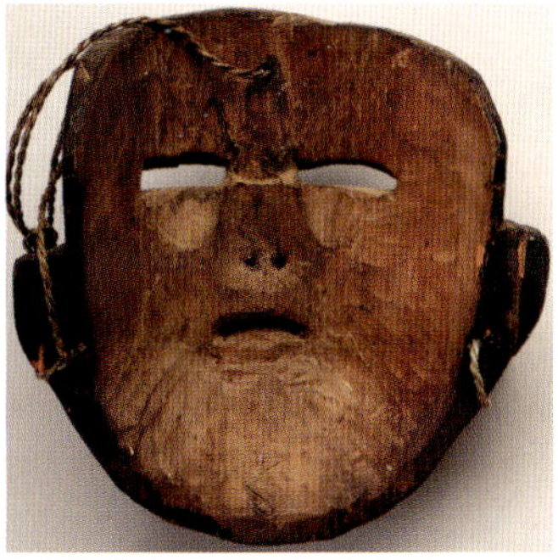

Left: This is a handsome Negrito mask; 7½" × 7". Circa 1990. Note the typical ear design of this carver. Rating: known carver, good condition, well carved, good patina, and not rare, ****. *Collection of the author.*

Above left: The side view of this mask, showing the elaborate ear design.

Above right: The back of this mask. It shows good wear.

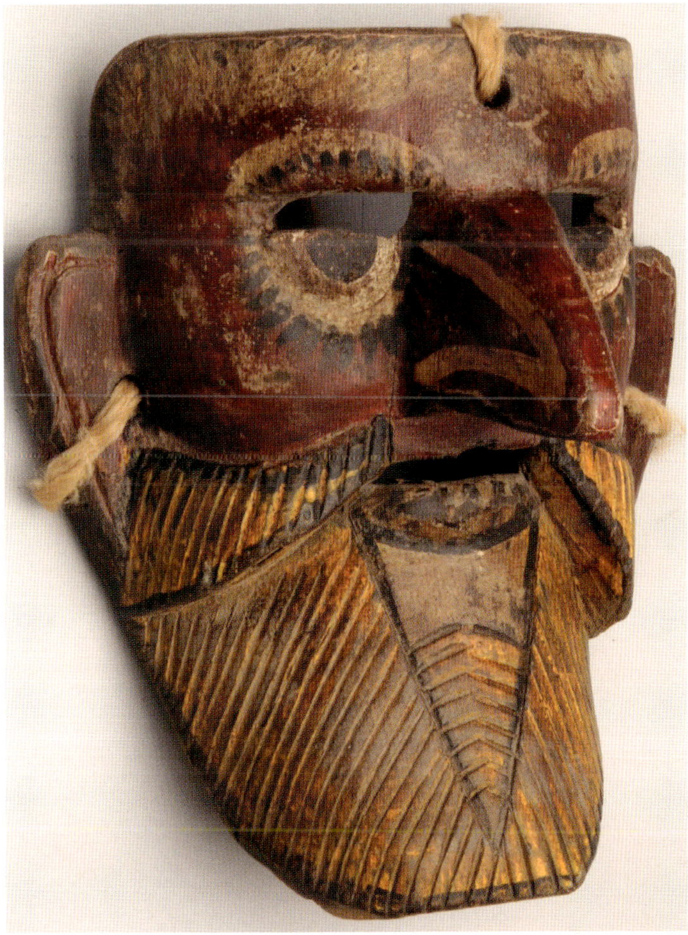

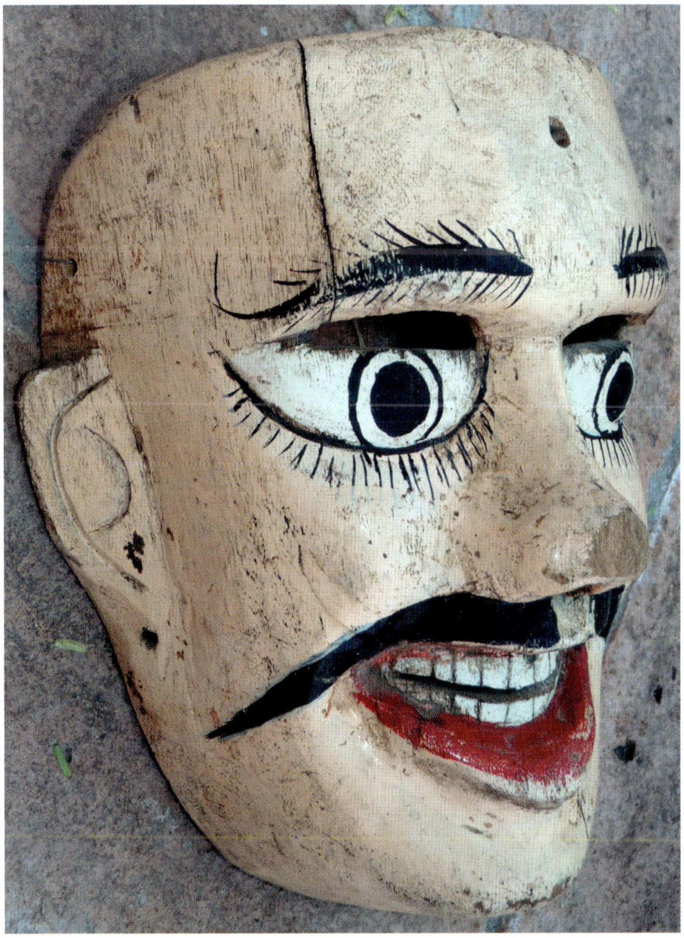

Opposite page:
Teodoro Tacuepián Galvan, Don Teodoro, at the door of his workshop, in Tatoxca, just outside of Zacapoaxtla, Puebla. He is holding an unfinished Pilato mask. *Photo included with permission of Don Teodoro.*

Above: A Pilato mask by Don Teodoro; 7¼" × 8". Circa 1990. Rating: known carver, good condition, well carved, good patina, and not rare, ****. *Collection of the author.*

A male Huehue mask by Don Teodoro; 7½" × 7". Circa 1980. His female Huehue masks can look much the same, minus the mustache. The truly constant feature across all of his masks is the ear design. With open mouth and a toothy grin, this mask could be a Payaso, but it lacks the embellishments that would mark it as a clown. Rating: known carver, good condition, well carved, good patina, and not rare, ****. *Collection of Bill LeVasseur.*

Francisco Tino

Francisco Tino was born on February 2, 1958. He is currently the principle carver in Olintla, Puebla. When Vernon Kostohryz, Carlos Moreno Vásquez, and I visited Olintla in March 2010, we saw his masks and puppets in use. We attempted to meet with the carver, but he was actively involved in the fiesta; I did visit him in December 2010. I have seen male and female Huehue masks and masks of dogs by Francisco. He appears to be a popular and talented carver. I will discuss his puppets in Chapter 7.

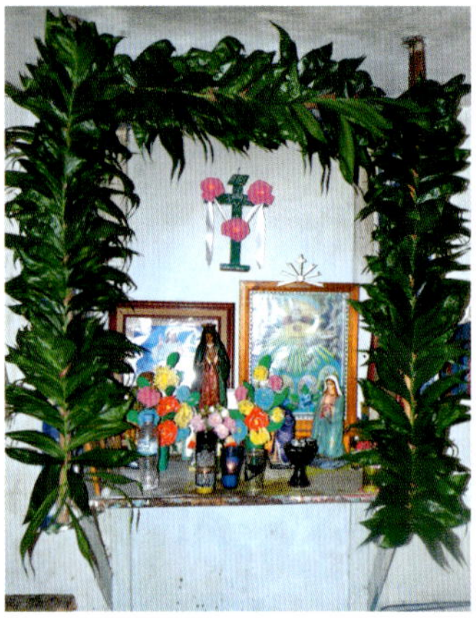

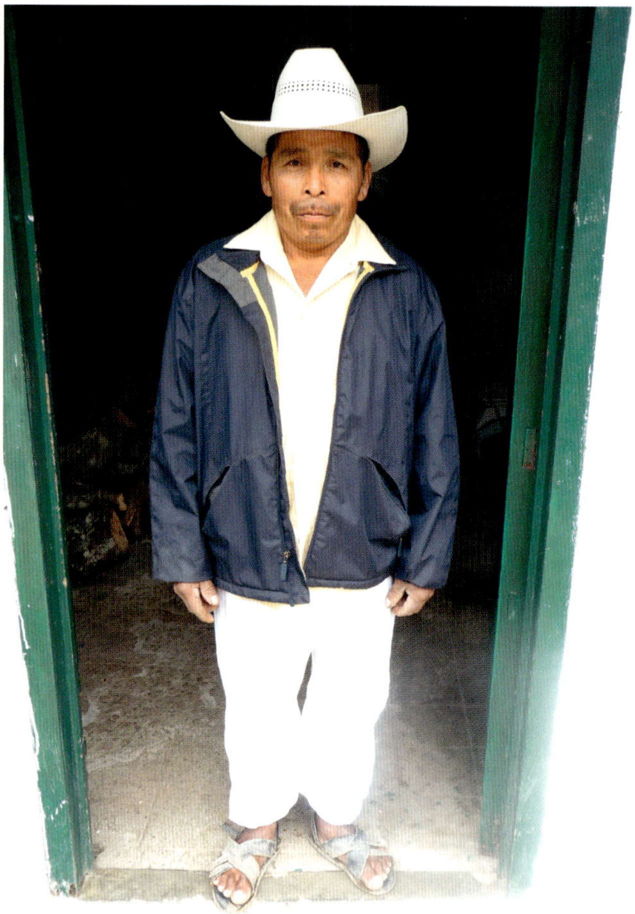

Right: Francisco Tino standing at his doorway in Olintla, Puebla, in December 2010. *Photos of Francisco and objects in his house are included with permission from Francisco Tino.*

Left: Francisco Tino's family altar.

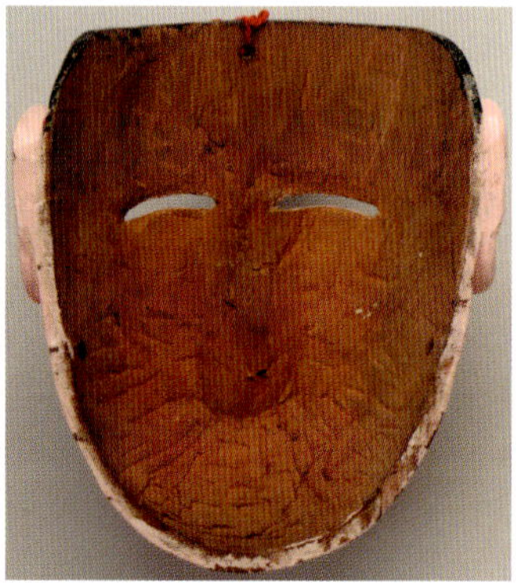

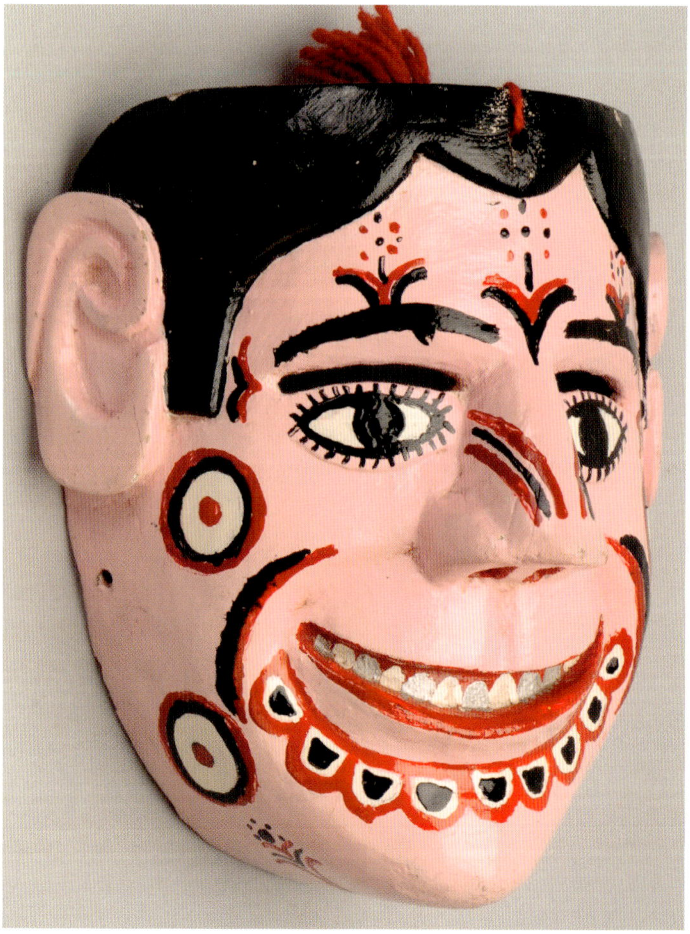

Right: A Payaso mask in Francisco's characteristic style; 7" × 7¾". Circa 2000. It was carved with an open mouth, and it has been vividly painted by the carver. It has Francisco's typical ear design. Rating: known carver, excellent condition, well carved, good patina, and not rare, ****. *Collection of the author.*

Above: The back of the mask. In this instance Francisco has not carved a hollow for the dancer's nose; as a consequence we see considerable staining in that area where the nose and mask made contact.

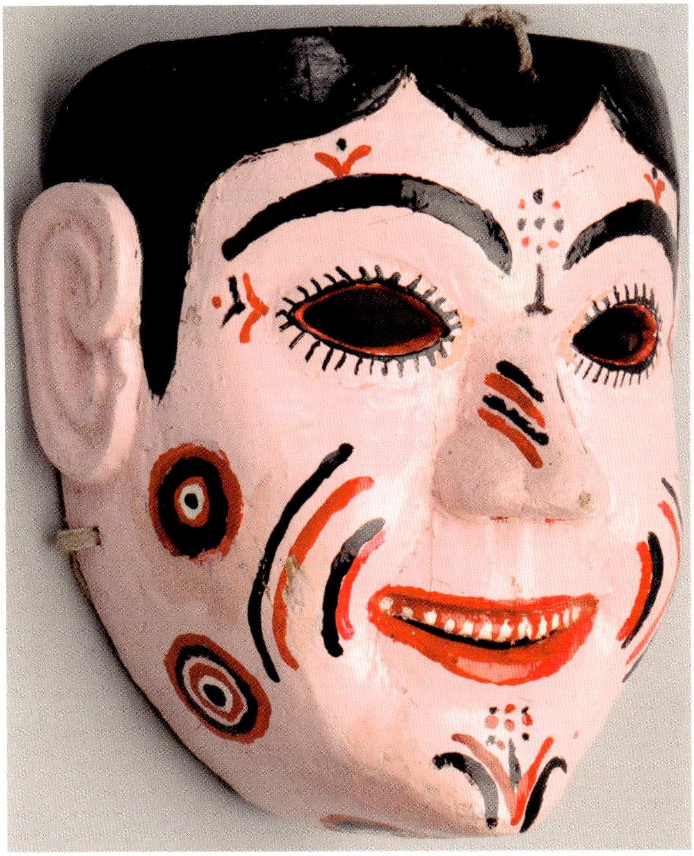

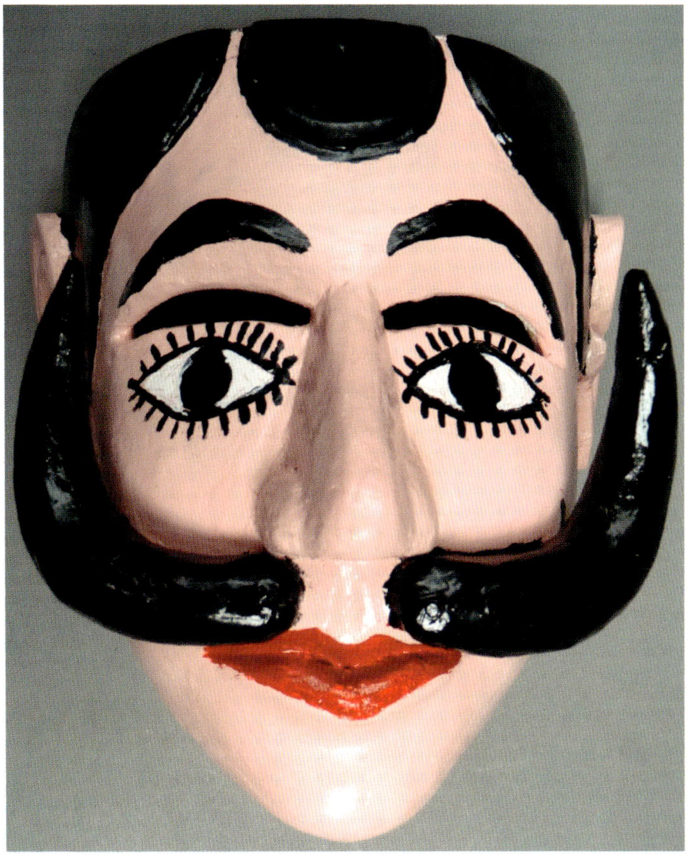

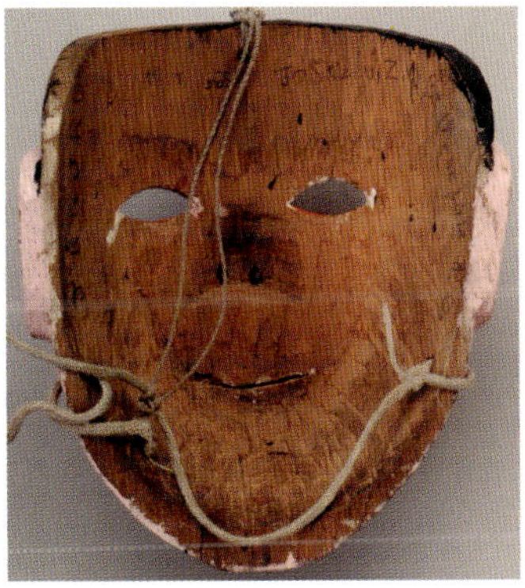

Above: A Payaso mask carved by Francisco Tino that was danced for 7 years; 6¾" × 7½". 2003. Rating: known carver, excellent condition, well carved, good patina, and not rare, ****. *Collection of the author.*

Left: The back of this mask. Here Francisco has carved a hollow to accommodate the dancer's nose.

This undanced male Huehue mask was made to order for the author by Francisco Tino in 2010; 7" × 7". Rating: known carver, excellent condition, well carved, undanced, and rarity unknown, ***. *Collection of the author.*

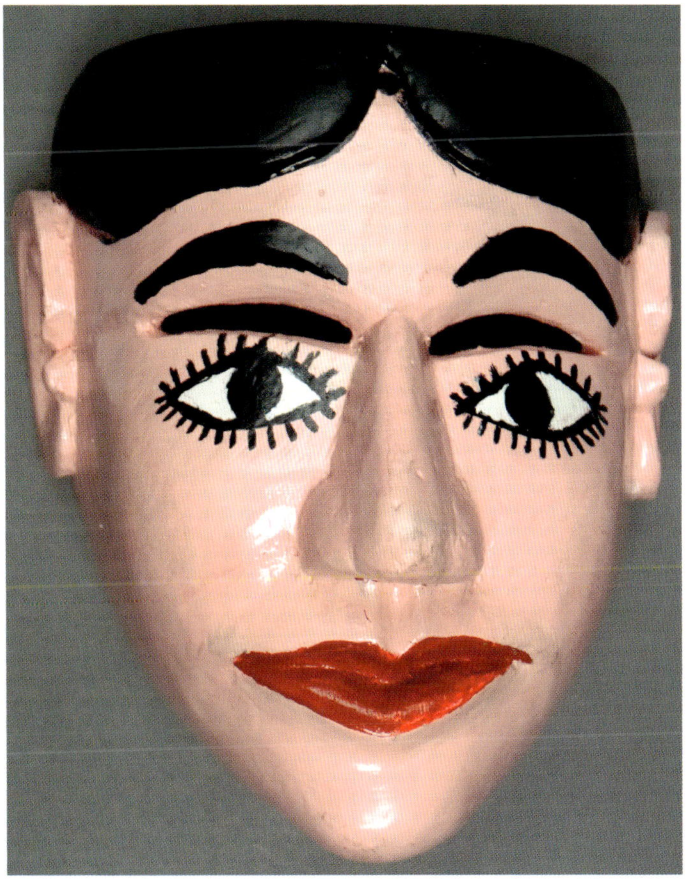

This female Huehue mask was also made to order by Francisco Tino; 7" × 7". It too is undanced. Rating: known carver, excellent condition, well carved, undanced, and rarity unknown, ***. *Collection of the author.*

Ernesto Tóral Hilario

Ernesto Tóral Hilario was born on April 11, 1934, though he looks younger. He lives with his wife and children in San Miguel Tzinacapan, Puebla, just outside of Cuetzalan. He has recently been ill, but he is a determined man who somehow has kept on doing what he needed to do. He has been the proud manager for a Quetzalines dance group, composed of elementary school-aged boys. He himself has danced in the Santiagueros dance in his community.

As a mascarero, Ernesto seems to mainly carve Santiaguero masks, in the style and proportions that seem generic for Cuetzalan and the surrounding villages. His masks are nicely carved, well finished, and truly notable for the attention that he pays to the carving of the backs. There is a deep, smooth hollow to accommodate the nose, and all of the edges inside the mask are carefully smoothed and sanded. This treatment of the back surface of these masks is as good as a signature for this carver.

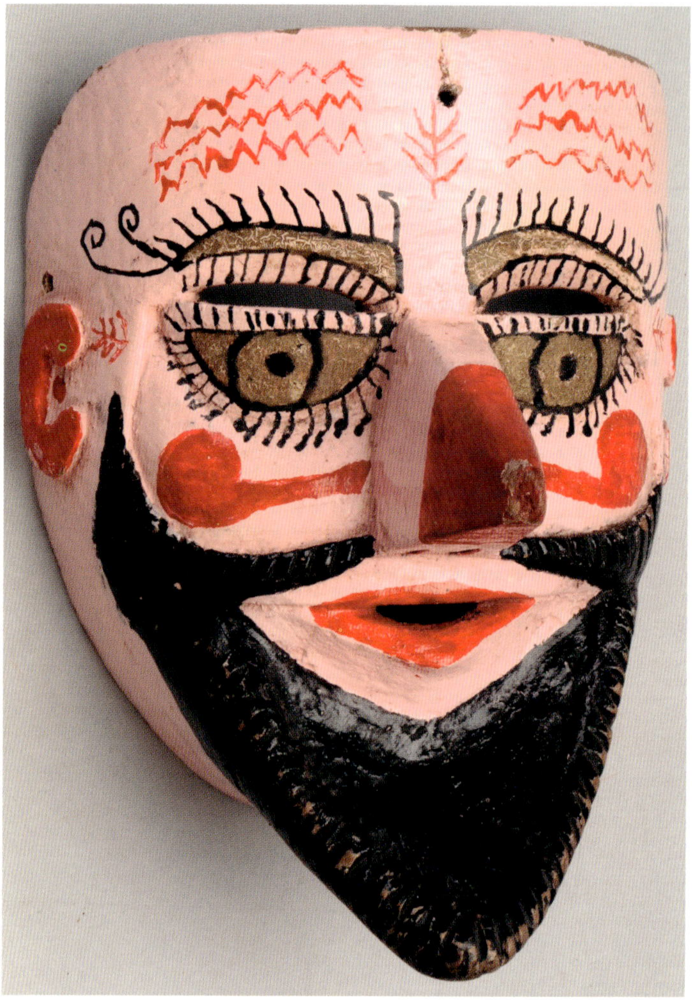

Right: This mask is identifiable as Ernesto's due to the usual C-shaped ears and a beard similar to the old Santiaguero below; 6¾" × 8½". Circa 1990. Rating: known carver, excellent condition, very well carved, good patina, and not rare, *****. *Collection of the author.*

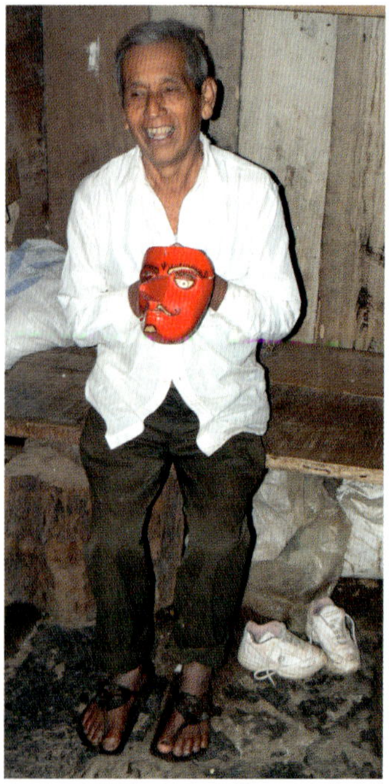

Ernesto Tóral Hilario holding his own Santiaguero mask; this mask is highly typical of his work. Note the design over the nose and the flat chin.

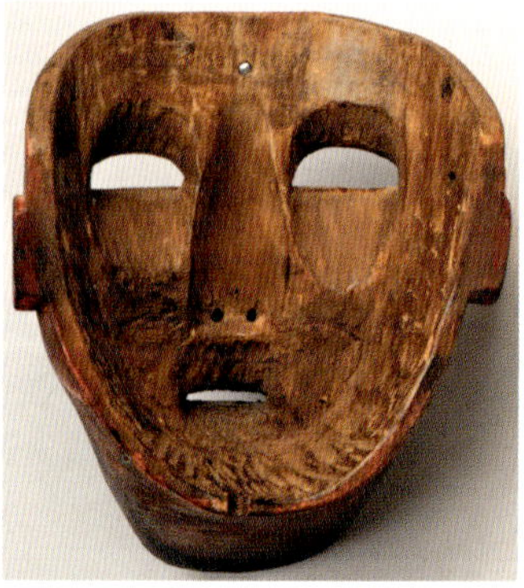

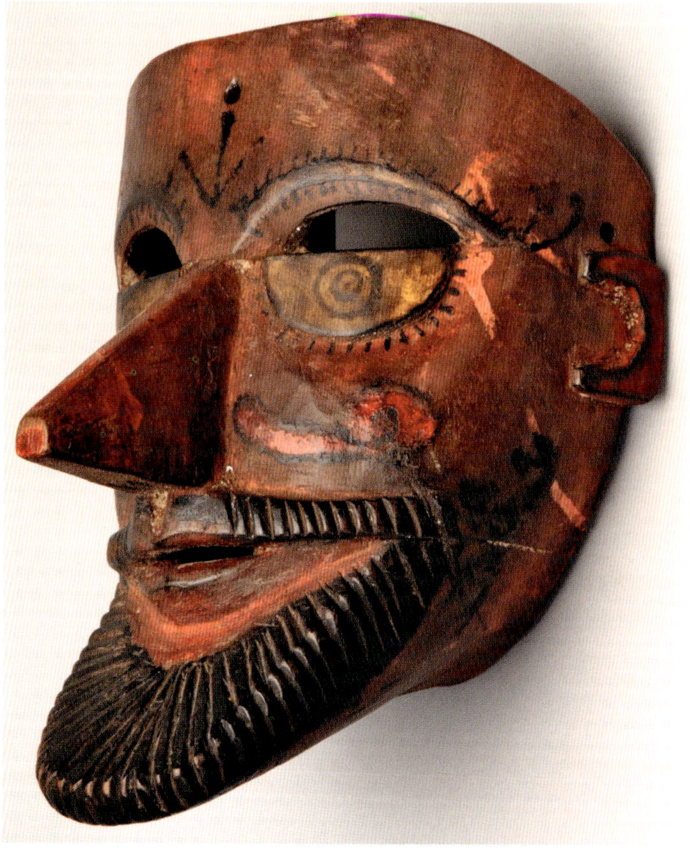

Right: An older Santiaguero mask, recognizable as Ernesto's due to the C-shaped ears, the mark over the nose, and the nicely carved back; 7" × 8½". Circa 1980. Rating: known carver, excellent condition, very well carved, excellent patina, and moderately rare in this condition, *****. *Collection of the author.*

Above: This view demonstrates the extreme care that this carver devotes to the contours and smoothness of the back.

Aurelio Vásquez

Aurelio Vásquez lived in the area near San Juan Ozelonacaxtla, Puebla. The little that we know about this carver was provided by Roberto Villegas Santiago. Roberto identified Aurelio as the maker of a very beautiful Huehue mask that Vernon had purchased nearby. Roberto estimated that Aurelio had died in about 1960. On the basis of this single mask alone, I would say that Aurelio was one of the great master carvers of the twentieth century for this region. I have identified a second mask that also seems to have been carved by Aurelio.

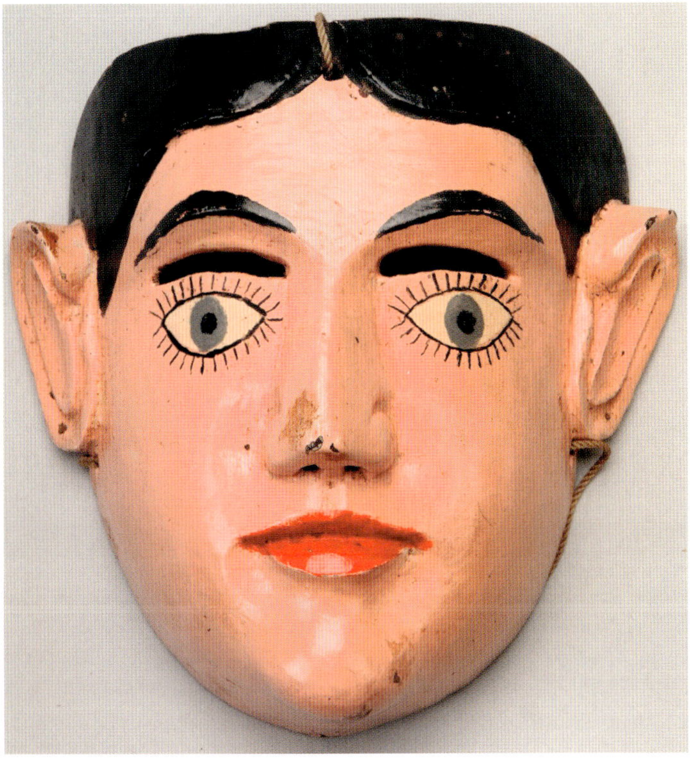

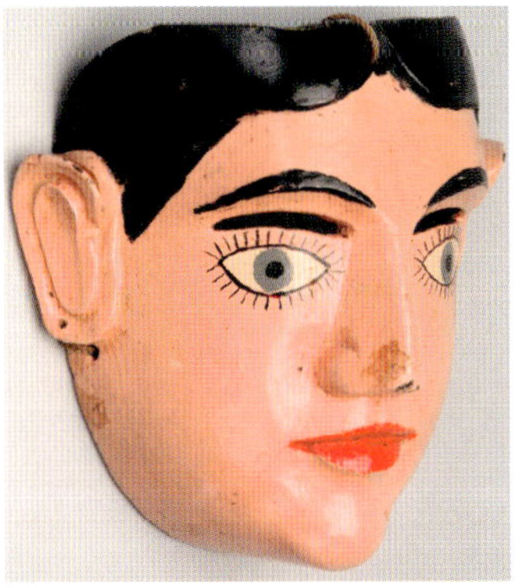

Above: This mask of a female Huehue by Aurelio Vásquez has a remarkably beautiful face; 7" × 7". It is very well carved and carefully painted. Rating: known carver, good condition, extremely well carved, excellent patina, and very rare, *******. *Collection of the author.*

Left, above: The ears are carved in a particularly delicate design, somewhat like those of Benito Juárez, his father, and his grandfather, but yet a little different. A striking quality about the ears is that they are rotated in an anterior direction, so they appear to be unusually prominent.

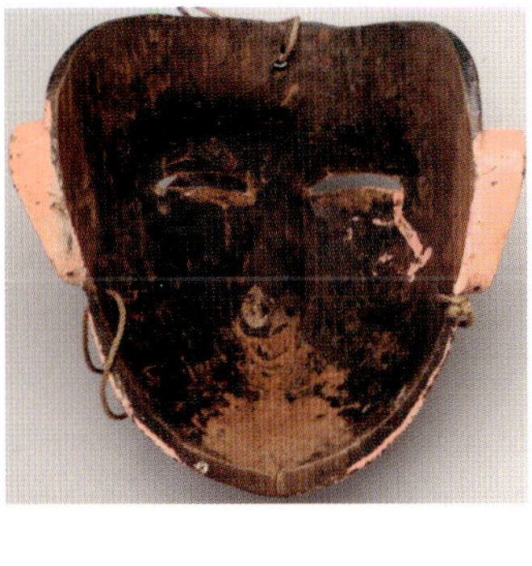

Left, below: The back of this mask appears to have great age.

Germán Vega Pérez

Germán Vega Pérez was born on January 30, 1926. He lives in Chumatlán, Veracruz. We are certain that he was a talented carver in the past, but it seems that he is no longer carving. Several years ago Vernon purchased a pair of really unusual masks from Germán that he had carved—a male mask of a Payaso and an accompanying female, "María Loca." I had obtained an attractive Perro mask with an articulated jaw from Vernon that was also carved by Germán. When we visited his house in March 2010, we also saw a very nicely carved Santiaguero mask and a charming child's hobbyhorse that Germán had carved from a crooked stick.

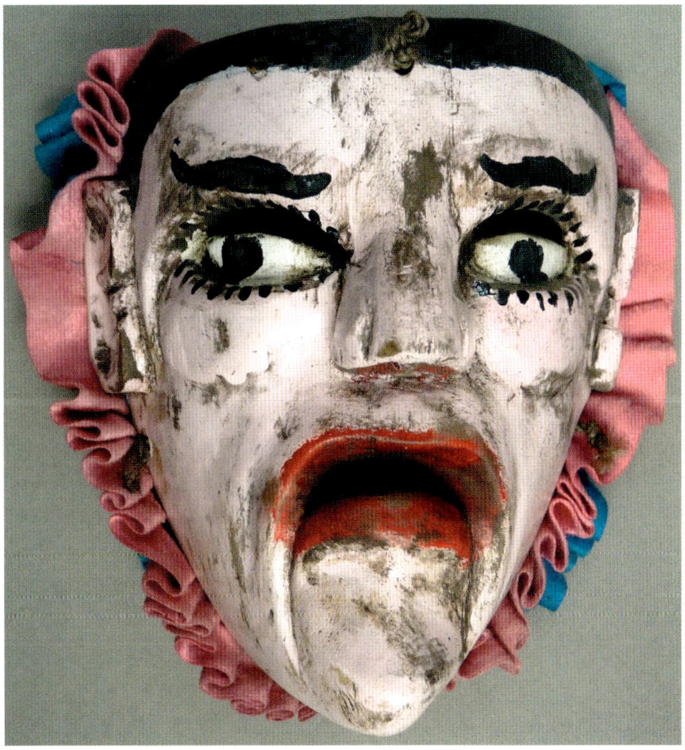

This mask by Germán Vega depicts a female Payaso from the Huehues dance; 7½" × 7". Circa 1980. The carver named her *María Loca,* which, in this context, probably means Wild Mary. This mask was purchased directly from the carver by Vernon Kostohryz. Rating: known carver, good condition, vividly carved, excellent patina, and rare, ******. *Collection of Vernon Kostohryz.*

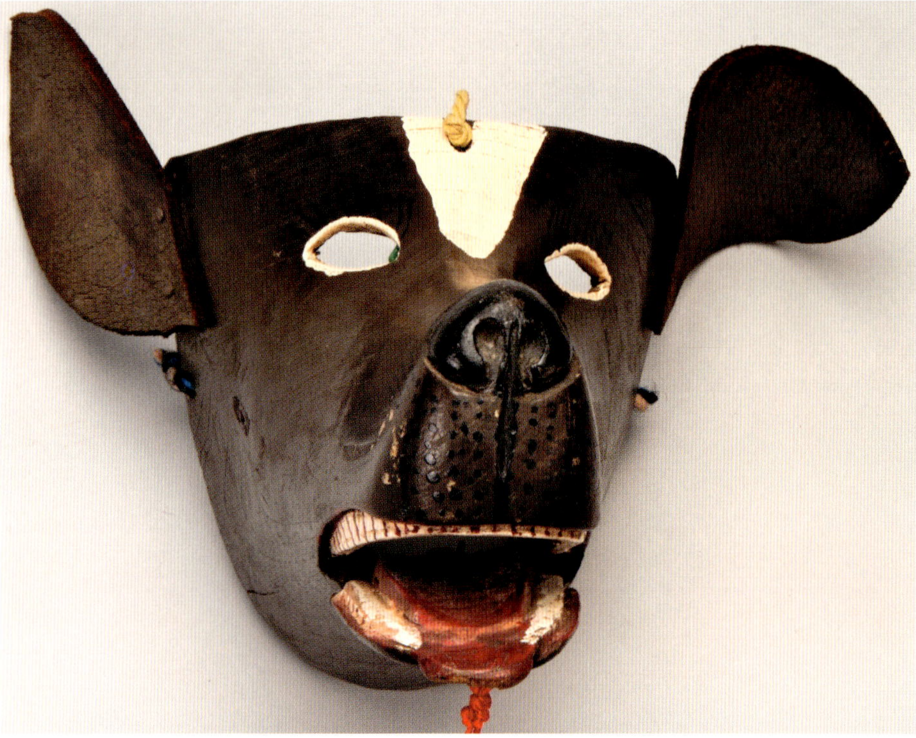

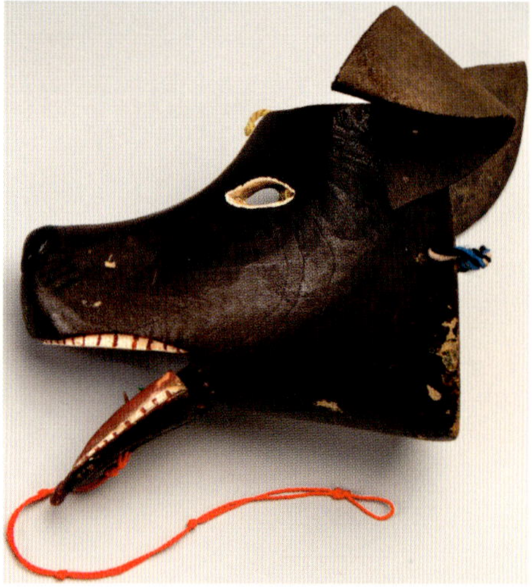

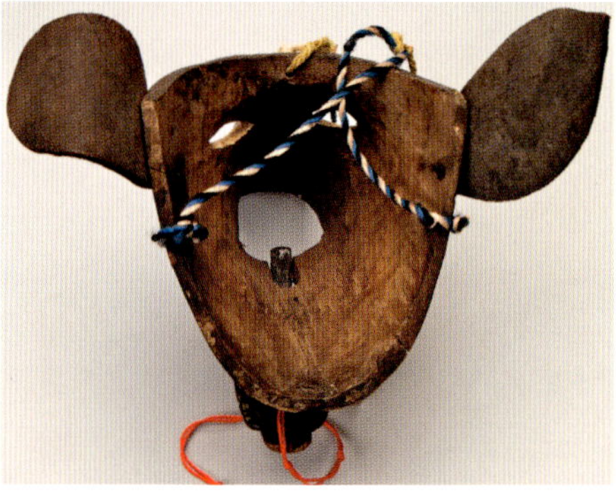

Above: Perro mask by Germán Vega for the Huehues dance; 6" × 6¼", 9" long. Circa 1980. The articulated jaw is original to the mask. Rating: known carver, excellent condition, very well carved, good patina, and rare, ******. *Collection of the author.*

Top right: The side view, showing the open jaw of the Perro.

Bottom right: The back of this mask reveals the unusually excellent view that results from the use of the open mouth for the vision slit; this is a common arrangement in masks of jaguars and dogs.

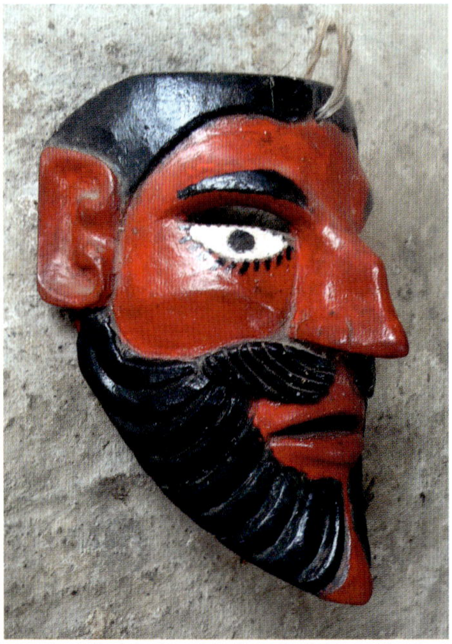

A very handsome Santiaguero mask by Germán. Rating: known carver, excellent condition, very well carved, good patina, and rare, ******. *Collection of the carver. Photos of Germán's carvings are included with the permission of Germán.*

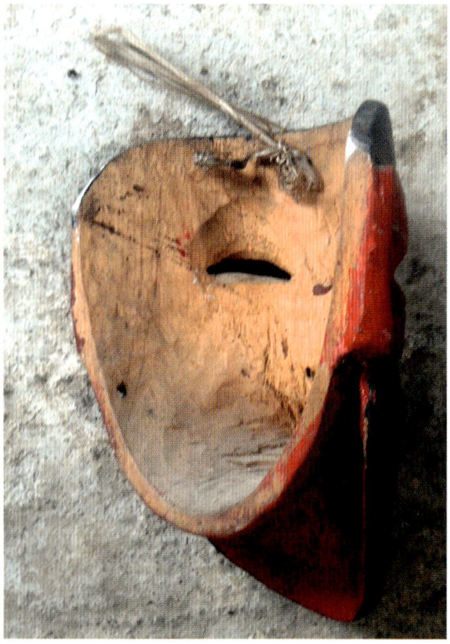

Note the separation of the back of the beard from the back proper, with the hollowing of the beard. The patina on the back is mild. As far as is known, this is the only mask photo in the book that includes a live insect.

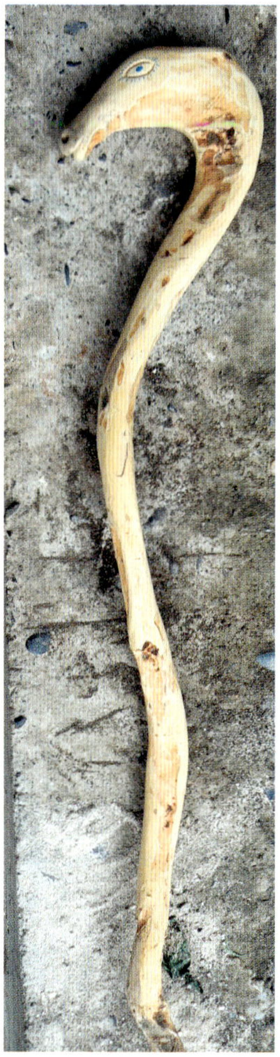

A hobbyhorse carved by Germán from a crooked branch, for a young girl living in his household. The face of the horse is very appealing. Unrated.

Mateo Vega

Mateo Vega is a carver who only recently came to our attention. His masks are of average or slightly above average quality. He seems to be using an ear design of an older and now deceased carver from Olintla, Puebla, Leopoldo "Polo" Cortez González. I have included a female Huehue Payaso by this carver.

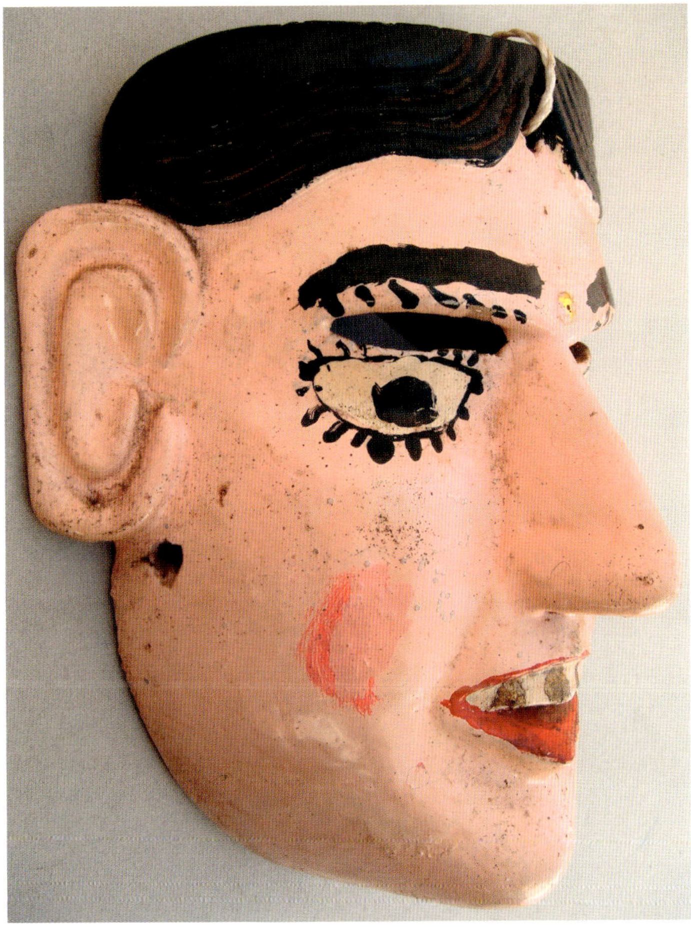

Above: The female Payaso mask referred to in Chapter 4 on the subject of female clowns; 7" × 7". Circa 2000. This character is recognizable by the treatment of the mouth, in this case open and with buckteeth. This mask is very nicely carved, with an attractive ear design, grooved hair, and careful definition of the area around the mouth. It has an unattractive face because this was the carver's intention. Rating: known carver, excellent condition, well carved, good patina, and not rare, ****. *Former collection of Vernon Kostohryz.*

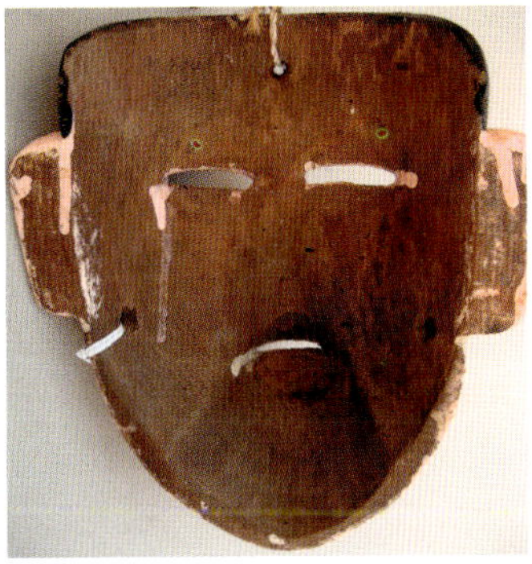

Right: The back of this female Payaso mask by Mateo Vega. The treatment of the back is similar to the style of Polo Cortez.

Roberto Villegas Santiago

Roberto Villegas Santiago was born on May 14, 1930. He has long lived in San Juan Ozelonacaxtla, Puebla, a small Totonac village that is not very far away from Huehuetla, Puebla, by mountain trails, but quite a few miles by paved roads. He has worked as a farmer, a mascarero, and a carpenter.

Roberto is one of the finest living mask makers in the region of study, for the following reasons: He has developed elegant design elements for the masks that he carves, he carves these elements with great precision, and yet he creates a great variety of characters. He also paints each mask with care. The result of all this is that his masks are very beautiful and interesting. They certainly appear to be popular among dancers in his area. He also carves saints and puppets with equal skill and taste.

I was fascinated in my initial visit to Roberto's house to see that he had a wooden workbench that he had apparently built for himself. It was lower than what we would expect in the United States, but well matched to Roberto's stature. He also had a combination table saw/tenoning machine, hand built entirely of wood except for the electric motor, arbor, and saw blade. It seemed so ingenious and appropriate.

In Chapter 5, I introduced you to my discovery that Roberto was using an old Hormega mask that was carved by Benito Juárez as a model to carve a set of Santiaguero masks. His approach to those masks taught me something about his style that I had not previously understood. It is quite common for a mask maker in this region to use a mask by another carver as the model for a new mask. But what was so different in Roberto's case was that he was using Benito's mask to provide the shape and form for the new masks, yet providing these masks with his traditional, highly sculptural ear design and converting some of the painted design elements by Benito into relief-carved detailing. I hadn't anticipated that he would be so ambitious in his approach, but of course it is this intensity of artistry and detail that causes his masks to be so impressive.

When I saw Roberto in December of 2007 I was concerned for him, because it seemed that he was losing his vision, and consequently he had stopped carving. I was so pleased to see, during my most recent visit in March of 2010, that he had obtained eyeglasses and, with the enhanced vision that resulted, was carving very well. In fact, he was busy completing a set of about eight Santiaguero masks that someone had ordered.

I was so impressed with Roberto's continuing artistry that I asked whether I could buy one of these newly carved Santiaguero masks. Roberto explained that he was filling an order for a local dance group, and he was unwilling to sell one of them as this would delay their delivery. I was able to order one, which subsequently arrived several months later. With that mask Roberto included a sun shield for the Santiagueros dance, also newly completed.

Until I saw Roberto carving that set of Santiaguero masks in March 2010, I would have said that he carved only masks and puppets for the Danza de los Huehues. It was his Huehue carvings that initially convinced me that Roberto was a master carver. To briefly review, the Huehue dance includes dancers wearing male and female human-faced masks, and there is also a Viejo figure, Payasos, and one or two dancers wear Perro (dog) masks. All these characters perform around the Telón, a decorated curtain that surrounds a tall pole. A male and a female puppet perform from behind the curtain, clapping their hands. A wooden Chénchere (woodpecker) climbs the pole while mechanically pecking. In the illustrations that follow we will see masks and puppets for all of these characters or roles.

Roberto's male and female puppets for the Huehues (or Green Woodpecker) dance are very finely carved, and they are among the most beautiful puppets that I have ever seen from this region. His woodpecker puppets are also very nice, although they don't stand out in the way that his human puppets do, as it seems that many carvers take great pains when they carve these Chénchere figures. These will be discussed in detail in Chapter 7.

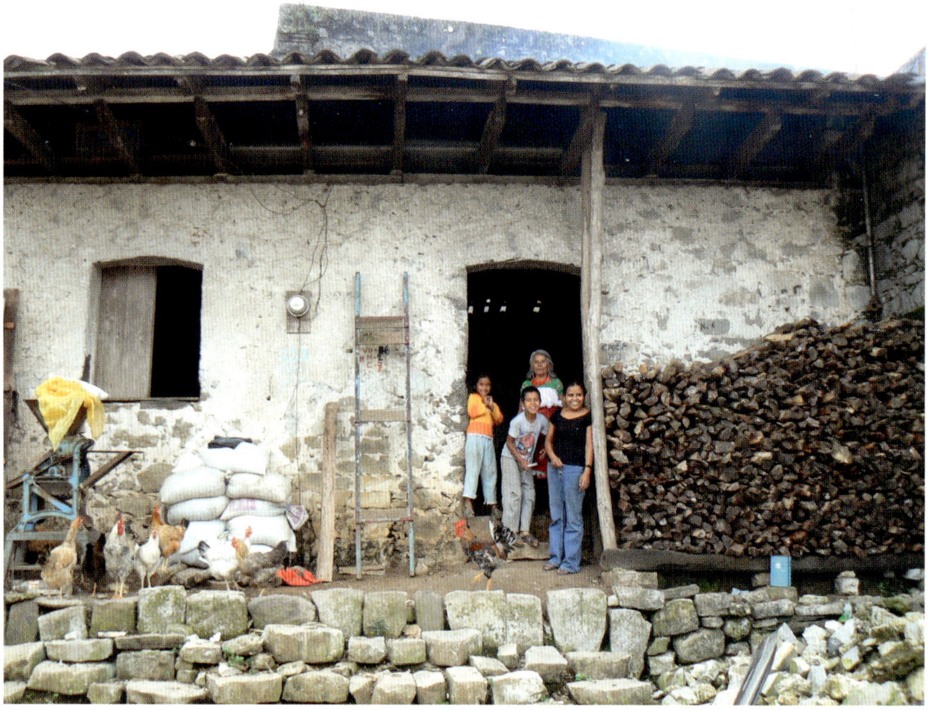

Right: The wife of Roberto Villegas Santiago stands in the doorway of their house in December 2007, with several grandchildren. *Photos of Roberto, his family members, his workshop, and masks are all included with permission of Roberto Villegas Santiago.*

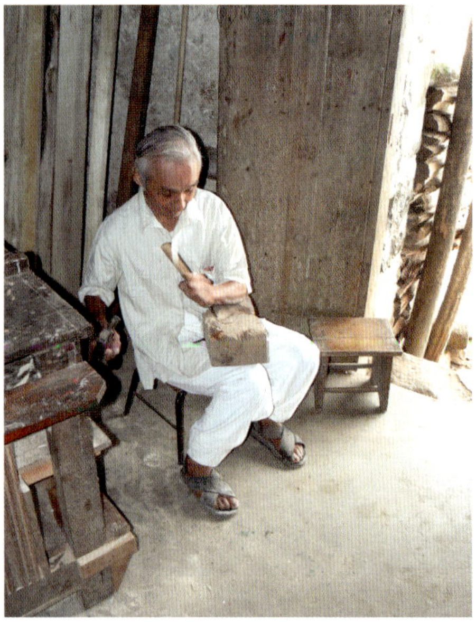

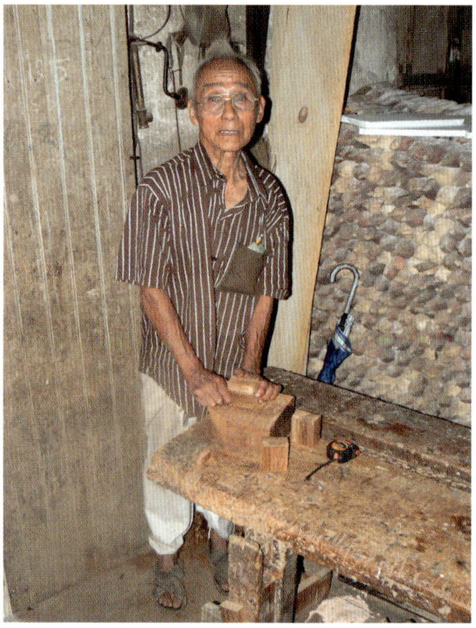

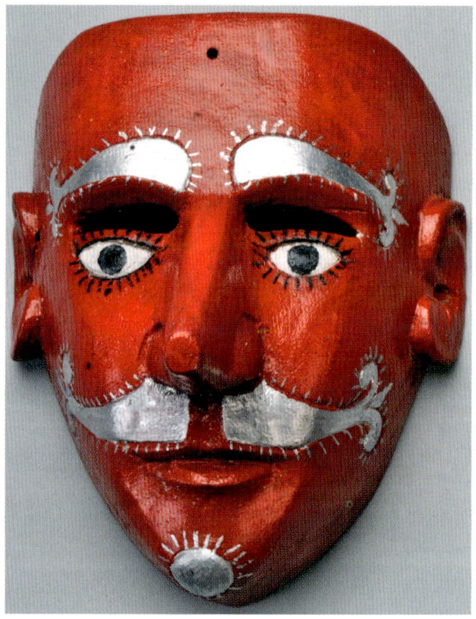

Above: Roberto at his workbench in March 2010. He is gluing a block for the nose onto a Santiaguero mask that he is roughing out. Note his recently acquired eyeglasses.

A Santiaguero mask that Roberto carved to order in 2010; 6½" × 7¾". The brows, mustache, and goatee have been carved in very low relief, while the ears demonstrate Roberto's usual bold and beautiful design. Rating: known carver, excellent condition, well carved, undanced, and not rare in this state; one that was old and worn would be very rare, ***. *Collection of the author.*

Top left: Roberto Villegas Santiago poses in his workshop in December 2007. Note the typical stool to Roberto's left; two boards form a shallow valley. His workbench is to the viewer's left.

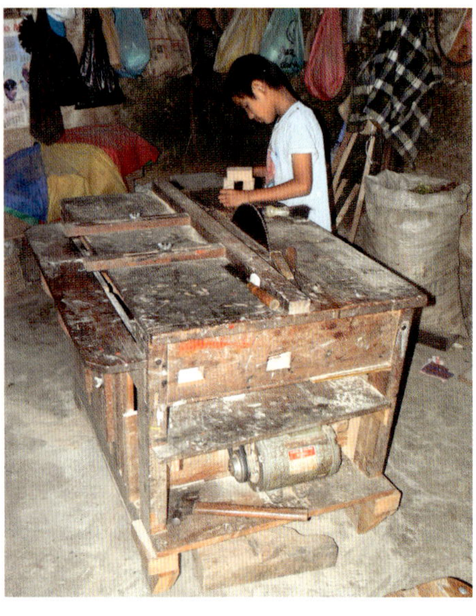

Left: Roberto's table saw. The saw blade height is not adjustable and there is no guard to cover the blade. Note the adjustable fence. The tenoning drill extends from the left side under the shelf, but it is not visible in this photo.

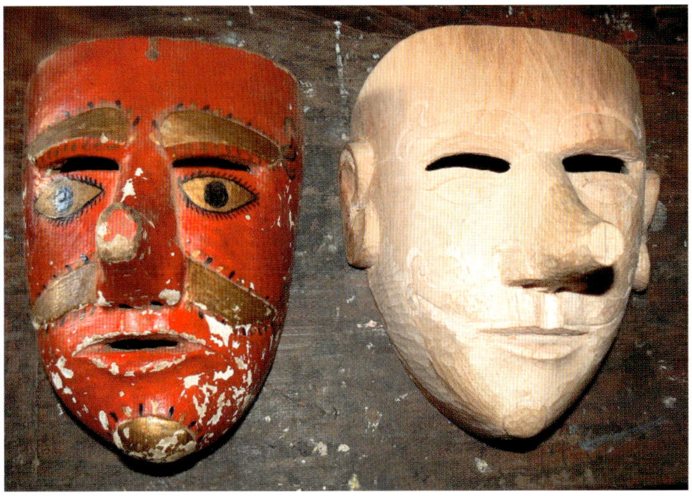

An old Hormega mask carved by Benito Juárez Figueroa provides the model for a newly carved Santiaguero mask in Roberto's workshop. Note that the older mask lacks ears, but Roberto has provided his mask with ears that conform to his usual design. He has copied Benito's relief-carved brows, mustache, and goatee; however, he has substituted relief-carved curling tips for the painted swirls at the ends of the brows and mustache on Benito's mask.

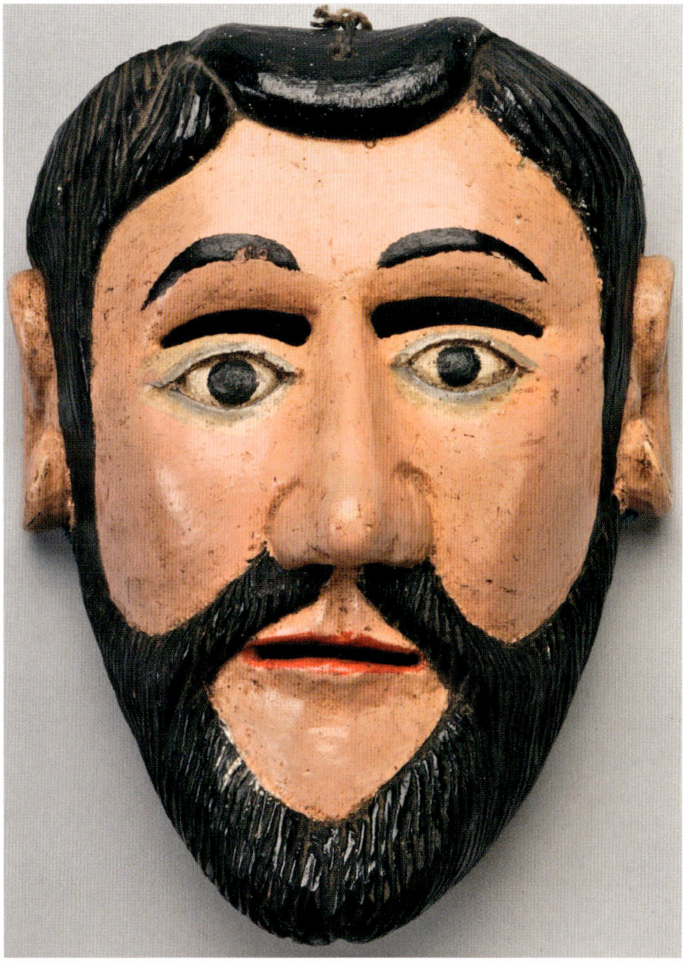

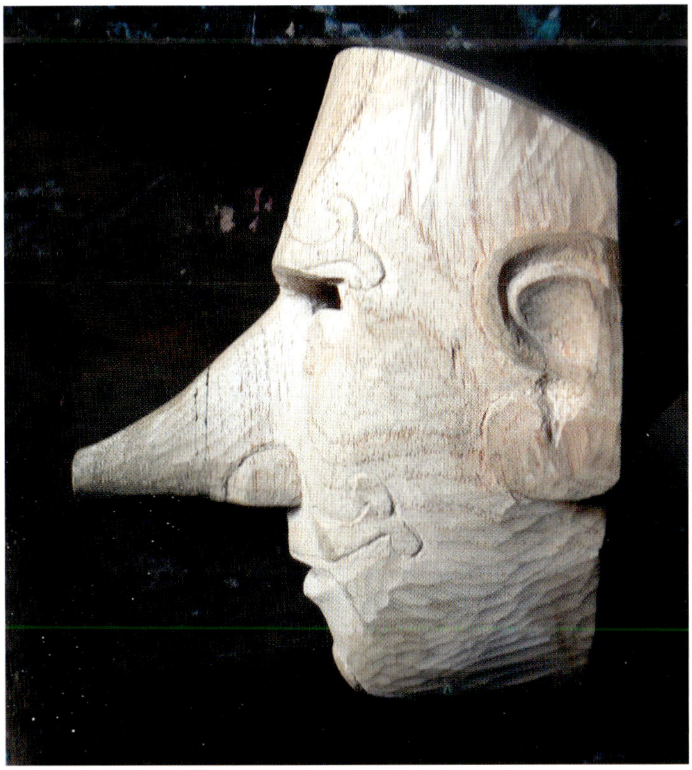

A side view of the same new mask, just being carved. The fine lines of Roberto's typical carved ear are just emerging in this photo.

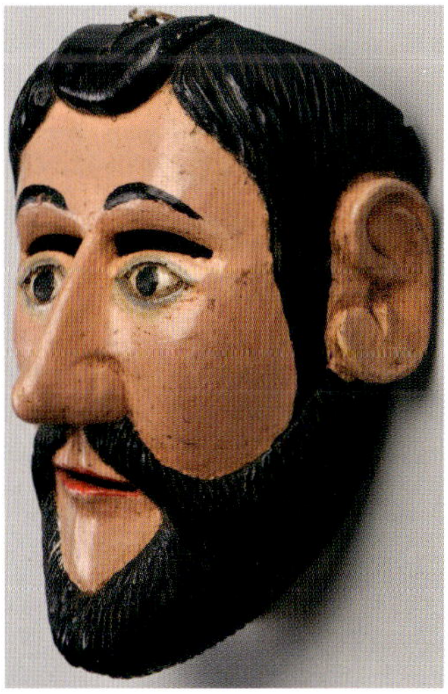

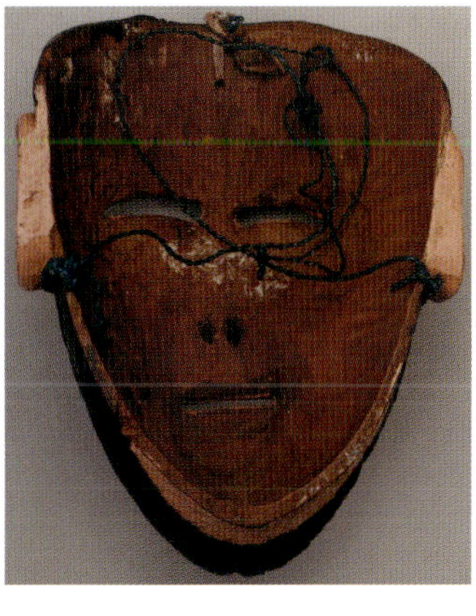

Above: An extremely fine mask carved by Roberto Villegas Santiago to be worn by a male Huehue dancer; 6¼" × 7¾". Circa 1975. On the one hand, this mask demonstrates Roberto carving at his best. All the elements of the mask are beautiful. On the other hand, one may observe that the two carefully carved eyes are not on the same level, nor are the ears. This tendency to asymmetry is not uncommon on Roberto's masks, which is a bit of a paradox. Rating: known carver, excellent condition, very well carved, excellent patina, and now becoming rare, ******+. *Collection of the author.*

Center left: The side view of this mask, which provides a better view of the carving of one ear as well as the fine carving of the nose. The management of the carving of the hair is, of course, sensational.

Lower left: The view of the back of this mask, where fine chisel marks remain. There is good patina. This view makes it particularly clear that Roberto carves the ears from the same block of wood as the rest of the face; that is, the ears are not added on.

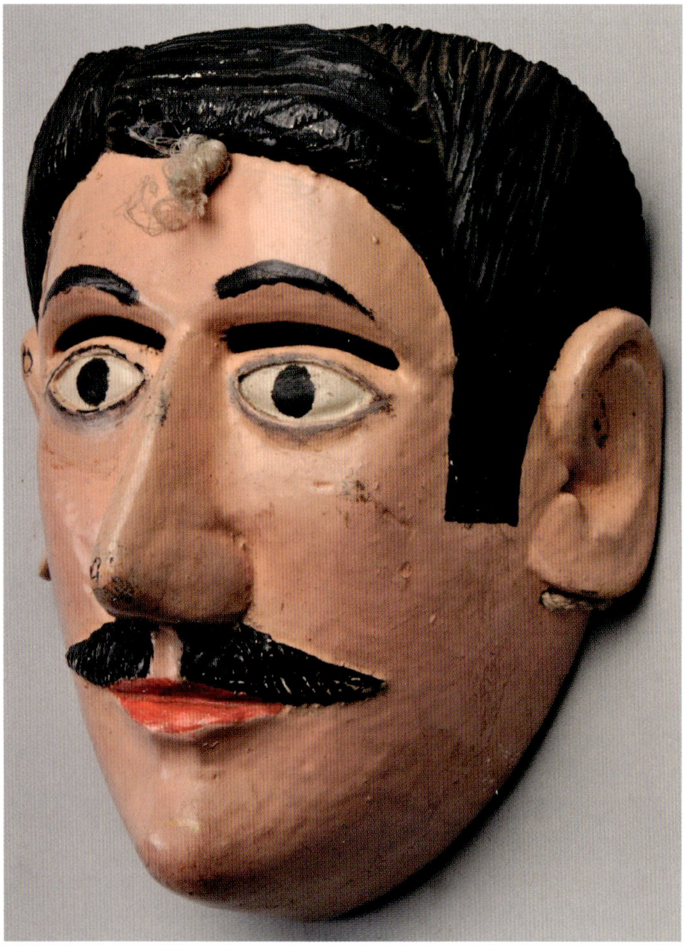

A similar Huehue mask by Roberto, with relief-carved mustache but without the extended sideburns and beard; 6½" × 7¾". Circa 1975. The eyes are appropriately aligned. Roberto always carves the eyes in relief, in contrast to many other carvers who only paint in the eyes with minimal or no carving. The presence of these characteristic eyes and ears will invariably identify a mask as Roberto's work. Rating: known carver, excellent condition, very well carved, excellent patina, and rare, ******. *Collection of the author.*

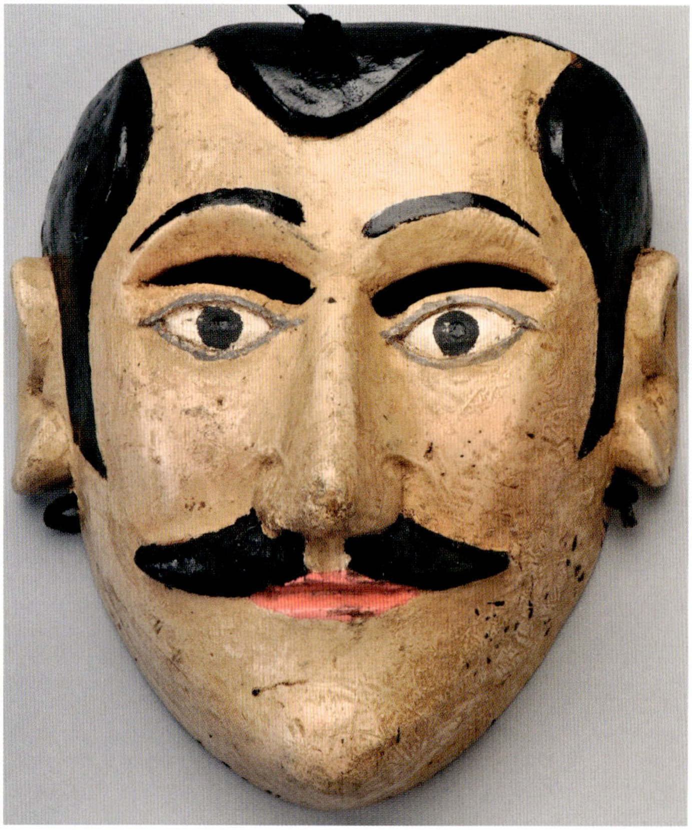

Another very similar mask, but the hairline is indicative of a gentleman with early balding and the hair is not detailed with grooved carving, nor is the mustache so decorated; 6½" × 7½". Circa 1975. The eyes and ears retain their usual designs, on the other hand. The overall effect of this mask is very strong, as usual for masks by this carver. Rating: known carver, excellent condition, well carved, excellent patina, and rare, ******. *Collection of the author.*

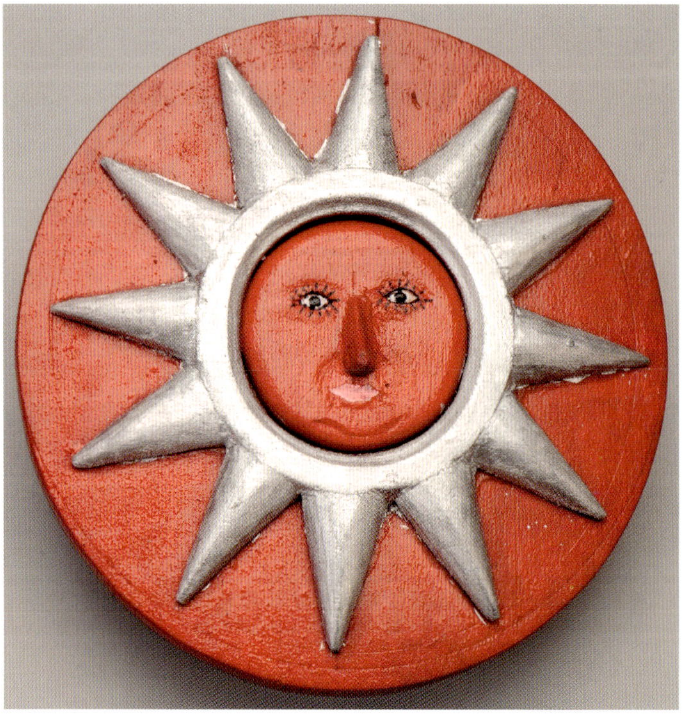

A wooden Sun Shield for the Santiagueros dance, newly carved by Roberto in 2010; 8½" in diameter. This would be carried by Captain Sabario, the leader of the Santiaguero subgroup. Rating: known carver, excellent condition, well carved, undanced, and not rare in this condition, although danced shields are very rare, ***. *Collection of the author.*

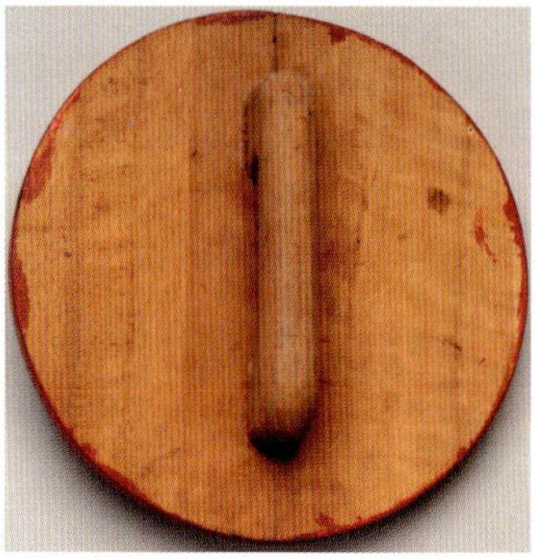

The back of the Sun Shield. Note the vertical seam, partly hidden by the handle, where Roberto has glued two boards together to obtain sufficient width. He would have squared these boards on his table saw.

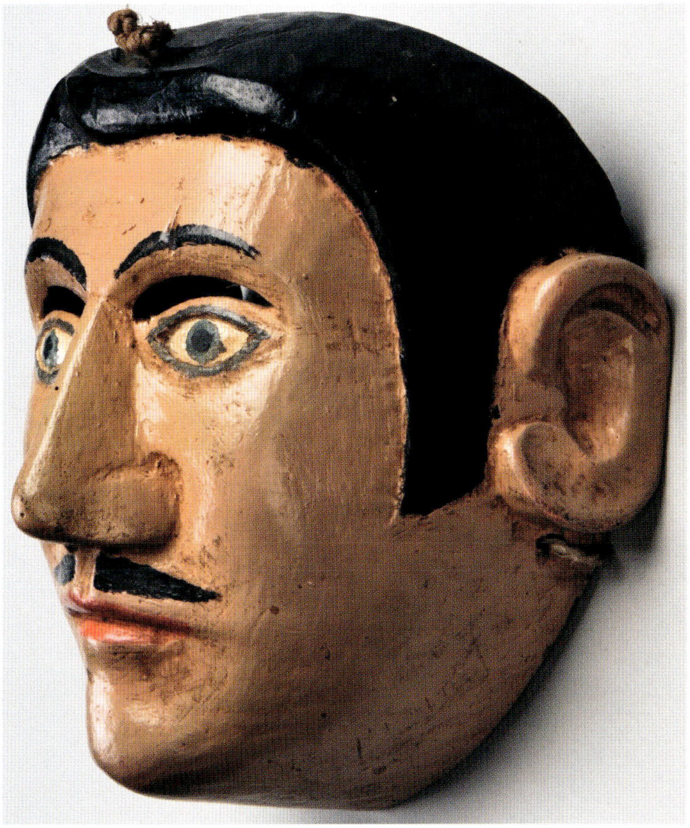

In yet another variation, this mask of a male Huehue was apparently carved without a mustache; later one was painted on. In contrast to the flat surface of the mask under the painted mustache, one sees that the sideburns are carefully carved by Roberto in low relief; 6¼" × 7½". Circa 1975. This is another mask where the eyes are not exactly on the same level. One begins to notice that Roberto has gone to great lengths to achieve variety in his Huehue masks. Rating: known carver, excellent condition, well carved, excellent patina, and rare, ******. *Collection of the author.*

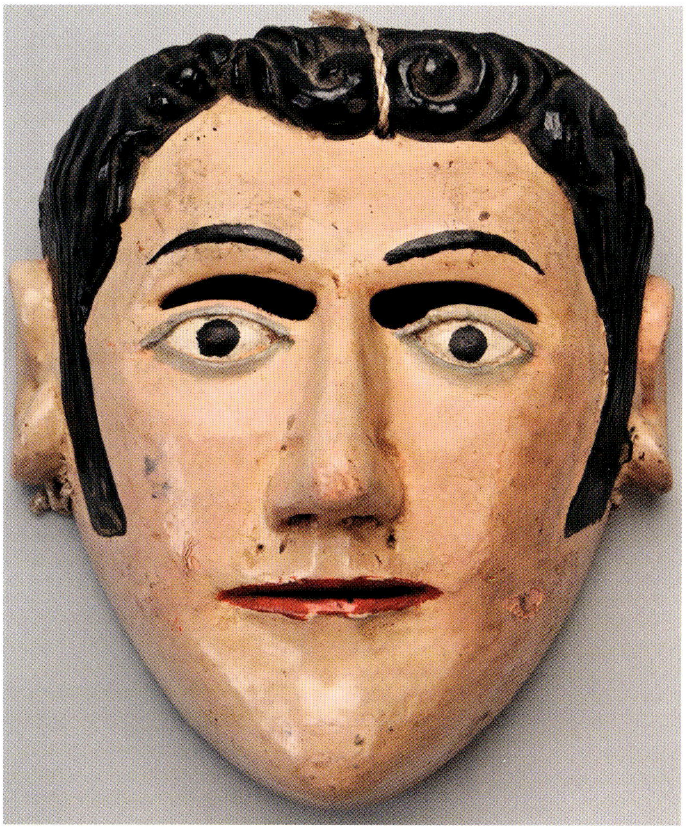

A very handsome male Huehue mask. Though lacking any mustache, his gender is clearly indicated by relief-carved sideburns that extend from his finely carved hair; 6¼" × 7½". Circa 1975. It is interesting to see such masks as this one and the last; male Huehue or Tejonero masks without mustaches are unusual. Rating: known carver, excellent condition, very well carved, excellent patina, and rare, ******. *Collection of the author.*

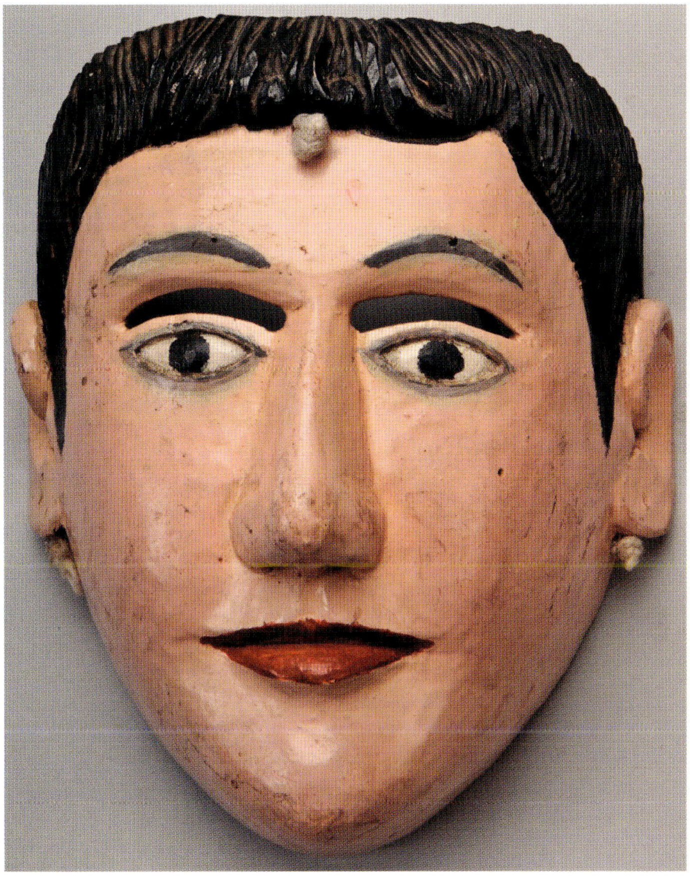

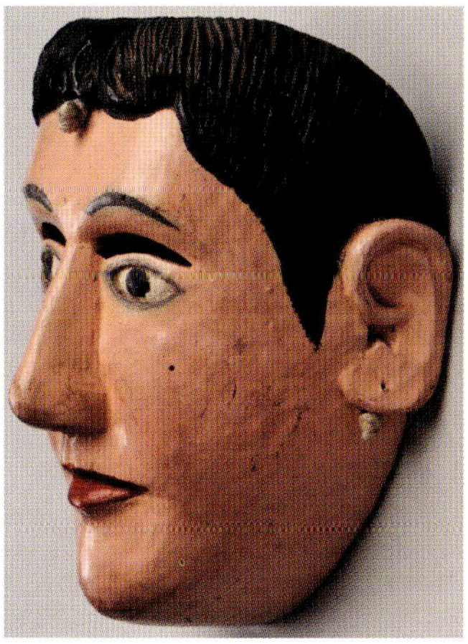

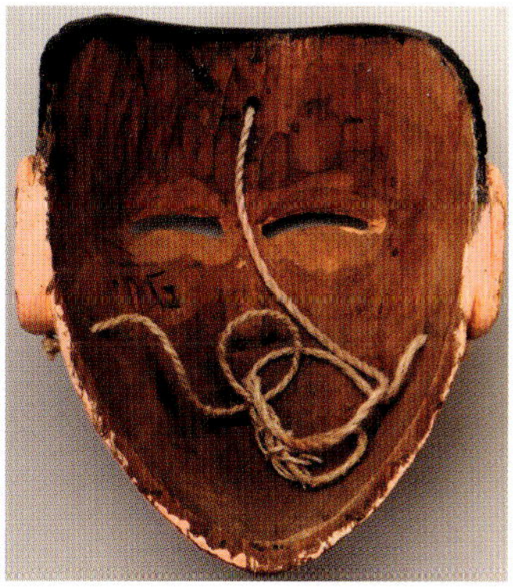

Left: A superlative female Huehue mask, which could easily be paired with one of the male Huehue masks above in terms of the quality and style of the carving; 6½" × 8". Circa 1975. Rating: known carver, excellent condition, very well carved, excellent patina, and rare, ******+. *Collection of the author.*

Above left: Side view of the same female Huehue mask by Roberto. Again one sees his typical ear design. Notice how Roberto has defined a distinctive shape for the hair on this mask but then someone has extended the hair with paint, past the carved area. Also we can notice that many masks of females have their ears pierced for earrings, as in this case.

Above right: The back of this female Huehue mask, with the chisel marks Roberto left showing when he delivered the mask. The darkening of the wood demonstrates the way that sweat and skin oils gradually mark the back of a danced mask to show its history of use, which is often interpreted to demonstrate the mask's age.

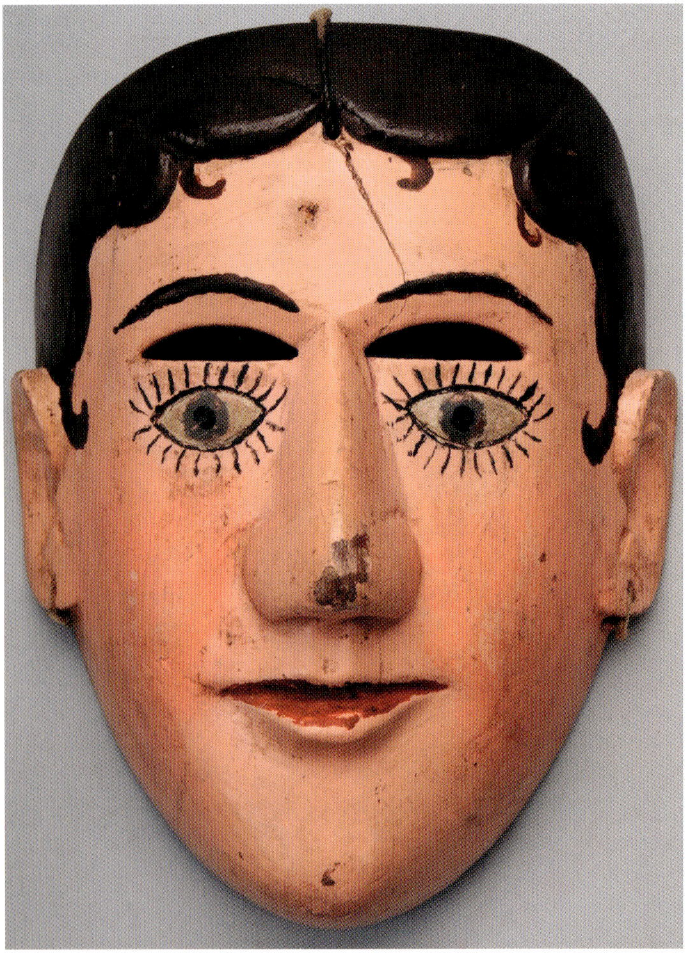

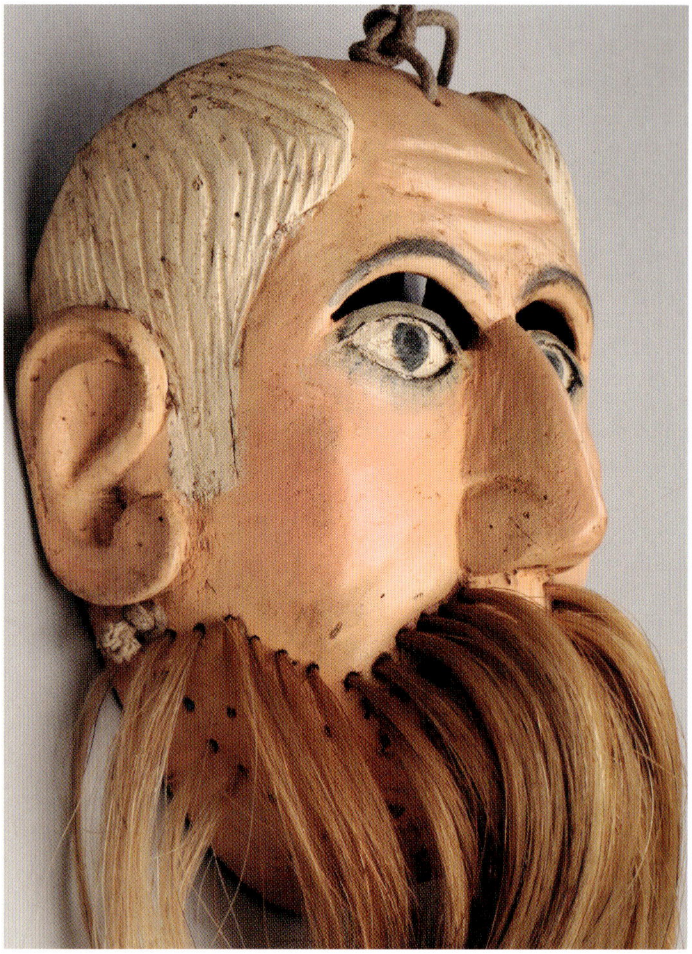

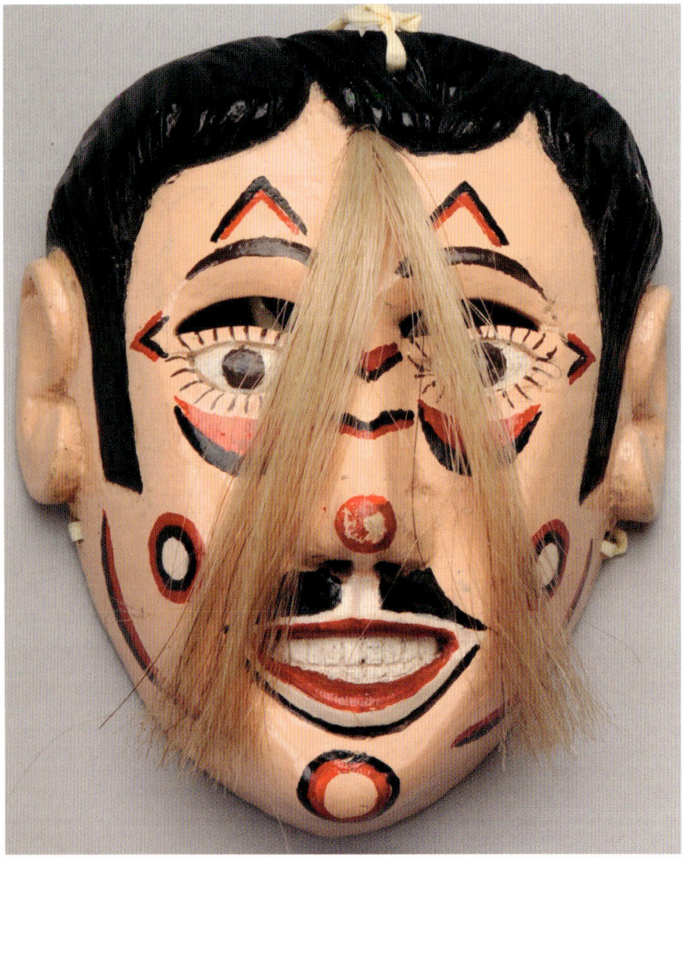

Above left: Just as we saw variations in the detailing on the male Huehue masks of this carver, here we see the same thing for one of the female masks. Also someone has repainted the mask in a rather different style from that used by Roberto; 6" × 7¾". Circa 1975. This mask does illustrate the appearance of typical wear; the paint is scuffed on prominent points that would be most vulnerable, such as the end of the nose and the chin. Rating: known carver, excellent condition, well carved, excellent patina, and rare, ******. *Collection of the author.*

Above right: When I showed a photo of this Viejo mask to Roberto, in March of 2010, I expected him to identify it as the mask of Pilatos in the Danza de los Voladores; instead he told me that this was the Viejo in the Huehues dance. So I learned that those two characters wear virtually the same mask. Of course there was no ambiguity about the identity of the carver of this mask, looking at the design of the carved ears, the carved eyes, and the carefully grooved hair. The beard is made from cow-tail; 6½" × 8", 20" with beard. Circa 1975. Rating: known carver, excellent condition, well carved, excellent patina, and very rare, ******. *Collection of the author.*

Left: A mask of a clown for the dance of the Huehues, carved by Roberto; 6½" × 7½". A Payaso mask has an open mouth with the teeth showing, a tuft of horsehair emerging from a hole in the forehead, and characteristic face paint. Note the finely carved hair on this mask. These painted decorations are typical for Roberto's Payaso masks; other carvers use their own combination of painted elements. Rating: known carver, excellent condition, well carved, excellent patina, and rare, ******. *Collection of the author.*

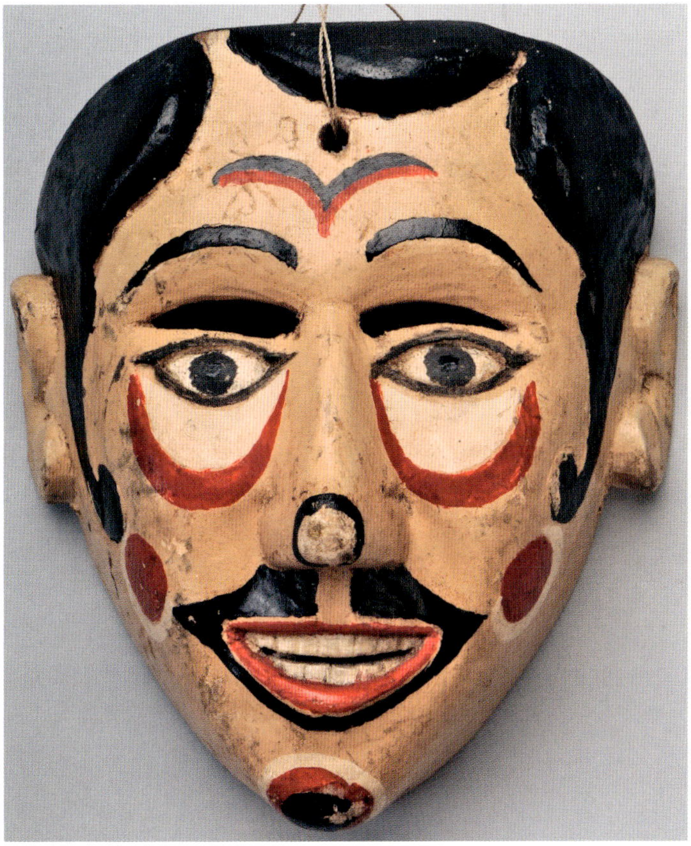

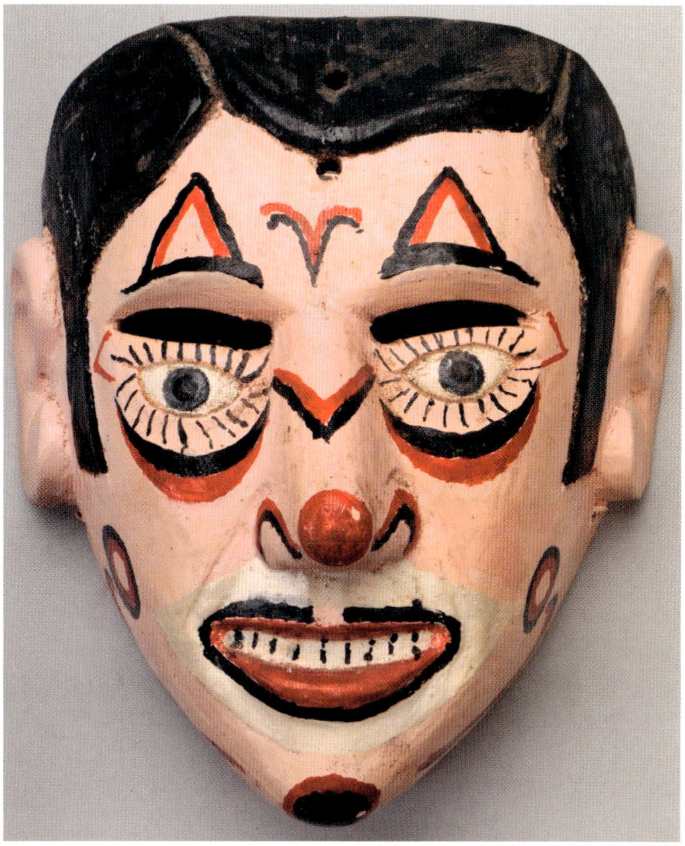

Above: A second example of a Payaso mask by Roberto Villegas Santiago; 6½" × 7½". One sees the same variations in the treatment of the hair that we observed in the male and female Huehue masks above. The sideburns on this mask are carved in mild relief, right down to the rounded ends, but the hair is not grooved. This mask has lost its hair tuft. In this case the teeth are slightly separated; they were together in the previous Payaso mask. Rating: known carver, excellent condition, well carved, excellent patina, and rare, ******. *Collection of the author.*

Above right: A Payaso mask proportioned for a child; 6" × 6½". This was carved by Roberto Villegas in 2010 and is undanced. I was pleased to see that Roberto could still carve so well, even though this mask is not quite as carefully painted as his earlier examples. This is the only child's mask that I have ever seen by this carver. Rating: known carver, excellent condition, well carved, undanced, and possibly rare in the child's form, ***+. *Collection of the author.*

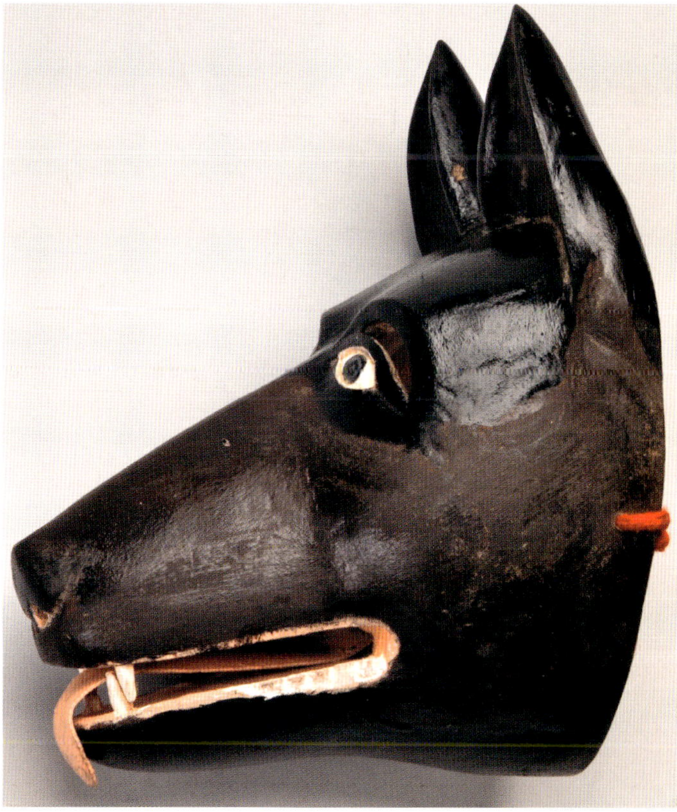

Above: A Perro mask for the Huehues dance that was carved by Roberto; 7" × 11". He had carved this mask about 5 or 10 years ago and then it hung in his shop, unpainted and undanced, before he painted it. The tongue is leather. This is a very handsome mask with finely carved teeth and dramatic upright ears. Rating: known carver, excellent condition, well carved, undanced, and not rare in this condition, ***. *Collection of the author.*

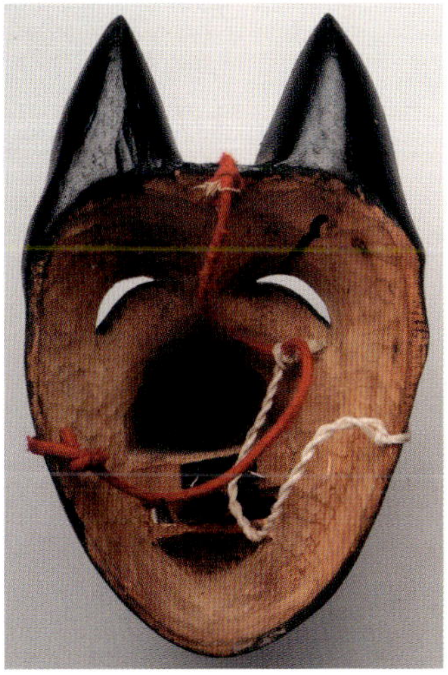

Left: The wearer's view of the Perro mask.

Artemio Zaragoza Zaragoza

Artemio Zaragoza Zaragoza was born on June 6, 1943. He lives in Xochiapulco, Puebla. Artemio is definitely an entrepreneur. He operates a trout fishery beside his home, and cooks these fish to serve patrons in his restaurant. We would never pass up an opportunity to have lunch there, based on repeated positive visits.

Artemio appears to approach mask making with similar resourcefulness and energy. He may be the most prolific carver that we have encountered in this region, and we have often seen his masks in distant towns, either new ones for sale or others being danced. These masks are traditional in design, well carved, and inexpensive, which explains why they are so popular. Therefore I think of Artemio as a mask maker who serves a wide region and not just his local community.

Artemio is one of very few carvers we have visited who regularly uses power tools to finish his masks. He carves in the traditional manner with chisels, but then he smoothes the masks in front and behind with a handmade power sander, sometimes leaving telltale circular marks.

Several years ago we became aware that Artemio possessed an extremely worn copy of a famous book about Mexican masks—*Máscaras: La Otra Cara de México/Masks: the Other Face of Mexico*, by Victor José Moya Rubio (1986). Recently Artemio sold a group of heavily worn masks that he subsequently told us he had carved in the 1980s. I asked Artemio about the possibility that his masks were copies of some he had seen in the Moya Rubio book and Artemio acknowledged this as the source. As a test of the theory, I examined Artemio's copy and found that a number of pages were marked with pieces of string; on those pages there were pencil notations next to a number of the mask photos. One could sometimes match up a mask carved by Artemio with one that was marked in the book. For example, two of these masks carved by Artemio closely resembled the mask for the Dance of the Fish in Plate 139 (Moya Rubio, 115, 130–131), and another looked like the mask of Christ in plate 201 (160); Artemio had marked both of these photos.

Then Artemio showed us the masks that he was currently carving in his workshop. These closely resembled plate 132, a photo in the book of a mask for the Dance of the Marquis (Moya Rubio 1986, 112); this plate was not marked. This mask has the baroque beard design that I associate with masks in Donald Cordry's book that have been questioned (Lechuga 1988, 218–243) as possibly decorative, such as illustration 16 (Cordry 1980, 13), illustration 21 (19), illustration 32 (27), and illustration 188 (138–139).

I am including all this information in order to make the following point: We have learned in recent years to think of certain mask designs as inherently false or decorative, but here we see that a carver has unknowingly adapted such apparently false designs for use as danced masks, in effect recycling these designs into new traditions. Something like this was actually predicted by Lori Jacobsen and Donald E. Fritz, writing in the book that initially blew the whistle on the decorative masks for English speakers: *Changing Faces: Mexican Masks in Transition*. There Jacobson and Fritz write (1985, 11–12), "The picture can become even murkier if some of the newly created masks are used in actual dances. But even disregarding that possibility (believed by some researchers to have happened already), the existence of the new masks is an irritation to anyone attempting to understand established mask use in Mexico." Ironically, the *Changing Faces* book was published in 1985 and Artemio might have obtained his copy of Moya Rubio's book (1986) as early as the following year!

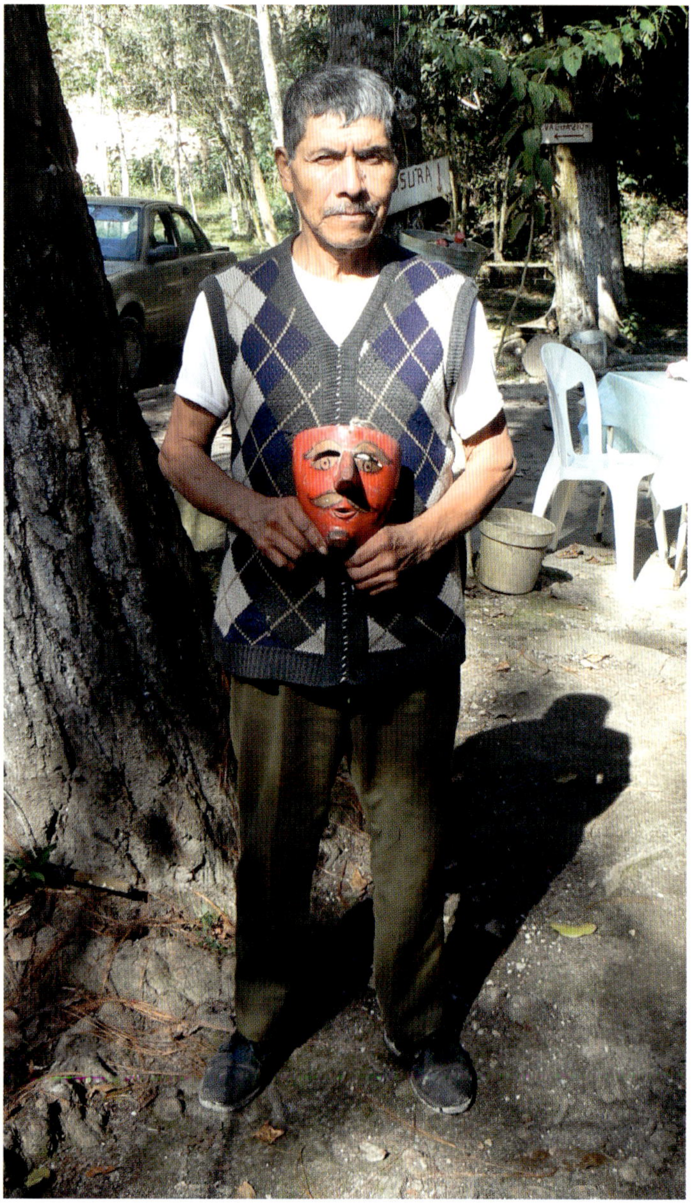

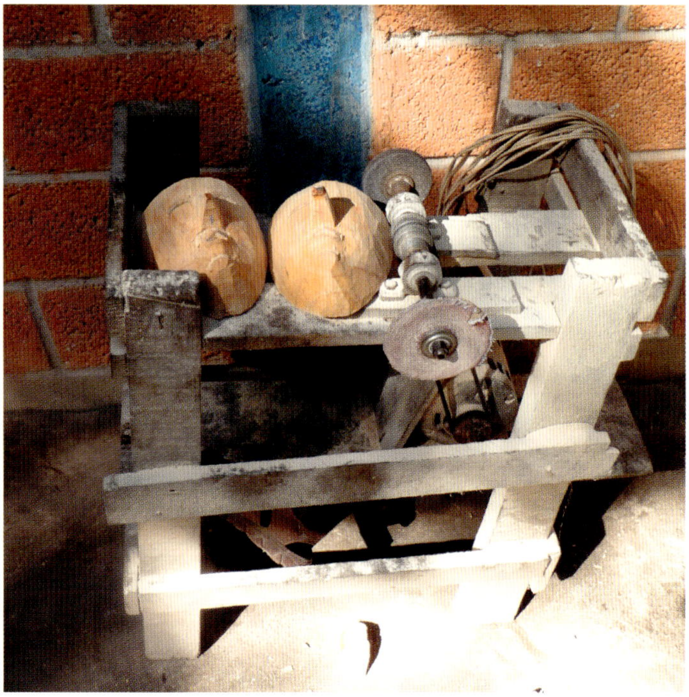

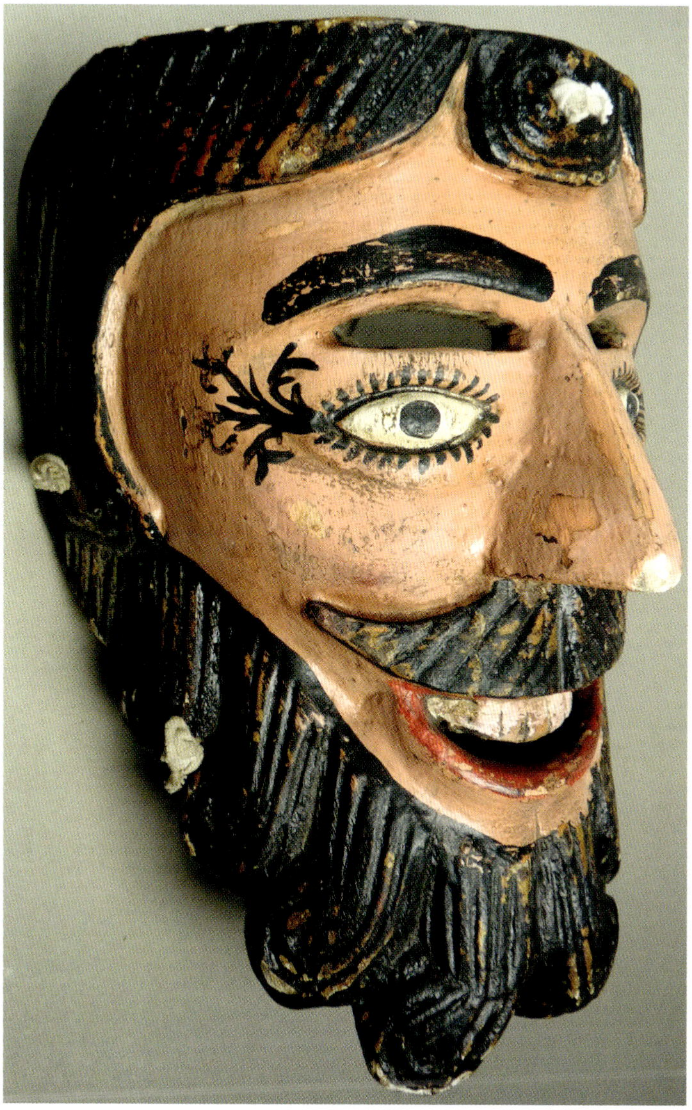

This Pescado mask is one that Artemio had carved in the 1980s, from models in Moya Rubio's book; 8" × 10". The vine-like paint next to the eyes is typical of decorative additions that have been acknowledged by Ernesto Bernabé Sánchez on other masks. I have no knowledge of the context or purpose of these additions. I suppose that he buys masks, "enhances" them in some fashion, and resells them, but this is simply conjectural. Rating: known carver, good condition, well carved, good patina, and rarity unknown, ****. *Former collection of Vernon Kostohryz.*

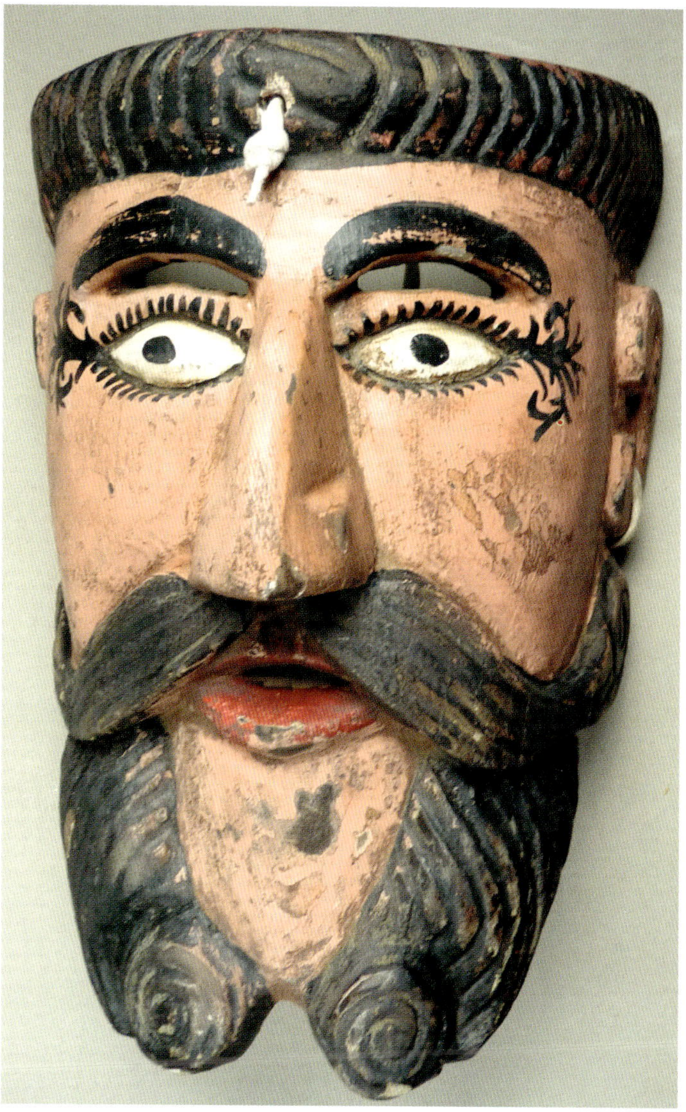

This mask appears to be a close copy of the mask in plate 201 (Moya Rubio 1986, 167) of Jesus Christ; 8½" × 10½". Circa 1986. Rating: known carver, good condition, well carved, good patina, and rarity unknown, ****. *Former collection of Vernon Kostohryz.*

Opposite page top: Artemio Zaragoza in December 2008, holding a traditional Santiaguero mask that he had carved. *Photos of Artemio, his tools, masks, and other carvings are included with the permission of Artemio Zaragoza.*

Opposite page bottom: The wood-framed electric sander used by Artemio Zaragoza to smooth the front and back surfaces of his masks. Two masks to be sanded are lined up in readiness.

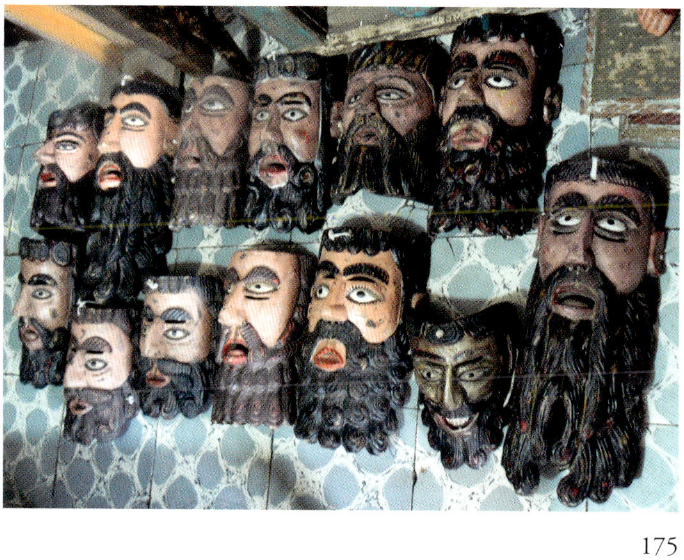

This is a group of masks carved by Artemio Zaragoza Zaragoza in about 1986 that were apparently modeled on various masks in Victor José Moya Rubio's book (1986). Most of these are masks of the so-called Dwarf or Marquis forms (Cordry 1980, 13, 138–139), although one of these is another example of the Pescado copies. *Collection of Carlos Moreno Vásquez.*

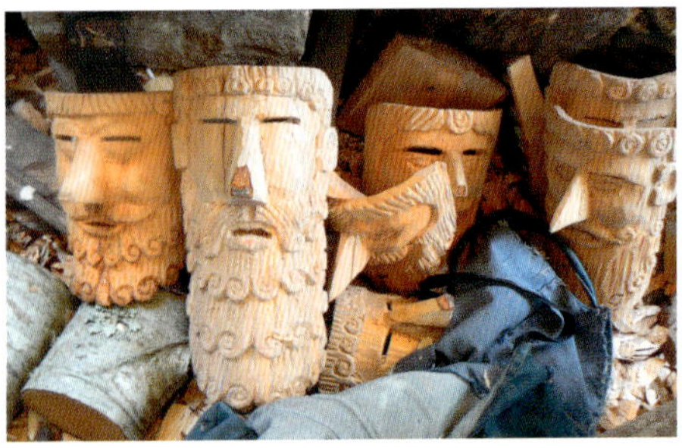

Some masks that were in the process of being carved, in the workshop of Artemio Zaragoza Zaragoza, when we visited him in March 2010. These are the ones that remind me of so-called Dwarf and Marquis masks.

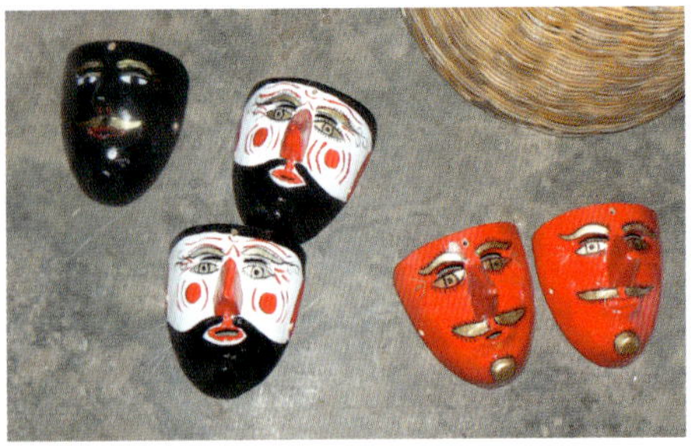

A group of completed traditional-style masks for sale at Artemio's in March 2010. They include a Negrito mask, two Pilato masks, and two Santiaguero masks. *Collection of Artemio Zaragoza.*

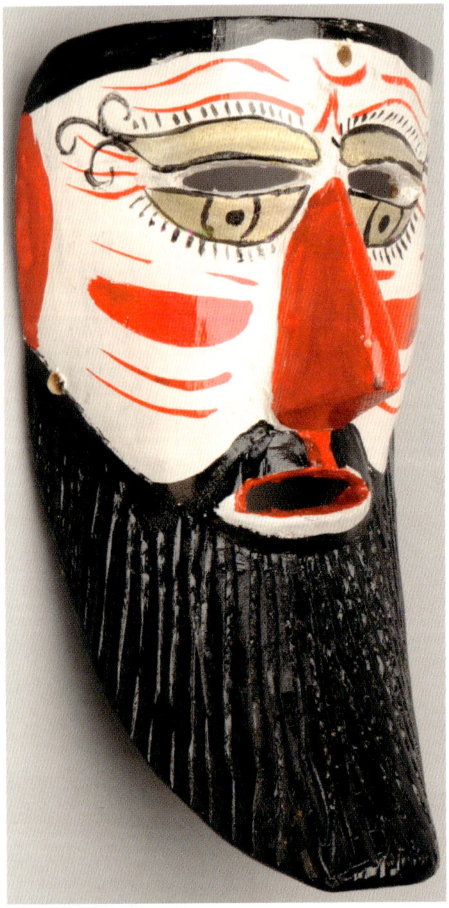

A new, undanced Pilato mask from the Santiagueros dance, purchased from the carver in March 2010; 6¼" × 10½". Rating: known carver, good condition, well carved, undanced, and not rare, ***. *Collection of the author.*

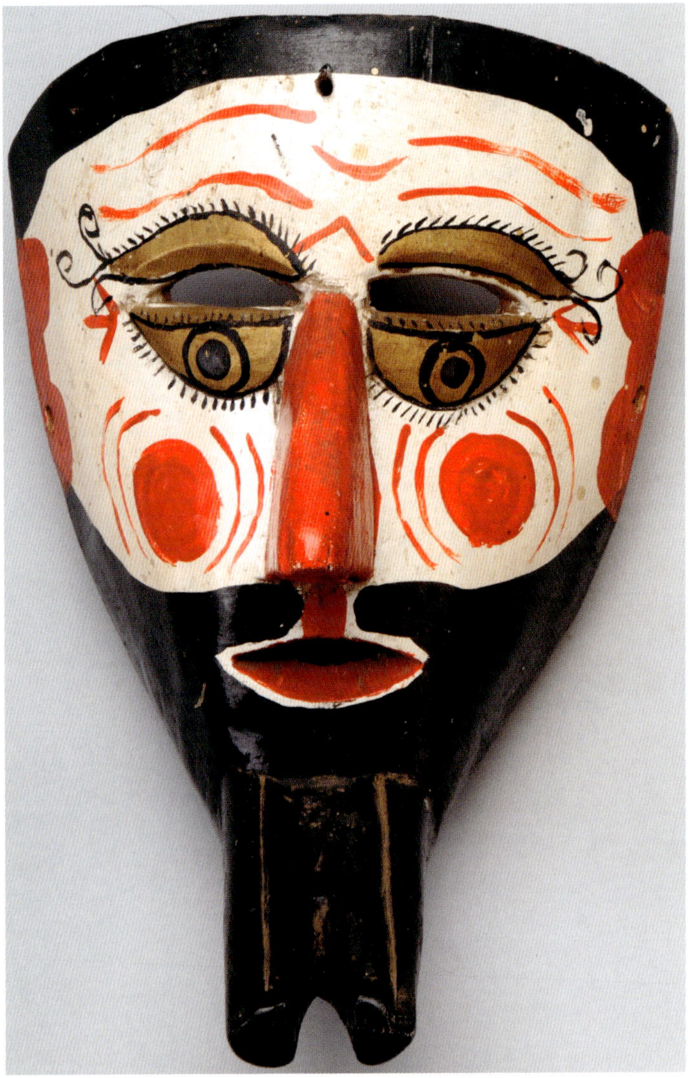

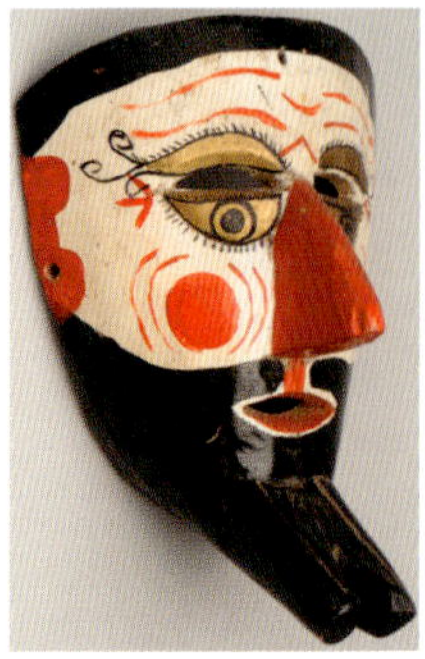

Left: A danced Pilato mask by Artemio from the Santiagueros dance; 7" × 10". Circa 1990. The design is quite stylish with the slim bifurcated beard. Rating: known carver, good condition, well carved, good patina, and rarity unknown, ****. *Collection of the author.*

Above: The side view of this danced Pilato mask. The ears are painted but not carved in relief.

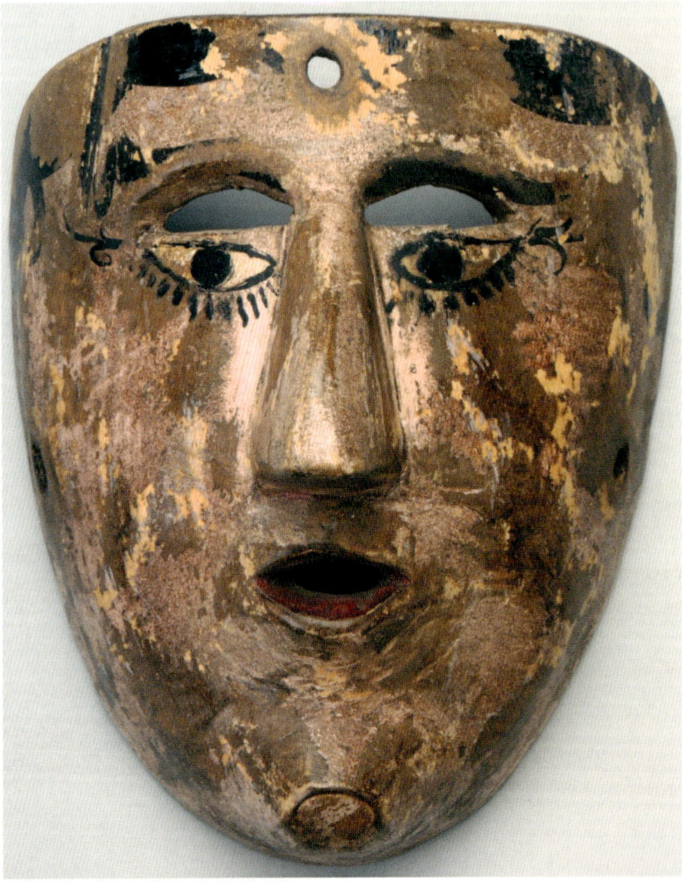

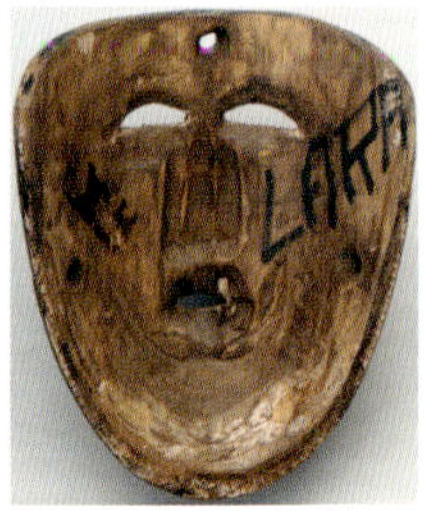

Left: A female Huehue mask carved by Artemio, old and worn; 6" × 7". Circa 1980. The mask has a flat spot on the chin that is found on a number of older masks by Artemio. Rating: known carver, good condition, well carved, good patina, and rarity unknown, ****. *Collection of the author.*

Above: The back of this female mask.

Anonymous

Despite our efforts, a number of masks remain that are beautiful or interesting, of moderate to great age, but whose maker remains unidentified. I'll begin this section with some masks that have such distinctive ear designs that one is tempted to label their anonymous carver according to that trait.

The "C-ears carver" may still be alive and actively carving. One sees old and well-worn masks as well as undanced, apparently made-for-sale masks by this carver. All of these masks have a number of shared features. Of course, the most obvious one is the shape of the ears, which look like capital C letters with an internal dividing line that starts near one end and extends almost to the other end. The noses all share one shape; likewise the chins all resemble one another. The vision slits are uniform in placement and shape. The shape of the mouth tends to also follow a particular design. We have everything we need to define an individual carver's hand except for his name. These are attractive masks.

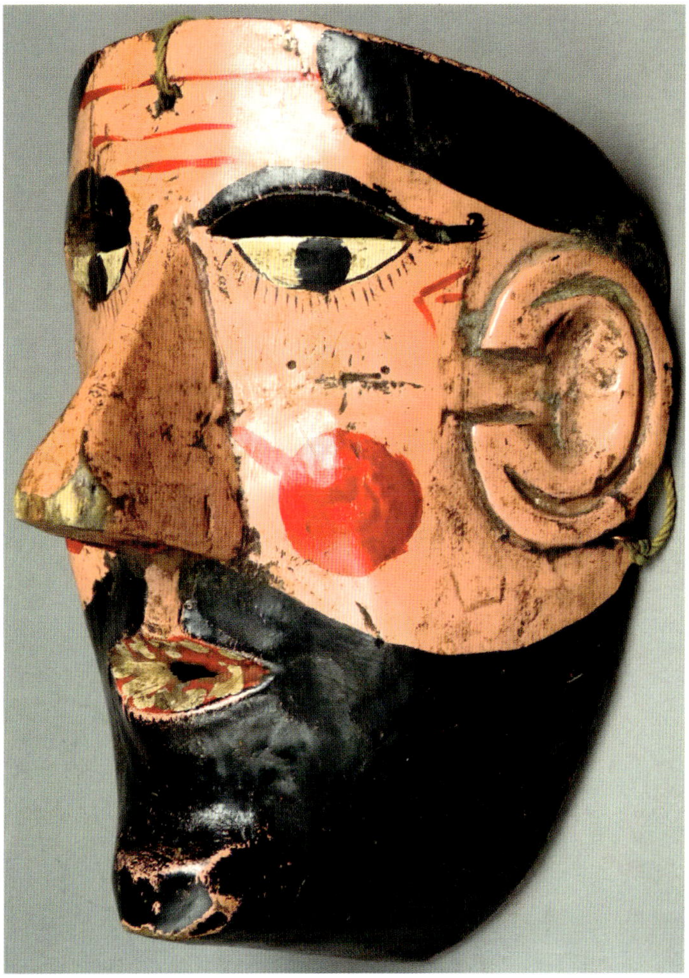

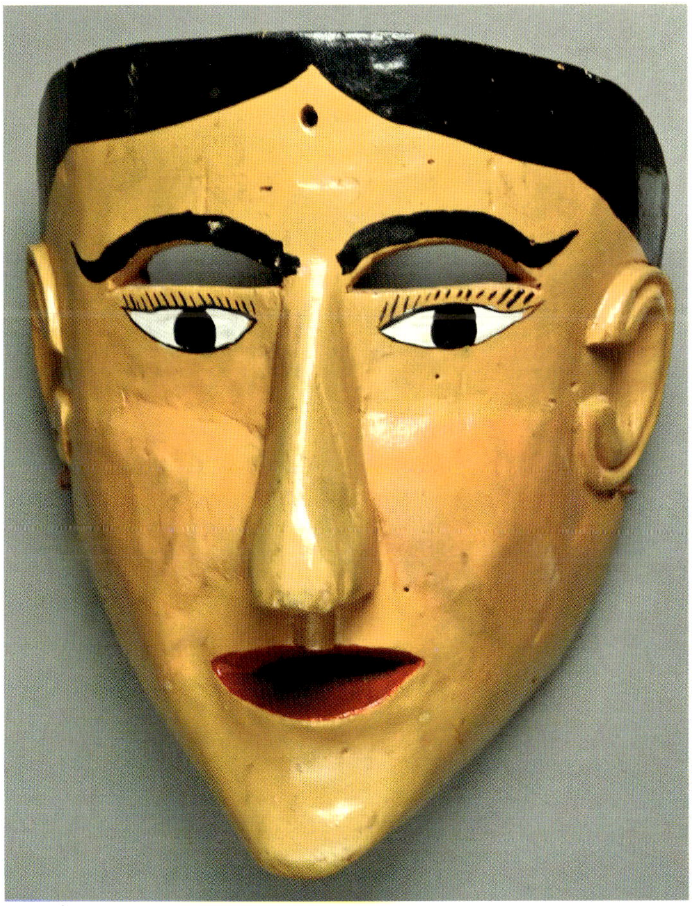

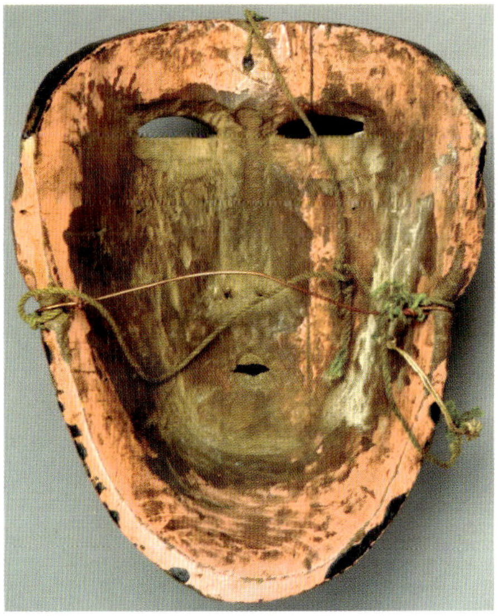

This female Huehue mask with C-ears was purchased from Bob Ibold in November 2006; 6½" × 7". It was identified as a mask from Cuetzalan, Puebla. Rating: unknown carver, good condition, well carved, mild patina, and rarity unknown, ***. *Collection of the author.*

Top: I obtained this mask with the C-ears from a dealer in Mexico City in January 1998, with little information; 6" × 7". Circa 1980. When I began to study the masks of the Sierra de Puebla, I recognized that the red painted markings on the cheeks were highly characteristic of the masks traditionally found in Cuetzalan, Puebla. Rating: unknown carver, good condition, well carved, great patina, and rarity unknown, ****. *Collection of the author.*

Bottom: The back has beautiful wear.

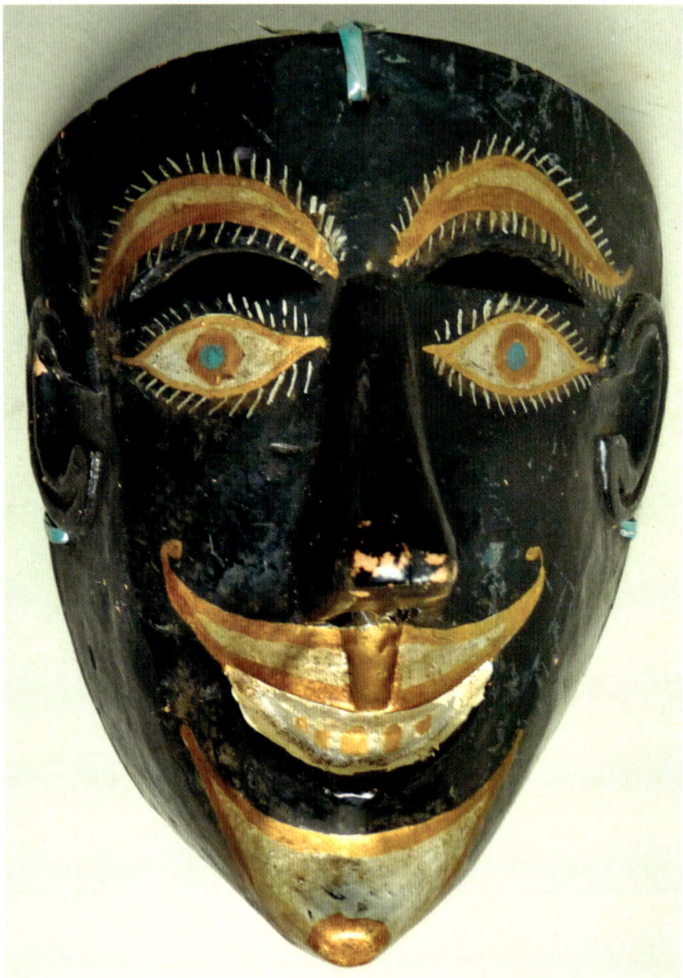

The mascarero whom I will call the "Complex-ears carver" is represented by two masks that were collected in the area near the border of Puebla and Veracruz. Both have the same remarkably unusual ear design. Otherwise they are fairly similar in some features although they lack the identical triplets quality of the C-ears group.

The next group of masks for our review consists of Tejonero or Huehue masks of varying quality. No two of them appear to be by the same carver.

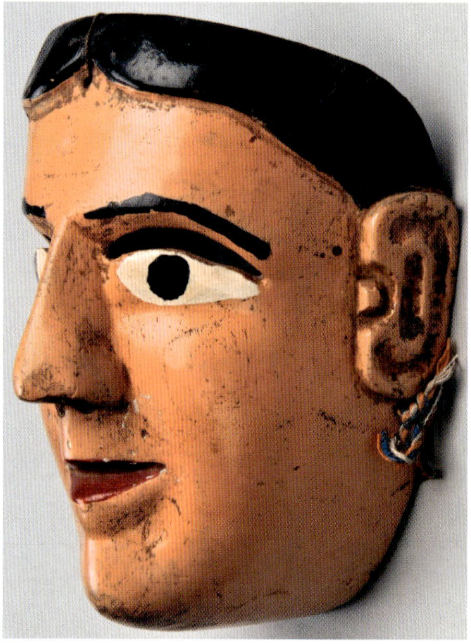

This attractive female Tejonero mask with complex ears was found by Vernon Kostohryz in El Chacal, Puebla, a community that lies just inside the state of Puebla, southwest of El Espinal, Veracruz; 5¾" × 7". Circa 1960; this mask is old and worn. *Collection of the author.*

Vernon Kostohryz found this Negrito mask with C-ears in Yancuitlalpan, Puebla, a small town that is not very far down the road from Cuetzalan; 6" × 7½". Circa 1980. Where the paint has flaked off one sees an underlying layer of pink paint. Probably this mask was a near duplicate of the previous mask, before it was repainted as a Negrito for the Danza de los Negritos. Rating: unknown carver, good condition, well carved, great patina, and rarity unknown, ****. *Collection of Vernon Kostohryz.*

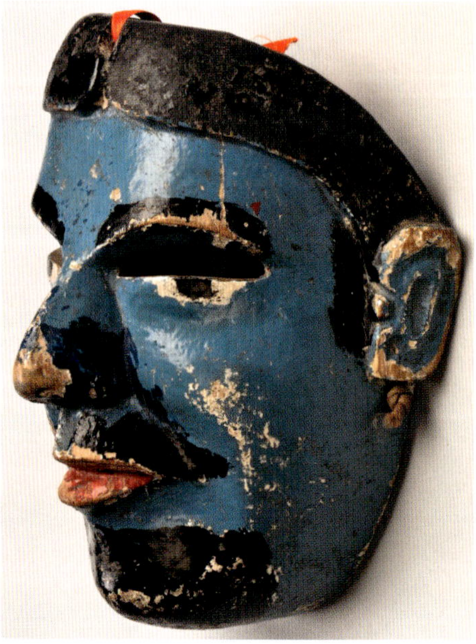

This equally old and worn blue Huehue mask with complex ears was found in a private collection in La Union, Veracruz, a town to the east of El Espinal; 6" × 7½". Circa 1960. It was probably a female Tejonero mask when it was first carved, although it has long been painted blue, along with black painted sideburns, mustache, and goatee. It has the same hairline as the other mask with this ear design; it lacks evidence of pierced ears, so really we would have to conclude that its initial gender is uncertain. It is my theory that masks that have been painted blue or green represent the dead. Not rated. *Collection of the author.*

The first of these is most puzzling. It was found in Zozocolco de Hidalgo, but it fails to conform to that local pattern of design. Based on many unusual details such as the design of the eyes, the shape of the sideburns associated with the lack of ears, the shape of the back, and notched corners at the top, one is inclined to think that this mask is from farther north in the state of Veracruz, the area known as the Huasteca.

Next comes another very well carved mask by an unknown carver. The ear design suggests Manuel Pérez, but Don Lillo denied that attribution; he said that it was carved by some unnamed carver from Zozocolco de Hidalgo, Veracruz. It was found in Filomeno Mata, Veracruz, in November of 2008.

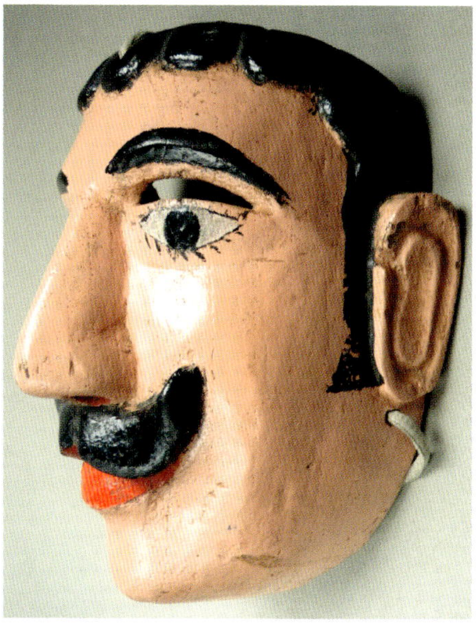

This well-carved male Tejonero mask has an unusually ornate hairline; 6½" × 7½". Circa 1950, based on patina. The back shows dark staining and is not in the style of Benito Juárez. The ear design resembles that of Manuel Pérez, but Don Lillo denied that Manuel was the carver. Rating: unknown carver, good condition, well carved, great patina, and probably rare, *****. *Collection of Vernon Kostohryz.*

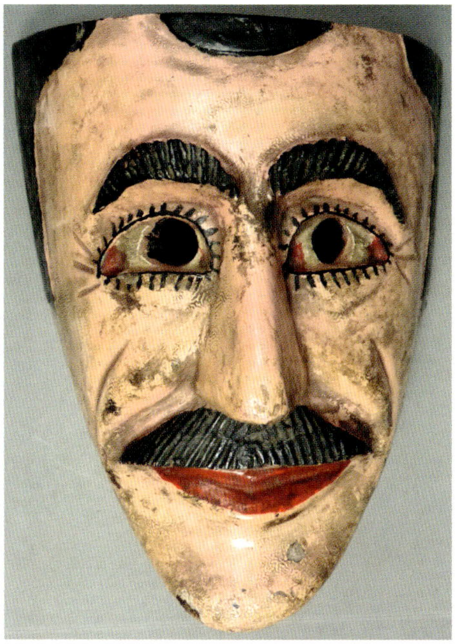

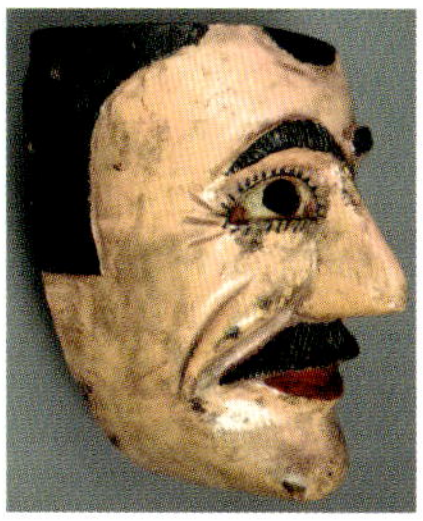

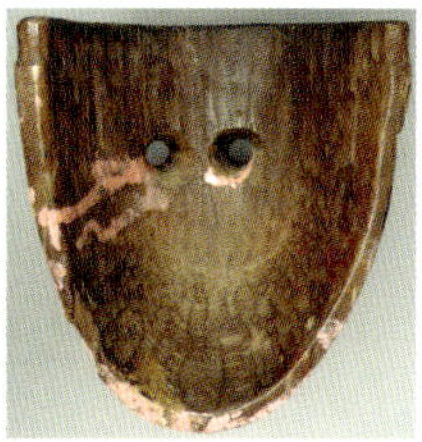

Above: An anonymous masterpiece, this unusual male Tejonero mask is very well carved; 6½" × 7½". Circa 1950, based on patina. The eyes are carefully shaped, the hair is carved in relief, brows and mustache are relief carved and nicely grooved. Instead of vision slits above the eyes the wearer looks through the open pupils, an unusual solution for this region, more commonly found on masks of animals. It lacks ears, also unusual. Rating: unknown carver, good condition, very well carved, great patina, and probably rare, *****. *Collection of the author.*

Above upper right: The side view reveals a telltale detail that one finds on some masks from the Huasteca, the curved notch at the upper corners. The sideburns have the typical shape seen in that area as well.

Above lower right: The shape of the back is unlike the usual pattern for our area of study. Again one can see the curved notches at the corners where the sides meet the top of the mask. The patina is lovely; it has significant age or wear.

Here is a male Huehue mask with a delightful expression. The ears seem to be carved with significant dishing; various carvers do this to some extent, but it is more prominent on this mask.

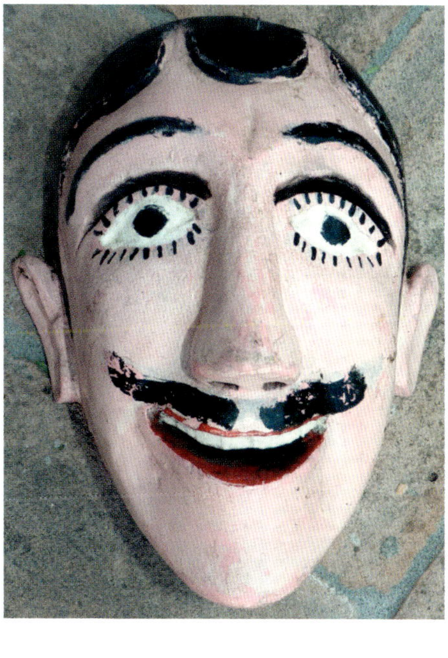

This male Tejonero mask with dished ears has an amusing expression. Age unknown. Rating: unknown carver, good condition, well carved, good patina, and rarity unknown, ***. *Collection of Bill LeVasseur.*

Now we will consider a few anonymously carved female masks from the dance of the Huehues or Tejoneros. The first, found in Filomeno Mata, Veracruz, has an unusually animated expression. Thinking it a male, I called it "Puck." Later I noticed the pierced ears and realized that the apparent sideburns were really curls, and the mask was of a female clown. The level of carving is very high; this is an anonymous masterpiece. What else by this carver will be discovered? But on the other hand, this is a mask that gives a false impression of its age. On the face and also on the back one sees what appears to be extreme patina, including green streaks as if from a crayon. I used a solvent, meaning to remove the green pigment, and all of the darkening on the face dissolved. Looking again at a photo from before the cleaning I can even see brush strokes from the application of the darkening agent. I did not apply the solvent to the back, but I suspect that this too has been artificially darkened. So this is a paradoxical situation—a masterpiece that has been artificially aged in order to make it seem more valuable.

One may choose to collect masks for a particular trait, for instance, because they are beautiful, or humorous, or even horrifying. This mask seems to fall into the humorous category. The hair across the forehead has been decorated with small scalloped indentations, and then the hair sweeps down into dramatic curls. The design and execution of the ears is particularly unusual. This mask, which would appear to be the work of an ambitious amateur carver, was collected in Filomeno Mata, Veracruz.

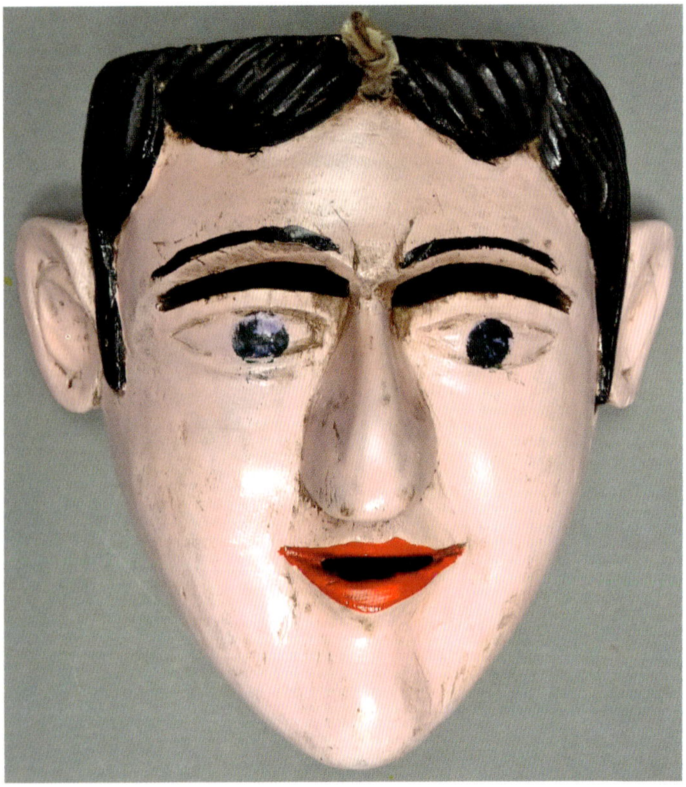

Left: This female Tejonero mask has an animated and saucy expression, as if a female clown. Her curls make one think of sideburns, although atypical. On the other hand, her ears are pierced for earrings, she has no mustache, and her mouth is quite feminine; 6¾" × 6¾". Age unknown. The eyes, ears, nose, mouth, and hair are all very finely carved. Ordinary female Tejoneros are more solemn in expression, with closed mouths. Rating: unknown carver, good condition, extremely well carved, uncertain patina, and rarity unknown, ***. *Collection of the author.*

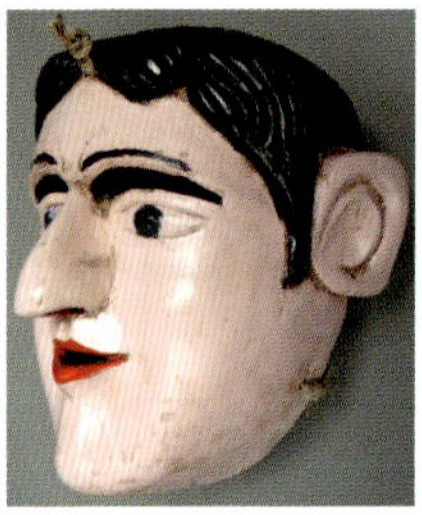

Above: On the side view of this female clown, the elaborate carving of the ear is quite evident.

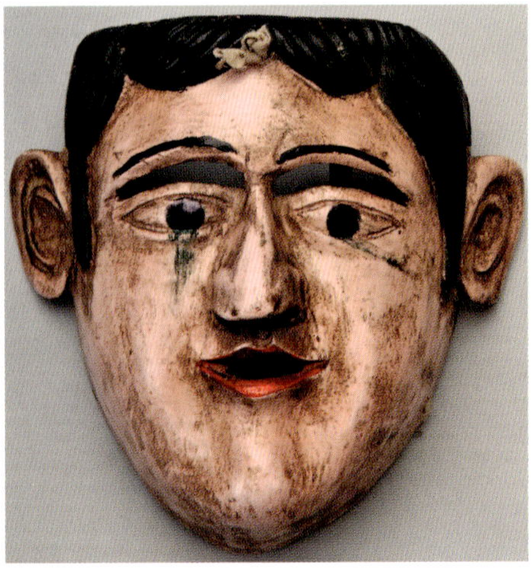

Left: A second view from the front, prior to cleaning. Note the area over the left eyebrow, where diagonal brush strokes seem to confirm the application of a darkening agent.

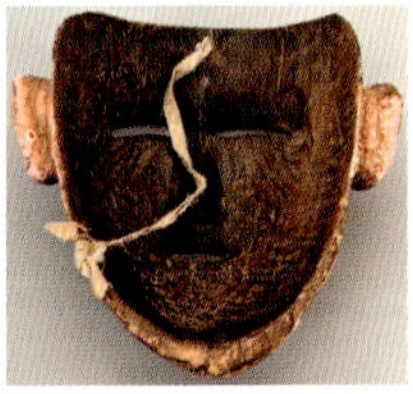

Above: The view of the back suggests that this is an old and heavily used mask, with extreme patina. But this may well be a false impression.

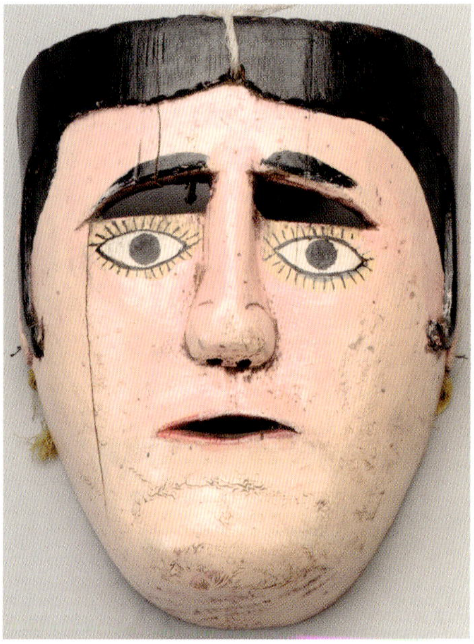

Top: An extremely naïve carving of a female Tejonero mask, from Filomeno Mata, Veracruz, showing a chip-carved hairline; 6½" × 8½". Circa 1950, based on patina. Rating: unknown carver, good condition, well carved, excellent patina, and rarity unknown, ***. *Collection of the author.*

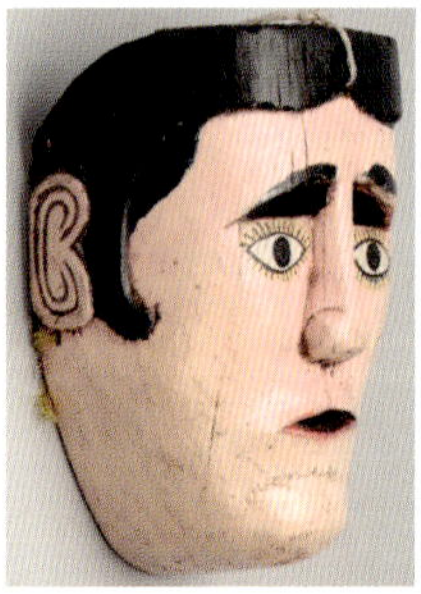

Bottom The curling hair and the ear design are charming. Both ears are pierced, and loops of black thread in the piercings apparently once held earrings. At the last repainting the hairline was distorted.

I will conclude the discussion of anonymous Tejonero masks with two Payaso masks.

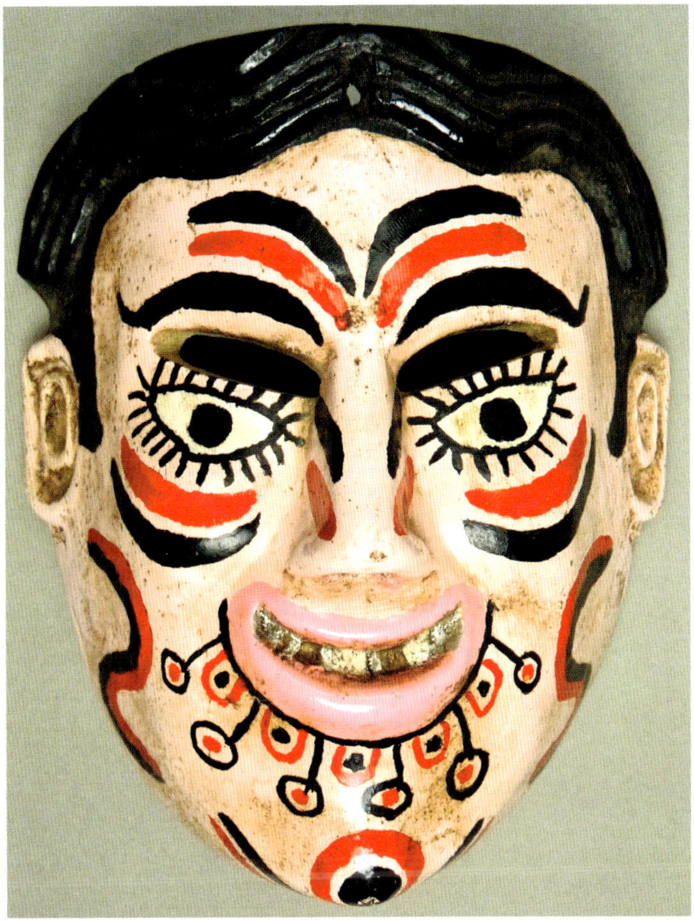

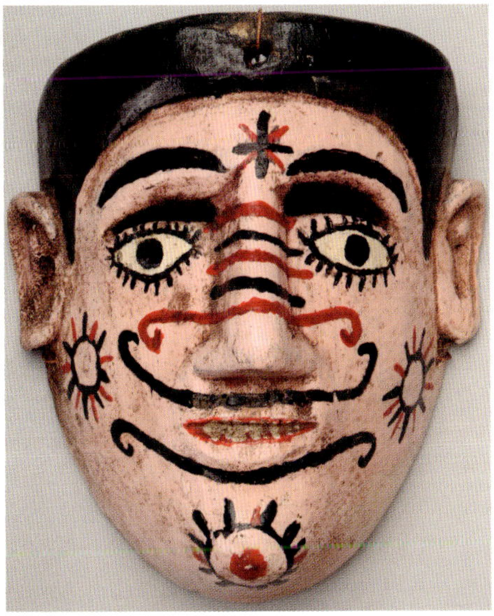

Above: This vigorously carved and painted clown mask, from the Tejoneros dance, was found in Mecatlán, Veracruz; 5½" × 6½". Circa 1960 based on patina. The carving of the hair is particularly striking. Rating: unknown carver, good condition, very well carved, great patina, and rarity unknown, ***. *Former collection of Vernon Kostobryz.*

Left: This vividly painted clown, whose ear design is notable, was found in Chumatlán, Veracruz; 6½" × 7¼". Circa 1980. Rating: unknown carver, good condition, well carved, good patina, and rarity unknown, ****. *Collection of the author.*

Other Carvers

Over the years several other carvers have come to our attention, usually on the basis of just one mask. Unfortunately, I lack photos to illustrate their work. I will list their names here for future reference.

- Amador Juárez Juárez of El Arenal, Veracruz.
- Hermelindo Mariano Lucas, of Zozocolco de Hidalgo, Veracruz.

Chapter 7

Tejonero and Huehue Puppets

To begin with, the puppets used in the Huehues or Tejoneros dance are referred to as *títeres* (puppets) or *muñecos* (a word that can be used for dolls or puppets). We have identified examples of puppets that were made by many of the mask makers in this area. Few if any are signed by their respective makers, but some can be identified as the work of a particular carver on the basis of stylistic details, just as we have seen for the masks. In this chapter I will present what I have been able to learn thus far about these puppets and their distinguishing characteristics.

A Few Facts and Observations

To briefly review, puppets have been traditionally used in La Danza de Los Chénchere*s*, also known as the Dance of the Huehue*s*, Tejoneros, or Matlachines. According to one legend (Lane, *Notes on the Text of The Tree of Knowledge* nd) from Huehuetla, Puebla, all the wood used to make the masks, the puppets, the poles holding up the puppets' curtain, and the pole that the Chénchere climbs represents the spirits of the trees in the forest, important deities from the time prior to the arrival of the Spanish. According to this legend, these spirits taught the Indians about the natural world.

The ideal puppet set consists of a male puppet, a female puppet, a wooden *Chénchere* (woodpecker) puppet and a wooden box to contain them. The associated apparatus includes the *telón* (curtain), 8 or 12 wooden posts to support the telón, and a tall bamboo pole that has been specially prepared; the interior partitions between the sections of the pole have been removed so that a cord to raise the woodpecker up the pole can run down the inside space. At the top of the pole there is a *guajillo*, a hollow chamber in the shape of a gourd that can be released to fall open by the pull of yet another rope, revealing a Mexican flag, streamers, and formerly flowers when the woodpecker reaches the top.

According to the carvers I have consulted, the male character is commonly called San José; according to Stresser-Péan (2009, 297), he can also be called Francisco, a possible reference to Christ and the Spirit of Maíze. The female character is commonly called the Virgin María; Stresser-Péan has also collected an alternative name for this puppet—*Xochitl* (flower)—that can also refer to the mother of the Spirit of Maíze. So the two are named as if they might represent Christian or indigenous deities. But the contemporary explanation collected by Bruce Lane (*Notes on the Text of The Tree of Knowledge* nd) was that they are Mestizos who are inviting the Indian onlookers to give up their identity and to become Huehues (meaning Mestizos, in this context) themselves. It seems that the puppets have traditionally had idealized features, which would reinforce the idea that they represent noble characters. There is a certain tension between the Indians and the Mestizos; if the puppets do represent the latter, we might expect them to be portrayed in a less flattering or idealized fashion. As a matter of fact, a shift in this direction seems to be occurring in recent decades. I don't know whether this reflects a weakening of the concept of the sacred nature of the puppets or a conscious shift towards strengthening the camouflage of the puppets as alleged Mestizos. I suspect the latter, because when I have photographed puppets that were still being used, I was directed to treat them with respect because they were considered to be sacred. Also I have seen that they continue to be stored on the home altar of the lead dancer. As I have explained at length in other parts of the book, the dances of this region seem to demonstrate parallel and shifting layers of meaning, as in this case.

The Chénchere, or woodpecker, appears in myths regarding the origin of Maíze (Medina Jiménez 2005, 63–66) as the bird that assisted the Spirit of Maíze in his work to release corn to the people of the Sierra de Puebla. In the process he was struck by a falling stone, which caused his head to bleed. The legend goes on to explain that this is why the woodpecker has a red crest to this day.

Medina Jiménez (2005, 68–69) has described the three puppets as the "*dueños de la danza*" (masters of the dance of the Huehues or Tejoneros); he also referred to them as "*dioses naturales*" (gods of the natural world). In her glossary, Cora Govers provides some further helpful information: According to the residents of Nanacatlán, Puebla, dueños are "owners or supernatural custodians of natural elements, animals, or crops" (Govers 2006, 306). We have already learned that, because they are living wood, the puppets may represent the spirits of the trees. Don Felix Ramos informed Govers that in the Tejoneros dance, "The bird [in the dance] is the Patron of Maíze" (Govers, 162). He repeated the legend that the Chénchere had played a vital role in bringing Maíze to humans to use as food. So we see again that a dance element can appear to be European while it may actually represent something indigenous and pre-Hispanic in another level of meaning.

Medina Jiménez (2005, 68–69) explained that for the period of months following the last performance until the period of preparation for the next, the three puppets traditionally would be kept in their closed wooden box. At the beginning of the period of dance rehearsals they are removed from this box and "revived" with great ceremony, then they are kept out on the home altar of the leader of the Huehues or Tejoneros dancers until they appear in the actual dance performance. Afterwards, at the end of the fiesta they are returned to their box. I have seen aspects of these practices myself. In Tuxtla, four weeks before the fiesta, the puppets were visible on the house altar of the local dance leader. In Sabanas de Xalostoc, at a time when the fiesta was far off in the future, I found the puppets in their closed box on the altar of that dance leader.

In the actual dance ceremony the male and female puppets gesture to onlookers from behind the telón (the painted curtain); however, their traditional activity is to clap their oversized hands together while whirling about. So they produce the sound of wood striking wood, potentially another reference to the spirits of the trees. An unseen operator, animating one puppet on each hand, moves quickly around the inside of the four (or eight) sides of the curtain. The space enclosed by the telón represents the *monte*, the mountainous forest world of the tree spirits. The *tarro* (bamboo) pole, wrapped in banana leaves to represent a stalk of corn (and thereby the *milpa* or cornfield), rises in the middle of this space. The woodpecker puppet is raised and lowered on the pole with cords, and another cord causes his neck to extend and retract so that his beak raps the pole. So the woodpecker too makes a sound, one that we invariably associate with woodpeckers and trees.

According to Stresser-Péan (2009, 292), the dance originally had three Chéncheres of graduated sizes who each pecked their way to the top of the pole in turn; in our area of focus there is just one bird. When the woodpecker reaches the top of the pole the guajillo is manipulated to open, releasing its contents.

There is another puppet-like character used in this dance (although not considered to be a titere or a dueño)—the *Tejón* (wild animal, referring to a coati). A live animal might be released to run up the pole, although more commonly nowadays an animal carcass is raised and lowered, as with the Chénchere and using the same ropes. One of the dancers pretends to shoot the marauder in order to protect the corn crop. In the past the shooter was a hunter character, dressed in Indian clothing; now this task often falls to one of the clowns.

A Word about Names

For those who may be reading about the puppets first, I will repeat the reminder about the names of the carvers that was provided in Chapter 6. In Mexico an individual has a given name (first name) followed by the father's surname (last name) and then frequently the mother's surname as well. So for example there is José González Galindo. We can refer to him by his full name or we can call him José González for short. We would not properly refer to him as José Galindo or simply Galindo. But among the carvers included in this book there are three who could be addressed as José González. These are José González Diaz; his father, José González Galindo; and the unrelated José González Hernández. Furthermore, there are a number of carvers who share the same father's surname, such as Juárez. In any part of the book where the discussion is obviously about just one carver, I will refer to him initially by his full name and thereafter by either the short form or simply by his first name or nickname. Only when it is absolutely necessary to avoid confusion will I repeatedly refer to a carver by his full name.

After leading off with the puppets of Lorenzo Ciriaco García, I will discuss the rest of the carvers in alphabetical order, arranged according to the father's surname. That is, Manuel Aldana Valencia will come before Francisco de Aquino.

A Parade of Puppets, Beginning with El Kalimán

I will discuss the features of a number of puppets by many of the carvers whom you have already met in Chapter 6, in order to reveal the variety that can be observed and to illustrate the possibility that some puppets can be attributed to their respective carvers on the basis of style. As in the case of the masks, we shall see that the style of the carver is revealed both in the parts of the puppets that are usually visible and also in those parts that are usually hidden by the costumes. Likewise for the woodpecker puppets there are also two aspects to notice: the external shaping versus the manner of the mechanical arrangements, usually visible on the underside of the Chénchere.

Lorenzo Ciriaco García: El Kalimán

In 2005, Vernon Kostohryz and Carlos Moreno Vásquez first met Lorenzo Ciriaco García. He was bedridden due to complications of diabetes mellitus, but he greeted them warmly. Vernon recalls that Lorenzo had a radiant smile. The visitors asked him about his masks, and he directed them to a former dance group that still owned some masks that he had carved. Vernon purchased those masks, along with a set of puppets. They learned that Lorenzo had the nickname of "El Kalimán" (see Chapter 6). Vernon and Carlos also met Leonel Lecona at that time. Leonel and Lorenzo had been friends from childhood.

I met Vernon soon after those events, and quickly agreed to buy the set of masks and puppets that were carved by Lorenzo. We planned to visit the carver together in the fall, but in the end Vernon arranged for me to travel there with Carlos instead. On our arrival we learned that Lorenzo had suddenly died, just days before we came.

Thus in December 2006, in the company of Carlos Moreno Vásquez, I visited the family of the recently deceased carver. They were gracious hosts, clearly pleased to have visitors who were interested in Lorenzo and his work. I was permitted to photograph his set of tools, along with masks and puppets that he had made. The tools and masks are presented in Chapter 6; here I will introduce the puppets. There were two of them, a male and a female, and neither had any costume. I was not shown a woodpecker puppet, nor did I see a box for their protection and storage. What I did immediately see was that these were wonderful carvings. At that time I felt highly respectful of the family's loss and associated grieving, and I made no effort to purchase any of these things.

Carlos and I had also visited Leonel Lecona at that time. To my surprise, Leonel showed us a movie, on a DVD, of Lorenzo performing in the Huehues dance. This was our introduction to Bruce Lane's movie *The Tree of Knowledge* (Lane 2005). When I later obtained this DVD, I saw that Leonel had also played a prominent role in the film, appearing as Manuel.

Several years later I commissioned Carlos to approach the family about one of the masks, and they proved to be interested in selling the one that I wanted. Then in 2010 the family approached Carlos, offering to sell the puppets. There was even a Chénchere, but still no box. In the interim the puppets had apparently served as children's playthings and they had lost more of their paint; they looked battered. I purchased them, Carlos arranged for costumes to be made, and I had the paint restored by a specialist in Pennsylvania.

Restoration to a museum-quality standard involved infilling with the appropriate paint along with the use of a stabilizing synthetic varnish. Much of what you see is the original paint; the surface is restored but the patina suffers. I'm always sorry when the situation dictates such a terrible choice. I much preferred the minor chipping and wonderful patina that I saw in 2006.

In the illustrations we see the wooden elements of two puppets by this carver. Please note the following points about these puppets:

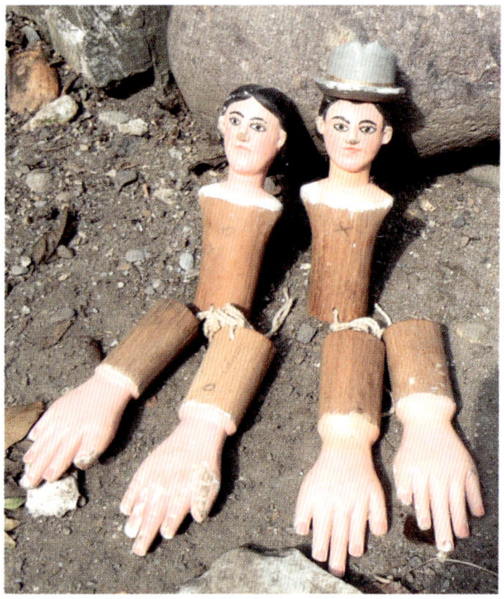

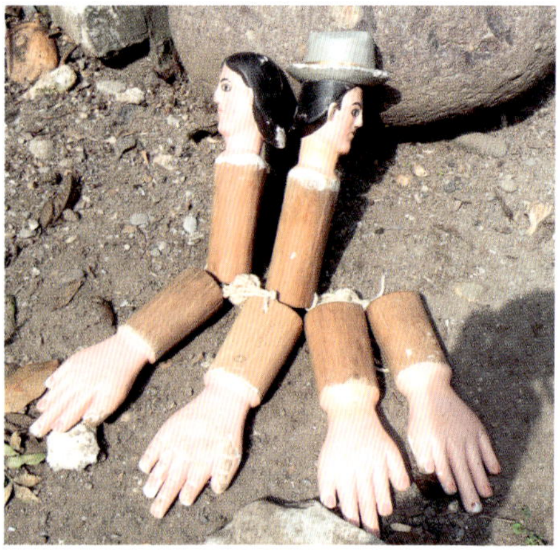

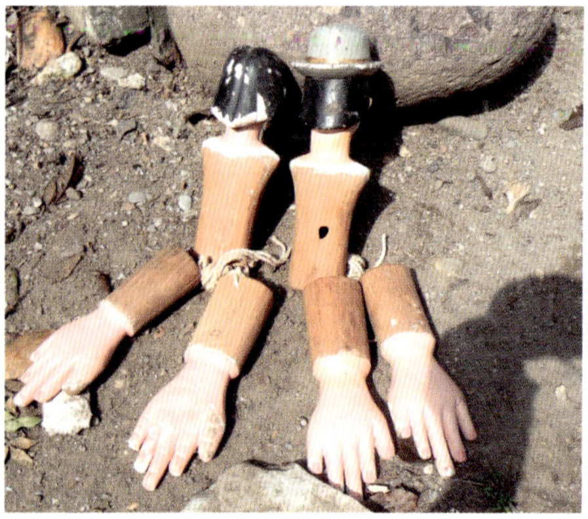

Top: This set of puppets was in the possession of Kalimán's family when these photos were taken in December 2006; they were made circa 1980. The hat on the head of the male puppet was carved in place; it is not separate from the head. Even when these photos were taken there was some chipping of the paint. Rating: known carver, good condition, excellent design, moderate chipping of paint with good patina, and very rare, *******. *Collection of the author. Photos permitted courtesy of Kalimán's family.*

Center: The side view allows us to see how elegantly carved is the hair; both puppets have carved ears. They have attractive faces.

Bottom: The back view of these puppets.

1. A puppet of human form from this region consists of three separate elements—a torso of some sort that includes a head, plus two forearms with oversized hands, one right and one left.
2. Carved and painted fingernails often mark the backs of these hands.
3. These three elements are usually tied together with cords, to reduce the possibility that a head or hand will fly off during the vigorous motion of the puppets. In this case the carver has coded the parts with "x's" and "o's" in order to maintain their groupings when untied.
4. Despite their apparent identity as gods, these human puppets have the appearance of *catrines* (dandies or city dwellers). They are depicted as light-skinned; the male is wearing a jaunty hat. Thus they appear to represent Mestizos.
5. Each carver has developed a stereotyped design for the hands; in the examples that follow you will observe a remarkable variety. One can see the wear on the palm side of the female puppet's left hand, the result of so much clapping.
6. The puppets would ordinarily be dressed in smock-like costumes. The costumes become worn and must be periodically replaced. In this case the costumes were apparently discarded and not replaced; this set was clearly no longer in use.
7. It is helpful for the puppet torsos to have some sort of shoulders, as in this case, to support the costume so that it does not slide down the torso. In the absence of this feature, sometimes the collar of the smock is attached to the puppet's neck with metal tacks.
8. Likewise it is helpful to have a ridge (or a dramatic change in the circumference of the limb) where the hands and wrists meet, to anchor the sleeves, usually secured by drawstrings.
9. What these photos fail to show is that the three elements of each puppet have hollow bases, permitting two fingers to support the torso in an upright position, while the thumb on one side and the two smallest fingers on the other side manipulate the clapping hands.
10. One might think that each carver would develop characteristic faces for his puppets. However, as you will see in the survey that follows, the faces can vary from one set to the next by the same carver, while the hands more often follow a standardized design for each carver. What is more consistent is the quality of the carving, such as a tendency to include carved or constructed hats or not, or a tendency to carve the ears on the puppets in a style that may mimic the ear design used for that carver's masks.

A puppet set will ordinarily include a Chénchere or woodpecker. When I purchased the set from the family in 2010, the beautiful Chénchere emerged as well. These puppets are constructed to mimic the pecking of a live woodpecker. A cord that is attached to the front of the neck passes down over the bird's breast. Then it tunnels through the lower body and emerges under the tail. When this string is pulled downward, the neck extends to create a pecking motion. Rubber tubing attached to the back of the neck causes it to retract again, ready for the next "peck."

Strangely it is not uncommon to find a Chénchere in the absence of the human puppets, although usually when the puppets are present there is also a woodpecker. In this case there was not the traditional box to hold the set of puppets.

El Kalimán was an excellent carver and he had a real flair for design. This is nowhere more apparent than on this set of puppets and another set that follows later.

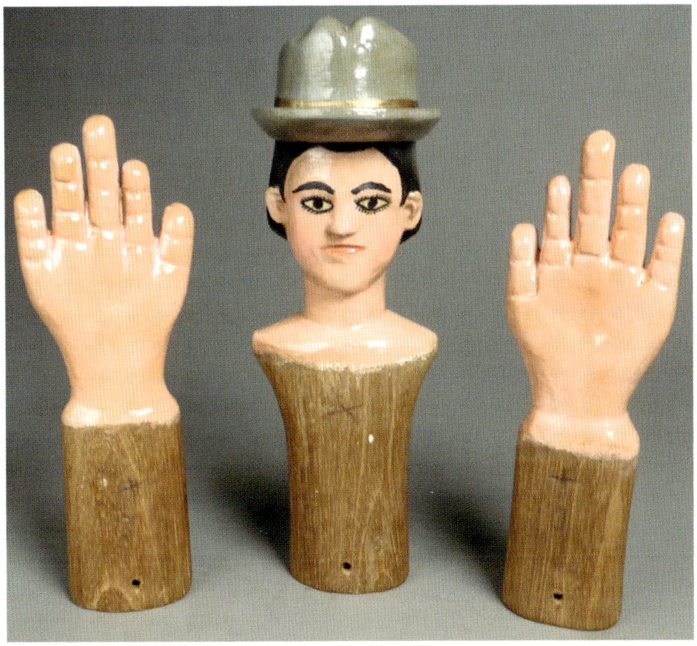

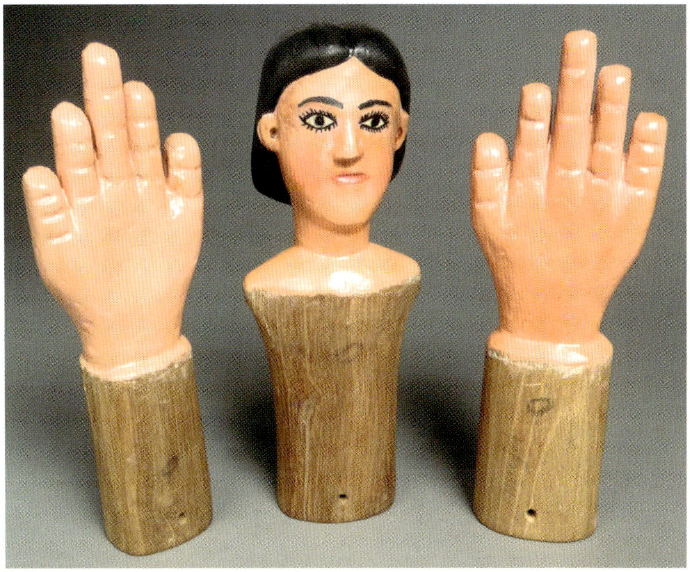

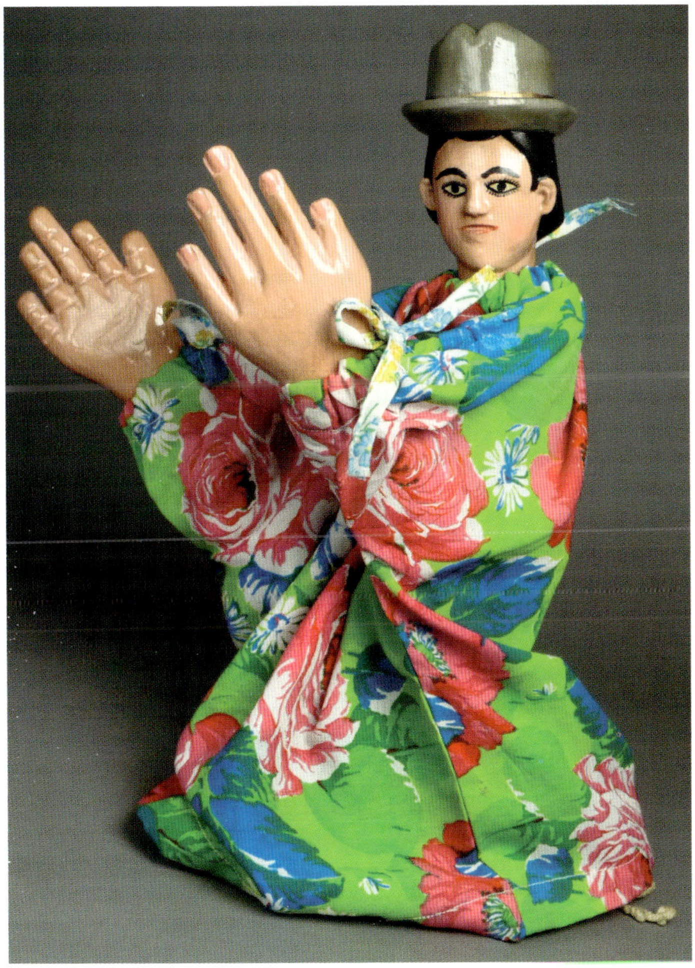

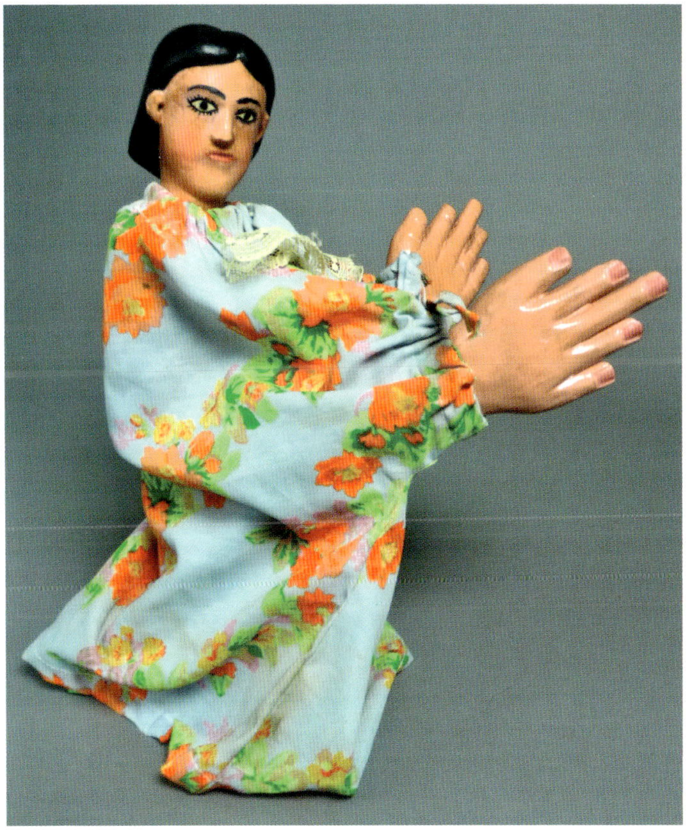

Top left: The male puppet by Kalimán, following expert restoration; the torso is 9" tall, limbs 7¼". Note the lines marking the folds on the fingers. Rating: known carver, good condition, excellent design, restored paint and good patina on the unpainted areas, and very rare, ******+. *Collection of the author.*

Bottom left: The male puppet in his replacement costume.

Top right: The female puppet by Kalimán from the front view; the torso is 9" tall, limbs 7¼". On her left wrist, in pencil, is the word *mujer* (woman); this further links the limbs marked with the letter "o" to the female torso. Rating: known carver, good condition, excellent design, restored paint and good patina, and very rare, ******+. *Collection of the author.*

Bottom right: The female puppet dressed in a modern replacement costume.

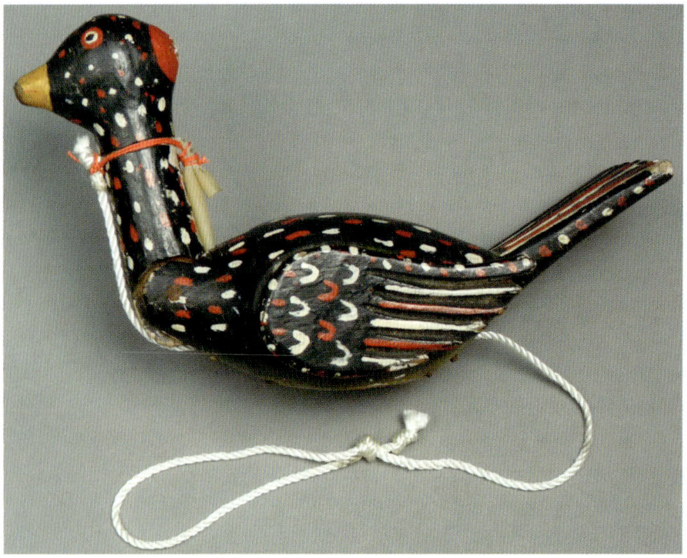

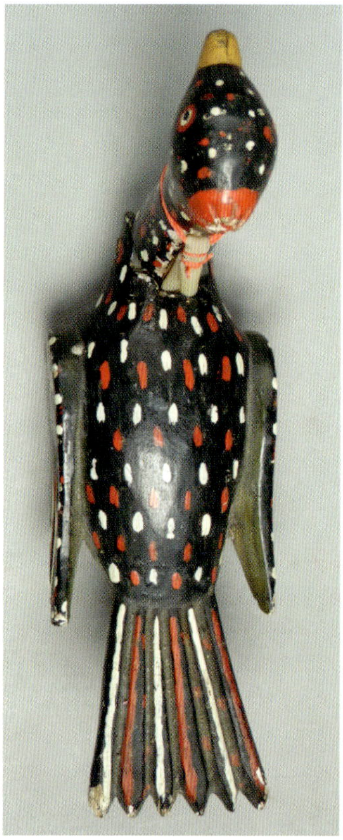

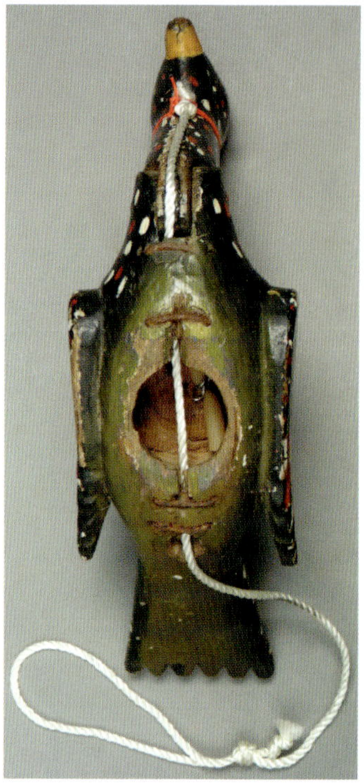

Above left: The Chénchere that is part of this set; the extended length is 10½". From this side view we see the cord from the neck that tunnels through the lower body and emerges under the tail. When this string is pulled (to the viewer's right in this view), the neck extends to create a pecking motion. The rubber tubing attached to the back of the neck can also be seen. Kalimán created the crest with a small rounded prominence that is painted red; other carvers often create a more elaborate crest. Note the nicely grooved wings and the graceful shape of the body. Usually, as in this case, there is a nail attached to the tip of the beak; its flat head raps the pole when the bird "pecks." Rating: known carver, good condition, excellent design, good paint and patina, and very rare, *******. *Collection of the author.*

Above center: The Chénchere positioned as if climbing. We can see the grooved tail and the rubber tubing that flexes the neck.

Above right: This ventral view of the woodpecker shows the full course of the string that causes the neck to extend. This design, with rounded contours and an access hole, is one very common variant. It is not so easily seen, but this Chénchere is very worn on the base; the four metal staples are there to span a lengthwise split in the wood. This puppet lacks the necessary tie-in loops for cords that extend up and down the pole to raise and lower the bird; these remain attached to the second Chénchere by Kalimán that follows.

Another Chénchere

For comparison we will examine a rather large Chénchere by another carver; this woodpecker was said to have been used for at least 15 years in the Huehues dance in Buena Vista, Puebla. It was carved by Guadalupe Ortiz González of Buena Vista, Puebla, the maker of a root serpent shown in Chapter 6.

Right: The base of the Chénchere is flat and rectangular, in marked contrast to that of Kalimán above. Readily seen is a strip of rubber tubing that has been tied to the back of the neck and then anchored through a hole in the base of the carving. This holds the neck in a retracted state. Also seen is the string that follows the front of the neck and then tunnels through a hollow portion of the base before exiting out the back. This is another bird that has lost the attachment points on the base for strings to pull the bird up and down the pole. Probably a strong cord was looped around the bases of the two wings in a figure eight centered over the opening; then the ropes to raise and lower the bird would tie into the crossing of the figure eight.

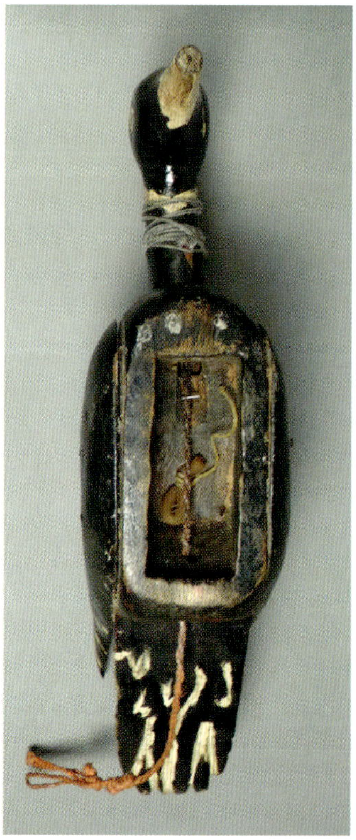

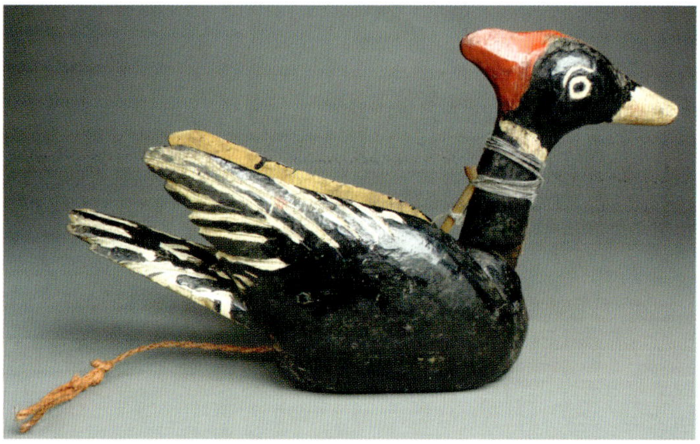

A large woodpecker puppet made by Guadalupe Ortiz González. The extended length (from tip of bill to tip of tail) is 15½". The shape of the comb is more developed for this carver. Rating: known carver, good condition, excellent design, good paint and patina, and rare, ******. *Collection of the author.*

A Second Set of Titeres by Kalimán

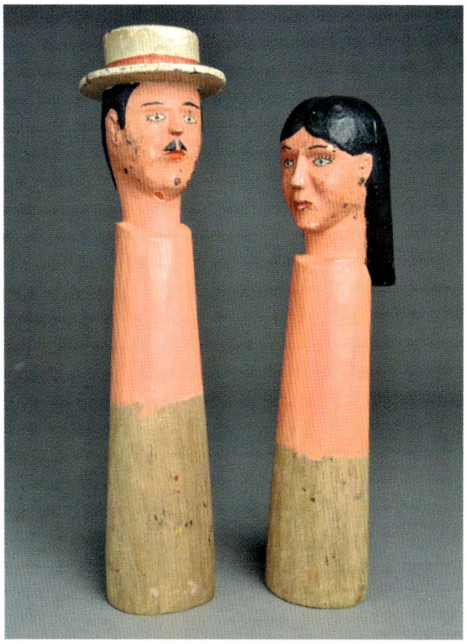

A second set of puppets by Lorenzo Ciriaco García was collected from a dance group in Huehuetla, Puebla, in 2005. Kalimán specifically told Vernon Kostohryz that he was the carver of these puppets. They have very minimal shoulders, just sufficient to prevent the drawstring at the neck of the garment from slipping down. Their hands resemble those of the first set, and both sets have relatively long torsos, compared with puppets by some other carvers. The elements of these puppets are sculpted in dramatic proportions, as if they had been carved by some artist like Modigliani.

One would not say that the faces of this set closely resemble those of the other, but the quality of the carving is quite similar. I am particularly struck by the very graceful carving of the hair on both female puppets. The theme of stylish hats has certainly been maintained on the male puppets.

This puppet set also came with a beautifully carved Chénchere. As we shall see, this woodpecker is a little different from the first. The set did not come with a box.

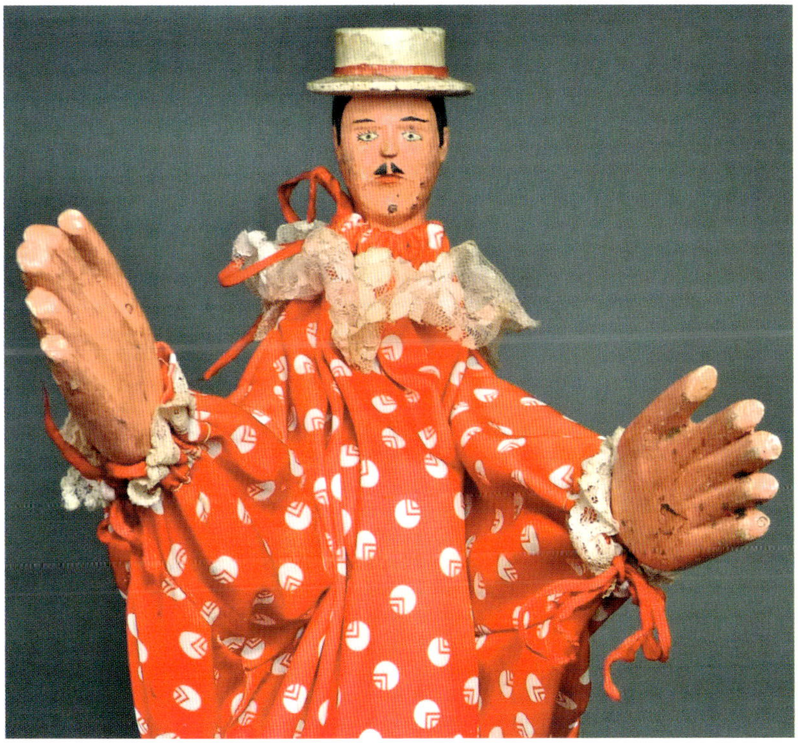

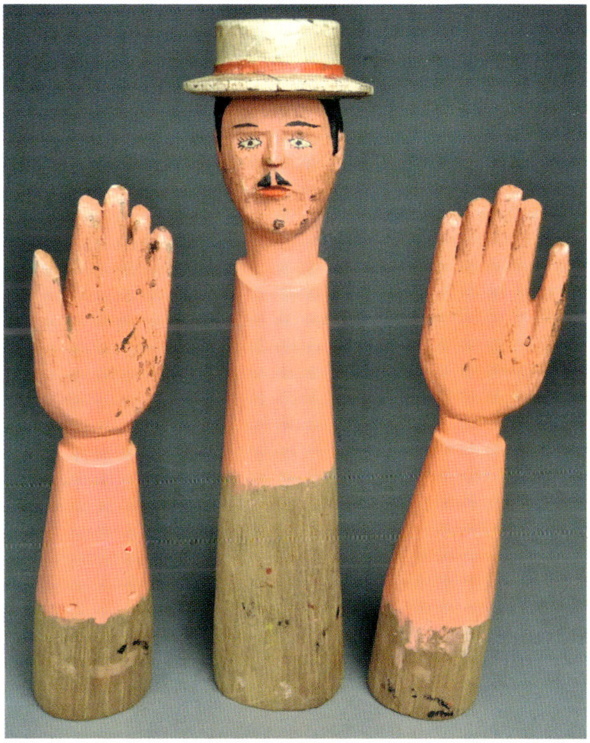

Top right: The torsos of the two puppets in this set by Kalimán; the torsos are 9" and 10" tall. Circa 1975. Rating: known carver, good condition, excellent design, good paint and patina, and very rare, *******. *Collection of the author.*

Above left: The male puppet in costume.

Above right: The wooden parts of the male puppet by Kalimán; the torso is 10" tall, the limbs are 8". We see minor paint loss and normal patina. As in the first set, the carver has created a step, almost a groove in this case, at the neck and wrists to anchor the collar and sleeves of the costume. The straw hat was carved as part of the head. The hands resemble the previous set but lack the fold lines.

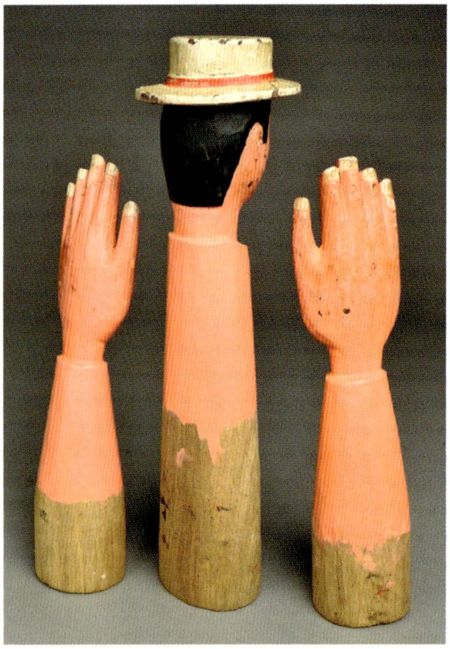
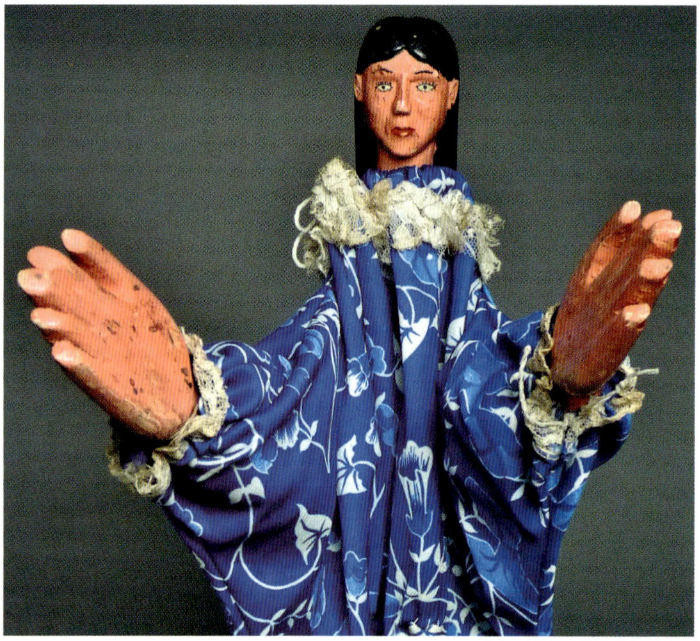
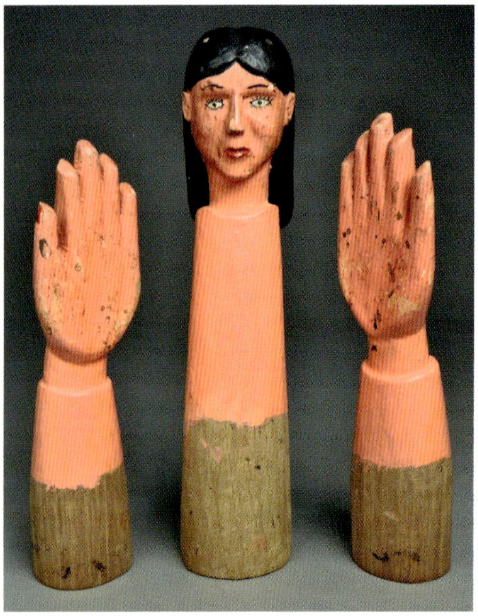
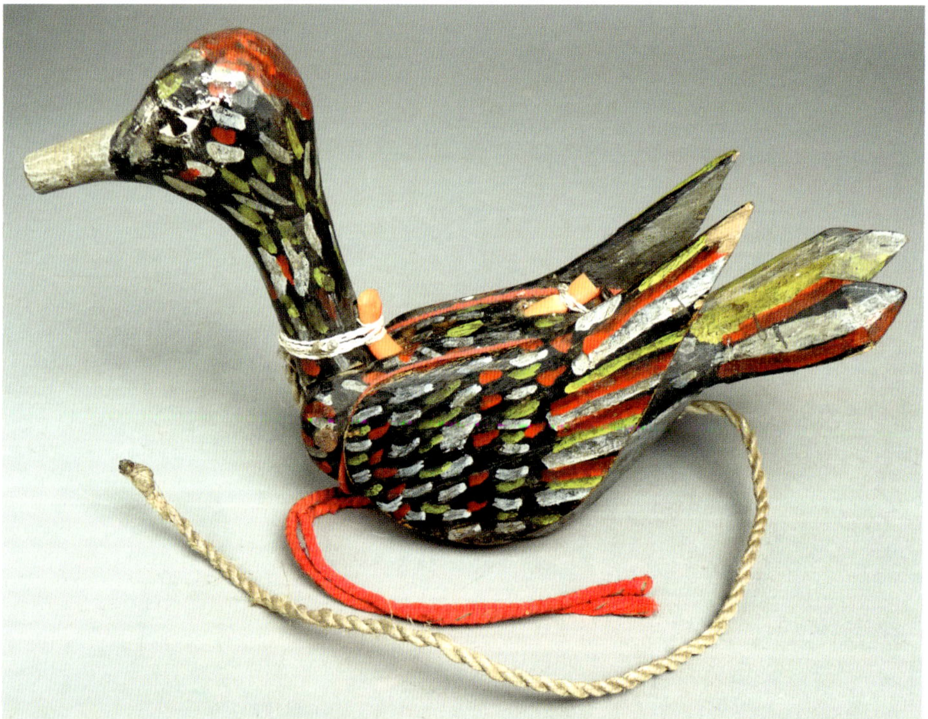
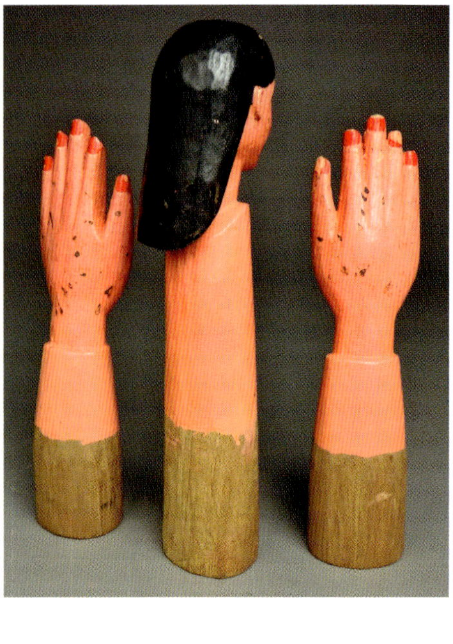
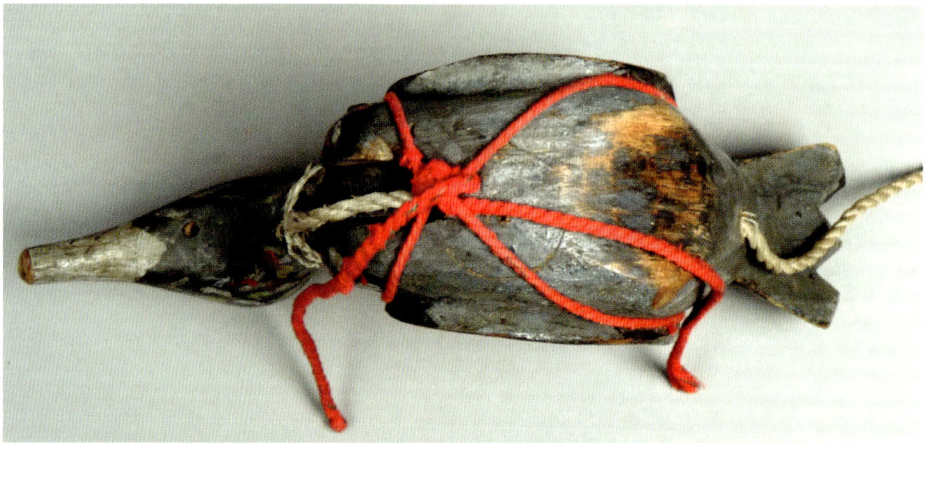

The Work of Leonel Lecona, of Huehuetla, Puebla

I'll include the work of Leonel Lecona with that of Kalimán, not only because their lives were so closely linked but also because this will introduce an example of a telón, the dance curtain necessary for the presentation of the puppets. When Carlos Moreno Vásquez and I visited Xonalpú, Puebla, in December 2010 we were pleased to discover that the Huehues there, led by Andrés Juárez García, were using a telón that had been painted by Leonel Lecona.

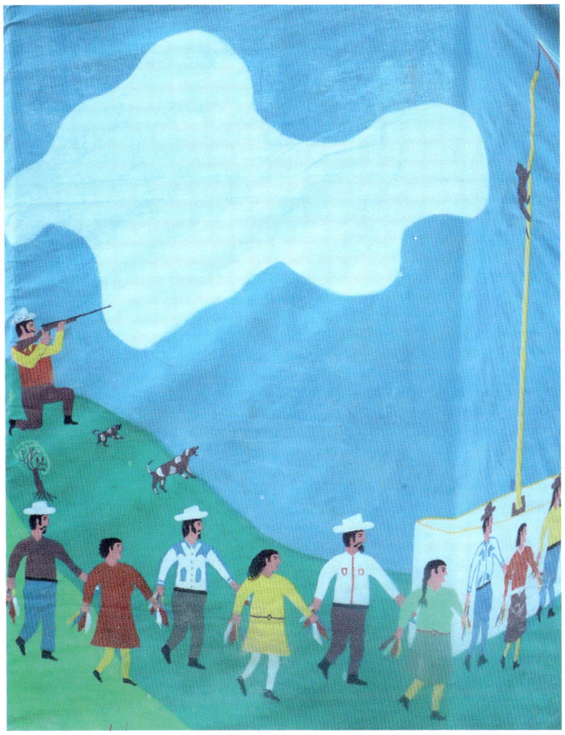

A panel from the telón that was painted by Leonel Lecona, which is current used by the Huehues dance group in Xonalpú, Puebla. On this panel the hunter shoots at the Tejón or coati, treed by two dogs. The colored ribbons at the top of the pole indicate that the Chénchere has already been up and down the pole, causing the opening of the guajillo. Often, but not in this case, the painting on the telón will show the Chénchere and the Tejón on the pole together, with a hunter or Payaso seeming to aim his rifle at both.

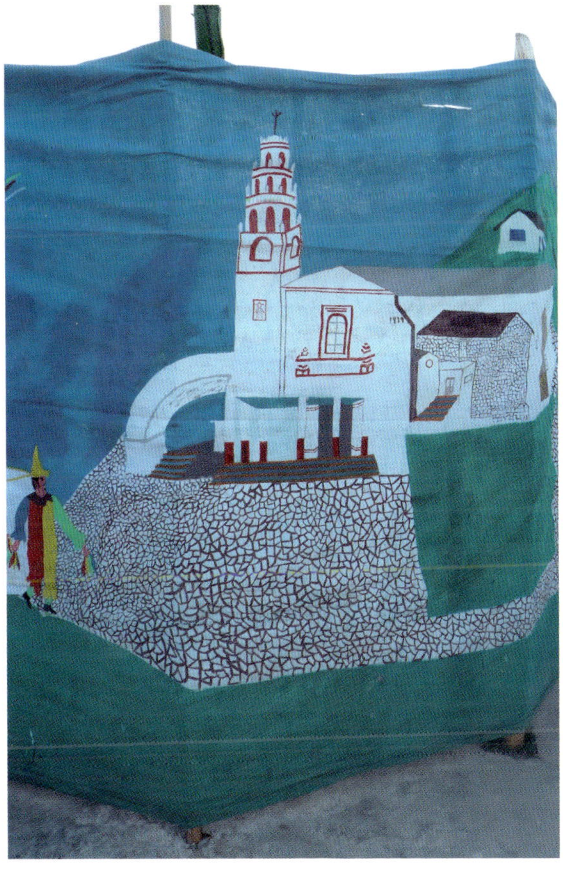

The dance area is customarily located in front of the church.

Opposite page, left:
Top: The view from the back, showing the same points.

Center: The wooden parts of the female puppet by Kalimán; the torso is 9" tall, the limbs are 8". Her appearance is dramatic, almost severe.

Bottom: The back view of the female puppet.

Opposite page, right:
Top: The female puppet from the same set by Kalimán, dramatic and stylized. Rating: known carver, good condition, excellent design, good paint and patina, and rare, *******. *Collection of the author.*

Center: The Chénchere from this puppet set; the extended length is 10". The form is again elegantly simple. The paint is vivid, in the absence of the grooves on wings and tail that we saw on the other Chénchere. On this side view you can see a red cord that is tied in a figure eight around the two wings. Rating: known carver, good condition, excellent design, good paint and patina, and rare, *******. *Collection of the author.*

Bottom: A bottom view of the same bird. The red string is wrapped around the wings in a figure eight and knotted at the Chénchere's breast, providing two red string-ends to tie to a hoisting loop. The white string that causes the neck to extend and peck goes through a drilled hole rather than through an exposed space, so it is not visible from the bottom. The base has a flat spot and lacks the round porthole. So this woodpecker is different from the other one by Kalimán in several details.

Manuel Aldana Valencia (Don Lillo)

In December 2007 we visited a man in the small village of Sabanas de Xalostoc, Veracruz, which is near Coxquihui. He had a set of puppets that were carved by Manuel Aldana Valencia, known as Don Lillo, but he was unwilling to sell this set. However, on a subsequent visit in December 2008, he did agree to sell them. They had been made 25 years earlier.

In these puppets by Don Lillo we see a general form which resembles that of the puppets of Kalimán, but much simpler in design and finish.

The figures themselves are pleasing but not particularly elegant.

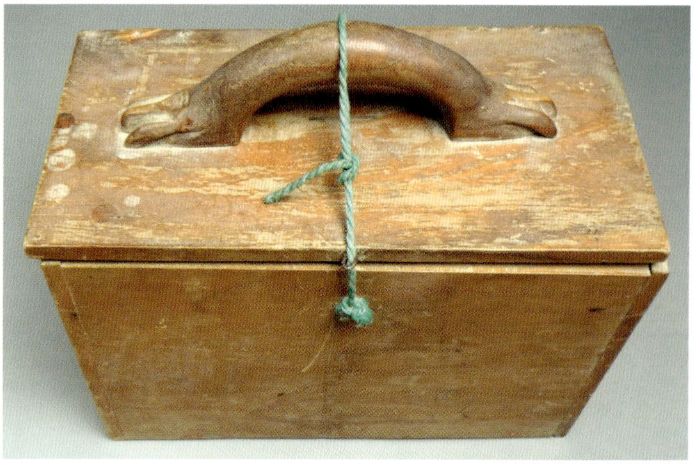

The original box for the Don Lillo puppet set from Sabanas de Xalostoc, Veracruz; the length is 11", height 8", and depth 6½". Note the unusual latching arrangement and the beautiful handle. Rating for this set: known carver, good condition, good design, good paint and patina, and rare, *****. *Collection of the author.*

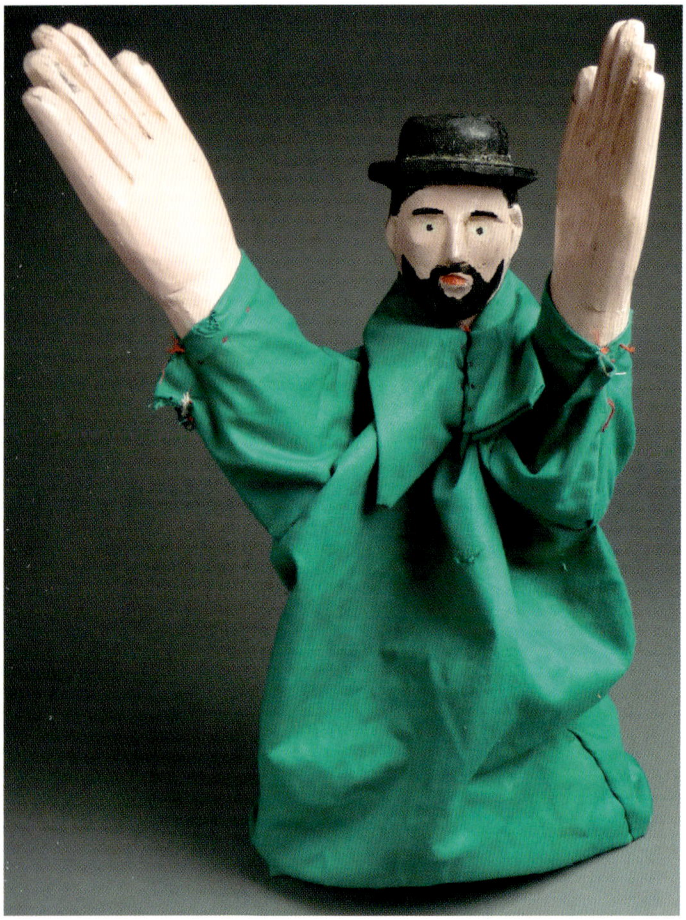

The male puppet in costume, which is stitched in place around his neck; the torso is 7", limbs 7". Circa 1983. Both the male and the female puppet have very simple torsos, with a narrow shelf below the neck to hold the costume up.

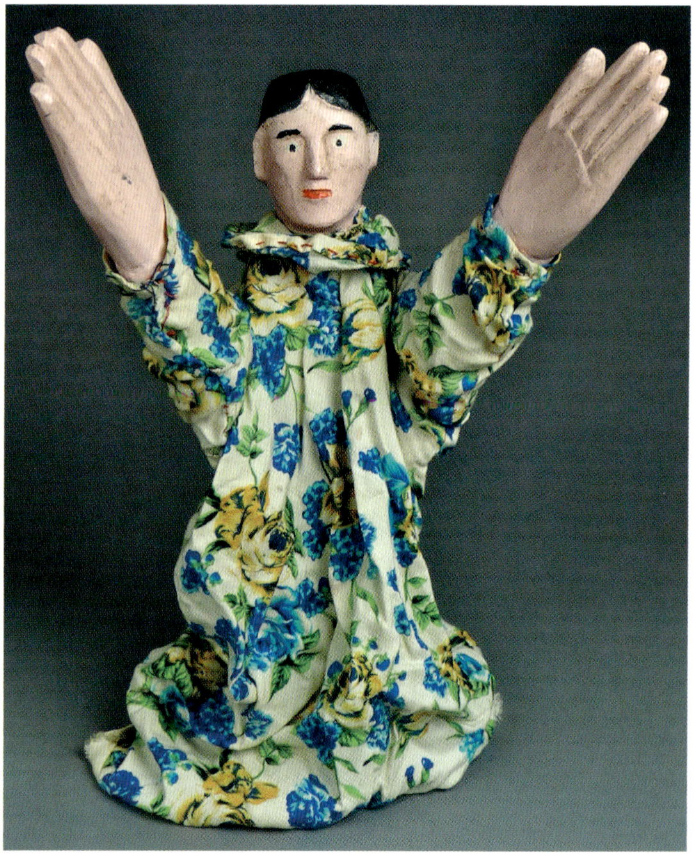

The female puppet from this set. Her costume is also stitched in place around her neck; the torso is 7", limbs 7". Like her partner, she lacks shoulders. A flat rim around the base of the neck supports the costume.

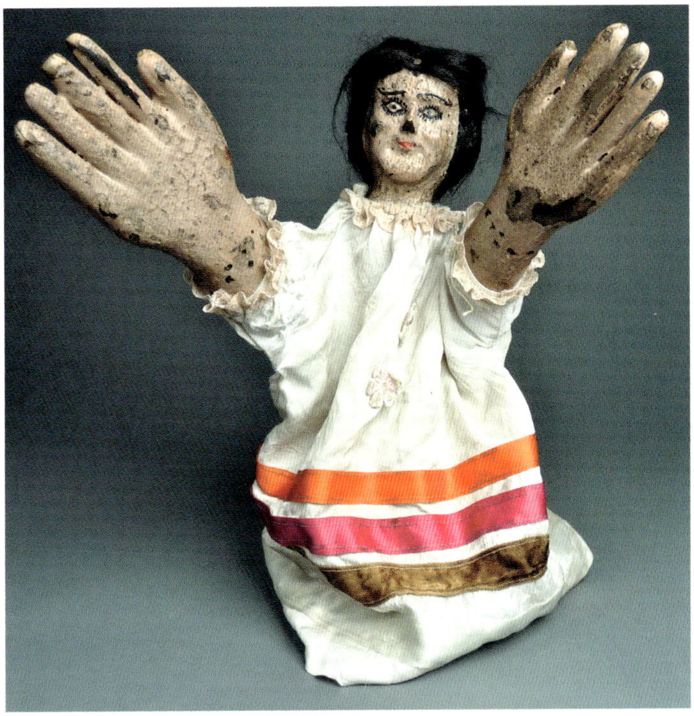

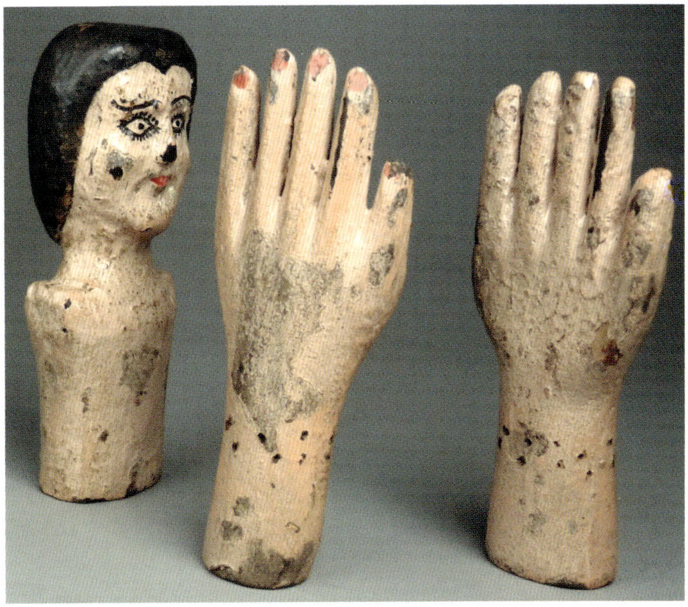

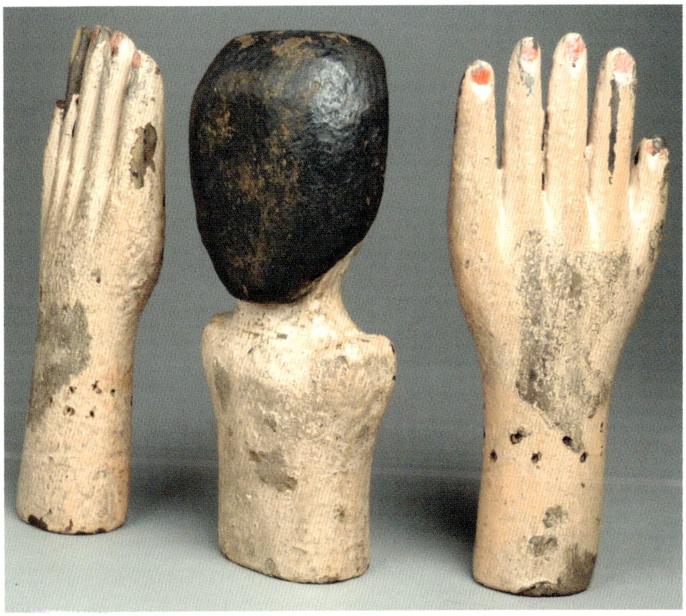

Above: The female puppet from the old Coxquihui set in her costume; the torso is 7", limbs 7". A wig is attached to her head with many tacks. Her old paint is unstable.

Upper right: The wooden parts of the female puppet from an angle. I have removed her wig, revealing a nice painted hairline.

Lower right: The wooden parts of the female puppet from the back. The shoulder stubs are present, though subtle.

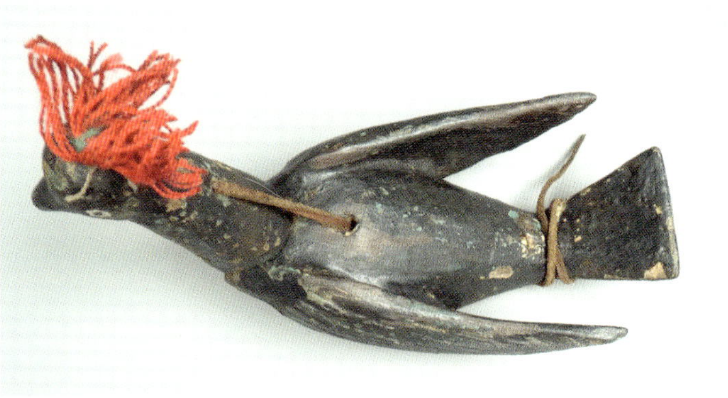

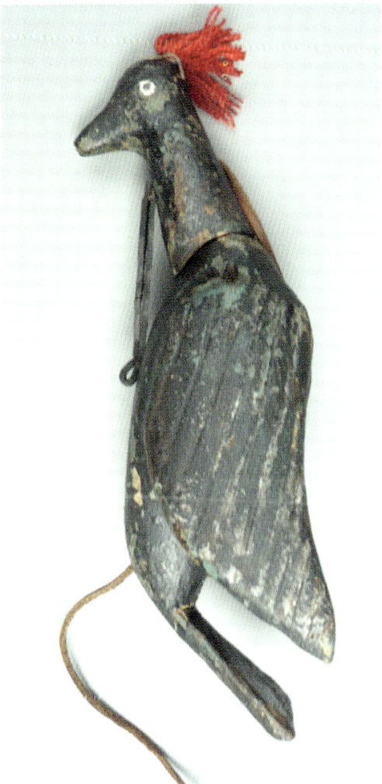

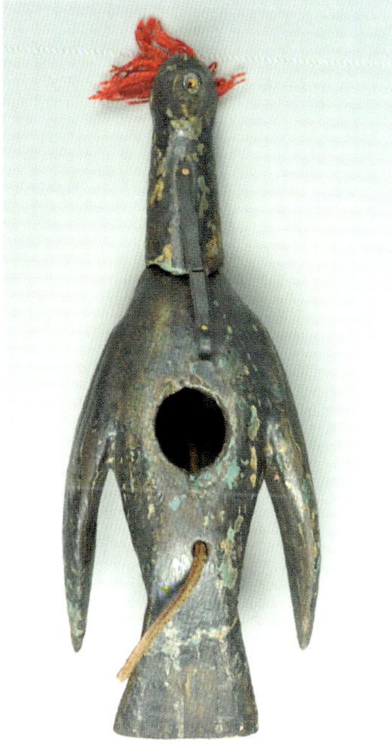

Above: The Chénchere seen from above. I have lashed the leather thong around the tail to photograph the woodpecker in the retracted position.

Near right: The Chénchere positioned as if pecking; 10" extended length.

Far right: The Chénchere, seen from below, has a very graceful shape. The nail in the bill has been lost. The strange arrangement of the thong and the rubber band can be observed.

Puppets by Francisco de Aquino

In late 2010 Carlos Moreno Vásquez located a set of puppets that were said to have been carved by Francisco de Aquino, of Xochitlán, Puebla. There was no Chénchere and no box.

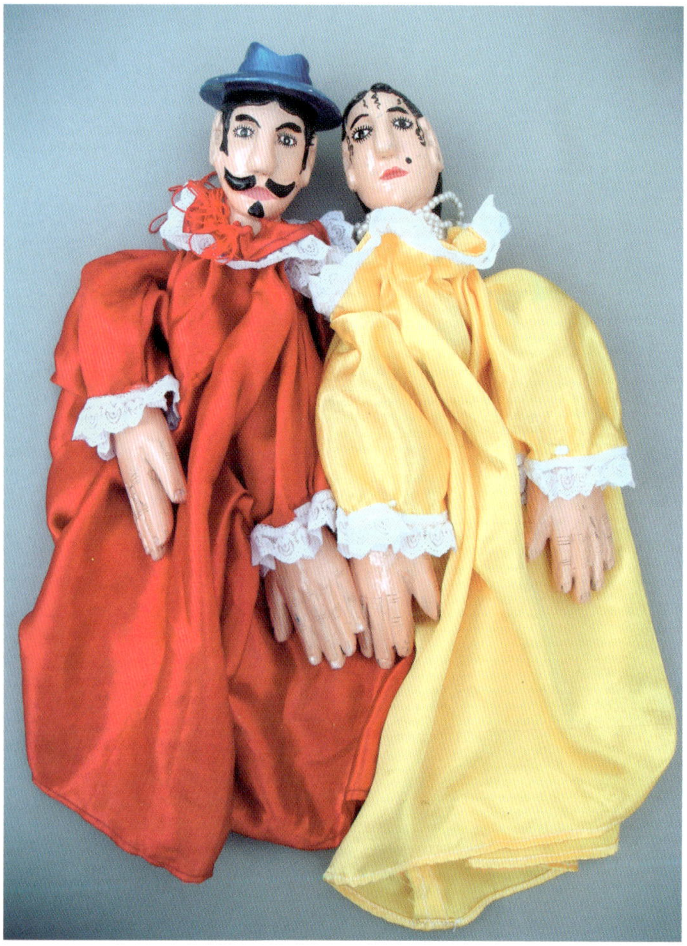

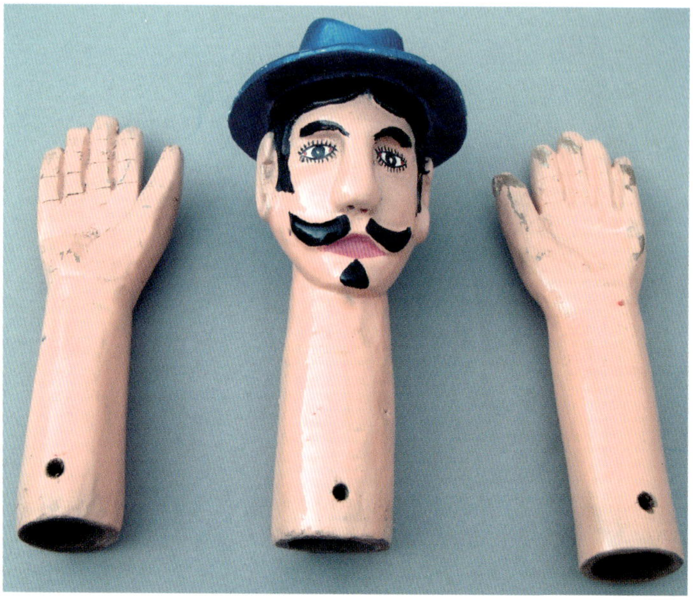

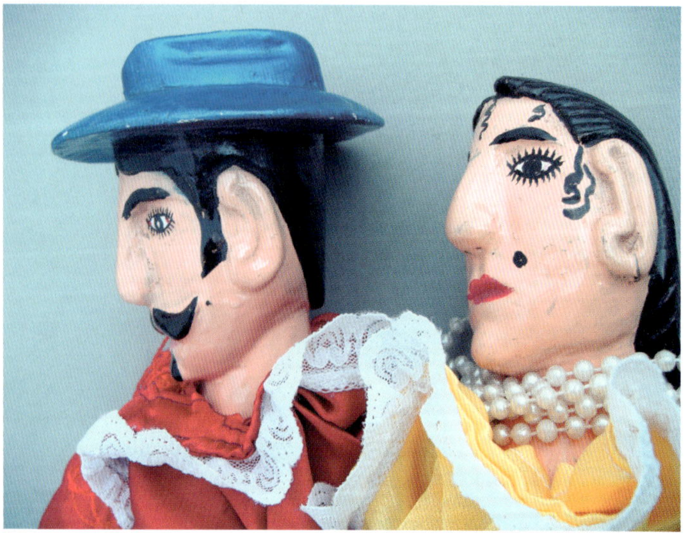

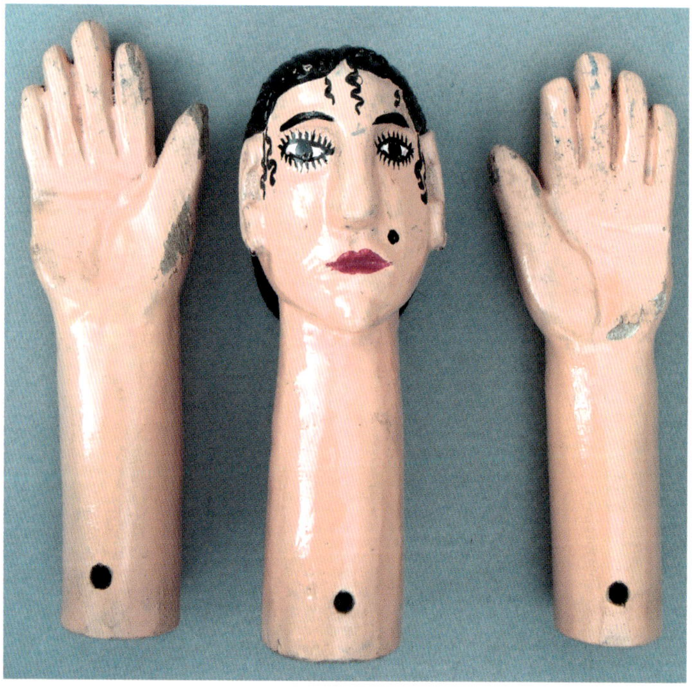

Top left: The pair of human puppets by Francisco. They appear to be new, having been repainted in 2005; they were made circa 1990. One's initial impression is of very modern features and a high level of carving. Rating: known carver, good condition, excellent design, recent paint with mild patina, and rare, *****. *Collection of Vernon Kostohryz.*

Bottom left: A close-up view of the faces of the two de Aquino puppets. We see dramatic carving details, including relief carving of the hair, ears, and mustache on the male and relief-carved hair and ears on the female.

Top right: The wooden elements of the male puppet by Francisco de Aquino; the torso is 7¼" tall, the limbs are also 7¼". There is wear on the hands, evidently from clapping.

Bottom right: The wooden elements of the female puppet; the torso is 6¾" tall, the limbs are 7¼". Again we see wear on the hands.

The Puppets of Simón Fernando García of Tuncuhuini, Veracruz

"Don Simón" sold us a set of puppets when we visited him in December 2007. We were as charmed by the box as by the puppets themselves.

The puppets themselves were simple in design, but effective. The hands have a quality of folk carving that is quite charming.

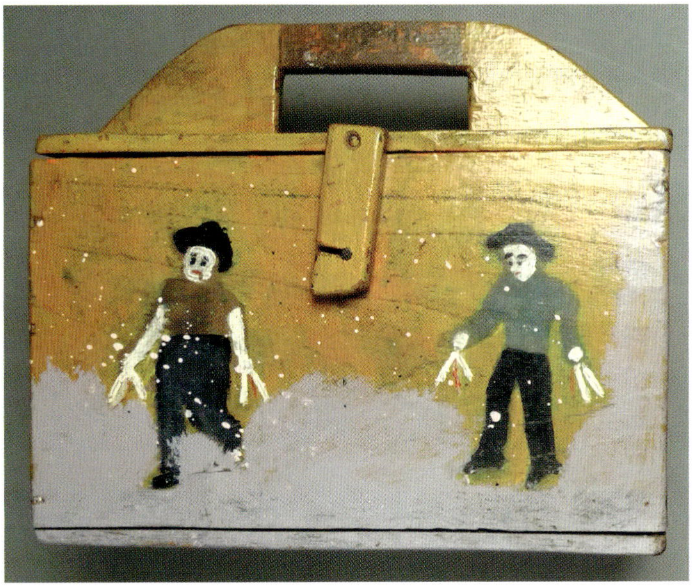

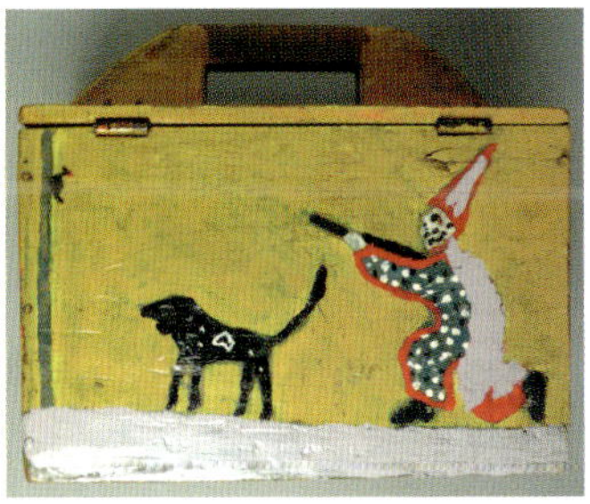

Above: The front view of Don Simón's puppet box, showing Tejonero dancers with scarves hanging from both hands. The design of the latch is ingenious. Circa 2000. Rating for this set: known carver, good condition, good design, good patina, and rare, *****. *Collection of the author.*

Left: On the back, a Payaso pretends to shoot at the Chénchere as it pecks its way up the pole.

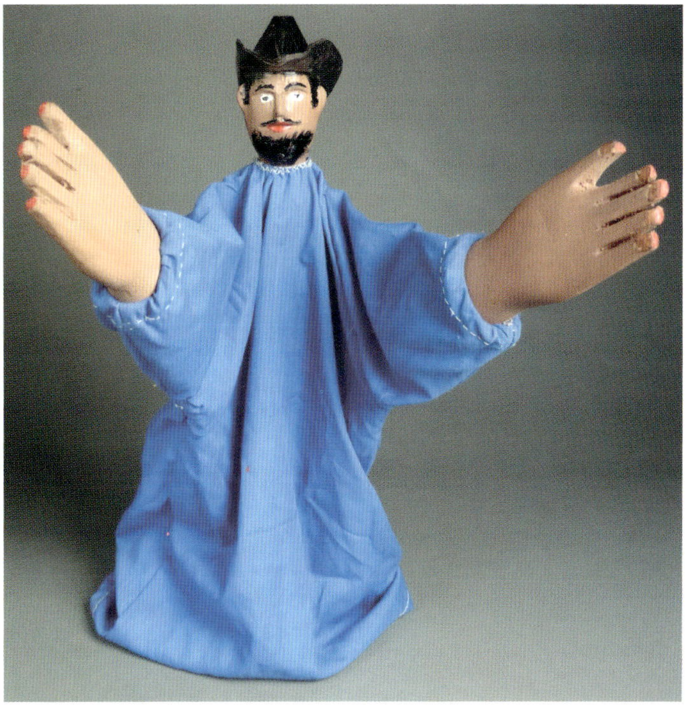

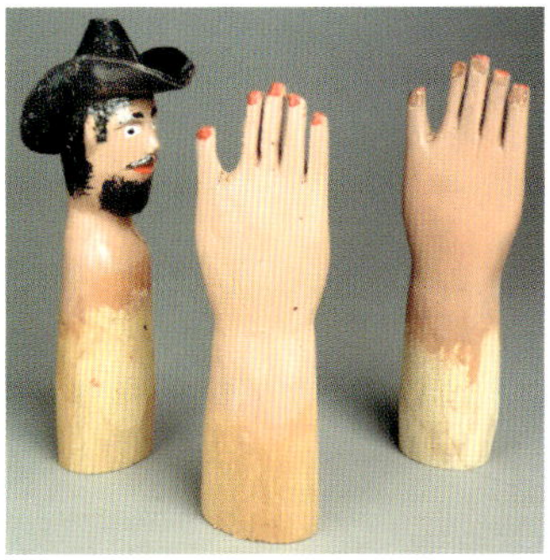

Above: The male puppet from Don Simón's set in costume; the torso is 7" tall, limbs also 7". His hat, constructed of leather or cardboard, is applied.

Left: The wooden elements of the male puppet.

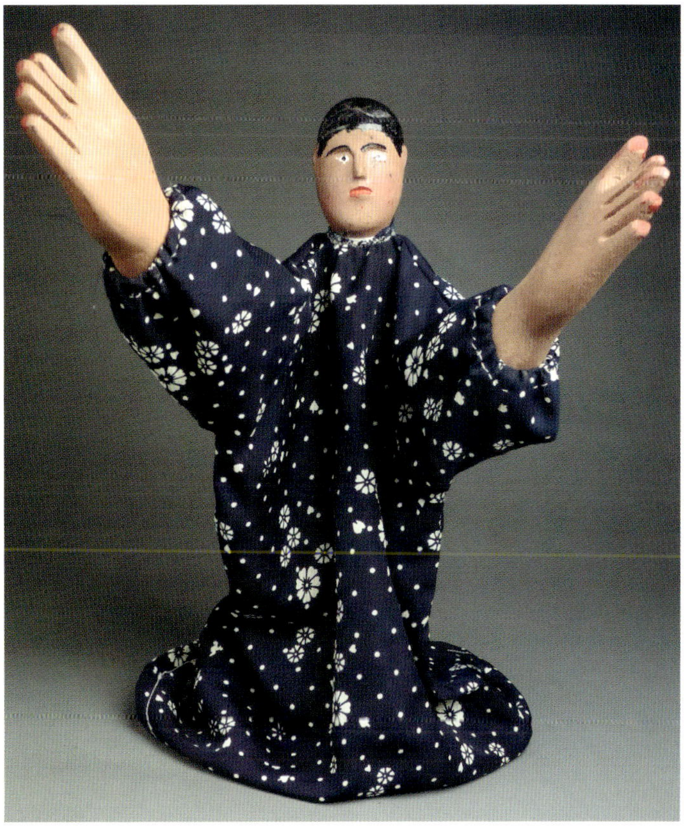

Right: The female puppet from Don Simón's set in costume; her torso is 6½" tall, limbs also 6½".

Below: The wooden elements of the female puppet.

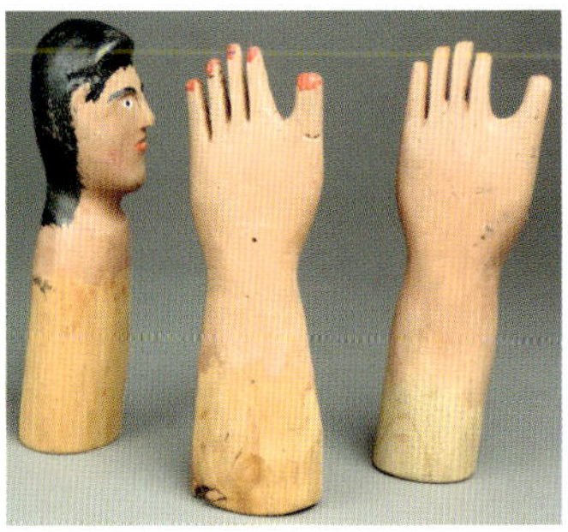

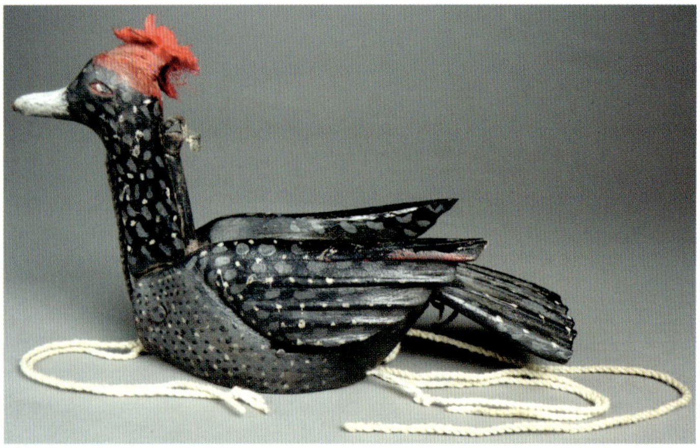

The Chénchere from this set is very nicely carved. The tail is hinged, permitting it to flap. The bottom of the bird is flat and oval. This puppet provides a particularly clear view of the string arrangement. On the bottom, a string loops from the center cavity to the front to provide a connecting point for the lifting string, while another loop around the back anchors a string that drops down to stabilize the woodpecker. The string that extends the neck tunnels through the breast, crosses the open area, and then tunnels out the back, to tie to a descending string.

In December 2010 Carlos Moreno Vásquez and I visited the Tejoneros dance leader in Sabanas de Xalostoc, where we found another set of puppets by Don Simón. These were in their closed box on the household altar. Once again Simón had painted designs on the box that were related to the dance.

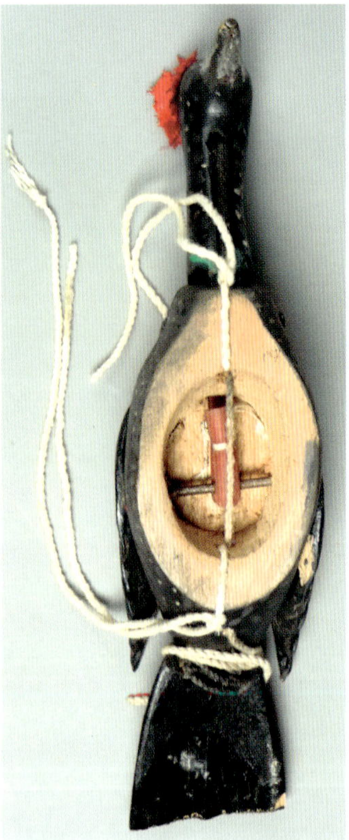

Above: Viewed from the side, one finds very attractive carving on the Chénchere from Don Simón's set, with grooved wings and tail: the extended length is 12". On close inspection one can see the usual rubber tubing that pulls the neck back after each peck, and the string that runs down the front of the neck.

Left: Here we see yet another variation on the design of the base of a woodpecker.

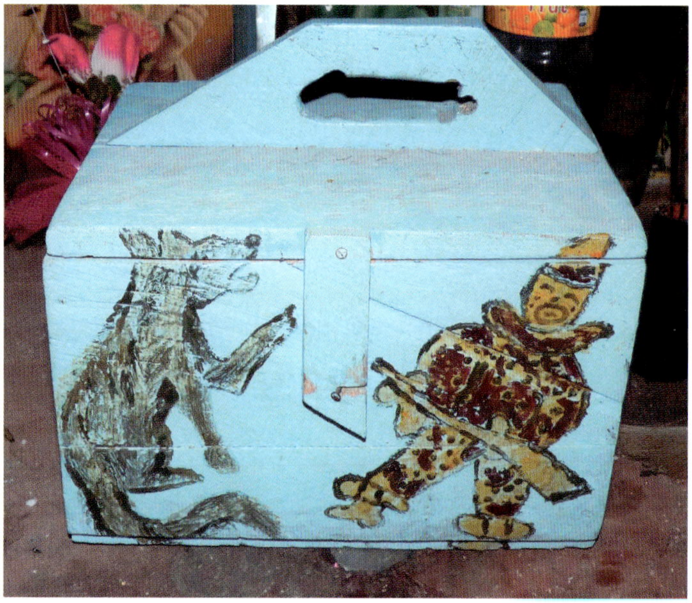

A closer view of the puppet box from Sabana de Xalostoc. A Perro and a Payaso are apparently preparing to hunt the Tejón.

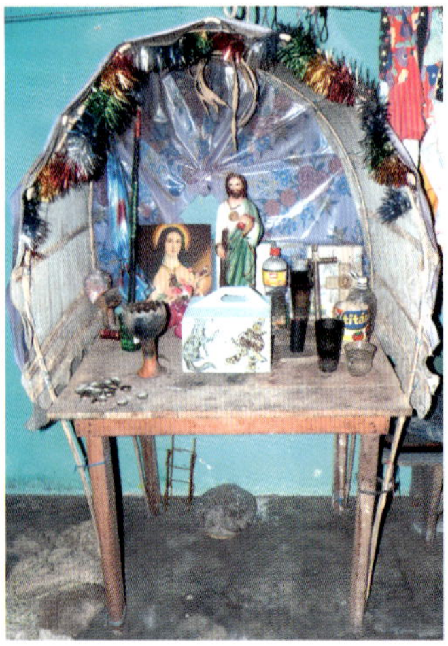

The altar at Sabanas de Xalostoc with the puppet box. *Photos courtesy of the dance group.*

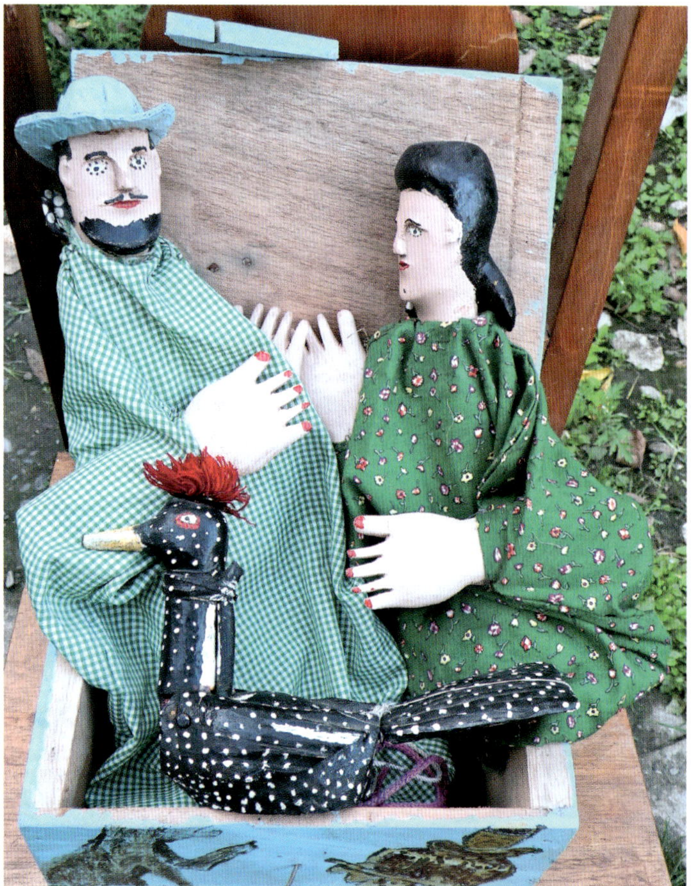

The Chénchere at Sabana de Xalostoc has a hinged tail, laced to the body just like the previous one. The male puppet has a hat made of cardboard. The female puppet has a remarkable hairdo.

José González Galindo Puppets

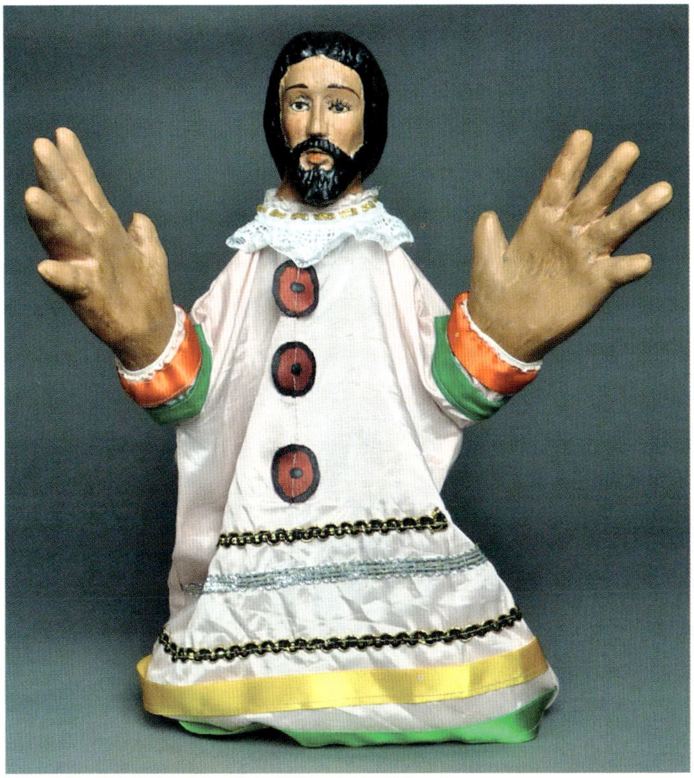

Several years ago Carlos brought Vernon Kostohryz an old and unusual set of puppets that he found in Tuzamapan, Puebla. They were very well carved, at the level that made one think of Roberto Villegas; however, Roberto denied being their maker. Furthermore, the hands are unlike those of any of the other puppets described in this chapter, including those of Roberto, in that the fingers are widely separated and naturalistically carved. The Chénchere in this set did not resemble those of Roberto either.

Also anomalous was the fact that the finely carved male puppet had been provided with a carved wooden sombrero, though Vernon and I both suspected that this was a later addition. It was nailed firmly to the head of the puppet, but under the edge of the hat one could see that the hair was carefully carved, as if the figure was originally bareheaded. Indeed, the male puppet had the appearance of a saint; it was difficult not to think that this was a rather literal representation of San José or even Christ. To find such a head wearing the hat of a clown or *campesino* seemed to represent excessive artistic license.

Another problem was that prior costumes had been repeatedly attached to the puppets with metal tacks; the puppets were riddled with holes. The most recent costumes were worn to shreds, so Vernon had arranged for new costumes. The seamstress elected to dress the puppets as clowns.

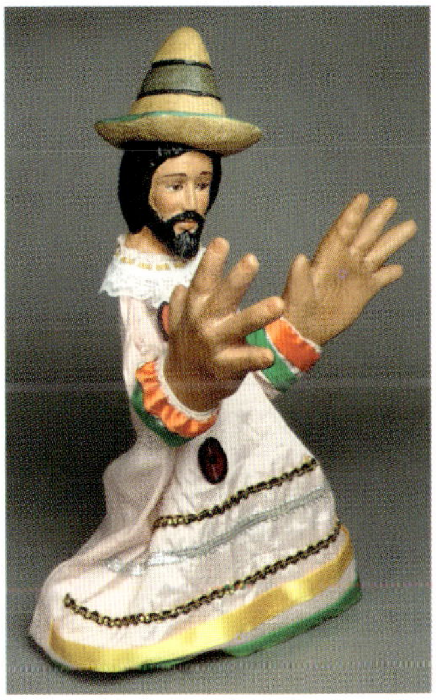

For a year I simply pondered these puppets. I knew that, if I acquired them, I would feel compelled to have the hat removed and the tack holes patched. Eventually I purchased them from Vernon and immediately turned them over to a restorer. As predicted, the pattern of the carved hair extended to the top of the head. The female has painted hair under her wig.

I'll show the male puppet with and without his hat because I believe that both presentations are relevant. We could think of this puppet as a transitional sculpture, a traditional design that has been adapted in the modern era. The puppet was apparently created in the image of San José or Francisco (Christ); but for some reason this identity has become less important.

The set, which was last used to teach schoolchildren about local dance traditions, was housed in a typical box. However, this was painted with very fanciful decorations, obviously the work of Germán Guerrero.

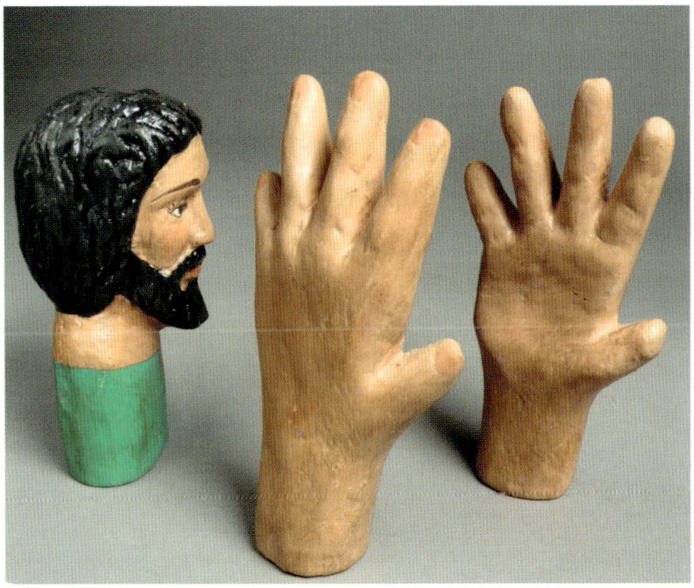

Top: The male puppet from a set probably carved by José González Galindo, in his clown costume; the torso is 6" tall, limbs 6". Age unknown, circa 1970 or older. Note the unusual design of the hands. They look so strange in comparison to the hands found on other puppets from this region. Ironically, this is because they are more realistically carved than any of the others; the carving closely matches normal anatomy. The head of this puppet looks like the head of a traditional carving of a Roman Catholic Saint. Rating: probably known carver, good condition, excellent design, marked patina, and rare, ******. *Collection of the author.*

Center: The male puppet wearing his sombrero; the sombrero itself is 4" tall. This angle provides different views of the puppet's head and hands

Bottom: The puppet's wooden elements, seen from the side. This is the head that emerged when the sombrero was removed.

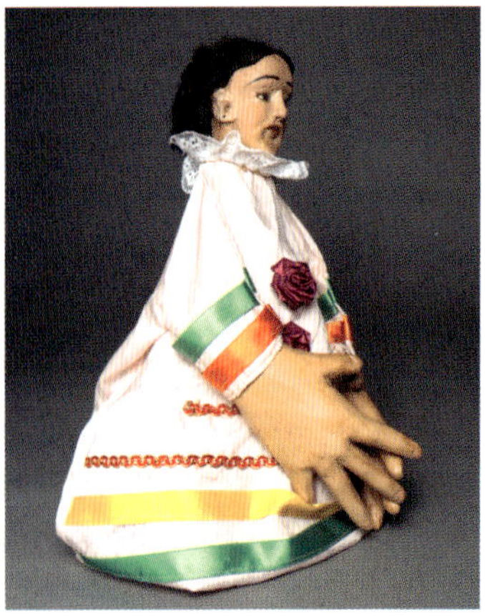

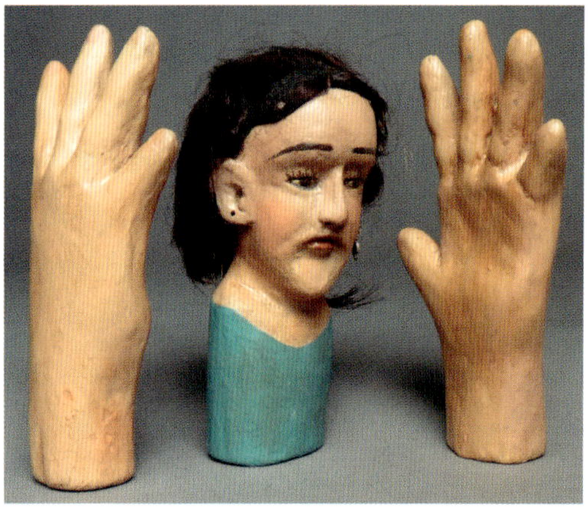

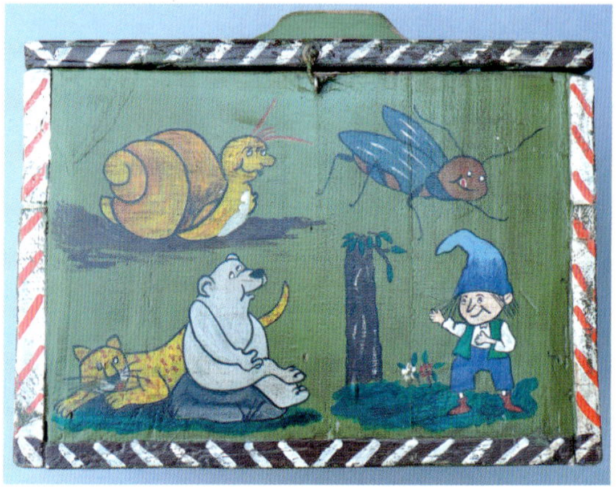

Above left: A female puppet from the same set in her clown costume; her torso is 6", limbs 6". Again it seems that her expression is that of a saint and not that of a clown.

Above center: The wooden parts of the female puppet.

Above right: The front panel of the box for these puppets, painted by Germán Guerrero. The width is 14", the height 10", and it is 9" deep.

The Chénchere that came with these puppets is nicely carved and unusual in form.

When we visited the workshop of José González Galindo in March 2010, we were shown a small but attractive Chénchere, as yet unfinished. I took photographs, although at the time it didn't seem very striking, being unpainted and incomplete. Later we realized that the brown Chénchere in the mystery set was essentially identical to the little one, but larger and, of course, much older. So we have concluded that the set was probably made by Señor González Galindo.

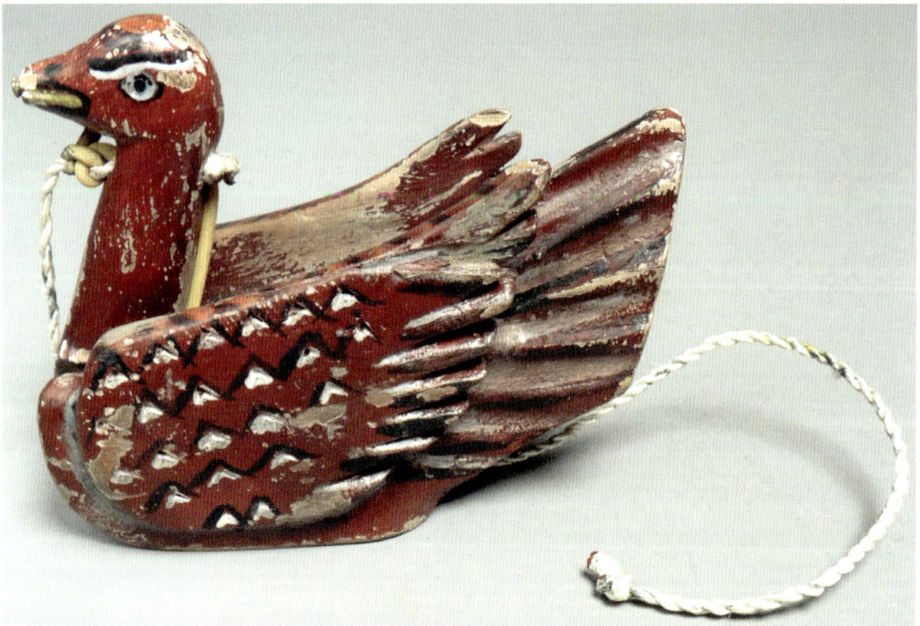

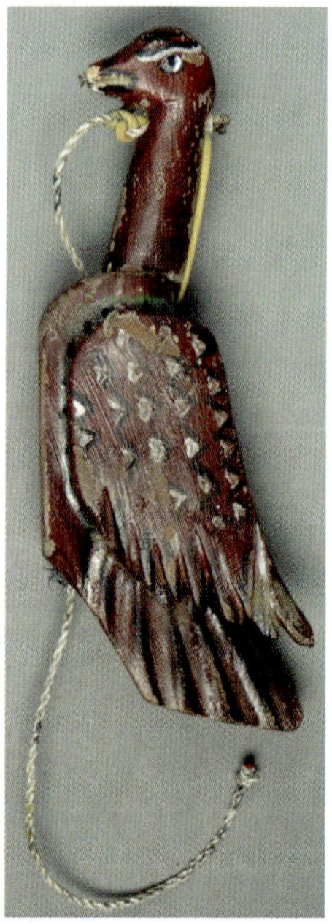

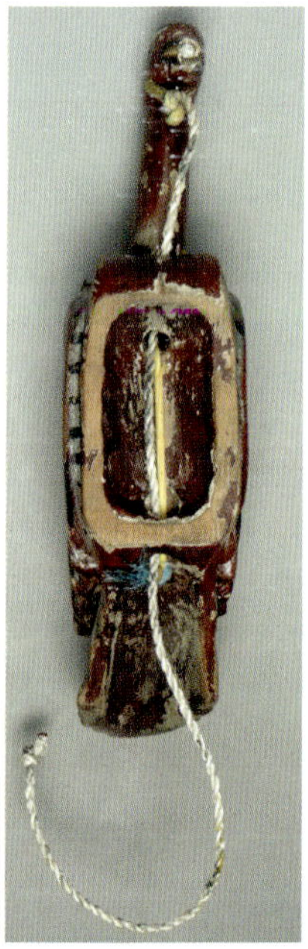

Above left: Seen from one side, the woodpecker from the José González set has the usual mechanical design; a rubber piece retracts the neck while a string pulls the head forward. The decorative grooving is dramatic and unusual. In this photo the wings appear to be applied, but actually they were carved in place, from the same block.

Above center: Here the neck is extended as if ready to peck; length extended is 10".

Above right: Seen from below, the base is flat and rectangular. The tail is V-shaped and hollow.

You may wonder why we haven't simply asked José if he was the carver of these puppets. Actually we have asked him such questions in the past. We discovered that Don José will quickly claim many masks, apparently because he means to convey his willingness and ability to duplicate anything that a customer might desire. We came to believe that such answers were more confusing than helpful, so I decided to concentrate on observed stylistic details to identify José's work. In this case I think that the new Chénchere in his workshop provides fairly solid evidence.

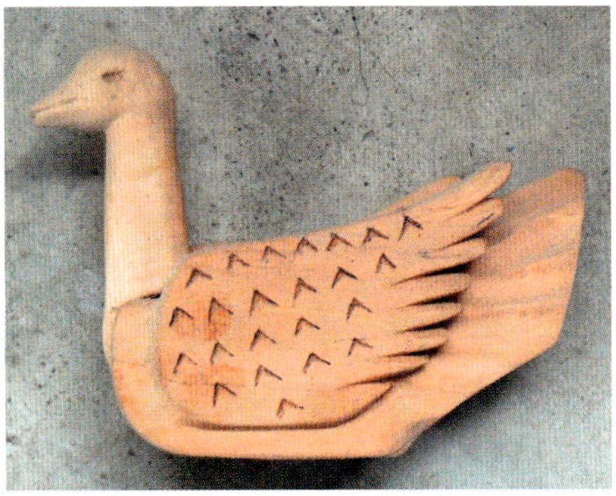

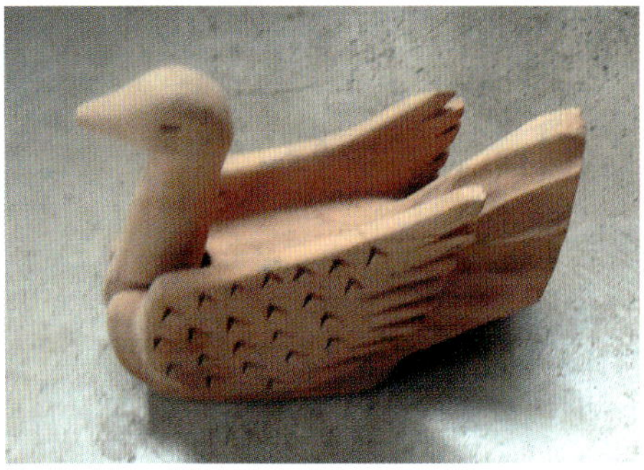

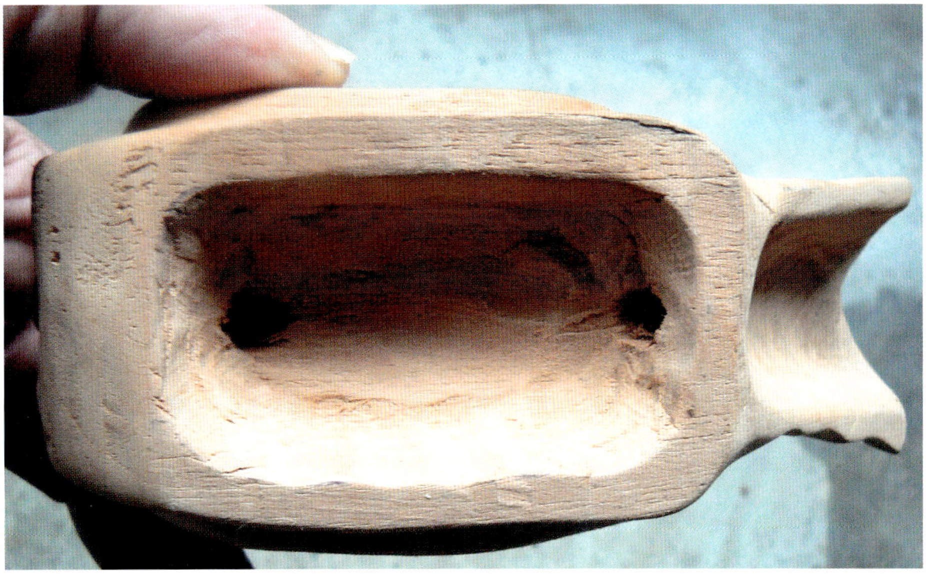

Upper left: A side view of the small, unfinished Chénchere at José González's workshop in March 2010. Note the shape of the head, neck, body, and wings, all identical to these elements in the older brown Chénchere. Likewise note the very distinctive V-shaped carvings on the wings and the grooves on the tail, also exactly the same.

Upper right: The Chénchere viewed from an angle. The image is poorly focused but it does demonstrate that the wings are carved as a part of the body of the bird, just as for the larger brown one.

Right: The bottom of this woodpecker is also carved with exactly the same design as the other. Because it is smaller, the hollow underside of the tail has a slightly different appearance.

Andrés Juárez García and Pedro Juárez García

Also in December 2010 I saw puppets dance in Xonalpú, a small mountain town near Huehuetla, Puebla. You have already seen the telón, painted by Leonel Lecona. The male and female puppets were carved in about 2006 by Andrés Juárez García; the Chénchere was carved about 20 years ago by the father of Andrés, Pedro Juárez García. I can report that this Chénchere functioned very effectively during that fiesta. This set had no box.

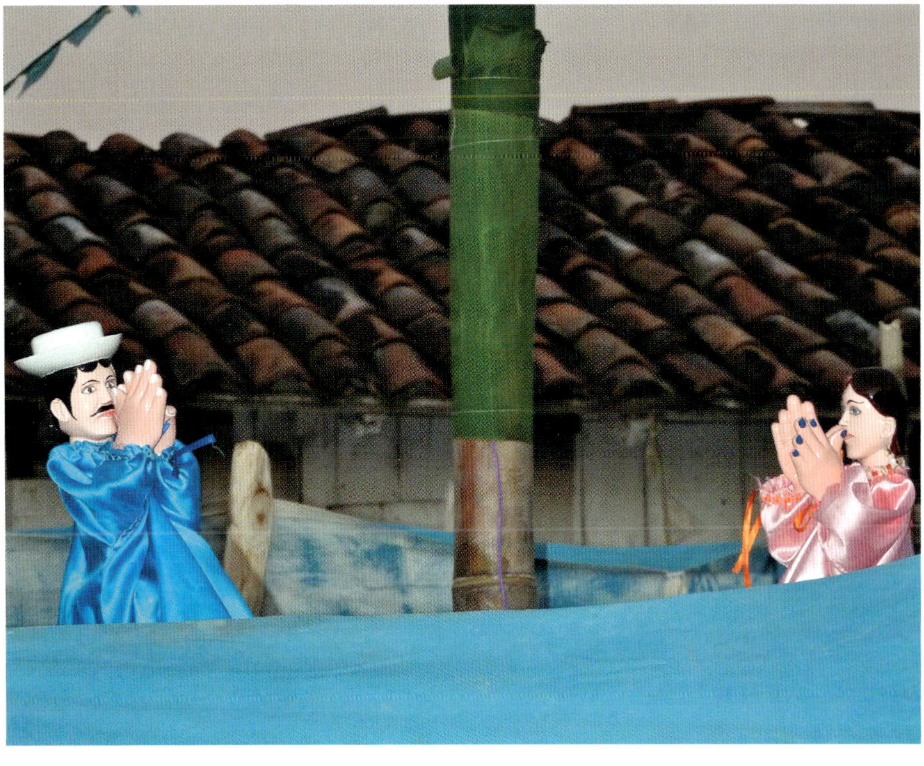

The Andrés Juárez García puppets dancing and clapping their hands at Xonalpú, Puebla, in December 2010.

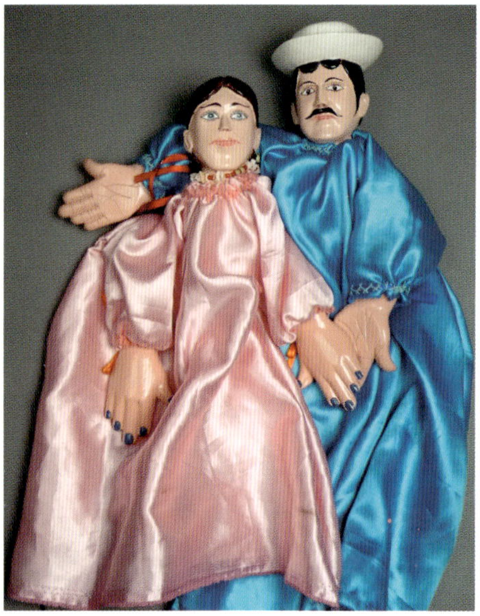

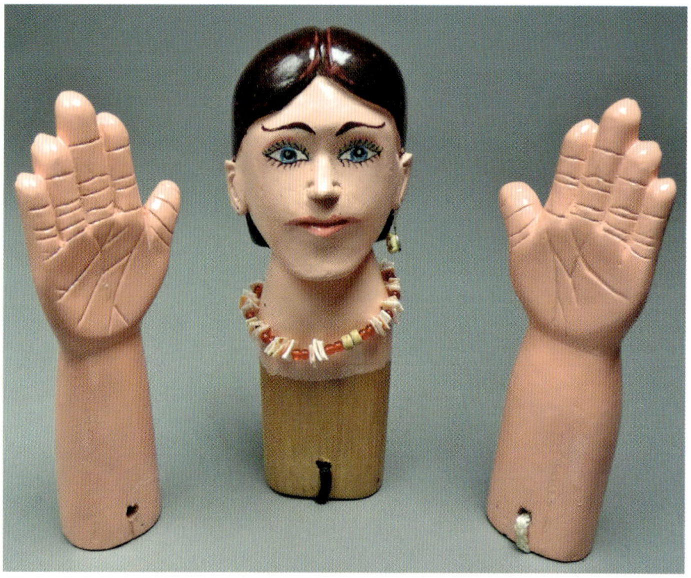

Far left: The two puppets in costume. They are very well carved, beautifully painted, and stylishly dressed. Circa 2006. Rating: known carver, good condition, excellent design, good paint and patina, and probably not rare, *****. *Collection of the author.*

Near left: The wooden elements of the beautiful female puppet by Andrés; the torso is 7" tall, limbs 6½".

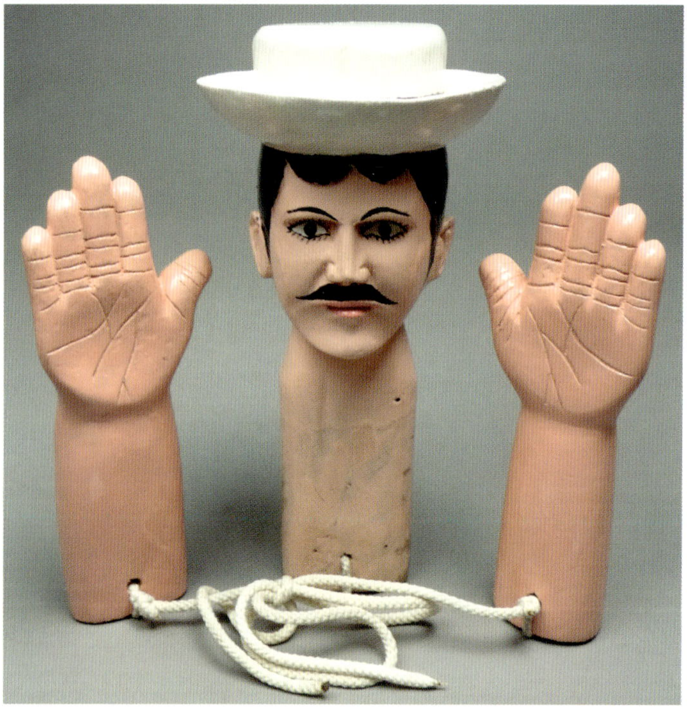

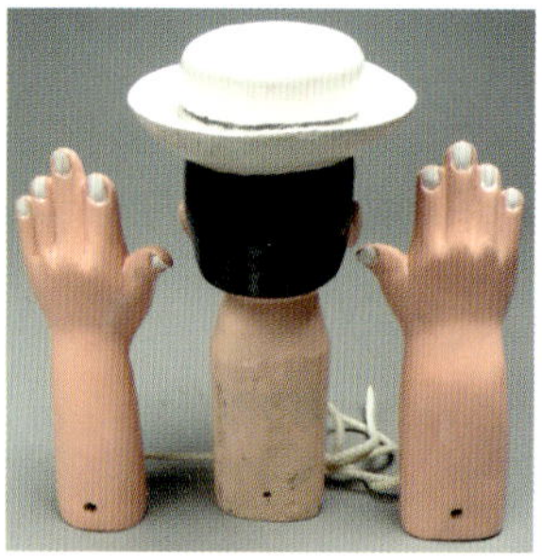

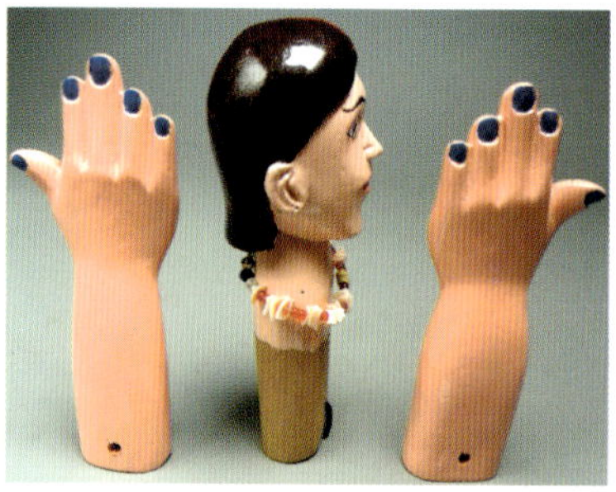

Left: The wooden elements of the male puppet; the torso is 8" tall, limbs 6½".

Above left: The wooden elements of the male puppet from behind. His hat is carved in place.

Above right: A view of the female puppet from the side; even the carving of her hands is highly stylized.

Lower left: The Chénchere that was carved by Pedro Juárez García, viewed from an angle. Rating: known carver, good condition, excellent design, good paint and patina, and probably rare, ******. *Collection of the author.*

Below left: The same Chénchere, viewed from above. The wings are applied.

Below right: The Chénchere from below. The string to extend the neck tunnels though the body without the usual porthole. The loop of string to attach the hoisting ropes is in place.

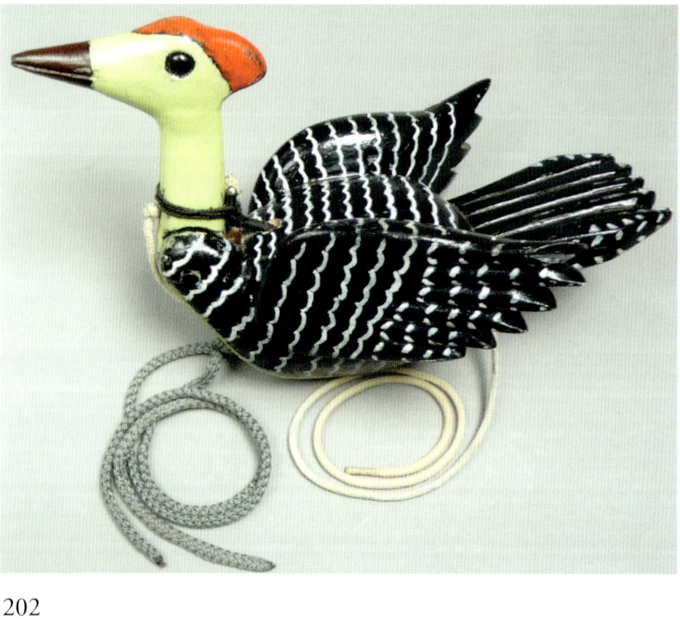

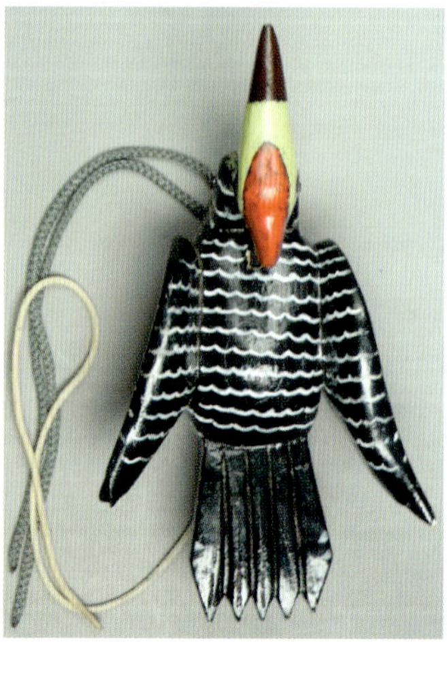

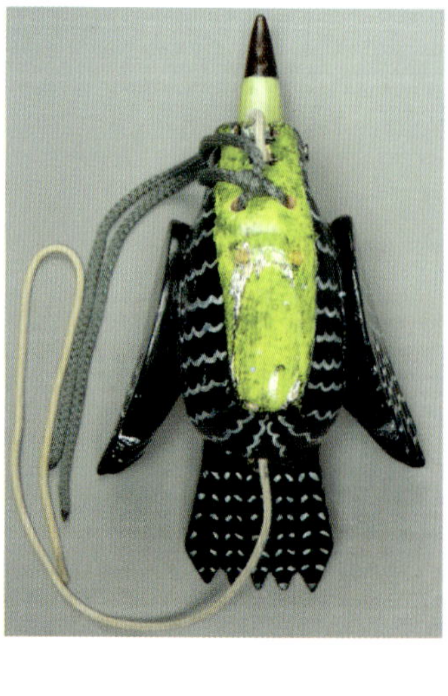

Puppets by Benito Juárez Figueroa

For several years Vernon, Carlos Moreno Vásquez, and I had been searching for a puppet set by Benito Juárez Figueroa because we hold his masks in such high esteem and hoped that his puppets would be equally impressive. Eventually Vernon commissioned Benito's daughter Alina to find a set in Filomeno Mata, and she was soon successful.

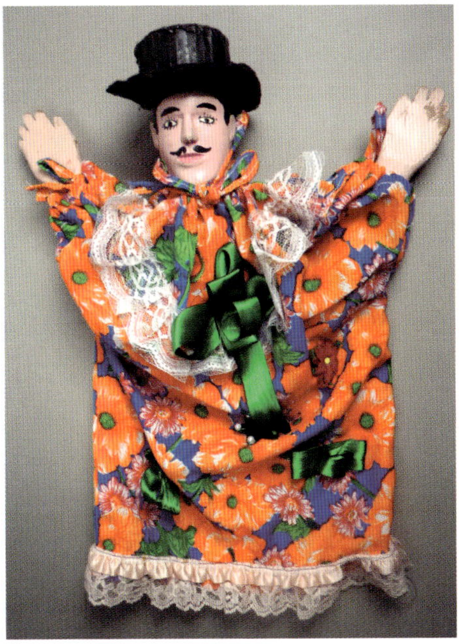

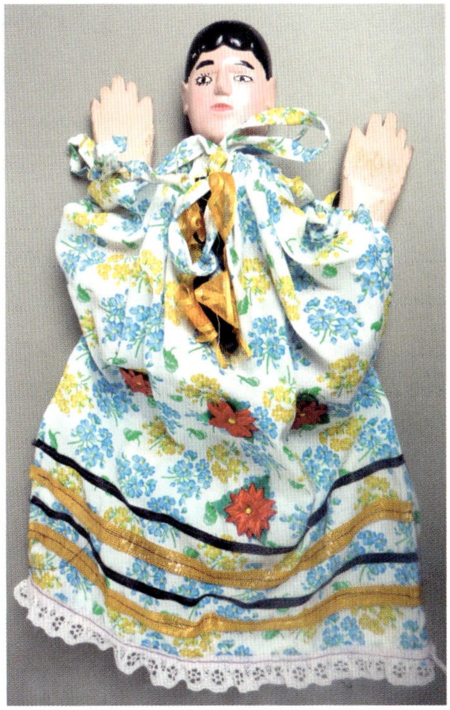

Left:
The male puppet by Benito Juárez in his costume; the torso is 8½" tall, the limbs 7¼". The costume is a new replacement, but the paper hat came with the puppet. A notable feature is that the palms are flat. Rating: known carver, good condition, excellent design, good paint and patina, and extremely rare, ******. *Collection of Vernon Kostobryz.*

Right:
The female puppet by Benito Juárez; the torso is 8" tall, the limbs 7¼". We can observe wear on both palms. Her hair is carved in relief for the full circumference of her head. Rating: known carver, good condition, excellent design, good paint and patina, and extremely rare, ******. *Collection of Vernon Kostobryz.*

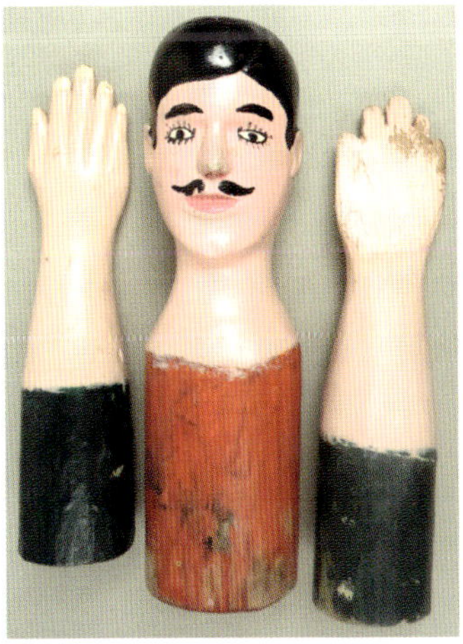

The wooden parts of the male puppet by Benito Juárez. One observes that the back of the right hand is very nicely carved, and has the usual carved nails. The hair is carved, with a part, in low relief across the brow. One assesses wear or patina by looking at the areas that, being hidden by the costume, are less likely to be repainted. In this case we can see that the paint is worn on the lower ends. Also there is wear on the left palm, apparently from clapping.

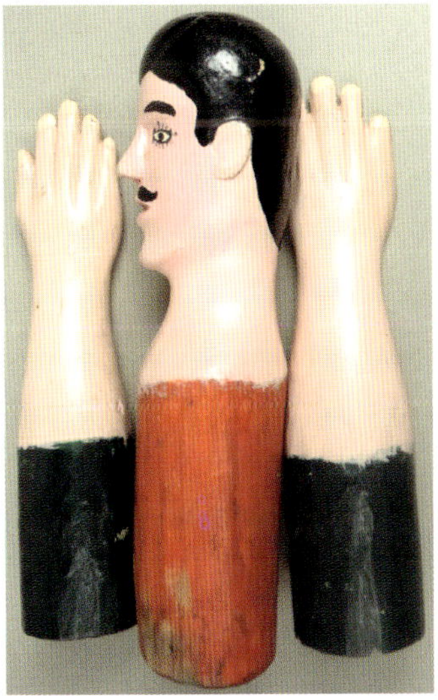

From the side, the ears are carefully carved.

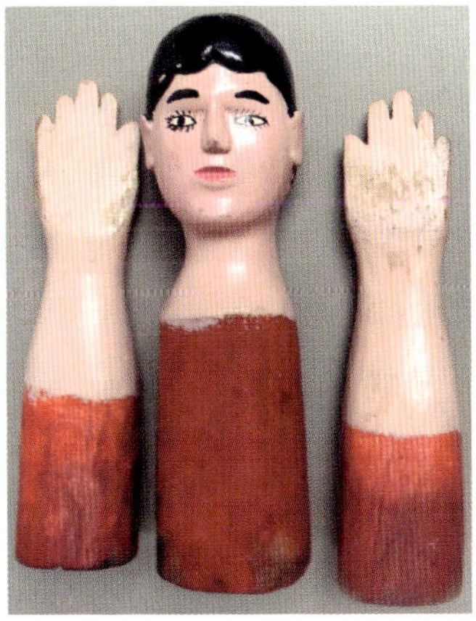

The wooden elements of the female puppet. We see simple lines, very smoothly carved.

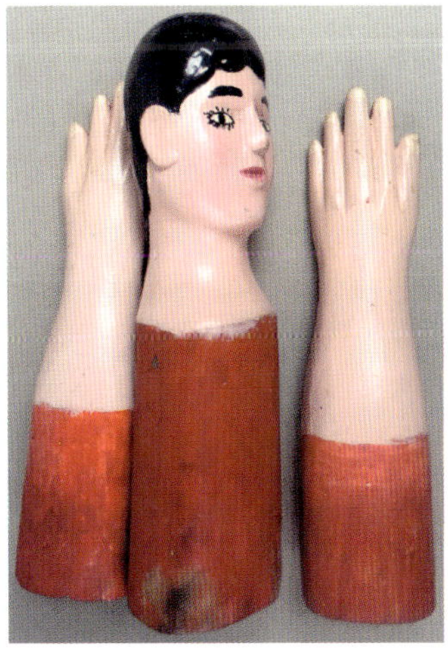

From the side, an elegant little puppet. The ears are carefully carved. We see worn red paint at the bottom of the torso.

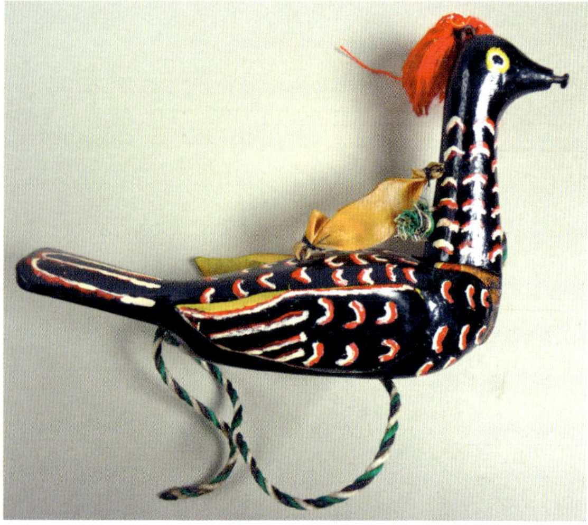

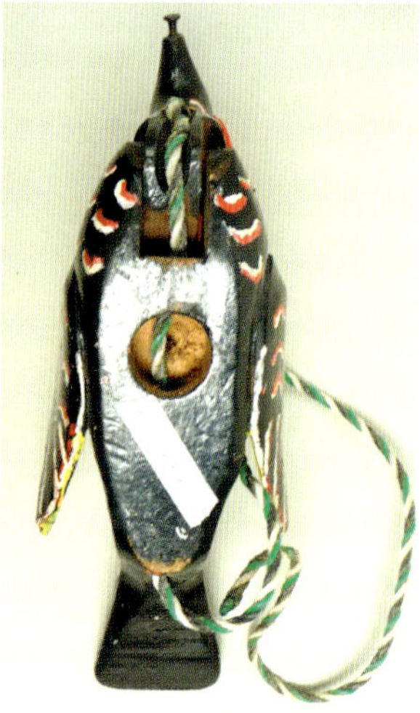

Far left: The Chénchere by Benito Juárez from this set; extended length is 12". The very graceful wings are applied. It is rather standard in its layout, only unusual for the use of metal staples to anchor the rubber tubing and the red yarn topknot. Rating: known carver, good condition, excellent design, good paint and patina, and extremely rare, ******. *Collection of Vernon Kostohryz.*

Near left: The Chénchere viewed from below, notable for the long flat spot on the bottom. Otherwise it could have been carved by Don Lillo.

A Puppet by José Juárez García

José was the father of Benito Juárez Figueroa and the grandfather of Alina Juárez Pérez. From Alina we obtained this old string puppet that had been made by her grandfather. I have no idea whether it was used in the Tejoneros or Huehues dance. So little is known about the history of the use of puppets in these dances that I am including it.

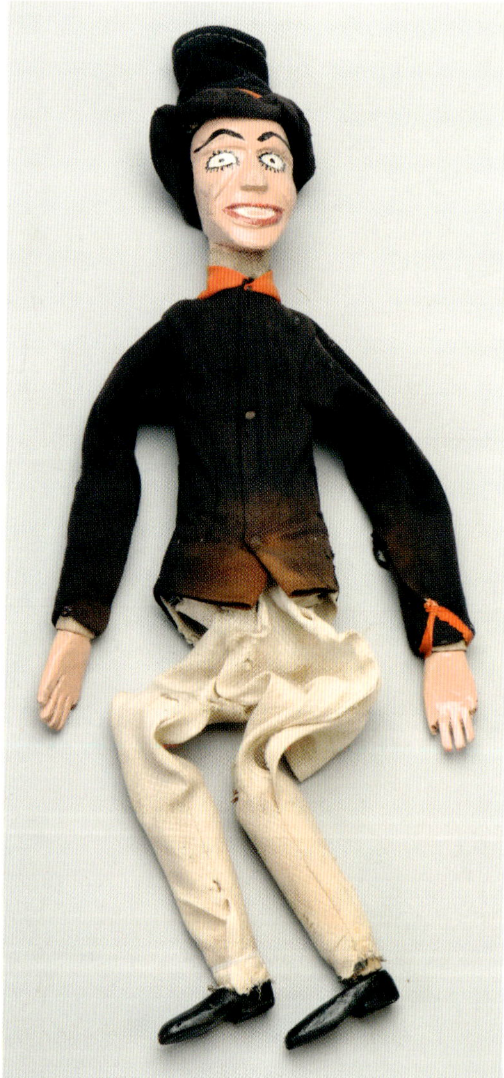

A string puppet that was reportedly made by José Juárez García; the length is 19". Circa 1900. The face was recently repainted; I believe this was by Alina Juárez Pérez.

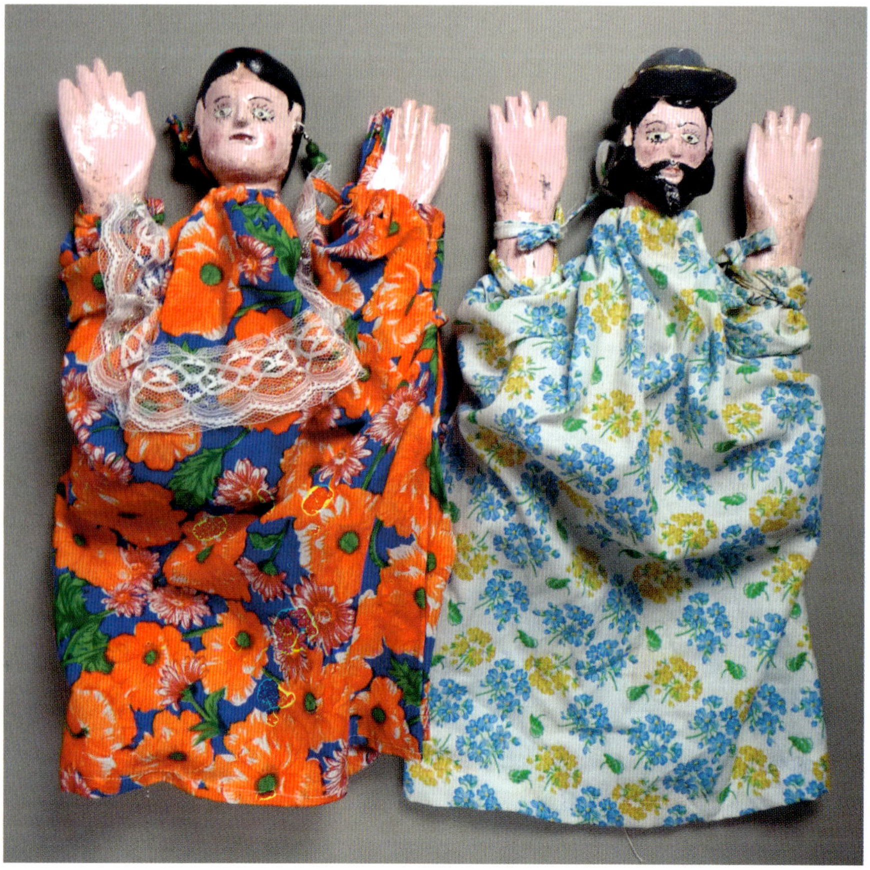

Daniel Ramos Ramos

In 2010, Carlos Moreno Vásquez purchased an old set of puppets from Daniel Ramos, of Nanacatlán, Puebla, for Vernon Kostohryz.

The male and female puppets by Daniel Ramos, wearing new costumes; they were obtained from the carver without clothing. Circa 1990. Rating: known carver, good condition, interesting design, good paint and patina, and probably rare, *****. *Collection of Vernon Kostohryz.*

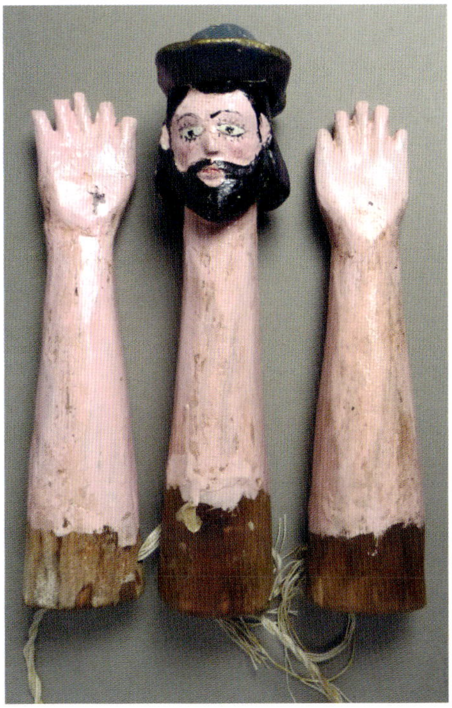

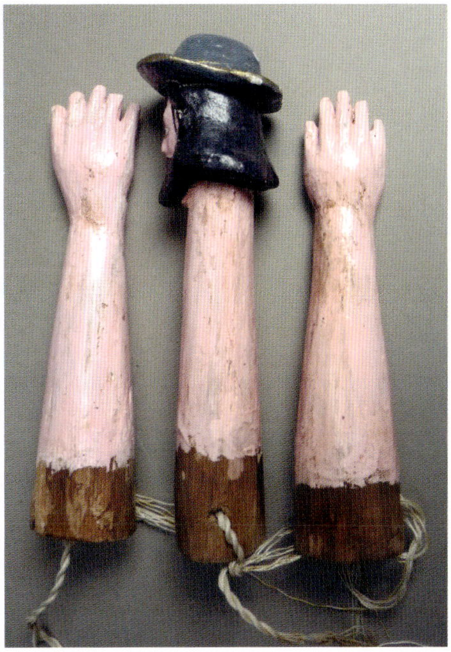

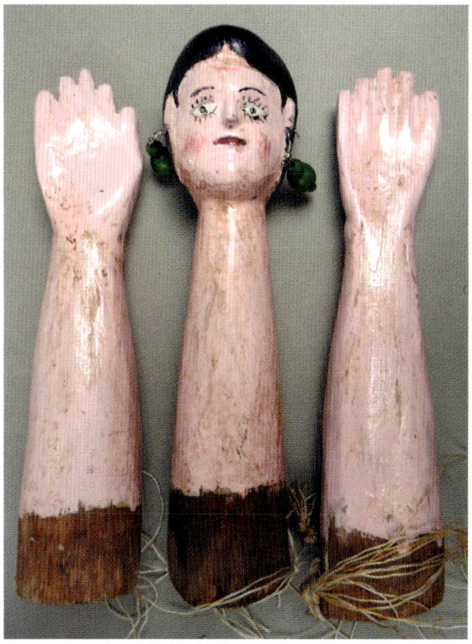

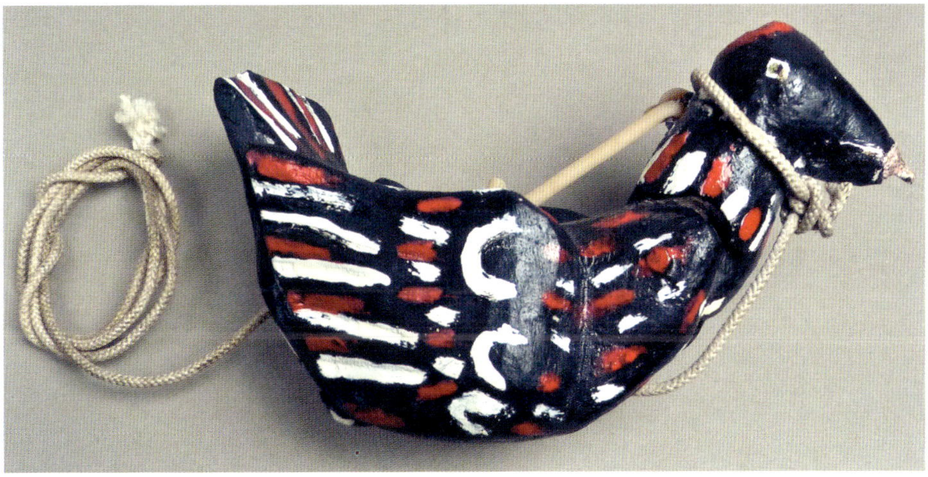

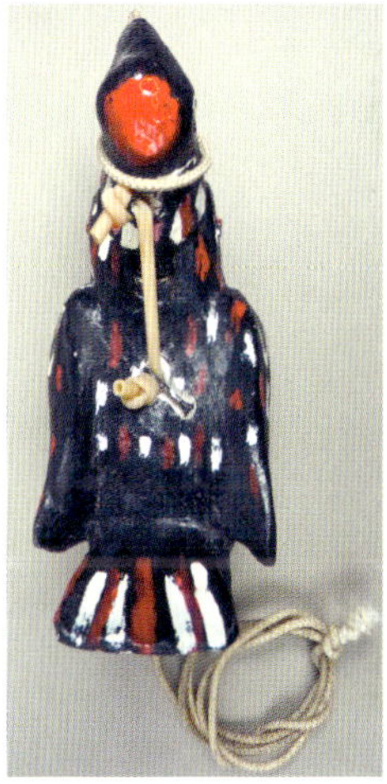

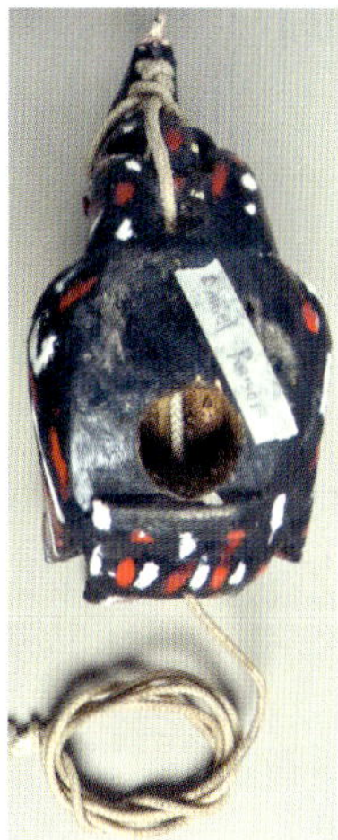

Top left: The three wooden elements of the male puppet by Daniel Ramos; the torso is 10¾" tall, the limbs 9½". These lack any ridge or groove to secure the costume to the neck and wrists. The torso and wrists are very long. The hat is carved as part of the head. The figure has a full beard that is an extension of his shaggy hair. All three parts have obvious and marked patina.

Top center: The three wooden parts, seen from behind. I like the shaping of the hair and beard.

Top right: The three elements of the female Daniel Ramos puppet; her torso is 9¾" tall, her limbs 9½".

Bottom left: The Chénchere from this set by Daniel; the extended length is 8¼".

Bottom center: The Chénchere seen from above. The carving of the bird is much like that of the puppets, with interesting rounded shapes.

Bottom right: The bottom view of the Chénchere.

Francisco Tino

When Vernon Kostohryz, Carlos Moreno Vásquez, and I visited Olintla in March 2010 we saw puppets perform that had been carved by Francisco Tino. Soon afterwards I commissioned Francisco to make a new set for me. These proved to be very similar in appearance and design to the puppets that we saw perform. These are dynamic carvings, but they lack polish. In other words, they are ideally suited for their purpose. Francisco's Chéncheres are typically bulbous in shape and larger than expected. One is initially astonished to see one of these birds in action. Vernon has an older Chénchere by this carver of the predictable shape but very large; the extended length is 18" and it weighs 5 lb. It was retired because it weighed so much.

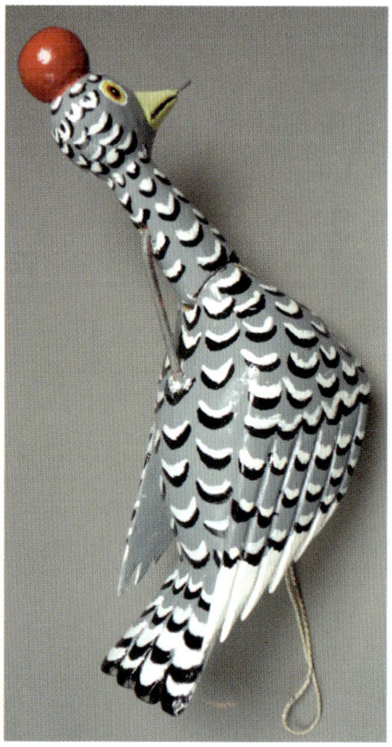

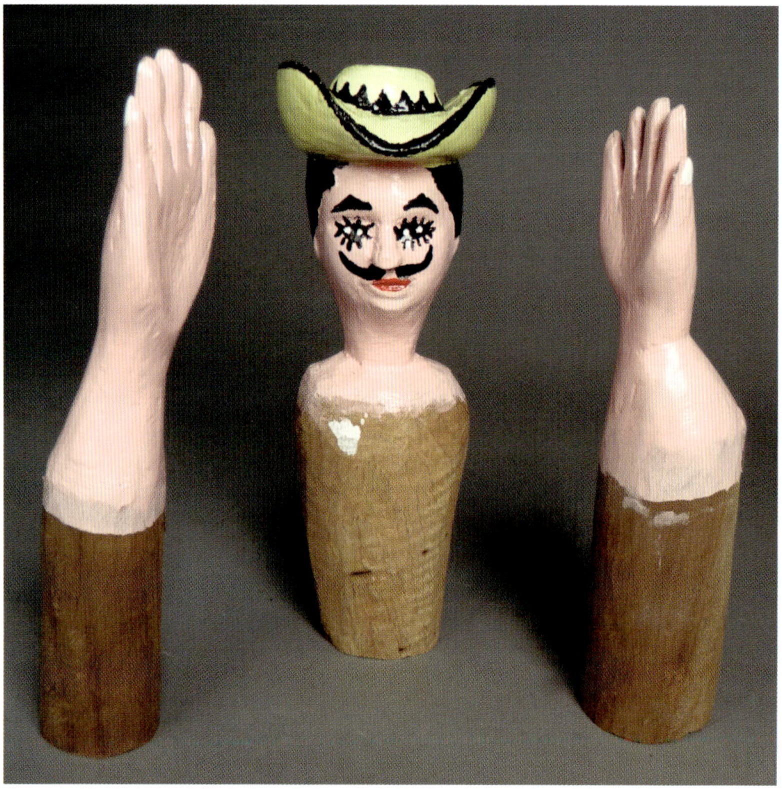

The wooden elements of the new Francisco Tino male puppet; the torso is 8½" tall, limbs 8". The hat is carved in place. The abruptly tapering wrists of Francisco's puppets are a unique feature. Rating for this set: known carver, good condition, adequately carved, unused, and probably not rare, ***. *Collection of the author.*

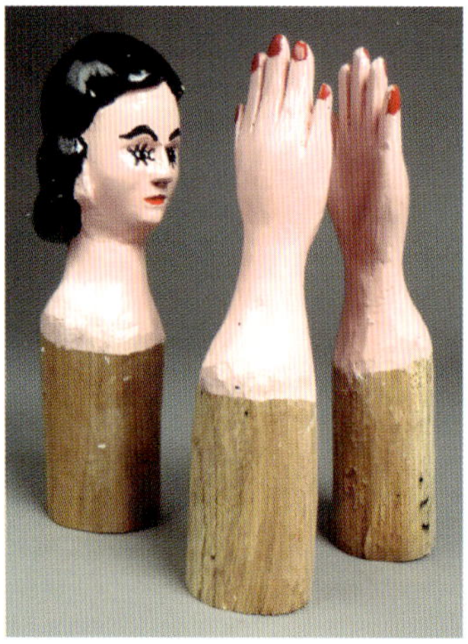

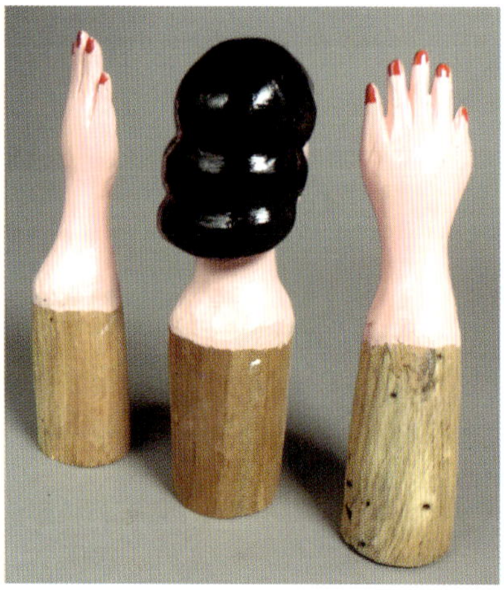

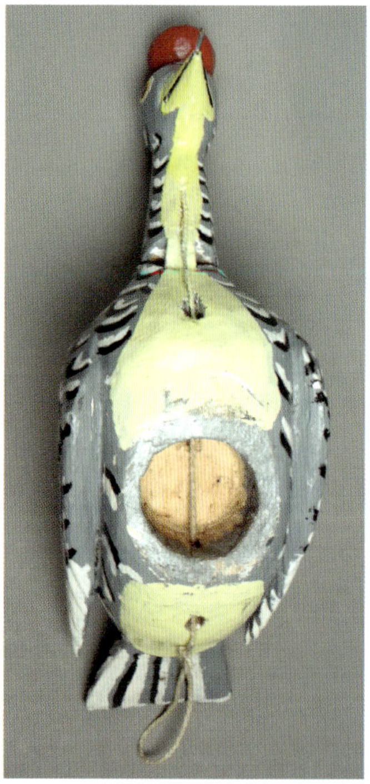

The wooden elements of the female Francisco Tino puppet; the torso is 8" tall, limbs 8". Both puppets have simple relief-carved ears.

The wooden elements of the female puppet from behind, to illustrate the typical waves of hair on Francisco's female puppets.

Top: One of Francisco's oversized Chéncheres in position for hoisting; the extended length is 17". The round crest and the style of painting are typical for this carver. The wings are carved in place.

Bottom: The bottom view of the Chénchere, showing the usual arrangement.

The Puppets of Roberto Villegas Santiago

In 2007, Roberto Villegas told Vernon Kostohryz of a dance group that had a number of Roberto's masks. Vernon discovered masks and puppets that were no longer in active use, and he was able to purchase a number of these carvings. They dated back to about 1975. Here is the spectacular puppet set that he collected with that group. These are remarkable carvings. If you compare the heads of these puppets to the masks by this carver in an earlier chapter, it will be apparent that Roberto modeled the puppets' faces on his masks, even using his typical ear design on the female puppet. The set included male and female puppets and a Chénchere, but came without a box.

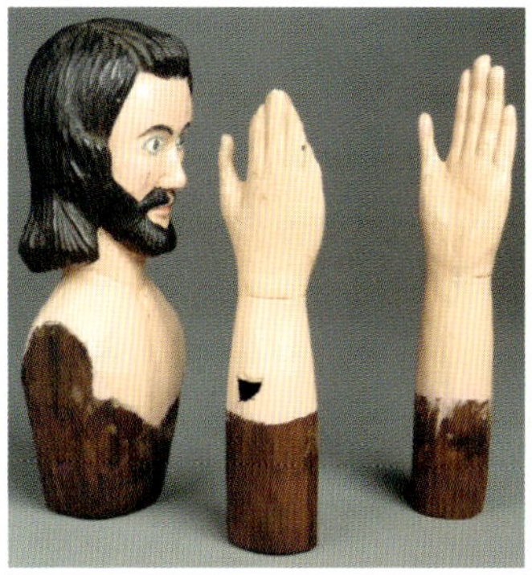

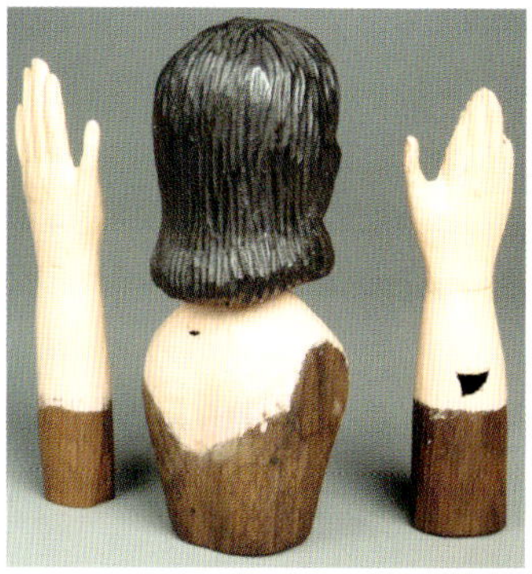

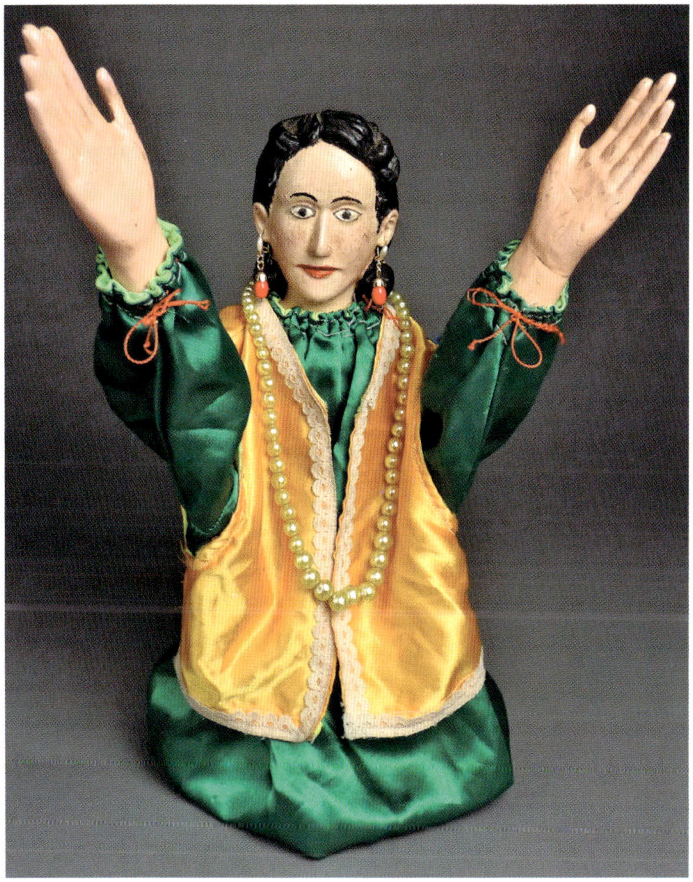

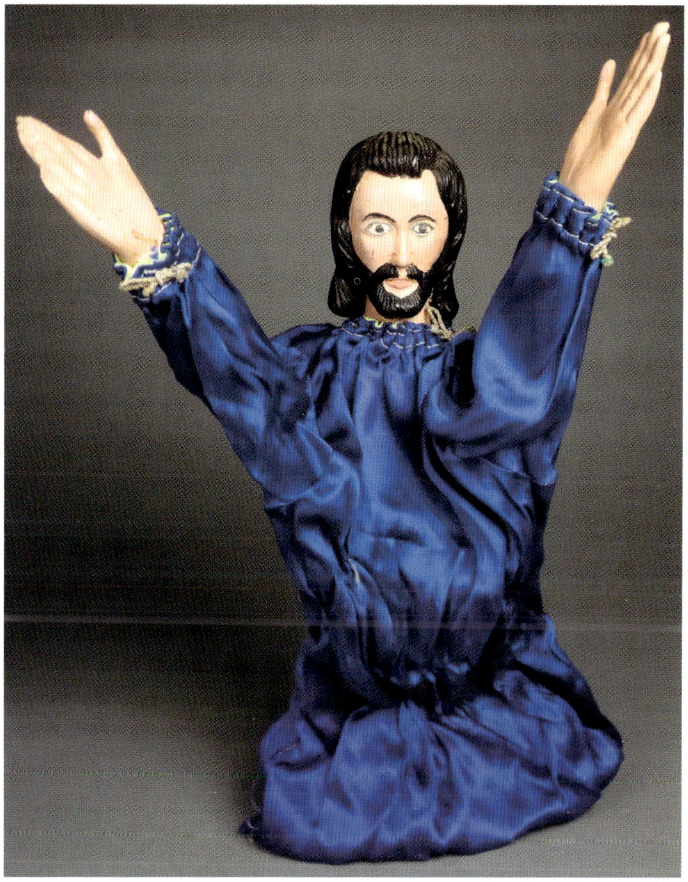

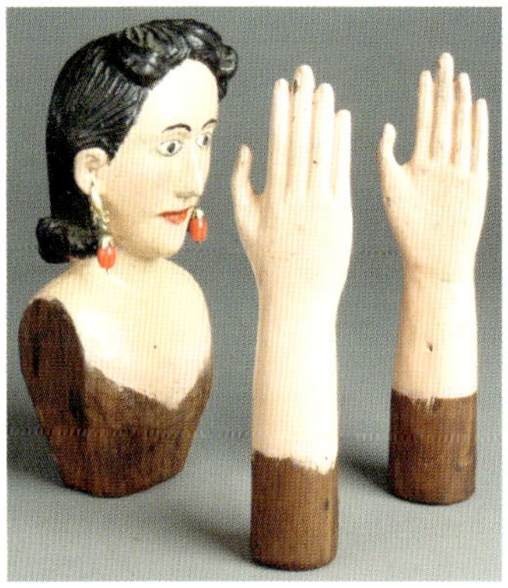

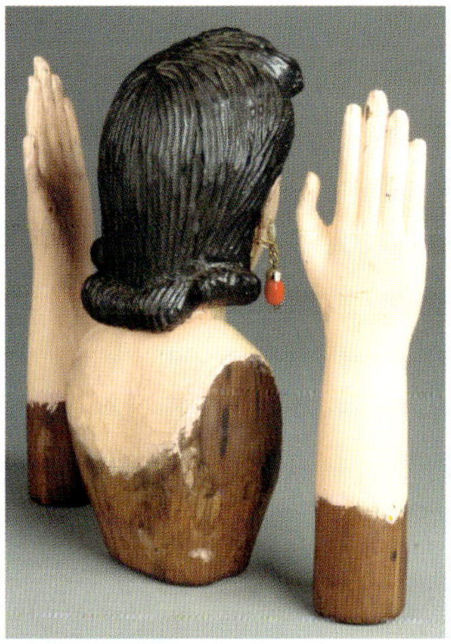

Left, above: The female puppet, whom Roberto identified as Santa María, in her costume; her torso is 7" tall, limbs 6½". Once again note the very fine carving of the puppet's hair, face, and hands.

Far left: The wooden elements of the female puppet, seen from an angle. Note the detailed carving of her left ear.

Near left: The rear view of the female puppet. Even the back of her hair is finely carved.

Above: The male puppet, which the carver, Roberto Villegas, identified as San José, in his costume; the torso is 7" tall, limbs 6½". Notice the very fine carving of the puppet's hair, face, and hands. Also note that the fingers of his right hand are broken at the ends, apparently the result of heavy use (clapping). Rating for this set: known carver, very good condition, excellent design, good paint and patina, and very rare, *******. *Collection of the author.*

Top left: The wooden elements of the male puppet, seen from an angle. The damage to the palm side of the right hand is even more dramatic in this view. There is also a hole in the right wrist.

Top right: The rear view of this puppet. The carving of the hair is remarkable in this view.

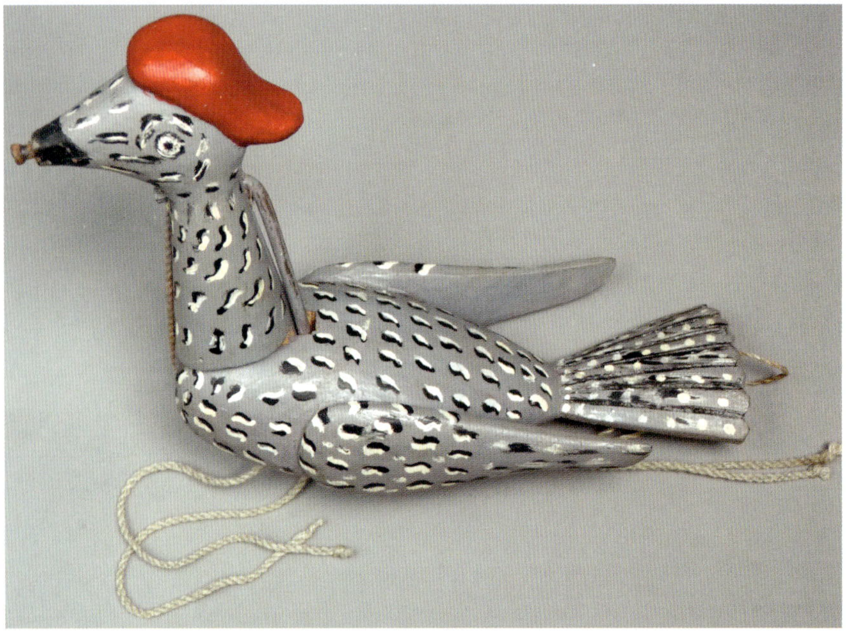

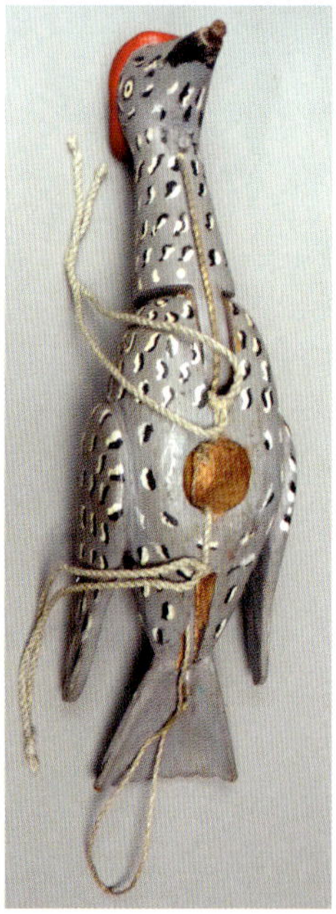

Far left: The Chénchere or woodpecker puppet carved by Roberto; the extended length is 11½". It follows a very typical design for this carver; Another example, seen below, is virtually identical. The inflated red crest of this woodpecker, which is rather distinctive, seems to be an exclusive design of Roberto's. The wings are applied. Often, as in this case, a small nail or screw is installed at the end of the beak, to tap more sharply while protecting the wooden end of the beak from the impact.

Left: The Chénchere seen from below. The looped strings to attach the bird to the hoisting ropes have been preserved on this woodpecker. The string to extend the neck emerges under the tail, as usual.

Recently Vernon Kostohryz found a very large Chénchere, decorated with chip carving to indicate the feathers. The comb or crest of this woodpecker is of the design that I have seen in three Chéncheres known to have been carved by Roberto, so I felt fairly certain that he had carved this one. I visited him with a photo of the giant woodpecker in December 2010. Roberto confirmed that he was the maker. He recalled that in about 1985 he had made six of these oversized woodpeckers—three for Caxhuacan, two for Tuzamapan, and one for San Miguel; all three are villages in Puebla. The idea was that such large birds would be visible if used on very tall poles, perhaps 10 to 12 meters (40 feet) high. It seems that he was never asked to make any more.

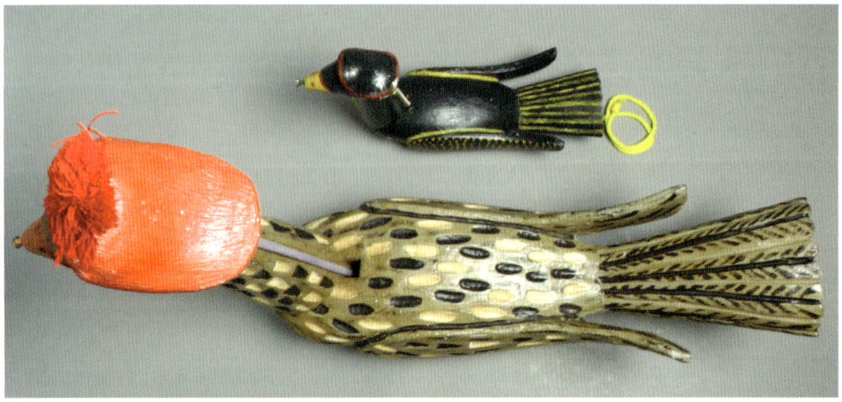

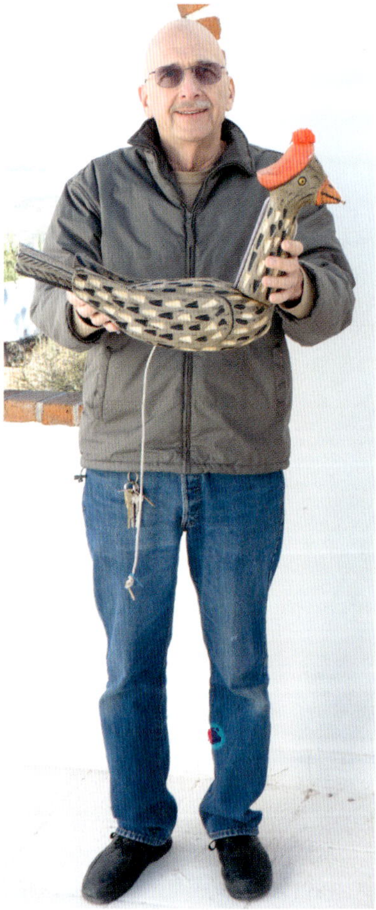

Vernon Kostohryz holding the oversized Chénchere, to indicate its surprising size. The extended length is 28". This was the photo I carried with me to my visit with Roberto Villegas. Rating: known carver, good condition, interesting design, good paint and patina, and rare, *****. *Collection of the author.*

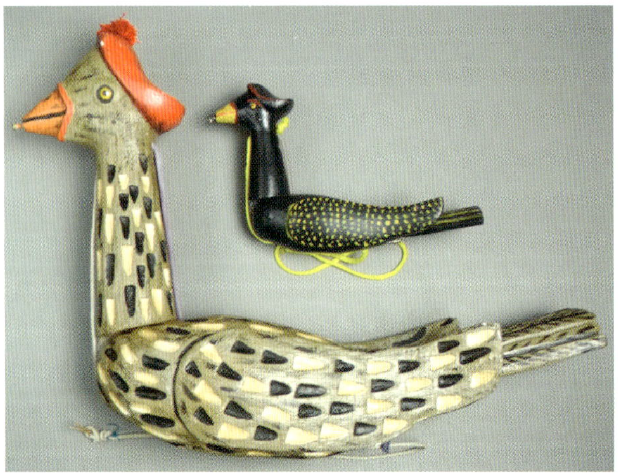

Above: A comparison between the large Chénchere and a normal size example, both carved by Roberto Villegas. Note the chip carving to create the pattern on the larger bird.

Left: The same comparison from the side. The chip carving on the top of the Chénchere has oval depressions, different from the triangular depressions on the side. The small woodpecker has been fitted by Roberto with a steel spring in place of the usual band of rubber to retract the neck.

Artemio Zaragoza Zaragoza

In March 2010, when we visited Artemio Zaragoza Zaragoza, we began to ask everyone we visited about puppets. I don't believe that we had ever raised the subject before with Artemio, although we had visited him repeatedly over the years. He replied that he was currently carving a set of puppets and that he had an old Chénchere that he had carved about 25 years ago. He allowed us to see the ones being carved, which were as yet pretty rough, and of course I jumped at the chance to buy the old woodpecker.

Several months later Carlos Moreno Vásquez found a puppet set that was attributed to Artemio. In December 2010, Carlos and I visited Artemio's house; his daughter stated that Artemio was the carver of the two human puppets, but not of the Chénchere that accompanied them. So it happened that I was able to assemble a set of puppets by Artemio, by adding the old Chénchere to the more recently confirmed pair. Looking at these puppets, one sees again how each carver can have his own very specific style.

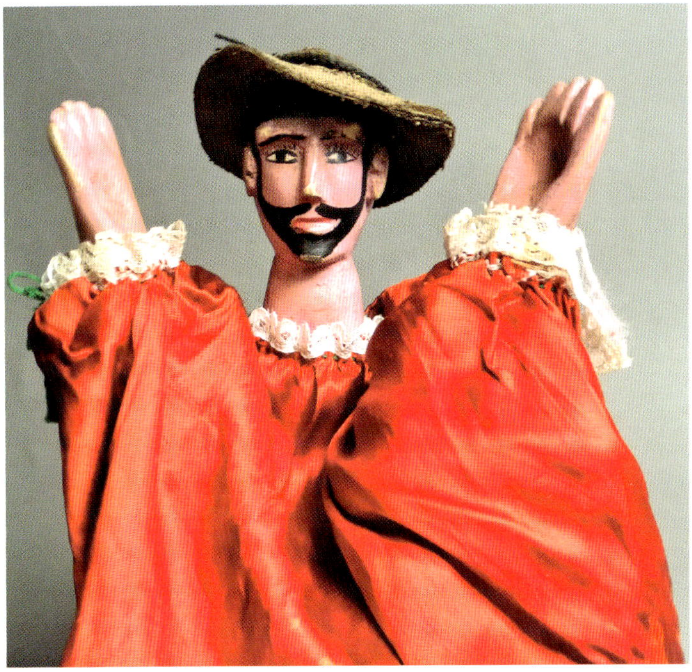

Top left: The male puppet by Artemio Zaragoza Zaragoza in costume; his torso is 6½" tall, his limbs 7". His straw hat is tattered. Both puppets have hollow palms. Rating for this set: known carver, good condition, well carved, good paint and patina, and probably rare, *****. *Collection of the author.*

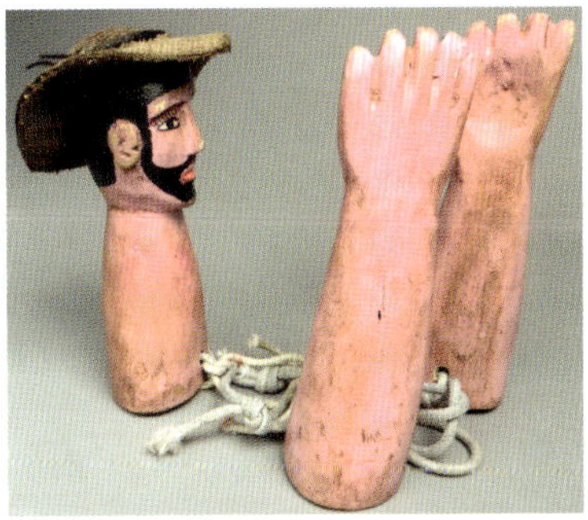

Far left: A side view of the wooden elements of the male puppet. Artemio doesn't carve separate fingers, except at the tips. Both puppets have the same stereotyped ear design.

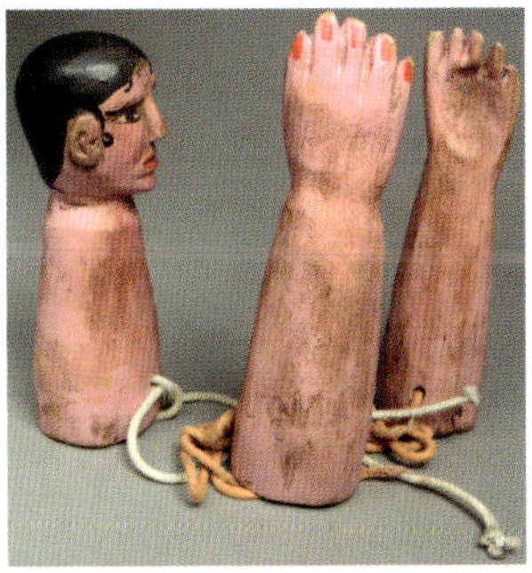

Near left: A side view of the wooden elements of the female puppet.

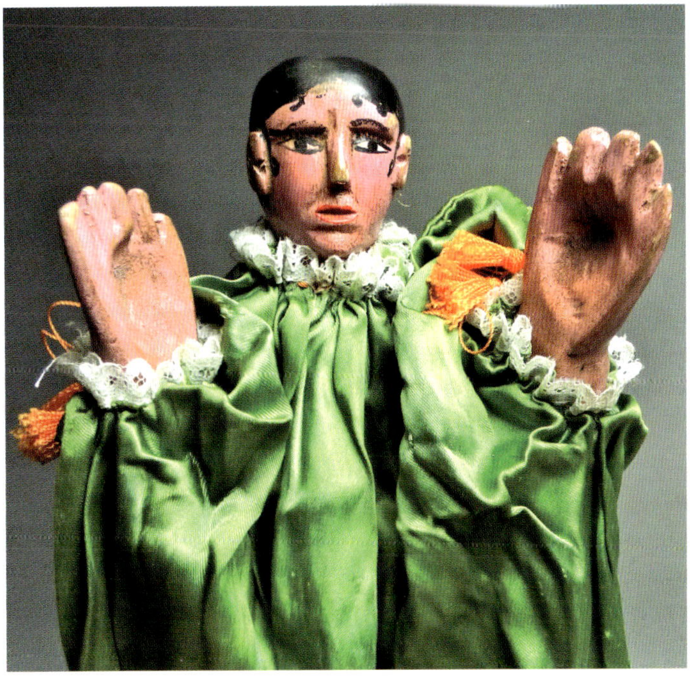

Bottom left: The female puppet by Artemio in costume; her torso is 6" tall, her limbs 7". She has elaborate ears for a puppet.

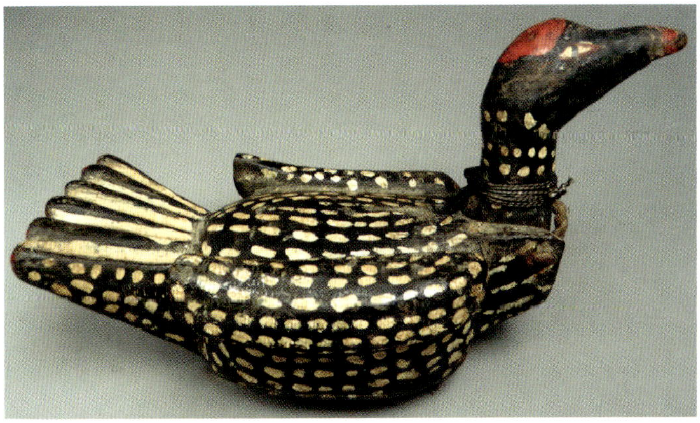

Bottom right: The 25-year-old Chénchere from Artemio Zaragoza Zaragoza; the extended length is 10". This has wonderful patina.

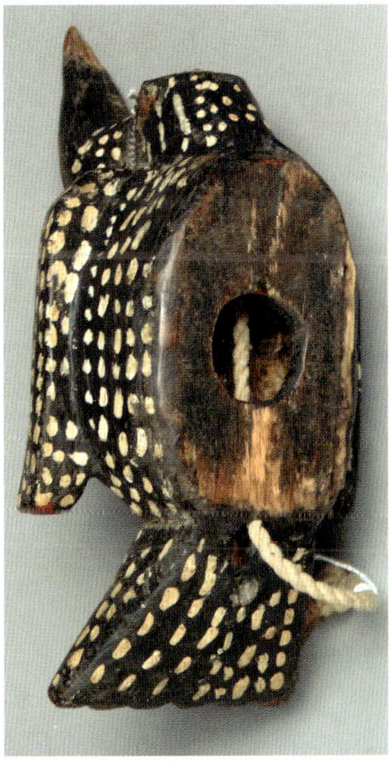

Below: The bottom of this Chénchere looks different from the norm because it is so short and broad.

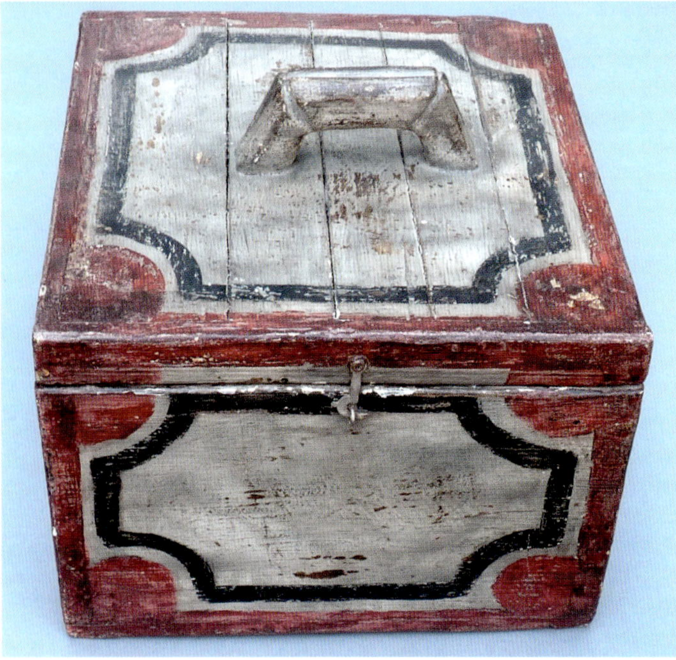

This traditional puppet box is very deep; the width is 8", the height is 11", and the depth is 12". The style of the painted decoration is antiquated. Age unknown. Rating: unknown carver, good condition, well made, good paint and patina, and probably rare, ****. *Collection of the author.*

Puppet Boxes

I will end this chapter with a further discussion of the boxes that have been traditionally used to store the puppets. You have already been shown instances where the apparently original box had remained with the puppet set. The ones that come to mind are as follows:

- The very old set, recently identified as the work of Don Lillo, where the male puppet wears a top hat; this fits nicely in its original box.
- Don Lillo's personal puppet set, kept in its original box that is painted with scenes of a hunter with his dog.
- The Don Lillo puppet set from Sabanas de Xalostoc, kept in a plain box with a nicely carved handle and a string to secure the lid.
- Don Simón's boxes painted with scenes related to the Tejoneros and their puppets.
- The set of puppets attributed to José González Galindo came in a box decorated in the style of Germán Guerrero.

Some other sets came without any box, and I have found replacement boxes to be assigned to these puppets, as follows.

The two sets of puppets by Kalimán fit nicely in a very large older box. This has traditional paint that resembles the paint on the box for the oldest Don Lillo puppets.

I have a beautiful old domed puppet box that I suspect of having been made by Don Lillo. It has box joints at the corners and traditional paint like the old green box. It has a nicely carved wooden handle; Don Lillo provided the box from Sabanas de Xalostoc with a very finely carved handle, although he often makes his handles from adapted hardware.

In January 2008, I obtained the vividly decorated box that houses my old and beautiful set of Roberto Villegas puppets from Carlos. It was Vernon's opinion that the box, of cedar, was likely to be old while the painted decoration was more recent. Since then we have identified the painter as Germán Guerrero, of Tuzamapan, Puebla. I suspect that Don Lillo might have made the box originally, but I have never remembered to ask him. I'll present multiple views of that box to illustrate this painter's style. He commonly covers his boxes with scenes from various regional dances, as in this case. In his scenes, he mixes characters from more than one dance. During a fiesta the various dances do occur adjacent to one another, so that Quetzales wander through the circle of Huehues and vice versa.

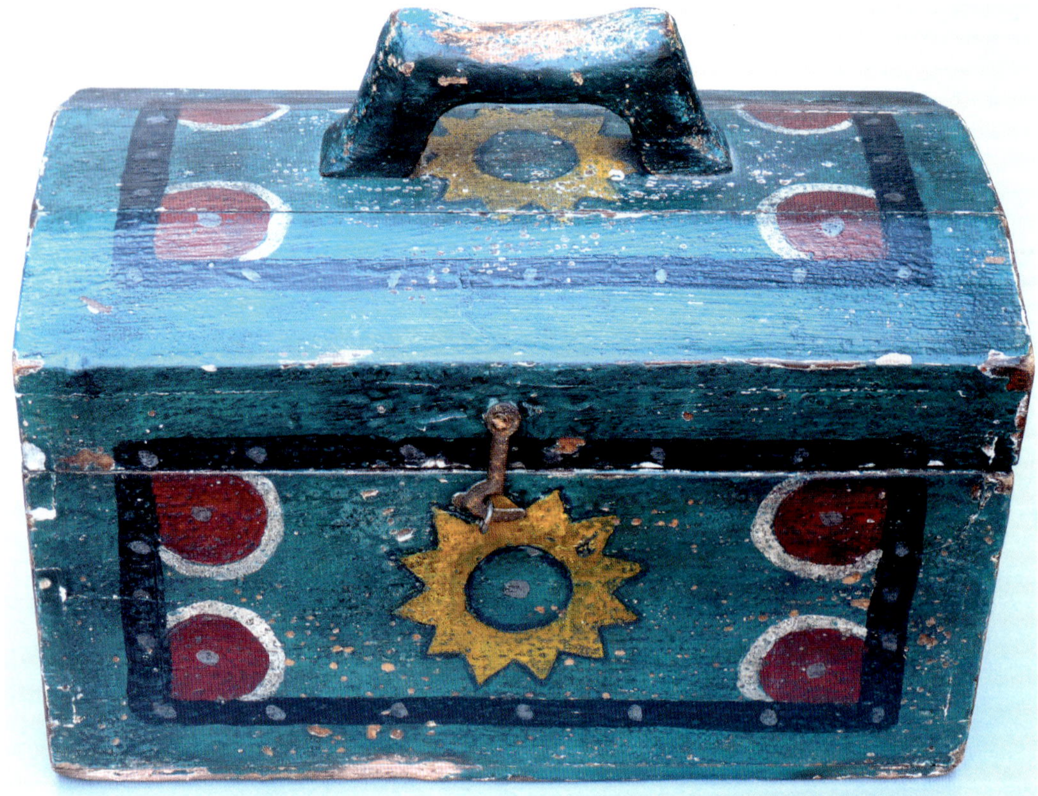

This attractive domed traditional puppet box is 12" in length, 10" high, and 7" deep. It is nicely painted and with obvious patina. Rating: uncertain carver, good condition, well made, good paint and patina, and probably rare, ****. *Collection of the author.*

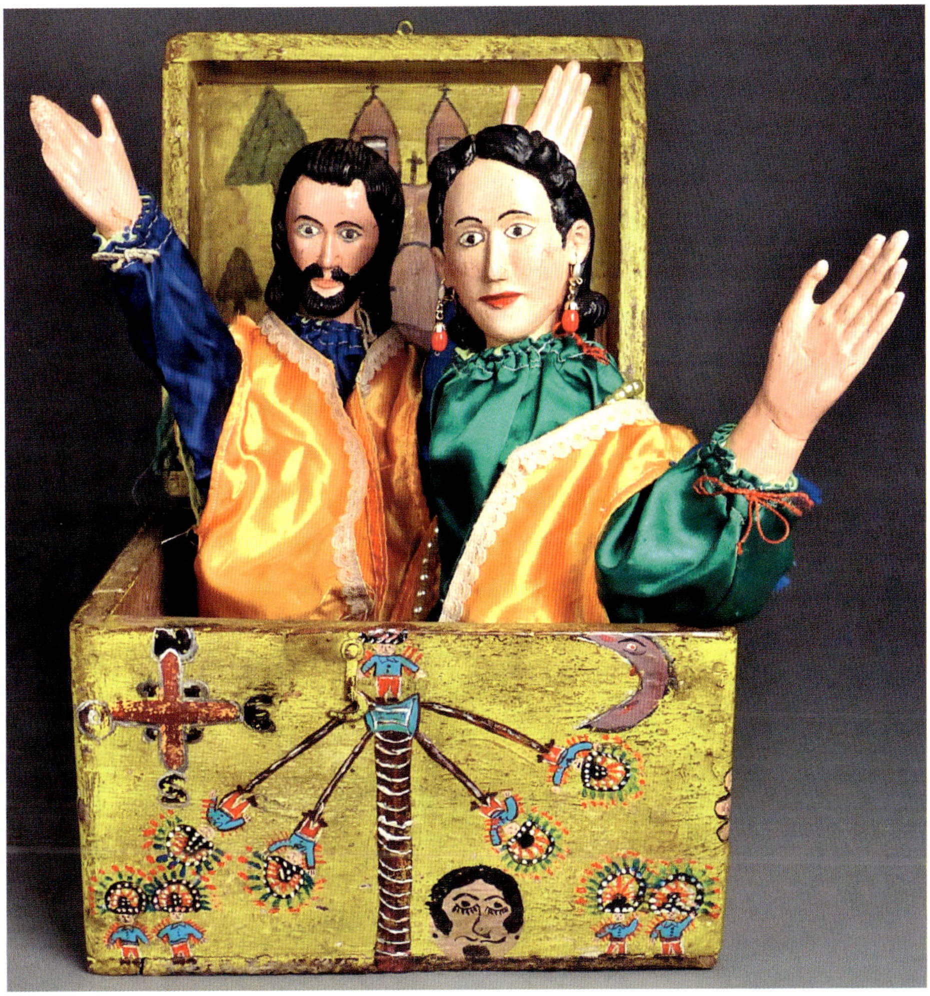

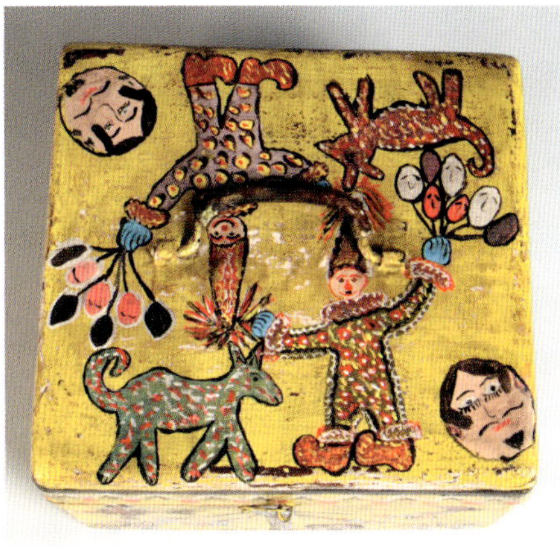

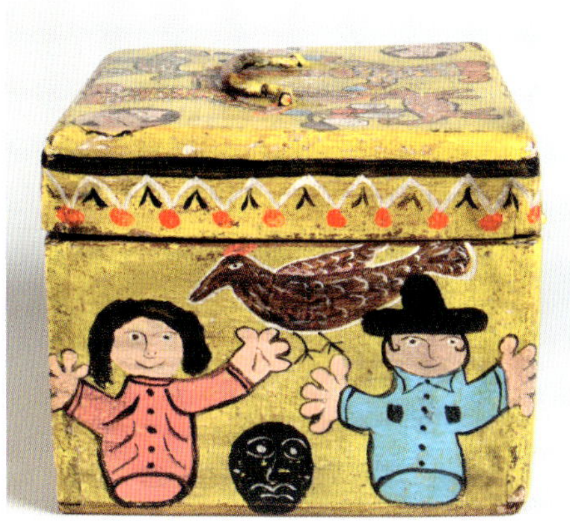

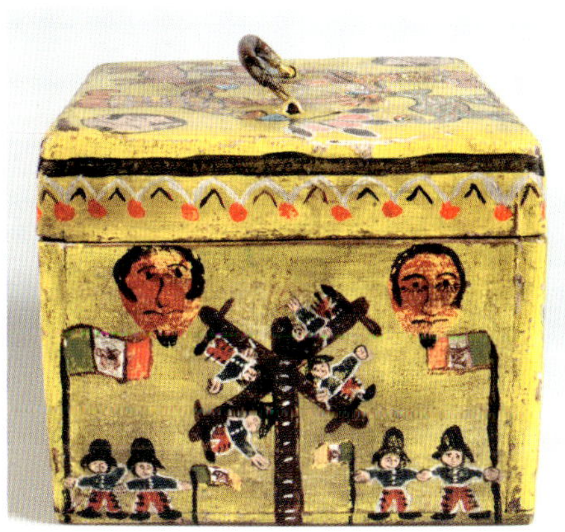

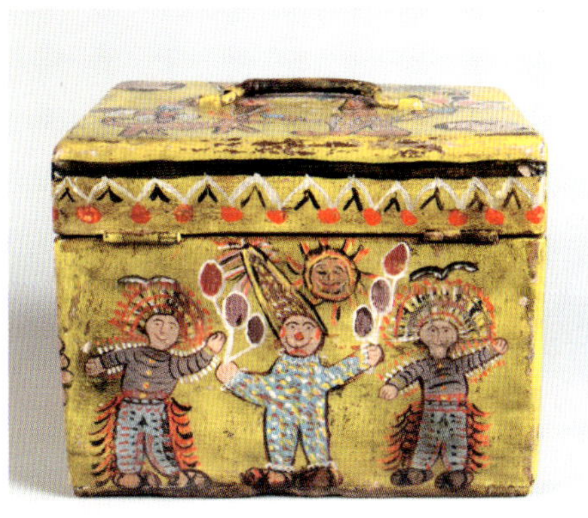

Above: This box, painted by Germán Guerrero, currently holds the old puppets by Roberto Villegas; the width is 10½", the height is 7½", and the depth is 9½". The theme is Voladores. On the upper left one sees the four cardinal directions; this may also represent the cross or wheel of the Quetzales dance. Rating: uncertain carver, good condition, well made, excellent paint and patina, and probably rare, *****. *Collection of the author.*

Right from top:
The top panel of this box. The handle looks like those of Don Lillo. The theme is Huehues or Tejoneros, including Payasos and a Perro.

The side on the viewer's right. We see a set of puppets, plus a brooding Negrito mask.

The side on the viewer's left definitely shows the wheel of the Quetzales.

The back panel of this box presents a Payaso from the Huehues flanked by two Quetzales dancers.

Chapter 8

Afterword

Persistent Mysteries

This book began as a testament to the carvers of the Sierra de Puebla and their beautiful masks. In such a work, it was necessary to briefly describe the dances in which these masks appeared. However, the subject did not lend itself to brevity; there were too many inconsistencies. The search for the true essence of each dance revealed an unexpected pattern of layered meaning. As these layers emerged again and again, one became aware of persistent mysteries across many of the dances. In this chapter I will identify and explore just one of these questions.

We begin by underscoring a fundamental issue. When the Spanish priests taught the Indians of this region about Christianity, the Indians were clearly able to learn the basic outline of these teachings, including the names of the various characters, whether Satan, the Saints, the Apostles, the Archangels, or the Holy Trinity. In this respect they appeared to participate in a process of religious conversion, as if accepting many Christian elements within an organized system of beliefs. What was much less apparent, at the time of teaching and over the intervening years, was that the Indians were likely to have attributed their own meaning to these characters, concepts, and symbols. The resulting mixture of Christian and Indian beliefs, which might or might not be called syncretic (because "syncretic" implies that the conqueror's religion prevailed over that of the conquered), presents the non-Indian observer with apparent dissonance or contradictions. Indeed, it is these moments of dissonance that call our attention to the underlying complexity of these beliefs and religious elements.

Who Is Pilatos?

Within these puzzling constructions there are several dance personages who stand out as particularly jarring, namely the Devil and his apparent alter ego, Pilatos. I can still recall the feelings of anxiety that were aroused within me when I began researching these dances and read about those dances in which Pilatos, who could also be called Satanás, appeared to be a major figure, but in an apparently benign role. I had been raised within a North American Christian tradition, with the usual European roots. From that perspective, the Devil was unambiguously evil, menacing, and bad. When his name appeared, my radar went up.

For example, in the Danza de los Negritos there is a central character, el Pilato or Pilatos. In his article about this dance, as performed in the area of Papantla, Veracruz, Aguilera Madero (2005, 119–120) states that Pilatos can be called by various other names, including *Rey* (king), *Satanás* (Satan), *Scores* (meaning Viejo or old man) and *Padre de la Danza* (father of the dance). Acosta Báez (2005, 113) makes the same point. Although this character is most often called Pilato or Pilatos, it seems that those other names were all at one time considered to be equivalent.

In his article about the Santiagueros, José Xochihua Ibarra (2005, 88) listed the usual characters for that dance, including the "Presidente (Pilatos)," while another character in the dance was "Pilato," whom he described as often playing the role of the father of the dancers. The presence of Pilatos (Pontius Pilate) is obviously necessary due to his role in the death of Christ, but it seems that the other Pilato is necessary as well, and that the two characters are defined as separate entities or manifestations.

Writing about the characters in the Danza de los Tejoneros, Rubén Croda León and Domingo Francisco Velasco (2005, 72) describe a Viejo figure that represents the devil, but they don't specify whether he is also called Pilato or Pilatos. We have seen masks for this character by Roberto Villegas Santiago and by Andrés Juárez García (Chapter 6).

The Pilatos/Pilato figure, in the guise of a benign, aged clown dressed in ragged clothes, seems to be a staple character in other dances as well, but not labeled as the devil or Satanás. For example, Pilatos appears in the Carnaval dance in Joloapan, Veracruz. There he wears old worn-out clothing and a wooden mask that is painted red or black. He is clearly described as a clown (or bogeyman, from a North American perspective), and someone who behaves in an unconventional manner. He chases children who have deliberately provoked him. This Pilatos does not seem significantly different from the one in the Negritos dance, in dress or style, but the author does not state that he might be called by any other name, such as Satanás or el Diablo (Aguilera Madero and Márquez Hernández 2005, 169).

Additional dances that can include a Pilatos figure, named as such and appearing as a Viejo and/or a Payaso character, are the dance of the Voladores and of el Matarachín. I have shown the Pilatos of the Voladores in a dance photo from Huehuetla (Chapter 4). There is no positive evidence that Pilato/Pilatos appears in the dances of Navidad or in the dance of the Scarlet Macaws/Guaguas/Quetzales, although we don't know whether this was the name of the former clown in the latter dances.

You may recall the myth that was included in Chapter 2 regarding the creation of all of the dances by Jesus, just prior to his death (Aguilera Madero 2005, 120). Jesus was said to have provided to each dance a representative to continue his teachings. To the Danza de los Negritos he provided Pilato, who was to represent San José; Maringuilla was to represent the Virgin Mary. So one might ask, is this the true identity of Pilato? I briefly struggled with this idea.

The possibility that Pilato is really San José in disguise seems initially appealing. San José could readily symbolize the father of the dancers, having served in the role of the earthly father of Jesus in biblical accounts. But there are several problems with this. First, why would one need to disguise the identity of San José, when he was a legitimate and beloved Christian saint who could readily appear under his own name? Second, how could it be possible for San José to carry the alternate names of either Satan or King? Neither could ever be appropriate! So here we see once again an instance of dissonance, to alert us to the likelihood of layered meaning and subterfuge.

On reflection, there is a comic aspect to this myth about the creation of the dances. In reciting the hidden identities of the characters, the myth actually demonstrates the techniques used to introduce a hidden transcript within a public performance. At the same time, this "explanation" is apparently designed to hide such an element under this new myth.

Pilatos as an Aspect of Tezcatlipoca

It is my impression, based on suggestive evidence, that Pilato/Pilatos is now or once was an extension or representation of the important Aztec god Tezcatlipoca. I also believe that Satan was attached to Tezcatlipoca, such that the devil, Pilatos, and Tezcatlipoca together represented one entity. This multidimensional personage stood opposite another that was quite similar, combining Quetzalcoatl, the Spirit of Maíze, the sun, and Jesus, as described by Stresser-Péan (2009, 515). These two deities or clusters would have functioned within the Sierra religious perspective to balance one another in a duality.

It is absolutely clear that Pilato/Pilatos was at one time either very important in his own right or represented some power or deity who was very important. This is self-evident, in that we can identify five dances in which this figure clearly appears, compared to three others where he apparently does not; across the spectrum of Sierra dances no other character appears with such frequency.

I am inclined to doubt that Pilatos represents a discrete, independent figure, because he is provided with such a fluid identity. A personage who has so many names is unlikely to actually be just one of them, to the exclusion of the rest. Furthermore we have seen that Pilato*s* appears to be a generic false name, apparently used to mislead, such as in the Santiagueros dance. This leaves me to think that, despite all his names, Pilatos probably represents some other figure who is unnamed.

One of his alternate names is Satanás/Satan. An obvious hypothesis would be that he was or is a manifestation of the devil. However this does not seem a very satisfactory explanation, in that he fails to behave in the manner that we would have associated with Satan, at least the Satan of the Christian tradition.

From my perspective, the most satisfactory answer to this puzzle involves the hypothesis that Satan and Pilatos are interchangeable names because both names refer to some other power. The fact that they don't more closely resemble one another would be consistent with the possibility that both are projections of a deity whose nature was chameleon-like.

If "chameleon-like" is our marker, then the name that suggests itself is Tezcatlipoca, the sorcerer and trickster, an apparently friendly and harmless old man who offers Quetzalcoatl medicine that is really something else (Sahagún 1952, Book 3, 15–16), but then he is "a bundle of ashes… rolling, groaning and billowing," or he is a skunk, or he is a disembodied head (Sahagún 1957, Book 5, 171, 177–180). In his manner Pilatos closely resembles Tezcatlipoca's friendly old man persona, except sometimes he wears a mask that is said to be either horrifying in appearance or mocking (García García 2005, 116). This was puzzling and disconcerting until I became aware of his possible identification with Tezcatlipoca, and then it all fit; horrifying and mocking are words that one reads in the writings about that god (Sahagún 1970, Book 1, 5). Tezcatlipoca had many manifestations as an Aztec god, and others were added, it seems, following the arrival of the Spanish.

Earlier I mentioned the idea that the devil might have been attached to Tezcatlipoca, because the two tend to be described in similar terms. For example, both Tezcatlipoca and Satan have been portrayed as particularly associated with the night (Olivier 2003, 23). Furthermore, the Spanish priests had apparently taught the Indians that Tezcatlipoca and Satan were one and the same (Sahagún 1970, Book 1, 67–69).

In the Danza de los Negritos, where the most explicit connection is made between Pilatos and the devil, there are several elements that seem particularly evocative of Tezcatlipoca. To begin with, the dance is said to have been originally about slaves, and according to legend those slaves were permitted to dance on only one day each year (Medina Jiménez 2005, 111). We know from Sahagún that all slaves were assigned the day sign of "one death," the day sign of Tezcatlipoca, and that slaves were especially well treated only on that day of the year, in order to avoid offense to this god (Sahagún 1957, Book 4, 33–36). In the Negritos dance, which is allegedly about slaves, Tezcatlipoca would appear to be the leading candidate to be called the father of the dancers or the dance.

Furthermore, the Negritos dancers dress in black, which is a color that was associated in legend with Tezcatlipoca. The Negritos demonstrate a stamping rhythmic step in their dancing, which may mimic the enchanted dancing that in legend was caused by Tezcatlipoca, in order to bewitch the men of Tula so that they fell to their deaths (Sahagún 1952, Book 3, 21–22). Thus there are elements present in the Negritos dance to remind its viewers of this god. The speculation by Rocío Aguilera Madero that the Totonacs may have adopted this dance in order to disguise and maintain earlier dance elements dedicated to Tezcatlipoca rings true, in this light (Aguilera Madero 2005, 122–123).

The dance would not have needed to dramatize Tezcatlipoca; it might have been sufficient to suggest his persistent presence. Again recalling Sahagún (1952, Book 3, 11–12), this god was described as "invisible—like the darkness; [like] the wind. When sometimes he called out to one, he spoke like a shadow." This makes one think that there was a time in the past when Tezcatlipoca was very highly feared, such that an individual might have strained to be constantly alert for this god's possible presence, and scrupulous to maintain an attitude of worship and respect. But to maintain worship of this god was forbidden by the Spanish conquerors; for this necessary practice to continue, it needed to be covert.

Duality as a Perspective for Understanding

Knowing the prior central place of the concept of duality, we could hypothesize that when one power was represented in a dance, we might expect to find the opposing power there as well. The well-known legends of conflict and duality between Quetzalcoatl and Tezcatlipoca (Olivier 2003, 274–277) permit us to expect the hidden presence of Tezcatlipoca in any instance when the other deity appears to be a manifestation of Quetzalcoatl, such as Jesus, the spirit of Maíze, or the sun. In the case of the Negritos dance, Maringuilla is likely to represent the Virgin Mary (a member of the Holy Family and thus a manifestation of Jesus), so the presence of Pilatos as the representative of Tezcatlipoca would complete the duality. Then this dance could be interpreted as once exemplifying the eternal struggle between this pairing of Quetzalcoatl and Tezcatlipoca.

We might examine the possible correlation between the sun and Quetzalcoatl on one side balanced by either Pilatos or the devil on the other. Do we see this linking in the other dances? That is, does the impulse to maintain this duality appear to explain the presence of Pilato/Pilatos or the devil in other dances? We can examine this question, dance by dance.

In the dance of the Santiagueros, if Santiago and the Santiagueros are secretly considered to be agents of the sun, then of course we might expect to find Pilato to maintain the duality, along with Pontius Pilate/Pilatos. We don't necessarily require both, and the literature on this dance frequently fails to mention Pilato as a member of the cast, while of course Pilatos el Presidente (Pontius Pilate) is invariably present. Ichon (1973, 395) described the Santiagueros dance in Pantepec, Puebla, where Pontius Pilate actually wore a mask of Satan. In Chapter 6, I described a Pilato Malo mask that was used in the Hormegas dance in Olintla, Puebla; it had been carved by Magno León. I expressed my view that this was a mask of Satan, disguised as Pontius Pilate.

In the Migueles dance there is an obvious duality between the Migueles, as agents of Jesus, versus the devil.

In the dance of the Chéncheres, Huehues, or Tejoneros, the Spirit of Maíze was said to be the architect of the cornfield, so once again we are not surprised to find a Viejo (said to be the devil) present to complete the duality (Croda León and Francisco Velasco 2005, 72).

The Voladores appear to be flying in pursuit or support of the sun and the Spirit of Maíze; at the foot of the volador pole, with no apparent role, we find Pilatos (Aguilera Madero and Cano González "La danza ritual del volador," 36).

The Scarlet Macaws/Guaguas/Quetzales dancers are also said to be flying towards the sun, so where is Pilatos to complete the duality? We don't know, but was that the identity of the clown or clowns described by Stresser-Péan (2009, 283) who were formerly attached to this dance?

In the case of the dances of Navidad, we find a variation on this pattern. Rather than there being the expected duality within a particular dance, the tension is between dances; the dance of Lakapíjkuyu seems to occur in apposition to that of Lakakgolo (as if they represent two separate groups of worshippers who evidently reflect some duality), while both the Lakapíjkuyu and the Posadas performances occur in apposition to the dance of el Matarachín. In the latter pairing, as noted in Chapter 4, there is a striking duality between Jesus versus demons who include Pilatos, or alternatively between light and darkness. Furthermore, by his movements the Matarachín is said to physically demonstrate the duality that is within him.

In Conclusion

Having drawn all these ideas together, I will add two cautions.

First, I should note that despite the convincing nature of this line of speculation, one would be wise to maintain an attitude of humility and uncertainty in the absence of more positive confirmation of these theories. The history of mankind is littered with incorrect ideas that at one time appeared to be true on the basis of logic—for example, that the world was flat. Nevertheless, if one measure of an idea's validity is its enhanced power to explain the unexplained, then perhaps we have indeed discovered something useful and interesting.

Second, there is an important mystery that remains. If indeed the plots of these dances reflect powerful beliefs about ancient Nahua and Totonac gods, at what point in the recent or remote past might these beliefs have diminished, causing the dances to lose their old meanings and purposes? Stresser-Péan's research (2009, 351–3), for instance, regarding the sudden loss of prestige of the "learned men" and the near abandonment of the ancient calendar by the end of the second quarter of the twentieth century, certainly suggests that this diminution had occurred by that time. Such calendrical practices would have remained urgently necessary for as long as beliefs were maintained about the dangerous omnipresence of Tezcatlipoca.

Hoping to shed further light on this question, in August 2010, I asked Carlos Moreno Vásquez to once again interview Manuel Aldana Valencia ("Don Lillo"), whom we had come to regard as a particularly helpful and knowledgeable informant. What follows is their dialogue about Pilato, as translated from the Spanish by Vernon Kostohryz, based on Carlos' report.

> Carlos: Who was Pilato?
> *Don Lillo: He doesn't have a name. He is bad and forms a group of seven Pilatos.*
> Carlos: Was Pilato important?
> *Don Lillo: In the past and now they are important.*
> Carlos: In some regions was Pilato called Satanás?
> *Don Lillo: No. The diablo that dances with the San Migueles is called Satanás.*
> Carlos: When Don Lillo was small, was the Pilato a diablo?
> *Don Lillo: No, never.*
> Carlos: In the dance of the Guaguas, are there payasos that dance?
> *Don Lillo: No, only in the dances of the Tejoneros or Huehues.*
> Carlos: A long time ago, did they include payasos?
> *Don Lillo: Not in Coxquihui, only in Espinal or Papantla.*
> Carlos: Do the payasos have names?
> *Don Lillo: No. In los Tejoneros it is said that they are consejeros (counselors of the tribe) and the tribe consists of the descendents of Maíze."*

For me, the most intriguing part of this dialogue occurs in the first two lines, when Don Lillo states that Pilato "doesn't have a name." Thus he seems to indicate that the connection has been lost between the Pilato el Presidente character and Pontius Pilate or the devil. The Pilato characters have become generic symbols of evil. As such they continue to play an important role in the dance of the Santiagueros.

Don Lillo's responses suggest that if Tezcatlipoca was ever considered to be the hidden presence behind the Pilato/Pilatos figure, this connection has been long forgotten. Instead, it seems that Pilato has taken on a simpler meaning, as with Halloween characters in the United States. We can notice that Don Lillo does not make a connection between Pilato and San José either. It may be that the old myths have slowly and inexorably lost their former power, and that newer layers of meaning have actually supplanted the older beliefs. This would explain the observations in earlier chapters that would be consistent with such changes in meaning, for example, my observation that Negrito masks are no longer considered to be necessary during the performance of the Negritos dance.

Bibliography

Acosta Báez, Francisco. "Danza de los negros." In *Entre los hombres y las Deidades: Las Danzas del Totonacapán*, edited by Rubén Croda León, 112–114. Mexico City, Mexico: CONACULTA, 2005.

Acosta Báez, Francisco, and Zeferino Gaona Vega "Danza de San Miguelitos." In *Entre los hombres y las Deidades: Las Danzas del Totonacapán*, edited by Rubén Croda León, 94–102. Mexico City, Mexico: CONACULTA, 2005.

Acosta Báez, Francisco, and Zeferino Gaona Vega "Danza de voladores de la sierra." In *Entre los hombres y las Deidades: Las Danzas del Totonacapán*, edited by Rubén Croda León, 38–42. Mexico City: CONACULTA, 2005.

Adams, Richard N., and Arthur J. Rubel. "Sickness and Social Relations." In *Handbook of Middle American Indians.* Vol. 6, *Social Anthropology*, 333–356. Austin: University of Texas Press, 1967.

Aguilera Madero, Rocío. "Danza de los negritos." In *Entre los hombres y las Deidades: Las Danzas del Totonacapán*, edited by Rubén Croda León, 117–120. Mexico City, Mexico: CONACULTA, 2005.

Aguilera Madero, Rocío. "Negritos de la costa." In *Entre los hombres y las Deidades: Las Danzas del Totonacapán*, edited by Rubén Croda León, 121–123. Mexico City, Mexico: CONACULTA, 2005.

Aguilera Madero, Rocío, and Carlos Márquez Hernández. "Carnaval en Joloapan." In *Entre los hombres y las Deidades: Las Danzas del Totonacapán*, edited by Rubén Croda León, 168–169. Mexico City, Mexico: CONACULTA, 2005.

Aguilera Madero, Rocío, and Onésimo Cano González. "La danza ritual del volador." In *Entre los hombres y las Deidades: Las Danzas del Totonacapán*, edited by Rubén Croda León, 34–37. Mexico City, Mexico: CONACULTA, 2005.

Alberto Popoca, Juan. "La danza de los quetzales." In *Entre los hombres y las Deidades: Las Danzas del Totonacapán*, edited by Rubén Croda León, 49–51. Mexico City, Mexico: CONACULTA, 2005.

Álvarez Boada, Manuel. "Danza de moros y españoles." In *Entre los hombres y las Deidades: Las Danzas del Totonacapán*, edited by Rubén Croda León, 83–84. Mexico City, Mexico: CONACULTA, 2005.

Álvarez Boada, Manuel. "Danza de santiagueros." In *Entre los hombres y las Deidades: Las Danzas del Totonacapán*, edited by Rubén Croda León, 90–91. Mexico City, Mexico: CONACULTA, 2005.

Andrade, Mary J. *Day of the Dead in Mexico: Through the Eyes of the Soul.* San José, California: La Oferta Review, 2001.

Arizpe Schlosser, Lourdes, and Vera B. Kandt. "La Sierra de Puebla." *Artes de Mexico* XIX, no. 155 (1972).

Bello Pérez, Miguel Ángel. *Crónicas De Hueytamalco Y La Region.* Puebla: Unidad Regional Puebla de Culturas Populares y Indígenas, 2004.

Carillo Azpeitia, Rafael, et al. *Lo Efímero y Eterno del Arte Popular Mexicano,* vol. II. Mexico City, Mexico: Fondo Editorial de la Plastica Mexicana, 1971.

Cassidy, Joseph L. *Mexico: Land of Mary's Wonders.* Paterson, New Jersey: St. Anthony Guild Press, 1958.

Cervantes, Fernando. *The Devil in the New World: The Impact of Diabolism in New Spain.* New Haven, Connecticut: Yale University Press, 1994.

Champe, Flavia Waters. *The Matachines Dance of the Upper Rio Grande: History, Music, and Choreography.* Lincoln: University of Nebraska Press, 1983.

Cordry, Donald. *Mexican Masks.* Austin: University of Texas Press, 1980.

Cordry, Donald Bush, and Dorothy M. Cordry. "Costumes and Textiles of the Aztec Indians of the Cuetzalan Region, Puebla, Mexico." In *Southwest Museum Papers*, No. 14. Los Angeles, California: Southwest Museum, 1940.

Cordry, Donald, and Dorothy Cordry. *Mexican Indian Costumes.* Austin: University of Texas Press, 1968.

Croda León, Rubén. *Entre los hombres y las Deidades: Las Danzas del Totonacapán.* Mexico City, Mexico: CONACULTA, 2005.

Croda León, Rubén. "Danza de los guaguas." In *Entre los hombres y las Deidades: Las Danzas del Totonacapán*, edited by Rubén Croda León, 57–60. Mexico City, Mexico: CONACULTA, 2005.

Croda León, Rubén. "Danza del volador. Leyenda totonaca." In *Entre los hombres y las Deidades: Las Danzas del Totonacapán*, edited by Rubén Croda León, 27–28. Mexico City, Mexico: CONACULTA, 2005.

Croda León, Rubén. "El matarachín y los viejos." In *Entre los hombres y las Deidades: Las Danzas del Totonacapán*, edited by Rubén Croda León, 149–152. Mexico City, Mexico: CONACULTA, 2005.

Croda León, Rubén, and Domingo Francisco Velasco. "Danza de tejoneros." In *Entre los hombres y las Deidades: Las Danzas del Totonacapán*, edited by Rubén Croda León, 70–73. Mexico City, Mexico: CONACULTA, 2005.

Croda León, Rubén, and Francisco Acosta Báez. "Introducción." In *Entre los hombres y las Deidades: Las Danzas del Totonacapán*, edited by Rubén Croda León, 17–22. Mexico City, Mexico: CONACULTA, 2005.

Dow, James. "Sierra Otomí Carnival Dances." In *Behind the Mask in Mexico*, edited by Janet Brody Esser, 172–189. Santa Fe, New Mexico: Museum of International Folk Art and Museum of New Mexico Press, 1988.

Durán, Fray Diego. *Book of the Gods and Rites and the Ancient Calendar*, translated and edited by Fernando Horcasitas and Doris Heyden. Norman: University of Oklahoma Press, 1971.

Erickson, Kirstin C. *Yaqui Homeland and Homeplace: The Everyday Production of Ethnic Identity.* Tucson: The University of Arizona Press, 2008.

Espinosa, Aurelio M. *The Folklore of Spain in the American Southwest*, edited by J. Manuel Espinosa. Norman: University of Oklahoma Press, 1985.

Esser, Janet Brody. *Winter Ceremonial Masks of the Tarascan Sierra, Michoacan, Mexico*, 2 parts. Ann Arbor, Michigan: University Microfilms, 1978.

Esser, Janet Brody. *Máscaras Ceremoniales de los Tarascos de la Sierra de Michoacán.* Mexico City, Mexico: Instituto Nacional Indigenista, 1984.

Esser, Janet Brody, ed. *Behind the Mask in Mexico.* Santa Fe: Museum of International Folk Art and Museum of New Mexico Press, 1988.

Fergusson, Erna. *Fiesta in Mexico.* New York, New York: Alfred A. Knopf, 1934.

Fernández de Calderón, Cándida, ed. *Great Masters of Mexican Folk Art: From the Collection of Fomento Cultural Banamax.* New York, New York: Harry N. Abrams, 1998.

Francisco Francisco, Salvador. "La danza de toreadores." In *Entre los hombres y las Deidades: Las Danzas del Totonacapán*, edited by Rubén Croda León. 109–110. Mexico City, Mexico: CONACULTA, 2005.

Francisco Francisco, Salvador. "Origen de la danza del volador." In *Entre los hombres y las Deidades: Las Danzas del Totonacapán*, edited by Rubén Croda León: 25–26. Mexico City, Mexico: CONACULTA, 2005.

Francisco Velasco, Domingo. "Carnaval en Arroyo Florido." In *Entre los hombres y las Deidades: Las Danzas del Totonacapán*, edited by Rubén Croda León, 157–160. Mexico City, Mexico: CONACULTA, 2005.

Francisco Velasco, Domingo. "Danza de los toreadores." In *Entre los hombres y las Deidades: Las Danzas del Totonacapán*, Edited by Rubén Croda León, 106–108. Mexico City, Mexico: CONACULTA, 2005.

Fuentes Aguilar, Luis. *Regiones Naturales del Estado de Puebla.* Mexico City: Universidad Nacional Autónoma de México,1972.

Furst, Peter. "Forward". In *Mexican Masks,* by Donald Cordry, ix–xx. Austin: University of Texas Press, 1980.

Galinier, Jacques. *The World Below: Body and Cosmos in Otomí Indian Ritual*, translated by Phyllis Aronoff and Howard Scott. Boulder: University Press of Colorado, 2004.

Gaona Vega, Zeferino. "Danza de malintzin." In *Entre los hombres y las Deidades: Las Danzas del Totonacapán*, edited by Rubén Croda León, 78–79. Mexico City, Mexico: CONACULTA, 2005.

Gaona Vega, Zeferino, and Facunda Juárez Hernández. "La danza de lakapijkuyu en las posadas del municipio de Coxquihui, Ver." In *Entre los hombres y las Deidades: Las Danzas del Totonacapán*, edited by Rubén Croda León, 134–139. Mexico City, Mexico: CONACULTA, 2005.

Gaona Vega, Zeferino, and Francisco Acosta Báez. "Danza de los ormegas." In *Entre los hombres y las Deidades: Las Danzas del Totonacapán*, edited by Rubén Croda León, 85–87. Mexico City, Mexico: CONACULTA, 2005.

García García, Domingo. "La danza de los guaguas." In *Entre los hombres y las Deidades: Las Danzas del Totonacapán*, edited by Rubén Croda León, 52–54. Mexico City, Mexico: CONACULTA, 2005.

García García, Domingo. "Los negros." In *Entre los hombres y las Deidades: Las Danzas del Totonacapán*, edited by Rubén Croda León, 115–116. Mexico City, Mexico: CONACULTA, 2005.

García García, Domingo. "Los voladores." In *Entre los hombres y las Deidades: Las Danzas del Totonacapán*, edited by Rubén Croda León, 29–33. Mexico City, Mexico: CONACULTA, 2005.

Gillmor, Frances. "Symbolic Representation in Mexican Combat Plays." In *The Power of Symbols: Masks and Masquerades in the Americas*, edited by N. Ross Crumrine and Marjorie Halpin, 102–110. Vancouver: University of British Columbia Press, 1983.

González Callado, María de los Ángeles, and Alejandra Cerdeño Lance. *El Arte de Ser Totonaca.* Veracruz, Mexico: Gobierno del Veracruz, 2009.

Govers, Cora. *Performing the Community: Representation, Ritual and Reciprocity in the Totonac Highlands of Mexico.* New Brunswick, New Jersey: Transaction Publishers, 2006.

Griffith, James S. *Rio Mayo Pascola Masks: A Study In Style.* Ann Arbor, Michigan: University Microfilms, 1967.

Gutiérrez, Electra, and Tonatiúh Gutiérrez. *Mexico Magico.* Mexico City, Mexico: Salvat Editores, 1974.

Gutiérrez, Tonatiúh, and Electra L. Mompradé. *Danzas y Bailes Populares.* Mexico City, Mexico: Hermes, 1976.

Halpin, Marjorie. "Confronting Looking Glass Men: A Preliminary Examination of the mask." In *Ritual Symbolism and Ceremonialism in the Americas: Studies in Symbolic Anthropology*, edited by N. Ross Crumrine. Occasional Publications in Anthropology, Ethnology Series 33:41–61. Greeley: Museum of Anthropology, University of Northern Colorado, 1979.

Harris, Max. *Aztecs, Moors and Christians: Festivals of Reconquest in Mexico and Spain.* Austin: University of Texas Press, 2000.

Harris, Max. *Carnival and Other Christian Festivals: Folk Theology and Folk Performance.* Austin: University of Texas Press, 2003.

Harris, Max. *The Dialogical Theatre: Dramatizations of the Conquest of Mexico and the Question of the Oth*er. New York, New York: St. Martin's Press, 1993.

Harris, Max. "Moctezuma's Daughter: The Role of Malinche in Mesoamerican Dance.*" Journal of American Folklore* 109, no. 432 (Spring 1996): 149–177.

Harvey, H. R., and Isabel Kelly. "The Totonac." In *Handbook of Middle American Indians.* Vol. 8, *Ethnology,* Part Two, 638–681. Austin: University of Texas Press, 1969.

Hernández Orea, Eva. "Carnaval en Cuyuxquihui." In *Entre los hombres y las Deidades: Las Danzas del Totonacapán*, edited by Rubén Croda León, 161–163. Mexico City, Mexico: CONACULTA, 2005.

Hernández Vázquez, Ygnacia. "Danza de quetzales." In *Entre los hombres y las Deidades: Las Danzas del Totonacapán*, edited by Rubén Croda León, 46–48. Mexico City, Mexico: CONACULTA, 2005.

Hernández Vázquez, Ygnacia. "La danza de lakapijkuyu." In *Entre los hombres y las Deidades: Las Danzas del Totonacapán*, edited by Rubén Croda León, 132–133. Mexico City, Mexico: CONACULTA, 2005.

Hernández Vázquez, Ygnacia. "La danza de matarachín." In *Entre los hombres y las Deidades: Las Danzas del Totonacapan*, edited by Rubén Croda León, 130–131. Mexico City, Mexico: CONACULTA, 2005.

Ichon, Alain. *La Religion des Totonaques de la Sierra.* Paris, France: Centre National de la Recherche Scientifique, 1969.

Ichon, Alain. *La Religion De Los Totonacas de la Sierra.* Mexico City, Mexico: Instituto Nacional Indigenista, 1973.

Jacobson, Lori, and Donald E. Fritz. *Changing Faces: Mexican Masks in Transition.* McAllen, Texas: McAllen International Museum, 1985.

Jiménez Morales, Jacobo. "Relatrio de la danza de los negritos." In *Entre los hombres y las Deidades: Las Danzas del Totonacapán*, edited by Rubén Croda León, 124–127. Mexico City, Mexico: CONACULTA, 2005.

Lane, Bruce. "The Making of *The Tree of Life*." Quaker Theology 4, no. 2, issue 7 (Autumn 2002). http://www.quaker.org/quest/issue7-4-lane03.htm.

Lane, Bruce. *The Tree of Life*. In *The Tree of Life: Three Films on Indian Mexico*. Rochester, New York: Ethnoscope Film, 2005.

Lane, Bruce. *The Tree of Knowledge*. In *The Tree of Life: Three Films on Indian Mexico*. Rochester, New York: Ethnoscope Film, 2005.

Lane, Bruce. *The Tree of Knowledge: English Text*. http://www.docfilm.com/webpages/Mexico/TOK_txt.html.

Lane, Bruce. *Notes on the Text of The Tree of Knowledge*, http://www.docfilm.com/webpages/Mexico/trOfKnidg.html.

Lane, Burce, *Warriors of the Sun*. Rochester, New York: Ethnoscope Film, 2011

Lechuga, Ruth. *Máscaras Tradicionales de México*. Mexico City, Mexico: Banco Nacional de Obras y Servicios Públicos, 1991.

Lechuga, Ruth D. "Mask Making in Guerrero." In *Behind the Mask in Mexico*, edited by Janet Brody Esser, 214–243. Santa Fe: Museum of International Folk Art and Museum of New Mexico Press, 1988.

Lechuga, Ruth D., and Chloë Sayer. *Mask Arts of Mexico*. London: Thames and Hudson, 1994.

de León, Imelda. *Calendario de Fiestas Populares*. Mexico City, Mexico: Dirección General de Culturas Populares, 1988.

Leyenaar, Ted J. J. "Some Dances of the Nahuas and the Otomies of Sierra Norte de Puebla, Mexico." In *Behind the Mask in Mexico*, edited by Janet Brody Esser, 190–213. Santa Fe: Museum of International Folk Art and Museum of New Mexico Press, 1988.

Madsen, William. "Religious Syncretism." In *Handbook of Middle American Indians. Vol. 6, Social Anthropology, 369–391*. Austin: University of Texas Press, 1967.

Madsen, William. *The Virgin's Children: Life in an Aztec Village Today*. Austin: University of Texas Press, 1960.

Mauldin, Barbara. Photographs by Ruth D. Lechuga. *Tigers, Devils, and the Dance of Life: Masks of Mexico*. Santa Fe: Museum of New Mexico Press, 1999.

Medina Jiménez, Alejandro. "Origen de la Danza de moros y españoles." In *Entre los hombres y las Deidades: Las Danzas del Totonacapán*, edited by Rubén Croda León, 80–82. Mexico City, Mexico: CONACULTA, 2005.

Medina Jiménez, Alejandro. "Origen de la Danza de los negros de plumaje." In *Entre los hombres y las Deidades: Las Danzas del Totonacapán*, edited by Rubén Croda León, 110–112. Mexico City, Mexico: CONACULTA, 2005.

Medina Jiménez, Alejandro. "Origen de la Danza del quetzal." In *Entre los hombres y las Deidades: Las Danzas del Totonacapán*, edited by Rubén Croda León, 43–45. Mexico City, Mexico: CONACULTA, 2005.

Medina Jiménez, Alejandro. "Origen de la Danza de San Miguelitos." In *Entre los hombres y las Deidades: Las Danzas del Totonacapán*, edited by Rubén Croda León, 92–93. Mexico City, Mexico: CONACULTA, 2005.

Medina Jiménez, Alejandro. "Origen de la Danza de tejoneros." In *Entre los hombres y las Deidades: Las Danzas del Totonacapán*, edited by Rubén Croda León, 63–67. Mexico City, Mexico: CONACULTA, 2005.

Medina Jiménez, Alejandro. "Rito ceremonial de la danza de tejoneros." In *Entre los hombres y las Deidades: Las Danzas del Totonacapán*, edited by Rubén Croda León, 68–69. Mexico City, Mexico: CONACULTA, 2005.

Méndez García, Sara. "Danza de los 'Viejos' o lakakgolo." In *Entre los hombres y las Deidades: Las Danzas del Totonacapan*, edited by Rubén Croda León, 140–141. Mexico City, Mexico: CONACULTA, 2005.

Méndez García, Sara. "La danza de los huehues o carnavaleños." In *Entre los hombres y las Deidades: Las Danzas del Totonacapán*, edited by Rubén Croda León, 164–167. Mexico City, Mexico: CONACULTA, 2005.

Moya Rubio, Victor José. *Máscaras: La Otra Cara de Mexico. Masks: the Other Face of Mexico*, 3rd ed. Mexico City, Mexico: Universidad Nacional Autónoma de México, 1986.

Nájera-Ramírez, Olga. *La Fiesta de los Tastoanes: Critical Encounters in Mexican Festival Performance*. Albuquerque: University of New Mexico Press, 1997.

Ogazon, Estela. *Máscaras*. Mexico City: Universidad Nacional Autónoma de Mexico,1981.

Olivier, Guilhem. *Mockeries and Metamorphoses of an Aztec God: Tezcatlipoca, Lord of The Smoking Mirror,"* translated by Michael Besson. Boulder: University Press of Colorado, 2003.

Ontiveros Peña, Bonifacio. "Carnaval en Solteros de Juan Rosas." In *Entre los hombres y las Deidades: Las Danzas del Totonacapán*, edited by Rubén Croda León, 152–156. Mexico City, Mexico: CONACULTA, 2005.

Palacios Sánchez, Alejandra. *Material Etnografico del Grupo Lingüístico Totonaco: Catálogo de las Collecciones Etnograficas del Museo Nacional de Antropología*. Mexico City, Mexico: Instituto Nacional de Antropología e Historia, 1992.

Rael, Juan B. *The Sources and Diffusion of the Mexican Shepherd's Plays*. Guadalajara, Mexico: Libreria La Joyita, 1965.

Ravicz, Marilyn Ekdahl. *Early Colonial Religious Drama in Mexico: From Tzompantli to Golgotha*. Washington, D.C.: The Catholic University of America Press, 1970.

Reyes Palma, Francisco, and Carlos Monsiváis. *Los Méxicos de Mariana Yampolsky: Ritos y Regocijos*. Mexico City, Mexico: Lunwerg Editores, 2005.

Rodríguez, José Antonio. *Ruth D. Lechuga: Una Memoria Mexicana*. Mexico City: Museo Franz Mayer, Artes de México, 2002.

Rodríguez, Sylvia. *The Matachines Dance: Ritual Symbolism and Interethnic Relations in the Upper Rio Grande Valley*. Albuquerque: University of New Mexico Press, 1996.

Sahagún, Fray Bernardino de. *Florentine Codex: General History of the Things of New Spain*, 13 vols., translated and edited by Arthur J. O. Anderson and Charles E. Dibble. Santa Fe, New Mexico: School of American Research and University of Utah, 1950–1969. Page references are to the first edition except for Books 1 (1970) and 2 (1981), 2nd ed. rev.

Salas García, Luis. "Los guaguas." In *Entre los hombres y las Deidades: Las Danzas del Totonacapán*, edited by Rubén Croda León, 55–56. Mexico City, Mexico: CONACULTA, 2005.

Scott, James C. *Domination and the Arts of Resistance: Hidden Transcripts*. New Haven, Connecticut: Yale University Press, 1990.

Sepúlveda Herrera, María Teresa. *Catálogo de Máscaras del Estado de Guerrero de Collecciones del Museo Nacional de Antropología*. Mexico City, Mexico: Instituto Nacional de Antropología, 1982.

Stone, James S. *The Cult of Santiago: Traditions, Myths, and Pilgrimages*. New York, New York: Longmans, Green and Co., 1927.

Stresser-Péan, Guy. *The Sun God and the Savior: The Christianization of the Nahua and Totonac in the Sierra Norte de Puebla, Mexico*. Boulder: University Press of Colorado, 2009.

Toor, Frances. *A Treasury of Mexican Folkways*. New York, New York: Crown Publishers, 1947.

Williams García, Roberto. "El matarachín, rito del dios dual." In *Entre los hombres y las Deidades: Las Danzas del Totonacapán*, edited by Rubén Croda León, 148–149. Mexico City, Mexico: CONACULTA, 2005.

Williams García, Roberto. *Los Tepehuas*. Xalapa, Veracruz: Universidad Veracruzana, 1963.

Xochihua Ibarra, José. "La danza de santiagueros." In *Entre los hombres y las Deidades: Las Danzas del Totonacapa*, edited by Rubén Croda León, 88–89. Mexico City, Mexico: CONACULTA, 2005.

Index

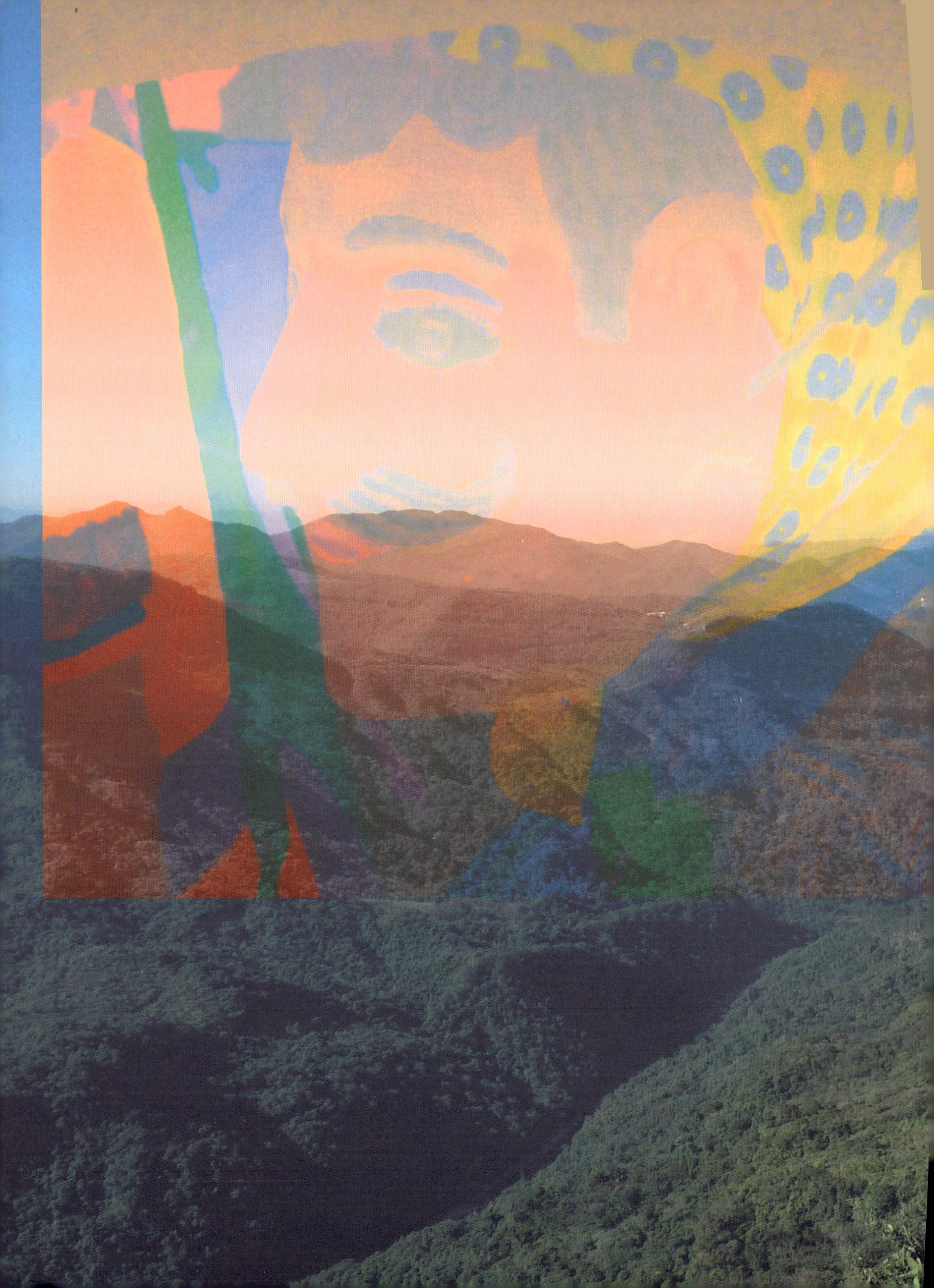